The Caste Question

The publisher gratefully acknowledges the generous support of the Asian Studies Endowment Fund of the University of California Press Foundation

The Caste Question

Dalits and the Politics of Modern India

Anupama Rao

UNIVERSITY OF CALIFORNIA PRESS
Berkeley · Los Angeles · London

)

University of California Press, one of the most
distinguished university presses in the United States,
enriches lives around the world by advancing
scholarship in the humanities, social sciences, and
natural sciences. Its activities are supported by the
UC Press Foundation and by philanthropic contributions from individuals and institutions. For more
information, visit www.ucpress.edu.

University of California Press
Berkeley and Los Angeles, California

University of California Press, Ltd.
London, England

Library of Congress Cataloging-in-Publication Data

Rao, Anupama.
    The caste question : Dalits and the politics of
modern India / Anupama Rao.
        p.   cm.
    Includes index.
    ISBN: 978-0-520-25559-3 (cloth : alk. paper)—
    ISBN: 978-0-520-25761-0 (pbk. : alk. paper)
    1. Dalits—Political activity.   2. India—Politics and
government—1947–   I. Title.
DS422.C3R365   2009
305.5'688—dc22   2009004280

Manufactured in the United States of America

18   17   16   15   14   13   12   11   10   09
10   9   8   7   6   5   4   3   2   1

This book is printed on Natures Book, which contains
50% post-consumer waste and meets the minimum
requirements of ANSI/NISO Z39.48–1992 (R 1997)
(Permanence of Paper).

For my grandparents,
Dr. D. A. Lakshmana Rao, Malathibai,
C. Gopinath Rao, and Tarabai,
who taught me the value of words
and the power of stories.

Contents

Illustrations

Preface

This book tells the story of how untouchables became Dalits. It is an account of how the stigma of being "untouchable" was redefined as an identity about historically specific forms of suffering and exclusion, and of how this identity eventually became politically powerful. It is also a story about the reorganization of caste under political modernity. *The Caste Question* thus addresses the constitutive relationship between Dalit emancipation and Indian democracy.

Dalit emancipation is an unfinished project, initially conceived by the Mahar Dalits of Bombay Presidency who challenged both colonial and nationalist ideas of personhood and political subjectivity in fundamental ways. Their struggle for rights and social recognition utilized diverse strategies, ranging from the demand for separate political representation to conversion to Buddhism. These strategies produced the Dalit as a specific political subject, a non-Hindu, a political minority, and finally, as a suffering subject who required state protection. Efforts to redress complex cultural forms of discrimination thus produced a unique set of religiopolitical resolutions to the problem of Dalit suffering. The signal efforts of a key figure, the political thinker and activist Bhimrao Ramji Ambedkar (1891–1956), were critical in resignifying a political universal, equality, as *caste equality*.

The history of Indian democracy is thus inseparable from the politics of caste and from the activism of anticaste radicals who struggled to render caste, a culturally and historically specific form of embodiment, universally salient as the practice of inequality. This explains why caste has grown rather than diminished in significance as democracy has taken root in India, producing a form of politics that forefronts collective rights and group emancipation rather than individual autonomy. The alternative genealogy of the political subject proposed in this work thus poses a challenge to received accounts of democratization. The latter assume liberal individualism as the goal of enfranchisement even when political action centers on demands for group recognition and the protection of minorities. Instead, I propose to examine how caste subalterns influenced the distinctive career of India's secular modernity.

The received account of India's modernity equates politics with the oppositional consciousness of anticolonial nationalism. Scholarly efforts such as those by the Subaltern Studies Collective to counteract explanations of non-Western political forms and social processes as derivative of, or deviating from, hegemonic narratives of Euro-American transition do not satisfactorily resolve the problem. The subaltern is often conceptualized as an anachronism, a political subject from a precapitalist past, rooted in forms of social life and community that appear to be the source of oppositional consciousness. Subaltern agency is thus posited in opposition to the state and its institutions, while the failure of subaltern protest is attributed to a failure to capture state power. Instead, my focus is on how caste subalterns creatively transformed key political categories, such as rights, equality, and citizenship, through recourse to constitutionalism and the franchise. Focusing on Dalit subject-formation allows us to write an alternative history of democratic liberalism, instead of exploring alternatives *to* hegemonic (Western) political forms.

History from the perspective of the Dalit subaltern reflects a persistent effort to convert the Dalit's structural negativity within the caste order into positive political content, and to make historic suffering and humiliation—the experience of being "ground down" and "broken"—central to the identity of Dalit as both a non-Hindu minority and an inaugural political-ethical subject. This book's title, *The Caste Question*, is thus a provocation to rethink India's political modernity from the perspective of Dalits as they simultaneously pursued religious, social, and political emancipation. Such a position goes beyond the perspectives of writing "histories from below," though the paucity of serious social and cultural histories of Dalit life makes this a valuable and necessary effort. Instead, this book focuses on the crucial role of Dalit subalterns in redefining organizing terms of colonial liberalism such as religion, community, rights, and equality, and interrogates the multiple and often contradictory outcomes of Dalit emancipation.

Caste, once a modal form of social organization identified with backwardness and underdevelopment, is today a vibrantly contested political category and identity. Dalits—Scheduled Castes in government parlance—have been crucial to the elaboration of India's civil rights regime after national independence and figure in the governmental imaginary as vulnerable subjects and victims of historic discrimination. While Dalit enfranchisement through affirmative action is compelling and subversive, the affective force of Dalit identity politics derives from the myriad ways in which the Dalit body continues to be the site of recurrent stigmatization, making it a historical and a contemporary object of suffering. Rising Dalit militancy has been offset by new formations of anti-Dalit violence: brutality against intercaste liaisons, land grabs, and other forms of economic violence, especially against more prosperous Dalits, sexual humiliation of Dalit women, ritual murders, and the desecration of Dalit commemorative sites.

The conceptual elaboration of Dalit emancipation (and the politicization of Dalit identity) returns us to an enduring question for political liberalism: to what extent can the social differentiation and ascriptive identifications of civil society avoid becoming politically salient? If the separation of private interests (or beliefs) from public rights is impossible, under what terms and conditions are social identities politicized? The paradoxical coexistence of (Dalit) political militancy and the politicization of (upper-caste) violence is a crucial phase in the "untouchable" subject's continued struggle to *become Dalit*. The transformations of caste and of untouchability attest to a corporeal politics premised on the continued salience of embodied difference, and not its transcendence. They forefront as well a more general paradox of political recognition: seeking emancipation by identifying with historical vulnerability. As cultural practices and social forms are redefined as civic disabilities, and as the inequities of caste are equalized through political intervention, the terms of "politics" itself have become politicized: the social antagonisms and violence of everyday life structure the political field, even as politics heightens the agonistic character of social life. Efforts to convert the negative centrality of the Dalit into positive political content have also emphasized the Dalit's unique place in the political unconscious of Indian society.

Dalit history is not merely of concern to those with interest in the subcontinent, but also forms a key chapter in the global history of political emancipation. If democracy is predicated on the figure of the citizen and the idea of equality, it is also a historical form and a cultural concept, the terms of which are subject to political negotiation and revision. The transformation of subjects into citizens is contingent on historical circumstance, while the idea of equality has developed in relation to efforts to overcome the inequities produced by various forms of embodied "difference." Just as there is nothing in the logic of social formations that guarantees an automatic transformation of subjects into citizens, there is no unitary definition of equality or of citizenship around which political subjectivity coheres. Thus it is fair to say that the form of democracy is closely connected to the forms of inequality that define a social order at any given point in time. From this it follows that the logic of democracy neither excludes a redefinition of political citizenship nor precludes historico-cultural formations of suffering and discrimination: the pursuit of rights and recognition have the capacity to expand what we recognize as the field of politics.

Dalit emancipation is a significant (if unacknowledged) chapter in the history of an idea: democracy. But it is also a prism through which to address the critical role that Dalit history has played in the translation of caste into a complex form of inequality that undercuts analytic distinctions between "the social" and "the political" and between "religious" and "secular" domains of social life. The continued reverberations of the "problem of freedom" are today reflected in social forms and political practices that place the Dalit at the center of democratic struggle. *The Caste Question* traces this intersection between Dalit emancipation and the development of distinctive practices of political recognition, and offers a way of understanding how a deep logic of democratization relies on (rather than dissolving) derided cultural forms and social practices in the effort to refashion selves and to remake politics. *Dalit history is the history of India's political modernity.*

Acknowledgments

This book began as a dissertation at the University of Michigan with support from a Junior Research Fellowship from the American Institute of Indian Studies; a grant from the Joint Committee on South Asia of the Social Science Research Council and the American Council on Learned Societies; and a Hewitt Dissertation Grant from the University of Michigan. A Summer Stipend and a Faculty Fellowship from the National Endowment for the Humanities, together with a research leave from Barnard College, allowed me to revise and rewrite much of the manuscript.

In India, my greatest debt is to the men and women who allowed me into their lives. Many remain unnamed for obvious reasons. Others include Pratap Bhangar, Arjun Dangle, Namdeo Dhasal, Vishnu Dhoble, Sunil Dighe, B. K. Gaikwad, Sudhir Gawhane, the late Shankarrao Kharat, Subodh More, Madhukar Nerale, Urmila Pawar, Rekha Thakur, Shantaram Pandhere, and Prakash Sirsat.

Ram Bapat saw the ethical contours of this project well before I did; Umesh Bagade, Kishore Dhamale, Pratima Pardeshi, Ranjit Pardeshi, and other *karyakarthas* of the Krantisingh Nana Patil Academy introduced me to Marx-Phule-Ambedkarvad; Gopal Guru encouraged me to challenge Ambedkarism by rereading Ambedkar, and Kumud and Motiram Pawde shared their deep knowledge of Dalit history and social life in Vidarbha. Each has shaped my thinking in critical ways.

I am grateful to the following institutions and their staffs: the Indian Office Library and Records; the Maharashtra State Archives; Bapusaheb

Mane at Shivaji University; the Khairmode Collection, Bombay University; the Prabhodankar Thackeray Collection (Kakadwadi); Shashikant Bhagat at Mumbai Marathi Grantha Sangrahalaya; Sanjay Hadkar at the Vidhan Bhavan library; the Bombay High Court Judges' Library; the Bombay High Court Archives; the PCR Cell of the Maharashtra Police Headquarters; the Bureau of Police Research and Development (Delhi); and the Sardar Vallabhai Patel Police Training Academy (Hyderabad).

It would be impossible to write Dalit history without the private collections of the late Vasant Moon, Dr. Gangadhar Pantawane, and Ramesh Shinde. I am especially grateful to Arati and Milind Moon, and to Bharati Wakode for hosting recent visits to Nagpur. Professor Gangadhar Pantawane shared handwritten notes and printed material, all while extending his legendary hospitality. Ramesh Shinde shared his invaluable collection of books and journals, as well as his considerable knowledge of the movement. To them, my deepest thanks.

Professor V. S. Kadam introduced me to Kolhapur city and to Shivaji University. Professor Krishna Kirwale shared his knowledge of Dalit popular culture and facilitated recent stays in Kolhapur. Aroon Tikekar shared his extensive knowledge of nineteenth-century Maharashtra—and his library. Medha Kotwal-Lele, Nirmala Sathe, and Simrita Singh made me feel at home in Alochana, Pune, during earlier visits. I am grateful to each for their friendship and affection.

Jayashree Borhade provided invaluable help with Marathi-language data entry. Ninad Pandit helped with the Khairmode Collection. Shailaja Paik and Mrinal Patnekar tracked down sources in Bombay and Pune, respectively. And Balaji Gharule was a wonderful research assistant in the last phase of this project.

Friends helped me survive the sometimes painful process of research. Tulsi Parab, Wandana Sonalkar, Ojas and Daryan have been thick friends from the first day we met in Aurangabad on Ambedkar Jayanti in 1996. They have accompanied me on many adventures and taught me more about politics than anyone else. Aniket Jaaware and Urmila Bhirdikar inspire with their fierce intelligence and challenge with their brilliance, from music to Marathi and "theory." More importantly, they are friends who make me laugh and live fully. Kabir and Sharmistha Mohanty are instructors in the art of the possible. They have taught me to "see" and "hear" differently, and to understand time and narrative in altogether new ways. Amrita Sabnavis and Surabhi Sharma have known me since my first visit to Bombay in 1989. Vasant Samant gave us his home in Pune, while Raji and Sushma Sharma hosted me on many a visit. Their love has meant a great deal. V. V. Modak and Nirmala Modak are surrogate grandparents, their presence even more precious now that I have lost my own. To them, my enduring respect.

In the United States, my first and deepest debt is to my teachers. Bernard Cohn and Ronald Inden introduced me to the historical an-thropology of South Asia at the University of Chicago. The paths they opened were critical, and the lessons they taught invaluable. The Anthro-History Program at the University of Michigan shaped my intellectual world in profound ways. I have learned greatly from Val Daniel's work on political violence. Ann Stoler's theorization of race and gender gave me the courage to address the gendering of caste. Her continued guid-ance and support have helped me navigate the strange world of acade-mia. Nicholas Dirks has believed in this project at every stage—from Michigan to Columbia. This book could not have been conceived with-out his signal rethinking of the historical anthropology of caste. Partha Chatterjee's theorization of an Indian genealogy of "the political" has inspired my own small efforts in that direction.

Eleanor Zelliot shared contacts, boxes of material, and stories, all while debating the changing shape of "the movement" about which she first wrote nearly forty years ago. I can only hope to repay her exemplary generosity through similar gifts.

Fellow travelers at the University of Michigan—Laura Bear, Anjan Ghosh, Pamila Gupta, Riyad Koya, Mandana Limbert, Rama Mantena, Setrag Manoukian, Gita Rajan, Parna Sengupta, and Dina Siddiqi—have inspired with their elegant intelligence and deep integrity. To Gita and Mani, I owe special thanks for all the good counsel during the New York years.

I am grateful to friends and colleagues who read and gave critical feed-back on the manuscript as it took shape: Janaki Bakhle, Antoinette Bur-ton, Dipesh Chakrabarty, Saurabh Dube, Ranajit Guha, Sumit Guha, Thomas Blom Hansen, Ira Katznelson, Dorothy Ko, Rama Mantena, Karuna Mantena, Uday Mehta, Brinkley Messick, Mrinalini Sinha, M. S. S. Pandian, Neni Panourgia, Gyan Prakash, Gita Rajan, Lee Schle-singer, Rachel Sturman, Kaushik Sunder Rajan, Milind Wakankar, Luise White, and Eleanor Zelliot. Sumit Guha has been generous to a fault in sharing his considerable knowledge of western India. To Rachel Sturman I owe special thanks for being a discerning critic and a trusted interlocutor for many years now.

The manuscript was fundamentally transformed by the incisive comments and supportive feedback of its reviewers. Stan Holwitz's unflagging support and enthusiasm for the project mean more than he knows.

I am grateful to Provost Elizabeth Boylan and to my colleagues at Barnard who have extended guidance and support at every step, especially Joel Kaye, Herb Sloan, Lisa Tiersten, Deborah Valenze, and Carl Wennerlind. At Columbia, Janaki Bakhle has been an inspirational presence and force of nature, her coruscating intelligence matched by her indefatigable energy. I am grateful for her good advice and fierce loyalty.

Lila Abu-Lughod and Dorothy Ko are co-conspirators and fairy godmothers who have watched over me from the start. Thank you . . . for *everything*.

Students at Barnard and Columbia have been the testing ground for many ideas and arguments. They have humbled me with their intelligence and invigorated my thinking in the "problem space" of the classroom. Special thanks to Aparna Balachandran, Manmeet Bindra, Rosie Bsheer, Jesse Chanin, Nadia Guesseous, Andy Liu, Cassidy Luitjen, Golnar Nikpour, Meha Priyadarshini, Ravi Rajendra, Marina Smith, and Andrea Stanton. Thanks to Aparna and Ravi for research assistance, and to Ashley Walls for help with the notes.

I could not have finished without six wise and wonderful friends who held on during the hard times and kept me honest with their tough love. Rajeswari Sunder Rajan is my most cherished interlocutor. Her exemplary integrity is an impossible ideal, and her gentle solicitude is unmatchable. Over the years she has given endlessly of a radiant brilliance that takes my breath away. Jared Stark asked whom this book was for and reminded me of the deep responsibility we bear others. He inspires with his words and energizes with the force of his friendship. Steven Pierce knew what this book was about before I did. He is a native of my person, my altogether more brilliant double, and a force to reckon with. Tanya Fernando knows the craziness within better than anyone else. She has been a shimmering presence in my life for over twenty years now, teaching me that the glass is, indeed, half full. Riyad Koya has kept me afloat with his good sense, hard questions, and powerful editing. Carin McCormack reentered my life when I needed her most and showed me the way. Her keen eye for argument and her exquisite narrative sense fundamentally transformed this book.

My parents, Manjula and Prasanna Rao, are true artists who nurtured my desire for self-expression from the start. Their sacrifice has enabled the boundless possibilities of my own life. No words can describe the intensity of their love, pride, and support. Thank you for all you have given me, especially the music.

My brothers Dileep and Kiran have long known that "love and hate come in moods." Hema and Purnima form a haven of sanity and good sense. My thanks to Dilli and Purnima for sharing Cuddles (Anjali) with her *atthai*, and to Anjali for the change she will bring. My extended family—Jayi, Sheela, Harsha, Madu, Ninette, Usha, Ananth, Sunder, and the beloved Venkatesh Murthy—have cajoled, prodded, supported, and loved me like only family can. P. C. Rajagopal and Padma Rajagopal have extended virtual love and support on a daily basis. Thanks to Lakshmi and Ravi Rajagopal for putting me up. My fond affection goes to Anu and Niranjana.

Arvind Rajagopal has lived and breathed this book—from arguing with me about ideas to asking me to "ventilate" my prose. He is my fiercest critic and my most demanding interlocutor. But most of all, he is the love of my life, who makes it all worthwhile.

An early version of chapter 5 first appeared as "Understanding *Sirasgaon:* Notes Towards Conceptualizing the Role of Law, Caste, and Gender in a Case of 'Atrocity,'" in *Signposts: Gender Issues in Post-Independence India,* edited by Rajeswari Sunder Rajan (New Delhi: Kali for Women, 1998): 204–47. A shorter version of chapter 6 appeared as "Death of a Kotwal: Injury and the Politics of Recognition," in *Subaltern Studies 12,* edited by Shail Mayaram. M. S. S. Pandian, and Ajay Skaria (New Delhi: Permanent Black, 2005): 140–86. Early arguments about Ambedkar's political thought are discussed in "Ambedkar and the Politics of Minority: A Reading," in *From the Colonial to the Postcolonial: India and Pakistan in Transition,* edited by Dipesh Chakrabarty, Rochona Mazumdar, and Andrew Sartori (Delhi: Oxford University Press, 2007): 137–58. I am grateful to the publishers for permission to reprint later versions of these essays.

Author's Note

This is a work of academic scholarship. To make Marathi and Hindi terms accessible to nonspecialist readers, I employ transliterations without diacritics and offer the translation in parentheses so that the sense of a word or expression is immediately clear. The many terms used to describe ex-untouchables are drawn from archival sources, colloquial speech, and interviews. None is meant to hurt or offend anyone. In addition to their caste names—for example, Chambhar, Mahar, Mang—members of the untouchable communities are referred to colloquially as *asprushya* (untouchable), *bahishkrit varga* (excommunicated classes), Anarya (non-Aryan), and *atishudra* (lowest among the *shudra* or laboring classes).

By 1911, the British government was using the term "Depressed Classes" to refer to the untouchable communities, though there were demands for replacing this derogatory term with "noncaste" or "nonconformist" Hindus. From 1935, the term "Scheduled Castes" has been in use. This refers to the state-wise list of untouchable communities who are eligible for constitutional safeguards.

In addition to governmental nomenclature, M. K. Gandhi adopted the term "Harijan," or "people of god," in 1933, to atone for the sin of untouchability. Some years later, a mass conversion of ex-untouchables to Buddhism in Nagpur in 1956 gave rise to the category *nava Boudha* (neo-Buddhist).

However, the term commonly used today by those who have suffered the stigma of untouchability is "Dalit," which means "ground down" or "broken to pieces" in Marathi and Hindi. The term first made its appearance during the late 1920s, but gained prominence during the 1970s, at a time of literary and cultural efflorescence among Dalit youth in Maharashtra. Today, the term is used across India in recognition of Dalits' claims to a history of suffering and resistance against caste inequality. I use the word "Dalit" throughout this study, even when that usage is anachronistic (for the colonial period, for instance), when writing about general or conceptual matters pertaining to the untouchable communities. I use the expression "Mahar Dalit" (pl. Mahar Dalits) to detail the activities of this particular caste, which was at the forefront of political conscientization in Maharashtra. I capitalize the word because I believe that 165 million Indians are entitled to a capital letter.[1]

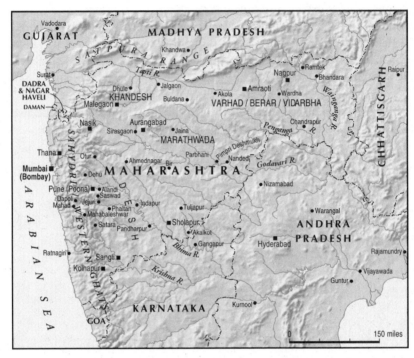

Figure 1. Map of Mahrashtra and adjacent areas, with state boundaries as of 2008. Courtesy of Philip Schwartzberg, Meridian Mapping, Minneapolis (MN), with editorial assistance from Joseph E. Schwartzberg.

Introduction

Untouchables, usually known by degrading names such as Chamar, Mahar, Mang, and Paraiyar, were dehumanized by the caste Hindu order. Caste subalterns' efforts to overturn prevailing relations of caste and community through the creative transformation of existing social categories and practices thus challenged caste Hinduism and the privileges that reproduced it. Dalit emancipation was predicated on the existential, political, and ethical reordering of Indian society, but it also presupposed the imagination of the Dalit as a specific kind of political subject. It is the contention of this book that by examining how people without rights came to possess them, and how stigmatized subjects were transformed into citizens, we can also learn something about the enabling conditions and constitutive contradictions of India's political modernity: the *becoming Dalit* of the stigmatized subject is also a genealogy of the Indian political.

"Dalit" is a word for a community and an identity that are in the making. To call oneself Dalit, meaning "ground down," "broken to pieces," "crushed," is to convert a negative description into a confrontational identity and to become a particular sort of political subject for whom "the terms of exclusion on which discrimination is premised are at once refused and reproduced in the demands for inclusion."[1] Dalit history traces the paradoxical manner in which an identity predicated on a future outside or beyond caste was conceived with historical humiliation and suffering as its enabling ground; it is the narrative of how a new political collectivity was constituted by resignifying the Dalit's negative identity within the caste structure into positive political value.

The historical conditions under which the untouchable subject became *Dalit* are critical,[2] for it was largely (though not exclusively) through the activism of Dalits that untouchability was secularized and politicized, or, that certain socioreligious practices were redefined as forms of civic and political exclusion. The institutional and discursive shifts that enabled these processes also affected the trajectory of Indian democracy, especially the contemporary development of a constitutionally mandated field of civil rights law (rhetorically) committed to caste equality. Taking up a number of distinctive moments in Dalit political engagement from the 1880s to the 1990s, *The Caste Question* weaves together a history of community formation and the remaking of the caste self with an account of India's secular modernity.

This is no heroic history, but one beset with reversals, failures, and contradictions produced by caste subalterns' engagement with colonial, nationalist, and upper-caste power. Tracking the formation of the Dalit political subject from the colonial into the postcolonial period leads us to ask how persons once stigmatized succeeded in creating political visibility and social worth for themselves. More significantly, it poses the question of why Dalits continue to be afflicted by violence and marginalization. In fact, I suggest that the terms of Dalit enfranchisement and the forms of governmental reparation for stigmatized personhood have produced new forms of vulnerability, together exacerbating the relevance of conjunctural violence to contemporary Dalit identity.

The broad strokes of this narrative are not hard to delineate. The story begins with the unique relationship between colonial modernity and anticaste thought that was forged in western India. Spurred by colonial experiences and ideas, members of the Mahar caste led a regional movement in the last decades of the nineteenth century, which for the first time produced a political response to the association of untouchability with Hinduism. They did not demand Hindu inclusion, but instead conceived the untouchable as a unique political subject, as *non-Hindu* and Dalit. In the 1920s, caste leaders, led notably by Bhimrao Ramji Ambedkar, were able to nationalize the Dalit question and to coalesce around the enfranchisement of Dalits as a particular kind of minority, exceptional subjects of historic suffering and discrimination. Although a bid for separate representation failed in 1932, Dalits ultimately found an important place in India's 1949 Constitution: Article 17 abolished the practice of untouchability. Over the next decade, the government implemented laws to protect Dalits from caste violence and instituted affirmative action policies, known as reservations, to redress inequities. The legal status of Dalits was transformed. As a consequence of these changes over the course of a century, once-stigmatized Dalits came to occupy new subject positions: they became members of a political minority and vulnerable citizens constitutionally encoded as objects of state protection. Thus did erstwhile untouchables become central to the development of a distinctive democratic order.

If the details of the story are political common sense, their longer-term implications remain poorly understood. Why did a centuries-old practice of deprivation become the focus of intense debate and intervention from the late nineteenth century, leading eventually to its formal abolition? How did a putatively religious ordering of persons come to be redefined as a form of social inequality and historic discrimination that demanded state action? I approach these questions through interwoven threads that acknowledge the complexity of Dalit political subject-formation. One line of inquiry follows ideas and practices developed by Dalits themselves, caste subalterns who pursued what I call *caste radicalism*. Their politics of recognition and rights comprised an original critique of the caste Hindu order, and it was accompanied by the creation of a distinctive political counterculture. Eventually, these made Dalits visible to the Indian political-legal order as exceptional subjects. Thus, Dalits altered the shape of Indian democracy as they creatively redeployed founding assumptions regarding the subject of rights and the terrain of politics. The broader consequences of their actions can be gauged by the manner in which accounts of Dalit emancipation stand to amend the global history of liberal secularism. For this, a second and complementary thread of analysis tracing policy directives, governmental debates, and legal-juridical action around untouchability is helpful. State practice, colonial policy, and the agency of upper-caste reformers and nationalist elites are of great interest here insofar as they made it possible for untouchability to move to the very center of concerns about political recognition and rights. These conjunctural shifts proved crucial to the elaboration of the caste question in the late colonial period even as they illuminated productive alliances between the colonial constitution of "the political" and the nationalist reconstitution of politics. Examining contradictions within political liberalism will contextualize the issues involved.

Liberalism combines two distinctive histories. One is the history of political rights, and the other is the transformation of moral sentiments in the growth of human freedom.[3] Liberalism's narrative of political subject-formation typically aligns the subject of rights with the subject of freedom and rationality. However, colonial power was effective precisely because of its mode of justification for inequality and domination. The tension between universalism and difference, an organizing binary of liberal universalism (and of capitalist modernity more generally), when adapted to projects of imperial governance and control, manifests as a distinction between normative subjects and "politically inadequate" ones who are seen to suffer the stigma of culture, race, religion, or, indeed, sexual difference. These politically inadequate yet excessively embodied subjects have been objects of a peculiar and perverse fascination: they have constituted sites of moral-political intervention, even as they have been subject to violent control and discipline. Indeed, the anxiety to control such forms of alterity reflects a broader logic of liberalism generally, and of colonial liberalism in particular: the manner by which the production, recognition, and distribution of social difference serve as the explicit predicate for the state's authority to govern legitimately.

In India, social forms that were the product of colonial intervention were instead viewed as artifacts of precolonial social life and impediments to the modern bureaucratic state. Meanwhile, some forms of community and collective life—for example, caste and religion—were invested with political value. Thus religious and political domains, though theoretically separate, were practically intertwined. This contradiction crucially defined the colonial state form: religion was secularized and defined as community, while community gained political salience as constituency. This was the route whereby religion was politicized. A paradox of political commensuration followed: religious communities were seen as *quantitatively incommensurable* but *qualitatively equivalent*. In turn, colonial state intervention resolved the paradox, mediating between communities as neutral (external) arbiter. We might thus extend Philip Abram's famous deconstruction of the political realism of state theory to examine what might be termed the "colonial state effect."[4] Abrams argued that "the state" was an enabling fiction for masking decentralized practices of power, and that the putative materiality of the state as a thing or a place was in fact the effect of practices of power that produced the state as an autonomous whole. Misrecognition plays a critical role in Abram's account of the state effect, as it does in my description of the colonial state. However, the colonial state effect is derived from an opposite set of moves to what obtains in Abrams' account: colonial power was repeatedly denied, dissimulated, and devolved onto native social and political forms to produce the effect of dispersion and dis-aggregation rather than of cohesion. This enabled colonial authoritari-anism and the emergence of a distinctive politics of identity.

For those defined as Hindus, caste also played a mediating role, defin-ing identities, demarcating the boundaries of community, and regulating exchange. The British complemented their colonial perspective on caste as social totality with perceptions of caste as a unique, unchanging form of Hindu social stratification. Enumerative technologies like the census took caste and religion as modal forms of social categorization and ef-fectively gave them political pertinence. By fixing tribe, race, religious groups and especially caste as modes of social categorization, the impe-rial census of 1871–72 instigated complex interactions between indige-nous class-caste formations and colonial classification. Requiring people to identify themselves by governmental categories, census technology em-phasized the differential electoral weight of religious communities, pro-moted identification with caste, and facilitated lower-caste demands for rights and representation. Rather than yielding political individuation, new investments in community-based claims changed prevalent norms of status and respectability. By treating caste as both traditional and po-litical, then, the colonial state inadvertently enabled a (new) politics of caste.

Nicholas Dirks has argued that an enhanced politicization of civil society took shape after the Mutiny of 1857, when culture became an explicit category of colonial government.[5] Social and ascriptive identi-ties such as religion and caste became sites of political conflict and com-petition, leaving the colonial state to arbitrate between good and bad, deserving and undeserving forms of politics. This pointed to a hierarchy of colonial political forms, where native agency was stigmatized as re-quiring colonial correction. Anticolonial nationalists challenged precisely this denigration of native social forms and resignified them as sites of cultural authenticity and collective sovereignty. From 1885, the Indian National Congress explicitly challenged the colonial state's sovereignty over native subjects. Like the British, nationalists and upper-caste re-formers understood caste to be religiously derived. Their response to caste hierarchy differed, however, in that they saw it as a matter for Hindus to negotiate, *not for colonial policy to determine.* In turn, untouchability was incorporated into the political project of anticolonial nationalism as a religious problem of reforming Hinduism. Though they challenged the legitimacy of colonial domination over the intimate lives of natives, na-tionalists left intact colonially derived distinctions between the social and the political, even as they asserted their right to define the *content* of those categories. If colonial state practice politicized social forms and practices while denigrating them as signs of human backwardness, nationalists reinvested the social with a capacity for ethical and political regeneration. Thus the growing significance of untouchability reform derived from the divergent meanings (and deepened salience) of the social-religious domain for colonial *and* nationalist thought. By 1920, the Indian National Congress under its creative and unconventional leader, M. K. Gandhi, had acknowledged untouchability as a "reproach to Hinduism" and made it something of a test case for reforming Hinduism, from exhorting upper-caste Hindus to perform stigmatized labor to renaming untouchables Harijans, or "people of god," by 1933. Untouchable reform became central to the identity of a confessional Hinduism and to the consolidation of Hindus as a majority political constituency representative of the nation as a whole.[6] Equally, locating untouchability wholly within religion effectively limited the colonial state and legal apparatus to little more than delegating to Hindus the problem of untouchability. Thus if the religious solution of inverting negative stereotypes affirmed the primacy of the "social" for anticolonial mobilization, it also reproduced upper castes' hegemony by deflecting attention away from the victims of caste discrimination.

Scholarly accounts of the politics of untouchability typically chart a move from a social reformist phase to the Congress's politicization of untouchability as a problem for Hindus, which effectively limited participation in social reform to upper castes.[7] *The Caste Question* departs from such treatment to track the manner in which the violence of untouchability became a central element of Dalit critique, which enabled stigmatized subjects to be defined initially as *non-Hindus* and later as a cultural and political minority. Dalit critique exposed the doubled nature of the caste question. As colonial abstraction, caste was externally manifest in a demographically based politics of number and in the reliance of upper castes on untouchables to constitute a religious and political majority in Indian society. As a category of everyday life and a form of stigmatized existence, untouchability shaped the "inside" of community, and thus its reform became central to the ethical and affective reconstitution of Hinduism. By politicizing the principle of structural negativity that underwrote Dalit identity, caste radicals also redefined the social totality of caste as a form of historical violence crucial to the constitution of the caste community. In turn, Dalits used the contradiction between their religious status as untouchable and their political status as minority to leverage a powerful demand for political rights and social recognition.

A *Dalit* history of caste politics brings into view a wider set of relationships—those between state, caste and community, between nation and minority, and ultimately, between the religious and the political. The history of how untouchables became Dalits is the story of how alterations in the social relations of caste became central to debates about equality and discrimination. It is also the story of how a geohistorical universal, equality, became historically and culturally specified as *caste equality*. Ultimately, an account of Dalit political subject-formation illuminates the colonial (and postcolonial) trajectories of secular liberalism and explains why it is marked by a permanent tension between "the religious" and "the political."

QUESTIONS OF CASTE, COMMUNITY, SUBJECT

Far from being the "unthought" of Indian society, caste is overwhelmingly visible to scholars of South Asia as the overdetermined site of Indian "difference." If it was long seen through Louis Dumont's account of caste as a religious principle and social totality, the intellectual labor of the last three decades has consisted of rescuing caste from religion to reveal its political entailments. I should note at the outset that my interest in the development of *anticaste thought* extends and reprises such concerns at the levels of both "history" and "theory."

As is well known, in Dumont's formulation of caste society a purity-pollution opposition structured a sacral order that subsumed politics.[8] In the process, potential conflict was ritually defused so that caste relations could appear consensual. Dumont argued that political ideas of individualism and distinctions between equality and inequality—the major achievements of European political thinking and institutions—were missing in hierarchical societies. This was because the idea of equality was bound up with the capacity for abstraction and equivalence, rather than the encompassment of politics by religion as was the case with hierarchy. The epistemological significance of Dumont's argument cannot be emphasized enough: because hierarchy is about ritual binaries that divide social space, secular conceptions of equality (concerned with the operation of abstraction and of commensuration) are *logically* impossible. Early ethnographies of untouchable communities accepted the Dumontian opposition between Brahmin and untouchable and examined the partial integration of impure castes into the ritual hierarchy, thereby assuming

the putative consent of the untouchable communities to their own exclusion, as well as lower castes' mimicry of the ranked relations of caste.[9]
While such works focused on the social practice of distinction and discrimination, they also assumed the ideological power of dominant castes'
conception of social order. That is, they equated *power* with the *power
of upper castes*. To maintain that "impurity is a relative concept" *and*
that the untouchable's stigma is inherited and irreversible, as Robert
Deliège has argued, reveals a gap between the description of caste stigma
at the level of practice and scholarly reproduction of upper-caste ideology as a descriptor of social reality.[10] Instead, a subaltern theory of caste
would begin by examining the production of social analytics as a reflection of the politics of knowledge formation; it would focus on how caste
radicals theorized caste as historically specific *and* as a geohistorical universal, and then examine the implications of anticaste thinking for alternative histories of political subject-formation.

More recently, historicized analyses of colonial power and knowledge
formation have followed from Nicholas Dirks's signal critique of Dumont's totalizing, ahistorical treatment of caste. Dirks argues that Dumont's orderly caste structure headed by Brahmins was an artifact of colonial power; that caste and religion were always political. By dissolving
crucial connections between caste, kingship and territory, the colonial
state was able to take caste and religion outside the domain of politics
and to redefine them as social categories and associational civic forms.
Though newly created divisions between the domain of politics occupied
by colonial power and the domain of civil society defined by aberrant
forms of political authority were constituted through practices of power,
these divisions were reified by colonial (and nationalist) sociology as a
set of existing analytic distinctions between the religio-ritual and the political, the material and the symbolic.[11] The subsequent appearance of
caste politics within the Indian social domain was taken to be a category
mistake reflecting Indians' political backwardness. In a further twist, it
was the colonial version of caste that was defended as being authenti-
cally Indian by colonial administrators, native elites, and even lower-caste
activists.[12] Thus did a colonial category become an "ethnographic real," a
modern identity and a naturalized representation around which Indians
developed a range of discursive positions, political claims, and alignments
in the colonial and postcolonial periods.

Dirks's arguments provide key analytic openings for scholars recon-
sidering caste in terms of history and power relations. They influence my
efforts to address the discursive separation and conceptual entailments

of religion and politics as central elements of colonial (and postcolonial) knowledge formation, and allow me to extend those concerns to consider the novel manner in which Dalit critique emphasized the perennial and unresolved tension *between* these two realms and focused attention on their mutual entailments. If the ambiguous relationship between religion and politics has long been a preoccupation for colonial and postcolonial history, Dalit political thinking and action upset the neat binarism between these two domains of social life by inviting attention to the political consequences of the split, and instead emphasized the relationship of supplementary opposition (and mutual constitution) that obtained between them. Such duality persists, however, and it is reflected in postcolonial efforts to resolve the caste question on two fronts: through the reform of Hinduism to produce religious equality and the institution of a legal regime to mitigate civic inequality. As I argue in later chapters, an important result of these moves has been to provoke localized anti-Dalit violence and the reenactment of ritual humiliation, which underscore the continued salience of divisions between the political and the religio-ritual domains of social experience for Dalits. My own scholarly position situates caste radicalism within discursive and institutional contexts of the colonial-modern as a distinctive form of secular criticism, which recognizes social/religious and political designations as duplicitous, misleading, and complicit with colonial knowledge. Remaining attentive to *how* such distinctions have been deployed means accepting necessary ambiguities as these categories shift and interpenetrate in politics through time. (Ironically, such critique is enabled by another intellectual trajectory associated with imperial practices, namely colonial liberalism.) Addressing the formative conditions of caste radicalism takes us away from an epistemology of caste toward the existential lifeworlds of caste subalterns, and the critique of everyday life that emerged from within the experiential domains of stigmatized selfhood. Ultimately, caste radicals' analysis of caste Hinduism as a justification for structural and transacted violence, together with their range of experiments with social practice and political forms, exposed the founding contradiction of the caste order and underscored the paradoxical centrality of the stigmatized subject to the project of freedom. It is this genealogy of Dalit emancipation (and its aftermath) that concerns me.

My focus diverges from studies of untouchable community formation that have focused on Dalit struggles for a respectable place within the Hindu order or for escape from hegemonic Hinduism through novel social and religious practices. Important recent works by Sekhar Bandyopahdhyay, Saurabh Dube, Dilip Menon, and Vijay Prashad examine how regional caste groups developed oppositional consciousness through political critique as well as forms of religiosity and self-fashioning, refusing caste stigma while imagining alternative forms of community. Menon and Prashad are keenly attentive to the Gandhian resolution of the untouchable problem as a problem of personal hygiene and unfairly degraded labor. They rightfully evaluate this as a most innovative, yet politically compromised upper-caste response to the problem of untouchability.[13] These recent works situate earlier studies—such as Mark Juergensmeyer's analysis of the thought of the Ad-Dharm movement and R. S. Khare's study of Chamar Dalit intellectuals, which took seriously the historical and political explanations of caste stigma produced by organic intellectuals—within the shifting discursive and institutional contexts of anticolonial activism.[14]

Community is a misleading rubric under which to examine changing forms of power and political subjectivity, however. Like caste, it is a putatively primordial entity resignified under colonial conditions as the enabling form, or receptacle, of an aberrant politics. The political salience of community derived from its resembling religious communities, which were invested with political recognition and juridical authority by the colonial state.[15] By the turn of the twentieth century, the transfer of localized authority from caste *panchayats* and religious bodies to homogenously defined Hindu and Muslim communities regarded as quasi-sovereign entities meant that community was both the site of embodied religious particularity and a parastate entity.[16] Hence, community cannot be backgrounded as the "context" for Dalit subject-formation, as many studies do, but must be incorporated as a simultaneous dimension of its politics. Alone among subalterns, the Mahar Dalits of western Indian conceptualized a collective exit out of colonial religion and community. Remaking the self challenged the colonial-nationalist reification of community and anticipated a new political and ethical subject, the Dalit, and a new community of Buddhism. Relating anticaste thought with Dalit activism takes us beyond a focus on critical praxis into the domain of a novel theorization of the political subject. It is precisely this imagination of a new political collectivity, contingent on the conceptualization of the Dalit subaltern as both stigmatized subject and revolutionary figure, that illuminates Dalit history as something *other* than the history of community.

Inseparable from considerations of caste and community is the Indian subaltern, usually viewed as a precapitalist subject rooted in forms of social life that became sources of oppositional consciousness. The Subaltern Studies Collective made a sustained argument for tracking the specificity of anticolonial nationalism and nation-state formation, even as it underscored the political complicities between colonial and nationalist elites. This allowed the Collective to expose nationalists' institutional reliance on colonial infrastructure, on the one hand, and to criticize nationalism's ideological dependence on culturally coded, or "traditional," forms of authoritarian power on the other. If anticolonial nationalism's difference lay in the enhanced political currency of culture and tradition, as Partha Chatterjee has argued,[17] then it has long been the contention of the Collective that a hegemonic, mainstream (Hindu) culture was conflated with the distinctive lifeworlds and aspirations of the subaltern, enabling epistemic violence and antidemocratic politics on the part of nationalist elites.[18] Thus, in as insightful an analysis as Ranajit Guha's study of insurgent peasants as revolutionary political actors, community unhistoricized is simply the locus of a traditional moral order while the subaltern appears negatively, what is left over outside the axial political equation of colonial state and elite nationalists.[19] In these accounts, the political culture of caste and the intellectual history of radical anticaste thought appear for the most part as residual rather than as intrinsic and necessary to the development of political critique.

Drawing inspiration and yet departing from such work, *The Caste Question* expands caste, community, and subaltern historiography across the religious-political and colonial-postcolonial divides and beyond its usual focus on the figure of the peasant, indigenous idioms of protest, and on a clean opposition between an anthropological conception of community and a Marxist distrust of state power. At the heart of my analysis are caste subalterns who positioned themselves at the center of debates about inequality and discrimination in India from the late colonial period, and who transformed conceptions of nation, citizenship, and political rights by working *within,* rather than outside, state institutions. Their conceptions of power, like their desire for rights, derived from colonial liberalism, yet enabled Dalits to step outside the suffocating embrace of a cultural nationalism dominated by upper-caste elites. Addressing caste radicals' understanding of caste as a distinctive form of power allows us to see how, in western India, caste radicals articulated a critique of Brahminical hegemony and religious superstition with a powerful socioeconomic evaluation of caste as a material structure of exploitation, to develop a theory that traversed the realms of the experiential, the political, the epistemological, and the ethical. Their focus on the existential aspects of caste subalternity—on questions of the caste body, violence, language, and experience—addressed matters of personhood and self-making typically elided in critiques of colonial and anticolonial thought. Analysis of caste radicals' thinking and action animates this book because it is their unique understanding of the manner in which the caste Hindu order was reproduced, coupled with vital efforts to bring into being a new political subject, that defines the trajectory of Dalit emancipation.

Writing "history from below" is a worthwhile venture in view of the scarcity of serious historical studies of Dalit life.[20] I shift away from movement-centric accounts, however, using *The Caste Question* as a provocation to rethink India's political modernity from the perspective of Dalit enfranchisement. Tracing long-term developments in the thought of radical anti-casteism that culminated in the political philosophy of B. R. Ambedkar during the interwar years allows me to illuminate distinctive aspects of the caste question and their potent translation into categories of democratic thought and practice. Subalternity itself stands to be reconceived in the process of understanding how Dalits' ideas, actions, and political interventions altered the content of caste and challenged the organizing principles of colonial liberalism and democratic processes in India.

CASTE RADICALISM: DALIT SUBJECTS AND DALIT POLITICS

A vital inaugurator of anticaste discourse was Jotirao Govindrao Phule (1827–90)—from the non-Brahmin Mali, or gardening, caste—who developed one of the earliest critiques of caste and Brahmin religious domination.[21] In a number of books, such as *Ballad of Raja Chatrapati Shivaji Bhosle* (1869), *Priestcraft Exposed* (1869), and *Slavery* (1873), he began to construct a counterhistory for the lower castes that drew heavily on the prevalent idea of an Aryan invasion to explain the millennial suppression of the *shudras* (lower castes) and *atishudras* (untouchables). Rereading Hindu mythology as a historic battle between Aryan Brahmins and Dravidian others, Phule endowed elements of popular culture with a radical caste consciousness, connecting economic, social, and political domination to the outcome of a race war. His story revolved around the defeat of Dravidian Kshatriyas (warriors), who constituted the *bahujan samaj* (majority community) through the trickery of Aryan Brahmins. Indeed, Phule's rewritten history of caste conflict and his sustained offensive against the inhuman and inegalitarian caste order became political common sense.

Undergirding this meaningful alternative history was Phule's use of slavery as concept-metaphor for the complex structure of exploitation organized around embodied difference. Published in 1873, his book, *Gulamgiri (Slavery)* was inspired by radical freethinkers such as Tom Paine and the ideas of Protestant Nonconformism. Phule invoked the exemplary structure of modern unfreedom, Atlantic world slavery, to reframe caste relations in idioms of exploitation and inequality rather than religious order. Because the caste subaltern, like the slave, was defined by the historical experience of oppression and exploitation, recovery of the lower-caste self was intimately connected to a critique of caste power. This was a key strategy that allowed caste radicals to resignify caste subjugation as a process of subject-formation by transposing political antagonism from social space onto the plane of mytho-historical time.

Caste radicals generally understood the religious and the political aspects of caste as formally differentiated, but systemically interdependent and mutually constitutive. For them, history and politics, the past and the future, were conjoint in the rewriting of history as the work of imagining the caste subaltern as a revolutionary political subject. As a social movement, however, caste radicalism was contingent and conjunctural, a product of encounters between the critical intellectual traditions of anticaste thought and the institutions and infrastructure of colonial society. Missionary discourse and colonial institutions, as well as new ideas and experiences of civic space and public property, empowered Dalit and lower-caste struggles. New educational opportunities, urban migration shaping new contexts of life and labor, a distinctive public sphere of print and performance, and a colonial legal order accommodating debates about of public equality all contributed to Dalits' newfound ability to demand civic and political rights regardless of the traditional rules governing caste segregation. Simultaneously, caste radicals also developed a nuanced understanding of how colonial policies deepened caste distinctions. The new Brahmin, for instance, was seen as a product of colonial bureaucracy, his sacerdotal position enhanced by secular positioning. Phule's critique—and that of anticaste polemics and activism more generally—focused not only on the ideology of Brahminism, but on the overrepresentation of the Brahmin minority in educational and bureaucratic contexts.

Caste-radical thought was forged around a critique of Brahminism as

a historically located ideology that justified caste power in all its manifestations—religious, sociopolitical, and economic, as Rosalind O'Hanlon's important work on Phule's thought attests.[22] I add to this scholarship a perspective on how Dalit and lower-caste subject-formation relates
to colonial and anticolonial thought and politics. Around the turn of the
twentieth century, Dalits in Bombay and the Central Provinces, led by
members of the Mahar caste, began organizing to demand civil and political rights and recognition as Hindus. They gradually enlarged their
target from caste Hinduism to colonial classification and mainstream nationalism, especially the upper-caste bias of the Congress. Partha Chatterjee has clarified the way in which anticolonial nationalism positively
valued those forms of spiritual and cultural life derided by British colo-
nizers.[23] Instead, I draw attention to the conflation of spirituality with
the practices of upper-caste Hindus and its (re)deployment as public discourse. Caste radicals specifically politicized this aspect of nationalism
by arguing that caste inequality was reproduced through practices that
straddled spiritual and material domains. Beginning with Phule, they
framed caste hierarchy as a form of exclusion and inequality and, by the
1920s, translated it into terms such as "public exclusion," "segregation,"
and "civic disability"—secularized terms with expanded political range.
Indeed Dalit and anticaste activists challenged the terms of religious *and*
political inclusion and telegraphed the inadequacy of either a reformed
Hinduism or the enumerative solution of colonial liberalism, with its focus on primordial community. In this way, Dalit critics made rights claims,
even as they sought to extend the range and signification of a "right" to
include forms of life without prior political visibility.

In contrast to earlier anticaste struggles, the Dalit-led movement during the interwar years pressed not only for separate political rights but
also for conversion out of Hinduism. Dalit conversion made sense for a
community whose history, since Phule, was written as the narrative of historical antagonism between Brahmins and first peoples, or between Aryan
and Dravidian races for whom emancipation could only happen *outside*
forms of identity produced by Hindu society. Imagined simultaneously
along two distinct registers—political minority and socioreligious *non-
Hindu*—Dalit identity combined seemingly incompatible modes of experience. Yet the complex nature of caste inequality meant that political
emancipation required religious conversion, and that conversion could not
be rendered salient without civic and political protections. Equally important, individual freedom was contingent on collective emancipation.
"Dalit" came to name an identity and a community, most importantly an

imagined community outside Hinduism—and outside religion itself—
as a strategy of political emancipation.

This political posture matured in the interwar years, when B. R. Ambedkar, the Dalit movement's most significant thinker and national political leader, reconceived Dalit activism in terms of democratic thought
and action, and positioned Dalit disenfranchisement as a complex, experiential structure of oppression, exploitation, and dehumanization. At
his death on December 6, 1956, Ambedkar left behind a rich legacy as
a political thinker and Dalit activist who nationalized the Dalit question
more effectively than any other leader; as a scholar, commentator, and
modernizer of Hindu law; and as the architect of India's Constitution.
Ambedkar's centrality to popular history and academic scholarship
poses unique challenges for the historian-anthropologist, however. Insofar as Ambedkar has an important place in popular memory, there is
a fierce investment in tracking his life and his movement through highly
valued written records, archival sources, and documentation that suggests extra-Dalit significance. Dalit intellectuals—few are professional academics, most write exclusively in Marathi—have assiduously collected,
recorded, and produced accounts of the Dalit past. If they have played
a central role in producing a Dalit past, it is very often a past oriented
toward a personal and political *telos*. Scholars have tended to reproduce
the personality and community-centric content of these narratives. Or they
have positioned Dalit history along caste/class or Buddhist/Marxist bi-
narisms, taking as objective fact debates and divisions that structure
polemical positions. Thus, in my view, popular histories tell us much about
the existential axes of Dalit subject-formation and about how the figure
of Ambedkar has been constructed as totemic of the Dalit past and future. Ambedkar is iconic of Dalit struggle and symptomatic of the social
field and ideological forces that enabled Dalit political visibility at a
particular historical conjuncture. My interest is to critically assess the
contradictions and paradoxical outcomes of an emergent theory of the
political subject connected to cultural history and to political action.

Simply put, Ambekar provided the set of political idioms that most
effectively converted the negative identity of the untouchable into the political potentiality and historical agency of the Dalit. Ambedkar first used
the term *dalit* in his journal, *Bahishkrit Bharat* (Outcaste India), in 1928,
where he characterized being Dalit as the experience of deprivation,
marginalization, and stigmatization.[24] "Dalit" indexed both subject of
suffering and revolutionary agent, and it was posed against "Harijan"
(people of god) or "Hari," first used by M. K. Gandhi in 1933 to describe

"men of God abandoned by society," a term abhorred by many Dalits for its paternalism.[25] Indeed, the politics of naming is deeply consequential for the politics of recognition. If names are also "claims to certain identities, properties, or entitlement," it is through the "reiterative process of naming" that those identities become fixed and meaningful in the first place.[26] The politics of naming thus secures new relationships between words and bodies, between ways of being and ways of seeing and speaking within the social field.[27] In this case, the politics of the name also reflects a deeper paradox of Dalit politics that derives from the fact that the term "Dalit" is both analytic and prescriptive: *it defines the historical structures and practices of dispossession that experientially mark someone as Dalit and simultaneously identifies the Dalit as someone seeking to escape those same structures.* In other words, the name indexes an analysis of caste inequality and the terms of resistance that can augur its annihilation.

Far from naming a consummated subject, then, "Dalit" signifies a process of becoming and a community-in-the-making: these are difficult horizons of potentiality. History from the perspective of the Dalit subaltern anticipates and overturns a powerful Dumontian paradigm for understanding untouchability as the *negative* axis of the caste order. As untouchability is the constitutive outside to the ranked social relations and symbolic transactions that define the practice of "caste," the untouchable is dialectically related and diametrically opposed to the ritually pure Brahmin, the common object of revulsion from whom all "touchable" castes derive their identities. The Dalit history I recount here reveals a sophisticated attempt to make historic suffering and humiliation central to Dalit identity in a way that converts this structural negativity into positive political content. By infusing a negative identity with positive or revolutionary potential, caste radicals—including Ambedkar—looked to end historic discrimination and suffering. This is why, unlike the peasant subaltern, the Dalit could become a figure of the future, necessarily disconnected from prior community and existing practices that reproduced historic humiliation. This decisive move toward what we might call a revalued or positive negativity, which Ambedkar articulated most powerfully, produced an inbuilt tension in Dalit identity that, when activated on constitutional and political fields, has had important consequences. Briefly put, discourses of state protection and the legislation of Dalit vulnerability resymbolized Dalit identity around the axis of political violence.

It is important to note that while Ambedkar maintained continuity with most traditions of radical anti-casteism, his genealogy of the Dalit rejected the biological/racial distinction between Aryan and Dravidian that distinguished Phule's vision of the non-Brahmin Dalit, though Ambedkar maintained that sociopolitical conflict between Dalit and Brahmin was the structuring antagonism of Indian history. And though Ambedkar addressed the experiential dimensions of untouchability, he also exceeded them by converting a Dalit problematic into an inquiry into the nature of social relations and political ethics. He did so through a sustained engagement with liberal thought and democratic discourse to position the Dalit as a unique cultural and political subject of historic suffering. His caste radicalism took shape at a time when the political language of equality, freedom, and historical agency—legacies of colonization—presented political opportunities and new strategies with which to challenge marginalization. My contention is that the historical conjunction of Dalit political thought, language, and activism, together with the changing character of the late colonial state, influenced the career of India's political modernity. The twentieth-century course of Dalit political recognition and enfranchisement explored in *The Caste Question* illuminates how Dalit struggles to address the distinctive inequities of caste simultaneously, and necessarily, expanded the historical provenance and discursive range of democratic liberalism.

QUESTIONS OF DEMOCRACY, MINORITY, AND VIOLENCE

Examining how untouchables become Dalit reveals a surprisingly productive alliance between caste, liberal institutions, and democratic ideals. Against the grain of a tradition that takes caste and democracy as antithetical,[28] my examination of Dalit emancipation tracks the relationship between the political enfranchisement of stigmatized subjects and India's political modernity, between the Dalit and democracy. As the experience of stigmatized existence intersected with ideas of democratic equality, caste was secularized through a sustained problematization of the religious/political divide. This meant neither that caste became completely political, nor that models of equality for a bourgeois subject of freedom adequately addressed Dalit enfranchisement. But it did mean that, ultimately, liberal forms such as constituency and minority became means through which Dalits imagined community and pursued equality.

Dalits' incremental, regional struggles for civic and political rights through the early twentieth century matured on a national stage in the interwar years. There were key developments in this period: a shift in the political economy of empire; distinctions between "white" Dominion colonies and nonwhite imperial possessions; the emergence of the United States as a counter to British hegemony; experimentation with interme-diate forms of political organization between empire and nation; and finally, challenges to the legitimacy of empire as a political form by al-liances of colonized peoples. Most importantly, the period reflected a re-newed focus on, and redefinition of, "the political."

World War I provided an opening for Indians, like Britain's other col-onized subjects, to press for limited political representation in return for their participation in the war effort. The gap between liberal ideologies of progress and improvement and illiberal government practices became the target of critique, and the focus for new modalities of political ac-tivism and mass protest. The British responded by devolving power to the natives in stages.

Lord Ripon's 1882 Resolution on Local Self-Government made pro-vision for the inclusion of a few elected members in municipal commit-tees and proposed the establishment of rural local boards. An advocate of Gladstonian liberalism, Lord Ripon, who was viceroy from 1880 to 1884, saw limited self-government as "an instrument of political and pop-ular education" and encouraged the expansion of self-government from locality to provincial and central legislatures.[29] Unlike Ripon, John Mor-ley and Lord Minto entertained no illusion of democratization. The Morley-Minto reforms of 1909 entrenched dyarchy as a system of con-stitutional autocracy whereby the "natural leaders" of India's multiple religious and caste communities would be trained in self-governance.[30] British officials maintained control over revenue and taxation, army and police, while elites received a limited franchise and some provincial au-thority over education, health, agriculture, and local governing bodies. Without administrative funds, however, native representatives faced ac-cusations of corruption and nepotism that the British then attributed to the "Indianization" of politics. Dyarchy brought no substantive political change to the exercise of autocratic power. The confrontation between nationalist demands for expanded political representation and the colonial government's racialized dyarchy instead emphasized limits to colonial democratization and produced a charged field of constitutional politics. Under pressure from nationalists, the government established the South-borough (1918) and Simon (1928) commissions to consider the terms of native franchise and the functioning of dyarchy. Constitutional reforms led to the Government of India Act of 1919. A revised Government of India Act of 1935 rejected Indians' demand for Dominion status, created a federation of British India and the Princely States to dilute the political strength of the Congress, and was colonial India's first constitution. These political experiments were deeply compromised by racial practices of rule and by the reproduction of traditional authority by the colonial state.

Throughout this period, enfranchisement was illusory, "a semantic sleight" as Ranajit Guha has observed, "used to dignify measures for imperial control over the subcontinent by a spurious parallelism with the radical constitutional initiatives of nineteenth-century revolutions."[31] If democratic institutions came slowly to the subcontinent, ideas of equality and individual rights introduced by British forms nevertheless became a recognizable political rhetoric and a formalized political ideology. In positing noncongruence between colonial policy and democratic ideology, I take inspiration from scholars of postemancipation societies who have powerfully argued for a distinctive *colonial genealogy of rights*, for example, the arguments of C. L. R. James in his powerful classic, *The Black Jacobins,* that Haitian revolutionaries redefined the Declaration of the Rights of Man as a founding document of *racial equality.*[32] Such contingent, conjunctural demands—whether by caste radicals or by the enslaved—have lasting effect: they expand the repertoire of rights claims even as they situate them within particular sociohistorical contexts of inequality and exploitation.

A genealogy of democracy, then, incorporates multiple instances where discourses of democracy and equality confront diverse forms of difference and are called upon to ameliorate contingent instantiations of inequality. If race constituted the form of embodied difference that exposed the constitutive paradoxes of republican thought in the late eighteenth century, then in colonial India in the early twentieth century, the problem of caste minority exposed the fundamental authoritarianism of colonial rule, as well as anticolonial nationalism's complicity with colonialism's culturalization of the state.

Examining minority as a political form in the interwar period extends and challenges prevailing analyses. Scholars associated with the Cambridge School have played a significant role in historicizing the colonial state by drawing attention to the expansion of its infrastructural and administrative complex, the restructuring of India's colonial economy, and the entry of Indian elites into politics proper.[33] They associate the interwar period with the simultaneous retreat of the (colonial) state and an indigenization (and regionalization) of political power that made elites mimic men, mere political conduits between center and region. While this sheds light on the extension of state power into new domains of native life, it portrays native elites as power brokers jockeying to convert status into interest and runs the risk of positing envy and self-interest as adequate representations of historical agency. By mistaking effect for cause, therefore, such political sociology renders historical explanation subservient to empiricism and economism.

It is more helpful to consider Dalit interwar politics in the context of a shift in colonial governmentality. "Governmentality," Michel Foucault's word for the combined and uneven powers exercised from above together with dispersed, capillary forms of power exercised by subjects through self-regulation, is a concept-metaphor useful for attending to changing permutations of sovereign and rationalizing power.[34] From this perspective, the state itself appears as a complex, internally fissured entity ruling through ideology as well as coercive power or, in Philip Abrams excellent formulation, as an effect of overlapping practices of power rather than a unitary object.[35] Colonial governmentality is that mix of autocratic and infrastructural power that worked, initially, by politicizing the domain of culture. Culture constituted a form of civic disability even as it enabled, in Partha Chatterjee's words, "the rule of colonial difference."[36] Historicizing colonial governmentality makes it clear, however, that there are significant differences between a late nineteenth-century version characterized by the culturalization of politics and enumerative technologies such as the census, and a twentieth-century phase organized around the political technology of the franchise and procedures of representative government. The colonial politics of minority is an exemplary case for considering how the politics of commensuration transformed colonial liberalism.

The political theorist Ernesto Laclau has described democracy as an exercise in political commensuration that produces equivalence between unlike persons, objects, or qualities. Thus the presumed equality of citizens is the product of strategies of equalization and comparison. The tension inherent in commensuration is most apparent in demands by minorities for recognition *on their own terms* as the precondition to substantive equality.[37] This is the case where politically "inadequate" subjects such as untouchables seek to become citizens. Because the ground of their inadequacy is taken to be non- or prepolitical difference—whether sexual, religious, racial, or cultural—it must be *rendered* politically consequential. Here, because particularity is the basis of political recognition, such claims are precarious and reiterative. This was certainly the case for India's Dalits. From the early twentieth century, the Indian National Congress had dominated the political-moral space of nationalist thinking

and political action, complementing many critiques of colonial oppression with the pursuit of power in a national state. Regionally, by 1930,
the Congress in Bombay was dominated by non-Brahmins, including key
activists of the anticaste and non-Brahmin movement. The rural base of
non-Brahminism was thus incorporated into the Congress. It is at this
conjuncture, and against the closures in nationalist thought, that minority
status became a focal point around which Ambedkar attempted to articulate the specificity of Dalit as a distinctive community, a constituency.
Dalit equality and enfranchisement increasingly came to be associated
with their difference from, rather than similarity to, other communities.

Within the colonial framework that mapped community and constituency onto religious identity, Muslims were India's modal political
minority. The enumerative principle of weightage, first accepted for the
Muslim separate electorate in 1909, was introduced to acknowledge their
"historic and political importance" and to compensate them for future
demographic changes.[38] Simultaneously, caste Hindus discovered an interest in claiming untouchables as Hindus, especially after the 1908 census, when colonial officials began to emphasize untouchables' separate
identity. In 1911, untouchables became "Depressed Classes," a term that
described persons suffering ritual exclusion and stigmatization as "lesser
Hindus." Initially, colonial officials used the politics of number and quota
to argue that untouchables were extraneous to a demographically defined
national Hindu majority. From 1919, the Indian National Congress
worked against these efforts by arguing that the community of Hindus
included the stigmatized untouchables. Yet colonial categorization facilitated Dalits' self-identification as a discriminated community; their
move toward formal political demands for rights reflected awareness of
the constraints and possibilities of liberal institutional logic. If during the
1920s Ambedkar struggled to bring visibility to the Depressed Classes
through the demand for adult franchise and protection, by 1932 he would
defend his position that they constituted a socially vulnerable and separate political minority.[39] Earlier forms of activist mobilization, such as
regional temple entry *satyagrahas* (lit., "struggle for truth"; here, peaceful mass mobilization challenging the status quo, whether colonial policy or, in this case, Hindu exclusion), reached closure as Ambedkar led
activism toward new demands for juridical rights for a historically exceptional and ethically normative community.

The British Communal Award of August 16, 1932, allowed the Depressed Classes a double vote, one for their own candidates wherever
these voters predominated and another vote in the general (Hindu) elec-

torate.[40] Here, colonial sociology amplified the paradoxical nature of minoritarian claims: Dalits' collective status as a stigmatized community within Hinduism was the basis for recognizing them as a separate entity. Indeed this period, which culminated in India's first constitution, the Government of India Act of 1935, saw sustained action by Dalits and Muslims to establish political identities through new arrangements of power.[41] Electoral politics became an arena for performing minority social and political interests, with the franchise conceived as a technology of political self-fashioning.[42] There was one significant difference between the identity of Muslims as minorities (which enabled subsequent claims to separate nationality) and the impossible task that Dalit emancipation set for itself: to maintain historical antagonism to hegemonic Hinduism—rather than a claim to absolute religio-cultural difference—as the grounds for Dalit claims to minority recognition. Colonial knowledge formation amplified the paradoxical nature of Dalit demands, for it was Dalits' collective status as a stigmatized community within corporate Hinduism—itself a reified category and the product of colonial intervention—which enabled claims to separate entity.

Here, it is helpful to examine how the colonial constitution of "minority" differed from theoretical constructs in the classical literature. Indeed *The Caste Question* is a provocation to contrast Dalit emancipation against the classic problem of minority as articulated, for example, by Karl Marx in "On the Jewish Question."[43] In that text, Marx stages the internal tensions of liberal thought by emphasizing the troubled dependence of the citizen, a figure of political universality, on forms of embodied particularism. Minority is thus a political form that exposes the internal tensions of liberal thought, and the mechanism by which liberalism incorporates difference. Minority is a mediating term between civil society and state that converts religious distinction into political lack. As Marx presciently argues, it is the secularization of religion that makes religious difference politically consequential. By asserting that minority is "the political manner of emancipating oneself from religion," Marx prescribes freedom *from* religion as the first step toward a human emancipation, with liberal distinctions between religion and politics mirroring the material contradictions that anchored the liberal state form.

For Marx, it was necessary to annihilate (religious) particularism by transcending embodied difference and to move toward a new universality. In colonial India, however, religious difference was the ground of inclusion and exclusion, immanent rather than extraneous to the political field. In a political sphere permeated by "prejudice" (Marx's term for nonpolitical difference), caste radicals saw that it was through the exacerbation of difference *within* religion, and not its transcendence, that Dalits could realize political selfhood. For Dalits, individual freedom was contingent on the emancipation of the community, rather than separation from it. Since individual freedom was contingent on the emancipation of the community from caste stigma, and not on a separation from community as in the liberal narrative of freedom, Dalits identified themselves as a community of suffering and as a special kind of political minority negatively defined as *non-Hindus* in antagonistic relation to the Hindu order. A negative identity became the basis of collective political rights and also converted the democratic political field into a space of agonistic combat.

Ambedkar's activism and political thought together played a crucial role in making a negative identity the basis of substantive rights claims. His critical engagement with, and creative transformation of, liberal democratic norms and practices produced new idioms for untouchability as a form of historic discrimination and enabled experimentation with a range of ameliorative measures. Insofar as caste did not map along a single axis of conflict and contradiction, and because untouchability was manifest through the complex articulation of religious, economic, and social forms, caste radicalism redefined the caste order as a form of historical violence and inequality. In turn, Ambedkar imagined the Dalit as a vulnerable and violated subject lacking political worth, whose entry into full humanity required two specific modes of redress: political adequation (or equalization) and recognition of cultural exception. Caste discrimination required a rewritten history of the Dalit and redress through modern political measures, such as the franchise and a constitutionally mandated regime of affirmative action.

By the end of the 1930s, Muslims had begun to shed their minority status and demand recognition as a separate and distinctive nationality. During the same period, Ambedkar posited Dalits as subjects of suffering defined by a permanent antagonism to the caste Hindu order. They required: (1) a political resolution to the problem of religious exclusion through a separate electorate for Dalits as non-Hindus; (2) a religious resolution to political inequality by conversion out of the Hindu fold; and (3) a constitutional resolution recognizing Dalit disenfranchisement and making the abolition of untouchability central to Indian civil rights. Indian society and politics would be democratized through caste, with constitutional measures placing Dalits at the center of an emergent civil rights regime. Ensuing legislation included a new juridical category, the "caste atrocity," to apprehend and prevent anti-Dalit violence.

As a consequence, Dalits' enfranchisement bound them to state structures and bureaucratic mechanisms, entrenching debates and policies on
caste deep within the postcolonial state. However, both popular ha-
giography and scholarly accounts of untouchable community formation
scant the discursive centrality of untouchability to the development of a
range of political initiatives, from the establishment of a separate electorate to the Indian Constitution. This book exposes the constitutive relationship between untouchability and democratic ideas in India, and argues that their relation mirrors the centrality of slavery to the elaboration
of capitalist regimes and to the development of ideologies of freedom and
equality in the Atlantic World. In particular, I examine the role of legislation, especially reservations policy, in equalizing Dalits' social status
and explore how the Indian state has played a critical role in practicing
a kind of restitutive justice that has made exceptional subjects rhetorically indispensable to constitutional policy and debate.

Unlike remedial civil rights regimes in the West, which are perceived
as special, intentionally temporary and ostentatious state interventions
into civil society, exceptionalism is written into the Indian Constitution
to protect vulnerable subjects. Addressing the Constitution as a historical and cultural text clarifies why Dalits are legally encoded as exceptional subjects, and how legal exception functions as a form of political inclusion. Such a reading strategy can indicate how the Constitution
came to function as a restitutive measure for colonial underdevelopment
through the far-reaching transformation of Indian society. On the other
hand, it also positions constitutionally mandated civil rights policies as
a critical node in contemporary transformations of the social relations
of caste. Utimately, the redefinition of untouchability via constitutional
policy and legislative action transformed relations between Dalits, caste
Hindus, and the state in postindependence India. Once a form of social
experience identified with tradition, religion, and stigmatized labor, Dalit
identity was redefined as a form of vulnerability that constituted the
grounds for political recognition. Indeed this was a paradoxical outcome
of minoritarian enfranchisement: *the civil rights regime produced not
the emancipated citizen but the vulnerable subject (at risk of conjunctural violence)*. Affirmative action policies and protective legislation recognized caste discrimination and anti-Dalit violence as social harms, but
they also restricted identity by classifying Dalits as vulnerable subjects
at risk of injury.

The paradoxical exacerbation of identification around injury and vulnerability as a symptom of the emancipation of cultural and political mi-

norities alters assumptions about the politics of recognition. Instead of achieving purely political status Dalit identity balances between a purely relational and historical identity and a more essentialist or embodied one. By forefronting what Dorothy Ko calls the "stubbornness of bodies"— forms of embodiment and experiences of stigmatization that require a range of political interventions—Indian democratic processes highlight the incomplete politicization of caste.[44] In part, Dalit politics operates through a dynamic where stigma, constantly repeated, enables new sets of claims. As I noted earlier, the fact of stigmatized existence secures the ground of political struggle even while politics anticipates its disappearance. This supplementing of the Dalit's political body with something outside politics and history—the natural body, religion, culture—suggests why Dalit and state efforts at political commensuration consistently reengage the social degradation and nonrecognition Dalits experience at the edge of the Hindu social order. This is the point of failure for commensuration and the limit case of the Indian political. This limit on the full politicization of stigmatized existence suggests not the cessation, but the permanence of politics. The "anthropological limits of the political" are marked by forms of excess and insufficiency that must constantly be brought into the field of political commensuration.[45] Thus the political field is constantly made and unmade in response to external constraints and conditions outside the field of politics. Just as the symbolization of cultural practices and social forms identified with Dalit life is an ongoing process, so too are attempts to symbolically annihilate Dalits' identity through political violence an indicator of the reconstitution of caste sociality.

Changing forms of Dalit politics and more general shifts in discourse and policy around caste and untouchability distinguish the Indian resolution of minority: this is characterized by an exacerbation of difference in order to obviate it. The legislative invention of the "caste atrocity" as a special category of crime in order to identify and thereby thwart anti-Dalit violence; the growing power of Dalits in electoral politics; and, from the 1950s, the emergent cultures of Dalit protest, including religious response to the caste question through Buddhist conversion—all have become compelling if contradictory aspects of Dalit emancipation. They have also provoked new ways to stigmatize Dalit bodies through physical and symbolic violence. The constant reiteration of difference balances Dalits between a purely historical, relational identity and an essentialist one. The tension within an identity doubly derived from stigmatized essence and state classification is a structuring aspect of Dalit existence that unavoidably complicates schemes for redress and restitution. Dalit, like blackness, appears as the experience of suffering and exclusion for which, despite requisite political restitution, there can never be adequate compensation. Dalit militancy around this ambivalent identity has also incited newly ritualized structures of anti-Dalit violence. Modes of political recognition dependent on identification with Dalitness as a form of life have also enabled new practices of violation.

The "Dalit question" has long been organized around the stigmatized body as historical and present object of suffering. What distinguishes Dalits is their millennial, religious stigma and the unique dilemma untouchability poses to the state. While the underlying force of Dalit identity has been a critique of the dehumanization of bodies labeled "Dalit" and deemed incommensurable with caste Hindu bodies, we also see that postindependence idioms and practices designed to redress stigmatized, embodied experience are part of an infrastructure that makes Dalit suffering appear timeless and historically specific at once. Dalits continue to be burdened by a historical susceptibility to violence and marginalization despite the legal frameworks constructed to protect them. The coexistence of the subject of rights and the violated subject is replicated in formal and informal politics by efforts to redress historic injuries through corresponding structures of material and symbolic reparation. Thus a crucial phase in the *becoming Dalit* of the "untouchable" now involves the paradoxical co-constitution of recognition and violence, and the politicization of violence.

Instead of a triumphalist emancipation story, then, *The Caste Question* traces the contemporary implications of identifying Dalits as minority subjects burdened by historic vulnerability. In attending to the ways in which postindependence politics perpetuates violence against Dalits and reproduces suffering bodies, this alternative history of Dalit identity sheds critical light on the historical field of Indian democracy as a political form distinguished not by the elimination of caste discrimination, but by its implication in new forms of violence and the emergence of new means of regulating the caste order. The civil rights regime, the constitutional classification of the Dalit, and the creation of the juridical category of "caste atrocity" together comprise a set of bureaucratic measures to define and protect exceptional subjects. Ironically, they reproduce vulnerability as the condition of possibility for continued protection and legal recognition.

Caste violence must be distinguished from studies of collective violence in South Asia, for example, the anti-Sikh riots, Sinhala-Tamil conflict, and Hindu-Muslim conflict.[46] Instead, the acceleration of violent sociality and its proximity to postcolonial lawmaking I discuss resemble processes of identity formation that Jean and John Comaroff eloquently describe for contemporary South Africa. There, the legislated visibility of African lifeworlds has renewed the "standoff between liberal universalism and the pragmatics of difference" and has provoked intense attachment to ritual-archaic forms (witchcraft in their case), as the result of a specifically postcolonial politics of multiculturalism. In South Africa, moving problematic practices from criminal to civil courts has been a way to counterpose cultural alterity to liberal reason. Instead, we see the aggressive criminalization of untouchability in postcolonial India. While each constitutes a structurally distinctive mode of engaging difference, they are symptomatic of new relationships between the postcolonial state and its citizens. The Comaroffs' argument about the co-constitution of political violence and cultural forms productively echoes my understanding of the accelerated symbolization of caste violence.[47] Caste violence spans a range of acts that reproduce caste stigma: spatial segregation; technologies of the body from rules governing physical proximity to the comportment of the physical body and its appearance; sexual violation; the use of insults and epithets demeaning caste labor and the caste body; caste massacres. When it erupts as spectacular violence, caste violence coalesces around symbols of Dalit militancy and signs of Dalits' sociopolitical advancement.[48] Anti-Dalit violence is anticipated, named, described, and is a specific focus of governmental intervention. The praxis of caste radicalism was distinguished by efforts to theorize *the violence of caste* from the perspective of an embodied subalternity. Today, caste violence is a ritualized form of political violence that stages the Dalit as an exceptional subject.

By joining community formation, political formation, and subject-formation, I hope to encourage consideration of caste/untouchability as both political category and perceptual field. Because the emergence of the Dalit as a political subject has altered the social field and political practice of caste, the deeper ethical force of Dalit history and politics derives from continually highlighting the tension between culture and politics, the religious and the political, and its consequences for persons and bodies named Dalit.

FRAMEWORK AND METHODOLOGY

"Dalit studies" is a recognizable field of inquiry today. This is due to the growing presence in the Indian academy of self-identified intellectuals from the Dalit and non-Brahmin communities who emphasize the continued relevance of caste as a form of inherited privilege and challenge its erasure in debates about social justice, economic redistribution, and electoral politics. Their effect in shaping conversations about the continued if transformed presence of caste in public life has been profound.[49] Beyond the academy, conjunctures in culture, politics, and economy have renewed a focus on Dalit culture and political assertion that compels us to rethink the historical anthropology of caste. A presentist orientation—gauging critical practice and intellectual production in terms of contemporary relevance—must be distinguished, however, from a history of the present or historical ontology, phrases Michel Foucault used to describe the refracted relevance of texts, objects, words, and persons across time. I believe that a history of the present can chart the afterlives of discourses and practices, their peculiar and unexpected hauntings, and their contingent transformations. It is in this spirit that I address the discursive context and the sociopolitical field in which contemporary debates about caste are situated.

My interest in the contiguity between Dalits' long-term struggles for rights and social recognition and their continued vulnerability to physical and symbolic violation requires some combination of ethnographic and historical methods, for I seek to historicize the symbolic forms of life defined by the term "untouchability" and to approach democracy and political citizenship as cultural categories. If anthropology examines culture as symbolic constellations significant for people in their daily lives, history addresses their formation and transformation. Historical anthropology thus explores the supplemental relationship between genealogy and archeology, methods that privilege form and depth, respectively. Historical anthropology is not primarily about synthesizing archival research and participant observation to comprehensively analyze social reality. It is a critical practice that considers how disciplines such as anthropology and history construct their objects of knowledge within fields of power. The supplemental relation between culture and history is discernible in the very words "culture" and "time." Taken to identify the keywords of two disciplines, they turn out to be terms that assume, require, and replace each other, their instability revealed when we examine, say, the cultural construction of time or the historicity of the culture concept. This "supplementarity" signals the openness of dialectical structures and the provisional nature of syntheses.[50] As a critical strategy, historical anthropology can defamiliarize objects and idioms of analysis, inserting them into new frames of reference and creating novel semiotic connections. It is this set of intellectual moves that has allowed me to stage the paradoxical centrality of the Dalit to Indian democracy.

IN MAHARASHTRA

North and east India have been the focus of much South Asia scholarship. My research moves attention toward the west where a nineteenth-century tradition of caste radicalism provided fertile ground for the development of Dalit critique. Over the course of two and a half years of research between 1996 and 2004, I talked with people and worked in the state archives of Maharashtra; in the archives of the police and both district and high courts; at the India Office Library; and in four private libraries and collections. This experience helped me see how caste radicals adopted the vernacular, Marathi, as their main language for an entire corpus of texts such as ballads, mythic histories, plays, pamphlets, memoirs and autobiography, as well as journalism that was crucial to a counterculture that sustained a public critique of caste oppression. My regional focus and unique archival sources affected how I perceived the field of inquiry, and underscored my appreciation of contingent historical practices and developments that have received limited attention. They also guided the arguments this book advances.

The state of Maharashtra, formed in 1960, unified the Marathi-speaking regions of what had earlier been the Bombay Presidency, the Central Provinces and Berar (or the Vidarbha region), and the Marathwada region of the former parts of the Hyderabad state. Its 118,717 square miles include a 300-mile coastal strip between the Sahyadri Mountains and the Arabian Sea, an area of wet-rice and garden cultivation, small landholdings, and a greater degree of landlessness than the Deccan, the large lava plateau east of the mountains. Marathi, the language most commonly spoken in various dialectal forms across Maharashtra, is categorized as Indo-Aryan but has Dravidian elements. In terms of rules and structures of marriage and kinship, the region is characterized as Dravidian, predominantly featuring forms of cross-cousin marriage.[51] Maharashtra thus is a bridge area of cultural mixing between north and south, organized around the geopolitical region of the Deccan. The "idea" of Maharashtra managed to unite diverse sections of society divided by political ideology and divergent interpretations of the past around a shared pool of core symbols for Maharashtrian uniqueness, especially the figure of Shivaji, who asserted autonomy from the Mughal center,[52] headed the Maratha polity at its apogee, and was coronated as *Chatrapathi,* or lord of the royal canopy, in 1674.[53] Also supporting historic claims to a common regional identity were exclusionary idioms, especially anti-Muslim ones drawing on recurrent tropes of Maratha valor resisting the Mughals.

Indeed, an unlikely populism of class and caste emerged in the immediate postindependence period amid long-standing cultural and political tensions, especially between Brahmins and non-Brahmins, which transferred to struggles over ideology and leadership in political parties from the Indian National Congress to the Communists.

Central to the politics of identity in this region, as we will see in the following chapter, is the category of Maratha-*kunbis*, or soldier-farmers, who were central to the emergence of political non-Brahminism across the nineteenth and twentieth centuries, and the charged (and often conflictual) relationship between political non-Brahminism and an emergent Dalit movement dominated by the Mahar community.

Mahars, 9 percent of the population, are by far the most numerous Dalit group in the region. Unlike other untouchable communities, which tend to be localized, they are to be found in every district, from forming 5 percent of the coastal population to almost 20 percent in the east. Mahars consider themselves superior to Mangs and inferior to Chambhars, who do not hold the ritually inferior position in Maharashtra that they do in northern India. Mahars' distinctive use of a stick marked them as *kathivale* (those who carried a kathi, or staff), as did use of the greeting *johar,* accompanied by suitable deformation of the body and maintenance of physical distance from caste Hindus; the suffix *nak* on the first name did the same, indicating the Mahars' military past as watchmen and soldiers of the Maratha polity. An inherited *balutedar* (village servant) position entitled its Mahar holder to a fixed amount of land known as the *vatan* and dozens of rights to such things as cattle hides, the clothes of corpses, left-over food, and various ritually degraded "gifts." Mahars were inferior village servants, watchmen, and messengers who arbitrated border disputes, tracked thieves, performed burial-ground duties, and removed cattle carcasses. They also lit the first fire at the Holi festival and kept the shrine and palanquin of Mariai, the goddess of smallpox.[54] Under the British, Mahars served in the British Army until racial typologies and martial race ideology provoked army reorganization in the aftermath of the 1857 Mutiny, leading to Mahars (and Chambhars) being pensioned off and retrenched from military service by 1892. In the aftermath of military exclusion, Mahars, many with English education and lacking a defined occupational niche in the village economy, migrated to urban areas such as Nagpur and Bombay, where they formed a significant constituency of cotton-mill laborers, railway workers, and sanitation and dock laborers in the early twentieth century.[55]

The sociopolitical transformations induced by colonial modernity shaped the two major caste movements that overtook the region during the late nineteenth and early twentieth centuries. Both responded, in part, to the hegemony of a very small Brahmin population, which was consolidated in the eighteenth century, when state intervention hardened caste practices and prohibitions, particularly those controlling women and regulating caste purity.[56] This was preceded by the cultural and political dominance of the Chitpavan Brahmins, who displaced the then-dominant Deshastha Brahmins to create the seventeenth-century Peshwai, a Brahminical state.[57] Brahmins' ritual power was in constant tension with fluid processes of caste and class formation in the Deccan from the sixteenth to the nineteenth centuries, which provided openings for itinerant, nomadic and low-caste communities to become a part of the Maratha patrimonial state. A combination of the Brahmin's symbolic centrality and the social mobility afforded by the military-agrarian order produced repeated challenges to Brahmin hegemony across the nineteenth and twentieth centuries. By then, memories of Brahmin political dominance together with their predominance in the colonial bureaucracy associated Brahminism with caste power even as it made the Brahmin a potent figure of ridicule.

Colonial critique of the Indian social, missionary intervention and Enlightenment ideologies of natural rights and freedom together influenced a small but influential group of upper-caste reformers. As Rosalind O'Hanlon has shown, Protestant Nonconformism in western India united ideas about human equality and rationality advocated by thinkers such as Volney, Voltaire, and Thomas Paine with missionary-styled critique of Hindu superstition.[58] A combination of these ideas was reflected in the secret society, the Prarthana Samaj (Prayer Society), established in 1862, which grew out of the Paramahansa Mandali (Society of the Supreme Being), a secret society established in 1849 with a fervid message against religious superstition and idolatry. Across the late nineteenth and early twentieth centuries, Maharashtrian social reform took strong positions on caste and gender reform in response to colonial critiques of the Hindu domestic. However, social reform also produced new configurations of Brahminical patriarchy and of heteronormative conjugality, even as it reproduced upper castes' secular power through institutions associated with colonial modernity. Another response to colonization can be seen in the emergence of a radical Hindu nationalism articulated in the political thought and activism of Bal Gangadhar Tilak (1856–1920), the inaugurator of *melas* (festivals) in the mid-1890s that aggressively staged Hindu identity and politicized public space through processions, songs, and virulent anti-Muslim rhetoric. V. D. Savarkar's (1883–1966) early enthusiasm for a multireligious, quasi-nationalist upsurge against colonial power was offset by his growing advocacy of political Hinduism, correlating religion, territory, and racial identity in *Hindutva: Who Is a Hindu* (1923). The Hindu Mahasabha, formed in 1915 with Savarkar as president, played a key role in taking up the untouchable problem in the interest of crafting Hindu unity. Mahasabha activists were centrally involved in the Parvati temple *satyagraha* of 1928, while noted Dalit leaders from the Vidarbha region of Maharashtra responded to exhortations to Hindu unity and broke with B. R. Ambedkar in the 1920s and 1930s over his position on Hinduism.[59] Social reform of the (Hindu) intimate, political practices of crafting Hindu community, and the institutional contexts of colonial modernity, together with the imperatives of colonial extraction and underdevelopment, framed the emergence of political non-Brahminism and, later, of Dalit politics in the region.

The two-part structure of *The Caste Question* reflects the dissonance between Dalits' successful struggles for rights and social recognition, on the one hand, and their continued experience of being vulnerable citizens subject to violence, on the other. Though related, these two areas of inquiry necessarily draw on different materials and methods and engage different modes of argument.

In part 1, "Emancipation," I adopt the methods of political and intellectual history to examine how Dalits developed a public critique of stigmatized existence, joined it with self-fashioning and social activism, and ultimately won recognition as a political constituency. I draw on archival sources, private papers, and political writings to examine the connections between a movement and an ideology, between organized efforts to challenge caste stigma and the development of a discourse of minority connected to fields of power and meaning informed by imperial rule and Indian nationalism. This section covers more than half a century, from the late nineteenth century to the period of constitutional law making between 1947 and 1950, when Dalits struggled to transform the social relations of caste and remake themselves as minoritarian citizens, only to be reconstituted within state and legal discourses as vulnerable persons living a form of stigmatized existence.

Chapter 1 follows the creation of a Dalit public sphere and a new political identity out of traditions of anticaste radicalism by a nineteenth-century generation of Mahar Dalit activists who brought ideas of rights and social recognition to bear on addressing caste humiliation and discrimination. The chapter explores how two divergent formations, political non-Brahminism and Dalit critique, emerged out of the public critique of Brahminism generated by activists of the Satyashodak Samaj (Truth Seeking Society). Caste radicals established a fundamentally secular understanding of the artificial distinctions between the religious and the political and the failure of "religion" to encompass the totalizing character of caste oppression. A domestic focus, reforming stigmatizing practices and uplifting women's status to refashion the community, also resituated authority within the Dalit community. Concurrently, activists fostered associational forms for protesting and petitioning in new idioms of segregation and public exclusion, inciting activism around public space. Two such spaces were the school and the temple, where I show how Dalits made novel interventions and incited new exclusionary tactics.

Chapter 2 follows Dalit activism to the water tank and temple door, symbolic sites where Indian nationalists and Dalits pursued caste democratization in the 1920s. I show how water and temple entry *satyagrahas* exposed the contradictions between nationalist and Dalit conceptions of rights and inclusion, religious and civic frames, and modes of political action. A close look at legal cases around the *satyagrahas* reveals how Dalit demands for social inclusion couched in terms of civic rights and natural justice were recast by courts as claims upon private property. This enabled British legality to supplement the accepted right of Hindus to regulate customary caste practices and to translate caste privilege into liberal practices of exclusion founded on the exclusionary right to (private) property. This shifted untouchability in two ways: (1) bringing it under a language of liberal property that could legitimize exclusion, and (2) rendering caste into a property of the self, and real property (such as temples) an extension of persons. Untouchability was again interiorized as an ineffable quality of the caste body, and Dalit attempts to secularize untouchability remained incomplete. To further illustrate the elasticity of liberal discourse, I examine a counterbalancing kind of legal reasoning (leavened by practical considerations different from those of temple entry) applied to a traditional Mahar property, the *vatan*, that processed another version of custom as law and Dalits as necessarily, if unfortunately, stigmatized persons.

Chapter 3 moves to the nationalization of the Dalit question within the politics of colonial governance and anticolonial nationalism and, finally, its resolution by the postcolonial state. The chapter underscores the remarkable political theoretical contributions and the practical political actions of B. R. Ambedkar, the Mahar lawyer, political scientist, and organizational leader of Dalit activism from the 1920s onward. In centralizing Ambedkar, I try to balance a dual focus—one eye on how his thought and activism contributed crucially to Dalit recognition and enfranchisement, the other on how his critical encounter with liberal democratic ideas defined major aspects of Indian democracy and brought something novel to liberal visions. In brief, Ambedkar placed untouchability center stage as a form of historical discrimination requiring redress by drawing on traditions of anticaste thought. And in recasting untouchability as historical inequality, Ambedkar also reconstituted Dalits as a distinctive political minority with a right to separate enfranchisement. In an unusual act of political emancipation challenging colonial apprehension of Hindus as a natural political constituency, he also created a Dalit identity outside the Hindu fold through conversion to a putatively originary Buddhism. The chapter considers Ambedkar's intellectually compelling yet politically paradoxical resolution of the caste question: the institutionalization of Dalit identity within the state and constitution, which prepared the way for significant legal protections. Both have had profound implications for a continuing politics of recognition and rights around a Dalit subject encoded as essentially vulnerable and susceptible to violence. I also suggest, however, that Ambedkar's distinctive resignification of Dalit identity in cultural-historical and political terms made the Dalit integral, rather than peripheral, to a genealogy of democratic political modernity.

Part 2, "The Paradox of Emancipation," turns to the organizational shape of Dalit politics and changing structures of Dalit life in Maharashtra over the last forty years to consider new forms of political violence related to Dalit identity that arise despite—and sometimes due to—legal-bureaucratic frameworks designed to end caste discrimination regulating the caste order. This section shifts the scale and tenor of previous argument. Beginning on the national stage of the constitutional-legal framing of Dalits, it then returns to regional and local scenes, placing political renarrations and legal adjudications of singular acts of violence in relation to state discourses and new mechanisms of caste regulation.

Chapter 4 is a theoretical inquiry into the connections between caste, social recognition, and protected minorities. It looks at how the postcolonial state has underwritten new and sometimes violent practices of caste sociality through bureaucratic regimes developed to address caste inequality. Recalling how violence figured in caste historical consciousness and politics, most particularly as an issue between Gandhi and Ambedkar, I suggest ways to consider the significance of both structural violence and its enactment as forms of political communication. Keeping this in mind, I discuss Indian constitutional-legal measures, especially the criminalization of untouchability, which embeds assumptions about Dalit personhood in democratic processes. I argue that constitutional categories, in particular, have produced a discursive-structural context in which vulnerability and protection, conjuring the specter of violence, become key dimensions of the Indian state's caretaking profile and an aspect of Dalits' subjectivity. From this perspective, vulnerability becomes a Dalit form of life perceptible as an artifact of state intervention and juridical convention, and an unanticipated product of the government-defined caste atrocity.

Chapter 5 begins to historicize the relationships between the state practices discussed in chapter 4 and the dynamics of Maharashtrian Dalit life and cultural politics in the 1970s. Offering longer-term reflections on symbolic politics, this approach provides a model for relating historical process and cultural transformation while leaving room for the incommensurability between the experiential domain of everyday life and its objectification in institutional practice and political discourse. Set into the scene of postindependence political developments in Maharashtra, the nodal points for examining these dynamics are new configurations of political violence, particularly around symbolization of the Dalit past and the Dalit self by the Dalit Panthers, who challenged extant Dalit leadership even as they contested Dalits' exclusion from symbolic representation. By examining Bombay riots between the Dalit Panthers and another emergent political formation, the Shiv Sena (Shivaji's Army), as well as a symbolically charged struggle to rename Marathwada University after B. R. Ambedkar, this chapter examines the interplay between Dalit countercultural forms and new formations of anti-Dalit violence.

Chapters 6 and 7 directly address local denouements of Dalit emancipation: the exacerbation of anti-Dalit violence known by the term "caste atrocity." Moving between intimate portraits of social life afforded by the case study and analysis of political forms and social structure, I hope to replicate, rather than to resolve, the tensions and ambivalences of Dalit existence within structuring regimes of law, bureaucracy, and governance. Two focal incidents took place in Marathwada, an area once in the former colonial princely state of Hyderabad until it joined Maharashtra during the 1960 linguistic reorganization of states. Chapter 6 explores the intersection of local caste and family relations with the legal apparatus through a well-known 1963 case in which village residents in Sirasgoan abused and humiliated four Dalit women. Chapter 7 looks into policing, legal action, and publicity surrounding the 1991 killing of a Dalit *kot-wal* (village-level police officer) at a village temple entrance. A running theme throughout these chapters is the management of anti-Dalit violence by state functionaries at both national and local levels, and an examination of how state action intersects with the complex semiotic registers through which anti-Dalit violence signifies as ritual degradation as well as political backlash. While these chapters examine the consequences of Dalits' legal vulnerability, they also explore the performative nature of caste violence, which manifests aspects of ritual archaic and political discipline.

   In the epilogue, I reprise the concerns of this book by addressing broader themes in the politics of identity and recognition, and by revisiting the contemporary perils and possibilities of a *corporeal politics* of caste.

PART ONE

Emancipation

CHAPTER I

Caste Radicalism and the Making of a New Political Subject

In colonial India, print capitalism facilitated the rise of multiple, distinctive vernacular publics. Typically associated with urbanization and middle-class formation, this new public sphere was given material form through the consumption and circulation of print media, and characterized by vigorous debate over social ideology and religio-cultural practices. Studies examining the roots of nationalist mobilization have argued that these colonial publics politicized daily life even as they hardened cleavages along fault lines of gender, caste, and religious identity.[1] In western India, the Marathi-language public sphere enabled an innovative, radical form of caste critique whose greatest initial success was in rural areas, where it created novel alliances between peasant protest and anticaste thought.[2]

The Marathi non-Brahmin public sphere was distinguished by a critique of caste hegemony and the ritual and temporal power of the Brahmin. In the latter part of the nineteenth century, Jotirao Phule's writings against Brahminism utilized forms of speech and rhetorical styles associated with the rustic language of peasants but infused them with demands for human rights and social equality that bore the influence of nonconformist Christianity to produce a unique discourse of caste radicalism.[3] Phule's political activities, like those of the Satyashodak Samaj (Truth Seeking Society) he established in 1873, showed keen awareness of transformations wrought by colonial modernity, not least of which was the "new" Brahmin, a product of the colonial bureaucracy. Like his anticaste, non-Brahmin compatriots in the Tamil country, Phule asserted that permanent war between Brahmin and non-Brahmin defined the historical process. This was the foundation for politicized non-Brahmin communities identifying themselves as members of a political and ethical community, the *shudra-atishudras,* who shared a common identity across *jati* specificities, *jati* being the term to describe regionally distinctive caste clusters (e.g., Maratha, Mahar, Deshastha Brahmin) associated with long-term processes of state and society formation.

By the late nineteenth century, there were significant continuities between the new forms of sociopolitical critique and historical identity that Phule established for Dalit and non-Brahmin communities and a distinctively Dalit (largely Mahar) discourse of stigmatized existence. Dalit discourse, however, highlighted the *instability* of a collective *shudra-atishudra* identity (and the unique disabilities of being an untouchable) as Dalits confronted efforts to align non-Brahmin (especially Maratha) identity with the *varna* category, or the prescriptive pan-Indian category, of Kshatriya. Print journalism nurtured this Dalit public sphere. Between 1877 and 1929, many newspapers explicitly addressed the disabilities of caste while fashioning a new sense of Dalit identity.[4] In their pages, Dalit reformers and publicists depicted the practice of untouchability as contingent and wrong, and associated the religio-ritual stigmatization of Dalits with their illiteracy, poverty, and social backwardness: upper-caste perceptions of untouchability as ritual transcendental were countered by an immanent, sociopolitical critique of caste relations. Exploring the intellectual formation I call caste radicalism, and the contexts in which it arose, clarifies how a Dalit critique initially allied with radical anti-Brahminism separated from it in the first decades of the twentieth century, with Dalit critique pursuing its own trajectory of distinctive analysis joined to activism.

MARATHAS, BRAHMINS, MAHARS

Over the last two decades, studies of the Maratha polity have moved away from frameworks wherein the Marathas were viewed as either predatory hordes of men from low-caste and nomadic communities relentless in their pursuit of revenue extraction or Hindu warrior-nationalists pitting their "Maratha" valor and manliness against Islam and the Mughal Empire. Revisionist historiography on the Marathas has long roots, for example, in the writings of the liberal economic nationalist, Mahadev Govind Ranade, who proposed a genealogy for Indian nationalism through Maratha history in *The Rise of Maratha Power* (1900), and in S. N. Sen's *The Military System of the Marathas* (1928), which traced overlaps between Mughal and Maratha military regimes. While these works challenged the depiction of Maratha history as the unfolding of Hindu history, they nonetheless suffered from the malaise of claiming the Marathas for a contemporary anticolonial nationalism.[5] However, recent scholarship has addressed the significant continuities between Mughal and Maratha political idioms, while studies of the Maratha polity have focused on those sociopolitical aspects that distinguished Maratha state formation: sophisticated structures of revenue contracts and collection, monetization of services, a market in patrimonial tenures, expansion of agriculture from the Deccan heartland into the frontier regions of middle India in the interest of settled revenue collection, and finally, an elaborate legal-bureaucratic regime distinguished by a system of fines and punishments.[6] This Maratha polity accords with developments in various parts of the subcontinent between the sixteenth and eighteenth centuries, when new groups—Jats, Rajputs, Marathas—arose out of the contexts of military service and tenurial holdings under the Mughals (1526–1707).

"Maratha" was an expansive category (and an identity) that was intimately related to early modern patterns of labor mobilization for land and military markets, and included a range of persons whose bids for political and economic power had succeeded, from the lowly *kunbi* peasant-cultivator to the ninety-six elite Maratha families, the *shahannavkuli*, who claimed a genealogical link with the Rajputs. *Thus, state formation in the Deccan region was characterized both by the increased salience of the category Maratha in signifying emergent patterns of power, and by a growing number of persons laying claim to Maratha as identity.* Entry into the category Maratha was possible through marriage, political-economic control over land, and over time, through the fabrication of genealogical affinity with the *varna-jati* combination of the Kshatriya-Rajput. The inherent plasticity of Maratha social formation was tied to the redistributive economies of Old Regime polities: by embedding holders of service tenures within locality, Old Regime paradigms of land and power also enabled imperial service to function as a mechanism of localization.[7] The Maratha polity transformed in the eighteenth century into what the historian Hiroshi Fukazawa has termed a "Brahminical" state ruled by Chitpavan Brahmins, the Peshwai.[8] It suffices here to note that the state-society linkages of the Peshwai produced a unique collective memory of Brahmins' political domination and not merely their ritual authority. This situation and the tripartite caste structure of the Deccan—comprising Brahmins, untouchables, and especially that loosely defined middle group, Maratha-*kunbis*—enabled an unusual critique of caste oppression.

The consolidation of a Maratha polity was symbolically marked by Shivaji's coronation as Chatrapati in 1674. By then, the Deccan was characterized by a sedentarized populace, monetization of the economy, and a highly organized regime of revenue collection, though Maratha suzerainty was initially achieved through practices of social banditry and guerilla warfare. Significantly, Maratha dominance provoked challenges to Brahminical authority conducted within ritual idioms. The most famous illustration of the pattern is Shivaji's coronation as Chatrapati, or lord of the *chhatra,* a large parasol or canopy placed over Hindu gods and kings to signify grandeur and dignity. The controversy over Shivaji's claims to Kshatriya lineage—he came from a family of *patils* (village headmen) near Pune who acquired power through military service to the Nizam Shah of Ahemdnagar—arose when a section of Deccan Brahmins rejected the possibility of allowing Shivaji to be coronated with Vedic rites reserved for twice-born Kshatriyas. A Brahmin from Benares, Gaga Bhatta, supported Shivaji's claim to Kshatriya status after much persuasion and traced the Bhosle lineage to the Sisodia Rajputs of Udaipur. Though Brahmin authority sanctified temporal claims, ritual was powerful only when supported by idioms and practices of political sovereignty. The belatedness of Shivaji's coronation and its ritual recognition of Shivaji's consolidation of real power over the Deccan (and other Maratha families) are noteworthy. Even more important are the multiple significations of the term "Maratha" and growing conflict around efforts to align Maratha *jati* with Kshatriya *varna.*

Brahmins continued to deny the Bhosle royal family's claim to Vedic rites and thus rejected their identity as twice-born Kshatriyas. Instead, they argued that the Bhosles were Shudras entitled to rites performed according to the Puranas. Symbolic insults to Maratha identity gained traction across the nineteenth century as the Chitpavan Brahmin community gained political visibility as a consequence of the Brahmin *peshwa,* or prime minister's increased centrality in political affairs. By 1749, the transfer of real power from the Chatrapati to his Brahmin ministers was an established fact, and Shahu I had been banished to Satara from Poona and confined to his fort, almost a prisoner of the *peshwa.* The declining political fortunes of the Bhosle family popularized the growing perception among upwardly mobile Maratha-*kunbis,* that a repetitive structure of Brahmin insult and non-Brahmin humiliation was *the* governing logic of history. Indeed Brahmins had long maintained that the genocide of Kshatriyas by the Brahmin Parashurama, the sixth incarnation of the Lord Vishnu, as related in the Dasavatara, or the ten incarnations of Lord Vishnu, was proof that there were only three castes in the Kali Yuga: Brahmins, Shudras, and untouchables. Thus the Vedokta controversy between Pratapsingh and the Chitpavan Brahmins of Poona between 1820 and 1830, and again in 1900 between Shahu Chatrapati of Kolhapur and his *rajopadhyaya* (priest to the royal family), resuscitated the long-standing battle over Maratha demands for recognition as Kshatriyas in the face of Brahmin efforts to reiterate their Shudra identity. Shahu's response was distinctive, however, and it is a symptom of the extent to which conflicts between Brahmins and non-Brahmins (and the emergence of political non-Brahminism) defined the sociopolitical landscape: in 1913, he challenged Brahmins' exclusive control over scriptural knowledge and ritual performance by establishing a school to train non-Brahmin priests, and by 1921 he had established an alternative locus of Kshatriya ritual authority.[9]

By then the Deccan had undergone significant political transformation, and both Brahmin and Maratha responses were mediated through a powerful new presence, the East India Company. The Peshwai ended when East India Company forces defeated Peshwa Bajirao II in 1818.[10] From then, the colonial state increasingly played a significant role in defining the meaning and social experience of the term "Maratha"; produced a set of affective attachments and institutional investments in history and (caste) identity, and enabled the rise of a newly salient, oppositional term, "non-Brahmin." Ironically, colonial intervention accelerated two seemingly contradictory processes: the secularization of caste *and* its novel association with Hindu religion. The colonial government abdicated direct responsibility for adjudicating issues of ritual status, religious rights, and community standing, though these were important realms of state intervention under the Old Regime.[11] While this produced new openings for challenging caste discipline and Brahminical norms, the mediation of Brahminical knowledge (and the secularization of the Brahmin's power as state functionary) played an important role in colonial knowledge formation. Power was no longer exercised through explicitly hierarchical registers, but through binary distinctions between "religious" and "political" arenas that respected neither social experience nor popular categorization. The emancipatory possibilities and the novel closures of colonial modernity thus produced a distinctive conjuncture.

For non-Brahmin communities, colonial modernity had a twofold effect. It produced new investments in history and caste identity, and it provoked affinity with a new range of modern institutions—schools and colleges, law courts, hospitals—spaces through which social mobility for the downtrodden and exploited might be accomplished. Colonial infrastructure, and its multiple and dispersed effects in the form of a colonial "sensorium," was inextricably linked to new experiences of the self and enabled radical egalitarian ideology to percolate through caste radicals' discourse, from ideas of self-respect and equality among intimates to a critique of the structured political-economic inequities of Brahminism.

A distinctive Mahar history was the ground from which other claims to social inclusion emerged and on which differences from non-Brahmins set a divergent trajectory for Dalit politicization. In drawing on a racial theory of conquest to explain the subjugation of non-Aryan Kshatriyas, the Shudras and *atishudras,* by Aryan Brahmin invaders, Jotirao Phule transvalued colonial-national fascination with theories of Aryan conquest to argue that a permanent and irreconcilable hostility between Brahmin and non-Brahmin had characterized caste society from its inception.[12] Phule never used the term "Hindu" in his writings, lest it appear that he was describing a consensual religio-cultural formation. He always wrote of Brahmin interests antagonistic to the *bahujan samaj,* the "majority community." However, by the time Phule was writing the terms "Arya" and "Aryan" had come to symbolize a set of associations between language and territory and between territory and religion, enabling a particular vision of the national-archaic: the civilizational history of India was now aligned with a territorially bounded, geographically distinctive protonational (Hindu) space, Bharat or Bharatvarsha.[13]

Reversing European narratives about the divergent civilizational status and material development of Indians and Europeans, both Hindu reformer Bal Gangadhar Tilak and Arya Samaj leader Dayanand Saraswati positioned Aryan society as coeval with Vedic religion, even as they posited Bharat—expansively defined by B. G. Tilak as spanning the North Pole to the subcontinent[14]—as the home of modern-day Hindus who had exported their religious values to the European world long ago.[15] Even the downtrodden communities had a place in this reconstituted Vedic past: because their degraded lifestyles were a consequence of forgetting their Aryan identity, they could be redeemed through *shuddhi* (purification).[16] Indeed, the desire to reconstitute a glorious Aryan past in India's present was evident across the board. Phule's conception of *history as caste conflict,* however, recuperated a non-Aryan Kshatriya past for Maharashtra's downtrodden. Arguing that the word "Kshatriya" originated in the Sanksrit *kshetra* (field), he imaginatively linked agricultural labor with military service, fields of cultivation with battlefields, and the humble peasant-cultivator with a past of military prowess. Then he went even further, asserting an exceptional role for the downtrodden, the Mahars and Mangs, who had offered the strongest resistance to the Aryan-Brahmin invaders.[17] Interpreting the term "Mahar" as Maha-ari (Great Enemy), Phule argued that the Mahars had twenty-one times freed their Dravidian brothers from conquest by Aryan Brahmins but were finally defeated through chicanery and cunning.[18] Subsequently, the *bhat* Brahmins, Phule's pejorative term for these ritual specialists, composed sacred texts—the Smritis, the Samhitas, the Shastras, and the Puranas—to justify their ill treatment of vanquished Dravidian Kshatriyas: "So that [the Maha-ari, or Mahars] would never lift their hand against the brahmins [Parashurama] had a black thread tied around their necks, and prohibited even their Shudra brethren from touching them. He [Parashurama] started the practice of calling these Maha-ari Kshatriyas by the names ati-Shudra, Mahar, antyaj, Mang, and Chandal."[19]

As punishment for resistance, the Mahars were defined as untouchables and banished from society, condemned to poverty, feeding on dead carcasses and wearing the black thread as a symbol of servitude.[20] A *pada* (poem) written by the president of the Bombay Shri Somavanshi Mitra Samaj (Association for Friends of the Somavanshi),[21] Pandit Kondiram, who was influenced by Phule, drew on this imagery to communicate the continued effects of past horrors.[22] In addition to wearing the black thread, Mahars could own no new clothes or jewelry. They dressed in clothes taken from corpses, wore iron jewelry, ate from broken clay pots, and owned only "dogs and asses; rats and mice."[23] They were dispossessed, shadowy figures reduced to begging and eating food unfit even for animals.

> The [Mahars'] condition is so deplorable, that they come begging
> For the rotten food scraps that have been thrown to the cows [lit.
>   "thrown into the cow shed"]
> Which even the cattle will not touch[24]

Kondiram ended with the powerful image of Mahar children sitting on a dung heap, their bodies covered with ash, sores on their eyes, rags covering their buttocks, their stomachs "sunken and empty."[25] Kondiram's imagery echoed the detailed prohibitions of texts such as the Manusmriti, which relegated untouchables to the very edge of human society, near graveyards and on dung heaps.[26] While Pandit Kondiram, like Phule, agreed that the *shudra-atishudras* were Dravidian Kshatriyas, he presents here a very specific set of images of Mahars' destitution. Though Phule had argued that the *shudra-atishudras* were a political collective, he had also held Brahmins responsible for creating divisions among them. Coached by wily Brahmins to "hate the Mahars and Mangs," Shudras had forgotten that the untouchable communities were once brave Kshatriyas.[27]

Early Dalit activists such as Gopal Baba Valangkar (?-1900) and Shivram Janba Kamble (1875–1942) drew on Phule's recuperation of a militant history for the Dalit communities.[28] Both, however, hitched a martial Mahar identity as Dravidian Kshatriyas to a new goal—a claim to continued employment in the British Army. Army service and its suspension deeply affected the first generation of Dalit publicists who had experienced social mobility and relatively little discrimination in the military. The significance of military service for Mahar Dalit is best understood by examining Valangkar, whose experience in the army, combined with immersion in Phule's Satyashodak ideology, resulted in a systematic Dalit critique of caste injustice. Gopal Vithalnak Valangkar was a Mahar native of Ravadhul, about five miles from the town of Mahad. He was an active member of the Satyashodak Samaj while in the military. In 1886, he retired as army *havaldar* (native sergeant) and went to Dapoli in the Ratnagiri district of the Konkan to become a schoolmaster. Dapoli was a unique settlement of Mahar and Chambhar military pensioners. According to the 1872 census, Dapoli had a population of 8,513 Mahars. In the Ratnagiri district, 2,180 Mahars were on the military rolls, 1,150 of whom were listed as pensioners. In fact, Mahars were described as "owning much land" in Dapoli.[29]

By 1892, however, Mahars were collateral damage of a decision by the British government to stop recruiting untouchables. They were victims of the "martial races theory" adopted by the British Army after the Mutiny to justify reorganization of the military along caste lines by excluding Dalits and Brahmins (as well as South Indians, communities from east India, etc.), who were regarded as weak, effeminate, and incapable of martial courage.[30]

If the British army justified military exclusion, Mahar Dalits mobilized Phule's concept of history as race war to emphasize their martial identity.[31] Educated up to the Normal School examination in Poona's Shri Ganesh School, Valangkar was deeply influenced by Phule's critique of Brahmin hegemony and the radical egalitarianism of Satyashodak thinking.[32] Subhedar R. S. Ghadge, a military pensioner who later became a member of the Poona branch of Vithal Ramji Shinde's Nirashrit

Sahayyak Mandal (Depressed Classes Mission; DCM), recalled that when he was stationed in Poona along with Valangkar, they heard Jotirao Phule lecturing the Mahar regiment about the bravery of the Chambhars, Mahars, and Mangs who had valiantly fought the Aryan Brahmins in ancient times.[33] Another member of the Satyashodak Samaj, Govind Ganpat Kale, recalled that Phule was a frequent visitor to Valangkar's home in the Maharwada in Bhavani Peth and that Phule often tested members of the Samaj by seating them in the same *pangthi* (row) as Valangkar, while food was served.[34] While the Samaj might have tolerated such experiments in Phule's lifetime, Valangkar himself became a victim of caste prejudice a few years later. In 1895, five years after Phule's death, the Samaj decided to ban Dalits—Chambhars, Dheds, Mahars, and Mangs— from their meetings.[35]

Valangkar's activism manifested both significant continuities with and new departures from Satyashodak thinking. In 1888, Valangkar wrote a *Vinanti Patra* (Petition Letter) in which he offered an extensive critique of caste exclusion in the form of a series of questions regarding the divine rationale for *jati* and *varna* distinctions, and for the practice of untouchability.[36] In this text, as well as in his reply to Census Commissioner H. H. Risley's questionnaire regarding the origins and practices of various castes, which he composed in 1894, Valangkar provided a genealogy of Dalit humiliation and suffering and framed arguments for Dalit rights and social recognition in the language of humanitarianism and social justice.[37] Elaborating upon Phule's account of the defeat of the Shudra-*atishudras,* Valangkar argued for a repetitive structure to the outcasting of the untouchable communities after their original defeat by Aryan Brahmins, and he historicized Dalits' social stigmatization to the *peshwa* period, when lower castes and untouchables had faced severe religious exclusion and social violence. Valangkar argued that the Mahar Kshatriyas had been stigmatized after eating meat to survive the Mahadurga famine of 1396. Again during the Peshwai, the lower-caste and untouchable communities had found themselves subject to severe caste discipline under a Brahminical state. As in Phule's account, the abject position of the Dalit was historically produced through the foundational conflict between Aryan Brahmins and the autochthonous Dravidian communities of western India. In Valangkar's account, however, originary conflict was overlaid with an argument that specified a key element of Dalits' degradation, their eating of carrion. This became a recurrent theme in Valangkar's explanations of Dalit stigma, which drew on the real-life experiences of Mahar communities.[38]

In addition to founding the first Dalit organization in the Bombay Presidency, the Anarya Dosh Pariharak Mandali (Society for the Removal of the Misdemeanors of the Non-Aryans) (ADPM),[39] Valangkar was a frequent contributor to the newspapers *Sudharak* and *Din Bandhu*. In the 1890s, he toured western India performing *kirtans* (religious songs) against the ill treatment of the Dalit communities.[40] When he was nominated to the Mahad Local Board in 1895, caste Hindus and Muslims boycotted the board's meetings. This provoked a series of reports in the *Din Bandhu* criticizing Valangkar's treatment.[41] Ironically, this incident occurred in the same year that the Poona branch of the Satyashodak Samaj decided to ban untouchables from their meetings.

Valangkar was adept at the organizational practices of the Satyashodak Samaj, but he was also familiar with the workings of colonial institutions such as the school, the army, and finally, the colonial bureaucracy. When faced with evidence of social exclusion and stigmatization specific to the untouchable communities, Valangkar responded by seeking colonial intervention to safeguard Dalits' historical rights. In July 1894, Valangkar drafted a petition on behalf of the ADPM to the Bombay government demanding equal employment and civil rights for the untouchable communities.[42] This inaugurated a spate of petitioning from other Dalit activists, including petitions from 1905 and 1910, drafted by Shivram Janba Kamble, demanding Mahars reinstatement into the British Army and employment in police forces.[43] None of these petitions received a positive response.[44] However, the petition became a crucial forum for writing Mahar Dalit history and for self-representation. In this genre, Dalits positioned themselves as supplicants and pleaded that historical wrongs to proud warriors required redress, while drawing on new discourses of social inclusion and civic equality to make their case.[45]

Phule's historical conflict between Brahmin and non-Brahmin produced the *shudra-atishudra* as a revolutionary subject. Like the Dalit to come, *shudra-atishudra* named a community that did not exist: it signaled a potentiality, but also defined that group historically by valorizing their military prowess and indigeneity while challenging their defeat at the hands of wily *bhat* Brahmins. The power of Phule's narrative lay not only in the refusal of Brahminical hegemony but also in the claim to self-representation by the *bahujan samaj* (majority community) of the downtrodden and toiling castes, now valued as key political actors against alien interlopers. They were the Rakshasas, the protectors of the land, who, once vanquished, appeared in Hindu mythology as *asuras,* or demons.

History was a counter to historical forgetting, an antidote against religious superstition and ideological indoctrination. Valangkar took up the narrative of *shudra-atishudra* bravery and military valor and the critique of Brahmin chicanery and cunning. Unlike his notable predecessor, Jotirao Phule, whose investment in Enlightenment rationality and humanism was combined with efforts to reinterpret Hindu popular culture, especially the Puranic tradition, Valangkar turned to the Rg Veda and the Bhagavad Gita, and argued that they put forth competing views on the origins of untouchability: the former relied on a model of descent codified in the Manusmriti, while the Gita (and the Vayu Purana) were based on a theory of *karma*, or doing.[46] Valangkar's argument regarding a key contradiction between caste as religious transcendental and caste as derived from a theory of action gave the practice of untouchability a more specific history, even as it allowed Valangkar to challenge religious ethics from *within* the scriptural tradition. This was distinct from Phule's rationalist humanism, belief in a formless Universal Creator, and his efforts to propagate his Sarvajanik Satya Dharma (the True Religion for All), each of which verged on atheism. It allowed Valangkar to specify the nature of Dalit stigma and to seek its redress through a set of sociopolitical strategies, from petitioning to challenging the religious bases for untouchability through an alternative reading of a humanistic *bhakthi* Hinduism.

If Valangkar's critique was enabled by forms of anticaste critique popularized by the Satyashodak Samaj, the Samaj's expulsion of its Dalit members in 1895 was an early sign of fissures within this imagined community of the *shudra-atishudra*. By the early decades of the twentieth century, anti-Brahminism had transformed into political non-Brahminism with a focus on converting the demographic predominance of the non-Brahmin into political power. By the time the movement was incorporated into the Indian National Congress in the early 1930s, non-Brahminism had moved from ideological critique to political contestation.[47] Concurrently, the once expansive, incorporative Maratha identity associated with anti-Brahminism became an exclusive identity tied to the realization of ritual Kshatriya status, or to forms of peasant populism.[48] As non-Brahmins poured into the Congress, Dalits' conflicts with the Congress were increasingly inflected with a Dalit/non-Brahmin antagonism.[49] Crucially, emerging distinctions between Dalits and non-Brahmins were played out on the field of intimate life and familial relations, gender and genealogy. The regulation of sexuality, in particular, was an important axis for the politicization of caste identity.

GENDER, SEXUALITY, ANTI-BRAHMIN POLITICS, AND THE DALIT HABITUS

Widows are cursing the religion that prohibits a woman from remarrying
Those who persecute women shall find themselves in hell
The Peṣhwas created this ignominious treatment of women
And for that reason their kingdom was destroyed

> GOPAL VITHALNAK VALANGKAR,
> DB, July 19, 1896, Akhand 5, verse 1–3

Hindu scriptures, especially the Manusmriti, defined both lower castes and women as impure, polluting, and subject to detailed regulation. It is not surprising that Phule and Valangkar equated the plights of these groups. Phule's earliest reform efforts addressed both lower castes and women: he opened a school for untouchable students in 1852 and a home for upper-caste widows in 1854. Placing gender and sexuality at the heart of caste distinctions enabled a powerful critique of the reproduction of caste through the regulation of gender.

Enforced widowhood, an important target of caste radicals' critique, focused on the inhuman treatment of the widow, who was tonsured, subject to severe sartorial codes, prohibited from wearing jewelry, and forced to observe dietary restrictions to control her passions.[50] Sexual anxieties about the widow were long-standing, but Hindu reformers' and caste radicals' renewed focus on the treatment of widows coincided with the colonial state's efforts to reform the Hindu joint family.[51]

Caste radicals were distinctive and vociferous in emphasizing the importance of caste respectability and sexual purity to the reproduction of Brahminical patriarchy. Thus, when Phule and his wife, Savitribai, opened a home in 1854 for upper-caste widows who faced intimate violence ranging from physical abuse to impregnation, they were criticizing a Brahminical order that sanctioned such practices, even as they were challenging upper castes' capacity to protect "their women."[52] Tarabai Shinde extended their critique in *Stri-Purush Tulana* (A Comparison between Women and Men), written in 1882 in response to the conviction of an upper-caste widow, Vijayalakshmi, of infanticide.[53] Shinde attacked the hypocritical stance of criminalizing women rather than challenging the sexual excesses of men and argued that all men, not merely Brahmins, were implicated in the ill treatment of women.[54] The upper-caste widow also played an important role in Valangkar's critique. He compared the tonsure of widows with cows going to the slaughterhouse and argued that widows were deeply susceptible to sexual advances by "ascetics, mendicants, and priests" who congregated at holy places to take advantage of them.[55] Indeed, an established trope in anticaste polemic was Brahminism's ideological reduction of women and the lower castes to beasts of burden: their sentience and physicality were inversely related to their value as persons.

Because enforced widowhood exposed the structuring relationship between caste hegemony and control over female sexuality, the practice provided the occasion for early critiques of the caste order and of Brahminical mores in particular. A dialogue between a widow and her father in a Satyashodak *jalsa* (folk drama) uses the widow's physical disfiguration to stage a broader critique of enforced widowhood and to challenge its growing acceptance among non-Brahmin communities where *pat* (second marriages) had previously predominated.[56]

> I am your loved one [*ladki*], Anna,[57] your loved one
> How can you make me bald [*bodki*][58]
> My form
> Glitters [*chamchamki*]
> Like a dazzling diamond in a foil
>
> I am as delicate as a flower garland
> I ornament my plaits with flowers
> Give up your adamant behavior
> Hurry and fix my [second] marriage
> Allowed among lower castes
>
> Bhimrao says
> Don't cause sorrow
> Or you will be sorry [lit. "you will fall on your noses"][59]

In the first decades of the twentieth century, Satyashodak *jalsas* were the main vehicles for spreading the Samaj's message to the rural populace. Traditional *tamashas*, renowned for their word play and sexual innuendo interspersed with song, typically began with an invocation to Lord Ganapati. The stories centered on the theme of Lord Krishna's dalliances with his *gopis* (milkmaids). Instead, the Satyashodak *jalsa* invoked the *gana* (the people) as leaders (*pati*, or "the source of rule"). Satyaji's dialogue with Brahmin women on the irrationality of Hindu ritual, discussions about the exploitation of the peasantry, and critiques of the Brahmin-moneylender (*shetji-bhatji*) were popular.[60] The use of coarse and insulting language was standard. Bhimrao Mahamuni from Otur is credited with having staged the first *jalsa* with the support of Shahu Chatrapathi and Krishnarao Bhalekar. Ramachandra Ghadge (Kale, Satara district) started his famous *jalsa* troupe in 1915.[61] Colonial reports indicate the extent to which the Satyashodak Samaj relied on the *jalsa* and other popular cultural forms. A brief note by District Magistrate Satara, dated October 11–12, 1919, recorded: "It was found necessary in April 1919 to issue an order under Sec. 144 Cr. P. C., preventing the religious sermons, kirtans, and 'tamashas' of the Samaj at Karad for two months. District Magistrate reported that the so-called religious 'tamasha' and kirtans of the Satya Samaj consisted of coarse abuse and ridicule of the Brahmans and were rightly stopped."[62] By 1929, more than twenty-nine troupes were performing in southern Maharashtra. By 1932, however, the Bombay government noted a marked decrease of the performance of Satyashodak *jalsas,* but attested to their continued cultural significance: "The Satyashodak Samaj hit on tamashas as a means of propaganda amongst illiterate rustics and the points they make are probably coarse, but though the Brahmans have complained to me of the coarseness of the attacks made on them in these tamashas by the Satya Samaj, I have never yet been able to get a statement of any particular words they consider offensive. What happens, apparently, is that songs are sung containing offensive stories from sacred books and these are represented as Brahman morality."[63]

Satyashodak activists experimented with new social forms and countercultural strategies to challenge Brahmin hegemony and exploitation of female suffering. Like the jalsa, another important effort centered on politicizing Hindu marriage as the hinge between intimate and public political life, and as the site where ideologies of caste purity and gender respectability were articulated *as caste power.* Thus the Satyashodak marriage eliminated the need for a Brahmin priest and emphasized self-respect and equality within marriage.[64] This challenge to the social reproduction of caste through religious exploitation of the non-Brahmin communities, and the sexual regulation of (their) women, inspired Ambedkar, who urged Dalits to perform Satyashodak marriage. He even presided over one in Vidarbha in 1927.[65] Similarly, Self-Respect marriages in south India in the movement's heyday (1925–39), took the politicization of marriage to new heights. Self-Respecters, especially their leader, Periyar, or E. V. Ramasamy Naicker, urged activists to perform intercaste and widow remarriages and celebrated them in movie halls and theaters, where they were performed at ritually inauspicious times. By so doing, they staged the theatricality of politics and the significance of sexual politics for radical anti-casteism.[66]

The political import of the Satyashodak marriage is reflected by a legal case from Otur in Poona district, a site of radical Satyashodak activism.[67] A Brahmin *joshi* (priest) demanded his traditional fees for performing a marriage even though the Satyashodak marriage had eliminated his role.[68] On appeal to the Bombay High Court, Balaji Patil argued that his fellow caste members had performed his daughter's wedding in keeping with ancestral tradition. His legal representative recognized the novelty of the Satyashodak marriage, however, and argued: "The marriages were performed without any prescribed ceremonies, and no priest as such, was employed. There was no *ganeshpujan* (inauguration of the marriage ceremony through a prayer to Ganesha). There was nothing beyond the placing of garlands on the necks of the bride and bridegroom. There was no distribution of fees (*dakshina*); therefore the village joshis cannot claim any fees. *There is a separate ritual for the Sudras of the defendant's caste. That ritual was not performed.*"[69] The 1888 judgment by Justices Sargent and Candy supported the Satyashodaks' argument that because the wedding of Patil's daughter was not performed as a (legally) recognizable non-Brahmin or Shudra marriage, the *joshi* was ineligible for fees. By refusing to sacralize marriage *on the Brahmin's terms*, the Satyashodak marriage positioned itself as an explicit challenge to the social reproduction of caste through the sexual regulation of women. This was of a piece with challenges to Brahmin sacerdotal power and ritually "pure" status in important rationalist texts such as *Svayampurohit* (Your Own Priest) and *Gharache Purohit* (Household Priest) that empowered non-Brahmin communities to perform religious rituals without Brahmin intervention.[70] Schools for training priests were similarly established in villages, so that rituals could be performed without Brahmin intermediaries.

Though caste radicals were preoccupied with challenging caste ideology by rethinking marriage and sexuality, they were by no means immune to the extension of novel patriarchal practices into their own households. In the last quarter of the nineteenth century, enhanced regulation of women became a mechanism to resolve anxieties about social status among upwardly mobile, politicized Marathas.[71] Sociocultural practices such as Marathmola percolated down from royal families and landed gentry to young women from upwardly mobile families. This partial segregation of women involved withdrawing their labor and physical presence from public space and became a status marker for Maratha families claiming elite Kshatriya status. Meanwhile, Dalit publicists and reformers underlined the susceptibility of Dalit women to sexual violation according to "custom" and focused on enforced sexual servitude through womens' ritual dedication.[72] Even as Dalit publicists launched a severe critique of the interdependence of sexual compulsion and the material deprivation of Dalit communities, their efforts to modify Dalit intimate relationships also enhanced the authority of male Dalit reformers.

The contradictory effects of the social reform of gender by caste radicals can be explained by the fact that Dalit and non-Brahmin political subject-formation increasingly involved the politicization of Dalit and lower-caste men through the reform of family and female subjects. Earlier, colonial paradigms of social reform had intersected with (and enhanced) Brahminical models of caste and sexual purity to produce hegemonic ideologies of domesticity, female enfranchisement, and companionate marriage. They had been vigorously criticized by anticaste radicals, who drew attention to the supplemental relationship of gender and caste and the reproduction of caste norms through sexual regulation. In the first decades of the twentieth century, however, non-Brahmin critiques of the gendered character of caste were muted by emergent forms of caste conflict that increasingly framed the modernization of gender as dependent on the reconstitution of caste masculinity.

An important consequence of the discrete, if mutually entailed, trajectories of gender reform and the politicization of caste by anticaste radicals was that the subject of non-Brahmin and, later, Dalit politics was imagined as male.[73] Let me clarify that my argument in no way refuses the significant public presence of women and the centrality of female labor to the household economy of Dalits and lower castes. As well, bourgeois ideologies of femininity carried a very different valence for stigmatized communities, since coerced sexual labor constituted a key site of collective humiliation. While such developments speak to divergent genealogies of the feminist subject, they also help to explain the specific conditions that set the ground for a masculinist anticaste politics.

By the early decades of the twentieth century, Jotirao Phule's resonant narrative of Brahmin invasion and political usurpation was redirected to serve an argument regarding the impure, miscegenated origins of the Chitpavan Brahmins. Maratha masculinity was directly engaged in the resulting narratives, while Dalits—excluded from Kshatriya status—were rendered marginal to the conflict. The emphasis on Dalit and Maratha masculinity was the result of caste radicals' initial emphasis on the importance of gender and sexuality in the constitution of the (political) community of caste. Their divergent trajectories can be explained, however, through caste radicalism's intersections with the institutional contexts of colonial modernity and the discursive logics of an emergent cultural nationalism. Below, I address the polemical centrality of narratives of sexual violation for the justification of Brahmin hegemony *and* for counterarguments that challenged Brahminism by questioning the Brahmin's putative "purity." My focus is on two things: (1) the manner in which gender and genealogy discursively constituted the difference between Brahmin and non-Brahmin; and (2) how the renewed politicization of caste identities around the axis of gender and sexuality demarcated emergent non-Brahmin and Dalit public spheres.

In Maharashtra, it was said that there were only Brahmins and Shudras in the Kaliyuga (the present, corrupted age). This indicated a Brahmin-centric view of the degradation of the all intermediate castes to Shudra status. Constant conflicts over Shudra status were in evidence from the 1700s, if not earlier, and became especially virulent by 1830 with regard to Chitpavan Brahmins' determination to downgrade the Kayastha Prabhus to Shudra status.[74] But who were the Chitpavan Brahmins? Phule had framed them as aliens and interlopers. Valangkar embellished Phule's account: the Konkani Chitpavan Brahmins were Semitic people who had fled the Barbary coast, were shipwrecked off the Malabar coast, married low-caste women from the Konkan region, and became a caste of fishermen. They won power and Brahmin status through cunning.[75] Valangkar went further to explain the distinctions between Mahar and Maratha. He described the Mahars as *varnas* of mixed *jatis* who shared the lineage of other Dravidian Kshatriyas—Surya, Chandra, Shes, and Yadu. However, he defined Rajputs and Marathas as Turks who had been sent to annihilate Buddhism and Jainism in India. If Valangkar distinguished the Marathas from other Dravidian Kshatriyas, it is because this was a pronounced theme of Maratha genealogies produced in the early decades of the twentieth century, which sought to redefine Marathas' status as *Aryans* and as Kshatriyas.

Dalits *and* Marathas past felt compelled, however, to engage with the Chitpavan Brahmins' genealogy related in the Sahyadrikhand, a caste origin myth that referenced an act of genocide in the Dasavatara to explain the disappearance of Kshatriyas from the Deccan.[76] In the Dasavatara, the axe-wielding Brahmin Parashurama, an incarnation of Vishnu, is said to have exterminated all Kshatriyas during the Treta Yuga, in retaliation for his father's murder.[77] (Recall that in Phule's account, the Maha-ari had risen against Parashurama twenty-one times, only to be subjugated.) To extirpate his sins, Parashurama tried to perform penance. Unable to find Brahmins in the Konkan, he created the Chitpavan Brahmins by purifying a group of sixty fishermen at a funeral pyre. The Chitpavans were rendered pure *(pavana)* through funereal ashes *(chitta)*.

If this genealogy rendered Chitpavan Brahmins of dubious distinction, it created an even more compromising account of non-Brahmins. The Shudra-Kshatriyas of Kaliyuga, it was said, were the product of illicit intercaste unions between Brahmin sages, *rishis*, and enslaved Kshatriya women.[78] The term "Shudra," in both popular discourse and legal texts, conjured the dishonor of impure origins, a bastard identity born out of bondage, sexual degradation, and servitude. No less than B. R. Ambedkar was impelled by this account of sexual violence to argue that, "[i]n every case, the Kshatriyas are shown to have undergone an abject surrender . . . [in many stories] the surrender of the Kshatriyas was so to say purchased by them by offering their women to the victorious brahmins. The stories are all doctored with a view to glorify the brahmins and humiliate the Kshatriyas. Who can take such dirty, filthy, abominable and vainglorious stories of reconciliation as true historical facts? Only a supporter of Brahminism can do so."[79] Indeed, Maratha assertions in the early twentieth century challenged this foundational narrative of sexual violence and caste miscegenation by addressing the *Brahmin's* miscegenated identity.

In order to align themselves with region and nation, Marathas asserted that they were the original inhabitants of Maharashtra and thus true nationalists. To make their case they drew on colonial racial typologies inflected by regional caste conflicts and made sometimes confusing and inconsistent distinctions between Aryans and Dravidians, and Hindus and Brahmins.[80] By the turn of the century, Maratha purity had become a sensitive issue for Maratha activists and elite Maratha families alike. The latter distinguished themselves from Marathas of uncertain status, referred to by a range of terms—*kadu, akkarmashe* (lit. "miscegenated," "bastardized"), and *kharchi* (semi-legitimate)—and sought to legitimize status through ritual incorporation into varna hierarchy.[81] Marriage advertisements seeking pure alliances between elite, wealthy Maratha families began to appear in the pages of the Kolhapur newspaper *Vijayi Maratha* (Victorious Maratha) and the more conservative, Belgaum-based *Rashtraveer* (Patriot).[82]

Such practices were doubly inflected by the desire to challenge Brahmin hegemony and to claim for Marathas a distinctive Kshatriya identity by aligning *jati* with *varna* status. The net result was a shift away from Phule's tradition of radical egalitarianism and critique of religious orthodoxy toward an embrace of Aryan identity for Kshatriya Marathas, now increasingly represented as Hindus with full access to Vedic rituals in contrast to Brahmins, who were portrayed as being of questionable origin. Notable exceptions to this tendency are Mukundrao Patil, editor of the *Din Mitra* (1910-30), who repeatedly urged an expansive identity for non-Brahmin castes as non-Aryan Hindus ranged against Brahmin domination;[83] and the non-Brahmin activists Keshavrao Jedhe and Din-karrao Javalkar. They were increasingly confronted, however, by growing Dalit-Maratha conflict as an organized Dalit movement exacerbated economic tensions on a rural field polarized between Dalit laborers and non-Brahmin, especially Maratha, landlords.

Maratha assertions of pure Kshatriya origin positioned them as Aryan originators of Hindu scriptures with a first claim to Vedic authority, and Maratha polemicists urged non-Brahmins to take up the thread ceremony and other Vedic rituals to assert their superiority over Brahmins.[84] This erased the illegitimacy Phule had attributed to the scriptures as signs of Brahmin cunning and made for the Maratha Kshatriyas a central place *within* Hindu history. It also left intact the narrative of the defeat and humiliation of the Dravidian Shudra.

The reconstitution of the Maratha self (and of Maratha masculinity) was thus inherently unstable. At one level it constituted a challenge to Brahmin power (and Brahmin-centric history) across the *longue durée*. However by positing a direct correspondence between the uneven political regimes that produced Maratha as a resonant caste identity in western India and the ritually exclusive *varna* status of Kshatriyas, Maratha assertion relied on a genealogy that denied salience for Phule's imagined collectivity of *shudra-atishudras*. The rewriting of Maratha history left little room for Marathas of questionable status and increasingly rendered alliances between Dalits and Aryan-identified non-Brahmin groups difficult. As debates over caste identity intersected with narratives of sexual violence and structural analyses of the sexual reproduction of caste, complex political tensions between Brahmins, non-Brahmins, and untouchables were also staged. Between 1922 and 1926, an aggressively masculinized counterdiscourse became a major node of conflict for non-Brahmin challenges to Brahmin superiority.

Ganpati and Shivaji *melas* [festivals], started in the 1890s by radical Hindu nationalist Bal Gangadhar Tilak (1856–1920), had countered Muharram processions by politicizing public space and religion through everyday cultural symbols and historical figures associated with intimate practices of Hindu religiosity. The *melas* included street marches, singing, and the staging of plays that created a context for displays of anticolonial rhetoric and patriotic fervor. They also accommodated inflammatory anti-Muslim rhetoric and derogation of women and anti-Brahmin radicals.

In turn, Chatrapati *melas* counterstaged Maratha masculinity. Participants wore warrior costumes, carried spears and javelins, sang *mela* songs criticizing Brahmin hegemony, and asserted the true national patriotism of non-Brahmins.[85] The Peshwas were blamed for losing Maharashtra to the British. Insults were common.[86] By 1924, nightly fracases between Tilakites and non-Brahmin activists brought the *melas* under extensive police surveillance and caused the banning of many songs and publications by both sides.[87] The liberal organ, *Servant of India,* noted that the Chatrapati *melas* showed that "they [non-Brahmin activists] could beat the originators of the festival on their own ground, that is, in the employment of indecent language. Their attacks were directed against the very people who introduced this sinister element into the public life of Poona."[88]

This aggressively masculinized non-Brahmin political culture exacerbated caste antagonism through a sexual politics. Popular pamphlets made sexual innuendos about Brahmin women and represented widows as symbols of Brahmin tyranny. They cast aspersions on the sexual purity of Brahmin communities, characterizing them as the illicit offspring of Maratha men and Brahmin women. Brahmins were routinely described as *dasiputras* (colloq. "bastards") in polemical texts,[89] thus reversing the Brahmins' narrative of the Marathas as Shudras and the offspring of *dasis* (enslaved women). Indeed, Brahmins complained that one of the taunts employed by the activists was, "the Chatrapati *mela* has come; Brahmin women better run."[90]

Gender and genealogy were discursively central to this emergent non-Brahmin public sphere. Non-Brahmin activists emphasized the history of concubinage and Brahmin men's sexual exploitation of lower-caste women (and their own wives) through popular-cultural representations of the Peshwai as a period of sexual debauchery.[91] To suggest that Brahmins were foreigners and the offspring of caste miscegenation threatened the Brahmins' claim to caste purity and, therefore, to ritual authority. Government censorship of "inflammatory" or "obscene" texts illustrates the growing significance of a public sphere of print and performance in exacerbating Brahmin/non-Brahmin conflict in Poona, hotbed of Tilakite activism.

Let us begin with publication of *Deshache Dushman* (Enemies of the Country) in 1925, with an introduction by Keshavrao Bagade.[92] The controversy over the text was preceded by demands that same year that the Poona municipality honor Phule with a statue. The deep-rooted resistance of Brahmins and conservative non-Brahmins—including Phule's relative, Baburao Phule—who accused Phule of being a Christian convert who destroyed Hindu religion, intensified friction and set the stage for a spirited response. The Oriental Translator described the book as "written in the most intemperate and objectionable language; in places the violent fury of the writer has so carried him away that his whirling words are barely intelligible."[93] Bagade admitted that "the language and mode of expressing ideas employed in this book will not please Brahmans."[94]

Deshache Dushman branded Brahmin leaders as traitors sprung from a stock of foreign invaders of low status and questionable origins. The authors argued that Brahmins were well known for using any means to assert their superiority—from chicanery and cunning to falsifying history. Tilak and Vishnu Shastri Chiplunkar—the latter famous for his vitriolic criticism of Phule and the social reformer Gopal Hari Deshmukh, or Lokahitawadi, in his 1874 *Nibandhamala* (Garland of Essays)—were referred to as enemies of the country "born from the vomit of Brahmans" (in reference to Brahmins' claims that they were birthed from the mouth of Purusa, or "the original man").[95] Chitpavan Brahmins were generally described as "Satan," "cobras," "sons of prostitutes," and "mother goers."[96] Indeed the litany of complaints against Brahmin patriotism comprised an account of Brahmin treachery, sexual licentiousness, and female exploitation. This text, like others that followed, described Peshwa history as a period of maximal corruption, when Brahmins sold their daughters and loaned their wives.[97] Shivaji's protection of Brahmin women from the depredation of Muslim men was mentioned in conjunction with Brahmin hypocrisy about the behavior of their women—"the Bhat mind thinks religion is destroyed when a Shudra is crowned king but cannot comprehend when a Brahmin woman comes jumping from the bed of a Shudra.[98] Brahmins, it was noted, had the vile tendency to "suspect their mother's chastity," "shave women," and to allow widows to throw their illegitimate children on "crossroads eight times a week."[99] At the same time, the Brahmin priest "who calls the non-Brahmins Shudras an enemy is a badmash dacoit [bandit] who casts evil glances at their women."[100] Equating Brahminism with slavery, the text noted, "it is a sin to give alms to a Brahmin who smokes ganja, drinks wine and ascends the staircase of houses of ill repute. To get marriage solemnized by Brahmins is tantamount to polluting an auspicious occasion [and] writing the horoscope of a future slave generation."[101]

The controversy over *Deshache Dushman* was heightened by a set of parallel publications that challenged Brahmin hegemony and its ritual and material enslavement of non-Brahmins. R. N. Lad, the editor of

Mazur, and Annabhau Chavan, writer of "The Marriage Ritual of the Bhats According to the Shastras, or Their Foolish Foolishness," were sentenced to nine months rigorous imprisonment for promoting communal enmity.[102] In his piece of June 5, 1926, which described a marriage ceremony that took place in Masur on May 25, Chavan issued a challenge to "the extremely foolish, wicked, mean Bhats in Masur, the daredevil donkeys, the Bhat sons of prostitutes, who seek the evil of the benefactor, who give the form of untruth to truth, and truth to untruth, the cruel Bhats who put the barber's razor on the heads of their mothers and sisters." He called them hypocrites "intent on securing their own selfish ends," who despised Europeans, yet flattered them in "servile ways" and saluted them "by bending down again and again." Chavan argued that Brahmins refused to tolerate the reforms of the Satyashodak Samaj because it challenged them directly. He described Brahmin priests as Golaks, or the illegitimate offspring of "shaved widows," and warned of dire consequences if they cheated non-Brahmins or clamored for "more Dakshina" in the future.[103]

Antagonism between Brahmins and non-Brahmins was at an all-time high in Pune in August 1926—and the writers of *Deschache Dushman* were in jail—when a young Maratha man named Hari Narayan Dhanavade was accused of attempting to molest an eighteen-year-old Brahmin woman named Dwarakabai. An inflammatory newspaper article reported that a witness had seen "the accused in the act of moving his face towards her" when he was dragged away from his victim.[104] Dhanavade maintained that he had been standing in a doorway, far from the incident, when he was set upon by thirty to thirty-five Brahmin youth.

Tilak's *Mahratta* editorialized: "It is an insult to the womanhood of Maharashtra. . . . To the brahmans we have only to say one word. If they wish to live in honour then they must face the crisis with courage, manliness and bravery. They must take every step to defend the honor of their sisters and daughters. They will, we trust, prove equal to the occasion. . . . it is said that this assault is a most cowardly campaign that is being carried out through some leaders of the non-Brahman party against the Brahman community and their womanhood."[105] The newspaper noted the increased frequency of such incidents in the prior six years in southern Maharashtra, where a concerted campaign to boycott Brahmins had been taking place.[106] The *Vijayi Maratha* challenged this view and noted that "public rudeness to women was originally inculcated by the Tilakites and Brahman Ganapati melas and Tilakite and Brahman anti-feminist movements," and that there was an "old tradition" (among Brahmins) of "composing abusive song against educated women" and "reviling them at will." The paper went on to note that it was non-Brahmin men who had protected Brahmin women when they were abused and set upon by Brahmin men for supporting the Patel (Intercaste Marriage) Bill.[107]

In the first decades of the twentieth century, a set of mutually constitutive if deeply contradictory sociopolitical processes were at work: emergent forms of upper-caste female mobility and domestic modernity; the heightened centrality of Maratha genealogy and of Kshatriya status for upwardly mobile non-Brahmin families; a long-standing critique of Brahmin hegemony and Hindu history; and finally, a burgeoning anticolonial movement that sought political unity among disparate castes and classes and that took distinctive regional shape. Partha Chatterjee has argued that cultural nationalism revalued the Hindu domestic through women's alignment with the spiritual interior of the nation, even as it gave women a new place in public life and allowed them to navigate the public spaces of work and politics without imputation of sexual impropriety.[108] Chatterjee's argument describes the logic of anticolonial nationalism as *derivative* of colonial categories and *reactive* to the colonizer's discourse about the colonized, so that cultural nationalists could value the domestic intimate even as they sought to transform gendered relations within the family. Chatterjee's account addresses the affective centrality of the domestic sphere—and the Hindu upper-caste woman who symbolized it—for nationalist thought, but fails to take note of the political ambiguity that surrounded this figure. Given the centrality of gender and sexual regulation to the discursive hegemony of Brahminism in western India, the Brahmin woman had long personified elements of non-Brahmin critique, even as she became the rallying point for a renewed politics of Brahminism. Here, the historic conflict between Brahmins and non-Brahmins was staged through competing narratives of caste masculinity and differential claims over women.

In contrast to this public, explicitly confrontational, masculinist politics, Dalit reformers' masculinity was predicated on the reform of gender within their community and the defense of community honor against the disdain of outsiders. In 1908, the *Somavanshiya Mitra* published a letter from Shivubai Vallad Lakshman Jadhav-Sonkamble, who identified herself as a *murali*. *Muralis* were young girls from the Mahar, Mang, *kunbi*, and so-called nomadic communities who were married off to the god Khandoba at his temple in Jejuri in fulfillment of a vow.[109] *Muralis* wore a *mangalsutra* of seven cowrie shells[110] and, although human marriages were denied them, as nominal wives of the god they were obli-

Figure 2. Notice of a *tamasha* performance at Grant Road's New Elphinstone Theater in Bombay on June 28, 1898, with top billing to Tukaram Mahar Ture-wala Kundalwadikar. Namdev Vhatkar, *Marathi Loknatya Tamasha: Kala ani Sahitya* (Kolhapur: Yashashree Prakashan, n.d.), appendix. Author's collection.

gated to provide sexual services to men. *Murali* dedication was among a range of regionally distinctive practices involving women of all statuses, which came to be glossed by the colonial state as ritual "prostitution." The lives of dedicated women, however, were more complex. Many remained with one partner all their lives. As temple servants, others acquired property in the form of tax-free *inam* lands. Women from Dalit and nomadic communities were historically associated with the traditions of courtly performance, especially the erotic *lavani*.[111] By the twentieth century, they were more closely associated with *tamasha* performance, now depicted as a lewd and raunchy popular cultural form.[112]

The legendary Pavalabai was dedicated as a *murali*, though her exquisite beauty and performative skills brought her to the attention of the famous Brahmin *tamasgir* (tamasha performer), Patthe Bapurao, born Sridhar Kulkarni (1866–1948). Pavalabi joined Patthe's troupe and became his companion.[113] Though she was a famous performer, Pavalabai's career mirrored the reduced significance of traditional popular culture to an emergent Dalit politics and the growing presence of a reformist critique of (Dalit) female sexuality. Thus the new performative medium of the Ambedkari *jalsa*, which is discussed in chapter 2, was composed solely of men and reflected long-standing efforts of male reformers to break the association between *tamasha* and the sexual promiscuity of its (female) Dalit performers.

Shivubai's letter was written against this backdrop of male reformers working to abolish stigmatizing practices, especially ritual dedication and sexual servitude. She responded to a letter written by a Mahar *panch* (religious head) castigating *muralis* as social evils whose sexual promiscuity was ruining Dalit men and their families.[114] Shivubai objected that she was forced to do her job by the men of her community. She noted that many women converted to Islam and Christianity to avoid prostituting themselves.[115] Indeed, Shivubai held the men of her community responsible for perpetuating the practice and called for a campaign against fathers who dedicated daughters. Shivubai's indictment of the men who perpetuated the practice was distinctive. Her point was overwhelmed, however, by multiple and overlapping efforts to criminalize the practice.

The practice of *murali* dedication was strongest near Jejuri and in southern Maharashtra, where it was associated with a distinctive inheritance practice among the Mahar and Talwar communities. In 1906, the collector of Bijapur argued that "the prevalence of the practice of dedicating girls to prostitution among the Mahars is partly attributed to the fact that the male issue of prostitute daughters are allowed to succeed to a Mahar watan" when a man dies without male offspring.[116] Bomanji argued that even if the practice was customary, "this recognition of illegitimate children should be stopped."[117] What Bomanji failed to mention, however, was that the decision to allow a *murali*'s male heirs to inherit their mother's property had been reached *after a decision to disinherit muralis from directly owning ancestral property*. On February 27, 1857, the collector of Dharwad had "brought to notice the law of inheritance prevailing among Mahars and other low castes that a man dying without male offspring could leave property to a daughter only if she was a 'professional prostitute.'"[118] The collector noted that though it was practiced among "groups comparatively unimportant in numbers and social position," the "loathsome custom" encouraged women to lead a life of "privileged profligacy." The then Revenue Commissioner for Alienations, Sir Barrow Ellis, noted that "though prostitution was not expressly a condition for tenure, it was customary to retain one unmarried daughter to hand down watan to illegitimate offspring."[119] Government Resolution no. 6788, passed on January 22, 1858 barred ownership through illegitimates. Locally, however, the practice was clearly condoned. A complex case from 1873, involving a Talwarki *watan* in the name of "Vianki Talwar," brought up questions of whether a prostitute's adopted son, or her prostitute sister's biological son should inherit her estate. In this case, as with all other cases originating in the Dharwar district, it was decided that inheritance should skip the prostitute and go directly to her male illegitimate offspring.[120] Thus the depiction of the practice of ritual dedication as a form of sexual servitude (and social scandal) was only partially true: *murali* reform gathered steam after female inheritance was stigmatized and Mahar and Talwar men had become beneficiaries of governing paradigms that privileged patrilineal inheritance.[121]

By the 1890s, various missionary groups had taken up the issue and suggested punishing parents and priests who enforced the tradition and recommended the transfer of dedicated women to orphanages. N. G. Chandavarkar, a social reformer, famous justice of the Bombay High Court and a member of the Society for the Protection of Children, made similar recommendations.[122] By the time the noted Indologist R. G. Bhandarkar sent up a memorial from prominent Indian and European citizens of Poona in August 1906, it was found that an extensive discussion of the *devadasi* issue had already taken place in Madras in 1903.[123] The figures for dedication in southern Maharashtra for the period 1905–9, when the *murali* controversy reached its height, was as follows: 836 in Belgaum, 911 in Bijapur, and 876 in Dharwar district.[124] The Bombay government's inquiry into the practice encompassed more than four hundred pages of testimony by district magistrates in Bombay, extensive debate on whether *murali* dedication could be criminalized, as well as far-reaching transformations of Hindu law to prevent illegitimates from inheriting—whether male offspring of *muralis* or *dasiputras* customarily entitled to a half share from a Shudra father's estate.[125] The opinion of Dalit male reformers was not solicited, let alone the *muralis*.

Though sidelined by the government, Dalit reformers like Kamble applauded the effort and lobbied for community support. More significant, if rarely noted, is the fact that public attention to the practice of *muralis'* dedication shifted power within the community toward the viewpoint of male Dalit reformers and publicists. The degradation of Dalit women became a powerful issue around which they mobilized to demand gendered respectability through the abolition of customary practice. As much as intervention into *murali* practice was a means to reform the Dalit family, it was also the lever to move power away from figures such as the *panch* and male heads of household and toward Dalit publicists who wielded a normative conception of sexual vulnerability. Debates over ritual dedication—now recast as prostitution—became crucial to the reconstitution of Dalit masculinity even as it secured the social power of publicists, pedagogues, and community spokesmen.[126]

Shivubai's letter launched a furious debate in and beyond the *Somavanshiya Mitra*.[127] Efforts were made in Jejuri to educate families against dedicating their daughters.[128] Shivram Janba Kamble held a meeting in Jejuri where he made a speech against the practice.[129] *Muralis* like Shivubai held fathers responsible for pushing their daughters into the practice and criticized male customers for creating a market for *muralis'* sexual labor. But men castigated *muralis* for seducing them and breaking up families, thereby assuming *muralis'* "consent" to their dedication. This was tricky given the normal age of dedication and its representation as customary practice. And yet, *muralis* (and their families) were blamed for perpetuating a practice that stigmatized the entire community.

Increasingly, Dalit reformers—like missionaries—suggested criminalizing *murali* dedication. A 1909 reformers' petition demanded the registration of *muralis* and the prosecution of parents who performed new dedications.[130] This produced a climate among Mahars that was responsive to criminalization of the practice. By then, the Bombay government had reached a consensus that criminalizing the practice was the most direct means of curtailing it. No new legislation was passed,[131] but a proclamation banning the practice and reiterating the punishment for dedication was issued.[132] Subsequently, the *Somavanshiya Mitra* carried news of two men, Kisan Sadhu Mahar of Jejuri and Mahalu Mahar of Bombay, prosecuted for dedicating their daughter and sister, aged eleven and thirteen, respectively.[133]

Although some *muralis* supported criminalizing the practice of dedication, their primary focus was on redefining their position within the Dalit community. In addition to prosecuting *muralis,* Dalit reformers like Kamble also promoted *murali* marriage and sexual monogamy as the route to gendered respectability.[134] Shivubai argued that marrying *muralis* acknowledged men's responsibility for the practice, even as it enhanced *muralis'* self-respect and community standing. In fact, on April 18, 1909, the *Somavanshiya Mitra* noted that Shivubai had married the social reformer, Ganpatrao Hanumantrao Gaikwad.[135] Marriage offered protection in a context where men were actively involved in acquiring, dedicating, and frequenting *muralis.* For the women who chose to remain *muralis,* however, emphasis on marriage further stigmatized the practice and pushed it into a zone of shameful secrecy. *Murali* remarriage continued to have great public support.[136] At a meeting of men and women from the *devadasi* and *jogini* communities in Bombay in 1936, Ambedkar addressed women from Kamathipura, the red-light district of Bombay:

> The Mahar women of Kamathipura are a shame to the community. Unless you are prepared to change your ways we shall have nothing to do with you, and we shall have no use for you. There are only two ways open to you: either you remain where you are and continue to be despised and shunned or you give up your disgusting professions and come with us. . . . You will ask me how you are to make your living. There are hundreds of ways of doing it. But I insist you must give up this degrading life. You must marry and settle down to normal domestic life as women of other classes do and not live under conditions that inevitably drag you into prostitution.[137]

As the reform of the traditional practice of *murali* dedication came to be allied with the reform of the Dalit intimate, sexual monogamy and the production of family became appealing alternatives for Dalit men and women to whom this held out a recognizable model of respectability. Sexual respectability was achieved, however, through the stigmatization of "custom" and ritual servitude or dedication, categories of colonial legality whose paradoxical deployment and unforeseen consequences I explore in greater detail in chapter 2.

The fraught position of female subjectivity "between community and state" is an enduring binarism in South Asian historiography. An adroit colonial move allied women with caste and religious communities and simultaneously castigated communities for reproducing female backwardness and preventing female emancipation. As the relationship between women and community deepened, first in reaction to colonial intervention and later as a form of nationalist glorification, the possibility of gender equality was also precluded. By the turn of the century, upper-caste nationalists had recuperated women as symbols of a modernized "tradition" and relegated them to the inner recesses of community life, arguing that women would be enfranchised from within community rather than through colonial state intervention. An issue taken up largely by Christian missionaries and later by Dalit reformers, *murali* reform was distinct from this colonial-nationalist association of women with tradition. Here, the issue was the overdetermined association of Dalit female sexuality with sexual availability and degraded female value. The ill treatment of the upper-caste Hindu widow by scriptural injunctions is an apt comparison, although Dalit reformists differed in their efforts to create a set of secular associations between femininity and domesticity.

As the work of regulating Dalit women continued in more dispersed forms, the degraded status of women was seen to be closely related to the emasculation of Dalit men. Fifteen years after the *murali* issue died down, an editorial by the Dalit activist and thinker B. R. Ambedkar asked why Brahmin and upper-caste women enjoyed an exalted status as mothers when Dalit women's children were subjected to humiliation and denied basic recognition, negating all the desires that a mother might have for her child's well-being.[138] He went on to say, "You have given birth to [us] men, and when we are treated worse than animals, it hurts you." Thus linked to women's degradation, Dalit masculinity was simultaneously positioned as wounded and vulnerable. Importantly, however, the onus was on Dalit women to reform themselves and play a central role in modernizing the community. They had to resignify the gendered habitus: "You should wear your sari in the way that upper-caste women wear their saris. You incur no expense by doing so. Similarly, the many necklaces around your neck, and the silver and tin bangles you wear from wrist to elbow is a mark of identification [*olakhnyachi khun*]. . . . If you must wear jewelry, then get gold jewelry made. If you cannot, then don't wear jewelry. Pay attention to cleanliness!"[139]

What did these exhortations mean for women from a stigmatized community? On one hand, like upper-caste ideologies, they symbolically associated women's status with community status. On the other hand, they emphasized the significance of clothing, jewelry, and the right to ceremonial display as aspects of self-fashioning vigorously policed by upper castes. The right to a new habitus,[140] to good clothing, footwear, jewelry, and bodily comportment—standing erect while speaking, refusing to contort the body in an obsequious fashion—was critical to Dalit self-fashioning. Though discourses of sexuality and of female enfranchisement were caste-specific, the focus on the feminized body—how it was experienced and represented—was central to a range of political processes.[141] Women, marriage, and family remained irreplaceable sites for reproducing caste ideas and practices. Thus emergent forms of a caste-specific female subjectivity were directly implicated in the production of a social field where transformations of the non-Brahmin and Dalit habitus could occur, and they deeply affected emergent forms of caste masculinity. The politics of *caste and gender* complicated modes of political participation and of subject-formation associated with masculinization and community modernization. In a very real sense, however, the stage was set for a Dalit public sphere rendered male.

SEPARATE BUT EQUAL: SCHOOL, TEMPLE, AND THE DALIT SELF

We all drink water from the same tap, in hotels and Irani stores we sit at the same table and drink tea and eat bread and biscuits. On trains and steam boats we sit with our thighs and shoulders touching.

                                                                    DB, April 20, 1907

As a distinctive identity for Mahar Dalits was clarified in the late nineteenth century, so too were the emerging tensions of village life intensified—conflicts between Dalit and Maratha groups over provision of services, the exploitation of caste labor, and friction between claims to Brahmin proportional representation and anti-casteism increased. The situation made escape from the village highly desirable for Dalits. Indeed, the liberatory potential of machine and metropolis exerted a profound hold on the Dalit imagination and the Dalit modernity that developed in concert with the urbanization of Dalit communities.

Mahar Dalits migrated to cities like Bombay and Nagpur in disproportionate numbers.[142] According to the Indian census, between 1872 and 1881 the number of Mahars in Bombay rose 66 percent. By 1938, almost 92 percent of untouchable workers in the city were Mahars. Mahars performed unskilled labor under difficult and exploitative working conditions—40 percent of them were considered to be performing "coolie" labor, and they constituted more than 45 percent of the total workforce.[143] They were concentrated in particular industries: more than 60 percent worked in the railways or textile mills—the railways were the first and most significant mode of Mahar employment and drew a majority of workers from the Nasik and Ratnagiri districts. Significant numbers worked for the municipality, for factories , and for public works companies such as Bombay Electric Supply and Transport (BEST). Mahar migrants from Satara comprised the bulk of dockworkers and coal miners.[144]

Urban migration and urban infrastructure—especially everyday technologies of travel and communication that appeared to shrink, even obviate, social distance—provoked key transformations of Dalit selfhood. *Din Bandhu*'s commentator on urban life was clear that modern travel— "sitting with thighs and shoulders touching"—obliterated caste distinctions, because it was impossible to maintain caste taboos or regulate contact in public conveyances.[145] Lower-caste use of steamboats, trains, and trams opened a new dimension where touch was rendered anonymous even as it was secularized. However, these new spaces were in constant danger of being overwhelmed by social pressure to reproduce hidebound Brahminical beliefs and practices, as Valangkar's *abhang* warned.[146]

When a woman is polluted, even if she is a queen among the Mahars
She is shy of her husband and public gatherings
[Like such women] a Mahar or a Mang is not seen in public

Though the word is *sabha* [association] it is a sham because there is no
    place for a Mahar and Mang in it
Nobody knows what this *sabha* does
Why don't you ask a Mahar or a Mang who the members of this *sabha*
    are, give me an example of a Mahar who is a member of this public
    gathering

Clean your minds and bathe your bodies
Then, tie the bond of unity
If you get polluted by the touch of the Mahar
How will you achieve anything

[Respect] the name *sarvajanik* [public] of your organization and allow
    entry to Mahars and Mangs
Do the work by mutual agreement, by discarding shame . . .
There will be equality in society
Understand this fully, that only through the equality of Brahmin and
    Mahar
Will your unity look mature

Satyapreet [lover of truth] says embrace and accept the Mang and Mahar
And thereby achieve unity

Yours
A Vanquished Mahar[147]

It is likely that Valangkar's *abhang* was publicizing the Din Bandhu Sarvajanik Sabha, which was formed in 1884 by Krishnarao Bhalaker and others to counter what they considered to be a Brahmin-dominated, exclusivist Sarvajanik Sabha. Valangkar drew on a set of gendered associations between social stigma and public intercourse to challenge Dalits' civic exclusion. Like a woman naturally "shy of her husband and public gatherings" when she was menstruating, Dalits also experienced "shame" and self-revulsion. One was never to see a Mang or a Mahar in public. Valangkar's *abhang* challenged the Dalit's internalization of pollution and proposed that without equality between Brahmin and Mahar, between the excessively fortunate and the excessively stigmatized, there could be no true "public." For Valangkar, the organization of the world through the phenomenology of touch and smell also enabled an extension of stigma from biological bodies to the metaphorical collective of the body politic. In the interplay between literal touch and the imaginative democratization of the body he saw possibilities for self-fashioning and political transformation. Going further, Valangkar also suggested that only with a *caste mind* cleaned of impurities could the Sarvajanik Sabha (a regional precursor to the Indian National Congress) accept the Dalit castes.

Ironically, then, the institutional spaces and amenities of colonial urbanity exacerbated the experience of the caste body by highlighting the irrationality of caste segregation. As Dalit publicists—Valangkar, Kamble, and others—denaturalized the caste order, they also motivated caste Hindus to justify caste distinction in new ways that utilized the regulatory power of colonial institutions to produce new instruments of caste hegemony. Both dimensions, Dalit emancipation and new forms of subjection, were played out in schools and temples.

Access to education was a long-standing demand of Dalit publicists, as it had been for Satyashodak activists. Education was central to self-fashioning because it demystified the Brahmin trickery at the heart of the continued dehumanization of Dalits and non-Brahmins. There was also the material fact of Brahmin preponderance in colonial administration.[148] Conflicts over access to colonial schooling emphasized the built-in contradictions of colonial education. In 1882, the Hunter Commission asserted the government of India's commitment to untouchable education, reaffirming Wood's Dispatch of 1854, which opened government-funded schools to all castes in response to missionary pressure. The record of government-funded education for untouchables was poor, however. For instance, the first public schools in Poona's Purandhar district opened in 1836, but by 1839 only 17 of 759 pupils came from the untouchable communities. The numbers did not rise significantly in following years.[149]

The most famous case is of the Christian Mahar convert from Dharwar who petitioned the government in June 1856 after being denied admission into the government school. The Bombay government refused to compromise the education of the majority of caste Hindu students at a government school for the sake of "a single individual" by making caste Hindus associate with a Mahar student. Caste Hindus' right to exclusive education was thus reinterpreted as the colonial administration's respect for the religious sentiments of the majority.[150]

The Free Church of Scotland and the American Marathi Mission had supported Phule's Society for the Promotion of Mahars and Mangs, which established schools in Pune between 1848 and 1852. The extensive involvement of missionaries in the field of untouchable education was viewed as blurring the line between proseletyzation and social service, compromising the colonial state's explicit commitment to religious noninterference after the 1857 Mutiny. Colonial officials held missionaries responsible for politicizing untouchables who showed "independence and self-sufficiency,"[151] by inciting them to "claim a right" even when untouchables themselves chose not to exercise it,[152] thus exacerbating conflict between the majority of caste Hindu students and a few untouchable students.

Conflicts over equal education in the 1880s and 1890s confirmed government fears of unrest. Such an incident had taken place in Rajangaon, in Sirur *taluka*, Pune, in October 1886, when the village *patel* and *kulkarni* twice closed down a school run by the American Marathi Mission, using violence and intimidation to prevent the seven Mahar (and two Maratha) children from attending the school run by Indian teachers.[153] A similar report from Satara noted that Mahar boys were not allowed to sit in the school rooms with other boys, and that often a "few miserable Mahar boys are seen seated in the blazing sun outside scribbling on their slates and apparently entirely neglected."[154] Or else, as happened in Manmad, Nasik district, in 1884–85, caste Hindus financed an English class through private funds rather than sending their children to the Anglo vernacular school run by the Church Mission Society, which also admitted untouchable students. Often, the government's anxiety to maintain (and enhance) the population of students attending publicly funded English schools undercut the commitment to education for untouchables.[155] Increasingly, the colonial government faced a spate of petitions as untouchable students—who faced informal boycott by caste Hindus or the active enforcement of segregated education by colonial officials—petitioned for civic inclusion, while the parents of caste Hindu students wished to exclude untouchables from classrooms. The Bombay Education Department had considerable leeway in deciding issues on a case-by-case basis in this contentious atmosphere.[156] As government's general commitment to native education confronted its specific commitment to untouchables' education, a novel resolution arose: Dalit students were placed on the school's verandah at a distance from both caste Hindu classmates and the classroom, to fulfill the colonial mission of educational access.

Sitting on the verandah obstructed the untouchable students' vision and hearing and left them vulnerable to the adversities of climate. In 1916, Communist activist R. B. More attended classes on the first floor of a school in Tale, in the Mangaon district, sitting on a scaffold erected by school authorities.[157] Like the scaffold, the school verandah preserved the illusion of equal education even as it emphasized the liminal status of those Dalit students who had managed to secure a right to government education. Reinterpreting the caste Hindu position as the majority sentiment, colonial officials made the verandah a new technology of segregation that reproduced caste exclusion.

Dapoli, the hub of early Dalit activism, was also a significant site of struggles for equal education. After the Society for the Propogation of the Gospel closed down its primary school, military pensioners petitioned the government on July 1, 1892, to enroll fourteen of their children in the municipality's primary school.[158] After asserting that admitting Dalit children would cause caste Hindu students to leave the school, the Dapoli municipality agreed to open a separate class with a separate teacher if the Mahar and Chambhar pensioners could collect enough boys.[159] B. R. Ambedkar, who attended that school between 1894 and 1896, described how all the Dalit students sat in one room, placing their slates on the ground so teachers could examine them. The children were barred from the common water supply.[160] The right to education, when combined with new practices of segregation, paradoxically *intensified* untouchable students' experience of stigma.

The Dapoli petitioners protested on September 8, 1892, requesting that the students be included in the other classrooms. When their petition was rejected by the Dapoli municipality, the petitioners approached colonial officials, who asked the municipality whether the children could be accommodated on the verandah.[161] The municipality replied that the verandah was not large enough for all the children, but that the Dalit petitioners could pay Rs. 50 to enlarge it.[162] Stalled, the pensioners continued up the bureaucratic line until J. Nugent, commissioner of the

Southern Division, told Vishnudas Hari Barve, the chairman of the municipality, that he was required to open the school to the Dalit children.[163] The municipality responded that equal education should occur gradually in order not to offend orthodox sensibility, and by November 1894 the municipal engineer had not yet approved verandah extension.[164] After threatening repeal of the school's grant, Director of Public Instruction K. M. Chatfield instructed the Dalit children to maintain a safe distance from other Hindu children in the classroom.[165] A visit to the municipal school at the end of 1894 found "the Officers' children sitting in the same class rooms along with the other boys at the distance of three or four feet and receiving instruction with the class regularly." The Dapoli pensioners were said to be satisfied, because "they never wished that their children should mix with the other boys but they wanted that they should receive instruction along with them, separately in the same class rooms, and this is now done."[166] Though the collector of Ratnagiri decided to monitor the progress of untouchable education through quarterly reports, access to schools was a vexing one. Almost a decade later, in 1901, the president of the ADPM sent another petition to the Bombay government, claiming that Dalit students continued to be excluded from the school.[167]

As Dalit students tried to enter schools at the turn of the twentieth century, equal right to education was converted into the right to segregated education for untouchable students: caste restrictions were respected due to fear of boycott by caste Hindu students. The school verandah was a new mechanism of exclusion that encompassed overlapping structures of exclusion. One was based on Brahminical norms that replicated caste hierarchies. The other, grounded in liberal language, acquiesced to caste Hindus' refusal of mixed-caste schools as a matter of respect for the opinions of the majority community. Levels of education among untouchable students continued to be abysmally low: less than 0.48 percent were literate in 1911; by 1931, that number rose to 2.9 percent.[168] In response to segregated schooling, Mahar Dalits in Nagpur, Bombay, Poona, and Ahmednagar established separate schools and hostels for Dalit students in the first two decades of the twentieth century, complementing earlier work in Vidarbha and the Central Provinces.[169] Shivram Janba Kamble defended separate schools and argued that because Brahmin schoolmasters perpetuated caste distinctions, schools had to hire Muslim teachers.[170] By 1908, Vithal Ramji Shinde's DCM ran fifteen day schools, six Sunday schools, and four industrial schools in Bombay, Poona, and Ahmednagar.[171] By 1909, the DCM had even reached into Dapoli.[172] In 1916, of 1,600 Depressed Class students, 500 were enrolled in Shinde's schools. Though they were spurred by the failure of government schools to include Dalit students, separate schooling defined a powerful strategy for refashioning the Dalit self.

The Mahar community's growing refusal to countenance socioritual stigmatization produced new sites of contestation. Like separate educational facilities, efforts to build separate temples reflect an arc of Dalit critique. The economic enfranchisement of an important group of Mahar elites in the Vidarbha region enabled the institutionalization of a separate religious authority for Mahars. The 1877 opening of Empress Mills in Nagpur had provided a new source of livelihood for Mahar Dalits. In addition, a Mahar petty bourgeoisie of *malguzars* (landlords) financed the move into an industrializing cotton economy. This educated elite maintained links with rural areas, endowing schools and hostels and playing a role in shaping early Dalit politicization.

Born in 1864, Vithoba Raoji Moon Pande typified the new Mahar "small scale capitalist" first mentioned in an 1899 settlement report for the Nagpur district.[173] Educated in a mission school and influenced by critiques of caste hierarchy and Hindu superstition, he took advantage of his frequent travel as a cotton trader to act as a *pracharak* (preacher) for the Gorakshan Sabha (Organization for Cow Protection) which had links with the Arya Samaj.[174] In 1906, Moon Pande established the Antyaj Samaj (Society for the Outcastes), renamed the Loyal Mahar Sabha in 1912 and presided over by his close associate, the Reverend G. D. Philips. Before he died in 1924, Moon Pande had requested nomination to the Central Provinces Legislative Council. Like Valangkar, Moon Pande's life coincided with the emergence of the Dalit public and publicists in the crucible of colonial modernity.[175] Unlike Valangkar, however, Moon Pande's challenge to caste discrimination instituted an alternative source of religious hierarchy.

When Mahars were denied use of the Ambal tank at Nagpur's Ramtek temple in 1903,[176] Moon Pande mobilized a large group of Mahars who belonged to *bhajan mandalis* (groups that performed religious music). They went to the home of the temple owner, Raoji Raghuji Bhosle,[177] who gave Mahars permission to bathe at the Ambal tank on the condition that they stop eating beef and, more generally, desist from unhygienic practices.[178] Bhosle's response typified the upper-caste reformism that rationalized Dalits' degradation as resulting from their stigmatizing practices. Moon Pande appears to have supported this reform because he held meetings in villages near Nagpur to persuade Mahars to stop eating beef, even demanding that they take a public oath to that effect.[179] Although they did so, it was clear that relations with temple authorities had reached an impasse. The Ramtek Temple Committee asked Mahars to channel a portion of the fees paid to the *pande* (Brahmin priest) at the *ghats*—for services like shaving or making offerings of *pindadaan* to the ancestors—to the Gorakshan Sabha to fund separate Mahar bathing *ghats* at the temple tank. No Mahar *ghats* were built, however.

Moon Pande responded to the Brahmins' exploitation of Mahars at the Ramtek temple by establishing a separate Mahar priesthood to minister to the community's religious needs. To counter the Gorakshan Sabha's failure to build separate Mahar *ghats,* Moon Pande asked—and received—permission from the Ramtek Temple Committee to build a separate temple for Mahars on January 24, 1905. In March 1906, he acquired land for the purpose at a high price.[180] That same year the Antyaj Samaj committee took over management of the new Mahar *ghats,* established an independent Mahar priesthood, and gave Moon Pande *pandeship,* the right to perform rites and receive *dakshina* (charities) from Mahar pilgrims at the *ghats.*[181]

By 1907–08, this parallel structure of religious authority protected Mahar pilgrims from paying extravagant sums for *shraddha* (funeral) rites.[182] Moon Pande's use of Mahars' growing economic strength to assert a positive Hindu identity went further. Along with the Reverend G. D. Philips, he collected funds for a separate temple, a Shivalaya, near the Mahar *ghats.* Construction began on October 27, 1920, and was completed in 1924, shortly before Moon Pande's death.[183]

Separate institutions signaled failed efforts at civic and religious equality. They also indexed the changed discursive and political contexts of Dalit self-fashioning. Unlike the establishment of separate schools, Moon Pande's temple and Mahar priesthood reproduced religious hierarchy by legitimizing the priest's role. Instead of criticizing Hinduism in toto and envisioning a complete excision from Hindu religiosity, Moon Pande's critique of religious exclusion produced a mimetic structure of religious authority, a Mahar priesthood. At the same time, his work underscored the growing economic strength of an emerging Mahar elite whose power as reformers within the community allowed them to challenge the Hindu hierarchy. Moon Pande's actions were radical and reformist, and indicated the ambivalences of Mahar religiosity and the limits to Hindu inclusion.

Perhaps more pointed and problematic is the matter of thirteen Mahars who entered a temple dedicated to the god Meghnath, an incarnation of

जाहीर पत्र

खाली सही करणारा कडून सर्वे महार मित्रास जाहीर खबर कळवीण्यात येते की रामटेक देवस्थान श्री अंबाळातळावर्चे स्नान माहार ठोकास मुळींच नसल्यामुळें माझे पीस्याने खाली दीलेल्या कमेटीचा हुकूम आणून सर्वांस स्नानाची मोकळीक करून दीली.

नंतर त्यांचेच हुकूमावरून तेथें आपला घाट बांधणें सुरू केलें असतां त्या तळ्याचे पाण्यास लागलेली १०६ नंबर पाहाळाची जागा ती, खालील कमेटीचे अधिकारांत नसल्यामुळें, राजेश्री गोपाळ गणेश फडनवीस माळगुजार रामटेक यांचे कडून माझे पीस्याने खास खरेदी करून घेतली आणि स्वपूजेची शीव पिंडी तेथें स्थापीत करून घाटाचे काम पुरे केलें.

पुढें तेथें देवालय बांधले आहे अशा बेताचा १ जोता बांधून पुढें कामाची चाल करून ठेविला आहे—ता १३-४-१३ रोजी प्रती राजे श्रीमान व्हाईसराय सरकार प्रिव्हर्थी नागपुर टीनहॉल येथें मेहरबान रेव्हरेंड जी. टी. फीलीप साहेब यांचे अध्यक्ष ते खालां सर्वे महार लोकांची जनरल सभा भरून ईरोपीयन वगैरे लोकांस दी पारटी प्रांती सम्मान देऊन, बरील सर्वे गोष्टींचा उल्लेख सर्वांकडून मंजूर झाला त्यावर सर्वे पुढार्यांचे लेख. असून त्यामंजूर पत्रावर खालीं दीलेल्या ऑफिसर हुजूरांची न्याय सही आहे, खालां सही करणारा त्यांचा आश्रय धारक व पाळलेला असल्यामुळे मला त्यांचे स्मारक व पीठ्या चे ऊतराईपणे वरील कामाचे चाली प्रमाणे आपले एजेंस्यांनी खास देवालय बांधणे आहे करितां ता. २७-१०-२० रोजी आम्हा तर्फे काम करणारा हुसेनी व मनोराम प्रधान व तुझ्या महार म्हाळी याजला कांही रुपये देऊन वरील स्मारक देवालयाचे काम चालू केले आहे. वरील सर्वे प्रकरणी रजीस्टर लेख असून नागपुर माहार समाजीक मेंडळीने जाहीर प्रसिद्ध केलें की रामटेक येथें महार लोकांचा जो घाट आणि मुर्ती आहे त्या ऊज्या स्थानी लोकपणीवर शीवाळय बांधणे आहे असे छोहतात करितां त्यांना कींवा ईतर कोणासही लौकीक, स्वार्थे करणें असल्यास त्यांनी आमच्या खरीदकेलेली सह्हदीर्यां जागा खेरीज करून आपले इमारती वगैराची कामे कोठेंही चालविण्यास आमची कांही हरकत नाही. असे न करितां जाऊन आपलेच तोंम याने बंद ऊभारून आमेच कामांत हरकत आणील. कांबा त्यास स्थाय्बळावर अधिकारी वर्गांकडून पिंडग्न वगैरे सर्वे ऊज्या घेण्याचा हक्काधिकार नसल्या खेरीज वरील कामावर यात्रेकऱ्यांस फसऊन पैसे कादील. स्वायोम्य आम्हास धक्का पोहचेल तर त्यावर योग्य कारबाई केली जाईल. व त्याबद्दल मला त्या हुजुराकडेस लिहीणें कींवा खटपट करणें भाग पडेल—करितां आपले माहार बंधुत जाणून वाकिडवणा येकनये करितां हा जाहीर पत्र नामे नोटीस या वीनंती पत्र समजा. फ ता. १०-११-२० ई.

देवस्थान कमेटी अधिकारी वर्ग

हुकूम नंबर २१६   हुकूम नंबर २१६

राजे बहादूर रघोजी राव भोसले
गंगाधर राव चीटनवीस,
पांडुरंग राव गुजर
रामचंद्र राव शिरके.
दापोधर पंत पंडे

हुजूर त्या माहार कमेटीचे मंजुर पत्रावर न्याय सही देणार,

आनरेबळ सर, सी. ई. लो. साहेब बहादूर आय. सी. एस. ॲन्ड सी. आय. ई.
सेकेटरी, दु धी गव्हरमेंट ऑफ इंडिया.

आपला,
वामन विठोबा मून संत पंडे नागपुर
ड. नंबर २ द झु.

Figure 3. Public notice issued by Vaman Vithoba Moon Sant Pande, son of Vithoba Raoji Moon Pande, October 11, 1920. The notice outlines the exclusion of the Mahar community from bathing at the Ramtek *ghats;* Moon Pande's acquisition of a plot abutting the Ambala tank for the performance of funereal rites and plans to construct a Shiva shrine; and the support of British officials, including the viceroy at a meeting in 1913. It ends with a warning to "Mahar brothers" to beware of Mahars performing religious rites without proper authorization. Courtesy of the Vasant Moon Collection, Nagpur.

Shiva, in the village of Washer in Chanda district of the Central Provinces on September 22, 1922. They "slaughtered a goat there, sprinkled its blood upon the idol, put *shendur* [vermillion] on the image and adorned it with flowers."[184] Though staged as religious worship, this incident blurred distinctions between the sacred and the profane because anointing a deity with goat's blood could also be interpreted as an act of defilement. The ambivalence of the animal sacrifice arose from its signifying potential as worship and defilement. If upper-caste Hindus interpreted animal sacrifice as desecrating the temple, it is also true that temples to Shiva, a non-Brahmin god in Maharashtra, would have allowed the practice of animal sacrifice. Was it the sacrifice of the goat (as opposed to the more common buffalo), or the physical presence of Dalit worshippers in the temple that challenged its sacrality? Could the right to worship encompass the right to worship differently, as well as the right of Dalits to worship in a mixed-caste temple?

NEW DEPARTURES: THE EMERGENCE OF AUTONOMOUS DALIT POLITICS

By the late 1920s, conditions enabling Dalit activism were well in place. The distinctive ideological and institutional contexts in which Dalits' lives were enmeshed from the later nineteenth century facilitated an incipient discourse of rights and emergent conceptions of the Dalit self as a historical actor and a political subject. Nonconformist Christianity and imaginative alliances with radical Euro-American traditions of free thought had influenced ideas of self-respect, equality, and social justice, while the radical anti-casteism of the Satyashodak Samaj associated the stigmatized existence of Dalits and non-Brahmins with the Brahmins' ritual, economic, and social domination. Ironically, Dalits' experiences with the institutional infrastructure of colonial modernity amplified the impact of stigmatization and exclusion. Indeed, Dalit activism developed through the enhanced contradiction between the experience of stigma and the possibility of emancipation through the institutions and ideologies of colonial modernity.

The Dalit public that coalesced in the first decades of the twentieth century reflected the changed experience of Dalitness: by the 1920s, disparate and localized challenges to the caste order had coalesced into an explicit demand for civic rights. When three thousand people gathered in the town of Mahad on March 19, 1927, for nonviolent public action, a *satyagraha* to take water from the Chavdar tank, they were testing a

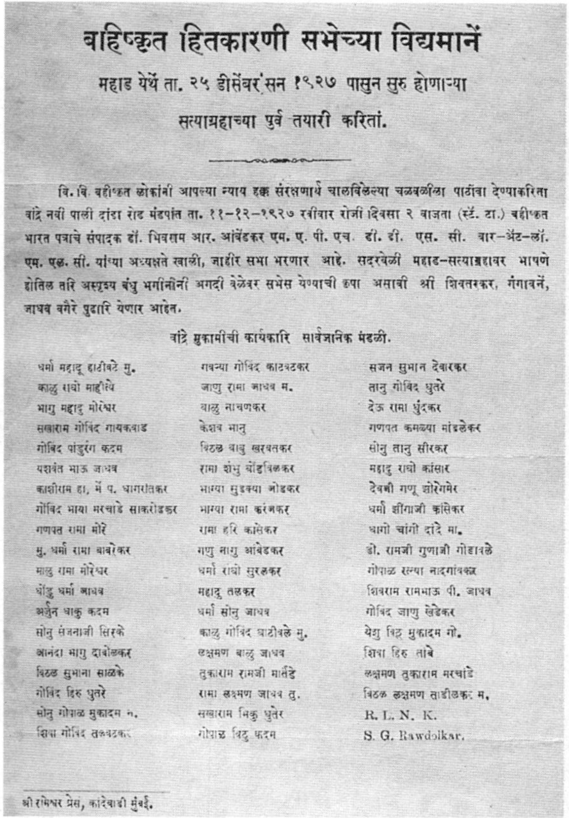

बहिष्कृत हितकारणी सभेच्या विद्यमानें

महाड येथें ता. २५ डीसेंबर सन १९२७ पासुन सुरु होणाऱ्या

सत्याग्रहाच्या पुर्व तयारी करितां.

वि. वि. बहीष्कत लोकांनी आपल्या न्याय हक्क संरक्षणार्थ चालविलेल्या चळवळीला पाठींबा देण्याकरिता वांद्रे नवी पाली दांडा रोड मंडपांत ता. ११–१२–१९२७ रवीवार रोजीं दिवसा २ वाजता (स्टँ. टा.) बहीष्कत भारत पत्राचे संपादक डॉ. भिवराम आर. आंबेडकर एम. ए. पी. एच. डी. डी. एस. सी. बार–ॲट–लॉ. एम. एल. सी. यांच्या अध्यक्षते खाली, जाहीर सभा भरणार आहे. सदरवेळी महाड–सत्याग्रहावर भाषणे होतिल तरि अस्पृश्य बंधु भगीनींनीं अगदी वेळेवर सभेस येण्याची कृपा असावी श्री शिवतरकर, गंगावनें, जाधव वगैरे पुढारि येणार आहेत.

वांद्रे मुकामीची कार्यकारि सार्वजनिक मंडळी.

धर्मा महादू हाटीवटे मु.	गवन्या गोविंद काटवटकर	सजन सुमान देवारकर
काळु रावो माहीरे	जाणु रामा जाधव म.	तानु गोविंद धुतेरे
भागु महादु मोरेश्वर	वाळु नाचणकर	देऊ रामा धुंदकर
सखाराम गोविंद गायकवाड	केशव भानु	गणपत कमळ्या मांडलेकर
गोविंद पांडुरंग कदम	विठ्ठ बाबु खरवतकर	सोनु तानु सीरकर
यशवंत भाऊ जाधव	रामा शंभु चोंडविलकर	महादु रावो कांसार
काशीराम हा. मे प. धागरतकर	भाग्या मुडक्या जोडकर	देवजी गणू झोरेगमेर
गोविंद भाया मरचांडे साकरोडकर	भाग्या रामा करंमकर	धर्मा झींगाजी कासेकर
गणपत रामा मोरे	रामा हरि कासेकर	धागो चांगो दांदे मा.
मु. धर्मा रामा बाबरेकर	गणु नागु आंबेडकर	डो. रामजी गुणाजी गोडावले
मालु रामा मोरेश्वर	धर्मा रावो सुरलकर	गोपाळ रस्या नादगांवकर
धोंडु धर्मा जाधव	महादु तलकर	शिवराम रामभाऊ पी. जाधव
अर्जुन धाकु कदम	धर्मा सोनु जाधव	गोविंद जाणु खेडेकर
सोनु संजनाजी सिरके	काळु गोविंद घाटीवले मु.	येशु विठु मुकादम गो.
आनंदा भागु दाबोळकर	लक्ष्मण बाळु जाधव	शिवा हिरु तांबे
विठ्ठ सुभाना साळके	तुकाराम रामजी मार्तंडे	लक्ष्मण तुकाराम मरचांडे
गोविंद हिरु धुतरे	रामा लक्ष्मण जाधव तु.	विठल लक्ष्मण ताडीलकर म.
सोनु गोपाळ मुकादम न.	सखाराम भिकु धुतेर	R. L. N. K.
शिवा गोविंद तळवटकर	गोपाळ विठु कदम	S. G. Rawdolkar.

श्री रामेश्वर प्रेस, कांदेवाडी मुंबई.

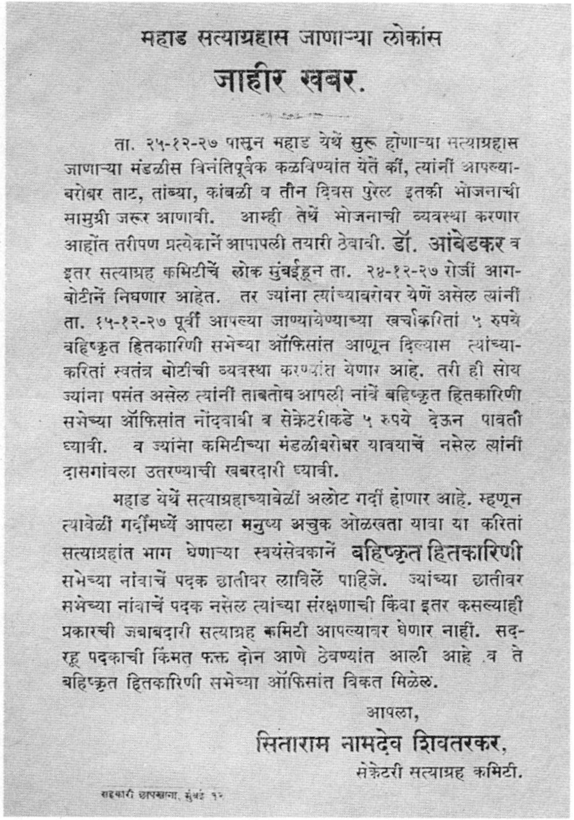

महाड सत्याग्रहास जाणाऱ्या लोकांस

जाहीर खबर.

ता. २५-१२-२७ पासून महाड येथें सुरू होणाऱ्या सत्याग्रहास जाणाऱ्या मंडळीस विनंतिपूर्वक कळविण्यांत येतें कीं, त्यांनीं आपल्या-बरोबर ताट, तांब्या, कांबळी व तीन दिवस पुरेल इतकी भोजनाची सामुग्री जरूर आणावी. आम्ही तेथें भोजनाची व्यवस्था करणार आहोंत तरीपण प्रत्येकानें आपापली तयारी ठेवावी. **डॉ. आंबेडकर** व इतर सत्याग्रह कमिटीचें लोक मुंबईहून ता. २४-१२-२७ रोजीं आग-बोटीनें निघणार आहेत. तर ज्यांना त्यांच्याबरोबर येणें असेल त्यांनीं ता. १५-१२-२७ पूर्वी आपल्या जाण्यायेण्याच्या खर्चाकरितां ५ रुपये बहिष्कृत हितकारिणी सभेच्या ऑफिसांत आणून दिल्यास त्यांच्या-करितां स्वतंत्र बोटीची व्यवस्था करण्यांत येणार आहे. तरी ही सोय ज्यांना पसंत असेल त्यांनीं ताबतोब आपली नांवें बहिष्कृत हितकारिणी सभेच्या ऑफिसांत नोंदवावी व सेक्रेटरीकडे ५ रुपये देऊन पावती घ्यावी. व ज्यांना कमिटीच्या मंडळीबरोबर यावयाचें नसेल त्यांनीं दासगांवला उतरण्याची खबरदारी घ्यावी.

महाड येथें सत्याग्रहाच्यावेळीं अलोट गर्दी होणार आहे. म्हणून त्यावेळीं गर्दीमध्यें आपला मनुष्य अचुक ओळखता यावा या करितां सत्याग्रहांत भाग घेणाऱ्या स्वयंसेवकानें **बहिष्कृत हितकारिणी** सभेच्या नांवाचें पदक छातीवर लाविलें पाहिजे. ज्यांच्या छातीवर सभेच्या नांवाचें पदक नसेल त्यांच्या संरक्षणाची किंवा इतर कसल्याही प्रकारची जबाबदारी सत्याग्रह कमिटी आपल्यावर घेणार नाहीं. सद-रहू पदकाची किंमत फक्त दोन आणे ठेवण्यांत आली आहे व ते बहिष्कृत हितकारिणी सभेच्या ऑफिसांत विकत मिळेल.

आपला,

सिताराम नामदेव शिवतरकर,

सेक्रेटरी सत्याग्रह कमिटी.

सहकारी छापखाना, मुंबई १२

Figure 4. Flyer for a public meeting on December 12, 1927, in Bandra (Bombay) to be addressed by B. R. Ambedkar in preparation for the December 25 Mahad *satyagraha* (left); and flyer asking for contributions of Rs. 5 to cover travel costs to Mahad and requesting all activists to wear badges of the Bahishkrit Hitakarini Sabha in Mahad (right). Courtesy of Prakash Vishwasrao, *Dr. Babasaheb Ambedkar* (Mumbai: Lok Vangmay, 2007).

resolution.[185] Three years earlier, the Mahad municipality had granted untouchables access to the town's public water sources. Apparently, civic inclusion threatened religious orthodoxy. The priest of the temple next to the tank ran through town announcing that the *satyagrahis* were not merely taking water from the tank, but were also attempting to enter the temple. Rumors of temple entry inflamed caste Hindu sentiments. A riot ensued. Caste Hindus attacked Dalits, many of whom were severely wounded and taken to the hospital, while others sought shelter in Muslim homes.[186] The Chavdar water tank was ritually purified soon thereafter to rid it of the polluting touch of Dalits.

One might have anticipated that such violent resistance to Dalits' claims would bring their struggle to a close. Instead, another *satyagraha* was started on December 25, 1927. A weekly letter from Mahad's district superintendent of police noted that "[h]andbills in connection with satyagraha of untouchables at Mahad are being distributed all over Mahad and Mangaon talukas [disrict subdivision]. The argument in the handbills is that . . . untouchables have a right to take water from the aforesaid tank. This right must now be established."[187]

Ten thousand people gathered in Mahad this time. They took considerable risks in participating in the *satyagraha* and faced retaliatory violence. Despite support from important non-Brahmin activists, tensions between Dalits and non-Brahmins persisted, and Keshavrao Jedhe appears to have participated in a call to impose a boycott against Mahars, even making a speech in favor of a boycott.[188] As Dalits asserted the right to participate in the *satyagraha*, tensions between non-Brahmins and Dalits assumed an economic dimension in rural areas where Maratha or non-Brahmin landlords directly exploited Dalit labor: "We had never imagined that these issues would be publicized so quickly. But like the waving of a magic wand begging for *bhakar* [millet bread], and eating dead meat has stopped in Kolaba district. But in those villages where these new programs have begun . . . [untouchables] are not allowed to come and go in the village, in some places wastelands given to them have been taken away."[189]

In a spectacular challenge to the orthodoxy of religious sanctions behind caste distinction, *satyagraha* organizers, who included caste Hindus and Dalits, agreed to burn the sacred text, the Manusmriti.[190] A longtime Brahmin associate of B. R. Ambedkar's, G. N. Sahasrabuddhe, moved the resolution to burn the text at Mahad. Ambedkar, who had read portions of the Manusmriti with a pundit in the months before the conference, had with him a copy of those segments concerned with the punishment and social exclusion of women and Shudras. Those portions were burned in public rejection of caste hierarchy and sanctioned violence. Ambedkar acknowledged the debt to the techniques and strategies of popular nationalism, comparing this rejection of the caste order with the burning of foreign cloth by Indian nationalists to challenge colonial exploitation. Both cases were examples of spectacular refusals of oppressive sociopolitical orders.

The events of 1927 marked a significant departure in Dalit politics and inaugurated urban-centered regional associational forms. The Bombay-based Bahishkrit Hitakarini Sabha (Association for the Amelioration of the Boycotted; BHS) was the organizational force behind the Mahad *satyagraha*.[191] Also known as the Depressed Classes Institute, the BHS was formed on July 20, 1924, to promote education and social reform among Mahar Dalits. In Bombay, it established a free reading room, a Students' Conference, and a Mahar Hockey Club.[192] The BHS also ran a free hostel in Sholapur; opened vocational schools, libraries, and community centers; and supported study circles and cultural activities. In its early phase, the BHS undertook joint programs with organizations such as the Social Service League dominated by caste Hindu reformers.[193] BHS activists intervened in village-level conflicts and held Bahishkrit Parishads (Depressed Class Conferences) across the Bombay-Konkan region.[194]

Throughout the interwar years, new conceptions of public access and civic inclusion animated Dalit public action. As radicalized Dalits made bold public rights claims and launched an attack on the symbols of caste orthodoxy, they enlarged their repertoire of activism as well as their conceptual vocabulary of politics.

CHAPTER 2

The Problem of Caste Property

In 1921, Kalicharan Nandagavli, a wealthy businessman and *malguzar* (landlord) from the Gondiya district, introduced a measure to open all civic water supplies to the Depressed Classes in the Central Provinces in the interest of realizing "ordinary human and civil rights."[1] The Arya Samaj reformer S.K. Bole introduced a similar resolution during the 1922–23 session of the Bombay Legislative Council, calling for opening all communal and municipal water supplies to the Depressed Classes.[2] In 1926, the Bombay Legislative Council added a proviso that municipalities depriving Depressed Classes of access to public amenities would suffer loss of government funds. Each of these resolutions preceded passage of the Mahad municipality's resolution that opened the Chavdar tank to all castes, and they were supported by Dalit and non-Brahmin provincial representatives (together with a few upper-caste reformers), who began to argue that access to government property was a *civic right protected by law*.

Taking advantage of the novel openings afforded by colonial modernity, nineteenth-century Dalit activism had focused on a variety of social spaces and had utilized diverse methods—from polemics to petitioning—to claim social recognition, with limited success. The interwar years brought about a significant change: Dalits began to organize around civic rights, especially the right of access to public and government property. As noted by V. Geetha and Rajadurai, "Streets, schools, temples and water points emerged as contentious spaces to which all sorts of people, individually, severally, and through their caste associations sought free and equal access."[3] In this second phase of emergence as a political community, Dalits aimed to subsume religious democratization under a more generous liberal paradigm of civic rights. This secularizing process was manifest in complex claims to public property and involved Dalits, upper-caste nationalists, and conservatives alike in a contentious debate about competing notions of equal access and civic inclusion.

Interwar political adjustments—limited representation for native subjects, non-Brahmin, and Dalit representatives—committed the colonial state to the rhetoric of public responsiveness, even as Dalit activism accelerated claims to public rights and access and adopted new modalities of collective expression, such as the nonviolent protest of the *satyagraha*. The result was that claims to public access began to draw colonial officials into adjudicating civic claims as Dalits increasingly came into open conflict with caste Hindus and the colonial state over the nature of those rights. Colonial law courts had played a crucial role in adjudicating claims to customary honors and privileges in the nineteenth century. Now, the claims involved the question of public access and use. That is, they were contingent on a conception of the colonial "public" rather than a colonial conception of community. The Dalit demand for public access was efficacious because it created equivalence between different practices of caste segregation and across sites of exclusion. Together and separately, such analogical efforts were supported by new conceptions of civic access. A rights claim required legal adjudication, however. As Dalit and caste Hindu conflict over practices of social exclusion increased, struggles moved from polemics and public action into the colonial law courts.

Central to this activity was the paradoxical outcome and political denouement of two temple *satyagrahas* (1928–35), as well as Dalit attempts to abolish a stigmatized property form, the Mahar *vatan*. In adjudicating these issues, I argue, colonial law courts mobilized discourses of private property to strengthen, rather than weaken, the power of caste Hindu claims that segregation was a customary practice dictated by religious custom. Case by case, the customary segregation of space was likened to the exclusive rights derived from the ownership of property. In this incremental alignment of custom with the contract-inflected regimes of private property, a new foundation for segregation was produced.

WATER TANK AND TEMPLE: POLITICIZING *AND* PRIVATIZING SPACE

The public response to the Mahad *satyagraha* was incontrovertible proof of the success of emergent associational forms in channeling critiques of Dalit stigma. However, Ambedkar called off the second water *satyagraha* scheduled for December 26, after burning the Manusmriti in public and comparing Dalit struggles with the demand for civic equality during the French Revolution. He explained his decision, noting, "The untouchable community is caught between the government and caste Hindus. One or the other is bound to attack the untouchables, and there is no shame in saying that [untouchables] do not have the strength to take them both on at once."[4] The Mahad *satyagraha* became a test case for issues of untouchable access and resulted in the only successful judgment in favor of Dalits' rights. The *satyagraha* raised troubling questions, however: Did Dalits already have the right to take water from the tank, or was this a "new" claim promoted by the *satyagrahis*? If Dalits had the right to take water from the tank, why hadn't they done so in the past? Could their possession of an unrealized right be mobilized against caste Hindu assertions that common access to water violated scriptural injunction?

As the debates over civic rights heated up and the ire of orthodox Hindus grew, the Mahad municipality quietly resolved, on August 4, 1927, to reverse their earlier decision opening the tank to all castes.[5] Some months later, on December 10, 1927, a group of orthodox Hindus sought a temporary injunction from the Bombay government barring untouchables from taking water from the Chavdar tank until a decision was passed in the court case challenging Dalits' access to the Chavdar tank.[6] The Office of the Remembrancer of Legal Affairs granted the injunction, noting that "if the injunction had not been granted and the suit decided in favour of the 'touchables' they will be put to considerable expense and inconvenience for 'purifying' the tank; while in the existing circumstances, *if the untouchables win the suit the only effect will be to prolong by a year or so the oppression that has lasted centuries*. I think most judges would have granted the injunction."[7] Local officials also supported caste Hindus' rights to exclusive use. The district magistrate, J. R. Hood, opined that the water *satyagraha* had been incited by outsiders stirring up trouble. "[People like Dr. Ambedkar] instigate the local depressed classes to enforce their claims by direct action and then appeal to me to save them from the resulting retaliation of the higher castes."[8]

Not all government officials subscribed to Hood's position, however, and there was a good deal of debate about Dalits' claims to the Chavdar tank. The tank was, after all, public government property. Shouldn't the government support the Dalits' rights claim? The government threatened to withhold funds from the Mahad municipality, but when that produced no results both the governor-in-council and the commissioner of the Southern Division demanded a clarification of Dalits' rights.[9] A directive from the General Department (GD) noted, "The Municipal resolution of 1924 gave the untouchables no new rights and the resolution of 1927 has taken away none. From the legal point of view both resolutions were superfluous."[10]

Though colonial officials might have taken a liberal view of Dalits' claims in their private correspondence, it was an altogether different matter to publicly recognize those claims. Caste Hindus maintained that they were prohibited by custom from coming into contact with untouchables. And as their position on the historical status of custom became hard to substantiate, they proffered an ingenious argument: the Chavdar tank was contiguous with the Vireshwar temple, which made it an extension of temple space and therefore a sacred site from which untouchables were definitively barred by custom. The distinction between, and the conflation of, sacred and civic space was creatively mobilized by caste Hindu plaintiffs. Because the tank abutted the Vireshwar temple, there was as much "sanctity about it [the tank] as about the temple under the Hindu law."[11] Sheer proximity transferred the temple's sacrality onto the tank.

The Dalits' position was that both civic and sacred spaces were already politicized. Both produced the same effect, Dalits' civic exclusion. In a passionately angry editorial in the *Bahishkrit Bharat,* B. R. Ambedkar argued that there was no difference between the tank and the temple. Reminding his readers that the Chavdar tank had been purified after the March *satyagraha,* Ambedkar acknowledged that prejudice against the untouchables was always manifest as a form of religious repugnance: "Some people think that untouchables went to take water from the Chavdar tank, and that the violence took place because of that. But we think it is more apt, appropriate, to call the riot a religious war. It is true that we wanted to establish whether or not we were on an equal with other Hindus. It has now become public [*jagajahirat zhale ahe*] that the caste Hindus have answered a resounding no to this question."[12]

Against such exclusionary tactics, Ambedkar skillfully conflated access to water with temple entry because the *general* right to public access included access to the temple. He argued that "public facilities should be open to untouchables like other Hindus," and noted that, "let alone the Chavdar tank, even if the untouchables had gone into the Vireshwar temple they would not have been going against the law."[13] Once the right of public access was acknowledged, Dalits could enter any institution they wished.

Ambedkar's argument rooted right of access in the public nature of a facility rather than in religious custom or precedent. A public institution, by definition, envisioned social intercourse across particularistic or exclusionary identities. This went against the equation of custom with social separation. Caste Hindus argued, for instance, that social intercourse with untouchables was inimical to "the principles of the Hindu religion and to the long-standing religious feelings and sentiments of the Caste Hindus."[14] The *satyagrahis* had "wounded" the religious feelings of the Hindus, forcing purification of the tank.[15] In contrast, Ambedkar defended temple access not because he supported religious worship, but because the public nature of the temple could only be manifested through the entry of the untouchable.

> The most important point we want to emphasize is not satisfaction you get from the worship of the image of God, but the plain fact that a temple is not defiled by the presence of an Untouchable nor is the purity of the image affected by it. . . . *The issue is not entry but equality.*
>
> Untouchables have as much claim [*varsa*, "inheritance" or "patrimony"] over Hinduism as do the touchables. If a right is established then the issue of usage becomes moot. When it concerns civic issues, no law gives rights to an individual. Even when use or enjoyment [of property] cannot be shown, or when it is interrupted, the right is not lost.[16]

Ambedkar derived the concept of public access from the definition of a public utility. Although his logic of association was the same one caste Hindus used to extend sacral authority from temple to tank, his conception of equal access depended on an expansive and inclusive, rather than an exclusive, definition of the public.

Dalits' political mobilization around public access was inspired by nationalist assaults on the racial exclusivity of colonial institutions. By emphasizing caste-based exclusion, however, Dalit defendants in the Mahad case encountered a major drawback: they could not prove long-term use of the Chavdar water tank. Instead, they asserted a right of use that existed regardless of whether or not it was realized. If caste Hindus resorted to custom as the grounds for exclusive right to property, Dalits argued that public access was premised on social inclusion. If custom was immutable, immune to the dictates of historical change or social transformation, so too was natural justice. The latter trumped the former because it was transhistorical, rational, and humanitarian, not religiously ordained. Two competing models of legality were in play here: one redefined customary practice as the exercise of law; the other redefined custom as the perpetuation of injustice contrary to a more encompassing standard of natural justice. However, the Mahad case was decided in favor of Dalit defendants on a far more constrained basis, and ultimately reflected the concerns of a colonial property regime that privileged private property rights. In the past, "the Muhur [Mahar] population of Mahad had promised to contribute towards the repair of the suit tank [i.e., the Chavdar tank under contention]." This meant that they were taxpayers.[17] The district court judge argued that the Mahad municipality was like a trust that held the tank as a property "for the whole public in general," all taxpayers, not for a particular section of the public.[18] The plaintiffs' appeal to the Bombay High Court brought a similar decision: there was little evidence of a right to exclusive use of a water tank that was maintained by municipal funds.

The success of the Mahad judgment belied troubling developments. Rights traced to custom were increasingly equated with the rights of private property. The scholarly literature on custom tends to counterpose custom and contract. Literal interpretation of analytic distinctions that were porous and context-dependent also tends to reify distinctions that took shape in the political contexts within which colonial legality developed.[19] Here, I examine the resemblances between custom and contract to reveal how two differently organized structures of exclusion—religioritual conceptions of differentiated personhood versus private property and contract regimes—could be productively aligned to support exclusion and spatial segregation.

The articulation between caste custom and property was not serendipitous, but tactical. According to Section 21 of the Bombay Regulation II of 1827, intercaste relations could come before colonial courts only if they were defined as conflicts involving property or physical injury. Internal caste matters—including issues of caste etiquette and ceremonial rights and honors—were to be decided by the caste *panchayat*.[20] The relations of property built into the Mahad case articulated mutually constitutive relations between person and property. First, there was a set of contiguous relations where the perceived repugnance to a person, the untouchable, transferred to property, especially property invested with sacrality. In turn, the contact with such property was associated with physical touch. This constituted a "structure of feeling," if you will, that enabled touching property to be redefined as touching persons identified with the property. So far as untouchables were concerned, their presence caused emotional repugnance on the order of physical harm.

More important, caste Hindu plaintiffs in the Mahad case not only asserted contiguity between temple and tank, or a shared sacredness, but also directly analogized custom to property. In other words, they equated social segregation with the right to exclusive use in the regime of private property. For instance, they pointed out that the Chavdar tank was surrounded by homes owned by caste Hindus as additional proof that the tank was caste Hindu property.[21] Homeowners had even built stone *ghats* (steps) leading to the tank, thus enclosing the tank as one would private property.[22] District Magistrate Hood agreed that the tank's geography supported claims to restricted access, even if caste Hindus were unable to provide written evidence to substantiate their position: "So far as I can ascertain at present the arguments likely to be put forward for excluding the Untouchables from the tank are; 1) The site of the tank is in the midst of the caste Hindu quarter 2) the custom of (untouchables) not taking water from it hitherto 3) the existence of a separate well maintained by the Municipality for the Untouchables of Mahad town at approximately a quarter of a mile from the tank 4) the existence of private ghats of the surrounding caste Hindus residing on all sides of the tank."[23] The tank's location thus became tautologous evidence of exclusive use and of the customary exclusion of untouchables.

Property logic could be used to justify violence against those who trespassed caste etiquette and convention. As in matters of property trespass, one had the right to self-protection and defense of private property—even at the risk of harming others—and one could argue that the right to private property protected one from contact with those who caused repugnance. We see here the complex closed circuitry that mapped the putative repugnance attached to certain categories of persons in the regime of custom onto the association between persons and places in the regime of property. The right to discriminate based on property ownership was inferred from the distinctions of custom proscribing contact between persons.

In deciding the Mahad case on appeal, the justices of the Bombay High Court, Broomfield and Wadia, noted that if caste Hindus actually proved a relationship between the Chavdar tank and the Vireshwar temple, they could have made a convincing case that the tank, too, was a sacred space historically out of bounds to the untouchable communities. A Chavdar tank shown to have a historic connection to the temple would obviate the need to establish a history of exclusive tank use, since it would be classified as a tank existing for the exclusive use of caste Hindus. This followed from the definition of a Hindu temple as a private or a limited trust held on behalf of caste Hindus who could restrict access as a matter of right.[24] Thus, if the tank was historically associated with the temple, the justices noted, it could have been argued that the juxtaposition of the two sets of persons in a sacred space like the temple was so "repugnant" to caste Hindus that "the entrance of one set into the temple entails the departure of the other, so that it is *as if it were trespass to the other person.*"[25] Because the rules protecting property permitted forms of discrimination that aligned with customary practices of exclusion, caste Hindus could just have easily claimed their exclusive right to a limited trust, the Hindu temple, instead of taking recourse to custom when they tried to exclude untouchables from access to the Chavdar tank. However, this required proof that the Chavdar tank was an integral part of the Vireshwar temple, and caste Hindu petitioners had failed to make their case.

Caste Hindus and colonial officials knew quite well that customary practices of caste segregation did *not* map neatly onto private property rights. Yet, despite a Dalit victory in the Mahad case, a perceived contiguity between exclusionary forms readied colonial courts to immunize custom from Dalit assaults upon caste exclusivity. By the 1930s, the consolidation of an active, visible Dalit public was matched by the emergence of a novel structure of exclusion in which colonial legality upheld customary forms of caste segregation by representing them as modern legal relationships. Nowhere was the contradiction between Dalit politicization and colonial regulation more acute than in the struggle over temple entry.

As the locus of Brahminical authority, the temple was a symbol of Dalits' exclusion from religious worship and the most potent site of Dalits' denigration by caste Hindus. Prior struggles to enter educational institutions and public facilities set the stage for demands for religious equality. By 1928, claims to public access focused on the Hindu temple as the frontier of Dalit efforts to democratize caste relations. Indian National Congress leaders, especially Gandhi, were responsible for inaugurating temple entry as a tactic for the realization of caste equality. Yet the major Congress-led temple *satyagrahas,* at temples in Vaikom (1924) and Guruvayur (1932), reflected the Congress position that caste inequality was a Hindu problem to be addressed by the upper castes. As Dilip Menon has argued, "Temple-entry continued to be seen within the paradigm of the 'purification of Hinduism' with the 'conversion even of the most orthodox' effectively limiting the political potential as well as the participation of anyone other than the upper-castes."[26]

Temple entry occupied a different position in the Dalit political repertoire. If nationalists framed the temple as an exceptional structure because it was a place of religious worship, Dalit activists equated temples with other enclosed public spaces, such as schools, hotels, and teashops, in their bid to clarify the legal principle of equal access. Their politicization of temple entry emphasized the resemblance between the temple and other public places, thereby refusing the a priori sacrality of the temple. Such a strategy allowed them to make an assault upon one of the most symbolically overdetermined spaces in the Hindu sociopolitical imaginary through the idiom of equal access, rather than through claims for equality of worship.

In making claims to the temple Dalits were identifying themselves, and demanding that caste Hindus acknowledge them, as Hindus. Their support for temple entry derived, however, from a political agenda radically opposed to Congress considerations: "We know that the deity in the temple is made of stone, and that neither our sight nor our worship of it will solve our problem. We are embarking on this *satyagraha* as a matter of principle to see if we can bring about a change in the Hindu mind."[27] Indeed, the two main Dalit-led temple *satyagrahas,* at the Parvati temple in Poona (1929) and the Kalaram temple in Nasik (1930–35), challenged the Congress-led temple *satyagrahas,* which positioned the temple, in a rather circumscribed manner, as the symbol of a shared Hindu religiosity. Instead, the Dalit-led *satyagrahas* exhorted *satyagrahis* to make claims to the temple as a public place—as government property that they could enter by right.

The use of shared terms—access, caste equality, and democratization of worship—obscured important differences in Congress and Dalit goals. Congress efforts to nationalize the temple as a place of Hindu worship also defined the temple as a Hindu structure outside the purview of colonial control. Dalit-led *satyagrahas* placed the temple within government control and imputed to it a "publicness" that dissolved distinctions between civic and religious space. Temple entry sharpened the conflict between differing *political* conceptions of rights by emphasizing conflicting interpretations of the basis for *religious* inclusion. These divergent positions on the right to enter the temple were finally played out on a judicial field that increasingly framed the temple as a form of encumbered property.

The *satyagrahas* of the late 1920s were not the first occasions of colonial government interest in Hindu temples. Prior colonial objectification of the temple affected the adjudication of temple-entry cases. From the nineteenth century, colonial regulation had orientalized the Hindu temple as the physical manifestation of Hindu tradition and religiosity. But colonial officials also defined the temple as a "religious institution of public utility," a space where ritual status was reproduced through worship and an economic institution for managing often-sizeable financial assets. Thus the Hindu temple emerged as a peculiarly bifurcated institution, an economic entity rendered amenable to colonial control also reified as a place of religious worship governed by custom. These incongruent frameworks for temple regulation would directly influence the impasse encountered by efforts to define the temple as public property, on the one hand, and to democratize religious worship, on the other.

In 1930, colonial administrators in Bombay noted that that "there could be no general policy concerning temples, and matters [of temple ownership and access] would have to be taken on an individual basis."[28] To understand this position, it helps to know something about established patterns of temple administration. The nineteenth-century temple had been transformed by colonial ideas regarding Hindu religiosity in conjunction with new articulations between capital, custom, and property. Bombay broadly followed the administrative pattern set in southern India, where temples had come under state regulation in 1873. At that time, the Hindu Religious Endowments Act brought temple administration under judicial control, but forfeited judicial intervention in issues regarding ceremonial rights and honors.[29] The colonial government assumed a regulatory power over the management of temple lands and began to make cash allocations for temple upkeep.[30] Temple worship was once at the heart of a redistributive process that converted the symbolic capital of prestige and status into material honors. But by the end of the nineteenth century these honors were themselves commoditized and the focus of legal disputes.[31]

The public and private dimensions of the temple came under separate legalities: the regulation of worship was carried out according to Hindu custom, while the colonial state regulated management of temple prop-

erty. The fiction of *Hindu* control over the temple was maintained, however. Administratively there was little difference between temples under
direct government control, such as Poona's Parvati temple, and private
temples like the Kalaram in Nasik; in most instances, the government
did not "interfere with the nomination of the Committee or with the management of the temple unless there was gross negligence, want of supervision, etc."[32] Indeed, public grants were made to temples regardless of
whether the management committee was appointed by the Bombay government. In the case of a public temple, "Govt. would be a party . . . having appointed trustees but even then would be neutral regarding worship"; they would only involve themselves in the affairs of a private temple
if "the point involved a question affecting allowances paid to the temple."[33] This did not preclude the involvement of colonial authorities in
the financial management of the temple, however.

The management of the Parvati temple, constructed in 1749, was well
documented and revealed two significant moments of colonial rationali-
zation. The first, between 1818 and 1842, involved aggressive intervention, and was led by the collector of Poona, H. D. Robertson. He gathered evidence of financial mismanagement and corruption, concluded that
government grants far exceeded monies needed for temple upkeep, and
appointed a Committee of Managers in 1842 to take control of the temple.[34] After 1860, the Parvati temple was maintained as an "established
religious institution" through native intermediaries, in this case the
Committee of Managers, with minimal government interference.[35] Like
Parvati, the Kalaram temple was also subject to colonial oversight, though
its management structure was a little more complex and was divided
between god as the temple's "owner," the *panches* (managers) who were
responsible for the temple infrastructure, and the *pujaris* (priests) who
had rights to offerings and responsibility for the idols and religious worship.[36] The Bombay government clarified that the temple was neither private in the sense of exhibiting individual ownership, nor public in the
sense of being open to all. "If it is public at all, it is a 'public Hindu temple.'"[37] So far as religious practice was concerned, "[government] would
remain neutral if the point at issue concerned the method of worship or
who should be allowed to worship."[38] Control over practices of worship
was thus ceded to the temple's caste Hindu congregation. Religious worship allied with that colonial artifact, custom, was rendered autonomous
from the domains of politics and economy with which it was integrally
associated, even as "the customary" was rendered ahistorical and de-

nuded of the context sensitivity of earlier articulations of religious authority and state practice.

Customary practice was supported by the definition of the temple as the exclusive property of caste Hindus. As temple records were rarely available, the government typically decided temple ownership through "the medium of inquiry of prevalent forms of congregational worship with respect to usage," that is, according to custom.[39] Such practices had produced the legal definition of the temple as a "limited trust" held on behalf of caste Hindu worshippers, meaning that any change in temple administration required the assent of all members of a temple congregation. A fiction of consensus thus supplemented the fiction of an original charter of temple ownership. If present usage constituted a record of ownership and if the possibility of expanding the community of worshippers also depended on the current congregation, this airtight construction promised little chance of Dalit entry into mixed-caste temples. The Bombay government explained its position of noninterference: "It is not in the power of individuals having the management of the institution to alter the purpose for which it was founded, or to say to the other worshippers 'we have changed our opinion and you who resort to this place for the purpose of worshipping in the customary manner shall no longer enjoy the benefit intended for you unless you conform to the alteration which has taken place in our opinions even to the extent of submitting to the presence of other worshippers who are prohibited by custom and the shastras from entering the temple.'"[40] Colonial authorities had struck a balance with caste Hindus in the peculiar power-sharing politics of dyarchic governance they had embraced, especially with regard to their nonintervention in the "religious" domain.

Increasingly, as interwar political pressures forced the colonial state to embrace the rhetoric of civic rights and public access, the earlier discourse of religious noninterference seemed insufficient. Legal conflict over the temple in the 1920s and 1930s registers the discursive turn to idioms of property to justify customary practices of caste segregation. Indeed the use of terms such as "segregation" and "trespass" created new associations between caste and property in the face of Dalit challenges. The awkward institutional history of the Hindu temple enabled Hindu worshippers to prevent Dalits' physical entry into the temple and later justified nationalist reformers' refusal to democratize the temple on the grounds that the temple was restricted property. Equating the repulsion of contact with the exclusivity of property materialized the repugnance that caste Hindus claimed to feel in sharing temple space with untouchables.

Thus, Dalit-led temple *satyagrahas* accentuated both the paradoxes of property and the embedded violence of the caste order.

TEMPLE ENTRY 1929–1935: NECESSARY VIOLENCE AND THE CUNNING OF CUSTOM

The Parvati *satyagraha* began on October 13, 1929, and brought together Dalit activists led by Shivram Janba Kamble, vice chairman of the Poona branch of the Depressed Classes Mission, as well as caste Hindu members of the newly formed Asprishyata Nivarak Mandali (Committee for the Removal of Untouchability; ANM).[41] The ANM had strong links with the Anti-Untouchability Subcommittee created by the Indian National Congress on March 29, 1928.[42] By June of that year, Congress came together with the Hindu Mahasabha to take up the project of temple entry in Poona.[43] When the *satyagraha* began in October, temple trustees immediately shut the temple doors and hired private guards. Soon after, a notice board outside the Parvati temple stating that the temple was open to all Hindus was changed and now forbade untouchables from entering.[44] The ANM withdrew its support of the temple *satyagraha* soon thereafter and sought a compromise solution: untouchables' partial entry into the temple or restricted access to the temple precincts for worship from a distance.

By January 19, 1930, the Parvati *satyagraha* was called off altogether at the insistence of Congress leaders. Gandhi and the leaders of the Anti-Untouchability Subcommittee argued that the *satyagraha* went awry because it had not been not under complete Congress leadership.[45] Seth Jamnalal Bajaj, secretary of the Congress Anti-Untouchability Subcommittee, had thrown open his own temple in Wardha to untouchables. But according to him, temple *satyagrahas* led by Dalits were problematic because "the existing conditions not only in Poona, but all over the country, do not warrant starting of *satyagraha* by 'untouchables' for asserting their right of temple worship."[46] Even when Dalit *satyagrahis* "stood the ordeal without in the least losing their temper,"[47] it remained Congress's prerogative to instigate and manage temple entry so that it did not "create internal jealousies among the Hindu communities and jeopardize Hindu unity."[48] A report noted: "The *Satyagraha* which the Bombay 'untouchable' leaders proposed to resort to was naturally different from the well-known methods of Mahatma Gandhi inasmuch as they did not make too much of a fetish of non-violence."[49] In fact, the report went on to blame the Dalit *satyagrahis* for marring the "good will" that existed for temple entry through their impulsiveness and impatience. By 1932, Gandhi was defending the Congress position on the temple *satyagraha* by arguing that the principle of religious equality had to be balanced against respect for private property: "[With] reference to temples like Parvati temple there is a difficulty about the trust. The trust deed itself lays an obligation on the trustees to prohibit the entry of 'untouchables' into the temple. Where such a disability exists, I would be able to understand the powerlessness of the trustees. *And Satyagraha in reference to such temples would be pure violence.*"[50]

In the sustained interrogation of violence that was crucial to his theorization of an indigenous ethics, Gandhi made a clear distinction between violence directed against oneself, resignified as self-discipline, and other-directed violence, which compromised the realization of truth. For the *satyagrahi*, the experience of violence only intensified the assertion of a moral claim. Ironically, the structural violence of caste remained invisible to the upper-caste activist who advocated violent suffering on behalf of untouchables. However, Narayanrao Gunjal, a temple trustee and a leader of orthodox Hindus opposed to *satyagraha*, distributed leaflets during a lull in the *satyagraha* demanding that caste Hindus "welcome" the *satyagrahis* with violence. Violence against the Dalit *satyagrahis* was a communicative medium newly developed to address Dalit efforts to secure right of entry. Gunjal castigated Dalits' growing politicization and associated it with transgressive sexual desire: "The untouchables wanted to marry girls from high-caste Hindu families, and therefore, it is unwise to give [them] any encouragement."[51]

In one of his last editorials in the *Bahishkrit Bharat*, B. R. Ambedkar wrote a long evaluation of the Parvati *satyagraha* addressing Gandhi's displacement of violence onto the Dalit *satyagrahi*. Ambedkar argued that acts of violence clarified the contradictions embedded in the very conceptualization of temple entry. Violence was the product of caste Hindus changing the "format of the *satyagraha*" by attacking the *satyagrahis*.[52] Reformist caste Hindus, half-hearted progressives (*navamatvadi*), were even more to blame. They had encouraged the *satyagrahis* to demand temple entry, backed off from the struggle, and then refused to condemn violence against the volunteers. When untouchables controlled the *satyagraha* they were blamed for inciting violence. Indeed the "*deva* [lit. "god," in this case the do-gooder Hindu] was actually a *devva* [demon] and his gift was poisonous." Even Gandhi's decision to suffer on behalf of the less fortunate was a patronizing and limited gesture. Ambedkar wrote: "Let me ask these people who would change hearts—how much change of heart [*matparivartan*] do you want to achieve? If every Hindu, then untouchables will wait forever. . . . No untouchable believes that his humanity will be recognized after independence just because caste Hindus argue that they can only live up to their humanity then."

Ambedkar argued that the true lesson of the Parvati *satyagraha* was that it taught Dalits the necessity for retaliatory violence. Rather than sitting quietly and getting hit with stones and bricks, the untouchables would also "take recourse to the brutal policy of causing harm to harmless people." Indeed, Ambedkar argued that the Gandhian criticism of violence was misperceived. The *satyagraha* form staged a necessary violence as the consequence of placing the weak in the direct line of violence, and yet *satyagraha* leaders feigned surprise when they became victims of violence.[53] For Dalits, acts of violence revealed the structural violence embedded within all forms of caste sociality. In contrast, for the Congress/Mahasabha alliance, the Parvati *satyagraha* redefined the *satyagraha* form altogether. First, *satyagraha* was to be performed under the guidance of caste Hindus. In other words, untouchable management of *sataygraha* exposed its inherent limits: *satyagraha* was a mechanism for the transformation of the upper castes, not a radical tool for caste equality. Secondly, *satyagraha* for challenging untouchability was seen to compromise the effectiveness of this "matchless weapon" for national independence and unity, since it intensified violence among Hindus.

The so-called aggression of Dalit volunteers gave Congress nationalists cover for withdrawing quietly from the Parvati *satyagraha*. Dalits did not enter the Parvati temple until 1932, after Gandhi's fast-unto-death. The Chambhar activist P. N. Rajbhoj led the effort, having rejected Ambedkar's leadership to join Gandhi in 1932, only to rejoin Ambedkar again in 1942, with the formation of the All-India Scheduled Caste Federation (AISCF).[54] In contrast to the reformism of caste Hindu leaders, the Dalit-led Nasik *satyagraha* exposed a new set of contradictions around the juridical status of "public access" and inaugurated Dalits' historic decision to refuse Hindu inclusion.

NASIK AND THE SPATIALIZATION OF PROPERTY

A priori an enclosed space is more private than an open one.
> Letter from Clayton, Commissioner, Central Division,
> to R. G. Gordon, December 10, 1931[55]

The ancient temple of Kalaram which is selected by the crusaders as the field of battle has been converted into a fortress by the Brahmin defenders.

. . . Each side has enrolled volunteers 500 strong, with distinctive colours
and slogans and there is an air of grim determination in both camps.

"Impressive Scenes," *Times of India,* March 4, 1930

Local leaders took the initiative in the Nasik *satyagraha* at the Kalaram
temple. It was organized by Nasik Mahar Sangh secretary Bhaurao Gaikwad and the group's president, Sambhaji Yesu Rokade.[56] They collected
Rs. 10 from each village in the region[57] in addition to large donations
from Dalit landlords of the Central Provinces.[58] By the end of February
1930, they had collected more than Rs. 15,000.[59] The Ambedkari *jalsas*
played a crucial role in mobilizing people for the Nasik *satyagraha.*[60]

Bhimrao Kardak and Dadasaheb Pagare, president and secretary of
one of the most famous Ambedkari *jalsa* troupes, the Nasik Yuvak Sangh
Sangeet Jalsa, explained their decision to use this form by describing the
Ambedakri *jalsa*'s continuities with its predecessor, the Satyashodak *jalsa,*
and with popular *tamasha* performance: "In tamasha there was fun
[*vinod*], and there was pedagogy [*upadesh,* i.e., to instruct or lecture]."[61]
The fun in *tamasha* was bawdy and risqué, but there was no ban on
women hearing it. Entire villages came out to enjoy a *tamasha* performance, and it was a significant medium of entertainment amongst Dalits. The Ambedkari *jalsa* also omitted the initial *mangalacharan* propiti-
ating a deity and instead recounted Ambedkar's glories. The Ambedkari
jalsas publicized important political events and problems internal to the
Mahar community, such as the performance of Maharki (degraded caste
labor), drinking and gambling, and the lack of education. Encounters
were staged between a *maushi* (lit. "maternal aunt," a familiar figure in
the *tamasha* who signified ignorance or tradition) and a *sudharak* (reformer). Dialogues, called *chakkad* or *saval-javab* (lit. "question-answer")
were interspersed with interludes of popular songs that would have been
familiar to anyone who had attended *tamasha* or *lavani* performances,
but that were rescripted with political rather than erotic content.

> *Maushi:* Is this *satyagraha* long or short, round or square? Is it some-
> thing to eat? I still don't know, so tell me.
>
> *Sudharak:* Mahar, Mang, Chambhar those of us who are defined as
> inferior and untouchable, why don't we have the right [*hakk*]
> to go to a Hindu temple when we are Hindus?
>
> *Maushi:* Arre, give us that right. I don't refuse it. That is not my ques-
> tion. My question is that for so long now we have been sloganeer-
> ing "Let's participate in the *satyagraha*." But first tell me clearly
> what a *satyagraha* is, define it and describe it, that is all I am
> asking!

श्री. अमृतराव धोंडिबा रणखांबे

भाऊराव कृष्णराव गायकवाड

श्री. बंदसोडे यांचा नवमतवादी जलसा व त्यांतील मंडळी

Figure 5. Special issue of *Janata*, 1933, with photographs of important leaders of the Nasik *satyagraha:* Amrutrao Dhondiba Rankhambe (left) and Bhaurao Krishnarao "Dadasaheb" Gaikwad (right). Shri. Bansode's Navamatwadi *jalsa* troupe is pictured below. Courtesy of Eleanor Zelliot.

Figure 6. Dalits entering the Kalaram temple, Nasik, n.d. Courtesy of Prakash Vishwasrao, *Dr. Babasaheb Ambedkar* (Mumbai: Lok Vangmay, 2007).

Sudharak: Alright, listen carefully. *Satyagraha* is composed of two words, satya means something that is true, and agraha means to demand something, such as to demand our human rights. Where is the 'satya' or truth here? Mahars, Mangs, Chambhars, we are all oppressed [*paddalit*, lit. "crushed"] though we are Hindu by religion. Why should we not enjoy the same religious, social, and civic rights that touchable Hindus enjoy?[62]

The Ambedkari *jalsas* were remarkably minimalist, focused mainly on rational critique and dialogue, while eschewing symbols of popular religiosity or folk belief as signs of tradition and backwardness. Each *jalsa* was described as a "farce," that is, a one-act play.

Between five thousand and eight thousand people attended the Nasik *satyagraha* when it began on March 2, 1930.[63] There was plenty of resistance to it as well. The president of the Kalaram temple trustees, a Brahmin lawyer named V. B. Akut, also happened to be the president of the Nasik Congress Committee. He resolved to prevent the *satyagraha* at all costs.[64] Gandhi said, "I have not approved of the Nasik *Satyagraha* about Kalaram Temple for the simple reason that I have *smelt a trace of violence* in that *Satyagraha.*"[65] Dalits themselves called off the *satyagraha* in 1936 and admitted the impossibility of Hindu reform.

By then, the issue of religious inclusion was moot. At a meeting of the Depressed Classes Conference in October 1935 at Yeola, a few miles outside Nasik, Ambedkar made the famous statement, "It is an unfortunate fact that I have been born a Hindu: it was not in my power to oppose or change that. But I can promise you this. I will not die a Hindu."[66] This statement was accompanied by talk of mass conversion from Hinduism and marked a major turning point in Dalit politics.

The entire *satyagraha* period of Dalit activism was inspired by Gandhian strategies of popular resistance, however. A photograph of Gandhi had hung in the conference hall during the Mahad *satyagraha* and activists called out his name as they undertook a procession around the Chavdar tank. But the split between Dalit activists and Congress nationalists was complete by 1930, with the latter pledging support for temple entry from afar. Still, symbols of Gandhian opposition to colonial rule had become ubiquitous and were portable signs of collective protest. Dalit leaders also borrowed the organizational methods of Congress leaders. During the Parvati *satyagraha,* for instance, volunteers were asked to sign pledges to follow strict discipline.[67]

1. Once untouchable brothers come to Parvati temple, they should sit at the foot of the temple where the volunteers tell them to, and behave/do as they are told.

2. Do not fidget or gather together in a crowd. There is no problem in hailing [*jayjaykar karane*] important men.

3. No one should bring *lathis, kathis,* or umbrellas with them.

4. Only those people selected by the Satyagraha Committee can climb to the Parvati temple.[68]

A fetish for order and bureaucracy was also evident in the focus on record keeping. Donations were to be documented with receipts. Handbills distributed throughout the Nasik district in 1932 exhorted, "*Chaupeel pauthi shivay deu naka!* [Don't make contributions without receiving a printed receipt]. Other handbills carried slogans in English such as "Untouchability is nothing but slavery," "Tell a slave he is a slave and he will revolt," and "Death is better than dishonour." Echoing Tilak's claim of freedom as a birthright, some handbills declared "*Manuski ha pratyek manasacha janmasiddha hakk ahe* [Human dignity is everyone's birthright]." For a largely illiterate community, the fascination with forms and receipts was an interesting mimesis of bureaucratic authority.

A police report on the Nasik *satyagraha* noted with unease the commingling of Gandhian and distinctly Dalit political symbols:

> In front of the main gate and close against it were collected nearly 100 depressed classes—mostly Mahars, seated on the ground singing songs and shouting war cries in loud tones at regular intervals. Included among them were a considerable number of women seated in the front rows. It would be utterly impossible for any person trying to enter the temple to make his way through their ranks. *Standing up at intervals were guards dressed in khaki and carrying sticks resembling the scout sticks. . . . It is noticeable that the satyagrahis were largely dressed in Gandhi caps and Khadar* [handspun, coarse cotton] *which have been recently served out to them. . . .*
>
> [N]ot a man would stand up, not even when I was speaking to them, and they are mostly village *watandar* Mahars! Yet the moment Ambedkar arrived they jumped up, salaamed, etc. It may also be noted that, judging by recent assumption of Gandhi caps, these unlawful actions are to be undertaken under the aegis of Gandhi as part and parcel of his campaign of Civil Disobedience.[69]

Dalit *satyagrahis* used symbols of Gandhian protest such as white peasant caps and *khadi* (homespun), as well as military outfits that signified the Mahar battalions. Shahid Amin has described the Congress volunteer as a hybrid creature whose commitments to Gandhian mobilization were processed through a Hindu religious idiom of asceticism and renunciation. In fact the *otiyar,* the local rendition of "volunteer," was a recognizable figure in the village as he came around demanding *chutki* [lit. "a handful," the alms given to holy men).[70] The Dalit scout became a similarly ubiquitous figure during the Nasik *satyagraha.* Initially a term used to describe a uniformed member of the highly disciplined Samata Sainik Dal (Army of Soldiers for Equality), "scout" came to describe any *lathi*-carrying volunteer in the front lines of conflict.[71] The Samata Sainik Dal even had a women's wing. At the start of the Nasik *satyagraha,* more

Figure 7. Annual meeting of twenty thousand members of the Samata Sainik Dal, organized by the ILP in Kamgar Maidan, Bombay, on January 8, 1939. Courtesy of Prakash Vishwasrao, *Dr. Babasaheb Ambedkar* (Mumbai: Lok Vangmay, 2007).

than five hundred woman marched at the vanguard "in martial array like disciplined soldiers," shouting slogans.[72] Drawing upon images of militarized masculinity as well as the status and respect that Mahars derived from a military past, the Samata Sainik Dal provoked a completely different set of associations—combat, armed resistance, virility—from those attached to nonviolent protest.

As the symbolic universes of Dalit and Gandhian protest collided, they revealed radically different perspectives on violence, as during the Parvati *satyagraha*. Temple *satyagrahas* were always meant to play a strategic role in politicizing Dalits. Ambedkar noted that he had launched temple entry not because he wanted "the Depressed Classes to become worshippers of idols which they were prevented from worshipping or because I believed that temple entry would make them equal members in and an integral part of the Hindu society . . . [but because it was the] best way of energizing the Depressed Classes and making them conscious of their position."[73] If the temple *satyagrahas* were supposed to mobilize Dalits to claim their rights, they did their job and did it well. Dalit *satyagrahis* came from diverse backgrounds—they were military pensioners, rural Dalits, and urban youth.

The extended duration of the Nasik *satyagraha* and its ultimate failure showed that though Dalits were partly successful in gaining some moral ground, they were ultimately unable to overcome the effects of a colonial legality that articulated custom with property and reinvested the caste habitus with the force of law and the fiction of consensus. And space, once politicized via *satyagraha,* became a more encompassing setting for political statements and acts, a stage for materializing new strategies of exclusion with the support of colonial officials whose stance of religious neutrality ultimately favored the status quo.

The Nasik *satyagraha* again posed the question: did Mahar Dalits have a right to temple entry? The district magistrate, R. G. Gordon, argued that the Mahars were not making a "legal" claim, but a "moral" one, a claim "as yet not . . . possessed or exercised."[74] His circular reasoning suggested that if Dalit *satyagrahis* had a claim to the temple through prior usage, they could have filed that claim under Section 147 of the Indian Penal Code concerning rights to disputed property.[75] Gordon noted, "It was on the ground that the case of the Mahars disclosed no allegation of a right of which a Civil Court would take cognizance that the [Remembrancer of Legal Affairs] held that S 147 would not apply to disputes arising from the alleged rights of the Mahars to temple entry."[76] Gordon argued that the *satyagrahis* were enacting new claims because they had not sought legal clarification on their right to temple entry by presenting it as a struggle over disputed property. As with Gandhi's ultimate capitulation to the property regime and the temple trust deed during the Parvati *satyagraha,* colonial officials articulated tensions between Dalits' right to religious worship and their right to the temple as private property. Both relied, however, on Dalits' uncertain status as Hindus.[77]

The Bombay government closed off access to the Kalaram temple to all Hindu worshippers, hoping to provoke clarification of Dalits' rights through the law courts. The *satyagraha* had settled into a pattern of daily confrontation between *satyagrahis* and caste Hindus at the temple entrance when the local organizer, Bhaurao Gaikwad, sent an urgent letter to Ambedkar on March 19, 1930. Gaikwad wrote that the priest of the Kalaram temple, the *pujari,* was allowing worshippers into the temple *through* his home: "Sir, I beg to inform you that though all the four gates of the Kalaram Temple are blocked by the *Satyagraha* volunteers a private entrance is being availed of by the touchables to get a *darshan* [glimpse of the deity]. This private door belongs to the *Pujari's* house and is situated very close to the Northern gate of the temple. . . . *though the entrance was private it was turned into a semi-public one by the fact that all the touchable public availed itself of it to enter and visit a Public Temple."*[78]

Gaikwad went on to note that the police officers on duty had refused to intervene. Furthermore, Gordon had warned the *satyagrahis* that preventing access to the temple would result in their removal by police. The *pujari's* ingenious method of allowing caste Hindus to enter the temple transformed the Kalaram conflict. Ambedkar said that "under no circumstance can we tolerate this new stunt of the *Pujari* and tolerate his rendering our *satyagraha* futile even if it [brings] us into conflict with the government."[79] Conflict it produced aplenty: the temple *satyagraha* was now diverted to the *pujari's* door.

In the meantime, Gordon defended his decision to allow the *pujari* to convert his home into a temple entrance and asserted that *all* caste Hindu worshippers could be viewed as guests who had been invited to a private gathering at the *pujari's* home. He even went so far as to erect a makeshift barrier of two dilapidated motor lorries at either end of the street to regulate Hindu worshippers' access to the priest's home during the *rath yatra* (a procession of Ram's chariot) in April 1930.[80]

Gordon appears to have internalized the legal debates about the status of Hindu temples that were raging at the time among colonial officials concerned with matters of law and revenue. His elaborate preparations to make sure that caste Hindus were not deprived of the right of worship suggest that he believed both that the temple was caste Hindu property and that it was his duty to protect property rights. His support for the *pujari* was an extreme interpretation of property rights. Gordon noted that "the question of what people do when they get inside it [the temple] it seems to me, is in law the business of the Pujari only."[81] Thus the Nasik district magistrate's commitment to private property transformed the *satyagrahis* into criminals: "If the *Satyagrahis* squat in front of the Pujari's house and prevent people whom the Pujari wishes to admit from going in, they commit wrongful restraint; if they go in while the Pujari opens the door to admit others, knowing that he objects to the entrance of the *Satyagrahis*, they commit house trespass. Both are cognizable offences."[82]

Gordon's attempts to regulate the flow of worshippers though the *pujari's* home during the Ramanavami celebrations, which commemorate Lord Rama's birth on the ninth day of the Hindu month of Chaitra, became something of a precedent. Two years later, the new district magistrate, L. N. Brown, proposed a similar method of crowd control: "Mr. Gordon allowed the pilgrims to enter the Temple through the *Pujari's*

house. . . . Mr. Robinson and I would like to substitute timber barriers
for those barriers of Mr. Gordon's. [These timber barriers consist] of two
strong timber walls, projecting from the walls at either side of the street,
and one slapping in the middle, in such a way as to allow one person to
pass through at a time. I have seen similar barriers in London, when big
crowds are expected."[83] Brown's superiors warned him against emulat-
ing Gordon's example: Gordon had been disciplined for his actions and
transferred out of Nasik.[84]

In the meantime, Bhaurao Gaikwad had filed a complaint with the
police noting that the *pujari* had made the entrance to his home semi-
public, converting it into "a public right of way."[85] The Home Department took a similar stand, saying that "if . . . the *Pujari* abuses this right
and uses his private entrance not for the entrance to his house proper
but as a passage to the temple, he is converting a private into a public
entrance."[86] The remembrancer of legal affairs, who had supported the
rights of private property until "prompted" by the home minister to reconsider his position, now argued that the *pujari* was a temple servant
who had abused his official position.

> There is nothing to show that the pujari's house is not part of the temple
> and besides it is not established that the entrance to his house which also
> leads to the temple is really a private entrance. Unlike a private individual,
> the pujari is a temple servant and his actions should be viewed from his
> state as such. Whatever rights and privileges he enjoys in this respect they
> are in virtue of this status and so long as he attempts to abuse them openly,
> the police could not give him any aid and protection to carry out his evil
> designs.[87]

The remembrancer's distinctions between public office and private
prejudice were quite slippery, since even in his official, public capacity
the *pujari* represented an exclusively caste Hindu public. He was under
no compunction to be more inclusive. The placement of his home beside
the temple marked his intimacy with the temple as public functionary
and custodian of ritual knowledge. The uncertain distinction between the
priest's status as merely a temple servant somewhat akin to a public official and his status as a religious specialist meant that he derived his authority from two sources, creating a confusing circularity so far as colonial officials were concerned.

The move to further enclose space and proscribe access to the Kalaram
temple and its environs indicates a radiating zone of conflict that politicized social interactions by spatializing them. This tactic was not restricted
to one priest. Other attempts to enclose public space clearly intended to

bring it within the ambit of proprietary claims. For instance, in December 1930 the *satyagrahis* asserted their right to use the four *kunds* (bathing ponds) outside the Kalaram temple. A caste Hindu aided by prominent members of the Nasik municipality won permission to erect a barbed-wire fence around each *kund*. Even Gordon, loath to support the *satyagrahis'* cause in any fashion, noted that the action verged on the illegal, as "this has been done without granting a lease" so that caste Hindus might avoid government scrutiny.[88] The government agreed that the ponds were a "part of a public river and unenclosed and though the Mahars do not claim ever to have bathed there it is certainly arguable that they . . . have as good a right to bathe in it as any Brahman."[89] Once enclosed, however, the ponds became legible as private property.[90]

Dalit-led actions exposed the limitations of temple *satyagrahas* as a route to caste equality. Thus it is not surprising that by 1933 Gandhi no longer advocated temple *satyagrahas* and argued that they compromised the *satyagraha* as a "matchless weapon" for national independence. In fact, Gandhi distanced himself from temple *satyagrahas* altogether and opted to instead undertake three personal atonement fasts against untouchability between 1932 and 1933.[91] He followed them with the 1933 Harijan tour asking caste Hindus to voluntarily impoverish themselves to become like the untouchables. Congress now acknowledged as a mistake the arc of temple *satyagrahas,* which began with violent encounters ranging Dalits and Congress activists against orthodox Hindus, but ended with almost immediate acceptance of partial access to the temple as a compromise solution, or complete cessation of *satyagraha* under threat of violence.

Dalits were only partially successful in presenting to the government religious rights folded into a generic claim to public amenities. If a moral right was the first step in establishing a new rights claim, how could it be recognized and where did its legitimacy lie? Accepting a moral right as a legal claim, the colonial government recognized, carried profound consequences. Such acceptance would overturn the legal status of custom: "if the courts recognized untouchable claims to temple entry, they would in essence be recognizing a moral claim as a legal or justiciable claim, and in the process they would be changing a fundamental principle of Hindu law, that 'custom has the force of law.'"[92]

Though the colonial government maintained the specificity of Hindu custom, it was easy to render custom compatible with contract, and to read into discourses of property a further equation of exclusive customary rights with the right to private property. In their distinctive ways, caste Hindus and the colonial government had used the productive tension between custom and contract to counter Dalits' rights claims. For caste Hindus, custom had the force of *law* precisely because the *force* of colonial law could be mobilized to extend and to regulate the domain of custom.

This is not to suggest that nothing had changed. As the remembrancer of legal affairs stated, "Even assuming that the untouchables had hitherto not worshipped in this temple, it might be simply because no one attempted so far to assert their rights."[93] This argument had found strong expression in Ambedkar's speech during another *satyagraha:* possession and enjoyment could be distinctive (and disaggregated) aspects of a "right." As colonial neutrality with regard to religious matters overlapped with the discourse of custom, however, arguments about unrealized rights failed.[94] The Bombay government might accept that "untouchables *as Hindus* have as much right to enter the temples as the touchables," but this position was treated as one requiring the consent of public opinion, that is, of caste Hindus.[95] Only then would it be possible to overturn custom and convert a moral right into a legal one.[96]

Caste Hindus' ability to manipulate the discourse of custom exposed the political nature of colonial legality. More significantly, it inverted the nationalist critique of the colonial propagation of custom. If nationalists blamed the colonial state for reifying custom, colonial officials explicitly devolved the responsibility for legal change upon caste Hindus whose customary rights stood to be compromised. As a result of the productive circularity between colonial interpretations of the temple as a peculiar property form, as a limited trust safeguarding caste Hindu exclusivity, on the one hand, and nationalists' interpretation of temple entry as a mechanism to transform Hindu morality on the other, temple entry was at an impasse. Congress representative Ranga Iyer's 1933 Temple-Entry Bill in the Central Legislature advocated a change in custom on a case-by-case basis with the assent of each and every temple worshipper as a means of breaking the deadlock.[97] The bill was described thus: "Shortly put, Mr. Ranga Iyer's Temple-Entry Bill empowers the trustees to widen the circle of beneficiaries under the instrument of trust—namely, the untouchables—and to do this by a referendum of the voters of the electoral roll of a municipality or of local boards in the vicinity of a temple."[98]

By equating caste Hindus with a political constituency with majority and minority opinions on temple entry, the Congress acknowledged, if inadvertently, that temple entry was a political issue and not simply the "religious problem" that Congress reformists, especially Gandhi, presented. Poised between orthodox and Dalit positions on temple entry, Congress reformism charted a highly compromised middle ground.

Congress reformism acknowledged the temple as a sacred space and simultaneously sought to make worship equitable. If equality of worship was about constituting a Hindu community, changes in the legal-political status of the temple indexed a secularization of temple space. This mirrored the governmental bifurcation that made the temple both property and place of worship. And it contrasted with the position of Dalit *satyagraha* leaders who demanded not a Hindu equality, but equality per se. For them, polling caste Hindus who had a right to be in the temple about untouchable entry was the worst form of paternalism; it maintained the right of the upper castes over the temple while procedurally appearing to make caste Hinduism compatible with the requirements of social inclusion and egalitarianism. It is interesting, therefore, to see advocates of Ranga Iyer's bill displacing responsibility for the negligible pace of legal reforms onto a colonial government accused of standing in the way of historicizing custom.[99] C. Rajagopalachari argued that "British courts and British law in India, by enforcing the established usages and customs of the Hindus, prevented the natural growth and evolution of Hindu customs."[100] Rajagopalachari was correct about the reification of custom, but appears to have forgotten that this was the result of a compromise between caste Hinduism and colonial legality.

Whether through colonial legality or nationalist law making, the end result was similar: the temple was affirmed as caste Hindu property. Even the passage of the Bombay Temple-Entry Act of 1947 was stymied by a constitutional guarantee of the freedom of religion, which proved useful for asserting sectarian rights over temple access, including prevention of Dalit entry. Only in 1956 did the Bombay Hindu Places of Public Worship (Entry Authorization) Act override all sectarian distinctions of temple usage by throwing open all Hindu temples to "all classes and sections of Hindus," finally aligning access to the temple with access to public places. Rather than a mechanism for producing Hindu inclusion, Dalit-led *satyagrahas* of the 1930s thus revealed the temple to be the most tangible manifestation of caste Hindu hegemony.

THE MAHAR *VATAN*: STIGMATIZED PROPERTY AND DALIT SERVITUDE

The temple was not the only place where custom and property met and conspired against Dalit rights claims. The Mahar *vatan*, a stigmatized property holding, was the scene of a familiar impasse regarding customary practices, this time of labor servitude and landholding. The Mahar *vatan* was a patrimony, a land grant as well as a hereditary office. Mahar *vatandars,* holders of the *vatan,* were obligated to perform extensive village duties, from ruling on boundary disputes and running personal errands for the village elite, to performing defiling labor such as removing carcasses. Mahar *vatandars* were "inferior" village servants appointed first by the Maratha patrimonial state and later by the colonial state. Their duties derived from their dual status as *balutedars* (village servants) performing necessary services for the village as a whole and as state functionaries. As one of the *bara balutedar* (twelve village servants), the *vatandar* was remunerated annually for duties performed, through a share of the harvest.

The Mahar *vatan* was unlike other rights and patrimonies, however. The stigma associated with it came from habituated forms of servility, such as begging for leftovers, to which Mahars had a *hakk* (right) that was associated with "payment" for services rendered,[101] and from Mahars' handling of defiled substances, such as dead cows. The Mahar's typical *baluta* (a customary share) was inedible food, used clothing, and the occasional handful of grain. Kardak and Pagare's description of Maharki (degraded caste labor) reflects the paradoxical position of *vatan* duties as a source of stigma and of livelihood.

> Untouchable brothers, renounce the ways of your fore fathers
>
> (According to) the customs of the past (we) eat carrion
> We have become degraded, and nobody touches us
>
> When cattle die in the village, they say "call the Mahar"
> When they ask us to take it away, we feel disgusted
>
> Taking a rope and stick in hand, four heroes get ready
> They start off happily, as if they are going to the council
>
> Lifting the stretcher on their shoulder, they say there is an
>   epidemic this year
> This is our traditional profession, how shall we leave it, Oh Govinda[102]
>
> Kardak Bhimrao urges you! Renounce this habitual beggary[103]
> We have become degraded, and nobody touches us[104]

Though characterized as a stigmatized property form, the Mahar *vatan* had been a sign of status and a mechanism of incorporation into Old Regime polities. The *vatan* and the rights associated with the *vatandari* office were coveted. The adjudication of *vatandari* rights had also been a source of revenue for the state, even as Mahars proudly asserted their rights to the ceremonial honors that accrued to the *bara balutedar.*[105] Indeed, histories of the late nineteenth and early twentieth centuries that recalled the precolonial Mahar military past counted the Mahar *vatan* among the fifty-two rights granted to the Mahar community in recognition of bravery and valor.[106] A popular twentieth-century account by Ambedkar's biographer, C. B. Khairmode, associated Mahars' historical rights with an originary, voluntary castration by the Mahar warrior Amrutnak, who was charged with conveying his master's queen to safety while preserving her chastity.[107] The practical significance of the Mahar *vatan* was rather different, however. As a land grant associated with Mahars' performance of caste-marked labor, it was, unlike other *vatans*, premised on relations of servitude and the performance of Maharki. All caste Hindus in the village had a right to the Mahar *vatandar*'s labor. Thus the Mahar *vatan* was a form of property that obligated Mahars to labor in ways that reproduced the very conditions of defilement and degradation that identified them as Mahar. It is no surprise that the remaking of the Dalit habitus in the 1920s and 1930s also sought to crystallize the exploitative nature of Mahars' "customary rights," since the regime of labor and property holding reproduced normative inequality and confirmed the socially negligent status of Dalits.

The Mahar *vatan* was a distressingly particular, stigmatized and stigmatizing property holding. The *vatan*'s standing as an encumbered or burdened form of property, not unlike the temple, is clarified when it is historicized through colonial efforts across the nineteenth century to rationalize exceptional property holdings and to bring them within a general regime of property relations. Described by the 1827 regulation, or the Elphinstone Code, as a "hereditary office," the *vatan* came under increased surveillance throughout the nineteenth century.[108] Offices were reified in the figure of native authorities such as *deshpandes* (district accountants), *deshmukhs* (district headmen), *patils* (village headmen), and low-level village servants such as the Mahar *vatandar*. The perquisites of their office, *inam* (tax-free) lands, were simultaneously brought within the purview of a normative property regime.

The Summary Settlement Act (Bombay Act II of 1863) released regional officers, *deshmukhs*, and *deshpandes* from their hereditary duties by levying reduced taxes on their *inam* land through a process the British called commutation. This normalized "exceptional" property holdings by turning tax-free lands into taxed lands to generate state revenue.[109] The Hereditary Offices Act (Bombay Act III of 1874) followed closely upon these changes. It regulated service rotation and the number of *vatan* co-sharers but left customary rights and duties untouched: because certain hereditary officers provided necessary services, their positions were viewed as useful to government. In a move of enormous consequence to Mahar *vatandars*, Section 16 of this act provided that the commutation of *vatans* should not be "held to affect any right of individuals or village communities to exact such service as may be customary from village servants who have been relieved of government liability to perform such services to the State."[110]

Thus were duties stripped away from the honor of holding an office. The hereditary village-level servants were simply localized without their links to the state. Why did this happen? After the Mutiny of 1857, consolidating the legal authority of the colonial state served, on one hand, to reify customary rights and duties such as the Mahar *vatan* and, on the other, divorced such duties from property and other perquisites that invested hereditary office with status and power. Property forms were thus imperfectly dissociated from the particularities of caste and kinship. The Mahar *vatan* thus continued to function as a stigmatized property form associated with degraded persons, but Mahars were denied the memory of military service and of centrality to the village economy.

Demands for change within the Mahar community articulated with political-economic changes already underway, including growing conflict between Mahars and peasants. Section 64 of the Hereditary Offices Act addressed conflict between Mahars, who claimed rights to dead carcasses, and cattle owners, who accused Mahars of poisoning cattle, with a provision for bringing the *vatans* of accused Mahars under the purview of the state.[111] Hiroyuki Kotani has written of the exponential rise in conflicts over rights to carcasses during the latter part of the nineteenth century and argues that a "new precedent" gave peasants ownership of the carcasses while Mahars were increasingly prohibited from claiming them as a customary right.[112] The next phase in the politicization of the Mahar *vatan* brought Mahars into direct conflict with agriculturalists, since the *vatan* tied Mahars to one village, where they were "required to do every sort of work, whether private or official, demanded by government officials or by any ordinary villagers.[113] They [were] required to do the work of carrying letters by running in the hot sun ten or twelve miles. If a Mahar [was] absent from a village, his wife or even minor children [were] forced to do his work."[114]

Vatan abolition became an important issue in the Bombay Legislative Council for five years between 1923 and 1928, but had no positive outcome. When D. D. Gholap, the first nominated Depressed Class member to the council, proposed on February 23, 1923, that the Mahar *vatan* be abolished, the *vatan* he described was already a colonial artifact.[115] R. S. Nekaljay inquired again, in February 1924, about the exact duties of a Mahar and introduced a resolution on August 14, 1924, seeking better pay for Mahar *vatandars*. He also demanded that *vatans* be considered tax-free lands to compensate for past exploitation. These resolutions were voted down, as was another effort four years later. Ironically, Mahar *vatandars* proved to be resistant to the efforts to abolish the *vatan*, since it was one of the only ways in which Mahars could acquire some semblance of status, even if it was a status that further stigmatized them.[116]

B. R. Ambedkar introduced Bill XI in 1928, which proposed that (1) Mahar *vatandars* give up their status as village servants and pay taxes upon *vatan* lands to escape the stigma of holding the Mahar *vatan*; (2) the Bombay government clarify the duties of the Mahar village servant so that he was not exploited by both state and village elites; and that (3) the government provide equitable cash remuneration for *vatandars* who opted to remain village servants. In essence, Ambedkar demanded that the Mahar *vatandar* be recognized as a salaried government servant. The bill followed intense discussion within the Mahar community, which was divided on the issue of giving up a customary right that provided a semblance of financial security.[117] However, Ambedkar was adamant about the necessity to modernize the community and emphasized that though the *vatan* was meant to be a subsistence holding, it bound its holders to the performance of exploitative labor. His effort to abolish the Mahar *vatan* identified the privatization of this property form with Mahars' escape from Maharki.

In a set of editorials in the *Bahishkrit Bharat*, Ambedkar queried the unclear distinctions between Mahars' "public" and "private" duties that led to their hyperexploitation.[118] "Instead of treating the *baluta* as payment [for services rendered] or a salary," he wrote, "villagers consider it as alms-giving and Mahars as beggars . . . even the snot-nosed children of upper castes—Brahmin, Maratha, *kunbi*—say what they feel like to a Mahar man or woman."[119]

Dependence on the *baluta* also made Mahars obsequious and helpless, Ambedkar observed. This was a form of slavery cultivated by the upper castes and premised on the Mahars' degradation.[120] Ambedkar also noted that the Mahar *vatans* had lost value. Or, where values had risen, Mahars had opted to sell their lands or subdivided them so many times that the lands were useless. This is confirmed by M. G. Bhagat's 1935 study of the state of the Dalit communities, which found that subdivision had rendered the Mahar *vatan* incapable of being a subsistence holding.[121] As well, although the Bombay government conveniently assumed that Mahars were adequately remunerated for their private services to village elites, their official salary of Rs. 5 to Rs. 6 per month was far below a subsistence wage. Ambedkar's efforts to transform the Mahar *vatan* into private property and to categorize Mahar *vatandars* as wage workers located the degraded identity of Mahars in their performance of defiling labor. For him, clarifying the conditions of labor while bringing it within the regime of contract would endow caste labor with monetary value. By altering the relations of labor, a transformation of caste sociality might also be produced.

Efforts to revise the Mahar *vatan* bill failed miserably. Bill XI, which was sent to a fifteen-member Select Committee, was characterized as "too exceptional" and was withdrawn two years later due to vociferous opposition.[122] Legislative Council members noted, "If . . . Dr. Ambedkar's proposal is to break up the organization of villages, as it inevitably would, his proposal stands condemned or at least must be regarded as too far in advance of the times."[123] This was an acknowledgment of the coercion through which Mahars' degraded status in the village was maintained.

Why not abolish the Mahar *vatan*? Why did this property form remain in place while the colonial government was only too happy to enfold other categories of *inam* lands into a homogenous regime of property? The Mahar *vatan* was remuneration for an office and it was *inam* (tax-free) land. The difference between the Mahar *vatan* and other offices, however, was its tie to labor servitude. Mahar *vatandars* were doubly stigmatized. They held an inferior form of property that rendered them susceptible to the performance of degraded labor. Efforts to abolish the Mahar *vatan* emphasized and elaborated this circularity between the Mahar's labor and the Mahar's stigma. Ambedkar's efforts to convert Mahar *vatandars* into property owners who relieved themselves of customary duties and gave up the privileges of the Mahar *vatan* anticipated a radical overhaul of the village economy. Ironically, *vatan* abolition produced great resistance within the Mahar community. Like the contexts of military service with which it was associated, the *vatan* was a bittersweet gift—it was a sign of prestige and of servitude.

There was also the difficulty of definition: how was one to separate the public and private duties of Mahar *vatandars*? When Ambedkar reintroduced his 1928 bill to the Legislative Council in 1937 in the hopes of encouraging "freedom of contract" between agriculturalists and Mahar laborers, his bill contained an important amendment: Section 19D stipulated that Mahar *vatandars* could refuse to serve *ryots* (peasants) and could forfeit "that portion of their money cess due to them for services to the *ryots*."[124] That is, Mahars could opt out of servicing villagers. The implications were extensive: Mahars' services could be disaggregated into discrete tasks, each carrying a separate wage, *and* Mahars had the right to refuse their labor, thus overturning the compulsions of Maharki.

A most telling contribution to the discussion was the Bombay government's admission that it was impossible to calculate the monetary value of Mahars' customary services. The Commissioner of the Central Division noted that Mahars performed purely government services, quasi-government services "for the general benefit of the community in which both the villagers and Government share," and purely private services. Mahars themselves would have to be responsible for collecting payment from private individuals, because "even if it were made legal the practical difficulties of classifying customary services rendered by Mahars under the head 'Private' and 'Government' would render the task of apportionment almost impossible."[125]

An even more dramatic issue was the significant financial losses anticipated if Mahar *vatandars* were classified as government servants, as Ambedkar proposed. In 1937, the Bombay Legislative Council noted that classifying Mahars as "stipendiary servants" in the employ of government would incur a huge loss to the Bombay treasury. It would be too expensive to remunerate Mahars' labor at market rate. Certainly, the failure of Ambedkar's bill signaled social resistance, but it also indicated government's devaluation of caste labor. It was calculated that 22,190 full-time servants would be needed to replace existing Mahar village servants, and that Rs. 29 lakhs would be needed to pay them at the rate of Rs. 10 per month. A full service assessment of Mahar *vatans* would only yield Rs. 5 lakhs, forcing the government to make up the balance.[126] The government's calculation revealed just how profitable it was to maintain Mahars as poorly paid "part-time village servants."[127] Their unequal status with respect to other village servants was also clarified in an explanation of how the lands of other hereditary servants were regularized. When district officers were relieved of their services, they were relieved of paying a one-time *judi,* or cess (tax), on their tax-free lands, and received extra cash in payment for government's undervaluing their services. In their case, "commutation . . . was made in view of a liberal policy of

Govt." As the remuneration of *kulkarnis* (village accountants) and *patils* was considered insufficient, they were also given a cash remuneration on the Wingate scale. "The *watan* lands of patils and kulkarnis were subjected to [a one-time] additional judi and ceased to be assigned as renumeration for service. . . . Thus when kulkarni service was commuted, it was not necessary to resume their lands."[128] In the case of "inferior village servants," however, *vatan* lands given in remuneration for service rendered could be reassigned to other impoverished Mahars.[129] This made the Mahar *vatan* a lucrative source of free labor for the government, and one that the government would not easily abolish. A government memorandum acknowledged as much. "In the cases of Hereditary District Officers and Kulkarnis the government themselves wanted to terminate the contract but the other parties were still willing to continue the service. Some consideration was therefore necessary to induce [them] to give up their source of livelihood. In the case of Mahars the position is the reverse and there is no reason why Govt. should make any sacrifice.[130]

If Ambedkar embraced the idea of the unencumbered personhood of the liberal subject, the Bombay government reasserted the coercive nature of the contract and its inherent inequality, and thereby also acknowledged the monetary value of stigmatized labor. Debates over the clarification of *vatandar* duties continued: government officials repeatedly asserted the impossibility of enumerating Maharki services, while the Backward Classes (BCs) officer demanded that Maharki services be brought within the domain of wage labor and pressed for reduction of Mahar *vatandars'* duties—for example, carrying the post long distances, being made to sleep on the porch at the *patil*'s home or outdoors in the village square, and performing free labor for government servants (including British officers) on visitation.[131] Dalit leaders continued to agitate against the Mahar *vatan* in the pages of *Bahishkrit Bharat* and *Janata,* and held Vatandar Parishads to demand regularization of the Mahar *vatan* as agricultural land.[132] The Mahar *vatan* was finally eliminated by the passage of the 1959 Bombay Inferior Village Vatan Abolition Act.

THE LEGIBILITY OF DALITS

Dalit activism in the interwar years reflects a transformed discursive context, as the category of "the public" itself became the site of conflict and new forms of political mobilization enabled Dalits' assaults on institutionalized practices of caste exclusion. Significantly, colonial commitments to public access produced a crisis in political discourse and colonial orders of legality. Standard frames of custom, tradition, and community no longer easily justified colonial authoritarianism. When Dalit struggles transmogrified into legal conflicts over water tanks, temples, and stigmatized labor, the idioms of private property were increasingly used to justify customary practices of caste segregation. The novel association between the regimes of custom and property that emerged during this period clearly responded to Dalits' success in presenting caste and untouchability as structured by institutionalized exclusion with material consequences. Although little changed for Dalits in the 1930s, the *rhetoric* of public access, as we have seen, was profoundly significant for the Dalit communities, albeit with paradoxical outcomes.

The issue of access to caste Hindu property was positioned within a social, political, and economic matrix very different from that of classical liberalism. Yet the odd referentiality between customary practice and the regime of private property thrived on the assumption that customary practices produced forms of exclusion like those that issued from the ability to alienate private property through the regulatory fiction of the contract. In fact, the logic of the contract itself went so far as to equate the practice of untouchability with a contractual agreement between consenting parties, as in this judicial opinion: "the uninterrupted observance thereof [the practice of untouchability] during the last 2000 years and over is a clear indication of the acquiescence in and the acceptance thereof by the untouchables themselves . . . as between private parties the said custom is perfectly legal and valid and hence enforceable."[133] If the practice of untouchability could be understood as a social contract between private parties, then untouchables could be viewed as complicit in their own exclusion from proscribed space.

It is the elusive, malleable, yet terribly material nature of what we commonly understand as property that enabled political liberalism to align property with personhood. From Hegel onward, the relationship between property and personhood has been described as one of supplementary opposition. The subject-object relationship and, more fundamentally, the identification of oneself as capable of possessing objects, of owning and alienating property, establishes subjectivity.[134] The owning subject converts objects into property and thereby also attains a certain self-reflexivity. The enabling fiction of property as the ground of recognition is then recast as the voluntary entry of propertied persons into a regime of *political legibility*. In classical, Lockean liberal terms, the act of enclosure that marks off private property instigates the social contract through which society, especially political society, comes into being. Thus, if the capacity to own property is the signature of personhood, it is also the foundation of the state, which exists to protect property.[135] The proprietary relationship thus "always also indexe[s] a set of political relationships between the holders of property, particularly real property, and the state."[136] For classical liberalism, then, the fiction of property is generative of both personhood and political orders.

Even though we associate property with real property and material objects, it is clear that "property" is a signifying apparatus that has the more general power of constituting persons as certain kinds of object-oriented subjects and of objectifying certain forms of personhood. So far as the Dalit communities were concerned, the strange dislocations of property and personhood, the customary and the contractual, invested terms such as "segregation," "trespass," or "disability" with new salience in describing traditional practices of exclusion and stigmatization. The spatial and property metaphors that organized the category of "the public" were generative of new justifications for caste exclusion.

Dalits' investment in expanding the category of the public in this interwar period and their claims upon public spaces such as schools, streets, trains and temples generated novel technologies of segregation that underscored the adaptability of modern disciplinary formations for reproducing caste norms and prejudice. Even as untouchability was interiorized as an ineffable quality of the caste body or recast in Gandhian paradigms of hygiene and cleanliness, caste exclusion and segregation were legitimized through a language derived from liberal property regimes. This rendered caste into a property of the self and (real) property an extension of persons. The implication of this was that demands for social inclusion were consistently recast as claims upon private property, enabling a legal defense of caste inequity in the language of liberalism, and *not* in the usual idiom of tradition. The secularization of untouchability was paradoxical: ritually inflected practices of separation inhered within liberal paradigms of exclusion and the legal discourses that justified them. So far as caste Hindus were concerned, the materialization/objectification of custom into a form of caste property (the temple) also supported a legally recognized caste Hindu personhood and agency. For Dalits, on the other hand, real property (the *vatan*) was converted back into a customary holding that justified the relations of caste servitude that underwrote it. The fiction of the social contract was perniciously interpreted to fix these forms of personhood and the social relations resulting from them as an originary agreement in which the untouchable communities acquiesced to their degradation. In the Indian public sphere Dalits were, in some more-than-metaphorical sense, "trespassers."

The political challenge of the 1930s, then, was to resignify the structural negativity and restigmatized existence of the Dalit into positive political potentiality and to make the stigmatized subject central to the imagination of caste equality.

CHAPTER 3

Dalits as a Political Minority

The untouchables are usually regarded as objects of pity but they
are ignored in any political schema on the score that they have no
interests to protect. And yet their interests are greatest. Not that
they have large property to protect from confiscation but they have
their very *persona* confiscated. The socio-religious disabilities have
dehumanized the untouchables and their interests at stake are therefore the interests of humanity.

> B. R. AMBEDKAR, *Evidence before the Southborough Commission,*
> in *BAWS,* vol. 1

I have accepted the Buddhist Dhamma. I am not a Mahar, nor an
untouchable, nor even a Hindu. I have become a human being.

> SHANKARRAO KHARAT, *Babasaheb Ambedkaranche Dharmantar*

B. R. Ambedkar's definitive and moving final gesture, his public conversion out of Hinduism together with almost half a million people, became
the symbolic core of a liberated Dalit identity. Ambedkar's conversion
emphatically affirmed a defining characteristic of Dalit emancipation: the
significance of the religious and the political as simultaneous axes of Dalit
subject-formation. Dalit conversion to Buddhism on October 14, 1956,
in Nagpur signaled this rejection of existing Hindu culture and ideology.[1]
It was anticipated by Ambedkar's famous statement at Yeola in 1935,
before a crowd of ten thousand people: "Because we have the misfortune to call ourselves Hindus, we are treated thus. If we were members
of another faith, none dare treat us so. . . . We shall repair our mistake
now. I had the misfortune of being born with the stigma of an untouchable but I will not die a Hindu for this is in my power."[2]

The 1956 rebirth into the Buddhist community consisted of a public
rejection of old memories and practices. Ambedkar's All-India Scheduled
Caste Federation was intensively involved in the preparations for the *diksha* (initiation ceremony). Buses were chartered to bring people to Nag-

pur, arrangements were made to house them on the grounds where the conversion took place, and cleanliness and hygiene were emphasized to underscore the spiritual significance of Dalit conversion.[3] Everyone dressed in white clothes for the *diksha,* while receiving the Buddhist vows.

Ambedkar was converted by Bhikku Chandramani Mahasthavir and then conducted the public conversion by administering the *tisarana,* the acceptance of Buddhist vows and allegiance to Buddhist precepts, to the gathered crowd. In addition to the *panchashila,* or the five Buddhist principles, the crowds accepted the twenty-two vows Ambedkar had specifically created for Dalit conversion. These amounted to a total rejection of Hinduism: a denial of the divinity of the Hindu gods, Brahma, Vishnu, Maheshwara (Shiva), Rama, and Krishna; refusal to perform *shraddha* (funeral rites) and to offer *pindadaan* (food for male ancestors); and rejection of Brahmin priests and denunciation of false propaganda that Buddha was an incarnation of the Lord Vishnu. These renunciations were followed by the positive acceptance of the fourteen oaths of belief in Buddhist ideals. Cries of *"jai* Buddha" (victory to Buddha) and *"jai* Bhim" (long live Ambedkar) filled the air. Ambedkar described the "enormous satisfaction" and "pleasure unimaginable" of the conversion and noted, "I feel as if I have been liberated from Hell."[4] The famous Dalit writer, Shankarrao Kharat, described it as a rebirth. Dalit conversion was a symbolic rebirth, but it also brought closure: Ambedkar passed away on December 6, 1956, hardly two months after his conversion. More than two million people gathered in the streets of Bombay as his body was brought from Delhi to his home in Dadar. It was the largest public gathering the city had witnessed to date.

Ambedkar's 1935 (Yeola) statement shocked Hindus and created alarm among members of the Hindu Mahasabha who feared the destruction of a Hindu political majority. Particularly troubling to them, perhaps, was Ambedkar's position that the reform of untouchability had nothing to with untouchables' "good conduct," since they were engaged in a permanent war with Brahminism, a conflict "without end."[5] Madan Mohan Malaviya was reported to have said "hands off the untouchables; none has a claim on Harijans [other] than the Hindus," and furious efforts ensued to prevent Ambedkar from converting to Islam, as he had initially intimated.[6] Even M. C. Rajah—president of the All-India Depressed Classes Association, who had clashed with Ambedkar over his demand for a separate electorate and signed a pact with B. S. Moonje, president of the Hindu Mahasabha, confirming the Hindu identity of the untouchables—felt compelled to respond. In a letter to Moonje, Rajah argued: "You view the whole problem of the Depressed Classes, in view of Dr. Ambedkar's proposal, as one of communal migration and not as a religious problem. One would expect the president of the Hindu Mahasabha to view it as a religious problem and not merely as a political problem. . . . *You are dissecting the Depressed Classes and affiliating them religiously with Sikhs while retaining them politically as Hindus.*"[7]

As always, Gandhi's response was more complex. He condemned conversion as a political tool. "Religion . . . does not lend itself to purchase in any shape or form. Or if such an expression can be used in connection with things of spirit, religion can only be purchased with one's own blood."[8] If Gandhi rendered the authenticity of Dalit conversion suspect, he also noted that this was because it precluded caste Hindu repentance: "The very existence of our religion depends on [untouchability's] voluntary removal by *savarna* Hindus in the spirit of repentance. It can never be a question of barter for me."[9]

While Hindus debated conversion from a political-demographic perspective or as a challenge to the very possibility of Hindu reform, Ambedkar's conversion to Buddhism twenty years after the Yeola statement was made on grounds of ethics and self-respect. Buddhism was a "civic religion" that met the need for social ethics and rationality that were missing in Hinduism.[10] Indeed, Valerian Rodrigues has argued that Ambedkar's Buddhism was a profoundly modern innovation that he adapted to the categories (and values) of Enlightenment reason.[11] The goal of Dalit critique was to challenge the violent exclusion, invisibility, and degradation to which the caste Hindu order consigned Dalits. The wretched material existence of Dalit communities, their susceptibility to the cunning and treachery of the *bhat* Brahmins, and their exclusion from cultural and political resources was central to caste radicalism. Ambedkar's distinctive contribution to this discourse was his critique of the caste order from the perspective of the Dalit subaltern, who was posited as a unique political, ethical, and historical subject. Ambedkar's creative reinterpretation of political terms and categories of democratic liberalism, especially the concept of minority, is a defining feature of his thought and the extended focus of this chapter. Buddhist conversion is equally crucial, however, to understanding the ethical-political reorientation of Dalit subjectivity.

Ambedkar's interpretation of Navayana (new vehicle) Buddhism was eclectic from the perspective of Buddhism's more traditional practitioners and was the direct result of Ambedkar's criticism of Hinduism. Inequality and dehumanization, he argued, were the "very basis of that religion [Hinduism] and its ethics." He argued that no "man must have his ancestral religion if he finds that religion repugnant to his notions of the sort of religion he needs as the standard for the regulation for his own conduct and as the source of inspiration for his advancement and well-being."[12] Buddhism condensed questions of state and nation, of rights and social recognition, answering both colonial domination and Hindu nationalism with an indigenous ethical alternative that manifested the highest orders of human compassion.[13] Ambedkar's *Buddha and His Dhamma,* completed a few days before his death in 1956, introduced Buddhism as the basis for a new society founded on the principles of equality, liberty, fraternity, and human compassion. The language of this text was markedly different from Ambedkar's earlier writing. "*The Buddha and His Dhamma* registers [Ambedkar's] experience of tiredness with the social science mode of reasoning. . . . *By giving up a certain kind of language I believe he was giving up the system that gave birth to it.*"[14] Ambedkar's rejection of the transcendental rendered his Buddhism an immanent critique of the social. Martin Fuchs writes that in central sections of the *Buddha and His Dhamma,* "Ambedkar launched an attack against 'religion,' putting Buddhism on a different plane . . . [as] superior to religion."[15] Not simply an act of religious conversion, Ambedkar's turn to Buddhism was an extraordinary, ultimate enactment of ethical conviction preceded by a forty-year struggle to understand the co-constitution of politics and religion that produced caste.

Ambedkar was multiply and actively engaged as a lawyer, scholar and theorist, publicist and activist, and as a notable Dalit participant in shaping India's representative democracy from 1917.[16] He was born in Mhow in 1891, into a family long affiliated with the British Army. He had advanced degrees in political science from Columbia University and the London School of Economics, and was called to the bar in England. A trenchant critic of the caste elitism and social conservatism of the Indian National Congress throughout his political career, Ambedkar played a central role in imagining the new India, first as chairman of the Drafting Committee of the Indian Constitution and later as independent India's first law minister (1947–51). He resigned from the cabinet over political intransigence regarding the Hindu Code Bill, which sought wide-ranging reform and codification of practices relating to Hindu marriage, divorce, adoption, and inheritance. Ambedkar had long maintained the centrality of sexual control to the reproduction of caste. "Social reform from its inception had a dual program: there was the reform of the Hindu Family, and social reform in the sense of reorganization and reconstruction of society."[17] Ambedkar considered the Hindu Code Bill "the greatest social reform measure ever undertaken by the legislature," and noted that leaving "inequality between sex and sex which is the soul of Indian society untouched and to go on passing legislation relating to economic problems is to make a farce of our Constitution and to build a palace on a dung heap."[18]

As India's first law minister and chief architect of the Indian Constitution, Ambedkar played a key role in imagining the Indian citizen as a political subject. The techniques of political commensuration that he devised rendered the historical denial of full personhood and political subjectivity to Dalits politically consequential. The almost half-million Mahar Dalits who converted with Ambedkar were citizens of a newly independent India where the adult franchise, the abolition of untouchability, and constitutional safeguards for historically discriminated against and disadvantaged groups sought to dismantle the old order of hierarchy and privilege.[19] Buddhist conversion, then, was preceded by the (political) conversion of Dalits into a *non-Hindu* minority. While most studies of Ambedkar focus on his demand for separate political representation for Dalits, which produced a historic conflict with Gandhi in 1932, such a perspective limits appreciation of the longer-term impact of caste radicalism on Ambedkar's thought and occludes his exceptional departures into democratic thinking and constitutional law.[20] It also scants the complex and seemingly contradictory actions that marked a political career accommodating multiple responses to the problem of Dalit dispossession: inclusion, political separation, religious conversion, emancipation through political citizenship, cultural alterity, and state protection of minority rights. Each of these strategies was an extension of Ambedkar's efforts to theorize the intimate violence of untouchability.

Ambedkar's evolution in thinking was symptomatic of broader shifts in Dalit politics even while his interventions produced a distinctly new Dalit identity. Caste radicals had long sought a language to describe the existential horrors of stigmatized existence. Indeed, untouchables were not invisible when Ambedkar rose to prominence; the term *dalit,* or *paddalit,* already had some currency. And while Ambedkar's critique of caste—from the sexual to the spiritual, from the political to the ethical—resembled that of Jotirao Phule, in whose critical tradition Ambedkar explicitly placed himself, there were distinct departures. Deeply committed to the category of the self-regulating, autonomous individual, Ambedkar committed himself to the creation of the Dalit self in response to a historically situated problematic: *collective emancipation* of the community from caste stigma and historical discrimination. The liberation of self was contingent on creating a community that was agonistically related to the community of Hindus and to the national community. Therefore, Ambedkar argued that a "fundamental and deadly antagonism" existed between caste Hindu and untouchable, that the Dalit communities constituted a "separate element in the body politic," and that the social stigma Dalits' suffered rendered them a very peculiar kind of political minority. His analysis reconfigured the field of signification named "Dalit."

By the third decade of the twentieth century, Mahar Dalits were organizing around rights claims. Their activities, in which Ambedkar played an important role, inhabited an Indian political climate increasingly focused on nationalism and government. As I have noted, the interwar years were marked by a global restructuring of the British empire and the emergence of anticolonial nationalisms. Some were inspired by the Bolshevik revolution of 1917 and by Marxist ideology more generally. Others interpreted Japan's success in the Russo-Japanese War of 1905 as the first successful national war of independence. In India, the Indian National Congress dominated the political-moral space of nationalist thought and action. Increasingly, as the ideology of anticolonial thought was transformed into majoritarian claims to state power, with Congress laying claim to being the rightful inheritor of the state, the question of minority was also sharpened to reflect awareness of the constraints and possibilities of liberal institutional logic.

Ambedkar's redeployment of Dalit identity crystallized in the 1930s around his representation of Dalits as a separate political minority. By then, colonial categorization, the (ideological) prominence of community as constituency and models for limited political participation intersected with Dalits' self-identification as a discriminated community to facilitate their shift into formal politics. Ambedkar's struggle to invest Dalits with human dignity and political legibility within a liberal framework required an act of ideological separation from colonial-nationalist paradigms, which shared the view of Depressed Classes as degraded Hindus, even if they differed on how to ameliorate their low status. Ambedkar undertook a complex task: to use existing political language and tools of redress to recreate Dalit identity by revaluing Dalit stigma. Ambedkar's critical rethinking of secular and democratic categories built political value into the dehumanized Dalit in a remarkable manner, making the Dalit minority, rather than the political majority, the bearer of emancipatory potential. At the same time, his articulation of an alternative principle of minority ultimately positioned him against the Hindu community and the Congress, while bringing him into conflict with the British colonial state. A more difficult political position there could not have been.

THE STRUCTURAL VIOLENCE OF CASTE

B. R. Ambedkar's political trajectory was distinguished by his lifelong effort to find a language into which the existential realities of Dalit deprivation could be adequately translated. He sought to elaborate the existential fullness of personhood historically denied to Dalits and to develop means of redress to counter the complex inequities of the caste order. If Gandhi was Ambedkar's foremost political rival, an intimate enemy who sought to transform the ethical conduct of caste Hindus, Marx was Ambedkar's intellectual adversary as Ambedkar thought about the Dalit as a universal historical subject with, against, and beyond Marxian categories of class and political subject-formation. It is no surprise that in one of his last works Ambedkar compared the nonviolent, compassionate community of the Buddhist *sangha* with the agonistic formation of class, acknowledging the two philosophies to be comparable in their depth of engagement with collective human suffering, inequality, and the struggle to remake the world in the quest for emancipation.[21]

Three distinctive moments can be distinguished in Ambedkar's quest to develop a discourse of the Dalit as political subject. They are less points in time during a linear development of ideas than intertwined dimensions of his reconsideration of caste, society, politics, and minority. First, in a sociolegal vein, Ambedkar constantly cultivated the ground of his thought and action through a comprehensive critique of Hinduism and the caste order. His efforts to politicize the boundaries of "the political" can be appreciated through his efforts to address the structural violence of untouchability as the secret of caste. In a second, formal political dimension, Ambedkar worked within liberal democratic thought to generate grounding principles for a new conception of minority. This began as an attempt to define untouchables as a political minority structurally similar to Muslims, that is, as a distinct community whose rights were certain to be diminished by the majority Hindu community. The third dimension of his thinking, however, challenged the very possibility of using liberal models of commensuration to equalize the Dalit. Dalits' status as a territorially dispersed, suffering minority rendered them incommensurable. As a figure of singularity, Ambedkar's Dalit was both a subject constituted by a hurtful history and a portent of the future, a constant reminder of the inadequcy of a merely political response to the violence of caste.

Nonetheless, as a practical matter, Ambedkar continued to try to incorporate Dalits as political actors within a liberal procedural logic of equalization, with the result that Dalits' anomalous position as *non-Hindu* minority—the positive political valuation of a negated identity—was embedded in the state as a permanent political contradiction, thereby acknowledging the impossibility of justice for Dalit suffering through mere political means. Ambedkar's signal transformation of the political consists, then, in investing the state with the protection of its minorities by using law to reveal state complicity in the extension of caste power. In Aniket Jaaware's powerful formulation, "This is what I would like to call the stamp on the forehead of the state. I mean stamp in the double sense of a bureaucratic seal of endorsement, as well as a mark of the contradiction that is, from now on, forever visible. This is, in a certain sense, an ironic inversion of the stamp of caste."[22] It is precisely this tension between political adequation and its ultimate insufficiency, I suggest, that produced the Dalit as political potentiality and a very particular sort of historical subject.

Ambedkar's early analyses emphasized two things that remained constant in his thinking about caste: Brahminism's centrality to the development of caste relations and the quasi-juridical basis of caste regulation. In a 1917 article in the newspaper *Indian Antiquary,* "Castes in India: Their Genesis, Mechanism, and Development," he theorized the social reproduction of caste along two axes.[23] The imitation of Brahminical mores across the caste order produced what he later referred to as a system of "graded inequality." Each caste in the *varna* (the fourfold prescriptive hierarchy of caste) was invested with reproducing its status in a system organized along "an ascending scale of reverence and a descending scale of contempt," a perverse ordering of persons along a hierarchy of dignities.[24] The Brahmin's quasi-juridical authority came from the Manusmriti, the compendium of the Hindus' "illegal laws . . . responsible for the acquiescence of the lower-castes to their subordination."[25] The second axis of caste was alignment of social and sexual reproduction through the control of women and their sexuality because, "in the final analysis creation of castes as far as India is concerned means the superposition of endogamy on exogamy."[26] Conflict within the caste system, from sexual violence to structural exploitation, was a conflict between intimates rather than between biologically distinctive races, as colonial sociology would have it. This intimate order, *chaturvarna* (the textually derived fourfold ordering of caste), sublated direct confrontation and dispersed conflict across the caste structure. As Ambedkar noted, "Inequality is not half so dangerous as graded inequality."[27] The point was to reorient conflict around this primary contradiction, a fundamental antagonism that structured history.

Ambedkar's theorization of caste and untouchability was influenced by Dalits' experience of civic exclusion. In the 1920s, as Dalit mobilization for civic access met violent resistance, Ambedkar's attention was drawn to the persistent, daily violence of the caste order. In particular, *bahishkar* (caste boycott) was a principle of structural violence, the generic form of caste antagonism working at physical, economic, and psychoreligious levels. It was also transacted violence, a disciplinary tool caste Hindus used to temporarily separate an errant member of the body politic or an entire community.[28] The exclusion of the untouchables was built into the structure of caste as a form of violence, which constituted a principle of segregation. Untouchability as practiced by the Hindus, wrote Ambedkar, "is not a case of social separation, a mere stoppage of social intercourse for a temporary period. It is a case of territorial segregation and of a *cordon sanitaire* putting the impure people inside a barbed wire into a sort of cage. Every Hindu village has a ghetto. The Hindus live in the village and the Untouchables in the ghetto."[29]

Ambedkar testified before the Simon Commission (1928) that *bahishkar* accommodated "modern" forms of civic exclusion:

> Dr. A: There are a great many villages where the depressed classes are not allowed to travel in these buses.
>
> Commission: Who prevents them?
>
> Dr. A: The driver would not take them.
>
> Commission: One would expect the driver to take anybody who pays. Why does he not take them?
>
> Dr. A: Because if he takes them the other people will not come into his car. For instance, the barber here would not shave my head even though I offered him a rupee.
>
> Rao Saheb Patil: According to the law the driver would be prosecuted if he refuses to take any passengers.
>
> Dr. A: That can be evaded by saying that all seats are booked.[30]

Perversely, the right to freedom of association could be used to justify the denial of services and social interaction. Social segregation could be perpetuated and legitimized through entirely modern ideas and contractual logic, as chapter 2 argued. Ambedkar repeatedly drew upon the meta-

phor of failed exchange to describe caste as a mechanism for withholding sociality. He argued that the threat of temporary outcasting drew its
force from the permanent outcasting of one community—the untouchables. This negative force held the caste order together, making structural violence integral to the molecular order of caste. Though despised,
untouchables formed the glue of the caste order, while untouchability
was its structuring negative principle; it was Hindusim's "constitutive
outside," its necessary yet excised animating force. Untouchability provided the single point of unification for the otherwise fragmented Hindu
castes. In every other respect, difference of practice and belief fractured
Hindusim irreparably. Ambedkar's critique of caste through theorization
of the violence of untouchability had ontological, existential, and political dimensions. His sophisticated analysis of caste as premised on the
systematic exclusion of untouchables inflected his thoughts about minority, class, and finally, the decision to effect a religious split away from
the Hindu majority.

To locate untouchability—readily seen as extraneous to caste Hinduism—as the secret of caste was perhaps the most powerful attempt yet
to critique caste from the perspective of the Dalit subaltern. It was a
difficult task for Ambedkar to defamiliarize what had been misrecognized
as consent and discipline rather than violence, however. Dalits and caste
Hindus alike acquiesced in mistaking violence for religious dictum. The
difficulty was exponentially intensified by Gandhi's brilliant attachment
of "nonviolence" to the Congress nationalist cause and, thus, to an ethical caste Hinduism. In fact, Gandhi foregrounded nonviolence by undertaking a fast-unto-death from September 20 to 24, 1932, in response to
the 1932 Communal Award, which allowed the Depressed Classes a double vote. In chapter 4, I return to that moment in detail as it relates to
understanding violence. Suffice it to say here that Gandhi's tactical use of
a technique Ambedkar considered violent was a practical success. Ambedkar backed down from a symbolically overdetermined and politically
potent conflict with Gandhi, describing his capitulation as an act of humanitarianism: "I responded to the call of humanity and saved the life
of Mr. Gandhi by agreeing to alter the Communal Award in a manner
satisfactory to Mr. Gandhi."[31]

The failure of political separation, together with a growing conviction regarding the inseparability of caste and Hinduism, was responsible
for Ambedkar's powerful 1936 text, *The Annihilation of Caste*. Described
as his "last address on a subject vitally concerning the Hindus," it was
written as a talk for the Jat-Pat Todak Mandal (Association to Break

Caste) of Punjab.[32] The text was incendiary—a total critique, arguing that there could be no equality in Hinduism until caste was destroyed: "You must . . . destroy the sacredness and divinity with which caste has become invested. In the last analysis, this means you must destroy the authority of the Shastras and the Vedas."[33]

The Annihilation of Caste was privately published after the Mandal, troubled by Ambedkar's decision to leave Hinduism, rescinded his invitation to speak. Ambedkar had described himself as a Hindu contemplating an exit from the Hindu religion and one of the conference organizers, Sant Ram, criticized him for this: "The object of our conference was to persuade the Hindus to annihilate castes but the advice of a non-Hindu in social and religious matters can have no effect on them. The Doctor in the supplementary portion of his speech insisted on saying that this was his last speech as a Hindu, which was irrelevant as well as pernicious to the interests of the conference."[34] Ambedkar expected this response and queried: "What can any one expect from a relationship so tragic as the relationship between the reforming sect of Caste Hindus and the self-respecting sect of Untouchable[s]."[35]

The Annihilation of Caste articulated Ambedkar's position on Hinduism as a juridical order: "Religion by the Hindus is nothing but a multitude of commands and prohibitions. . . . [W]hat the Hindus call Religion is really Law or at best legalized class-ethics."[36] Caste, a system of "graded sovereignties," reaffirmed the Brahmin's hegemony because each caste oppressed inferior castes and was in turn subject to the Brahmin's contempt. Hindus did not feel the need to justify injustice and inequality; each person was complicit because all identified with and desired the Brahmin's status. This was the hidden violence of the caste order. For those committed to abolishing caste and transforming Hindu society, the way forward was to democratize the priestly class and to kill Brahminism.[37] There was no escaping the essay's implication: the ethics of Hinduism subverted the principles of equality and self-respect. Hindu ethicality was impossible because Hinduism was premised on inequality. If caste was to go, Hinduism had to go. "There can be a better or a worse Hindu," Ambedkar argued, "*but a good Hindu there cannot be.*"[38]

In the 1940s, Ambedkar further refined his understanding of Hindu ethicality by characterizing untouchability as "an aspect of social psychology . . . a sort of social nausea of one group against the other."[39] A rare autobiographical description reveals the visceral nature of caste feeling. Ambedkar described traveling with his siblings as a child, revealing his Mahar identity to a kindly stationmaster who had assumed he was an upper-caste child. This produced "repulsion" in the man.[40] Ambedkar's difficulties in finding housing in Baroda on his return from the United States also revolved around counterfeit identity. He masqueraded as a Parsi to secure housing, only to be discovered and, this time, threatened with physical violence.[41] The troubled question of recognition for the stigmatized person, and Ambedkar's description of physical repugnance mirror Frantz Fanon's focus on racial and cultural violence in his analysis of subject-formation. Fanon argued that the racial gaze deforms recognition so that the colonizer is unable to "see" the colonized except as a (black) body. Blocked intersubjective processes of identity formation in the colonial context produced disgust, violence, and fear in the colonizer and self-hatred in the colonized. Like Ambedakr, Fanon used the term "nausea" to describe the visceral nature of racism: "In the train I was given not one but two, three places. . . . I existed triply: I occupied space. I moved towards the other . . . an evanescent other, hostile but not opaque, transparent, not there, disappeared. Nausea . . ."[42]

By defining group formation as a function of stigma and separation, and by describing social relations in the language of physical repulsion, Ambedkar suggested that only deformed social relations between castes existed in a structure that presented violence as law. Race and slavery were explicit axes of comparison. Elsewhere in his writings, Ambedkar noted that the slave was better off when compared to the untouchable. In ancient Rome slaves were educated as a sign of their masters' status and participated in the economy as scribes, performers, musicians, and skilled labor. Plantation slavery was brutal, yet slaves' status as a value-producing property meant that there was some incentive to protecting them: "Being property and therefore valuable, the master for sheer self-interest took great care of the health and well-being of the slave."[43] Untouchables, on the other hand, were not formally enslaved, but their social stigma reproduced their material deprivation. The comparison was polemical and it was meant to challenge the putatively consensual model of caste relations and caste labor that upper-caste reformers, especially Gandhi, had outlined.

Like race, the connection between caste and commodity logic is a suggestive axis of Ambedkar's thought. We have already seen this in Ambedkar's discussion of *bahishkar* as social segregation screened through free-market logic and laws of contract. I argue that Ambedkar theorized caste as a doubled structure of symbolic and material dispossession along the lines of Marx's argument about the commodity form as fetish and as a social hieroglyphic demanding to be read.[44] For Marx, abstract labor (la-

bor power) is realized in the exchange value of the commodity, which is
the misrecognized form of congealed labor. Capital thus necessarily includes labor even though labor is necessarily invisible, displaced onto the
fetish value of the commodity.[45] The untouchable was just such a social
hieroglyphic, one who provided a key to the animating logic of caste.

Unlike capitalist relations of production to which labor was central,
however, caste society was not organized on the model of bourgeois accumulation, but on ritual action as a form of symbolic expenditure, to
which the untouchables' labor was extraneous because it was defined
as being defiled and impure. In addition, caste was a complex symbolic
form whose antagonisms were dispersed across the social field and
whose accretive character forbade a systemic view of all of its historical layers in any synchronic formulation. This made it more difficult
for Ambedkar to centralize a historical antagonism between Brahmin
and Dalit as the motor of history. Caste society was internally contradictory, but in a nondialectical sense. Internal contradictions did not
propel the system forward in a holistic process of change. Rather, we can
see caste as a "structure in difference" whose various, discordant parts
bore a contingent, non-necessary relation to each other.[46] The Dalit subaltern was the negated and nauseating, if necessary, component of the
caste order, embodying the dehumanizing potential of caste in its most
acute form.

Even as Ambedkar developed this systemic theory of caste, he turned
his attention to specifically political mechanisms for making manifest the
position of structural negativity occupied by the Dalit communities. The
Indian National Congress, intent on incorporating majority and minority within a national community, formed the political and discursive context within which Ambedkar thought and struggled for a Dalit political
identity. What was the position of untouchable communities composed
of people who were essentially treated as subhuman or degraded Hindus? Was there a mechanism for recognizing them? Ambedkar's effort
to define the main characteristics of this political constituency built on
his critique of the Hindu community as a political/legislative entity that
excluded Dalits as a matter of principle.

THE POSSIBILITY OF MINORITY

Colonial conceptions of Dalits, or Depressed Classes as a community
of degraded Hindus, developed incrementally and oftentimes in opposition to caste Hindu efforts. The 1901 census established *varna* hier-

archy as an accurate descriptor of the caste system.[47] By 1908, when it became clear that the untouchable communities were sizeable—about 16–24 percent of India's population[48]—caste Hindus began to assert that untouchables were Hindus.[49] The colonial government decided not to rank caste communities in the 1911 census, a response to petitioning by caste groups looking to substantiate claims to high status in the *varna* hierarchy. At the same time, colonial officials began to emphasize untouchables' separate identity, recategorizing them in 1911 as "Depressed Classes," an altogether new category to describe degraded persons who suffered ritual exclusion and stigmatization as lesser Hindus. In that year, a circular from Census Commissioner E. A. Gait proposed a series of tests for defining membership in the Depressed Classes.[50] It caused consternation among caste Hindus because it enabled colonial administrators to classify close to a quarter of the Hindu population as Depressed Classes. It was reported in the *India Review* that Muslims were adamant that this strength of "outcastes [who] are beyond of Hinduism" should not "swell the numerical force of the Hindus."[51]

In 1931, Census Commissioner J. H. Hutton proposed a test for untouchability that essentially defined it as a form of social segregation characterized by exclusion from public amenities.[52] The translation of untouchability from religious to civic exclusion amounted to an official secularization of the category: "From the point of view of the State, the important test is the right to use public conveniences—roads, wells and schools—and if this be taken as the primary test, religious disabilities and the social disabilities involved by them may be regarded as contributory only."[53]

While this colonial understanding dovetailed with Dalits' own secularized perception of the consequences of caste stigma, a liberal truism posed a practical problem for forming a Dalit constituency: the idea that it was composed of free and equal contracting subjects. This liberal idea assumes what must be accomplished, that is, that procedures or processes be developed whereby incommensurable entities are rendered commensurable with each other. The political theorist Ernesto Laclau argues that political equality actually requires acts of commensuration, of creating likeness or similarity between persons or qualities that are dissimilar in some respects. He writes, "In the political field equality is a type of discourse that tries to deal with differences."[54] If commensuration presumes the logic of equivalence, minority is a political form that associates some ascriptive categories of civil society with political inadequacy. Thus, minority as a demographic category is never merely about number. It indicates a qualitative difference, what we might call a subject's singularity, which cannot be rendered fully commensurable within political space. It is precisely due to the qualitative and quantitative distinctions encompassed by the term "minority" that minority rights are such a fraught issue. When particularities typically considered to be outside the field of liberal political commensuration—because they are taken as pre- or apolitical categories—become sites around which demands for dignity and rights occur, they pose a problem for the abstract conception of citizenship. They also pose procedural problems insofar as rules and mechanisms are required to enable certain political results, for example equality. To locate commensuration as an active process, and liberal ideology as responsive to historical contingency and to political necessity, throws into relief two fundamental aspects of the colonial state: its externality to indigenous society as well as its interventions into Indian society through policies and procedures that blocked full political commensuration.[55] As we will see, religious difference was taken as absolute, but religious communities were balanced against each other as political majorities and minorities. This produced a politics of exception and demand for commensuration.

In a practical sense, Ambedkar confronted communities constituted as prepolitical, fundamentally religious structures of authority that regulated their members and, in turn, submitted to colonial regulation. Beyond the fact that these religious communities were recognized as political actors is the more significant issue of their recognition by the colonial state as *qualitatively equivalent*—Hindus were united to each other by faith and belief, as were Muslims, and each was subject to the laws of their respective communities. Yet they were *quantitatively incommensurable* as Hindu majority and Muslim minority. Hindus and Muslims were characterized by an unbridgeable absolute difference. Muslims were constituted as the archetypical political minority, acknowledged in a separate electorate. Once identified with the separate electorate, Muslims increasingly defined their interests outside of, and oftentimes in opposition to, the general interest. Hindus in turn saw the general constituency as Hindu and as a space where Muslims could expect "no extra" representation. The separate electorate designated Muslims as the political minority and normalized Hindus as a distinctive religious community (and a numerical majority) liable to dwarf any other electoral grouping. What did it mean to invoke the Depressed Classes as a "minority" under these circumstances?

Ambedkar's conception of a Dalit minority did not begin with the demand for a separate electorate for the Depressed Classes. He arrived there eventually, by working within, and trying to expand the boundaries of, liberal institutional logic to encompass recognition of the Depressed Classes as a constituency with the capacity to represent their own interests. In his vision of Dalits defined by social marginality, civic exclusion, and material deprivation, Ambedkar had already departed radically from the idea of untouchables as degraded Hindus. Specifying Dalits' minority status required engaging with caste as a complex form of inequality. To do so, Ambedkar made arguments about the primacy of the political to oppose preexisting organic definitions of community and to address Dalits as having a class interest that could be revealed as a *political* interest.

Specifying the conditions under which a socially and economically deprived collective could demand political recognition was an early step in Ambedkar's theorization of the Dalit as minority. He initially asserted the primacy of the political as the ground for human recognition. Through claims to a universal right to politics, he strove to bring attention to an unrecognized constituency possessing no distinguishing qualities but for the fact of its humanity. As he wrote, the Depressed Classes "have their very persona confiscated. The socio-religious disabilities have dehumanized the untouchables and their interests at stake are therefore the interests of humanity."[56] Thus was the humanity of the Dalit asserted through her right to political recognition.

In articulating a new Dalit identity, Ambedkar experimented with the Marxian discourse of class to distinguish a Depressed Class minority from a Muslim minority by specifying the materiality of caste. In 1918 and 1928, he testified before two British commissions, the Southborough and Simon commissions, which considered the extension of the franchise and the functioning of dyarchy, in both cases representing the Depressed Classes as a distinctive community with separate interests.[57] As he argued in 1918, "a minority which is oppressed, or whose rights are denied by the majority, would be a minority that would be fit for consideration for political purposes."[58] Noting that the caste Hindus could represent "the *material* interests of the Mohammedans and vice versa," Ambedkar distinguished the Depressed Classes as "educationally backward . . . economically very poor, socially enslaved."[59] Material deprivation and social stratification united them as a class.

Positioning untouchables as a distinct community and constituency was precisely what Gandhi contested. He offered a powerful reason why untouchables did not need special political representation. "Sikhs may remain as such in perpetuity," he pointed out, "so may Muslims, so may

Europeans. Would 'untouchables' remain untouchables in perpetuity?"[60]
In other words, it was self-defeating to dwell upon experiences of abjection to claim political representation. The history of caste subjection had to be transcended. Gandhi's question cut to the political conundrum of Dalit identity, which depended on exacerbating stigmatized identity to overcome it. Ambedkar answered that it was only along the axis of the historical, the ground of inherited subalternity, that Dalit identity could become salient. Caste was classlike, but also a form of embodiment; stigma carried upon the body was the perverse legacy of the Hindu juridical order. Thus Ambedkar attempted to render religioritual stigmatization politically salient and to ground political struggles in an identity that would ultimately be transcended. His was a sustained effort to transform the *structural negativity* of the untouchable into *positive political value*.

On what basis could a territorially dispersed minority, lacking social and economic status, become not only politically legible but politically consequential? Ambedkar took a principled and strategic stance: universal franchise was the common sense of democratic politics. It could be used proactively to reveal potential constituencies or groups such as the Depressed Classes, who required protection. Lowering eligibility criteria—property and taxation qualifications—and granting reserved seats in legislative bodies would address the unequal position from which the Depressed Classes entered the political terrain. Communal electorates had the best chance of representing the community's interest, however.[61] Instead of diluting particularity, adult franchise with reserved representation would position the Depressed Classes as political and economic, rather than religious, minorities. They required protection due to their low social and economic status; their small numbers required some form of compensation. A separate electorate with weightage could meet these goals.

Ambedkar developed his position through a sustained critique of the Muslim separate electorate. The enumeratively grounded principle of weightage was introduced in 1909 to acknowledge the "historical and political importance" of Muslims.[62] Some years earlier, in his representation to the viceroy, the Aga Khan had challenged the ratio between Hindu and Muslim communities, arguing that "the Mahomedans of India number according to the census taken in the year 1901, over sixty two millions or between one fifth to one fourth of the total population of His Majesty's Indian dominions, and if a reduction is made for . . . *those classes who are ordinarily classified as Hindus but properly speaking are not Hindus at all, the proportion of Mahomedans to the Hindu majority becomes much larger."*[63] For caste Hindus, the Hindu identity of the Depressed Classes became all the more important compared with the modal minority, Muslims. Ambedkar struggled, however, to define the Depressed Classes through an altogether different principle of minority. He emphasized that socioeconomic deprivation required legal safeguards, and argued that separate representation "was literally showered upon a community like the Mahomedans holding a stronger and better position in the country than can be predicated of the Depressed Classes. The Sabha protests against this grading of the citizens of a country on the basis of their political importance."[64]

In fact, Ambedkar acknowledged that Muslims represented the principle of nationality, rather than political minority. They were a demographic majority in Baluchistan, Sind, Bengal, Punjab, and the Northwest Frontier Provinces. The territorialization of number through the establishment of Muslim and Hindu majority provinces, a demand of the Muslim League from 1928, was a prelude for demands based on the territorialization of nationality.[65] Ambedkar thought these Muslim-majority provinces an "ingenious contrivance" involving "the maintenance of justice and peace by retaliation" and "a system of protection by counterblast against blast; terror against terror and eventually tyranny against tyranny."[66] The Muslim special electorate had created a false unity between communities of varying strength, displacing the question of equality onto (numerical) parity between communities rather than asking how representative they were: "It is contrary to all sense of political justice to approve of a system which permits the members of one community to rule other communities without their having submitted themselves to the suffrage of the communities."[67]

Nationality rendered number unimportant. Indeed, national affiliation was an affective bond of commonality, whereas majority and minority were structural positions that citizen-subjects inhabited *in relation to the state.* Against the reigning (oxymoronic) conception of Hindu majority and Muslim minority, Ambedkar posed political constituencies produced through the antagonism of competing class interests. The Depressed Classes were unlike Muslims, he argued, because they shared a set of social and economic disabilities *as a group.* Defining Dalits as a class that suffered material deprivation meant they constituted a minority in political terms, not a constituency united by primordial ties of community. Ambedkar also underscored the difference between the political interests of the Depressed Classes and Muslims. Muslims were a politicized community recognized by Hindus. Untouchables were unrecognized as political subjects and therefore also lacked social recognition. Distinguished by material deprivation, physical vulnerability, and stigmatized status in the caste order, Dalits represented an altogether different principle of minority. The thinking was ingenious. Ambedkar drew on a generic theory of representative government based on adult franchise to derive political value for a stigmatized community by claiming a universal right to politics.[68] In turn, he used the right to politics to redefine the meaning of minority and majority in India. Ambedkar noted, "A political majority is not a fixed or a permanent majority. It is a majority which is always made, unmade and remade." The Hindu majority, he continued, was a "communal majority [that] is a permanent majority fixed in its attitude. One can destroy it but one cannot transform it."[69]

Ambedkar was one of the last Dalit leaders to embrace the separate electorate.[70] His posture in favor of adult franchise along with reserved representation for the Depressed Classes was distinctive with regard to other non-Brahmin and Dalit leaders. The Depressed Classes Mission, the Servants of India Society, the Servants of the Somavanshi Society, non-Brahmin leaders, and the Depressed India Association all favored separate representation. Though they formed a similar proportion of Bombay's population, the Depressed Classes had managed to send only one nominated member, Ambedkar, to the provincial legislative council, compared to twenty-nine Muslim members. The Mahar Seva Sangh (Association for Service to the Mahars), represented by Dnyandev Dhruvnath Gholap, the first Depressed Class representative nominated to the council, in 1924, submitted a petition demanding separate representation to protect Depressed Class interests: "We reckon all Touchables as Bourgeois, feeding ruthlessly upon our innocence and getting themselves profited at our cost. We also make no distinctions between Brahmans and the non-Brahmans. . . . The non-Brahman Marathas, with a secret motive of giving a finer democratic touch to their movement, showed us some attractive signs of sympathy and fraternity; but past twelve years experience has proved that they have not only misused but abused the power that they obtained by our joining hands with them."[71]

Ambedkar, however, emphasized adult franchise and criticized education and property requirements, and demanded reduction of property and taxation qualifications for Depressed Class candidates. Acknowledging the power of separate representation, however, he noted that, "for the Depressed Classes, communal representation and self-determination are but two different phrases which express the same notion."[72]

If the Hindus, Muslims, and Depressed Classes were understood to constitute three distinct communities of interest, with the Depressed Classes forming 18 to 20 percent of the population, this third community disturbed the idea that only "fixed permanent communities" existed as political categories. By subverting the colonial discourse of community as constituency, Ambedkar was also strategically positioned to argue for a fundamental contradiction between Hindus and Depressed Classes on the basis of material exploitation and socioreligious stigmatization.

As early as 1920, Ambedkar argued that the Depressed Classes would remain powerless unless they used their political potential to threaten Hindu hegemony.[73] As an exceptional community, untouchables had to harness their latent political power to make Hindus realize that they were of greater significance than their mere numerical strength: "Our untouchable brethren will recognize their own strength once they realize that Muslims cannot win without us and equally Hindus cannot win without us. They [untouchables] alone have the power to bring about a decisive shift one way or the other."[74]

In a sense, then, Ambedkar saw the separate electorate as akin to the general strike. Ambedkar sought to mobilize the negative power of the Depressed Classes in the same way that the general strike revealed the secret of capital: that capital necessarily includes labor even though labor is invisible, displaced onto the fetish value of the commodity. By making caste Hindus "dependent upon the votes of Untouchables," the separate electorate would reveal the latent power of the Depressed Classes to withhold consent to Hindu hegemony.[75] By sharpening the antagonism between Hindu and non-Hindu, the perception that the Hindus constituted a consensual, quasi-natural community would also be challenged. Unlike workers in Western nations who could become visible as labor, Dalit structural negativity arose from their extraneous position in a system of symbolic labor. They could creatively make this visible only in the political arena: the emancipation of the minority subject was culturally specific, even if it resembled the trajectory of proletarian conscientization. Dalit emancipation required antagonism to religious identification, rather than a transcendence of religious identity.

Gandhi challenged efforts at political separation during the second Round Table Conference and bitterly resisted demands for a separate electorate for the Depressed Classes. Having agreed to a compromise solution on the stalled question of minority rights. Gandhi then went on a fast-unto-death to challenge Prime Minister Ramsay MacDonald's Communal Award of August 16, 1932, which gave the Depressed Classes separate electorates in areas where they were concentrated, in addition to a general vote. Indeed the Communal Award was a critical moment for Ambedkar insofar as it clearly marked the anomalous status of the Depressed Classes as a political minority *because* they were degraded Hindus. Despite Hutton's 1931 description of untouchability as social segregation characterized by exclusion from public amenities, the Communal Award reincorporated the Depressed Classes as a group of stigmatized Hindus whose status could be ameliorated through a claim upon caste Hindus in the form of the double vote. Sadly, the Award and its compromise successor, the Poona Pact, overwrote Ambedkar's redefinition of minority. The Poona Pact instituted reserved representation, with seats increased from the 71 granted by the Communal Award's separate electorate to 148 seats reserved for Depressed Class representatives in a two-tier election, a general Hindu electorate choosing from candidates who had been selected in a primary election for the Depressed Classes.

As the colonial state stepped back from interfering in what was characterized as an internal problem for the Hindu community in the aftermath of Gandhi's fast-unto-death, it became obvious that the majority of caste Hindus would not tolerate any form of internal regulation. If parity was established between religious constituencies, it was also the case that the colonial government had relegated the internal regulation of those communities to socioreligious elites, even if that contravened principles of justice or fairness. Whether the response was a politically motivated effort to plump Hindu numbers or whether it involved a sustained encounter between caste Hindu and untouchable premised on a "shared concept of humanity which means that the [Dalit] is a perverted version of the self,"[76] the Poona Pact was calculated to resist political separation because caste Hindus interpreted Ambedkar's demand for separate representation as an unspoken (religious) conversion. Even Prime Minister Ramsay MacDonald indicated that the Communal Award was based on the identity of the Depressed Classes as degraded Hindus: "The number of special seats to be filled from spec ial Depressed Classes constituencies will be seen to be small and has been fixed not to provide a quota appropriate for the total representation of the whole of the Depressed Class population, *but solely to secure a minimum number of spokesmen for the Depressed Classes in the Legislature* who are chosen exclusively by the Depressed Classes."[77]

The failure of separate representation haunted Ambedkar, despite the fact that the Poona Pact positioned the Dalit communities as subaltern

OUR CHARGE-SHEET AGAINST
GANDHIJI AND CONGRESS.

ENOUGH OF PATRONISING ATTITUDE AND LIP SYMPATHY.
WE ASK FOR JUSTICE AND FAIR PLAY.

1. In spite of the fact that the removal of the untouchability has been included in the constructive programme of the Congress, practically nothing has so far been done by that body to achieve that object, and in our fights against untouchability at Mahad and Nasik most of the local Congress leaders have been our bitter opponents.

2. The attitude of Gandhiji at the Round Table Conference in London with regard to the demands of the Depressed Classes as put forward by their accredited and trusted leader Dr. Ambedkar, was most *unreasonable, obstinate and inexplicable.*

3. Gandhiji was prepared to concede on behalf of the Congress special claims of the Mohamedans and the Sikhs including their demand for separate representation on " historic grounds ", but he was not willing even to concede reserved seats in general electorates to the depressed classes, although he knew, at least ought to have known, what sort of treatment they would get, should they be thrown at the mercies of caste Hindus.

4. Without giving reasons for his attitude Gandhiji opposed the demands put forward by Dr. Ambedkar at the R. T. C. and declared in meetings and at interviews that he would resist the claims of the depressed classes at the risk of his life. This obstinacy is rediculously fanatical. Heaven would surely not fall if the depressed classes were given separate representation or reserved seats in general electorates !

5. Gandhiji's attitude towards the political claims of the depressed classes was not only obstinate, but also vindictive, in that he privately asked the Mohamedan delegates and representatives of other minorities to formulate their demands and assured them that if they agreed among themselves he would accept them on behalf of the Congress, provided they did not support the claims put forward on behalf of the depressed classes. This trick was exposed by Dr. Ambedkar and Gandhiji was plainly told that such tricks did not become a "Mahatma." This is the head and front of the charge of rudeness towards Gandhiji levelled against Dr. Ambedkar by the Congress news-papers. Gandhiji tried to deny the fact afterwards but the evidence was overwhelmingly against him and *the fact has been indisputably proved.*

6. The greatest presumption on Gandhiji's part at the R. T. C. was that he claims that represented the depressed classes and not Dr. Ambedkar. This is an insult not only to Dr. Ambedkar but also to those millions of the socalled untouchables in the country who look upon Dr. Ambedkar as their foremost and trusted leader. *Leadership cannot be imposed, it must be accepted by those on whose behalf it is claimed.*

7. The Congress organs have been carrying on a campaign of vilification against Dr. Ambedkar. They have not had a good word to say about the brave fight put up by him on behalf the States' subjects at the Federal Structure Committee while Gandhiji had given up their case and betrayed them. Gandhiji's speech on that occasion though a sorry performance was published *verbatim* in the Congress papers, but no paper published Dr. Ambedkar's powerful plea on behalf of the States' subjects. The Congress papers have been slinging mud at the brave, learned doctor; attributing unworthy motives to him; boasting meetings of their hirelings and dupes, through mere family gatherings; suppressing the reports of monster meetings held for supporting Dr. Ambedkar; and supressing correspondence representing the other side and stating the real facts.

8. Under the pretext of espousing the cause of the depressed classes and removing their untouchability efforts are being made by the Congress people to wean away the followers of Dr. Ambedkar. *This is nothing but an attempt to purchase a leadership of the depressed classes.*

9. Gandhiji has said in opposing the claims of the depressed classes for separate representation that he does not want the Hindu community to be subjected to vivisection or dissection. But the Congress is now disecting the community of untouchables by playing one section of that community against another. Gandhiji and the Congress are not playing the game. *Open enemies are far better than treacherous friends.*

10. Attempts are being made to show that Gandhiji and the Congress alone represent the depressed classes by presenting addresses through the hirelings and dupes who are a mere a handful. Is it not our duty to demonstrate the fact by coming out in thousands and proclaiming the truth? *This is our charge – sheet against Gandhiji and the Congress.*

Let those who are not blind hero-worshippers and blind partisans judge and give their verdict.

General Secretary,
Depressed Classes Institute.

Figure 8. "Charge-sheet against Gandhiji and Congress," a response to the second Round Table Conference, produced by the Depressed Classes Institute prior to Gandhi's fast-unto-death and the Poona Pact compromise. Courtesy of the Khairmode Collection, Bombay University.

citizens. Ambedkar's faith in this political solution requires inspection. Why would someone who supported adult franchise, protective mechanisms, and inclusion of a marginalized community like the Depressed Classes in a common civic and political life advocate separation as a mechanism of political recognition? What did the demand for a separate electorate achieve? I have noted that caste was a complex symbolic form whose antagonisms were dispersed across a social field whose accretive character forbade a systemic view of all of its historical layers in any synchronic formulation. The status of the Depressed Classes as an impoverished, demographic minority made it difficult to centralize a historical antagonism between Brahmin and Dalit and to then render that antagonism politically consequential *without the support of the state* to counterbalance Hindu hegemony. Insofar as there was no single procedural mechanism or political form that could respond to the complexity of caste inequality, the separate electorate was an overdetermined political option from the start. What it revealed, however, was Ambedkar's sense of the necessity of working with and through the state to illustrate the limits of existing governmental procedures and mechanisms, instead of refusing to engage with democratic liberalism and embracing a religious politics, as Gandhi had done.

During the 1920s, Gandhi had skillfully articulated untouchability as a societal division of labor to which the untouchable's stigmatized labor was central.[78] In the aftermath of the Poona Pact, he began describing the relationship to untouchables in terms of a spiritual debt to Harijans (people of god) or Hari. This penitential model of citizenship required empathetic identification with the Harijan and repentance in the form of service, ceaseless labor for the Harijan cause, and complete identification with the untouchable.[79] We thus find Gandhi claiming to be a Hindu by birth and an untouchable "by choice." Equally troubling, he justified *varna* hierarchy as an ethical division of labor based on the principle of service and sacrifice, with the untouchable central to this economy of sacrifice.[80] Practical issues such as interdining and intermarriage were simply dismissed as matters of choice. No one was obliged to eat in anyone else's presence or to "give his daughter in marriage to anybody in particular."[81] Service and redemption were important, not equality and reciprocity. Gandhi argued, "If everyone regarded himself as a Shudra, religion would be well rid of the concept of high and low." The principle of (voluntary) manual labor, of service, that characterized Shudra dharma ought to be the governing principle of everyone's "varnadharma."[82] Gandhi's support for *varnashramadharma* (caste as a moral ordering based on the societal division of labor) left the laborer's stigma untouched and elided the question of inequality.[83]

In contrast, Ambedkar noted, "caste was a division of *laborers* and not just of *labor.*"[84] Violence was essential to the maintenance of the caste order: "One important requirement for the successful working of Chatur-varnya is the maintenance of the penal system. . . . The system of Chatur-varnya must perpetually face the problem of the transgressor. Unless there is a penalty attached to the act of transgression, men will not keep to their respective classes. . . . Not only is penal sanction necessary, but penalty of death is necessary."[85] Indeed, it was the effort to rethink the personhood of the laborer, not merely redefining stigmatized labor, that led Ambedkar to explore the adjacencies of race, class, and caste in the first phase of his political thought.[86] In contrast, anger at the insult of being referred to as Harijans was widespread among Mahar Dalits, as can be seen from this dialogue:

> *Congress supporter:* How sweet is the name, "Harijan." Oh Harijans, really you are lucky!
>
> *Ambedkarite:* Don't call me Harijan! That name is an affront to our self-respect. When the Congress government called us Harijans, all the representatives [of the Independent Labour Party] walked out. Not only that but our self-respecting untouchables are holding meetings to refuse that name, Harijan. Don't you dare call me Harijan! . . .
>
> Do you think changing our name can improve our status?
>
> . . .
>
> As soon as I hear the name Harijan I am on fire from head to toe, and I get so angry I start shaking.[87]

THE IMPOSSIBILITY OF MINORITY

You are fighting for Swaraj [self-rule]. I am ready to join you. And I may assure you that I can fight better than you. I make only one condition. Tell me what share I am to have in Swaraj. If you don't want to tell me that and you want to make up with the British behind my back, hell on both of you.

B. R. Ambedkar, *Bombay Sentinel*, April 28, 1942

Ambedkar's analysis of caste as structural violence required strategies to exacerbate the latent antagonism and conflict of Hindu society so as to harness Dalits as a political value. During the 1930s, such strategies took shape around the Dalit as a universal political subject and Dalits as the vanguard of broader struggles for material emancipation.

In her important account of Ambedkar's relationship with Communism, Gail Omvedt describes the 1930s as the "years of radicalism."[88] The election manifesto of the Independent Labour Party (ILP), formed on August 15, 1936, noted, "The word Labour was used instead of the words Depressed Classes because labour includes the Depressed Classes as well."[89] The party was to be sustained by a cadre of unpaid volunteers engaged in grassroots conscientization and fund-raising.[90] The Congress was characterized as a "capitalist party."[91] An editorial in *Janata* argued that it was impossible to have a party of capitalists, workers, and peasants.[92] The ILP was committed to state management and ownership of industry and supported credit and cooperative societies, tax reforms to reduce the burden on agricultural and industrial labor, and free and compulsory education.[93] However, the distinctive experience of caste labor was fundamental to the ILP.[94]

A twenty-thousand-strong meeting of the Manmad Railway Workers' Conference in 1938 saw critiques of Brahmanshahi and *bhandwalshahi*, or Brahminism and capitalism.[95] A workers' union of the Bombay municipality, the Mumbai Kamgar Sangh, was also formed in 1935 with help from the Samata Seva Sangh and represented about 5 percent of the fifteen thousand employees of the municipality.[96] Efforts were also made to organize dockyard workers and railway workers in 1948.[97] These organizational efforts sought to make caste a crucial focus for the working-class movement. Agitation against the *khoti* system and the power of landlords in the Konkan region saw joint ILP-Communist rallies in September and October of 1937; a strike and demonstration against the Industrial Disputes Bill in November attended by over one hundred thousand people; and a massive peasant protest in Bombay on January 12, 1939, attended by twenty thousand people. This was offset by Ambedkar's conflict with the largely upper-caste leadership of the Communist movement in India. Ambedkar threatened to break Bombay's historic mill strike of 1928 unless untouchables were employed in all departments, a demand to which Communists reluctantly agreed.[98] The strike of 1929 saw Ambedkar encouraging Dalit workers to return to work to avoid boycott and discrimination by powerful moneylenders.[99]

The exploitation of caste labor brought Ambedkar into alliance with the Communists, but Marxism was no substitute for an immanent critique of caste.[100] Though it remained a regional party, the ILP performed well in the 1937 elections and won eleven out of fifteen reserved seats.[101]

However, the period saw increased tension between Dalit groups: P. G. Solanki, a Chambhar associated with the Bahishkrit Hitakarini Sabha, and N. Shivtarkar parted ways with Ambedkar.[102] The latter rejoined as secretary of the AISCF. And by the end of the decade, the Communists were allied with Congress.

In the 1940s, the discourse on Scheduled Caste (SC) representation fundamentally changed: now, it was the Dalit's singularity as a historically stigmatized subject that justified her position as the subject of freedom. The unreconciled tension between universality and historical particularity was staged in spectacular fashion at the moment of postcolonial transition. On August 20, 1940, in a speech offering dominion status to India, Lord Linlithgow acknowledged the SCs as a separate political constituency whose consent was necessary for Britain's transfer of power to Indians.[103] Linlithgow's invitation to Ambedkar to join the viceroy's Executive Council coincided with Congress's Quit India movement of 1942 and led to charges that Ambedkar was an imperialist stooge.[104] The British continued to believe in the separate identity of the SCs. Even as late as 1944, Lord Wavell told Gandhi that the SCs constituted a "separate element in the national life of India," and made the granting of full freedom to Indians contingent on framing a constitution for India to which all major players, including the Depressed Classes, would assent.[105] Still, resistance to separate SC representation grew. Gandhi argued, somewhat disingenuously, "I know the fashion is to talk of the Hindus forming the majority community. But Hinduism is an elastic indefinable term, and Hindus are not a homogenous whole like Muslims and Christians. . . . In other words and in reality so far as India is concerned, there can only be political parties and no majority or minority communities. The cry of the tyranny of the majority is a fictitious cry."[106] While the Cripps Mission in 1942 supported separate representation for religious minorities, Sir Stafford Cripps's refusal to support SC demands for separate representation was described as a "conspiracy of silence" between "the Government, the Congress and even the Muslims."[107] It was the immediate trigger for Ambedkar's establishment of the AISCF, formed at a Nagpur conference in July 1942, which held that the SCs were "racially and culturally different from all."[108] The AISCF Working Committee even argued that Dalits were a religious minority and described Congress hegemony as leading to "the annihilation of our people as a political entity."[109] Ambedkar strongly objected to the Cripps betrayal, saying, "Up to the declaration of 8th August 1940 His Majesty's Government's view was that the untouchables were a distinct and a separate element and that

Figure 9. B. R. Ambedkar (seated, center) at the All-India Depressed Classes Conference (AIDCC), July 1942, pictured with workers and members of the AIDCC's Women's Conference. More than 75,000 people, including 20,000 women, attended the conference in Nagpur. Courtesy of the Vasant Moon Collection, Nagpur.

they constituted so important an element that their consent was necessary for any constitutional changes that may be desired."[110]

Although the SCs had once enjoyed Muslim political support, Ambedkar noted that recognition of Muslims as a nationality now pitted Muslims against all other communities. He saw the All-India Muslim League setting up "a new equation of values . . . that the Muslims, whatever their numbers, are just equal to the non-Muslims and therefore in any political arrangement the Muslims must get fifty percent."[111] The Muslim League had trumped number with nationality.[112] Now the problem was how to get untouchables recognized as "a separate element" in the national life of India. Physical separation was proposed through establishment of SC villages, on government wastelands and private lands, overseen by a government-established Settlement Commission.[113] Village committees would form the basic AISCF organizational unit and provide funds through a tax.[114]

Again, this was out of sync with the political proclivities of other Dalit leaders. M. C. Rajah, president of the All-India Depressed Classes Association and Ambedkar's most important rival, had demanded separate electorates all along. But he had also issued a joint declaration with the Hindu Mahasabha demanding reserved seats for Depressed Class candidates, noting that a separate electorate was only viable if the colonial government was the "special protector of Minority interests." Under changed political conditions, it was imperative that the Depressed Classes, who lacked an "effective percentage," amalgamate themselves into the Hindu constituency provided they got reserved seats.[115] Apparently, constituencies could play the game of parity only with the colonial state as ringmaster.[116]

Rajah's position apparently triumphed, since the SCs played no part in the critical Simla discussions of 1945.[117] The Cabinet Mission, which visited India from March to June 1946 to discuss interim government and the framing of a new constitution for India, defined the Indian National Congress as the chosen representative of all constituencies except Muslims. The Cabinet Mission Award of May 16, 1946, did recognize three main communities, however: general, including Hindus and others; Muslim; and Sikh. As the SCs had no separate representation, they would be accommodated within an advisory committee to the Constituent Assembly drawn from provincial legislatures.

This betrayal by the British government set the tone for Ambedkar's *What Congress and Gandhi Have Done to the Untouchables*, a vehement attack on Congress hegemony published in 1945, a few years before the violent onset of Partition. The text located the Poona Pact compromise as the root of the failures of the 1940s. Ambedkar wrote that the Communal Award had redressed the political weakness of the Depressed Classes by making Hindus dependent on their vote: "The second vote given by the Communal Award was a priceless privilege. Its value as a political weapon was beyond reckoning. . . . No caste Hindu candidate could have dared to neglect the Untouchables in his constituency or be hostile to their interests if he were made dependent upon the votes of the Untouchables."[118]

Although animated by an enormous sense of betrayal, this text was also one of Ambedkar's most important engagements with political liberalism. Moving from his earlier focus on redefining the colonial category of minority, he now targeted Hindu majoritarianism and its political representative, the Congress, for reproducing caste hegemony through the franchise. His immediate focus was the defeat of AISCF candidates in the historic elections of 1945–46, which resulted in Congress claims that they represented SC interests.[119] His broader concern, however, was how to demarcate a distinctive SC interest within the field of liberal politics.

Ambedkar's analysis began with the Poona Pact provisions regarding the selection of SC representatives. The pact dictated a two-tier process wherein SC voters selected a group of SC candidates in a primary election. Later, they voted together with the general electorate to choose the SC candidate for the reserved seats.[120] Ambedkar argued that because caste Hindus could ultimately swing their votes toward a palatable SC candidate, the initial selection of candidates by SC voters was rigged to produce candidates most acceptable to the general (Hindu) electorate. Even when SC voters elected representatives to reserved seats, their interests were not necessarily represented, since those interests would have to be rendered palatable to the general constituency, who voted for reserved seat candidates during the second vote. Ambedkar noted that the system of reserved representation worked in favor of Congress, which ran Depressed Class candidates in both the reserved and general elections. For the Congress, this substantiated their claim that untouchables were Hindus. What it actually produced, as Ambedkar noted, was concentration of political power in Congress's hands. The SC electorate remained a numerical minority subservient to Hindu interests, without having the separate electorate to transform the principle of minority into a logic of (political) exception.

Multi-member reserved constituencies were organized around two-tier elections. In the primaries, SC voters selected a roster of SC candidates most likely to succeed in the general election. This diluted Dalit self-representation because the process often produced "unrepresentative" tokens. Instead, under the system of distributed voting Ambedkar recommended, voters had the same number of votes as the number of candidates in the running: they could distribute their votes across candidates or bunch them up. SC and caste Hindu voters could swing their votes toward favored candidates, to produce more "representative" spokespersons to articulate competing political interests. SC and caste Hindu representatives would then confront each other on an *agonistic* political terrain.[121]

Ambedkar's critique of the electoral process and the Congress was interpreted as reflecting his pro-British, antinationalist stance. This rendered his efforts to position himself as *a nationalist critic of Congress politics* rhetorically untenable.[122] One Congress detractor, K. Santhanam, declared that *What Congress and Gandhi Have Done* was "an incoherent jumble" without order or justification, determined to represent Gandhi and the Congress as "wholly evil."[123] Though Ambedkar's text was structured to refute Congress claims to represent the nation through a step-by-step illustration of the oxymoron of Hindu democracy, his critique of Congress was ignored. C. Rajagopalachari argued that the SCs had no claims upon a separate democracy: "The Scheduled Castes are evenly distributed all over India and are about ten per cent of the population. . . . Thus distributed, they have to be part of the general population and cannot isolate themselves into a separate democracy. Nothing therefore follows from the argument even if conclusively proved that the Scheduled Castes do not stand behind the Congress and do not support its claim for political freedom."[124]

Ambedkar's critique of the unrepresentative character of the Congress was thus a moot point, since "it may often be impossible to get minorities to agree to the claims for self-government which is majority rule even though the minorities be fully protected in their civil and political rights."[125] Another text, K. Santhanam's *Ambedkar's Attack,* also discounted the SCs as a territorially dispersed minority: "Whether there are 50 or 60 millions, it is of minor importance. I may point out that they are distributed almost evenly in all the villages of India. In each village they constitute a minority."[126] Santhanam was emphatic that a community defined by neither demographic concentration nor cultural distinction must accept their position as Hindus. This was of a piece, of course, with Congress insistence on characterizing the AISCF as a communal organization. Ambedkar, not the Congress, was said to hold on to untouchability as a "precious possession," resisting assimilation and integration. SC representation was also posed as a "short cut" to political power for leaders who benefited from safeguards enjoyed by their community.[127]

As time went on, the Poona Pact was understood to be a political resolution of the caste question because it settled the problem of the religious status of the Depressed Classes. The politics of untouchability had once again foregrounded the relationship between "the religious" and "the political," while the politics of the 1940s demanded that the SCs join the political mainstream. The high politics of the transfer of power only exaggerated Dalit political negligibility. Ironically, Sir Stafford Cripps acknowledged as much, noting that "owing to the operation of what is known as the Poona Pact, they [Ambedkar's party] have been almost entirely excluded from the provincial assemblies."[128]

Ambedkar insisted that the political significance of the Depressed Classes derived from their status as an exceptional community defined by social exclusion. He adhered to the view that the Hindu majority was a communal, not a political, majority, since it could not be "made and unmade." He had repeatedly tried to transform political discourse by Dalits' oppression and their status as minorities. For a community that was stigmatized and territorially dispersed, self-representation was neither possible from within nor outside of the terrain of formal politics, however: the Hindu majority dominated both spaces. Though political community formation had been stymied in the 1940s, its necessary corollary, strong community and identity formation, remained for Ambedkar to rework and build upon. Increasingly, he elaborated a principle of Dalit personhood that lay outside of political commensuration.

THE BUDDHIST DALIT

For what is this sacred literature? It is a literature which is almost entirely the creation of the Brahmins. Secondly, its whole object is to sustain the superiority and privileges of the Brahmins as against the non-Brahmins. . . . Knowing that what is called the sacred literature contains an abominable social philosophy which is responsible for their social degradation, the non-Brahmin reacts to it in a manner quite opposite to that of the Brahmin. That I should be wanting in respect and reverence for the sacred literature

of the Hindus should not surprise any one if it is borne in mind that I am a
non-Brahmin, not even a non-Brahmin but an Untouchable.

B. R. Ambedkar, *Who Were the Shudras?* in *BAWS*, vol. 7

Ambedkar had repeatedly confronted the limits of liberal inclusion and
Hindu tolerance. He had shown that colonial governmentality enabled
Hindu majoritarian power. Yet he believed that Dalits could emerge in
their specificity: embodied particularism had to be justified as such. In
his later writings, Ambedkar rewrote the history of caste subjection as a
process of subject (de)formation by introducing Buddhism as a forgotten agent of history, thus locating religious *and* political antagonism at
the very heart of subaltern community formation. Ambedkar's genealogy of the Dalit Buddhist was located in the tradition of ideological critique favored by caste radicals, especially Phule. Ambedkar's focus on
Hindu juridicality (and on the Vedic basis of Brahminism) and his reliance on the methodologies of the human sciences—anthropology, an-
thropometry, philology—was distinctive, however. Ambedkar's attack on
Brahminism adopted the following major strategies:

1. Redefining the Vedas, Smritis, and Shastras, texts of social con-
    duct and political ethics with an imputed historical validity, as
    texts that justified Brahmin domination and thereby produced
    something like a *caste sociology of knowledge*.[129] (It should
    be noted here that Ambedkar reread the Vedic past to give the
    Kshatriya a distinctive history, even as he dated the distinctive
    stigmatization of the Dalit communities to the period between
    Vedic and Puranic history, thus implicating the Kshatriya com-
    munities in the defeat of Buddhism.)

2. Reading Puranic texts such as the Ramayana and the Maha-
    bharata as quasi-realist representations of the Hindu gods as
    corrupt, lascivious, and violent individuals. That is, turning
    myth into social realism by applying human standards of con-
    duct to divine actors and thereby exposing caste Hinduism as
    advocating violence and discrimination.

3. Examining Hindu law as political performative, that is, ad-
    dressing juridical texts as bringing desired forms of social order
    and regulation into being, rather than articulating existing
    domains of power and control. Legal categorization of peoples
    and communities thus became a crucial form of cultural pro-
    duction in Hindu society.

4. Engaging in a scientific and scholarly study of Indian society
   and history, using the methodological tools of comparative
   philology, archeology, and anthropology to describe the specificity of the Hindu social formation.

Ambedkar drew on each of these strategies in his genealogy of Dalits
as Buddhists and Broken Men.[130] Broken Men were a destitute, territorially dispersed community of suffering, and history's detritus. Because
they had resisted the movement of history, they symbolized obdurate
social forms and practices that were not subsumed by the mainstream.
Buddhism was the constitutive outside, the supplement, which inhered
within Brahmanism in the figures of these Broken Men, partially incorporated ethnic or political others who were the most vulnerable and
violated elements of caste society. The Broken Men were living symbols
of dehumanized existence and proof that colonization was integral to
Hindu historicity.[131]

The discovery of a new historical agent, Buddhism, allowed Ambedkar to argue that there had been a potent, though now-forgotten contender with caste Hinduism from the very inception of Indian society.
Buddhism was a religion that privileged rationality and ethics in contrast
to the ritualism and violence sanctioned by Brahmanism. Ambedkar's genealogy of the Dalit Buddhist was highly speculative, however. I attend
to it because of the political importance of Ambedkar's transposition of
political antagonism from the social space of caste onto the plane of historical time, which, like Phule's similar move, succeeded in anchoring
Dalit suffering to the deep structure of Hindu history. Such a reflexive
appropriation of history became a potential mode of political redemption.
History, translated into caste biography and thereby into a genealogy of
Brahminical hegemony, became the authorizing explanation of marginal
identity and of the experience of discrimination. It simultaneously offered
an alternative political mythology to the narrative, dominant among caste
radicals, of an enduring racial conflict between Aryan Brahmins and Dravidian Kshatriyas. Dalit Buddhist history was intimately bound up with
Ambedkar's desire for differentiating the genealogy of Shudra and Dalit,
and his focus on replacing Phule's narrative of collective *shudra-atishudra*
defeat with the distinctive narrative of Dalit Buddhism.

By the time Ambedkar was writing, the term "Aryan" had taken on its
association with race as a full-blown biological concept and had become
aligned with the horrors of National Socialism. Ethnonational, colonial,

and upper-caste accounts also privileged Aryan race theories. Ambedkar used the term to describe the racial stock of all Indians, drawing on methods adopted by Western proponents of the Aryan conquest theory to support his thesis of two originary groups in conflict.[132] Phule's racial-conquest narrative was now ingeniously transformed to locate political conflict *within* Indo-Aryan society, rather than *between* two contending races. In brief, Ambedkar found two origin myths in the Rg Veda, one supporting and one ignoring *varna* distinctions, and he mapped them onto "ideologies of two different Aryan races" who later "merged into one."[133]

Ambedkar's genealogy of the Shudras was based on rereading the Rg Veda and the twelfth book of the Mahabharata, the Shanti Parvan, as texts that staged a struggle between two (Aryan) Kshatriya lineages, the Solar and the Lunar.[134] The struggle between them was used to explain the production of the Shudra as a degraded identity, thereby overturning Phule's central thesis about the Shudras as *non-Aryan* Kshatriyas. The Shudras were vanquished Kshatriyas, but they were also Aryans degraded by vengeful Brahmins. With this move, Ambedkar offered the possibility of reading the Shudra as historically distinct from the untouchable, non-Brahmins as different from Dalits. Ambedkar went further and explained the repeated derogation of the Shudra as a consequence of Brahmins' withholding the *upanayanam* (thread ceremony inducting men into Brahminhood), recitation of the Vedas, and ownership of property.[135] What had earlier been an open system of induction into Brahminhood through scholarly learning was rendered a hereditary mark of status. The ban on intercaste marriage was also important in producing a Brahminical patriarchy. Ambedkar had long argued that "the absence of intermarriage—endogamy to be concise— is the only one [principle] that can be called the essence of caste when rightly understood."[136]

As should be evident from the discussion in chapter 2, Ambedkar's narrative draws on Maratha histories of the early twentieth century, which argued that Marathas were Aryan Kshatriyas, while *kunbis* were categorized as the offspring of Aryan conquest of Dravidian communities. There are also important continuities with Valangkar's argument that Maratha identity was coterminous with the Rajputs and Turks who were sent to western India to destroy Buddhism. Unlike late nineteenth-century efforts to challenge Aryan history through polemical counternarrative, Ambedkar's allegiance to the methods of scientific history and ethnology privileged the nation as the unspoken unit of political analysis, while his focus on history, and on ancient India in particular, resonated with anticolonial thought more generally.

These discussions had taken a specific turn in Maharashtra through the efforts of V. K. Rajwade (1863–1926), who legitimized disciplinary history and advocated for it a scientific method and philosophical basis. Rajwade attributed national sentiment to the resilience of Vedic Aryan civilization, its caste laws, and the dominance of Brahmins. Rajwade's Brahminism—and the institution he founded in Dhule, the Bharat Itihas Samshodak Mandal—was roundly attacked by caste radicals, most famously by Keshav Sitaram Thackeray. The focus on ancient India as the locus of incipient state-society formation became historical common sense, however. Veteran Communist leader Shripad Amrut Dange (1899–1991) published Rajwade's unfinished work, *Bharatiya Vivaha Sansthecha Itihas* (History of Indian Kinship), together with an introduction, in 1976. Dange himself wrote *India from Primitive Communism to Slavery* (1949) and drew on Friedrich Engels's *Origin of the Family, Private Property and the State* (1884). Dange was roundly criticized by the famous historian of ancient India, D. D. Kosambi for relying on faulty evidence.[137] But the debate continued. Ambedkar wrote *The Rise and Fall of Hindu Women* (1954) in response to A. S. Altekar's *Position of Women in Hindu Civilization* (1938). Whether Buddhism and Muslim invasion were blamed for the loss of women's previously high status in Vedic society, as Altekar argued, or whether it was Buddhism that enabled female enfranchisement, as per Ambedkar, gender and kinship came to play a central role in the evolutionary narrative of Indian state formation.[138] More recently, Sharad Patil's efforts to bring classical Indology into conversation with emancipatory thought, what he calls Marx-Phule-Ambedkarvad, makes state formation contingent on shifts in sex/gender systems.[139]

Ambedkar's creative re-reading of Indic texts and the specification of an *Indian* transition narrative together located the Shudra within history. It also explained untouchable identity by weaving together two distinctive models of historical causality: the evolution of settled society from nomadic communities and the religious-political conflict between Brahminism and Buddhism. Indeed, the Dalit Buddhist genealogy does not discuss Buddhist philosophy so much as it articulates Buddhism within the history of state formation. Buddhism was a religion of state supported by royal patronage, its rise coeval with a critical period of state formation and territorial consolidation in ancient India. Ambedkar described Buddhism's defeat by Brahminism as a "political revolution, a bloody revolution engineered by the Brahmins to overthrow the rule of the Buddhist kings."[140] In Ambedkar's account of the evolution of Hindu society, Indo-Aryan society was composed of Brahmins, Kshatriyas, and Vaishyas organized around the practices of Vedic sacrifice and beef eating. From this emerged the efflorescence of Buddhist thought, culture, and politics brought to a violent end by the Brahmin commander-in-chief, Pushyamitra, of the Buddhist emperor Brihadratha Maurya. This was followed by the institution of caste Hinduism by the Gupta emperors, who relied on the Manusmriti—Ambedkar dates its composition to 170–150 BCE—to justify *chaturvarna* and the stratification of Hindu society.

Ambedkar bypassed the tactic of asserting that untouchables lost high-caste status through their own actions, such as scavenging or eating beef or carrion. Instead, he historicized untouchables as a distinct group of Buddhists, wandering tribesmen defeated in battle as nomadic society gave way to settled agriculture and as blood affiliation gave way to territorial affiliation; that is, as clan and tribe gave way to the principle of nationality. Unlike the Shudras, with their militant Kshatriya past, untouchables had always been Broken Men, degraded, homeless, and fated to inhabit the margins as vestiges from the past. Guarding villages and their wealth, refusing to accept Brahminism, they had become dependent on eating dead cattle for sustenance. In the struggle between Buddhism and Brahmanism, Brahmins, originally meat eaters, had adopted the nonviolent policies of Buddhism and instituted the ban against meat. In turn, this stigmatized the Broken Men, who ate carrion to survive.

The contemporary fact of Maratha assertion clearly influenced Ambedkar's emendation of Phule's genealogy of caste conflict. In distinguishing between Shudra and untouchable to mark the singularity of the Dalit Buddhist, Ambedkar also positioned the Shudra both within and outside the caste order, an aggressor-turned-victim practicing the politics of resentment. As defeated Aryan Kshatriyas, Shudras were complicit in reproducing caste hierarchy through their desire for recognition within the *varna* order, even as they struggled against a Brahminism that denied them true status. The argument about Kshatriya resentment was organized around a rereading of the figure of Shivaji. Ambedkar's interpretation diverged, in fact, from almost all prevailing representations of this figure, including Phule's. It is a truism to say that Shivaji was one of the most powerful and multivalent symbols of non-Brahmin politics.[141] Shivaji's struggle for recognition as a Kshatriya and as a powerful and just ruler of the non-Brahmin communities was the single-most important node in the writing of alternative histories of Brahmin hegemony across the late nineteenth and early twentieth centuries. Instead, Ambedkar criticized the large sums of money that had been paid to the Brahmin priest from Benares, Gagabhatta, for "discovering" Shivaji's royal lineage and noted that "the decisions of the Brahmins on matters of status were open for sale like the indulgences of the Catholic clergy."[142] Ambedkar challenged the identity of Rajputs as Kshatriyas, the very legacy to which Shivaji laid claim, and argued instead that they bore no relation to the Vedic Kshatriyas. Instead, they were raised to the status of Kshatriyas "with the object of using them as means to suppress Buddhism in Central India."[143]

By positing Shivaji as desirous of recognition within the Brahminical order, Ambedkar was also noting that in the struggle against Brahminical domination, Shudras and untouchables had markedly different experiences of social exclusion. The most fundamental difference was between touchable Hindus (Savarnas) and those without caste (Avarnas). The Shudra was denied the privilege of being twice born, of being baptized into Vedic learning, but the untouchable was completely outside the *varna* order. Theirs was the dark side of the fairy tale, the story of "witches, goblins, and ogres."[144] This distinction illustrated Ambedkar's principle of graded inequality *internal* to the logic of *chaturvarna* that was encompassed by an earlier, more enduring conflict between caste Hindus and untouchables.

Ambedkar's genealogy of the Dalit Buddhist superimposed two temporal structures: the originary defeat and repeated degradation of the Broken Men fused with the enduring political-ethical challenge of Buddhism, forgotten but not vanquished. A developmental narrative alongside a redemptive one united historical with cosmological time. This dovetailed perfectly with Ambedkar's dual project of political emancipation and self-representation joined with remaking degraded Dalits into modern citizens. The recovery of a forgotten past furthered the emergence of a new political subject, the Dalit Buddhist.

In October 1935, Ambedkar declared that though born a Hindu, he refused to die one—his so-called Yeola statement.[145] At a Mahar Parishad held in May of that year, the only time he ever called a caste conference, Ambedkar broached the issue of converting out of Hinduism. He said that the weakness of the untouchable communities combined with efforts to challenge *varna* hierarchy would lead to eternal "conflict" and that there was no option but to leave the Hindu dharma.[146] The publication of *Annihilation of Caste* almost immediately followed the Yeola statement, but Ambedkar did not convert out of Hinduism until 1956, shortly before his death. This conversion was his final, most powerful challenge to Hindu inclusiveness after the Poona Pact. Though he described conversion as a Dalit *return* to the Buddhist past, it was perceived as Dalits' symbolic exit from the Hindu community, a final refusal to countenance Hinduism's historical degradation of the untouchables. Buddhism was significant insofar as it was personified in the figure of the Dalit Buddhist.[147]

Ambedkar connected again with Marxist thought at the end of his life when he justified his complete rejection of Hinduism through an innovative, eclectic reading of Buddhism. In his whimsical text, "The Buddha or Karl Marx," Ambedkar paid homage to Marx's revolutionary egalitarianism by arguing that Marxism came closest to Buddhism as an emancipatory ideology. Like Buddhism, it advocated the abolition of private property, aligned poverty with social exploitation, and offered redress, in the here and now, for social suffering.[148] Like the French and Russian revolutions, Buddhism was revolutionary, aiming to "reconstruct the world." The French revolution had imagined, but failed to materialize, equality; the Russian revolution instated equality, but sacrificed fraternity and liberty. "It seems the three can only co-exist if one follows the way of the Buddha," wrote Ambedkar.[149] Buddhism's achievement was to articulate egalitarian and compassionate guiding principles, something that Hinduism lacked, to gently reorient the behavior of individuals and the community. As Gauri Viswanathan notes, Ambedkar believed Buddhism capable of altering the disposition of men so that they "would be prepared, through a combination of rationality, morality, and social consciousness, to take action out of reasoned volition."[150]

Opposed to Marxism's reductive focus on material needs, however, was Buddhism's focus on the spiritual development of humanity. Ambedkar considered community and humanity mutually constitutive, each requiring the other, with Buddhism as the mediator. The defeat of Buddhism by Brahminism was significant precisely because Buddhism held out the possibility of an enlightened nationalism, one that joined the democratic principle with the desire for national unity. For Ambedkar, the return to Buddhism was a project of political self-definition. By linking nation with state through an ethical principle, Ambedkar's Buddhism offered an indigenous alternative to colonial domination and to Hindu nationalism. Ambedkar's statement, "I must undertake the work of conversion," thus profoundly expressed his conviction regarding the Buddhist Dalit as the universal subject of emancipation and a portent of India's future.

अखिल मुंबई इलाखा महार परिषद

जाहीर विनंती पत्रक.

अखिल अस्पृश्यांचे एकमेव पुढारी दीनबंधु डॉ. **बाबासाहेब आंबेडकर** यांनी तारीख १३ ऑक्टोबर १९३५ रोजी **येवले** (जिल्हा नाशिक) येथे भरलेल्या परिषदेंत सांगितले कीं, हिंदु धर्मांची समाज रचना विषमतेच्या पायांवर उभारलेली असल्यामुळें आपण हिंदु या नात्यानें माणुसकीचे हक्क मिळविण्याकरितां कितीही प्रयत्न केले तरी आपणांस यश मिळणें शक्य नाहीं. आपण महाड, नाशिक व इतर ठिकाणी सत्याग्रह करून समानतेचे हक्क प्रस्थापित करण्यासाठीं निकराचा व इरेचा प्रयत्न करून पाहिला, परंतु त्या लढ्यामध्यें आपलें द्रव्यबळ व मनुष्यबळ खर्च झालें. आणि त्यांत आपणांस यश मिळण्याऐवजी आपल्या बांधवांना खेड्यापाड्यांतून अनेक प्रकारचे हाल सोसावे लागले आणि दुःखे लागत आहेत. तरी आपणांस जर मनुष्य म्हणून जगावयाचे असेल व आपली सामाजिक, आर्थिक, शैक्षणीक व राजकीय परिस्थिति सुधारून आपले माणुसकीचे हक्क प्रस्थापित करावयाचे असतील तर **आपण या हिंदु धर्मापासून अलग झालें पाहिजे. म्हणजे धर्मांतर केलें पाहिजे** आणि त्यांतच आपणां सर्व अस्पृश्यांचे कल्याण आहे.

अस्पृश्यांच्या धर्मांतराचा प्रश्न हा अत्यंत महत्त्वाचा आहे. या प्रश्नाच्या बाबतींत अस्पृश्य जनतेनें धोरण निश्चित करणें हें अस्पृश्य जनतेचें कर्तव्य आहे, नव्हे जबाबदारी आहे. अस्पृश्यांतील निरनिराळ्या जातींच्या निरनिराळ्या परिषदां भरवून त्यांत या प्रश्नाचा खल करणें हा अस्पृश्य जनतेचें धोरण अजमावण्याचा मार्ग आहे असें डॉ. **बाबासाहेबांचें मत** आहे.

वरील सूचनेनुसार, मुंबई इलाख्यांतील सर्व महार बंधु भगिनींस विनंतिपूर्वक कळविण्यांत येतें कीं, मुंबई इलाख्यांतील सर्व महारांची प्रातिनिधिक स्वरूपाची परिषद मुंबई शहरांमध्यें येत्या **मे महिन्यांत** भरविण्याचें मुक्रर केलें आहे. परिषदेमध्यें आपले परमपूज्य पुढारी डॉ. बाबासाहेब आंबेडकर यांनी धर्मांतराची जी घोषणा केलेली आहे त्याबाबतींत आपल्या समाजांचे पुढील धोरण निश्चित ठरविलें जाईल. तरी या महत्त्वाच्या परिषदेमध्यें प्रत्येक जिल्ह्याजिल्ह्यांतून, ताल्क्या ताल्क्यांतून व ५०० गांवांगांवांतून आपणांला प्रतिनिधी पाठवून परिषद यशस्वी कराल अशी आशा आहे.

आपलें कार्य अतिशय मोठें व महत्त्वाचें असल्यामुळें, या कार्यास पैशांची व मनुष्यांची फार जरूर आहे तरी मुंबई शहरवासीयांस व इलाख्यांतील अखिल महार बंधुभगिनींस आग्रहाची व अस्पृश्यांची विनंती करण्यांत येते कीं, त्यांनी आपापसांतील वैयक्तिक मतभेद बाजूस ठेवून व एक दिलानें या परिषदेमध्यें भाग घेऊन ही परिषद यशस्वी करावी.

परिषदेमध्यें बहुजन समाजांस भाग घेतां यावा म्हणून सर्वांना रु. बांस्कर पडतील असें खालील प्रमाणे वर्गणीचे दर ठेवण्यांत आलेले आहेत.

[अ] स्वागत मंडळांतील सभासद	५ रुपये	[ब] सहकारी सभासद	३ रुपये
[क] साधारण सहकारी सभासद	३ ,,	[ड] सर्वसाधारण सभासद	१ ,,

टीप:— मुंबई शहर व उपनगर या खेरीज बाहेरील लोकांस स्वागत मंडळाच्या सभासदत्वाची वर्गणी ३ रुपये ठेवलेली आहे.

विशेष सूचना:— परिषदेकरितां वर्गणी किंवा देणगी देणे असल्यास अथवा काही सूचना किंवा इतर पत्रव्यवहार करणें असल्यास पुढील पत्त्यावर करणें.

जॉ० ८ सेक्रेटरीज:— **आखिल मुंबई इलाखा महार परिषद**
दामोदर हॉल, परेल मुंबई नं. १२

ता. क.:— छापील पावती घेतल्याशिवाय आपली वर्गणी देऊ नये.

आपले नम्र,

अध्यक्ष:- रेवजी दगडूजी डोळस   उपाध्यक्ष:- संभाजी तुकाराम गायकवाड
जॉ. सेक्रेटरीज:- १ दिवाकर नेवजी पगारे, २ मारुती बिठ्ठल धर्मे, ३ चांगदेव नारायण मोहिते.
खजिनदार:- सुभेदार विश्राम गंगाराम सवादकर.

=== सभासद ===

शंकर लक्ष्मण वडवळकर	देवराम चौखाजी आडांगळे	एम. सी. जगदळे	सोनू सज्जनाजी संदीसकर
केशव गोविंद आडेकर	मारूती भाऊदास साळवे	चनाप्पा नारायण गायकवाड	कृष्णाजी कमळाजी साळवे
प्रॉफेसराम नारायण गायकवाड	गणपत सहादेव जाधव	ताराचंद धनाजी गायकवाड	रामचंद्र बिठ्ठल मोरे
निळेस लिंबाजी गंगावणे	शिवराम गोपाळ जाधव	शंकर मुकुंदा अहिरे	शंकरदासुवा थरवे
भिवाजी हनवंतराय साळवे	शंकर श्रावण भोसले	धर्मो सोनू जाधव	आर. एच. अडांगळे
राणपत विठूजी निळे	शंकर महिनाजी भाळेराव	डी. पी. सावंत	गंगाचर सुसानराव दारोळे
गजोबा दगडूजी दुधवडे	अहिल्याजी तुकाराम फाले	महादू साधू पारधे	सखाराम सावळा विटेकर
मोगल साहिति गोयकवाड	कचर आबाजी डांगळे	सु० शिवराम सजनाजी घाटगे	भिमाजी सावकेराम आसींडकर

भारत भूषण प्रेस दादर-मुंबई.

Figure 10. Flyer for the Akhil Mumbai Ilakha Mahar Parishad (Bombay Province Mahar Conference) of May 1936, supporting Ambedkar's decision to convert and resolving to boycott Hindu deities, temples, and religious rites. Courtesy of Prakash Vishwasrao, *Dr. Babasaheb Ambedkar* (Mumbai: Lok Vangmay, 2007).

EMANCIPATION AND MINORITY

Ambedkar was a strategic and creative thinker whose efforts to address the violence and inequality of caste also reflected the heteronomy of caste, caste as a "structure in difference" whose various, discordant parts bore a contingent, non-necessary relation to each other.[151] His attempt to redress the inequities through political means was at some level an impossible project that emphasized the contradiction between caste and democracy, rather than resolving it. Ambedkar's critique was of a piece with caste radicalism's focus on the political consequences of religious ideology and its long-standing commitment to rational critique of Hindu superstition. Clearly, where Ambedkar differed with this tradition was in his sustained engagement of liberal categories—individual, minority, nation, rights—and their redeployment for the emancipation of community. Marx offered a strategy of "reading" the social. Ambedkar's immanent critique of caste ideology came closest to a creative deployment of such a reading.[152] In his thought as well as his activism, Ambedkar illuminated the persistent tension between the religious and the political and the manner in which this dichotomy structured modes of political commensuration and cultural exception. In this, he diverged from the classic account of (religious) minority.

Viewing minority identity as incomplete, caught between religious particularism and universal citizenship, Marx had noted that "minority" was a mediating term that converted the social categories of civil society into political lack. Asserting minority to be "the political manner of emancipating oneself from religion," he had prescribed political emancipation as the simultaneous freedom *from* religion. His solution was to annihilate religious particularism by transcending embodied difference. For Dalits, however, their negative relationship to Hinduism rendered full separation impossible. Instead, the Dalit relationship with Hinduism produced inclusion *and* exclusion. Religion was immanent rather than extraneous to the political field. Given the collective nature of caste stigma, freedom for the self was contingent on the emancipation of the community. In Ambedkar's view, this *required* identifying oneself as a stigmatized subject and as a special kind of minority, as *non-Hindus* defined by a permanent and antagonistic relationship to the Hindu order.

Ironically, the demand for political commensuration revealed that Dalits were incommensurable. They required political equalization as well as recognition as historically distinct subjects. Rather than transcending difference by transcending religion, the struggle for Dalit emancipation set up a universalized difference within an ethical religiosity. Dalit emancipation did not subsume the religious to the political. Rather, religion and politics were both redefined as sites of historic antagonism: Brahmanism versus Buddhism, Hindu majority versus Dalit minority, respectively. The turn to an ethical space outside Hindu law and its violent order marked the field of Dalit freedom. As regards political equality, Ambedkar's political experiments had positioned Dalits as a *non-Hindu* minority whose political strength derived from a claim to separation, and later, to state protection. This reflects the colonial context in which the question of minority arose and the specificity of the Dalits as minority: they had to be constituted as both a distinct community and a constituency with discrete political interests. In the case of Dalit emancipation, a negative identity became the basis of collective political rights, but it also converted the political field into a space of agonistic combat. *The model of Dalit identity was the model of permanent struggle through the exacerbation, rather than the resolution, of difference.*

There is certainly no material connection between Ambedkar's speculative history of the Dalit Buddhist and what was to come in the realm of state policy and politics. But the tense balance he maintained between the injurious history of the Dalit Buddhist and the political utopia of Buddhism, between the singular identity of the stigmatized subject and the need to redress historical suffering, left room for positioning Dalits as objects of positive remedies carried out by the state.

The irony of a Dalit law minister who played the role of the modern Manu, the eponymous law giver as the chief architect of India's Constitution, is central to Ambedkar's complexly ramified political career.[153] Yet Ambedkar's trajectory poses a problem for scholars seeking continuity and coherence. Sekhar Bandhyopadhyay has articulated a general unease with explaining Ambedkar's decision to accept a berth in a government led by Congress, an avowed political enemy.[154] Indeed, Bandhyopadhyay's response has been to address the "crisis" of Dalit politics at the moment of political transition (1945–47) as a problem of withdrawal of British patronage for the SCs, together with Congress's focus on religious difference as the site of minority recognition, both of which signaled failures for Dalit politics. He is right to point to the hegemony exercised by a majoritarian Congress version of nationalism. This was reflected in Rajagopalachari's and Santhanam's separate attacks on Ambedkar's *What Congress and Gandhi Have Done to the Untouchables,* where Ambedkar explained the demographic and political weakness of the Dalit constituency. Bandhyopadhyay is certainly right to argue that Congress hegemony was secured—in 1945 as in 1932—through a claim upon the political identity of the SCs as Hindu. Unlike Bandhyopadhyay, however, I would not focus on Dalits' organizational weakness—an issue Ambedkar explicitly addressed in his 1945 text on the nature of Hindu majoritarianism—or take recourse to a merely instrumental understanding of political constraint. By failing to relate Ambedkar's political thought with his activism, Bandhyopadhyay also fails to address the substantive critique of the nation form and majoritarian logic that was the hallmark of Ambedkar's thought.

Instead, I have underlined the impossible position in which Dalits found themselves as a territorially dispersed minority with *nowhere else to go;* the impossibility, precisely, of converting minority into nationality at the critical moment of postcolonial transition.[155] We might recall Ambedkar's moving statement at his first meeting with Gandhi on August 14, 1931, before they were to attend the second Round Table Conference: "Gandhiji I have no homeland. . . . How can I call this land my own wherein we are treated worse than cats and dogs, wherein we cannot get water to drink? No self-respecting Untouchable worth the name will be proud of this land. . . . If in my endeavour to secure human rights for my people who have been trampled upon in this country for ages I do any disservice to this country, it would not be a sin; and if any harm does not come to this country thorough my action, it may be due to my conscience."[156]

The moment of political transition straddles the moment *before and after* 1947. This was a moment when the "harm to the country" that Ambedkar threatened—Dalit violence—was instead transformed into an angry response to all manner of gender, caste, and socioeconomic privilege; it was a moment when Dalit conscience was channeled into a document with radical social implications, the Indian Constitution. We must concern ourselves with addressing Ambedkar's success in encoding Dalits in the Constitution and thereby fulfilling his project of inserting this universal-particular, revolutionary subject into the heart of Indian democracy as the place from which to remake society.[156] I therefore suggest a shift in focus from the high politics of negotiation and maneuver to Ambedkar's efforts to infuse the Constitution with his republican vision of transforming social practice through the state. Ambedkar's actions were undertaken from a position of defeat and the impossibility of inscribing Dalits' political separation into state structure. What Ambedkar managed instead was to predicate the development (and humanization) of society on abolishing the complex ritual, economic, and social inequities of caste. That is, he partially succeeded in making social reform and the change of habits—an interior transformation along the lines envisioned by Gandhi—contingent on the production of new laws (i.e., an external or *formal* transformation) that replaced the "illegal laws" of the Hindus. The specific terms of political recognition by the Constitution and subsequent legislation encoded the animating tension of Dalit identity and politics: their struggles for recognition came to depend on their identity as vulnerable subjects. This dynamic had much to do with the trajectories of Dalit—and Indian—politics to come.

PART TWO

The Paradox of Emancipation

CHAPTER 4

Legislating Caste Atrocity

The curse of untouchability is like a hydra-headed monster. You take away one of its heads, and two heads come out in its place. You remove it in one place, and it appears in another place. You try to cut it in one form and it appears in another form.

D. C. SHARMA, in *Lok Sabha Debates*, August 31, 1954

Untouchability is not a commodity, is not a thing that is visible.

N. RACHIAH, in *Lok Sabha Debates*, April 27, 1955

There is not a single political party in India today, which has got on its programmes an item that the practice of untouchability should continue.

G. H. DESHPANDE, in *Lok Sabha Debates*, August 31, 1954

The story of Dalit emancipation presents its share of violent incidents, from the policing of caste sociality to *satyagraha* clashes. The latent violence of the crowd and the undisciplined *satyagraha* volunteer were constant sources of anxiety for Gandhian civil disobedience. Gandhi castigated the violence of the Dalit *satyagrahi* who broke through police forces to enter temples and expressed fear of a more general Dalit violence. And he brought the problem of violence to the forefront when, in 1932, he responded to Prime Minister Ramsay MacDonald's Communal Award allowing the Depressed Classes a double vote. Although Gandhi had agreed to arbitration on the issue of minority representation, he refused to abide by the terms of the Communal Award. His letter to Samuel Hoare dated August 14, 1932, explained his decision to undertake a fast-unto-death by arguing that the Award offered a dangerous political solution to what was primarily a "religious and moral issue" requiring the "penance" of caste Hindus.[1] If Ambedkar conceived the separate electorate as a political weapon to reveal the latent power of the Depressed Classes to reject Hindu hegemony, Gandhi mobilized his power as an exemplary individual to change the rules of the game, posing the possibility of his death and hence his exit from the game. What would victory mean, after all, if the vanquished were also annihilated?

Gandhi had often undertaken fasts, including two famous ones in response to failures of nationalist mobilization.[2] A fast-unto-death in response to the political empowerment of the Depressed Classes appeared to be downright objectionable, however. Even Gandhi's supporters wondered how it could be justified, and indeed, who constituted the audience for this fast. Gandhi clarified, noting that the Communal Award thwarted Hindus from continuing a necessary repentance.[3] "The separate electorates are meant to perpetuate the sin or to make it impossible for the Hindus to repent," Gandhi argued, noting that political separation would encourage a violence akin to a civil war between caste Hindus and Harijans, and between Hindus and Muslims.[4] This was implicit confirmation of Ambedkar's position, which sought recognition for Dalits as a third political force. And instead of accepting that Hindu inclusion, too, could be understood as a form of violence, Gandhi attributed the threat of violence to a compact between untouchable "hooligans" and Muslim "hooligans" who would kill caste Hindus.[5]

Violence, its visceral presence acknowledged and sublated, was never far from Gandhi's experiments. For Gandhi, the body was a limit to be conquered and surpassed in the quest for ethical purification, even at the risk of self-violence.[6] Gandhi was well aware that like other individualized techniques of self-purification that formed a part of the ashram vows—celibacy, vegetarianism—fasting could appear to others not only as a form of denial, but also as self-directed violence. Redefined as a purification of bodily excess, however, such "technologies of the self" were mechanisms to sublate social violence. In one letter, Gandhi made it clear that one fasted against a loved one who was to be reformed, not to "extort rights" from an enemy.[7] The fast was terribly public and deeply private, both a spectacle of suffering and a disciplinary mechanism to vanquish desire: "All fasting and all penance must as far as possible be secret. But my fasting is both a penance and a punishment, and a punishment has to be public. It is a penance for me, and a punishment for those I try to serve. . . . The only way love punishes is by suffering."[8]

In Gandhi's own deeply embodied political practice, fasting, like the embrace of voluntary poverty or the performance of stigmatizing labor, was a form of upper-caste atonement.[9] Cleansing the upper-caste self of caste arrogance required a fast-unto-death even when it implicated others in the practice of one's ethics. Ambedkar noted that such penitential politics inflicted a violence of its own, and did so in two ways: first, by failing to recognize *Dalits'* quest for dignity and social recognition, and second, by redefining Dalits—in their quest for political autonomy—as the perpetrators of social violence rather than its historical victims.[10]

THE VIOLENCE OF RECOGNITION

However evaluated, Gandhi's orientation stands in stark contrast to Dalit views on violence. Dalit activists came to see the injustices of the caste order as intimate violence and as dehumanization; they used that language to criticize caste hierarchy and to indicate "a new form of social presence registered by Dalits."[11] The failure of Dalit-led *satyagrahas* showed that, when aimed at religious inclusion rather against the injustices of the colonial order, *satyagraha* heightened violent antagonism between caste Hindus and untouchables. Thus for Ambedkar, *satyagraha* was one way of sharpening Dalits' awareness of the daily injustices of the caste order, insofar as the *satyagrahis'* experience of physical violence, being hit with bricks and stones, was a reminder of more invisible forms of violation and dehumanization that defined Dalit identity. The Brahmin/Buddhist struggle had revealed Brahminism as a culture of violence euphemized as religious precept and social practice. A historical and collective memory of originary violence, the outcasting of the Broken Men, continued to be experienced in daily exclusion. As noted in chapter 3, Ambedkar understood *bahishkar,* permanent outcasting, as a sign of the structural violence of a caste Hinduism that disciplined through threats of outright violence and the quiet violence of cutting social ties. Indeed, the Starte Committee, which conducted a thoroughgoing inquiry into the status of the Depressed Classes in Bombay in 1930, declared the social boycott worse than physical violence because "it passes as a lawful method consistent with the theory of freedom of contract."[12]

For untouchables, *bahishkar* operated as a permanent principle of segregation internalized as a form of physical vulnerability. So far as Ambedkar was concerned, the boycott played an important role in muting the contradictions of caste society because it was euphemized as an occasional and lawful mechanism. Or, it could be used in a lawlike manner to reassert caste hegemony, as with boycotts against Dalit activists. In either case, the boycott was illegal and its violence was euphemized as discipline—"If you step out of line, then you are disciplined." Ambedkar defamiliarized this process to reveal its intrinsic violence and to argue that if caste boundaries were maintained through illegitimate violence, then Dalits required a radical remedy in the form of legal redress.

Ambedkar's repeated use of the phrase the "illegal laws of the Hindus" to describe not merely *bahishkar* but caste society connects him to important discussions about law and violence.[13] Max Weber defined the state through its monopoly on the exercise of "legitimate violence," a violence that cannot be named as such because it appears in another guise, as law. Walter Benjamin's distinction between lawmaking and law-preserving violence is helpful here. The first references an originary moment, when law and society are founded on violence—not on the social contract—as Thomas Hobbes argued. Law-preserving violence is the banal, regularized violence that passes for law, what Weber refers to as "legitimate violence."[14] Lawmaking and law preserving are manifestations of violence. But the temporal distance that separates law-preserving violence from its origins in violence makes law appear legal, rather than a species of violence. Violence is euphemized and rendered intrinsic, rather than external, to state power. The proximity of transacted violence and the invisibility of state violence is one reason why law is experienced as "not violence." Ambedkar's concerted efforts to address the violence of untouchability through the oxymoron of the "illegal law" resembles Benjamin's description of law-preserving violence as a violence that appears other than itself, as "law" and not "violence." The task of anticaste critique was to force recognition of the violence of caste as the geohistorical universal of Hindu history.

Despite fears to the contrary, Ambedkar did not imagine Dalit emancipation by physical acts of retaliation, but by the historical necessity to remake the self through the symbology of Buddhist conversion and through participation of the state as guarantor of social justice. The turn to a constitutional resolution of the violence of untouchability had to do with the situation Dalits found themselves in at the cusp of national independence: they were territorially dispersed and impoverished, and they were unable to escape their status as a *non-Hindu* minority, a minority framed by an agonistic relationship to the caste Hindu order without the physical separation of territorial partition. Indeed, Buddhism's status as an ethical force indigenous to the subcontinent was important proof of Dalits' political and ethical centrality to the redemptive project of remaking India. This articulation of an ethical response to Dalit suffering, together with a program of political enfranchisement, was operationalized at the moment of postcolonial transition through a set of efforts—from a failed radical transformation of Hindu law to constitutional safeguards and protective mechanisms for the specially disadvantaged—that were intended to remake caste personhood and the social relations of caste. These efforts culminated, ironically, in the articulation of the Dalit as an exceptional legal subject, marked by inherited subalternity and at risk of further violation.

Ambedkar's ambivalent victory, winning constitutional inscription for the Dalit, opens onto the organizing issue of part 2 of *The Caste Question:* politicized violence as a locus/symptom of state intervention into Dalit identity. Why violence? Whether it is physical or symbolic, woven into law or religion, used against Dalits or for militant self-fashioning, violence is neither aberration nor a simple reflection of existing social antagonisms. Indeed, the proliferation of violent forms following Dalit recognition and (state) protection suggests that violence is a historical and cultural formation that has played a distinctive role in the formation of Dalit personhood. By looking at instances of anti-Dalit violence as they articulate with the legal constitution of Dalit vulnerability and in terms of broader political dynamics, it will be possible to consider the ways in which violence reconstitutes social relations and political practice on the ground. The first aspect to consider is how violent acts against Dalits were centralized in the civil rights regime and in legal-bureaucratic mechanisms created to protect Scheduled Caste subjects.

BUREAUCRACY AND RECOGNITION: CREATING SOCIAL FACTS

Between 1947 and 1955, the Dalit citizen was conceptualized through legal equalization: the abolition of untouchability by Article 17 of India's Constitution and the institution of protective laws and affirmative action policies were meant as positive policy to produce equality. The subject of rights was simultaneously imagined as a universal subject and a historical subject defined by caste. As the nation came to be aligned with the Hindu community in the years leading up to and following Partition, state protection of Dalits' rights as minority rights was also placed on new footing through the regime of civil rights and the secularization of Hinduism.[15] (By then, the Gandhian project of self-reform had given way to the Nehruvian project of building the nation-state through public policy and infrastructural development.) Significantly, the practice of untouchability was criminalized, with stringent laws passed to punish caste Hindu perpetrators. Together and separately, these legal-bureaucratic measures defined the SCs as vulnerable citizen-subjects. The Indian Constitution set itself up as the ultimate guarantor of citizens' rights through acts of equalization via positive discrimination for socially marginal and

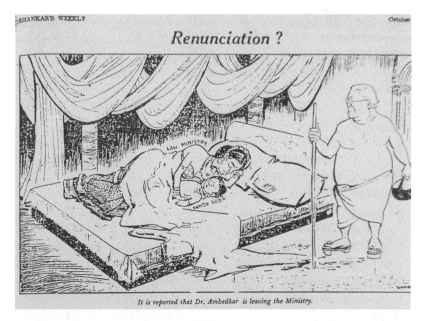

Figure 11. Cartoon caricaturing Ambedkar's decision to resign from the Law Ministry over the failure to implement the Hindu Code Bill and comparing it to the householder renouncing worldly living. Note the use of Hindu themes to represent what was, in fact, Ambedkar's *challenge* to Hindu hegemony. *Shankar's Weekly*, October 7, 1951. Courtesy of the Vasant Moon Collection, Nagpur.

deprived populations. Quite simply, it anticipated a significant transformation of civil society by the state, followed by shifts in (caste) sociality and conceptions of personhood.[16] Whereas a liberal democracy commits to the sanctity of specific procedures believed to guarantee unbiased outcomes, India's emergent democracy specified desired outcomes and committed itself to bridging the gulf separating them from the present.

Ambedkar's efforts to reform the Hindu family and intimate relations floundered not only because of the deep-seated resistance of Hindu orthodoxy, but also because of prejudice against a *Dalit* law minister who sought to change *Hindu* law.[17] When he resigned from his post as law minister in 1951 after a four-year rapprochement with Congress, Ambedkar was frustrated with upper castes' resistance to substantive reform beyond the abolition of untouchability and the institution of reservations, and thought it futile to remain part of the Congress government. Yet perhaps the attempts to redefine caste as a civic disability and a form of socioeconomic backwardness have been more successful than Ambedkar imagined. The reservations regime inaugurated a specific form of legal exception, what legal historian Marc Galanter calls "compensatory discrimination," that marked out a special place for the SCs in the constitutional vision. This vision heuristically divided social space into two zones, one governed by market principles of competition and putative merit and another that was an objectof social intervention, populated by subjects whose status was to be equalized. As a consequence, the substantive equality posited by the constitutional vision rendered the demographic majority—Dalits and lower castes—the object of social engineering, while a demographic minority retained its role as a social majority. This founding discrepancy between demographic weight and sociopolitical worth animates India's civil rights regime.

Another contradiction is produced by the discursive centrality of caste to civil rights, in contrast to the ban on enumerating caste identity in every all-India census undertaken after 1931. This posed a threat to national integration. Reservations in educational institutions and public sector undertakings were envisaged as temporary measures to be renewed a decade at a time. In addition, as castes advanced socioeconomically, they were to be removed from the roster of groups eligible for quotas, culminating in a final "descheduling" of Scheduled Classes (SCs), Scheduled Tribes (STs), and Backward Class (BC) communities by 1981, at the end of the sixth five-year plan. Today, however, the population of SCs, BCs, and Other Backward Classes (OBCs)—all those entitled to some form of constitutional protection—together exceeds 50 percent of the population even though the Constitution stipulates a 50 percent cutoff for reservations. The *majority* of castes are defined as suffering from some form of social deprivation and "backwardness." Indeed, caste has taken on a classlike terminology, while the term "class" has itself been interpreted by Indian law courts to subsume caste, now understood as but one indicator, if a significant one, of a group's socioeconomic development.[18] What political practices develop around the fissures between social domains, one occupied by citizen-subjects who are the beneficiaries of historical discrimination and the other inhabited by a demographic majority defined as socioculturally deprived? What happens when policies of equalization, usually viewed as temporary and exceptional measures, are the normative mechanisms of political socialization? What kinds of engagement with the state arise as new governmental categories impinge upon the reorganization of social life?

Indian political mobilization has been oriented around practices of social engineering implemented to challenge upper-caste hegemony and to transform deprived subjects into equal citizens. The relationship between social categories and (ensuing) social conflict becomes clear if we view them as effects of an animating tension between universalism and particularism in the Indian Constitution. Foreshortening what was for Western democracies a contentious, incremental process of franchise expansion, India granted universal adult franchise after national independence. The franchise was juxtaposed to an acknowledged long-term history of differential community rights and persistent, complex forms of ritual and cultural inequality. While "the people" do appear in the Indian Constitution in their general aspect as citizens of a sovereign nation-state, they are more often named in their particularity marked by class, caste, poverty, and religion. The putative equality of Indian citizens is achieved through embracing particularity. In the aftermath of Partition, Muslims lost their status as the modal minority, giving up the separate electorate "in the national interest."[19] Instead, from the Constitution's distinctive focus on social and economic equality came a new category of persons, "the poor." Caste, however, occupied the center of the constitutional commitment to social justice. Both a traditional category and a social evil, caste was to be excised from the body politic.[20]

The first front of caste equalization was the secularization of Hinduism. Article 26 of the Constitution guarantees that castes, in the form of sects, have the right to exist, to maintain their religious and charitable institutions, and to manage their own religious affairs.[21] Similarly, Article 30 gives religious and linguistic minorities the right to establish and administer educational institutions of their choice. Thus Indian secularism is committed to religious equality, not to religious noninterference, balancing rights to sectarian or particularistic forms of worship against a generic commitment to religious equality. It is Hinduism that has come under legal reform, however.[22] Article 25(2)(b) opens Hindu temples to all Hindus, placing the rights of subsects and the right of equal access to religious institutions at odds with each other.[23] And because the commitment to caste equality blurs the boundary between religious and secular rights, lawmakers and courts have implicitly acknowledged their right to intervene in and reorganize religious practice in the interest of caste equality.[24]

The second front of equalization was democratization through caste, insofar as equality was specifically conceived as *equality between castes*.[25] Marc Galanter notes that compensatory discrimination is "very much a domestic product, produced with little guidance or borrowing from abroad," a unique kind of civil rights law that addresses caste as a collective structure of deprivation and impoverishment.[26] There is thus a productive tension between a constitutional commitment to individual rights and the legislative focus on collective disabilities. Within this framework, the practice of untouchability has been singled out in a series of exceptional measures that reflect Dalits' distinctive place in the political unconscious. SC legislation is of two kinds: measures for protecting vulnerable subjects and policy measures supporting socioeconomic development. Article 15(4) empowers the state to make special provisions for the advancement of any socially and educationally backward classes of citizens, or for SCs and STs. Article 16(4) advocates "any provision for the reservation of appointments or posts in favour of any backward class of citizens which, in the opinion of the State, is not adequately represented in the services under the State." Article 46 of the Constitution, a directive principle, stipulates: "The State shall promote with special care the educational and economic interests of the weaker sections of the people, and in particular, of the Scheduled Castes and the STs, and shall protect them from social injustice and forms of exploitation." This has enabled several states to reserve seats for SCs and STs in technical, engineering, and medical colleges, and in police departments. Article 330 provides SC/ST reservations in the Lok Sabha (the lower house of Parliament), while Article 332 provides for reservations in state legislative assemblies. Recent constitutional amendments, the Seventy-Third and Seventy-Fourth Amendments of 1992, respectively, provide reservations in local government at the rural *panchayat* and municipality levels, and stipulate that one-third of those seats be reserved for women from the SC/ST communities. These provisions have enabled three kinds of reservation, each focused on the extension of dignified livelihood: (1) in legislative bodies, government service, educational institutions, and in housing and land allotment; (2) in programs granting scholarships, grants, loans, health care, and legal aid for SCs; and (3) special measures, mostly legislative, to protect SCs and STs from practices such as bonded labor, untouchability, and land alienation.

The presumed obviousness of the category of SC served as a model for defining groups entitled to "preferential" treatment by the state. As we saw in chapter 3, that definition merged the qualities of social exclusion suffered by the Dalit communities with their ritual status as degraded Hindus, so that the SCs were seen to suffer a unique combination of socioeconomic deprivation, occupational segregation, and educational backwardness combined with ritual stigma.[27] The definition of the BCs and OBCs presented lawmakers with a unique challenge. It was unclear who the BCs were, though their social advancement was enjoined by the Constitution. Mysore State first used the term "Backward Class" in 1918 to categorize everyone who was *not Brahmin*. Bombay included reservations for socially and economically backward groups in the Starte Committee Report of 1930. Since 1916, Madras had caste quotas for bureaucratic recruitment, while the princely states of Baroda and Kolhapur instituted similar policies at the turn of the nineteenth century to curb Brahmin dominance. The contemporary term "Backward Classes" does not map neatly onto the non-Brahmin politics of the colonial period, however. While a capacious use of the term includes those bureaucratically classified as SCs, STs, Denotified Tribes, Nomadic Tribes, and BCs, a precise definition of BCs and the related category of OBCs is at the heart of caste politics today.[28]

In 1953, a Backward Classes Commission headed by Kaka Kalelkar was convened to consider reservations for those OBCs who were excluded from earlier provisions. The commission's report was largely discredited for emphasizing the separation of castes, however. By 1965, individual states had been advised to develop their own socioeconomic indices for affirmative action policies. The 1975 Havanur Committee Report for Karnataka, followed by the Venkataswamy Report, and the Chinnappa Reddy Commission (1990), was perhaps the most ambitious: complex formulas were introduced to correlate low social status with the performance of degraded or marginalized economic functions in order to produce a quantifiable measure of cultural backwardness and deprivation. In 1978, B. P. Mandal was charged with heading a five-member commission to reconsider the Kalekar report. In 1980, the Mandal Commission Report supplemented the 22.5 percent reservation for SCs and STs in central government institutions with a recommendation of 27 percent reservation for the OBCs. Violent upper-caste resistance to the V. P. Singh government decision to implement the Mandal report in 1989 marked the apogee of these efforts. Widespread civil unrest and rioting spurred on by the Hindu nationalist Bharatiya Janata Party (BJP) eventually led to the removal of Prime Minister V. P. Singh from office in November 1990. However, in September 1991 the newly installed government of Prime Minister P. V. Narasimha Rao announced that it would retain the reservation scheme recommended by the Mandal Commission Report and would reserve an additional 10 percent for poorer members of the upper castes and non-Hindu minorities. In September 1993, the Supreme Court ruled the Mandal scheme constitutional in *Indra Sawhney v. Union of India*.[29] This brief overview illuminates the incremental manner in which the demographic majority has been enfolded into the reservations regime and contextualizes the violent conflict over redistribution of resources and privileges that has come in its wake.

Let me focus, however, on a unique set of legal measures through which Dalits came to be interpellated as injured subjects. I will focus on these laws to explore the legal constitution of Dalit vulnerability.[30] Article 17 of the Indian Constitution reads: "'Untouchability' is abolished and its practice in any form is forbidden. The enforcement of any disability arising out of 'untouchability' shall be an offense in accordance with law." Thus untouchability was underscored as an exceptional practice requiring measures beyond positive discrimination, including the provision of criminal laws to punish those who perpetrated untouchability, and it was secured by a new juridical category, the "caste atrocity."[31] These laws enabled judicial procedure to address specific forms of violation that comprised anti-Dalit violence, but they did so without a working definition of untouchability. As was noted in an early law case:

> It is to be noticed that the word 'untouchability' occurs only in Art. 17 and is enclosed in inverted commas. This clearly indicates that the subject-matter of that Article is not untouchability in its literal or grammatical sense but the practice as it has developed historically in this country . . . Art. 17 *which was intended to give effect to the decision to abolish the practice of untouchability, as mentioned above, does not define that term.* Nor is a definition contained anywhere else in the Constitution. *This omission would appear to be deliberate as the intention presumably was to leave no room or scope for the continuance of the practice in any shape or form.*[32]

The Protection of Civil Rights (PCR) Act of 1974—an amended version of the 1955 Untouchability (Offences) Act abolishing untouchability in public places[33]—notes, "'Civil rights' means any right accruing to a person by reason of the abolition of 'untouchability' by Article 17 of the Constitution."[34] This explicitly connects civil rights with the status of Dalits.

Why hesitate to define untouchability or name its victims? A broad consensus had emerged before passage of the 1955 Untouchability (Offences) Act that defining untouchability would risk reinscribing stigma.[35] Members of the Lok Sabha suggested that statements like "Whoever prohibits an untouchable from doing x and y" would emphasize the stigma of the name "untouchable."[36] Thus "the untouchable" as a name was replaced by "the practice of untouchability" as the focus of penal sanction.[37] During debates some members argued that it was necessary to define untouchability: "Otherwise this will be left to vague and complicated interpretations in the law courts, and even the law courts will not be in a position to say what is untouchability and what is not untouchability."[38] Others noted that a binding definition of untouchability opened anti-untouchability legislation to contentious and unnecessary litigation. A third group argued that the Constitution had already abolished untouchability: laws were required to punish perpetrators. Defining untouchability was unnecessary because courts would recognize the practice when saw they it.[39]

Progressive legislation thus generated a practical problem. Anyone might bar an agricultural laborer from a restaurant by arguing that he smelled or dressed badly. It was another thing if the laborer also happened to be an untouchable. In that case, regardless of the act—preventing entry, calling out an insult, or physical assault—motivation was predicated upon the victim's identity *as untouchable*. In fact, the connection between the person and the practice of untouchability was what distinguished anti-Dalit violence from other crimes against person and property. Thus "the practice of untouchability" targeted (and reproduced) the identity of persons already suffering stigmatized existence. Declining to name the untouchable in legal discourse left unattended the fact that in everyday social interactions people appeared to know the identity of their untouchable victims. By accepting the "I know it when I see it" model for defining untouchability, lawmakers also gave state officials charged with protecting untouchables great leeway in interpreting anti-Dalit crime. Laws meant to transform (existing) social relations became reliant on conventions of social categorization to apprehend the crime of untouchability.

The Untouchability (Offences) Act was a criminal law that took preventive action to reduce anti-Dalit offenses in order to enhance their sociability with other castes. It was not meant to guarantee equal rights. The Constitution already did that, according to minister of home affairs and states, Dr. Katju. The only issue was securing a "particular right," such as access to public amenities or private services that might be denied on the basis of caste: "Supposing a man is forbidden to draw water from a well in accordance with existing customs; we enforce the law and send the man to jail for six months. . . . The people in the village combine and say, this well has now become *brasht*, has become defiled, we will sink another well; so far as this well is concerned we won't use it. The result is that well is practically confined to the use of my brethren of the Scheduled Castes. Would that make them happy? . . . We want *equal use*."[40]

The major innovation of the Untouchability (Offences) Act was to shift the burden of proof to the accused, as a means of inculcating behavioral modification. N. C. Chatterjee described this to be contrary to cardinal principles of British, hence Indian, jurisprudence. He accepted it, however, as upper-caste "atonement."[41] Apparently, this view prevailed, since the relocated burden of proof became a defining feature of the Untouchability (Offences) Act. Legislators acknowledged that the legislation was coercive because it instituted a series of punishments for those who refused to obey the law. G. H. Deshpande argued:

> The moment you pass the law, the moment that [those supporting untouchability] find that the State machinery is behind you, they immediately come and obey everything, and they give everything they denied before the law was there. . . . So, what I want to say is that after you pass this law, the only thing that will be required is *to see that the entire State machinery and the organised and progressive public opinion is behind this law.* . . . It should be made *an obligatory part* of a District Superintendent of Police or a District Magistrate to see that whenever he receives a complaint, he *must rush to the village* and see that the Harijans are allowed to exercise their full rights. If that is not done, then this law will not be effective.[42]

After passage of the bill, the legislated abolition of untouchability became the bar against which the practice of untouchability was measured; increasingly, the discourse around untouchability (abolition) also described the social fact of untouchability. Each amendment to the Untouchability (Offences) Act brought more stringent punishments against perpetrators.[43] By 1989, the Prevention of Atrocities (Against Scheduled Castes and Scheduled Tribes) Act (POA Act) defined political, ritual, or symbolic violence as criminal acts. Section 3(1) placed humiliation—caste insults, coercion to eat or drink noxious substances, and ritual humiliation—on a par with denial of access to water sources, public property, and thoroughfares; sexual violence against Dalit women; economic dispossession such as land grabs or demands to perform bonded labor; and attempts to prevent voting or holding political office. All counted as atrocities.[44]

Amended laws eventually produced a definition of untouchability: a list of acts, public manifestations of the practice, which encompassed ritual and symbolic humiliation as well as physical violence. Equivalence between hurtful words and harmful deeds was assumed.[45] A complicated bureaucratic edifice grew up to monitor and manage instances of anti-Dalit violence. The post of commissioner for SCs and STs was created in 1950 by Article 338 of the Constitution. The commissioner had no statutory powers, however; this minister of the government of India could only make recommendations. His staff of seventeen field officers was placed under the Department of Social Welfare in 1967, compromising the primary activities of the commissioner's office—receiving complaints and grievances, keeping tabs on state and central government policies. The Department of Social Welfare, established in 1964, was responsible for most matters regarding SC/ST welfare until 1973, when the Home Ministry reclaimed that territory.[46] In the meantime, a watchdog parliamentary Joint Committee on Scheduled Castes and Scheduled Tribes was started in 1968 to recommend implementation techniques for the SC/ST commissioner's reports. Unlike the commissioner, the joint committee had investigative powers. Still, to deflect charges of negligence in addressing rising caste violence, Parliament set up a five-member commission for the SCs and STs in 1978; its activities mimicked the commissioner's.[47] Also expanded were the police infrastructure and programs to sensitize police to a new category of crimes, the caste atrocity.[48] Only in 1990 was Article 338 amended to give birth to the statutory National Commission for Scheduled Castes and Scheduled Tribes. In Bombay, a PCR Cell was formed in 1988 with a deputy inspector general of police to monitor cases of caste and gender violence.

The growing bureaucratic apparatus to monitor untouchability soon spawned a metamonitoring apparatus for watching over members of the Department of Social Welfare and the Office of the SC/ST Commissioner, and to recommend measures to amend the Untouchability (Offences) Act of 1955. For instance, in 1965 the government appointed R. Elayaperumal to chair a Committee on Untouchability, Educational and Economic Development of Scheduled Castes. The Elayaperumal Report, released in 1969, cited failure to enforce untouchability abolition, through official negligence, lax collection of detailed information on the workings of the 1955 act, lack of follow-up information on police action, and delayed hearings and decisions in untouchability cases. Even the PCR Cell was seen as a dumping ground for those "facing action for delinquency or inefficiency, or as punishment for refusing to toe the line of their political bosses."[49]

However ineffectively institutionalized, the atrocity—and the generation of actuarial knowledge regarding anti-Dalit violence more broadly—came to occupy a central place in state discourse as well as Dalit activism as a barometer of social relations. For caste Hindus, the threat of violence remained a crucial mechanism of social control. Focusing on the adjudication of violent acts thus becomes a point of entry into the transformed sociopolitical valence of untouchability as it intersected with governmental imagination.

If, overall, anti-Dalit violence prevention has been a story of failure, why attend in detail to the forms of Dalit personhood entrenched in legislation? What can dilemmas in definition really tell us? Michel Foucault argues that discourse is productive, initiating and transforming categories and practices by enfolding them within a new epistemic context.[50] Discourses are both ideational and material, enabling counterintuitive, unlikely connections between practices and spaces, institutional sites that bear a family resemblance to each other through some disciplining function. Thus school and bedroom, or prison and army, though very different kinds of spaces, share characteristics of regulating and normalizing bodies. Discourses about subjects can simultaneously constitute a predilection for surveillance, for monitoring and disciplining. In this sense, we can see how a certain field of "untouchability" was incrementally produced as an effect of the abolition of untouchability and the apprehension of violence against a stigmatized collectivity. Though atrocity laws are preventive, they are also productive: they reorganize social life around new governmental categories that themselves become available as objects of social and political attachment. By defining Dalits as injured subjects who are susceptible to continued harm, protective measures produced a more proximate relation between Dalits and the state and impelled the development of regulatory structures and disciplinary mechanisms to protect them. The effect of these measures, however, was both ironic and unanticipated, for the legislation of caste crime heightened the salience of caste conflict by drawing attention to the presence of anti-Dalit violence as a fact of everyday life.[51]

Although the term commonly used to describe anti-Dalit violence is *jatiya atyachar* (caste atrocity), this term was only defined in 1989 with the passage of the POA Act. *The Fifth Report of the Commission for Scheduled Castes and Scheduled Tribes* (April 1982–March 1983) noted "atrocity" as an everyday, not a legal term.[52] Our contemporary definitions of atrocity shuttle between an unnatural act, a crime against humanity, and a violation of civility, an offense to aesthetic sensibilities and cultivation.[53] Nowhere is "atrocity" confined to designating offense against a particular class or group of people. However, according to the Home Ministry, "atrocity" characterized offenses under the Indian Penal Code perpetrated on SCs and STs: "Where the victims of crime are members of Scheduled Castes and the offenders do not belong to Scheduled Castes, caste consideration[s] are really the root cause of crime, even though caste consciousness may not be the vivid and immediate motive for the crime."[54]

As "atrocity," a term with everyday usage, became a legal category, the legal implications of the term were clarified to suggest that all Dalits were at constant risk of violation by non-Dalits, that "caste considerations" alone were intense enough to motivate actions against Dalits. The catalog of violence, too, expanded. Acts from the everyday to the extraordinary, from the structural to the spectacular, from spatial segregation to ritual humiliation to political terror, became legible as practices of untouchability *because* the victim was an untouchable. Between the inception of preventive laws in 1955 and refining amendments completed in 1989, crucial aspects of everyday life and social relations between castes were brought within the ambit of this new juridical category, the caste atrocity.

A critical point is this: in providing punishments to deter the commission of caste crimes, the Untouchability (Offences) Act incorporated the Dalit's body as a kind of deformed or injured property that belonged to the state: "A crime is an offense against the public at large, for which the State as representative of the public, will bring proceedings in the form of a criminal prosecution. The purpose of such proceedings is to protect and vindicate the interest of the public as a whole."[55] The state could also bring a civil case against those who practiced untouchability if there were efforts to prevent use of public property such as wells or temples: "The social action for a tort on the other hand, is convenienced and maintained by the injured person himself and its purpose is to compensate him for the damage he has suffered at the expense of the wrong-doer. The State may never sue in tort in its political or governmental capacity, *although* as the owner of property it may resort to the same tort."[56]

Manifestations of individual acts of anti-Dalit violence could be ritual or secular, criminal or civil in nature. What bound them together was their generic status as acts perpetuating untouchability. This became the common denominator between different actions, with the untouchable's identity (*as an untouchable*) becoming the touchstone for anti-Dalit crime. As acts perpetuating untouchability gained public prominence and came to be identified as anti-Dalit violence, the social life of the category "atrocity" increasingly performed the work of making social relations between Dalits and others legible.

LAW, VIOLENCE, AND ATROCITY

Ambedkar had long argued that the violence of untouchability was manifest in the illegal laws of the Hindus, and that the molecular presence of structuring violence was misconstrued as caste law. The constitutional response was to articulate caste violence as a distinctive form of violence collectively practiced against a stigmatized group by individual perpetrators. This new moment of lawmaking embedded the violence of caste within law as a consequence of efforts to redress the historical violation of the Dalit. The effort to right historical wrongs by abolishing untouchability also cemented "untouchability" as a legal effect, as a category or practice that acquired salience and critical visibility through debate and discussion about its abolition. As "untouchability" was framed through contiguity with the juridical category of atrocity, its association with crime began to imbue the practice with a double reality, one in the context of everyday life, the other in the realm of performance and spectacle.[57] In contrast to practices of equalization that sought to bring Dalits within a *normative* framework of socioeconomic relations, the atrocity legislation was an *exceptional* legal measure that emphasized the Dalit's status as a historically stigmatized subject through the act of imagining justice for her.

No one believed that passing laws would abolish untouchability. Problems of implementation began almost immediately. What we can say is that the public life of untouchability and a new legal reality were mutually entailed processes. The incitement to declare oneself the subject of violation or the object of an authentic cultural practice must be a necessary first step in seeking recognition and redress. This requires strategic enactment of a belief in law: one must act *as if* legal structures are capable of delivering justice once harm and injury are presented in familiar legal idioms.[58] Such is the case even, maybe especially, when one knows the immense difficulties or impossibility of legal resolution. A peculiar quality of law has this effect: though law has the power to define, it also appears to be an external source of redress.[59] It is the seeming externality of the law to which people respond when they accept the force of law. This aspect of law—law as always already excessive, law experienced as the force of law—must be balanced against the self-sufficiency of law as a linguistic practice as well as a regime of punishment, as the legal theorist Robert Cover has argued.[60]

These combined aspects of law produced something like a force field around vulnerable subjects by generating new debates, bureaucratic forms, and most importantly, social relations between Dalits and others. As exceptional subjects, Dalits were excessively *visible* in bureaucratic discourses. That excessive presence, perhaps tautologically, called for state protection. It is especially noteworthy that social relations between caste

Hindus and Dalits came under intense regulation because these relations were perceived to carry the potential for violence. As customary practices of untouchability were subjected to punishment, incidents of caste inequality developed a politically explosive character. The past two decades in particular have witnessed a change from violence that prevents Dalits from claiming political rights to violence that responds to their perceived political militancy. This is the result, oddly enough, of criminalizing the practice of untouchability and penalizing its perpetrators. As upper castes and, increasingly, those referred to as BCs or OBCs enact violence against Dalits today, their violence in turn produces new forms of Dalit militancy and self-assertion. As "hidden" or invisible forms of violence gain public visibility, they also become the locus for further politicization. Containment of anti-Dalit violence is cemented into India's civil rights regime even as violence increasingly functions as a mode of public recognition between Dalits and caste Hindus.

This violence, then, is not a reflection of caste antagonism, which is how caste violence is often interpreted. It is counterintuitive but enlightening to address such violence as a form of social reproduction rather than as the destruction of social bonds. Anti-Dalit violence is a mode of representation and a material artifact that *stages* social life, as Allen Feldman has provocatively argued.[61] Certain performances of violence restructure the field of social action around violence, which takes on the aspect of a seemingly originary, structuring force from which cause emanates.

The outcomes of caste crimes are neither given in advance nor regulated solely by the state apparatus. The power of bureaucratic identification has to be reasserted, reclaimed, and renegotiated at local levels where it undergoes critical emendation and reinterpretation. As I will argue in the following chapters, antiatrocity legislation oversaw new forms of *localization* and a perceptual split between locality and state. This split mimicked the representation of the state as ideological unity *and* as a set of dispersed or divided bureaucratic powers. As a consequence, caste violence was increasingly processed at two levels: as local antagonism and as a structural entailment of Dalit politicization.[62] The following chapters, organized around critical localized events, examine the postcolonial legal discourse I have outlined here. In them I explore the governmental/judicial machinery operating in relation to, and elaborating, changed caste habitus, political assertion, and everyday identities in Maharashtra, where anti-Dalit violence moved to a central position in popular memory and public culture. Looking at the intersection between recurrent practices stigmatizing Dalits on the one hand and Dalits' continued pre-occupation with the experience of violation on the other, I discuss how anti-Dalit violence is also a locus for further politicizing Dalit identity. Untouchability's newfound visibility has incited new political formations rather resistant to the eye of the state. At the same time, efforts to use legislation regarding the caste atrocity as a model of justice and a form of social recognition raise critical questions concerning legal assumptions about Dalit personhood and vulnerability.

Taking violence as a constitutive element, a form of political currency in the postcolonial milieu of commensuration, also opens the intriguing possibility of writing the histories of postcolonial governmentality and Dalit personhood as explorations in the relationship between law and violence. In the chapters that follow, the violence of recognition, the puzzle of visibility and violence, marks a promising point of entry for under-standing changing configurations of the Dalit subject.

CHAPTER 5

New Directions in Dalit Politics

Symbologies of Violence, Maharashtra, 1960–1979

Well before the state of Maharashtra was formed in 1960, a linguistic state for Marathi speakers was enthusiastically endorsed by writers, academics, and activists who formed organizations for a united Maharashtra: the Samyukta Maharashtra Sabha in 1939, followed by the Samyukta Maharashtra Samiti in 1946. "The vernacular press and Marathi-speaking intellectuals had rallied around a single narrative of the emergence of the Marathi-speaking people," writes Thomas Hansen, "unique in their courage and independence, not to be subdued by Muslim invaders, indeed, the first real Indian nationalists."[1]

The demand for a united Maharashtra consolidated political common sense around Maharashtrian uniqueness and an unlikely populism of caste and class. The twentieth-century non-Brahmin movement had laid claim to Maratha standing, associating itself with martial bravery and manliness befitting Kshatriya status. In a separate Maharashtra lay the possibility of expanding non-Brahmin political and cultural dominance across caste, region, language, and history. For Socialists and Communists, affiliated with agrarian populism and working-class struggle, the *Marathi Manus* (the Marathi man) was identified with the urban laborer who was exploited by moneylenders and industrial capitalists from the Parsi, Gujarati, and Marwari communities. The ordinary *Marathi Manu* was thus entrusted with the historic task of reclaiming his essence, his Marathi *asmita*, against the depredations of "foreign" capitalists, Muslim invaders, and cunning Brahmins.

The consolidation of Maratha power enabled mobilization around a common linguistic and cultural identity. By 1930, the Indian National Congress was dominated by non-Brahmins, including key anticaste activists, so that non-Brahminism's rural base was translated into dominance over Congress networks of power and patronage. After independence, Marathas controlled a rural economy built on sugarcane agriculture and presided over educational and banking institutions as well as sugar cooperatives. The Congress came to be associated with Maratha power, while the Dalit was rendered marginal to the common regional identity on which organized politics was based after 1960.

Ironically, the growing regionalization of politics was the outcome of political reorganization at the center. At the national level, rising anti-Dalit violence was reinforced by upper-caste resentment of the reservations regime.[2] The increased visibility of violence was partly an effect of record keeping and the separation of caste violence from other forms of violence. But by the 1970s an increase in violence was also generated by the consolidation of Congress politics around a charismatic leader, Indira Gandhi; state-level politicians, chosen for their allegiance to New Delhi, were unable to control local tensions.

These shifts were concurrent with developments in Dalit political culture after B. R. Ambedkar's demise. The transformation of popular cultural practices, the creation of new institutional spaces, and the sedimentation of affective energies and political commitments around new objects and practices have defined the Dalit popular. In the postcolonial period, commemorative political symbology—flags, statues, naming and writing practices—materially signified the memory work through which a new community identity began to emerge. These acts of symbolization drew new objects and icons into an existing semiotic field that was organized around Ambedkar, the originary point of Dalit history and a political figure increasingly deified as community icon.

After the mass conversion to Buddhism in 1956, many people destroyed or threw away the idols of Hindu gods and goddesses.[3] Though every Dalit Buddhist home now contains a photograph of the Buddha and Ambedkar, Bhimrao Kardak and Dadasaheb Pagare's dramatic performance, the *Dharmantar* (conversion) *jalsa*, tellingly featured a resistant *maushi*, a maternal aunt who had to be convinced that Hinduism was hell and that Buddhism was the religion of equal respect.[4] If the Buddha became one axis of symbolic power, Ambedkar became an equally powerful one as the modern Manu, the eponymous lawgiver and chief architect of India's Constitution. In visual representations, Ambedkar is almost always depicted in a blue suit, a tie, and glasses. Often he is carrying the Constitution, hands pointed into the air in a defiant gesture. Plenty of hagiographical *charitra* (biographies) of Ambedkar have appeared.[5] Some "create a noble lineage according to which Ambedkar would belong to the Naga Buddhist clan."[6] Many, however, portray Ambedkar's life as contiguous with political thinkers like Socrates or with figures associated with collective emancipation—Lincoln or Lenin.[7] In a popular photographic collage, Ambedkar is depicted from youth to old age through images where he increasingly resembles the Buddha.

In chapter 3 I suggested that Dalit conversion marked a new temporal order outside Hindu history and cultural hegemony. Conversion also produced a distinctive Dalit culture. Organizationally, the Bauddha Jana Panchayat Samiti (Buddhist People's Council Committee), which grew out of the Mahar Jati Panchayat Samiti (Mahar Caste Council Committee), formed in 1941, transmitted knowledge about Buddhism to new converts through *bauddhacharyas* (Buddhist priests), educational activities, and by publishing on Buddhist Dalit history.[8] To guide the converts in Buddhist rituals, Ambedkar compiled the so-called Buddhist Bible, the Bauddha *Puja Patha,* a manual of how to conduct Buddhist rites. A new ritual calendar was organized around Ambedkar's life. It involved celebrating his birthday, Bhim Jayanti, on April 14; making visits to the *chaityabhoomi* in Dadar, Bombay, where Ambedkar was cremated on December 6; and commemorating Dalit conversion at Nagpur's *dikshabhumi* (initiation site). In the Ambedkarite calendar, called Krantiparva (Revolutionary Days), the new year begins on Ambedkar's birthday on April 14. Days of the week and the months are marked by Buddhist symbology. Pilgrims visit newly sacred spaces, including Ambedkar's residence, Rajagriha, in Bombay, and the Chavdar tank at Mahad, known as Krantibhumi (revolutionary site), sanctified through the use of Buddhist architecture, such as the *stupa,* the *dharmachakra,* and the distinctive portals that stand at the entrance to many Dalit institutions.[9]

These ongoing processes of sacralization certainly invested Ambedkar and the Buddha with affective energy, even as they produced a sacred topography of Dalit Buddhist imagery and institutions. Because such processes of symbolization were explicitly associated with the rejection of Hinduism and because they were contiguous with explicitly "political" claims to public space, these processes were interpreted by non-Dalits as militant forms of *political* commemoration.

This chapter examines Dalit political culture as it intersected with Maharashtrian sociopolitical transformations of the 1960s and 1970s to produce a new cultural politics around the identity "Dalit." Increasingly salient political violence distinguished this period, as new sites of antagonism developed within and outside of the domain of politics proper, including challenges to Congress hegemony by a new organization, the Shiv Sena (Shivaji's Army); growing conflict among Dalit groups, especially between the established leadership of the Republican Party of India (RPI), and the antiestablishment Dalit Panthers; Sena and Panther struggles over the control of neighborhoods and party cadres; emergent distinctions between urban and rural Dalits; and finally, rising political violence to counter Dalit militancy.

The ongoing struggle to symbolize the distinctive identity of the Dalit under changing circumstances produced a new focus geared toward accruing greater potency for the Dalit as political actor. If state legislation of Dalit identity had produced a particular interpretation of Dalit vulnerability, Maharashtrian Dalit politics countered with new forms of political subjectivity and of aesthetic self-making: the violence of recognition was met by violent demands *for* recognition on Dalits' terms. The net effect was to further politicize everyday life in Maharashtra, especially key symbols of Dalit identity.

POLITICAL VIOLENCE: RPI, SENA, AND THE DALIT PANTHERS

The general failure of an autonomous Dalit politics after independence was partly due to the marginal position of the Dalit vis-à-vis the common regional identity that formed the imaginative basis of organizational politics. Symbolic politics, a crucial axis of political subject-formation, was intimately, but not exclusively, connected with the demographically negligible position of Dalits and their exclusion from sites of social production. Still, the Dalit challenge remained: to expand the categories of who or what could be a political subject. In significant ways, this took place on symbolic ground: the maturation of Dalit politics was reflected in competing interpretations of Ambedkar's relevance for Dalit history. The initial struggles were over who had the power to represent the Dalit as political subject.

Having embraced the political universalism of the Constitution and the ethics of Buddhism, Ambedkar had little enthusiasm for a linguistic state based on equivalence among caste, region, and history.[10] He feared that a focus on language would only deepen caste dominance and argued that Dalit oppression would increase once rural elites from the Marathi-speaking regions united as a large bloc to preclude the developmental and democratic possibilities opened by positive discrimination and escape from village life.[11] Despite his skepticism, the RPI, formed soon after his death in 1956, was meant to represent his principles but allied itself not only with the Praja Socialists and the Shetkari Kamgar Paksha (Peasant and Workers Party), but also with the Samyukta Maharashtra Samiti. Together they used the demand for a separate Maharashtra state as a political opportunity in the elections of 1957 and 1961.[12] The RPI manifesto used the language of class and labor exploitation to position Dalits at the forefront of the struggle to unite the *shoshit* (exploited) classes for total emancipation—religious, sociopolitical, and economic. This continued earlier Independent Labour Party and All-India Scheduled Caste Federation strategies of building coalitions between Dalit labor—millworkers, municipal and railway workers, the rural poor—labor unions, and peasant organizations.[13]

The first RPI factional split came quickly, in 1958, as a young, urban, educated group broke away from the largely rural and illiterate, if charismatic, leadership of B. K. Gaikwad to form the *durustha* (reformed) RPI led by B. C. Kamble.[14] Generational differences, functional styles, and political ideology drove the acrimonious split. The symbolic significance of the RPI, however, remained. As Jayashree Gokhale-Turner notes, "Being a Dalit and specifically a member of the Mahar-Buddhist community, implied a visceral, if at the same time a vestigial, loyalty to the political form which Ambedkar left behind. . . . The RPI embodied a dual set of allegiances, to the figure and personality of Ambedkar which had become the transcendent 'myth' of the movement, and to their own history and the reworking of the history which the movement had brought about."[15]

While Ambedkar appeared to have rejected Marx for Buddha, significant strains of his thought resonated with Marxian critiques. B. C. Kamble hit a nerve when he warned—in a criticism of Gaikwad's group, the so-called *dhotare* (*dhoti*-wearing faction)—that an RPI coalition with the Communists would destroy Dalit autonomy. "When Congress got power they destroyed Ambedkar's organization," Kamble wrote, "and now the Communists are getting Dadasaheb's [Gaikwad's] support and they are conducting a mischievous smear campaign against Ambedkar."[16] Kamble thought the left's presence in the *bhumiheen satyagrahas* (*satyagrahas* of the landless) in 1956 and 1964 and in urban labor organizing, in which Gaikwad played a key role, compromised Ambedkar's vision of an autonomous Dalit party. Communists were using untouchables, drowning them in the proletariat. The RPI's Young Turks, described caustically by the Dalit writer Raosaheb Kasbe as anxious to "join the ruling class," focused on furthering the interests of an emerging Mahar urban elite, so-called Dalit Brahmins, through reservations, jobs, education, and political representation.[17] As the RPI began to move away from mass organizing in urban and rural areas, its dependence on mainstream political parties increased. By 1974, the party had split into four factions. Congress co-optation of RPI leaders exacerbated factionalism within the party and continued to produce splinter groups too numerous to outline here.[18]

Political factionalism underscored a deeper set of transformations: participation in democratic politics and demands for access to education and employment had exacerbated cleavages between urban and rural Dalits, between impoverished agricultural laborers and the upwardly mobile beneficiaries of the reservations regime (derogatorily referred to as *shasanache javai*, "government's son-in-law"). Although academic observers attribute Dalit political assertion to this vigorous, urbanized middle class, Dalit politics cannot be reduced to the politics of the vote bank. How, then, do we understand these fissiparous tendencies?

One standard argument understands politics in India to be the result of factionalism among local caste and landed elites, thereby temporally extending the political historians' tendency to equate ideology with material interest.[19] I want to reframe the discussion by recalling Ambedkar's prescient analysis of the impossibility of representing Dalits' political interests given their demographically negligible position and their exclusion from sites of social production and public self-representation. As noted earlier, symbolic politics became a crucial axis of political subject-formation partly due to the political weakness of the Dalit communities. Symbolic politics was also related to the crisis of leadership that followed Ambedkar's demise, as well as the inherent tensions at the heart of being Dalit: was Dalit an identity, or did it signal a political potentiality that exceeded the Dalit communities?

Both the RPI and a new political contender, the Dalit Panthers, laid claim to Ambedkar and made him a key symbolic site for reworking the Dalit past and the Dalit self. Ambedkar's very name and a consistent return to Ambedkarite symbolism—whether through installations of Ambedkar statues in rural areas, the proliferation of the *nila jhanda* (the RPI's blue flag), or the distinctive greeting, "Jai Bhim" (Hail Bhim, i.e., Ambedkar)—blessed Dalit political activism of all stripes even when such activism reflected significant divergence from his project. Ambedkar was a floating signifier attached to a diverse range of social practices and political demands that brought them all into a unified domain of action and visibility: Dalit politics. The name "Ambedkar" was a fetish object circulating through diverse arenas and accruing signifying power, as was his iconic representation. There was thus no easy distinction between the symbolic and the real in Dalit politics. Evoking Ambedkar's name and interpreting his legacy produced materially consequential responses definitive of Dalit politics.

A new form of Dalit militancy arose in an atmosphere dominated by the Shiv Sena, a social movement started in 1966 to challenge a ruling Congress party becoming increasingly centralized at the expense of regional party organizations. The Sena was also able to capitalize on elements of (Maratha) caste pride and regional identification predominant in the Maharashtra State Congress. Started to eschew *rajkaran* (organized politics), the Sena flouted public authority, flaunted the strength and courage of its youthful cadre, and staged violent displays of regional and ethnic chauvinism. The Sena took over the Marathi public sphere. Its rise was marked by its ability to organize "lumpen" elements in urban Bombay through hate speech, aggression, and displays of violence. Aggressively positioned against the political left, including labor organizers, the Sena became a useful, if embarrassing, Congress ally. It also harnessed the frustration and anger of the middle classes whose exclusion from white-collar jobs was attributed to Madrasis (southern Indians) and the power of a non-Maharashtrian financial elite. The Sena's main targets, however, were Muslims and Dalits. Muslims were the historically foreign "other" against whom the discourse of Maharashtrian uniqueness was constructed. Dalits were reviled for challenging their impure and stigmatized status through Buddhist conversion and political assertion.

Together and separately, southern Indians, Dalits, and Muslims were the hate objects of the Sena. Having laid claim to the symbolization of Maratha (and Maharashtrian) identity through the explicit exclusion of the Dalit Buddhist, the Sena focused Dalits' political energies around aggressive claims to self-representation. As a consequence, new performances of political violence ensued.

From the start the Sena's neighborhood units, called *shakhas* (branches), were politicized through religious festivals such as the Ganeshotsav and the Shivaji Jayanti as well as through an extensive financial infrastructure and allied patronage networks with petty traders, businessmen, and local politicians.[20]

In June 1972, the newspapers *Navakal* and *Prajasattak* noted the formation of the Dalit Panthers by organizers Arjun Dangle, Namdeo Dhasal, and J. V. Pawar. Another leader, Raja Dhale, had been politicized by the Socialist youth wing, the Yuvak Kranti Dal (Revolutionary Youth Movement), begun in 1969. The Panthers were critical of the RPI's political corruption, but their main focus was on the casteism of the Indian state. Raja Dhale's article in the Socialist journal *Sadhana*, commemorating the twenty-fifth anniversary of Indian independence, August 15, 1972, as Kala Swatantra Din (Black Independence Day), brought the Panthers notoriety. Dhale argued that a flag that could not protect the equality and dignity of Dalits was like a "piece of cloth to be stuffed up the savarna's [caste Hindu's] ass." The Shiv Sena and the Jana Sangh, precursor to the Bharatiya Janata Party, took a procession to the Sadhana office and threatened to burn it down if Dhale wasn't disciplined for his antinational views. This was a recurrent pattern: Panther militancy and abuse of establishment politics were met with the threat of violent discipline by Shiv *sainiks,* often with the support of state functionaries, especially police.[21] Increasingly, state policy mirrored the caste antagonisms reflected in the politics of the street.

The Sena and the Panthers recruited from the same base: unemployed, semi-educated lower middle-class and working-class youth. Some Panthers were involved in so-called lumpen or criminalized lifestyles.[22] As Sena control over central Bombay expanded into suburban neighborhoods, Dalit youth were recruited and even elevated to *shakha pramukh* (local branch leaders). Conflict escalated as Dalit *sainiks* (Sena cadres) from working-class neighborhoods began to join the Panthers in large numbers.[23]

The Panthers' challenge to the Sena, the state government, and ossified RPI leadership was persuasive, if measured by the spread of their *chhavnis* across Bombay. By using a term that recalled the march of the Mahar military unit, the Panthers signaled a militant urban presence. Within a year, they established thirty-two Bombay *chhavnis* of twenty-five members each and, by 1974, had branches all over Maharashtra. The hierarchical organization culminated in a central body that met annually.[24] In fact, *chhavni* organization resembled the *shakha* grid of the Shiv Sena. Despite the disciplined structure envisioned by the Panthers' Constitution, *chhavnis*—like the Sena *shakhas* and unlike the tightly disciplined RSS *shakha* on which both were modeled—were largely autonomous, often started on impulse, and loosely funded at public meetings and through journalism. Handbills or progressive newspapers such as *Navashakti* and *Navakal* published notices of impulsively organized meetings and *morchas* (processions). It was hard to coordinate the growing *chhavnis* and to control members.[25] Decentralized structure was their strength and their undoing: the Panthers had no single leader, no uniting ideology, and no long-term strategy. In fact, branches and leaders often clashed with each other. Nonetheless, public meetings served as ecstatic com-

memorations and public affirmations of a despised and denigrated identity now resignified as political potential.[26] But the capacity for storing
and accumulating the energy of these meetings was simply not built into
the Panthers' organizational structure.

What is clear is that the Panthers sought a new grammar of political
charisma. Rather than replicating existing symbologies of political virtue,
they challenged canonical representations of the Brahminical subject and
political leader. Without a developed alternative, however, their politics
remained experimental. The RPI-Panthers conflict, new forms of self-
representation, and anti-Dalit violence enhanced the sheer visibility of
Dalits in urban Bombay. The effects of such visibility had very different
consequences in rural areas, as we will see later in this chapter.

While the sociopolitical context of the 1970s transformed Dalit politics, internal polemics focused on Ambedkar's legacy. The war of words
between the Panthers and the RPI took place through privately circulated
pamphlets. RPI leaders were accused of "[filling] their pockets" while
trampling on the "Doctor's revolutionary heritage."[27] The RPI was "en-
tangled in the wheels of getting votes, reservations, reserved posts [and]
they ignored the issues of rural Dalits and their problems. . . . this is the
legacy of Ambedkar's party."[28] B. C. Kamble of the reformed RPI was a
favorite target. The Panthers inquired, "Are these leaders, especially B. C.
Kamble, even worthy of polishing Ambedkar's shoes? [*Babacha boot
pusaychi layak ahe ka?*]"[29] The Panthers declared, "If we give our futures
over to such neutered leaders then we will be destroyed. And therefore
we say, today, with bowed heads, that we and the Republican Party share
no blood ties."[30] The father had been killed and a new lineage begun.

Dalit Buddhism was a special point of tension. Kamble, positioning
Dalits in the vanguard of struggles for social justice, claimed that the "Shiv
Sena and the Communists have the same criticism of RPI—that it is a
Dalit-specific party."[31] Dalit Buddhists paid a price for conversion: a re-
strictive Dalit identity and the identification of the RPI as a party of and
for Buddhists. Likewise, the state's relationship to converted Buddhists
was a contentious matter.[32] A 1950 President's Order included Buddhists
in the Backward Classes and excluded them from Scheduled Caste reservations, even though Buddhism was legally defined as a Hindu sect.[33]
As courts equated conversion with loss of constitutional safeguards,[34] Dalit
Buddhists found themselves in the ironic position of claiming that though
changed in their "mind and manners," as Buddhists they were "despised
and disgraced" and continued to "suffer from stigma of untouchability." They had to qualify the aims of Dalit conversion, arguing, "the

Figure 12. RPI and Dalit Panther pamphlets, top to bottom, left to right: *Gair Republican Pudhari, Bichari Paddalit Janata, Ani Dalit Panther* (1974); *Dr. Babasaheb Ambedkaranchya Communist Nindemagil Rahasya va Artha Bodh* (1965); *Dalit Panthers' Constitution and Activities* (n.d.); *Itihasachi Chakre Ulti Phiru Naka Nahi Tar Khaddyat Jal* (1974). Courtesy of Dr. Gangadhar Pantawane, Aurangabad.

Conversion is mainly intended for spiritual and cultural elevation and not for any material gain or benefit."[35] The end result was that Dalits had a difficult time proving their conversion and, if they succeeded, they could not demand reservations as socioeconomically backward Buddhists.[36] As one pamphlet noted, they derived rights from remaining legible as stigmatized Hindus.[37] Due to political pressure, however, Maharashtra began treating Buddhists on par with SCs in 1972.[38]

Ambedkar's double legacy also divided the Panthers between Buddhist and Marxist interpretations of Dalit history, the Dalit self, and the best strategy for Dalit emancipation.[39] The Marxist critique was favored by supporters of Namdeo Dhasal, while Buddhism and an emphasis on the separate cultural and religious identity of Dalit Mahars predominated among supporters of Raja Dhale. In sum, Dhasal insisted that the broader significance of Dalit liberation was as a collective struggle of the dispossessed and marginalized, while Dhale argued that the fundamental conflict of Indian society was produced by the untouchable's degraded position within the caste Hindu order.[40] There were protracted, vituperative exchanges complete with personal accusations of wrongdoing—accepting bribes, womanizing, drinking. Despite both high-minded rhetoric and crass questing for power, this was at heart a struggle over Ambedkar's legacy. Dhale found Ambedkar's Dalit politics definitive and Ambedkar himself a "revolutionary leader" whose "greatness" lay in leadership and the Buddhist conversion.[41] Dhasal argued that Ambedkar's ideas had to be rendered adequate to changing historical circumstances, creatively reinterpreted to be relevant to the times. Firmly convinced of the material basis of caste exploitation, he wanted to minimize Buddhist identity and form coalitions with the left. His support for the Communist Party of India (CPI) in the 1974 elections became the most visible bone of contention. Dhale warned against trusting the Communists who were out to expand their political base, not to support the Dalit agenda, and argued that they were diverting Dalits from the fight against untouchability.[42] As one Panther wrote, "There cannot be a merging of Ambedkarvad and Marxvad."[43] Dhasal was ejected from the unified Dalit Panthers in October 1974.[44]

Overall, political violence steadily increased from the late 1960s, particularly through the Sena's cultivation of masculinity and associated street-fighting culture and the group's aggression against southern Indians, Muslims, and Dalits. This violence was symbolically potent even as it became politically efficacious for a social movement that castigated electoral politics as incapable of representing the distinctive majoritarian interests of the *Marathi Manus*. The Sena in the 1960s perfected the art of attacking opponents on train platforms, in alleyways, outside the entrance gates of mills and factories, and on the street, especially Communist labor leaders and union organizers. According to Thomas Hansen, "It [was] through ritualized destruction of property, the attacks on police, the hurling of stones, and the shouting of slogans that *sainiks* [were] produced, their identities formed and stabilized."[45] The climate of fear produced by riots and acts of retributive violence, often characterized as spontaneous outbursts of popular action, was essential to the Sena's image.

In contrast, Dalit politics definitively reentered the realm of public space and self-representation, what has been called a politics of presence with the Dalit Panthers.[46] Action to resignify space—streets and urban neighborhoods, institutional spaces such as universities and government offices, and the space of language and literature—brought Dalits visibility. These forms of assertion were readily perceived as violent claims upon public space and state institutions and, along with the containment of such assertions by the state, politicized Dalit identity around multiple significations of violence: symbolic, structural, transacted, and retributive. The threat of violence was also essential to the cultivation of an aggressive Panther masculinity. From the start, reports of atrocities against Dalits played a key role in the Panthers' advocacy of counterviolence.[47] Panthers often responded to news of atrocities by rushing to the scene with cycle chains, knives, and wooden staffs to threaten perpetrators. The Panthers' fearless demeanor and their readiness for street fighting were important components of their image.

There was intense street fighting (*prachanda mara-mari*) between the Panthers and Sena until 1980.[48] As *sainiks* attacked the Panthers during their public meetings, the Panthers challenged the Sena's casteism by noting that the Sena depended on Dalits as foot soldiers and front men in illegal activities.[49] The Panthers incited violence by insulting Hindu icons or by threatening to burn the Hindu scriptures. Due to the constant threat of street fights and sudden violence, Panthers Raja Dhale and Namdeo Dhasal were said to carry arms. The Sena's alliance with the police force, especially the constabulary, combined with the state government's interest in containing the Panther threat, had practical consequences. Hundreds of criminal cases were lodged against the Panthers. Leaders often hid from the police, making sudden appearances at public meetings and then disappearing again.

The salience of violence itself, if taken as an organizing locus of specifically political action, gives us the conceptual leverage to examine how Dalits and others were attempting to disaggregate structuring hierarchies of caste sociality and to redefine them as distinctions of power and privilege. This produced new arenas of conflict, from the literary representation of Dalit life and selfhood, to the right to lead processions or lay claim to public space through graffiti and political signage.

DALIT LANGUAGE, SPACE, IDENTITY, AND VIOLENCE

The Dalit challenge produced new loci of political antagonism not only within the space of politics proper but in civil society. The relationship between language and politics, violent speech and political visibility, and political visibility and claims to public space intersected with the dialectic tension—Dalit as a figure of general emancipation and Dalit as a historically restricted identity—that haunted Dalit politics. Violence reflected even as it exacerbated social fissures. As often as violence was performance, it was also a spectacle of power, particularly when it was channeled into speech. The use of epithets, slogans, and powerful wordplay became a defining characteristic of the Panthers, who verbally abused Hindu gods and goddesses and denigrated texts such as the Gita and Manusmriti. By August 15, 1973, when they demonstrated to protest the state's tolerance for injustice against Dalits and the exploited classes, the Dalit Panthers were well known for their public stunts, fiery language, and "extremist" views.

Panther discourse marked a shift from earlier rhetorical paradigms. Ambedkar's arguments were powerful illustrations of liberal/legal modes of argumentation substantiated with impressive documentation and flawless reasoning. The epithets and colorful language used by the Panthers were a sharp and unsettling contrast, even to potential followers. Many reacted against Panther modes of expression and left the organization.[50] The Panthers' efforts to disfigure language as a form of ideology critique resonated with a long-established tradition of anticaste critique—from polemics as acts of consciousness raising to the highly personalized, sometimes sexualized discourse of non-Brahman thinkers. Ironically, the Shiv Sena leader Bal Thackeray's clever wordplay and choice use of the double entrendre, not to mention his significant talent as a cartoonist, also traces back to this sharp tradition of non-Brahmin polemics through his father, K. B. Thackeray.[51]

Departing from Ambedkar's elegant arguments and realistic compromises, if not from his name, Panther politics was a politics of disturbing the status quo, unsettling categories and representational forms taken for granted. Certainly, Panthers' violent critique of bourgeois lifestyles and

TO BE A MAHAR...

Self-respecting Mahars hate the word "Harijan". They do not want the sympathy and the false pity implied by the word. The word "Mahar" has a history, a tradition. They want to live proudly as Mahars.

IRAWATI KARVE

I am proud that I was born in the Mahar caste. The Mahars are a brave people.

B. R. AMBEDKAR

The annihilation of untouchability was not to be achieved by the viewpoint of the great ones such as Mahatma Gandhi, but a beginning was made, and its echo had a good effect on the mind of the Caste Hindu people. We should respect this

SHANKARRAO KHARAT

Our aim and aspiration is to be a governing community. Let all of you bear that in mind and let all of your write it on the walls of your houses...

B. R. AMBEDKAR

It must be admitted that, at least in Maharashtra, the Scheduled Castes in general and the Mahars in particular are politically more conscious than many other high-caste groups.

V. M. SIRSIKAR

Goats, not lions, are sacrificed

B. R. AMBEDKAR

Hens and goats are not wealth, Mahars and Mangs are not castes.

OLD MARATHI PROVERB

"Get out!" says the Brahman to the Mahar. "One day," replies the Mahar. "I shall bring cowdung cakes to the ghat for your pyre."

OLD MARATHI PROVERB

In the beginning and in the end, only pollution is to be found. No one knows anyone who is born pure. Chokha says, in wonder, who is pure?

CHOKHAMELA MAHAR

The problem of the lower order is to remove from them that inferiority complex which has stunted their growth and made them slaves to others, to create in them the consciousness of the significance of their lives for themselves and for the country... Nothing can achieve this purpose except the spread of higher education

B. R. AMBEDKAR

Figure 13. "To Be a Mahar," quotations published at a moment of political conflict and cultural efflorescence, when the relationship between Dalit identity and the Mahar caste was being posed anew. *Illustrated Weekly,* April 2, 1972. Courtesy of the Vasant Moon Collection, Nagpur.

their focus on the aesthetics of daily life and survival under conditions of social and economic deprivation challenged the Marathi cultural establishment.[52] But theirs was an effort to distinguish Panther activity from a movement identified with a restricted social base and ideological orientation, and to create a different political discourse. The Panthers' political agenda, targets of critique, and strategies fluctuated to address the renewed marginalization of Dalits, displaying a tactical shift into a sociopolitical arena already highly structured around questions of identity— whether Maharashtrian, Maratha, or *sainik.* The Panthers' resymbolization of Dalit selfhood was political action in a situation where symbolic politics was genuinely consequential.

The Panthers came to be associated with the power of language to represent Dalit life and experience in new ways. New forms of Dalit self-representation were related to the intensified politics of locality and the association between the Panthers and a broadly defined left. Style became a part of that persona. By the time he started his little magazine *Vidroha,* Panther leader Namdeo Dhasal was recognizable by his "Castro"-type *topi* (cap) and a shoulder bag, imitated by many Dalit men. His open admission of his desire for liquor, *charas* (hashish), and women from Kamathipura, the famous red-light district of central Bombay, had earned him a fair degree of notoriety.[53] The Panthers also invited association with a global imaginary of progressive literature and politics—the Black Panthers, anti-Vietnam protests, the 1968 Paris student protest—as part of their antiestablishment aesthetic. Panther polemics, violation of linguistic conventions, and desecration of language tied into a politics of presence that gave rise to a new literary subject.

Many well-known Panthers—Dhale, Dhasal, Daya Pawar, Arjun Dangle, Yashwant Manohar—were identified with the Dalit *sahitya* (literature) movement, which crossed between literary and political registers. Neither an object of redemption nor purely a historical and cultural subject, the literary "Dalit" was an emergent form of life defined by destitution and poverty, but transformed into a militant force.[54] Dalit *sahitya* represented an "ethnographic" turn in the representational practices of self-narration or literary depiction. An earlier generation of Dalit writers who had participated in Ambedkar's movement—for example, Shantabai Dani's account of feminist activism in *Ratra Din Amhi* (1990); Vasant Moon and his account of growing up in a Nagpur slum, in *Vasti* (1995); or Narendra Jadhav's account of his father's life, *Amcha Baap Ani Amhi* (1994)—recalled the social and political upheavals of the 1920s into the 1950s as consonant with new forms of self-making. Their work is so closely tied to Ambedkar's movement as to make Ambedkar the protagonist of these narratives of a heroic struggle for self-respect and social recognition. Instead, Baburao Bagul's *Jevha Mi Jat Corli Hoti* (1963), Daya Pawar's *Baluta* (1978), and Shankarrao Kharat's *Taral Antaral* (1981) did not hesitate to reveal the painful histories of the Dalit self. These accounts did not merely indict caste Hindus, but also addressed the violence of the Dalit intimate, remarked on regnant cultural practices, and depicted the culture of desperation and self-degradation to which Dalits' low status had given rise. The richness of Dalit life was depicted in its contradiction; it was a cultural form that grounded an immanent critique of Dalit dispossession, but it was also the source of a militant urban identity. It was to be lived and transcended.

Thus the language of Dalit *sahitya* was not merely a form of social realism or a more "authentic" representation of Dalit life. Rather, it implicated the caste Hindu and constituted an ethical challenge. Daya
Pawar's autobiographical novel, *Baluta* (The Share), undercuts the presumed veracity, the "reality effect" of autobiography altogether via a tan-
talizing representation of the Dalit as society's secret sharer. The narrator,
Dagdu Maruti Pawar, characterizes his story as a secret that must not be
revealed to anyone because of the painful history he narrates.

> Dagdu Maruti Pawar
> Who carries as his portion, or share [*vatlya*]
> This *baluta* of pain
> Tied up in the folds of his *dhoti*
> Because of the structure of Indian society
>
> I am only the beast of burden [*bharvahak*]
> Who manifests his words [*shabdat shabdankan kela*]
>
> His desire was that
> No one should be told
>
> I also feel
> That we should not reveal this to anyone[55]

Begging for leftover food as *baluta* (remuneration for the performance
of stigmatized labor) is a quintessential symbol of the Dalit's humiliation. *Baluta* locates the stigmatized Dalit within an economy of humiliation and suffering, his share in life. *Baluta* acknowledges the Dalit as
the secret sharer of Indian society whose story cannot be related except
through an initial act of disavowal: his desire that no one should know.
The literary representation of the Dalit implicates the caste Hindu and
insistently poses the question of responsibility: what does it mean to con-
sume Dalit life, to witness Dalit life in all its brutality?

Simultaneously, the "Dalit Brahmin" is attacked for betraying the radical impulses of the Dalit movement, settling for the false security of upward mobility and mimicking of the upper-castes.

> Hey white collar Dalit Brahmin
> You have betrayed your own blood
>
> The people who have uprooted themselves
> Spilled their own blood to give you
> That plump and prosperous look
>
> You shouldn't keep it
> Like a terrylene shirt, uncreased and unwrinkled
> On that swivel chair in an air-conditioned office
> That reservations have brought you

And that two-room kitchen self-contained flat
That a clerkship has bought you
Don't think that this is the only form
that responsibility takes
Don't read the news that in the villages our mothers and sisters
Have been raped
Like a eunuch, between gulps of beer
The times are changing
You better learn the pattern of the times
And change

Or tomorrow's glowing embers will reduce
Your bungalow to ashes
Don't say you weren't warned[56]

The Panther literary-political aesthetic expressed a critique of the Dalit Brahmin's ethical position. The threat of violence against the Dalit Brahmin, who lacked the urge to protect his mothers and sisters from sexual violence, was also a statement about his effeminacy. The call to action is thus a critique of Dalits' co-optation into the administrative and institutional structures of the state as well as an indictment of Dalits' desire for power and recognition.

Panther self-representation also tied into a longstanding politics of the street, which had been defined by demonstrations, strikes, and tense relations between trade unions and the police in central Bombay.[57] These working-class neighborhoods had a definite identity from the interwar years, when housing contraction and overcrowding opened the streets to diverse social forms—*akharas* (gymnasiums), liquor shops, *mitra mandals* (friendship clubs), radical study groups, religious festivals, the performances of the Socialist and Communist *kalapathaks* (performing troupes) defined old working-class neighborhoods.[58] Criminal gangs and important members of the Bombay underworld lived and conducted business there.[59] The same streets saw intense political contestation among Communists, *sainiks*, the RPI, and the Panthers. Many politicians had electoral bases there and activists, including Namdeo Dhasal, displayed an intense affinity with working-class neighborhoods, red-light areas, and slums. These were sites of deprivation and destitution, but also of radicalized young people who made them spaces of political militancy. Reviewing Dhasal's collection of poems, *Golpitha* (1972), the progressive Marathi playwright, Vijay Tendulkar, noted that he could not understand the use of language by Dalit writers because he had no access to the life of everyday violence and sudden intimacies of which they wrote: "This is the world of days of nights; of empty or half-full stomachs; of the pain of death; of tomorrow's worries; of men's bodies in which shame and sensitivity have been burned out; of overflowing gutters; of a sick young body; knees curled to belly against the cold of death . . . of the jobless, of beggars, of pickpockets . . . Dhasal's *Golpitha* where leprous women are paid the price and fucked on the road, where children cry nearby, where prostitutes waiting for business sing full throated love songs."[60]

Literary depictions of the saturation of everyday life by violence, together with the spatialization of violent conflict in the neighborhoods of central and suburban Bombay, produced a volatile and violently symbolic political atmosphere that enabled the Bombay riots of 1974.

THE 1974 RIOTS

Riots in the Worli area of central Bombay, which began in the Bombay Development Department (BDD) chawls (tenements) on January 5, 1974, are an important landmark in Dalit politics. They pitched police and Sena supporters against Dalits, even as they brought to the surface political tensions between the RPI and the Panthers and among the Panthers. The BDD, formed in 1920, eclipsed the Bombay City Improvement Trust, which had been formed in 1898. The BDD chawls, 121 in number, were built as "sanitary dwellings for the poor and the police," organized in blocks of three to four chawls arranged around open fields.[61] Multiple families shared single rooms above ground floors rented out as shops; there was little management of infrastructure, especially toilets and access to water.[62] By 1974, however, the chawls were thickly inhabited. Seventy percent of residents were caste Hindus who most often supported the Shiv Sena, 20 percent were Dalits, and the rest were police constables.

By then, increased police surveillance had effectively curtailed Panther political activities.[63] RPI leaders had long wanted to crush the Panthers' growing power.[64] Sectarian differences took on a more broadly political character when the RPI allied with the Congress and the Shiv Sena for the 1972 and 1974 Bombay Municipal Council elections. The Panthers called an election boycott in protest and supported a January 1974 CPI-affiliated millworkers' union strike protesting Congress policies.[65] There were allegations that RPI members were responsible for attacks on Panthers and a proliferating number of police cases against them. The Congress offered to drop pending criminal cases if the Panthers called off the boycott.[66] Congress leaders attended a Panther public meeting in the BDD chawls on January 5, 1974, expecting the boycott to be withdrawn.

Instead, it was reported that the Panthers criticized the RPI alliance and made obscene comments about Hindu deities.[67] People in the audience began to throw stones; the violence escalated into a police charge with *lathis* and tear gas.[68] There was intermittent violence in the Worli BDD chawls the next morning, which, by January 16, spread to the BDD chawls in Naigaum, though the riots were more easily contained there.[69] The Worli riots continued intermittently until April.

One approach to investigating the continuation of violence in Worli is to look at relations of antagonism that manifested themselves in spatial strategies of boundary making and boundary destroying. Spatial proximity between police and citizens, between Sena and Panther supporters, made 70 of the 121 the chawls confrontational zones and contributed to the quick and continued intensification of violence.

The 1974 riots between the Hindus and "neo-Buddhists" were not simply riots, but were systematic attempts by Hindus to overthrow the neo-Buddhists and to destroy Buddhist establishments like the Buddha Temple and Memorial Hall, situated at Worli and Naigaum.[70] Describing the riots as a conflict between "caste Hindus and neo-Buddhists," the Bhasme Commission of Inquiry into the riots noted that the severity of the riots was due to the geography of the BDD chawls: "Caste Hindu chawls or Buddhist chawls face each other or they are the adjoining chawls. The riots started with the throwing of stones. The situation of the chawls is very ideal for stone throwing warfare. People just collect near about the chawls and throw or pelt stones at the opposite chawls. Even stones could be pelted easily from the terraces of the chawls. . . . During the riots Neo-Buddhists have suffered most because they are in a minority in terms of population."[71]

Alleys, corners, and terraces were places from which violence could issue. In my 1997 and 2000 visits to the BDD chawls, I was shown how windows carved into the stone structure were tactical points for throwing stones at crowds gathered for demonstrations, while the narrow walkways between chawls were like traps. The Bhasme Commission noted:

> We cannot forget the location of the chawls and the built-up area or the open space or gaps between the chawls. As observed by the police officers in the course of their evidence, it was not possible for them to prevent the people from gathering into crowds at various places. . . . Despite the arrangement, stones were hurled from the terraces of the chawls. The entrances to the terraces of the chawls were promptly closed. Missiles were collected from various chawls after their search. It appears that the partition walls of the common bath-rooms were demolished for using their bricks as missiles.[72]

The commission further noted that "the two communities [caste Hindu and neo-Buddhist] attacked each other with various missiles like stones, soda water bottles, and indulged in anti-social activities."[73] An old woman, Gangubai Jagtap, reported that the police entered her home after kicking her, as detailed in the commissiion's report: "Two pictures of Dr. Babasaheb Ambedkar were hanging on the door of the room. When they saw the pictures, they spent their anger on them. They broke the pictures by striking with lathis. When she again resisted, the policemen pushed and abused her."[74] Another witness noted that policemen "entered through the central entrance screaming 'Break the idols of these Mahardes.' So saying they struck their sticks to their heart's content on the photos of the revered Dr. Babasaheb Ambedkar, Bhagwan Gautam Buddha, and Mahatma Phule."[75] Another witness said that "residents of chawl Nos. 37, 36, 32, 58 and 57 continuously attacked chawl Nos. 39, 40, 60, 61 and 59 with stones, sodawater bottles, tube lights, fireballs of kerosene."[76] Indeed by January 7, according to one witness, this violence had assumed a "communal complexion." By Janury 18, "rival groups of forty-fifty persons and 8–10 people from the terraces were indulging in mutual stone-throwing. They were hurling missiles like soda water bottles, acid bulbs, fluorescent tubes. Acid bulbs were thrown from the terraces of Chawl 114 and 115, which exploded after hitting the wall of Chawl 98."[77]

Although much of the violence was indiscriminate, important markers between spaces—entryways, divisions between bathrooms and living areas, the privacy of homes—were invaded, and symbols of Dalit pride, such as Ambedkar photos, were targeted. Certain incursions into proscribed chawl space specifically crossed caste boundaries. The capture of Dalits' intimate space was a totem of victory, a sign of the reduction of Dalits' political presence. Seemingly indiscriminate crowd violence actually clarified broad distinctions between caste Hindu and Dalit; spatial differences mapped onto differences of political affiliation, *sainik* and Panther.[78]

Political rituals exacerbated the "communal complexion" of the riots. Demonstrations, processions, and the commemoration of Ambedkar's birthday on April 14 became charged events that produced further violence, much like communal riots of the colonial period when ritual occasions—religious festivals, historical observances, and public performances—were used to demarcate and enlarge community space. Violence enacted claims over space, while spatial tactics of boundary maintenance and destruction materialized claims to history, community,

and identity. Unlike earlier clusterings of communal violence around ritual events, however, the Worli riots codified political and sectarian differences. Rather than the politicization of ritual, this was a ritual or commemorative aspect of politics formed by new acts of symbolization
through violence.

As a consequence, everyday objects—lightbulbs, stones, bottles, cycle
chains, doors, electricity itself—took on new symbology as weapons. Justice Bhasme noted that "the situation of the chawls is ideally suited to
the stone-throwing warfare."[79] An assistant commissioner of police who
was on duty at the BDD chawls told the commission, "Later on in the
evening he [the commissioner] came to know that the residents of B.D.D.
Chawl No. 59 (NB) had connected a live wire to the main iron door of
the chawl." By the end of January, "Chawl Nos. 54, 59, 60, 80, 91 and
98 were frequently attacked by caste Hindus. The iron door of Chawl
No. 81 was removed by Hindu *goondas* [thugs, lumpen elements] and
thrown in front of Chawl Nos. 113 and 114.... The policemen residing in Police Chawls 32 to 40 and LA-Divn. 3 were also helping the Hindus in their attack on Neo-Buddhists."[80]

Public conflict complemented daily violence. On January 10, Raja
Dhale was arrested as a Panther *morcha* protesting police atrocities
wound its way through the mill district. Demonstrators started to stone
buildings and ransack a snack food shop. Police constables testified before the Bhasme Commission that the people in the crowd brought stones
to throw at police and at onlookers standing on top of buildings, who
were said to be Sena supporters.[81] The Panthers and their supporters also
carried Molotov cocktails.[82] A subinspector and six constables were injured, and the police tear-gassed demonstrators. Some months later, in
April during the Ambedkar Jayanti celebrations, caste Hindus "attacked
different gatherings of Neo-Buddhists when they were busy preparing
for Jayanti celebrations" with the help of police. The role of the police
was especially troubling. They knew the chawls well because many of
them lived there. In the Bhasme Report, witnesses testified to police brutality in numerous guises. The complaints against the police included: (1)
that a majority of them supported the Sena and were anti-Dalit; (2) that
their sons had dressed in uniform and threw stones; (3) that off-duty police were part of the violent crowd; and (4) that they used excessive force
to quell mob violence.

The commission concluded that there might have been instances where
the police used excessive violence or targeted Dalits, but that they had
for the most part behaved impeccably: "Caste Hindus have dubbed them

[the police] as pro-Neo-Buddhists, while the Neo-Buddhists have branded them as the champions or saviours of caste Hindus. Apart from other facts and circumstances, this one circumstance exonerates the police from charges of partiality, bias, communalism or one-sided behaviour during the riot period. The charges levelled against them by both the fighting communities is in a sense a tribute to the police force."[83] In fact, "the targets were always the police," the commission reported, going on to note that "when faced with a riotous mob indulging in stone-throwing, the police personnel have the same right of self-defence as any other citizen has under the relevant portions of the Indian Penal Code." Of course, the difference is that the police were armed with crowd-control technology, revolvers and tear gas. They used the tear gas extravagantly: "[The] only limit on the number of shells to be fired [was] the dispersal of the crowd."[84]

Evidence of police partisan behavior was overwhelming. Some members testifying before the Bhasme Commission described a "police riot" against Dalits. Interestingly, the Shiv Sena was nowhere mentioned in the commission report or newspaper accounts, although Communists were accused of inciting violence between Dalits and caste Hindus. Justice Bhasme commented, however,that "there [was] no doubt that amongst the residents of the Worli and Naigaum chawls, a large number of people are Shiv Sena minded or sympathizers of their cause.[85] He argued, however, that it was necessary to consider "the roles of the Dalit Panthers and the Sena party almost in juxtaposition."[86] By attributing reciprocity to the performance of violence, state functionaries reasserted control over the domain of representation. Bhasme also blamed "anti-social elements operating *matka* [numbers game] dens, illicit liquor trade centers, gambling dens, and their associates or supporters or patrons" for indiscriminate violence. "On account of their participation the riots continued for a considerable length of time despite the police intervention."[87] The commission report noted "large numbers of unemployed teenagers, school-drop-outs who had nothing to do but to organize themselves into street gangs."[88] Anxiety about social life in working-class neighborhoods was nothing new, but this attempt to tie the Worli violence to loosely brutal but nonpolitical gangs was important.[89]

Low voter turnout due to a general climate of fear in central Bombay led to the defeat of the Congress alliance later in 1974. The victory came at a cost: political violence desymbolized was redefined as criminal activity and urban warfare between rival gangs. The result was a further spatialization of violence. As boundaries in and between neighborhoods were redefined through violence, they became contested targets capable of inciting further violence. Thereafter, incursions into caste Hindu spaces and institutions and responding efforts to contain such transgressions through violence became a defining feature of the dynamics of Dalit activism. Symbolic politics was intensified as the result of Dalit claims to power.

Despite an obstinate universality of conception, whether in Ambedkar's articulation of the Dalit Buddhist or in constitutional paradigms of the suffering citizen, heterogeneous social-political forms and cultural practices produced a different Dalit in Maharashtra, where the deepened significance and symbolization of region and caste incited new mappings of political violence and new spatializing strategies. The form of politics described here most closely approximates what Partha Chatterjee has characterized as a politics of the governed, which manifests as a persistent demand for recognition from the domain of organized politics, oftentimes through creative use of discourses of democracy and moral inclusion. The politics of the governed cuts across properly legal, associational forms of civil society to produce "a constantly shifting compromise between the normative values of modernity and the moral assertion of popular demands."[90] It works through connections with "other groups in similar situations, with more privileged and influential groups, with government functionaries, perhaps with political parties and leaders."[91]

Chatterjee's is an important response to the devaluation of postcolonial politics, which, from a Euro-American liberal perspective, appears as "corruption," "nepotism," "factionalism," or "religious fundamentalism." By presenting the governed—a contextually defined category akin to the subaltern—as a form of alterity, Chatterjee also risks anthropologizing them, however. We might extend his analysis to examine how the charge of "violence" further stigmatizes the politics of the governed. Indeed, the spectacle and ethicality of different kinds of violence are critical aspects of the performance of the politics of the governed, producing a range of political forms, from the authoritarianism of the Shiv Sena to Dalit demands for social recognition. The Shiv Sena drew on the "presence of formal, institutional politics, violent street-level agitation, informal networking, and local brokerage" to become politically efficacious.[92] The Dalit's marginal social identity—his or her exclusion from the theaters of social production and political value—together with the legal-constitutional definition of the Dalit as a vulnerable subject, made the political symbolization and desymbolization of crucial icons and indexes of Dalit identity acts of enormous material consequence. Even as semiotic density amassed around the word "Dalit" and around violent interventions into Dalit selfhood, subjectivity was advanced. The multiple meanings of the word "violence"—from acts of linguistic defilement to masculine self-fashioning and claims to symbolic space—gesture to the range of activities through which a new Dalit public was being reconstituted, this time through an active engagement with Marxian categories of political subject-formation and support for revolutionary counterviolence.

Allen Feldman has argued that "the growing autonomy of violence as a self-legitimating sphere of social discourse and transaction points to the inability of any sphere of social practice to totalize society."[93] If violence represents and seeks to perpetuate the fragmented character of the social, it does so through its distinctive materiality. Dalit politicization and, for that matter, anti-Dalit politicization, challenged ideas of what was within and outside of "politics" and did so through specifically material practices of political violence. In Maharashtra, new sites of symbolization—space, institutions—were created through spectacles of desecration, defilement, and purification. It is precisely through political violence and the symbolization of political forms that the Dalit presence attained visibility and significance in the contexts of everyday life. As Dalits staged this politics of presence, state and casteist forces attempted to desymbolize sites of meaning by enacting forms of symbolic annihilation that would be experienced by Dalits as forms of social death and invisibility.

Organized politics and political violence intersected, but they were also discontinuous. This is to argue for the *relative autonomy* of violence from effectual causes, whether the behavior of political parties, election violence, or material circumstances of deprivation. Indeed political violence produced new acts of symbolization. The polysemous character of violence and its distinctive materiality hold the promise that social relations can be restructured, new discursive-structural contexts produced around acts of violence, and new axes of political subjectivity created. Another instance of political violence, this one an apparent Dalit incursion into caste Hindu semiotic space, takes us a step further into the ritual aspects of symbolization through violence.

NAMANTAR AND POLITICAL COMMEMORATION

The backward classes have come to realise that after all education is the greatest material benefit for which they can fight. We may forego material benefits, we may forego material benefit of civilization, but we cannot

forego our right and opportunity to reap the benefits of higher education
to the fullest extent.

> B. R. Ambedkar, "On the Bombay University Act
> Amendment Bill," *BAWS*, vol. 2, 62

Radical student politics was a defining feature of the 1960s and 1970s—
from the free-speech, antiwar, and civil rights movements in the United
States and the Paris student protests, to India's Naxalbari peasant rebellion of 1967, which attracted a generation of Calcutta's middle-class
youth to Marxist-Leninist politics. By the early 1970s, student politics had
generated a critique of the university as an institution for the reproduction
of bourgeois ideology. The *namantar* (renaming) movement to change
the name of Marathwada University in Aurangabad, Maharashtra, was
energized by these broader trends in student activism and the politicization of the university. Unlike the effort by conscientized middle-class
youth to criticize institutional ideology, however, *namantar* was a demand
for the right to be represented in the symbolism of the institution by renaming the university after B. R. Ambedkar. Organizing around Ambedkar as the origination point of Dalit history and identity, the *namantar*
movement represented the university as a particular symbolic place, a
site of political commemoration.

A majority of students in Aurangabad, regardless of caste identity, came
from nearby rural areas. All castes were severely affected by Marathwada's
drought and famine of 1972, which contributed to a strong student movement on the university campus for social justice.[94] The concentration of
Dalit caste groups in Marathwada's five districts was higher than in any
other region of Maharashtra. Dalit castes constituted 16.25 percent of
Marathwada's population and Mahar Dalits constituted 6.5 of the total
Dalit population, though in the districts of Beed and Osmanabad their
numbers were higher.[95] Higher education in Aurangabad remained segregated at the college level, but Marathwada University was better integrated. Almost a quarter of students came from the Dalit castes.[96] The university also had two Dalit vice chancellors in the early 1970s, R. P. Nath
(1972–75) and Shankarrao Kharat (1975–76).

Most Dalit students in Aurangabad attended institutions affiliated with
the People's Education Society (PES), established in 1945 with the intent
of "promot[ing] higher education among the poor middle classes in general and the Middle Classes in particular."[97] The PES had established the
Dr. Babasaheb Ambedkar College of Arts and Commerce, the Dr. Am-

bedkar College of Law, and Milind College on land provided by the nizam of Hyderabad.[98] These colleges formed a complex of institutions proximate to Marathwada University. Although initially only 200 of the 800 students at PES institutions were Dalits from the Mahar community, this changed during the 1960s when Dalits from Nagpur began to enter, especially at Milind College. In 1975, over 90 percent of the students attending PES institutions in Aurangabad could be classified as BC students.[99] The PES colleges were widely identified as Dalit institutions: "Milind Mahavidyalaya's English initials M.M. are popularly taken to mean Mahar-Mang college. The students call Saraswati Bhavan the Shetji Bhatji [merchants and Brahmins] college; Maulana Azad College is known as the Mohammedan College, and Vasant Rao Naik College is called Vanjari College [Naik's caste]. . . . When Babasaheb Ambedkar's follower Shankarrao Kharat [the eminent Dalit writer] became the Chancellor of Marathwada University, the students disparagingly referred to it as *Maharwada* University."[100]

In a segregated educational environment, the PES institutions had produced a very strong sense of unity among students. "Perhaps in no other city are the Scheduled Caste and Nava Bauddha students as well organized as in Aurangabad town. . . . It is quite possible that the caste tensions permeating the Aurangabad colleges have a tendency to spill over to other areas from where the students come."[101] The PES institutions symbolized Dalit pride. Staunch Ambedkarites on staff promoted a strong service ethic. Milind students were encouraged to conduct field surveys and sociological studies, and the Ambedkar College of Law ran a popular legal clinic for the impoverished. The focus on social work within the community came from the strong involvement of PES faculty and trustees in the Ambedkar movement. The PES curriculum showed a proclivity for Buddhist history and culture and for social justice issues. Students might have been oriented toward the socially and economically less fortunate, but they also showed a "willingness to work within the system in order to expand economic opportunities for the newly-developing 'middle class' within that community."[102]

In 1973, Marathwada students demanded an exemption from fees and tuition. The Dalit-led Republican Students' Federation did not support that movement, instead demanding a hike in government stipends for 1974. By 1977, student members of the Socialist-affiliated Yukrand (Revolutionary Youth) had widened the focus of the student movement to address poverty, rising prices, and the deteriorating economic situation of the region. Dalit students, initially joining with Yukrand, later accused them of hijacking the stipend issue initiated by Dalits. These student demands preceded the *namantar* issue.

Namantar agitation started in 1977 and culminated in the "Long March" of December 6, 1979, organized by Professor Jogendra Kawade from Nagpur and his Dalit Mukti Sena (Dalit Freedom Army), which brought activists from all over Maharashtra to Aurangabad to participate in a *jail bharo* (fill the jails) program.[103] Between 1977 and 1979, Marathwada was under siege, and random acts of violence as well as highly orchestrated attacks of murder, arson, and looting were carried out with the connivance of local authorities. Aurangabad was under curfew and the police were given shoot on sight orders. As the riots spread throughout the rural areas, it was clear that the violence had coagulated along train and bus lines. Police and state functionaries were prevented from reaching rural areas, however, because "the communication system and railway traffic were completely disrupted" and "track fish plates were removed and the signal actuating wires were cut" in many places. State authorities estimated "that they incurred a loss of Rs. 5–6 lakhs every day as more than 1,000 buses plying different routes in the region had to be withdrawn."[104]

The demand to rename the university was broached on July 18, 1977, at a meeting of the university's Executive Commission. A huge procession of more than ten thousand people comprising youth from political organizations, members of the Backward Classes University and Teachers' Association, and the Dalit Panthers confronted the university's governing body with their demands. The *namantar* movement from the first exceeded the control of the Aurangabad-based student leadership. Soon, internal differences on *namantar* strategy came to the fore between the Aurangabad, Bombay, and Pune branches of the Dalit Panthers.[105]

In *namantar,* control over space, real and virtual, was central to forming a new identity. Objects and icons—statues of Buddha and Ambedkar, the flying of blue flags, and the university as monument of self-definition and upward mobility—were imbued with an affective presence. These became objects of ritual veneration and signs of political commemoration as Dalits rejected the symbology of their earlier lives in toto and replaced it with a new cultural memory centered on Ambedkar and Buddhist conversion. When the chief minister of Maharashtra, Sharad Pawar, announced the legislature's decision to rename Marathwada University on July 27, 1978, severe riots broke out across the region.[106] Though many, including the mainstream media, thought *namantar* originated among urban, educated Dalits, a newspaper report failed to find the instigating center: "During the last decade there have been periodic student agitations in the region of Marathwada. They had a serious impact on the style of the functioning of political parties here. But there is a marked difference between this agitation and earlier ones. The present agitation is quite spontaneous, and no known student leader seems to be behind it. This is not only true of Aurangabad but also other parts of the region and no known student leaders seem to be behind it."[107] This statement captures the symbolic significance of the university for Dalits, for whom it was a space associated with their historical exclusion. The intensity of affect is well captured in the following statement: "The Milind campus in Aurangabad is now an educational and cultural centre thanks to the efforts of Dr. Babasaheb Ambedkar. We now want to convert it into a power centre."[108]

Because reservations were blamed for the presence of Dalits in the university and associated with the decline of academic standards, resistance to reservations became an important reason for the intensity of violence. Among urban and rural Dalits they also became an excuse to devalue broad-based support for the *namantar* position as merely instrumental. In contrast, as violence intensified, the university was being incorporated into an existing Dalit political symbology: "It is possible that rural Dalits did not fully understand the demands for *namantar*. But they definitely wanted to see a prominent institution named after their loved leader. And when the riots took place, the photos of Bhagwan Buddha and Ambedkar which can be found in each home [were] desecrated and destroyed. After this, *their demand for namantar has grown stronger.*"[109] Rumors flew among those university *namantar*: "The University degree awarded to students will carry the picture of Ambedkar. When the graduate frames his degree and hangs it on the wall, it may amount to image worship."[110] Ambedkar's name was the semiotic currency for pro and anti *namantar* positions in the struggle over Dalits' social mobility and right to self-representation in the postcolonial order.

Aurangabad's upper-caste intelligentsia, progressive on other issues, resisted the *namantar* demand, they said, to preserve the unique identity of Marathwada against the insensitivity of the Maharashtra state government. The editor of *Marathwada*, Anant Bhalerao, was quoted as saying, "*Namantar* makes it the university of one *dharma* [religion] and *jat* [caste]."[111] The depiction of Ambedkar as a Dalit icon and *namantar* as a casteist demand defined upper-caste resistance. An editorial claimed that "nobody wants to be seen as insulting Ambedkar, even those students who are angriest about *namantar,*" because of the vehemence with which Dalits protected his name. The editorial advised resistance to this censorship in order to reveal the antinational sentiments of Dalits. They had collaborated with the British and the *razakars,* Hyderabad's feudal landlords who had resisted national unification, and now made highly partisan demands unrepresentative of the majority's desires.[112]

Violence quickly spread into areas of commercial agriculture in the districts of Aurangabad, Parbhani, and Nanded.[113] Public works projects launched under the Employee Guarantee Scheme in response to the drought of 1972 had already politicized agricultural laborers around wages. The shift to sugarcane and cotton cash crops in these districts where landholdings were large meant that demand for agricultural labor was high. Dalit labor, the bulk of landless workers, experienced increased bargaining power and less economic dependence on upper-caste landlords.[114] On the other hand, the resuscitation of a government cotton scheme had depressed prices, partly explaining "why the extent of atrocities in the major cotton producing and marketing districts was markedly high in comparison to the other districts."[115] In these cotton-producing areas, signs of class mobility—bicycles, new pots and pans, good clothes—were specific targets of violence.

From July 27, 1977, through August 7, 1978, a reign of terror infected 1,200 of Marathwada's 9,000 villages. Fifteen thousand Dalits were affected in all, 1,200 homes were attacked, and 5,000 people were rendered homeless.[116] *"Photos of Bhagwan Buddha and Ambedkar which can be found in each home [were] desecrated and destroyed."* For Dalits, "this was the greatest insult to them."[117] Houses were torched, Dalit women were raped and molested, and in a few instances Dalits were set on fire and their property destroyed. Sexual violence was a great insult. Women were raped in Sonkhed village, Kandher *taluka* (subdistrict), tortured and raped in Bolsa village, Billoli *taluka,* and the ironically named Izzatgaon village (*izzat* is "respectability," "pride") was the scene of the brutal rape of four or five women who were running to escape attackers. The breast of one woman was cut off.[118] Brutal desecration of Dalit bodies, often by burning, was another distinctive feature of the anti-*namantar* violence. One instance was the killing of Fauzdar Bhurevar on July 31, 1978, in Jalgot village. When he took shelter in a home, he was beaten by a crowd and then burned alive at the police outpost.[119] In Sugaon village, in the Kanher *taluka* of Nanded district, Janardhan Mavde, a Dalit *upasarpanch* (deputy village head), was murdered and pesticide was poured into the Dalits' water well to poison them.

As violence spread across the region, some reports noted that changes to village structure had produced resentment. Filling the hereditary post of police *patil* (head of village police) with Dalits had become an especially sore point.[120] As educated Dalits competed with village heads for jobs, "those who were called 'Namya' earlier, now have to be called 'Namdevrao.'"[121] That is, those insulted in the past were now addressed with an honorific. Targets of violence were often these low-level village officers, police or politicized Dalits who had challenged village authorities in some fashion, each of whom represented the transformation of village caste relations through state policy. Symbols of economic accumulation and social advancement were also targets of violence, especially arson.

> [In Akola village] the first house that was set on fire belonged to Shri Kashinath Borde, a police patil from New Buddhists who is owner of 14 acres of agricultural land in the village. He had installed a flour mill in the village and was quite well off. He was the main target of the fury of the caste Hindus because in his official capacity he had been reporting the cases of harassment of Scheduled Castes. . . . His bullock cart and household articles were burnt. . . . The attackers set fire to the house with *Mashals* [lit. "candle," but here, "long torches"].[122]

The most infamous incident of all took place in Temburni village, Nanded district: the brutal killing of Pochiram Kamble, a Dalit from the Mang community who had embraced Buddhism. Kamble owned six acres of *gaayraan zamin* (common grazing lands, on which landless Dalits encroached in order to have the lands regularized later). He had assaulted a servant of the ex-*sarpanch* for grazing cattle on his land.[123] During riots on August 4, 1978, mobs ransacking homes and looting food grains and household goods found Kamble, who had hidden in a friend's home. "When they found the whereabouts of Shri Pochiram they chased him and brought him back to village Chouka where he was done to death and burnt his body."[124]

A parliamentary commission instituted by the central government's Home Ministry toured Maharashtra as it became apparent that there was a reign of terror in Marathwada. Its head, Ram Dhan, commented, "Many of the sarpanches and police patils instigated atrocities on Scheduled Castes and neo-Buddhists during disturbances and did not report the cases of arson, loot or burning of houses, etc. to local police stations or the higher authorities in their respective areas."[125] Brutal dismemberment was especially potent. The symbolic mutilation of the Dalit body underlined the threatened social existence of Dalits.[126]

Dalits were also held responsible for inciting violence. The Marathwada Nagarik Samiti (Marathwada Citizens' Committee) spread rumors that violence in rural areas came from anger against Dalits' abuse of the Protection of Civil Rights Act of 1974 and caste Hindus' resistance to the crude language and arrogance of Dalit leaders whose status had improved through reservations.[127] One *Samiti* founder argued that the legislation had become a "tool and weapon in the hands of the militants among the Dalits, for terror and black-mailing of non-dalits, giving rise to enormous discontent and conflicts."[128] Another article noted:

> The misuse of the PCR Act has been the cause of trouble in villages. It is a dangerous weapon in the hands of the Dalits. Anyone can make any charge. In many instances in order to squash the case the complainant agrees to remain absent (Offences under [the] PCR Act are noncompoundable) so as to have an *ex-parte judgment*. But this is only after extorting large sums of money. But villagers seething with anger at the treatment meted out against them have grabbed this opportunity to settle old scores with their Dalit opponents. All the caste Hindus, Muslims, Sikhs, Christians and other backward classes have got together against the Dalits.[129]

There was plenty of evidence that the police were unaware of the PCR Act or that they deliberately harassed victims by withholding information when filing cases.[130] The parliamentary commission suggested the need for greater representation of SCs and STs on the police force, as well as infrastructural reform to strengthen police intelligence at the *taluka* level and to improve communications with radios, telephones, and motor vehicles. Yet the media focused on allegations that the PCR Act was being misused by Dalits.

The *namantar* issue remained unresolved until 1994, when the *namavistar* (name enlarging) agitation succeeded in renaming Marathwada University as Dr. Babasaheb Ambedkar Marathwada University, satisfying Dalit *and* regional demands.[131] There was a great deal of violence again, largely restricted to the districts of Beed, Osmanabad, and Parbhani. At least four Dalits were stabbed, Dalit property was burned, and statues of Dr. Ambedkar were desecrated throughout the region. An important aftermath of the renaming was the withdrawal of atrocity cases in a deal brokered between some Dalit leaders, the then-ruling Congress led by Sharad Patil, and the incoming Shiv Sena government under Manohar Joshi. By September 1995, the Maharashtra state government had begun to withdraw more than eleven hundred cases registered under the POA Act, even though it is illegal to do so; only courts can dismiss atrocity cases. The Shiv Sena argued that cases were often falsely registered to settle old scores, and argued that the repeal would "promote communal harmony."[132] Newspaper statements were also issued saying that only cases of *shivi ghalne* (insult) would be retracted. Though the Committee for the Protection of Democratic Rights (CPDR), along with B. R. Ambedkar's grandson, the politician Prakash Ambedkar, filed a petition arguing that the state government could not summarily recall cases being fought by the state on behalf of Dalits, the High Court dismissed the petition. The irony of the state rejecting its own laws for protecting Dalits appears to have troubled no one. Clearly, unless state discourse and practice can become political leverage, they are empty exercises in legitimation. Politics accumulates around such performances; it is not internal to them. By the time I visited the Dr. Babasaheb Ambedkar Marathwada University (BAMU) in 1996, it had become another site of commemoration in an evolving lexicon. On my first visit there, I noted: "Busloads of people come from Aurangabad's environs to have *darshan* of the BAMU gate. The gate copies the gate surrounding the Sanchi *stupa,* to evoke the Buddhist sites in the region such as Ajanta and Ellora. People often take *darshan* at the BAMU gate and leave an offering, as though the university were a pilgrimage site."[133]

SYMBOLIC VIOLENCE AS SOCIAL FORM

Dalit victims of violence in Aurangabad were the collateral damage of the conflict between two orders of legality: the intimate hierarchies of caste in the village and the state's incorporation of caste antagonisms within its infrastructure. Though they diverged in scale, the state's connection with upper-caste cultural norms meant that there was little difference between repressive and ideological apparatuses of state.[134] As I will argue in following chapters, the (collapsed) distinction between repressive and ideological apparatuses produced a new politics of locality, with locality being the product, paradoxically, of a wider domain of publicity that staged local antagonisms and Dalit militancy. Dalits' symbolic claims to public space and institutions were devalued as sectarian (or casteist) by asserting equivalence between Dalits' (illegitimate) claims upon the university and the violence of upholding the caste order. The rhetorical commitment to the social distribution of economic opportunity and to legal protection for Dalits also created a schism between local caste culture and state law. This was reflected in the overlapping of two kinds of time and two distinct repertoires of violence: ritual violation, on the one hand, and the targeting of new symbols of Dalit pride and social advancement, on the other. Although the performative contradiction between the body of the state and the body of the state functionary often collapsed, it could occasionally produce openings for justice. Atrocity laws were themselves a barrier to arbitrary violence: anti-Dalit violence had a name, and it was a crime with victims and perpetrators. This is perhaps why allegations of "false atrocity" played such a significant role in justifying anti-Dalit violence. The balancing move was an effort to empty Dalit politics of its "ideological and historically specific intentionality and singularity."[135]

The *namantar* movement accelerated the symbolization of political figures and spatial logics. It also intensified political antagonisms and reflected them in transformations of caste sociality. Dalits' militancy produced violent repugnance in two registers: intensified ritualization of political violence, manifested in archaic forms of punishment, and crystallization of political antagonisms with substantial support from local state functionaries. This bifurcated structure of anti-Dalit violence—which enacted the recurrent tension between the political and the ritual-archaic—intensified affiliations with symbolic form, whether new symbolizations of Dalit identity or ritual degradation of the Dalit body. Understanding the relation between violence and politics, and between political violence and symbolic politics embedded in material and spatial practices, enables us to move away from the persistent binarism of depicting the *namantar* movement as a matter of either class antagonism or "purely" symbolic politics.

As the Worli riots show, this bifurcation was vivid in the 1970s, as limited avenues for social mobility and economic advancement through the reservations regime produced class fractions in the Mahar Dalit community. These mapped onto other divisions between the urban and the rural and between a universalist Dalit subject and an exclusivist Buddhist identity. These tensions seemed to become evident in a putative disconnect between the originators of the *namantar* demand and the victims who suffered its violence. An example of this view can be seen in the following statement: "The poor villagers whose properties were destroyed and whose life and liberty were threatened did not even know what this University was and whether there was any proposal to change its name. . . . [T]he caste Hindus did not attack them for the reason that the University was to be renamed; but did so out of jealousy, hostility and caste hatred and on account of the conversion of Dalits to Buddhism. . . . [One more reason] was the enmity on account of constant disputes between the landlords and agricultural labourers on the inadequacy of wages."[136]

In contrast was the effort to delink ideology from economy: "The implication that those who don't have 2 square meals a day should not be interested in the namaantar issue is patronizing. Does this mean that the poor don't have the right to exercise their civil rights, or to vote? 47% of the people in India get 2 meals a day. . . . Does that mean that [the rest] should not exercise their democratic rights? . . . Casteism does not have to do with economic standing."[137]

It is not within the scope of this book to explore the extensive and intense debates about caste and class from this period, which divided along idealist and materialist perspectives. Suffice it to say that many discussions addressed the possibility of adopting a class-caste model for the purposes of political mobilization and constituency building but were stymied by factional struggle and philosophical distinctions.[138] Nor can I address the range of localized political activity around caste and class issues. I draw attention to these debates to illuminate the binarism between material contexts and symbolic dimensions of Dalit life that were activated at a transformative political moment, and to suggest that the distinction—as one scholar noted, "objective class contradictions are masked by the intervention of varna ideology"[139]—is too emphatic. Materialist perspectives focused on production relations and the devaluation of Dalit labor. But the reproduction of antagonism was (and is) effected through other materialities—of language, space, and violence—that invest the stigmatized body with affect and value.

The symbolizing and desymbolizing of key dimensions of Dalit experience and identity became politically consequential and materially significant in the 1970s. But the politicization of everyday life beyond the realm of formal politics was itself central to postcolonial Dalit identity. Although this was partly an effect of the state and of the emphatic particular identity of Dalits, new forms of public self-fashioning were added to the mix by the 1970s. As the reservations regime became a conspicuous and highly conflictual space within formal politics, Dalits' representational practices produced new loci of conflict around ritual and socioeconomic exclusion in daily life. The experientially inescapable visibility of Dalits was the result of the accelerated symbolization of Dalit identity and the Dalit past. A more significant visibility came from the perception of Dalits as undeserving objects of government largesse whose additional claims upon the domain of representation had to be resisted at all cost.

As a consequence, violence became the hinge connecting the domain of formal politics and everyday life. As Dalits came to be stereotyped as militant, injured people with an insatiable appetite for government recognition, any effort to establish identity for self or community became a potentially incendiary demand. In this milieu, Dalit politics, from the formation of the Panthers to the *namantar* movement, enabled equivalence between political commemoration and political violence. The violence did not *stand for* other contradictions. Rather, it was a form of public communication and a material practice that staged political antagonisms. Violence became the pivot that articulated the spheres of production and reproduction of the Dalit body. This followed from the inaugural efforts of the Dalit Panthers to produce a public sphere where violent speech defined the Dalit as a revolutionary subject, even as such speech had the (limited) capacity to challenge the Sena's incursions into state power. As a practice of self-fashioning and as a strategy of political containment, violence embedded itself within the political during the 1970s, at a moment when regional relations of caste were undergoing great change due to emergent political actors, the Panthers and the Shiv Sena.

CHAPTER 6

The Sexual Politics of Caste

Violence and the Ritual Archaic

Political violence is a genre of emplotted events. An event is not
what happened but what can be narrated.

ALLEN FELDMAN, *Formations of Violence*

The alleged incident with Sonabai which is denied by the defence
took place some six months back. Yedu is said to have shown her
money and held her *Padar* [the edge of the sari that wraps around
the breasts]. . . . One cannot say that the thing must have happened
altogether.

JUDGE C. J. DIGHE, Judgment on Criminal Appeal no. 5/1965,
June 30, 1965

When I started fieldwork in 1996, almost everyone with whom I discussed
caste violence mentioned Sirasgaon. "Sirasgaon" was code for events that
had occurred in a village of that name, the site of a spectacular "atrocity" case of the early postcolonial period. As the unprompted recollec-
tions attest, the 1963 event was instilled in popular memory. In fact, I
first came to know the details from a government servant I call S., who
was extremely conscious of giving me information "off the record." Thus
I keep the description of place vague, emphasizing *what* I heard as I
recorded the story in my notes over two days. Taking this as a sample of
popular memory, I focus on how S. framed the sexual violation of Dalit
women, his acute sensitivity to how ideas about gendered respectability
were caste-marked, and finally, his political sensibilities regarding the case
as an instance of caste atrocity.

Day One:
I went in today [Thursday, May 16, 1996] to ask for permission to follow
up cases in district courts. I wrote up a visiting card, which the peon took in.
    When I finally meet S., he is very sparkly and interested in academic
research. His office has a photograph of Babasaheb [Ambedkar] on the

wall, and there are piles of registers on the floor. As is typical of administrative offices, his table is very large, and arranged in front of it are three rows of chairs. I briefly tell S. that I'm working on caste and law [my normal "cover," especially in government offices] and that I need permission to follow up on these cases. S. tells me that he will put my case before the chief justice, and that I should get the permission from the court in about three weeks.

I am getting ready to go, when S. says, "If I may offer you some advice . . . I don't know if I should presume . . . " I say, "Please, that would be very welcome." S. says, "You know there was a major case . . . " and before he can finish I ask, "Sirasgaon?" I don't know why this case came to mind, but I am glad it did because now S. seems pleasantly surprised that I have heard about this case. I say, "Can you tell me anything at all about the case? Everyone tells me that it was a big case, but nobody can give me any details because they were too young when the case took place!" [We both echo this last phrase together.] S. says, "I was involved in the case. I was an advocate in Aurangabad at that time." I am so excited I can hardly speak. I make an appointment to meet him the next afternoon.

Day Two:
When I go in the next day, someone else is already there. S. introduces me to him, and then launches into his story. I am getting used to this style of "interviewing" now. There are often other people in these big government offices, and the interview has the feel of a performance in a durbar, where my informant holds forth, and I listen, pipe in with questions hoping to get a debate going with the onlookers if I am lucky, or else just look on along with the audience, nodding occasionally and taking notes. Of course I give up the idea of taping anything under these circumstances. At one point early on, S. says, "You can listen, and write later." I ignore him and put the notebook on my lap rather than keeping it in his view, and scribble furiously as he speaks.

These are the details of the incident, in condensed form. [Recounted by S.; S. does not remember dates, the case number, or other details.]

"Five women tried to fill water at the common well at about ten AM. *Savarnas* [caste Hindus] tried to stop them, and Dalit men tried to resist. Twelve of the accused men went the next day and dragged the women out of their houses. The *sarpanch* [head of the village or governing body] and police *patil* were among the accused. They stripped the women and paraded them naked from street to street. Maybe 50–70 people were actually involved. The men were armed with sticks. RPI *karyakartha* [activist] and *taluka* [subdistrict]–level president Sakharam Khajekar went secretly to get the details. People were threatened before the police investigation began. Then our people came to Aurangabad to tell me [S.] about the case. I went to the SP [superintendent of police] and collector [Aurangabad]. The FIR [First Information Report] contains all details, but in the statements given to the police, people said 'We went to fill water, and they abused us [*shivya dilya*].'

"Joshi was the public prosecutor on the state's behalf. There was a lot of publicity in the papers. The accused filed an application to transfer the case. My brother-in-law, who was also an advocate, and I supported this move. Almost all the accused were Marathas. The star witness was a *sutar* [carpenter]. Justice P. E. Vani tried the case in Aurangabad. The Dalit *mandali* [community] was worried about whether Joshi would try the case properly, and an application was filed with the government of Maharashtra to give the case to someone else."

. . .

"Like others, I supported Laxmanrao Kulkarni's name, and suggested that the *vakil* [lawyer] should not be transferred just because of his caste identity [a demand that was made by other Dalit leaders at the time]. We appealed to Justice Dighe in the sessions court when the case came to sessions. Initially the sentence was six months plus Rs. 1,000 fine. The Bombay High Court upheld the ruling of the Aurangabad District and Sessions Court. Then the accused went to the Supreme Court where the sentence was lessened. [I have not been able to find the Supreme Court judgment, if it exists.]

"Ramrao Adik appeared on behalf of the criminals. At one point during the course of the trial, I asked Adik how he could have appeared on behalf of the accused, and whether it was because they were Marathas. In turn, Adik asked if this was a 'Dalit' case. I answered that if this had been a case involving the stripping of Maratha women, I would have been against the men."

S.'s story takes about an hour to narrate. Just as I am leaving, I ask about feminist intervention, and S. says there was none. Then he relates this anecdote: Soon after the Sirasgaon case, a report appeared in the *Maharashtra Times* regarding Swati Patankar, a woman traveling in a Bombay local train whose *mangalsutra* [necklace symbolizing a woman's status as wife] had been snatched.

S. mentioned that many activists and academics were incensed by this case and wrote to complain about the threat to the women's safety. S. says, "[I] wrote in to *Maharashtra Times* saying that a major case such as Sirasgaon had just occurred, and none of these academics had raised their voices. How was it that they were so angry about Swati Patankar. Was it because she was a Patankar [an upper-caste surname]?"

Like many other atrocity cases, Sirasgaon was publicized by local-level activists through formal and informal networks. S.'s account of the case reflects the Dalit community's vigilance regarding caste violence and their ability to intervene—S. had been an advocate in Aurangabad, the local RPI had been involved, and so on. Matters of gendered respectability and sexual humiliation made Sirasgaon an issue of community honor. S.'s caste-marking sensibility and atrocity perception were framed largely around questions of political strategy—which political parties defendants were allied with, how sensitive they were to caste issues—and around the un-

spoken caste prejudice that attended cases of caste atrocity. These produced what Ann Stoler has called "hierarchies of credibility," frames of
legibility that dictate what can and cannot be said and by whom. This was
a critical aspect of the framing of the Sirasgaon event as a legal case.[1]

Sirasgaon was part of popular memory, but it was difficult to get information about it. Once it was defined as a crime, the incident was transformed into a legal case available to researchers through multiple judicial
iterations.[2] Even though I had heard the story from S. in May 1996, I only
managed to track down case records near the end of my research stay, in
June 1997. After a series of frustrated efforts, I finally found the judgments
of the judicial magistrate first class and the sessions judge in the district
and sessions court's storage room in Aurangabad city. I was allowed to
take the case papers outside the courthouse to photocopy them the day
before my departure. Once I had the case number and other details, finding the oral judgments of the Bombay High Court became easier.

The Sirasgaon incident was not merely a legal case, however. Rangit
Guha has argued that redefining events into crimes "reduce[es] their range
of signification."[3] Legal redefinition is more than an act of epistemic containment; it is also a form of translation: quotidian practices are recon-
textualized and, in the process, rendered extraordinary. In this case, the
extraordinary aspect—the prominent individuality of Sirasgaon, we might
say—connected with and circulated through a larger force field whose
operations we can refer to as publicity.[4] The *Marathwada,* a newspaper
published in the city of Aurangabad and run mainly by Socialists, played
a significant role.[5] The Maharashtra Legislative Assembly (MLA) and the
Maharashtra Legislative Council (MLC) discussed the Sirasgaon case,
adding political ramifications.[6] The Republican Party of India held many
rallies across Maharashtra to protest the event. People composed songs
about Sirasgaon. The social circulation of information occurred at the
intersection of diverse rhetorical registers—legal, journalistic, activist—
of publicity around "Sirasgaon." These produced the multiple, refracted,
and incomplete narrative that constituted Sirasgaon as a scandal.

Why focus on the texts of law? What important labor did court judgments perform? As we will see, it was through the individualizing mechanism of the court proceedings that Sirasgaon gained notoriety as scandal.
Scandal straddles the terrain of secrecy and publicity, exposing routine
events that most people would know, yet about which they profess ignorance. Individualizing what is often a systemic issue, the scandal—like
the legal case—can make visible regnant structures of violence. According to S., the Sirasgaon incident originated in a quarrel over access to com-

mon water, one of the stereotypical "causes" of daily caste conflict. The sense that very little unusual had happened was initially promoted by the women victims themselves, who gave a first account describing only verbal abuse (*shivi dene*), and not sexual humiliation. Shame legitimized the public lie that "nothing happened," but it also offered a path for male activists of the Dalit community to focus on caste violation rather than multiple enactments of sexual humiliation. The court records, however, traced a complex circuit of desire, transgression, and retribution played out between a Dalit family, the Sirsats, and a Maratha employer, Yedu Kale. In fact, it is not far-fetched to cast this scene of seduction and subjection as a ritualized performance of sexual humiliation, which can be reconstructed as a form of political violence, as *caste violence*.

THE COURT, THE FAMILY DRAMA, AND EUPHEMISM

This is the story of Sirasgaon as a legal narrative, as a story created by and for the law. On December 22, 1963, four Dalit women were dragged out of their home, stripped, and paraded naked in the village of Sirasgaon, in Gangapur *taluka*, Aurangabad district. Six months earlier, one of the women, Sonabai Sirsat, had carried breakfast for her brother-in-law, Kishan, an agricultural laborer. She encountered Yedu Kale, a Maratha landlord who employed Kishan. Taking advantage of the fact that Sonabai was alone, Yedu Kale propositioned her. "Yedu is said to have shown her money and held her *Padar*."

Sonabai told her mother-in-law, Laxmibai, about the incident. Both went to see Yedu's wife, Shevantibai, to complain to her about her husband's misbehavior. She asked them not to make the matter public. Months later, Kishan decided to leave Yedu's employ. He visited Shevantibai at that time to remind her of the incident with Sonabai and asked Shevantibai "to imagine what she would have felt if Kishan himself was to touch her Sari or to outrage her modesty."[7] By asking her to empathize with a woman who had neither caste status nor privilege, Kishan drew attention to Shevantibai's vulnerability *as a woman*. He was also asserting that he, like Yedu Kale, could make a woman aware of her sexual vulnerability. Dalit laborer or not, Kishan appeared to be saying that he was capable of harassing Shevantibai as a man.

Shevantibai clearly felt insulted and "spoke about it to her husband with some relishments." On December 22, Yedu Kale and a group of men went to Kishan's hut armed with sticks, demanding to see him. Kishan was away. When his father asked the reason for the mens' visit, "He was told that Kishan had played mischief with his [Yedu's] wife."[8] Yedu began to beat Kishan's father, Vithal Amrita, as Kishan's brothers, Mohan and Lahanu, ran away. Kishan's mother, Laxmibai, was also beaten, and her sari was removed by Asaram Dada Agale. Two others, Tukaram Bhika Kale and Tukaram Dashrath Sirsat, removed Sonabai's sari. The two naked women were then dragged toward the village from their home in the so-called Baudhwada on its outskirts. About this time, another group of men, six or seven in number, rushed into Kishan's hut and dragged his sisters-in-law, Kadubai and Sakrabai, outdoors, where they were also beaten and disrobed. The women were paraded to the *ves* (entrance to the village) while being beaten with sticks. On the way, they stopped at Yedu's house so that his wife, Shevantibai, could see them. The four women returned home later that day covered by a single sari that one of the perpetrators had thrown toward them.

Yedu's act of revenge mirrors his initial act. He had touched or pulled Sonabai's sari, an action countered by Kishan's conversation with Yedu's wife, Shevantibai. Disrobing the women and exhibiting them to Shevantibai suggested that Yedu was quite capable of protecting his wife and humiliating the Sirsat women. This is the kernel of the Sirasgaon even. The scandal at whose core is a public secret that reveals underlying structure of caste sociality.[9] Rape, the stripping and parading of women, and other forms of gendered humiliation reproduce upper-caste male privilege. Sexual violence is particularly indecipherable as *caste* violence because it is normalized as upper-caste privilege and experienced as an unspeakable form of intimate humiliation. Secrecy around sexual violence is doubly inflected. Perpetrators do not conceive it as violation except when they encounter resistance, in which case they brutally assert their rights. Its victims experience humiliation as gendered violence and as collective punishment of the family and community.

The Sirasgaon scandal illuminated structuring violence—its role in producing and reproducing stigmatized existence—as the (hidden) ontology of caste, which became evident through the individualized theatricality of caste crime. The proper name "Sirasgaon" memorializes violence that was the result of deep structures of caste discrimination crystallized into a conflict between victims and perpetrators. Through the court case, seduction and subjection—or the ritualized performance of sexual humiliation—was also illuminated as a form of political violence, as *caste violence*. Thus the oddly reticent statement in the newspaper *Marathwada*, "*Sirasgavat ghadu naye te ghadala. Sarvanchi man sharamene khali zhukavi* [In Sirasgaon, something that should have never happened occurred. Everyone should hang their head in shame"].[10] This statement can be read as shame at the public acts of stripping and humiliating the women, and as acknowledgment that sexual violence solidified upper-caste patriarchal power. The peculiar structure of the public secret was also reflected in the judge's comments: first, that "one cannot say that the thing must have happened altogether," and later, that "[the motive] has come forward in a distorted manner."[11] The uncertain status of sexual violence as caste violence derived from the structures of caste patriarchy that justified it, and from its association with practices of secrecy and intimacy.

It is important that the Sirasgaon case was not registered under the Untouchability (Offences) Act and that its handling as a case shows only incipient awareness of the legal category of caste crime. Though cases involving anti-Dalit violence were categorized as caste crimes under the Untouchability (Offences) Act, public awareness of these laws was still underdeveloped. "Caste atrocity" had yet to become a full legal entity. In addition, as is apparent from official records, collusion between local police, bureaucrats, and caste Hindu participants meant that ultimately, caste crime could be obscured by local indifference and legal proceduralism. Finally, laws to protect Dalit victims could impart a spurious legitimacy to treating stigmatized existence as the status quo, further compounding the difficulty of perceiving differential forms of burdened personhood.

Two actions, however, reveal Dalit political sensibility about the Sirasgaon incident: first, Kishan's challenge to Yedu's harassment of Sonabai, and then the Sirsats' immediate move to publicize the event beyond the confines of the village by calling in the police, the law, and RPI activists. When the women returned home, they sent a neighbor to the village of Malunja, about a mile away, to contact their relatives. One relative rushed to Sirasgaon, and then went to Gangapur, the *taluka* headquarters about six miles away, to consult members of the RPI before writing an application to inform the police subinspector (PSI) of the violence. The subinspector entered the incident in the station diary and then went to Sirasgaon with the relative and an RPI activist.

In Sirasgaon, the subinspector drew up a *panchnama* (record of the incident and victims' testimony witnessed by at least five people). He recorded all four women's comments together as one consolidated statement. The *panchnama* contained no mention of the women's injuries and, oddly enough, repeatedly noted, "besides this nothing else happened." The subinspector then told his constables to escort the four women and Kishan's father, Vithal Amrita, to the medical officer in Gangapur. But they were not taken to Gangapur that night; the subinspector sent a message calling their bullock cart back. A constable by name of Salunkhe later testified that a meeting of caste Hindu notables at the *gram panchayat,* or village council, office that evening had resolved to bribe Vithal Amrita so that he would not register the incident with police.[12] Clearly the subinspector was aware of this meeting, since he called the cart back from its journey to Gangapur.

The cultural critic D. R. Nagaraj has described how Dalits' political awareness changes the political economy of village social life: "The crucial fact is that the upper caste society does everything in its imagination and power to seek solution of the dispute within the confines of the village, but the Dalits are stubborn in their refusal to accept this and they seek the active intervention of not only the instruments of justice, but the involvement of the activists outside the village."[13] The turn to state law is an act of delocalization that expands the domain of action and intervention, while simultaneously intensifying processes of localization through antiatrocity legislation and large-scale Dalit politicization. As I noted in the previous chapter, the split mimics the representation of the state as ideological unity *and* as a set of dispersed or divided bureaucratic powers, with implications for caste violence at two levels: violence understood both as local antagonism and as the structural entailment of Dalit politicization. After the Sirasgaon incident, the Sirsats used state law to circumvent village prejudice and community relations. That is, they drew the attention of the local RPI leader to the incident and sought access to law as a site of redress. Just as important, one of Vithal's sons, Mohan, suspected the subinspector's integrity and filed another application about the stripping. Only then, two days after the incident, did the subinspector investigate it as a cognizable offense that required a police inquiry and a medical examination of the injured women. Mohan's persistence, along with the support of RPI activists, led to the case being filed. The charges involved rioting, intent to hurt, house trespass, and outraging the modesty of a woman. By December 26, all ten accused were arrested.

The judgment of the *taluka* court magistrate notes, "The application which is registered by the PSI contains a paragraph showing that *the case of parading was not mentioned earlier because the ladies were bashful of disclosing the same.* However, it is the case of Mohan that this paragraph was added only at the insistence of PSI Patil."[14] Mohan testified that PSI Patil had made him change his original application to include a paragraph stating that the women had been too ashamed to mention the stripping to the subinspector who first investigated the incident. Patil then used the alibi of female modesty to cover up his own procedural lapse.

In court testimony, the accused introduced the scenario that S. recalled: the women had been injured while bringing water through the village. They suggested that a scuffle had ensued when *savarnas* (caste Hindus) had protested against the Dalit women walking through the village after taking water from the main well.[15] Yedu Kale made contradictory statements. At one point he said that he had visited Kishan to inquire about his absence from work and to retrieve a two-hundred-rupee loan. At another point, he argued that he had been home entertaining a potential bride's family. Six of the accused said they were in their fields or working outside Sirasgaon. All maintained that they had been arrested based on false allegations made at the behest of Asaram Bhusare, with whom Yedu Kale had a long-lasting feud and who was described as being in league with the "harijans." Asaram Bhusare, the *upasarpanch* (deputy village head) of Sirasgaon, had a sister who had been deserted by Yedu Kale some fifteen years earlier. Personal animosity between Yedu and Asaram Bhusare was suggested as the reason behind the Sirasgaon charges. By this point, intimate ties of kinship, marriage, and community were thoroughly saturated with local political signification.[16]

The magistrate of the *taluka* court rejected the alibi of factionalism and the argument that the Sirsat women were injured in a scuffle when they tried to bring water from the village. Although the case was not registered under the Untouchability (Offences) Act, the magistrate acknowledged the vulnerability of the "poor harijans" while chastising the subinspector's judgment: "PSI Patil had terribly erred in his duty when he tried to shelter the accused and minimise the offense as much as possible. The high principle of social equality for the poor harijans who were at the mercy of the other villagers was in my [the judge's] opinion trampled upon without any regard to modesty or humanity." The judge desired to put down this "animal instinct."[17]

C. J. Dighe, appellate judge of the Aurangabad District and Sessions Court, affirmed the ruling. The accused were sentenced to forty-three months imprisonment and a fine of Rs. 300. Vithal Amrita was to get Rs. 1,000 in damages. Dighe accepted the fact that the social world of Sirasgaon was casteist and that it was perfectly possible that the women had been disciplined for a caste infraction. He argued, "Actually the prosecution need not prove any motive. We have to look to the circumstances and other evidence for finding the guilt."[18] Sympathetic to the Dalit women, Dighe spent a great deal of his judgment addressing the social conditions that made anti-Dalit violence possible:

> It is said that it looks very unnatural that no person came forward and no human being should be there to help the poor ladies. It is further said that the case about parading the ladies is unbelievable, inasmuch as, they are alleged to have been taken through the streets lined with number of houses and it seems improbable that no inmate of the house not even a female one should come forward for their rescue. The argument is worth considera-tion. If the incident has happened, its tragic effect is heightened because no one has dared to come forward for helping the poor women. Instead of, therefore, coming to the conclusion that since no one came to their rescue, the whole story is concocted, it would be better to analyse the evidence on record . . . to find out why the bystanders could not have come ahead for succour. It is here that the complexion of communal tension or the com-munal aspect has to be rightly appreciated. However much one may say that Harijans are living in cordial atmosphere, the very suggestion given by the defence that they were subjected to attack because they used a pro-hibited road while carrying water pots goes to give an insight into the mind of the so called Hindus of higher strata.[19]

Dighe was comfortable with a general, sociological explanation of caste crime. But how did he interpret the complex family drama that ap-pears to have motivated the violence? Why were the women stripped and paraded? Dighe thought that explanation would prove difficult, but he did propose that when Kishan spoke to Shevantibai in a suggestive fash-ion, he "lower[ed] the prestige and status of an influential agricultural-ist [Yedu]." Dighe added that four of the accused were "rich and in-fluential" persons. He was skeptical, however, of the Dalits' claims about the origin of the incident:

> The social conditions of the Harijans could not be said to be as yet any way much better than what they were previously when they were called and believed untouchables. It is not unlikely, therefore, that Yedu should flurry up into a rage when a boy like Kishan had the audacity to enquire with Shevantibai in a straightforward manner making humiliating sugges-tions as to what she would feel if he were to outrage her modesty. . . . The alleged incident with Sonabai which is denied by the defence took place some six months back. Yedu is said to have shown her money and held her *Padar* [the edge of the sari that wraps around the breasts and hangs down]. According to Sonabai and Laxmibai they complained to Shevantibai [Yedu's wife] who asked them not to make the matter public. *One cannot say that the thing must have happened altogether.*[20]

Dighe was unwilling to believe that Yedu might have harassed Sonabai, but he was quite comfortable interpreting the transaction between Kishan and Shevantibai as an insult to Yedu's prestige. Imagining himself in the prominent agriculturalist's position of privilege allowed Dighe to interpret Kishan's actions as a challenge to Yedu's control over his wife and to his status as an upper-caste landlord. The sessions court judge may have professed some uncertainty about why the women were targeted for humiliation, but there was no doubt in his mind about tensions between Harijans and Hindus in Sirasgaon. He dissociated sexual violence from public practices of untouchability, however:

> Perhaps it is possible to interpret that both the sides are not making full breast of the previous incident if any. When one bears in mind that the ladies were more subjected to attack and humiliation, it is not unlikely that something connected with the females may have happened, and yet it has not come forward before the Court in so many words, I would be blamed for making a guess work but I am saying this only *to disprove the suggestion that the motive does not exist. Perhaps it has come forward in a distorted manner.*[21]

The distortion was an effect of the use and abuse of legal categories. Because they did not fit standard descriptions of caste crime—denial of access to roads or common water taps—sexual violence and expressions of caste masculinity were illegible as caste crime.[22] Dighe applied the "know it when I see it" model of untouchability practices. He saw clearly that the crime was committed in order to uphold caste stigma, affirming the commonsense understanding of the Dalit as someone who suffers disabilities because she/he is already a Dalit. As the judge noted, "It is here that the complexion of communal tension or the communal aspect has to be rightly appreciated."[23] He assumed the prevalence of a caste habitus, and his judgment hinged on the idea of a caste mind at work. Yet the crime against the Sirsat family was not quite a caste crime, not "in so many words."

What are the consequences of such reasoning? Like progressive judges, protective laws seek to render Dalit bodies commensurable, that is, to equalize them by redressing their stigmatized status. These efforts at commensuration fail, however, because the Dalit is not only a political or juridical subject. The Dalit's encoded identity as injured subject invokes elements outside politics, elements of the archaic—culture or religion—that cannot be legislated away. This creates an impasse in justice, which is also manifest at the level of the mundane and the procedural. Its effect is a denial of justice due to the inscrutability of sexual violence and humiliation *as caste crime*. Dighe's judgment reflects this impasse by shuttling between a sort of Gandhian moral outrage for protecting poor Harijans, on the one hand, and his focus on the technical and procedural missteps of the police, on the other. Thus, when we expect a judgment wholly based on procedural inconsistency, such as the errors of PSI Patil, Dighe suddenly poses the problem of how to do away with the social evil of untouchability or attempts to read motive by positing "caste mind" at work in rural Marathwada.

In fact, PSI Patil's missteps did become the defining feature of the case. Though he was animated by a sense of social justice, Dighe focused his arguments on behalf of victims confronted with an *errant police machinery* that colluded with the accused to produce *procedural inconsistencies*. A half-spoken understanding of the conditions of possibility for the Sirasgaon incident was transformed into a language of procedure and evidence inflected by moral outrage. Dighe's judgment couldn't comprehend sexual violation as constituting caste violence. Describing the Sirasgaon incident as a tragedy, he addressed untouchability as a moral rather than a political problem. As he noted, "If the incident has happened, *its tragic effect is heightened because no one has come forward for helping the poor women.*"[24] Condemning the immorality of stripping the women obviates a *political* reading of the relationships of caste privilege and patriarchy solidified through the humiliation of the women, an important matter to which we will return.

Does the invisibility of sexual violence matter when the courts produced a progressive judgment in favor of the Sirsats? From my perspective, it does, because the unique legal status of caste crime reveals a consequential bifurcation at the core of antiatrocity legislation. Anti-Dalit violence was conceived of as socially motivated against a vulnerable collective, the result of a prejudice so deep that it structured and normalized everyday social relations between Dalits and caste Hindus. Legislation against anti-Dalit violence challenged such social common sense. It was premised on the idea that law had the power to transform caste sociality because it could disarticulate the violence deeply embedded within social life and bring it to the surface as "crime." A crime, however, is adjudicated by individualizing victims and perpetrators and by following through on procedures that rely on a limited range of specifiably legal facts governed by ideas of what constitutes "good" evidence, especially with regard to motive. Though animated by a sense of social justice, Dighe was constrained by these limits: he focused on how an errant police machinery and the corruption of a PSI resulted in procedural inconsistencies and injustice against the Sirsats.

Here we might note affinities between the individualizing of the court case and the individualizing of the public scandal as shared forms of publicity: in each case, publicity has the capacity to render the banal exceptional, thus producing an almost illicit glimpse of the order of things. Both the court case and the public scandal individualize a stretch of human action as out of the ordinary, yet bring to the surface the "unknown well-known" of ever-present deep structures of caste sociality and violation.

The difference between everyday practice and expert knowledge is not only a difference in power, but also in perception. The contextual and the conventional are different semiotic dimensions: the former privileges perceptual distinctions valued in daily life, those of "common sense" or what Bourdieu refers to as *doxa*; while the conventional recesses singularity by privileging sequence, pattern, and regularity. The legal process of generalizing instances of violence into types of crime also incorporates singular acts into conventions of penal categorization.[25] In "Sirasgaon," governmental efforts to acknowledge social reality and translate the experiential everyday of caste violence into crime, was successful in generating publicity and visibility for the "new" category of caste violence. What we recognize clearly as ritualized humiliation and public exhibition of gendered vulnerability was occluded by judicial narratives of crime and victimhood in which the constitutive fact of sexual violation remained invisible and unsayable.

PERFORMATIVE VIOLENCE AT THE *VES*

If the sexualized frames of revenge and retribution found no adequate legal representation, could they be spoken at all? On May 4, 1997, I met with one of the Sirsat women, whom I call Y. She was living outside Sirasgaon in a government slum development where Dalit and Muslim homes sat side by side. An RPI activist introduced me, saying that I wanted to "discuss the incident [*ghatane baddal bolayca ahe*]," before leaving us alone. Y. was astonished and repeatedly asked why I was interested in something so old. How did I even know about it? When I told her about my extended search for the legal judgments, she sat down and looked off thoughtfully into the distance and then gestured for me to sit.

The Sirasgaon incident remained symbolically charged, thirty years after the fact. Y. wouldn't look at my face, her eyes fixed somewhere beyond me as she began to speak without any questions or interjections from me. She spoke about the men who had come to the Sirsat hut, and she pointed to her breasts and sari, saying "they removed this [*he sagale kadle*]," unable to speak directly about what happened. She talked about being dragged outside her house and through the village to the *ves,* her hands gesturing wildly to the various parts of her body that had been beaten by the men. The traumatic incident was vividly etched in the woman's memory, though none of her grown children knew about it. They knew, however, that she never wanted to visit the village of Sirasgaon and that they were also prohibited from doing so. Revisiting the incident resuscitated her humiliation and, more importantly, the fear of continued reprisal. At our first meeting, she noted bitterly that many people had come to speak with the Sirsat women when the incident first occurred, but that there had been hell to pay after the activists left. When I visited Y.'s home a few days later, she did not want to discuss the incident further.

As I demonstrated in chapter 5, when a political context enables violence to become a site for staging and challenging identities, such political violence can also transform context, creating and destroying frames of intelligibility. The semantic excess of political violence reveals and transforms symbolic formations of body, community, and history. I attend to an aspect of "Sirasgaon" almost overlooked in court in order to understand the women's humiliation as the performative violence of symbolic forms, where sexual humiliation represents the archaic within modern repertoires of violence. I do so by attending to the public exhibition of the women at the *ves.* By this route, we can explore the place of sexual humiliation within a social-symbolic order without compromising the specific identity (and traumatic experience) of the subject of violence.

In most villages in Marathwada, the residential area for Dalits, called the Maharwada or Baudhwada, is usually located at the southern end of the village, and it is almost always outside the village boundary. In Sirasgaon, the Maharwada abutted the southeast. A government primary school sat along the eastern side of the village boundary, along with a separate hand pump that was used by Mahar Dalits and other lower castes. I gathered, on my visit to Sirasgaon, that Dalits there were not in the habit of celebrating Ambedkar's birthday. Nor did his bust sit next to a figure of the Buddha, something I had come to expect from visits to other villages.

In most of the Marathwada villages I visited during 1996–97, the *ves* was close to a temple to Maruti or Hanuman. This was usually an open-air structure with a large stone image of Maruti installed at its center and painted a metallic saffron or dabbed with the *haldi* and *kumkum* (turmeric and vermilion) used for religious worship. In Sirasgaon, the *ves* was located in the northwestern quadrant of the village and required a walk through the village if one was to get to it from the Maharwada. The Sirasgaon *ves* comprised two large blocks of black stone about three feet apart. In conversation, I was told that animal sacrifices often took place at the *ves*, with the meat being shared between the villagers.

The *ves* is a ritually charged space. According to *Molesworth's Marathi Dictionary*, the *ves* (f) is "1. The gate of a village; 2. (Because it used to be enforced by closing the gates) payment of the government revenue; 3. A gate or door of a yard or other enclosure." Thus, a *veskar* is "the person appointed to keep the gate of a village. He is usually a Mahar. His nightly patrol around the village is known as *gast ghalne.*" This ties the Mahar caste to guarding the village boundary[26] and presents the *veskar* as the excommunicated figure who reinforces village solidarity.

The Sirasgaon incident resurrected the historically significant centrality of the *ves*, a symbolic boundary that both marked off the village from the public world and reaffirmed the Mahar's role in consolidating village solidarity. As the next chapter makes clear, the significance of the Mahar *veskar* as a boundary-marking figure was related to memories of a precolonial past when Mahars were sacrificed at the threshold of forts or villages to commemorate military conquest. Parading the women around the *ves* overturned this historical relationship between *ves* and Mahar. If the male *veskar* protected the village to guarantee the normal village order, the women's humiliation at the *ves* was a sign that things were out of place. At a moment of crisis, "tradition" was reversed. Marking the village boundary through the women's bodies and then parading the women around the *ves* in the daytime symbolically reconstituted a *threatened* village solidarity and performed a collective punishment of Dalits occasioned by improper interpenetration of the Kale and Sirsat family dramas. An especially humiliating form of public chastisement, the events at the *ves* also emasculated the men of the Sirsat family, who were unable to protect their women.

The Sirasgaon incident challenged the traditional order. Though upper-caste Marathas had shamed the women to reassert their hegemony, they deserted the village when the "atrocity" became public. Everyone did. The Sirsat family left Sirasgaon to escape the vengeance of the upper castes. They became migrant laborers working in the sugarcane fields of southern Maharashtra. The involved Maratha families left the village to live on their agricultural lands. Rather than preserving village solidarity at the *ves*, the incident transformed the social order because of its notoriety and the involvement of the police and Dalit activists. Instead of burying violence more deeply within a seemingly consensual structure of upper-caste privilege and Dalit subordination, the women's ritualized humiliation revealed deep social cleavages and politicized violence. The symbolic significance of the *ves* remained intact. However, the archaic siting of violent humiliation brought forth a response that reveals the effects of state and Dalit politicization in altering communal solidarities.

While this understanding of the Sirasgaon spectacle reminds us of the continued symbolization of the Dalit body through violence, it also points beyond itself. How do gender, caste, and sexuality together structure the inscrutability of particular forms of violence and humiliation?

CASTE AND THE SEXUAL ECONOMY

Where society is already well-knit by other ties, marriage is an ordinary incident of life. But where society is cut asunder, marriage as a binding force becomes a matter of urgent necessity. *The real remedy for breaking Caste is inter-marriage. Nothing else will serve as the solvent of Caste.*

B. R. Ambedkar, *The Annihilation of Caste*, in *BAWS*, vol. 1, 67

In arguing that intercaste marriage could eradicate caste, B. R. Ambedkar highlighted the critical role of female sexuality in the reproduction of caste.[27] In addition to the ban on intercaste marriage, *sati* (enforced widowhood) and child marriage regulated the lives of upper-caste women, all mechanisms Ambedkar thought maintained the ratio between men and women by ridding the system of "surplus" women. The structural functionalism of Ambedkar's early account of caste and sexuality notwithstanding, he saw that caste power was gendered and he addressed how sexual regulation reproduced caste relations. His profound investment in the Hindu Code Bill reflects Ambedkar's long-held views of the constitutive relationship between caste and sexual regulation. The call for intercaste marriage was an effort to reconceive the relationship between Hindu marriage and the caste order. It remains a radical intervention to this day.[28] Marriage was a hinge, articulating the social and sexual orders, but it also regulated sexuality through caste norms. Intercaste marriages were intrinsically political acts because they acknowledged desire between castes. Unlike informal sexual relations against which

Dalit activists had virulently campaigned, intercaste marriage was a sanctioned transgression.

Ambedkar's commitment to defining intercaste marriages as Hindu marriages, instead of as civil marriages registered under the Special Marriages Act, is significant. He envisioned that by breaking the association of women with the reproduction of caste community, intercaste marriage would annihilate caste distinctions. We can appreciate the strategic significance of keeping intercaste marriage as *Hindu* marriage when we recognize that intercaste marriage asserted the sanctity of marriage as a social form, but recalibrated the relationship between caste and gender from *within* the institution of marriage. Intercaste marriage would annihilate caste by rewriting the sexual contract.

The legacy of anticaste critique is heterogeneous and discontinuous: it contains critical as well as status quo perspectives on gender and sexuality. Despite Ambedkar's perspicacious discussion of the relationship between caste and sexuality, he also largely conceived the Dalit political subject as male. Female persons played important roles in political action and collective protest to be sure, but they were also held to bourgeois conceptions of respectability and female propriety.[29] The history of Dalit emancipation charted in this book addresses caste masculinity as a neglected issue, one pursued in powerful critiques by Dalit feminists today.[30] In chapter 1, however, I cautioned against assimilating this critique into existing paradigms of the feminist subject. As a consequence of appropriating colonial-Brahminical paradigms of autonomy and self-sovereignty that assumed an upper-caste, male subject of rights, Dalit and non-Brahmin political subject-formation predicated the upward mobility of Dalit and lower-caste men on the reform of family and of female subjects. Thus, Ambedkar's critique of caste and gender regulation, while it focused on the reproduction of upper-caste male privilege through the control of gendered bodies, also has important implications for challenging the historical association of gender control with community identity. Rather than proposing a model of female enfranchisement that posits the political rights of women against the authority of community—the general model of female suffrage—Ambedkar suggests a mechanism to dissolve the identity of "community" through intercaste marriage and thus secure the sexual rights of women *as political rights*. Ambedkar's focus on intercaste marriage is a foil against which to reconsider the sexual reproduction of caste power.

Upper-caste women were prominently regulated. What happened, however, to Dalit and lower-caste women who were not governed by ritually prescribed forms of social death and corporal violence? By what mechanisms were they disciplined? Dalit and lower-caste women have long suffered sexual violation as caste exploitation and forced sexual labor. As a Satnami (Chamar) said, "The upper castes would not touch us. They would never eat with us. But they were always ready to fornicate. For 'doing it' our women were not untouchable. . . . Even after licking the private parts of Satnami women, they would not lose their purity."[31] In fact, sexual violence performed a pedagogical function in socializing men and women, Dalit and caste Hindu alike, into caste norms. The specific relationship of stigmatized existence with sexed subjectivity accentuates the consistent illegibility of sexual violence as caste violence, even as it renders sexual violation a definitive aspect of gendered Dalit personhood. The paradox of sexual violation as constitutive of female identity and invisible to categorization is precisely what makes the Sirasgaon case so troubling. This is reflected in the event's performed specificity—the stripping and parading of Dalit women at the *ves*—together with its generic banality—another case of violence against women. One way to address the paradox is to examine the sexual economy of caste as a specific instance of the sexual contract.

The anthropologist Claude Lévi-Strauss famously argued that marriage lay at the interface of nature and culture and that it was animated by the logic of gift exchange, which produced a traffic in women between wife givers and wife takers: social status derived from sexual commerce. In traditional studies of kinship, the incest taboo is the origin of permissible sex, while sexual exchange produces social intimacy between strangers. As feminist critics of Lévi-Strauss have noted, the mythic charter for the emergence of sexual/social order in Western societies, the Oedipus myth, is a narrative of *family violence* through which the narrative of subject-formation and sexual difference are conjoint. For instance in the classic Freudian reading, the man's desire for the mother also propels identification (and conflict) with the father. Meanwhile, the lack of the penis and desire for the father force the daughter to accommodate herself to "lesser rights" from childhood. Jacques Lacan's argument that language is structured by desire and lack, and by the symbolic order of law, rendered virtual what in Freud remained a set of associations between biological difference and sexed subjectivity. This allows us to see that the Freudian family drama is less a literal description of existing conditions than the staging of a paradigmatic moment when nature is transformed into culture, a thought experiment through which Western societies produce a narrative about sociosexual order. One can remain agnostic, even critical about the implied universality of this form, while simultaneously acknowledging the model's power to connect sexual subordination with heterosexual desire.[32] One may also note that unlike—and in opposition to—commodity exchange, sexual exchange is typically read in two ways, as prepolitical *and* as inaugurating political society. Kinship is understood to be the chronologically anterior, primitive version of political citizenship.[33]

Of what use are theories of the relationship between sexual exchange and social formation in addressing the specific economy of caste? Caste is the effect of sexual regulation. Therefore, sexual relationships within and between caste communities are a nodal point through which caste supremacy is reproduced or challenged. Sexual desire and violence *across* caste is the constitutive outside to the regulatory order of caste and kinship. Thus the sexual economy of caste is complex: it prohibits all men from viewing all women as potential sexual partners, but also gives upper-caste men the right to enjoy Dalit and lower-caste women. Indeed, knowledge of this is a public secret, normalized as privilege by the upper castes and experienced as a shameful secret by its victims. Sexual violence is a negative but necessary effect of ideas regarding caste purity and social respectability that regulate the normative caste order. This is because caste hegemony is secured in two ways: by regulating caste respectability and by justifying flagrant transgression as a form of upper-caste privilege. The doubled economy of caste is at work in the exchange of women within the caste community and in an informal circuit of sexual liason with women seen as always-already amenable to sexual violation as a right. The putatively closed circuit of marriage and respectability is thus destabilized by this "other" economy of sexual violation/pleasure that equates caste privilege with the availability of lower-caste women as upper-caste property.[34] Although marriage regulates caste purity to some degree, the sexual economy of caste is intrinsically unstable. The problematic permeability of violence and desire, of rape and marriage, intimates that sexual violence *is* caste violence because it operates as the prerogative of upper caste men.[35]

The brutal violence against Dalit men accused of desiring upper-caste women further illuminates the double jeopardy of sexual violence as caste violence. If Dalits' political awareness has intensified caste conflict, the adjudication of the Sirasgaon incident suggests that a crucial but invisible consequence of Dalit politicization is that the desire for upward mobility was recast as a desire for sexual access to upper-caste women. Sirasgaon reenacted an archaic form of punishment for two small acts of resistance perceived as political challenges: Kishan's conversation with

Shevantibai, perceived as an insult to Yedu, and the Sirsat women's efforts to inform Shevantibai of her husband's misbehavior. In addition to everything else, exhibiting the women to Shevantibai reaffirmed the sanctity of upper-caste women as caste property, out of bounds to Dalit and lower-caste men. Just the hint of transgressive desire was catastrophic; it became an alibi for anti-Dalit violence.

The pernicious euphemization of sexual violence as a form of upper-caste, male desire also permits upper castes to imagine that fantasies of sexual possession, or of sexual violation of upper-caste women, are important vectors for consolidating Dalit caste masculinity. Remaining agnostic about the veracity of this assumption, I suggest, rather, that the perverse logic of caste's sexual economy is such that the violation of Dalit women as a matter of right and the violent disciplining of Dalit men are two sides of the same coin. As the Sirasgaon incident reveals, *both* are acts of sexual violence and indices of caste power. This duplicity of caste and sex makes apparent why the specificity of sexual violence is so often lost when it is redefined as caste violence, and why a feminist focus on sexual violence tends to ignore its specificity as violence against *Dalit* women. When sexed subjectivity is joined with stigmatized existence, sexual violence becomes existentially overdetermined and legally inscrutable. We can see below an illustration of the manner in which ideas of personhood and of property can be perverted by violence against Dalit women to reaffirm their identity as *Dalit* and as *Dalit women*. My aim here is to reflect on how a more generic set of arguments about sexual subordination might be operationalized to reflect the specific experience of Dalit women, who are marked by the disabilities of caste and gender.

Ideologies of accumulation →	*Dalit women*	← *Ideologies of caste purity*
Dalit women's sexuality is appropriated as the property of upper-caste men; sexual dispossession becomes an exceptional instance of the generic form of deprivation defining the Dalit family.		The Dalit body signifies a site of potential recurrent violation—a permeability to intimate violence that constitutes sexed subjectivity—because the invisibility of normalized violence arises from its redefinition as upper-caste power.

AFTER SIRASGAON: SEXUAL VIOLENCE AS CASTE VIOLENCE

Despite its scandalous existence as an exceptional event, "Sirasgaon" was not an anomaly. More recent examples of sexual violence show how dominant structures of sexuality and caste sociality—the structuring violence of caste—continue to be exposed in spectacles of violence. More poignantly, they remind us that violence can be reintegrated into social life even in the face of redress and more developed state discourses of "atrocity" than existed in 1963.

The ghastliest incidence of sexual violence in Maharashtra to date is perhaps the massacre of September 29, 2006, in the village of Khairlanji, Bhandara district. The incident began as a land grab by local agriculturalists—of the five acres the Dalit family owned, two acres had been taken over to make way for a road, and the remaining three were in danger of expropriation. It ended with the mutilation and rape of forty-four-year-old Surekha Bhotmange and her teenaged student daughter, Priyanka, and the brutal murder of Surekha's two sons, Roshan and Sudhir, aged nineteen and twenty-one. Again, Khairlanji highlights the paradoxical centrality of sexual violation as a mechanism of caste embodiment as well as the necessity of understanding the specificity of sexual violation through the signifying structures of Dalit stigma. Indeed the event addresses the complex materiality of violence as a political form and a perverse instance of (caste) intimacy.

By all accounts, the Bhotmanges were an upwardly mobile Dalit family. Priyanka was a school topper studying political science and sociology, and one of her brothers was a college graduate; both he and his visually impaired brother earned extra money by working as laborers. Surekha challenged the initial land grab with the help of a cousin. When he was attacked, Surekha identified the attackers and had them arrested. Sadly, these were the same men who returned with others to massacre the Bhotmange family. The family was paraded naked, beaten, stoned, sexually abused, and then murdered by a group of men from the *kunbi* and *kalar* agricultural castes. Surekha and her daughter Priyanka were bitten, beaten black and blue, and gang-raped in full public view for an hour before they died. Iron rods and sticks were later inserted in their genitalia. The private parts and faces of the young men were disfigured. "When the dusk had settled, four bodies of this dalit family lay strewn at the village choupal [square], with the killers pumping their fists and still kicking the bodies. The rage was not over. Some angry men even raped the badly mutilated corpses of the two women."[36] The bodies were later scattered at the periphery of the village.

It took more than a month for the news to spread. Internet discussion groups in the so-called Dalit blogosphere played a vital role. Web versions of the event circulated far and wide, as did photographs of the mutilated bodies of the victims, compensating for the lack of coverage by mainstream news media. Dalit and grassroots organizations such as the Ambedkar Centre for Justice and Peace and the Vidarbha Jan Andolan Samiti filed petitions with the government. By November, photographs of the victims' bodies were pasted on the walls of Dalit *bastis* (residential areas),and large rallies were held in Bhandara, Nagpur, Aurangabad, and Pune. Women's groups staged major rallies, and women came out in large numbers to protest. Police beat protesters and opened fire on crowds at these rallies and killed at least one person in Amravati. Dalit politicians were severely criticized for failing to intervene and seek justice for Dalit victims.[37] What came to light were police cover-up, bureaucratic mishandling, and utter disregard for justice for the victims.[38] Ultimately, all the eleven accused received bail on December 30, 2006, and three of them were acquitted on September 15, 2008. None were prosecuted under the POA Act.[39]

This time around two things were distinctive: the inaction of the Dalits associated with mainstream political parties, and the follow-up to anti-Dalit violence by the counterviolence of Dalits. Media exposure of the Khairlanji incident was closely followed by news that a statue of B. R. Ambedkar had been desecrated in Kanpur, in Uttar Pradesh, which provoked retaliatory violence in Mumbai and elsewhere in Maharashtra. We have seen already that Ambedkar images have played a crucial role in the constitution of a Dalit popular. At stake has been Ambedkar's singular individuality, the agentive power of self-determination to remake the Dalit self and thereby challenge the social invisibility and humiliation to which the community was relegated. Though Ambedkar statues are a social fact in almost every village in Maharashtra, the erection of statues in other parts of the country is more recent. In 1997 alone, fifteen thousand statues of Ambedkar were installed across Uttar Pradesh, provoking widespread conflict with caste Hindus who saw this as a challenge to their hegemony. Thus it is not important whether the Kanpur statue's desecration was indeed the cause of Dalit counterviolence. More significant is the statues' role as symbolic currency in the resignification of public space.

Dalit rage was described in a number of ways as it reverberated across state borders: as a response to the statue's desecration in far-away Kanpur; as retaliation for Khairlanji; and finally, as a symptom of Dalits' deep-rooted anger against an irresponsible and uncaring state. Dalit militancy was transformed from remaking the Dalit self to destroying the images and institutions of caste exclusion: protestors burnt the famous Deccan Queen, the Mumbai-Pune express train that ferries white-collar workers between the two cities and is a symbol of bourgeois, upper-caste respectability; suburban trains were burnt, as were a hundred buses; and there was stone-throwing in cities across the state. That violence was soon followed by an important commemorative event, the fiftieth anniversary of Ambedkar's death. Each anniversary is typically observed in Mumbai on December 6 by up to a million people: many travel ticketless or walk for hundreds of miles, braving hardship and hunger. The event is known for the highly disciplined crowds who visit the consecrated ground, the *chaitya bhoomi,* in Babasaheb's memory.

The portrayal of Dalit rage at this time is significant. The Maharashtra state government showed its deep ignorance about the solemnity of this occasion for Dalits across the country and anticipated further violence on that day. Though nothing happened, fear of a violent Dalit mob was fueled by news media: they predicted a siege of the city, warning that Mumbai residents could be potential victims of Dalit unruliness and random acts of violence. For Dalits, Khairlanji "was the end of imagination," as one activist put it—an apocalyptic event without any adequate frame of representation.[40] For the state machinery, however, the violence of Khairlanji was quickly replaced by the threat of Dalit counterviolence. Sexual violence, the desecration of a statue, Dalit counterviolence, and political commemoration produced a field of signification animated by acts of (symbolic) substitution and overdetermination.

Along with the power of violent reciprocity came heightened sensitivity to sexual violence against Dalit women. By the 1990s, Dalit feminists were arguing that it was impossible to understand the sexual violation of Dalit women except as a recurrent stigmatization of Dalits. They challenged upper-caste feminists for ignorning the central role of caste in regulating female sexuality and sexual access.[41] Sexual violence had thus attained semiotic density as a distinguishing feature of caste violence and a sign of its discursive centrality in framing Dalit identity, even when the meaning and interpretation of violence differed from victims to perpetrators. The violent excess of the Bhotmages' murder and the ritual desecration constituted caste punishment through the symbolic degradation of gendered Dalit bodies.

In attributing to violence a purely instrumental or utilitarian function—seeing it as a reaction to Dalit economic mobility or political mobilization of Dalits—we ignore the fact that violence continues regardless of efficacy because it is also pedagogical instruction in a symbolic order obscured by modern state forms and discourses. The brutal ritual desecration of the gendered Dalit body is a technology of violence that resurrects archaic forms of sexual violence and punishment in direct proportion to the politicization of Dalits. From Sirasgaon to Khairlanji then, the state action of defining the vulnerable Dalit subject and outlawing her violation has been met by counterresponse on the "creative" semiotic ground of violation and violence that relocates struggles over Dalit identity to streets, homes, and to spaces otherwise invisible to the state's modern, nonarchaic glance. From "Sirasgaon," an early atrocity in which the legal armature to name, contain, and control the field of popular representation was nascent, to this more recent case governed by the 1989 Prevention of Atrocities Act, the extremity of violence suggests that its symbolic significance and semiotic density are deepened as a consequence of the politicization of violence.[42]

CHAPTER 7

Death of a *Kotwal*

The Violence of Recognition

On August 17, 1991, Ambadas Sawane, a *kotwal* in the village of Pimpri Deshmukh in Parbhani district, Maharashtra, was bludgeoned to death on the steps of a Hanuman temple.[1] As police investigated, activists from political parties, from the Shiv Sena to Congress to the RPI, state government functionaries, and village locals produced their own contentious and often conflicting readings of the murder. All had one point in common: everyone agreed Sawane was killed because he was a Dalit. The brutality of the murder and its symbolic resonance with earlier instances of *mandir pravesh* (temple entry) generated a great deal of publicity. It was the first case in Maharashtra to be judged under the Prevention of Atrocities Act of 1989, which prescribes stringent punishment for caste violence.

In his judgment, delivered at the Parbhani Sessions Court, Justice Adharkar held that Sawane was the victim of a caste crime. Even though the immediate motive for the murder appeared to be upper-caste retaliation for Sawane's "desecration" of their Hanuman temple, Adharkar focused instead on Sawane's attempts to install an Ambedkar statue in the village, drawing attention to how Dalit politicization had affected the context of caste sociality. Out of ten accused, Adharkar found five individuals guilty of bludgeoning Sawane to death. He let them off lightly and argued that intent to murder could not be established. Of the five men acquitted, two were state functionaries charged with protecting citizens: the police *patil* (head of village police), Kishore Marathe, was accused of inciting the violence, and the *sarpanch* (elected village head) was accused of being negligent in his duties.

My analysis of caste atrocity comprises two arguments. First, the failure of justice derives not solely from the monumental problems of implementation, but also from the understanding of vulnerable personhood that drives exceptional laws, that is, from the fact that Dalit equality is set up to operate through legal exceptionalism.[2] Second, we can best make sense of the violence surrounding this exceptional subject by addressing the displacements between law, politics, and everyday life that make a violent act, an atrocity, the occasion for further politicization.

As we saw in chapter 4, the law produces objectified categories that are contested and thrown back into the legal arena in a cycle of exchange that grounds acts of recognition. To examine Sawane's murder and the publicity, trial, and judgment that followed is to address this meeting of progressive laws and local caste relationships, to show how juridical assumptions about Dalit vulnerability are refracted through political struggles that can unsettle the contexts and conventions of a caste civility created in the governmental imagination. The first zone of contact in the Sawane case was the policing function.

POLICE PROCEDURE, PUBLICITY, AND POLITICAL VIOLENCE

Unlike the Sirsat case in Sirasgaon, Sawane's murder from the start presented inescapable political implications within a milieu of increasingly confident Dalit political assertion. Like Sirasgaon, this case engaged the bifurcated nature of antiatrocity legislation that, on one hand, recognized anti-Dalit violence as springing from a prejudice so deep that it structured and normalized everyday social relations and, on the other hand, proposed to disarticulate such deeply embedded violence simply by redefining habituated actions as crimes. Communicative technologies such as police wireless (radio) records make visible an informational grid, a structure of publicity and internal communication that included discussion within the chain of command, responses to government functionaries in Bombay, and negotiations with political activists and the media that trace how the police developed the case.

On the night of August 16, Sawane's family found him lying in a pool of blood outside the temple. His brother Kachru took him to the police outpost at Tadkalas by bullock cart. A police constable then took Sawane to the Primary Health Centre, which referred him to Parbhani's Civil Hospital, where he died soon after arrival. The next day, Kachru filed a First

Information Report that was critical in bringing the murder to the attention of the authorities.[3] As a result, five men were taken into custody.
Two were Marathas and three were Malis. According to a September issue of the Marathi newspaper *Loksatta,* all five accused were identified
as Shiv Sena activists.

The police investigation began after Sawane's body was brought home
the next day, on August 17. Due to the severity of the crime, Subdivisional Police Officer (SDPO) Gopalshetty accompanied PSI Kolhapurkar
to conduct the police interrogation. They interviewed key witnesses:
Sawane's father, his brother, a neighbor, his wife Rukminibai, and a
cousin. The accused men from the Maratha and Mali castes were then
taken into custody. By August 19, Sawane's death was recorded by the
PSI under Section 302 of the Indian Penal Code (attempt to murder) and
linked to Section 3(x) of the Protection of Civil Rights Act of 1976. The
addition of the PCR Act's Section 3(x) was mandatory and signaled that
the case merited extra care as an atrocity.

Unfortunately, both Gopalshetty and Kolhapurkar were found to have
sabotaged the investigation by withholding crucial local knowledge. In
a public statement to the press, Gopalshetty had purposefully downplayed
the overdetermined symbology of Dalit homicide on the temple steps.
This was noted in this police wireless record of August 19:

> 7. SDPO from Sailu, S. B. Gopalshetty investigated the offence. After visit
> Gopalshetty saw me, and told me that the incident was not an outcome of
> casteism but it took place all of a sudden. *Gopalshetty also issued a press
> release which states that he met the witnesses, majority of whom were from
> Hindu community and that according to them, the incident took place all
> of a sudden and there is no communal past history to the village.* The press
> note further states that the incident took place due to misunderstanding
> which resulted in exchange of hot words followed by attack on the kotwal
> by the aforesaid five accused, injuring him seriously. . . .
> 8. I feel that . . . [the SDPO] did hurry in issuing the press note which
> was contrary to the very contents of the FIR and also to the facts subse-
> quently revealed during investigation. It was because of this press note
> that the Department and also the Govt. of Maharashtra were put in embar-
> rassing position. Not only this, but it resulted in unnecessary criticism by
> press and various political leaders that the police was partial and hiding
> the truth. From a bare read of the press note, it would be seen that the
> contents of para. 1 indicate that the incident of assault/murder took place
> due to temple-entry by a Mahar, i.e., Dalit, whereas para. 2 of the note
> speaks out all together different story that the incident took place all of
> a sudden due to misunderstanding. . . .
> On the spot enquiry revealed that Gopalshetty did not place true picture

of the incident before me . . . he admitted to not have stated the facts of temple entry by a Mahar kotwal resulting in his murder by caste Hindus [with] an intention of avoiding likely flaming of communal atmosphere and its repercussions.[4]

Gopalshetty told his superior, the superintendent of police in Aurangabad, that drawing attention to Sawane's homicide as a caste crime would have politicized the police investigation. Instead, he had tried to protect already fragile social relations in Pimpri Deshmukh. Ironically, Gopalshetty's own problematic public statement brought unwelcome attention to police practices. The news-reading public would have missed neither Sawane's identity as a Dalit nor the bizarre circumstances of his death. The press report implicated Gopalshetty, but it also placed the police investigation in a climate of suspicion. Together with this, there emerged evidence of complicity between police and a key accused, the police *patil*, Kishore Marathe.

SDPO Parab, who replaced Gopalshetty, conducted a new investigation into the homicide from August 28 to October 28, 1991. He met with witnesses who said that Kishore Marathe had incited the villagers to kill Sawane. According to them, Marathe remained near Sawane and refused to send for help once he was badly wounded. Sawane's father said that when he asked the police *patil* for help, Marathe sneered, "Why don't *you* take him home?" Sawane's father also gave evidence that Sawane had told him, "They have killed me, Bapu," and revealed the names of his killers, including Marathe.[5] Parab's investigation cast doubt on PSI Kolhapurkar's earlier investigation and suggested police negligence. An added irony was that Sawane was himself a *kotwal,* a low-level village police functionary. In Maharashtra, *kotwals* were drawn from the Mahar community, adding to their ritual function as *veskars* who had the duty of patrolling the village at night. Here, the police *patil* was implicated in Sawane's murder and later found to have used his position to protect himself from prosecution.[6] If Sawane's murder was politically motivated, then why did the police *patil* have such animus against him? More significantly, how did such deeply consequential lapses by local police come to light at all?

As we shall see, the contest over how to frame Sawane's murder was both an internal issue between government officers and an external battle of publicity. The local police stationed at the police outpost in Tadkalas reported to the SP in Aurangabad. However, caste and gender crimes were also monitored by the PCR Cell formed in 1988 and headed by a deputy inspector general of police (DIGP) sitting at the Maharashtra State Police Headquarters in Bombay. Sawane's homicide was overseen by the PCR Cell in Bombay, in addition to local police. On August 28, the DIGP sent a wireless to the superintendent in Aurangabad, saying: "One Kachru Sahebarao Sawane, brother of the deceased, was brought by Vivek Pandit [an activist] who says that the Police Patil of the village is the main accused in this case but is not shown as the accused. Similarly the harijans were not allowed to enter the said temple."[7] Another wireless of August 30 repeated this information and asked for a detailed report of the incident.

Such communication indicated a diverse and diffuse field of publicity adjacent to the police chain of command. There was a complex circuitry of debate, negotiation, and compromise among different departments of state and national government, and contingent responses to external political pressure. Bombay headquarters was under scrutiny from a host of interested parties: media, political activists, party leaders, nongovernmental organizations, members of the Legislative Assembly, and government functionaries (including from the National Commission for Scheduled Castes and Scheduled Tribes, from the state and central government's Social Welfare Ministry, and from Maharashtra's Home Department). Local police might have been driven by the dictates of local relations of power and their own position within a caste habitus inimical to Dalits. Starting at the level of activists and local political leaders, however, publicity could unsettle this enclosed world of police investigation. Responses by Bombay and local police illustrate multiple interests and pressures refracted through the police hierarchy.[8] The schisms reveal how contentious the categorization of Sawane's murder had become, but they also illuminate how such fissures enabled a productive space for political negotiation that engaged different strata of the state.

Debate among state functionaries and external political pressure produced this field of publicity. Police wireless reports were a crucial conduit. Their status as confidential communication offers us entry into the conflictual workings of the state apparatus and access to the politicized nature of bureaucratic knowledge. Together and separately, directives from police superiors and communication from local police illuminate "new" demands on the police to make caste crime visible. Thus, we see repeated demands from Bombay for SP Parbhani to provide details of the incident. "I contacted SP on phone yesterday and asked him as to why he has not sent the copies of his reports to me so far. He regretted and said he forgot to endorse a copy of his report to the DIG-PCR. Even now his report is not received."[9] These transactions show how procedural discussions either foreground or ignore the caste dimension of the killing, depending on political pressures exerted on the police. Insofar as wireless reports negotiate this wider social space, they make it apparent that the outcomes of state intervention were contingent products of debate and negotiation between apparatuses of state with divergent, often contradictory, interests.

Even though the police wireless records were constituted as a form of secret communication internal to the police, the information transmitted through these channels was susceptible to the broader worlds of journalistic publicity, rumor, and political activism. A brief exploration of this other circuit sheds light on how the wireless records articulated with, and inflected, police work.

Local police in Pimpri Deshmukh had come up with six potential "causes" for Sawane's murder in the course of their on-the-spot inquiry and witness testimony. These were:

1. something vague and ambiguous called "tradition," which explained why Dalits could not enter the temple and had to stand at the steps to take *darshan*;

2. Sawane's involvement in attempts to install a statue of Ambedkar in the village;

3. Sawane's consumption of large quantities of alcohol, which made him loquacious and gave him the courage to enter the temple and abuse the caste Hindus assembled there [the autopsy found no alcohol in his blood];

4. assertions of an "illicit relation" between Sawane and a woman from Pimpri Deshmukh, which led to a fatal assault on Sawane by the woman's two brothers;

5. Sawane's reported abuse of Maratha villagers, including the police *patil*'s wife;

6. a preplanned human sacrifice.

This set of motives constructed by local police took village rumors at face value and initially gave all possibilities equal weight. They meshed with various newspaper statements by political party leaders and with popular rumor regarding the event. For instance, Advocate Shri Bobde (a Shiv Sena member of the Maharashtra Legislative Assembly) suggested that

Sawane was killed due to an illicit love affair. In an interview with *The Indian Express*, Dalit Panther leader Rameshbhai Pandagale suggested human sacrifice, a view seconded by his colleague and Panther leader Gangadhar Gade in the *Maharashtra Times* on September 4. *Dainik Prabha* and *The Indian Express* published a story about the Ambedkar statue on September 1 and 5, respectively. Devidas Yashwant Deshmukh, who held a liquor license, came forward to say that he had served Sawane alcohol twice. Vishwanath Ganpath Dukre, participating in *bhajans* (Hindu devotional songs), noted that Sawane had been abusing Marathas in filthy language and had also insulted the *patil*'s wife.[10] Such motives began to locate Sawane's murder, for police and the public, in a context of caste and sexual enmity in a village that had been classified as "sensitive" by the Central Department of Intelligence.[11] As the police negotiated the thickets of rumor and publicity, their initial suggestions about localized political enmity were reinterpreted.

SDPO Parab, who took over the investigation ten days after Sawane's murder, focused on the location of Sawane's murder on the temple steps. His report noted:

> Dalits in the village even now do not enter the temple. If they want to worship or to take "Darshan" they offer it from the footsteps of the temple from the outside. It was raining in the village on the fatal night. Kotwal Ambadas according to the F.I.R lodged by his brother Kachru Sahebrao Sawane at P.S. Tadkalas on August 17 at 0700 hours was taking round as per the directions of Police Patil Kishore Marathe. When he reached in front of temple, he had to take shelter from rains inside the temple. Since he entered the sanctum of the temple the people gathered there for singing "Bhajan" got annoyed. Heated arguments were exchanged between kotwal Sawane and these villagers. . . .
>
> According to the complainant Kachru Sahebrao Sawane b/o [brother of] the victim, he . . . heard cries of Ambadas, the victim, at about 1030 p.m. near Hanuman temple. Hence, they rushed there and saw aforesaid persons attacking Ambadas with lathis [thick wooden staffs] and stones. Out of fear they ran towards their house and informed of the incident to the father . . . [they] went to the spot and found Ambadas lying unconscious in a pool of blood near footsteps of the temple. . . .
>
> It may be mentioned that the accused were saying that Ambadas Mahar entered into their temple and hence they were beating.[12]

This wireless report sheds light on local social reasoning. It centered attention on the spectacular circumstances of Sawane'a murder on the steps of a temple, allegedly due to temple entry. It highlighted Sawane's entry as a transgressive act—"since he entered the sanctum of the temple the people . . . got annoyed." It also offered an upper-caste villager's perspective on why violence ensued—"Ambadas Mahar entered into their temple hence they were beating." Finally, the report drew attention to local caste etiquette that called for Dalits to worship "from the footsteps of the temple from the outside." Thus, SDPO Parab presented Sawane's entry into the Hanuman temple as a sacrilegious act that led to his murder.

Where the Parbhani wireless report suggests that Sawane's murder should be seen as a ritualized observance of untouchability, the Bombay PCR Cell consistently demanded a more political reading of the murder. Officials in Bombay at the top of the chain of command were the ones who interpreted "local" information and concluded that Sawane's death was a caste crime. They were aided in this by newspaper reports of a long-standing political conflict in the village between Sawane, who wanted to install an Ambedkar statue in the village, and those who resisted this act.[13] In response to an August 20 query about the feud from the DIGP in Bombay, a wireless reply was sent from the subdivisional police officer in Parbhani to both Aurangabad and Bombay: "1) No previous dispute between the parties until incident 2) The facts came to be known to the police after the incident 3) The incident took place suddenly hence no preventive action taken in the matter [number 3 is underlined]." Handwritten at the top of the transmission is, "How does the SP say that this happened suddenly. Ask the SP for detailed report with a special messenger at once."[14]

This exchange between the DIGP and local police in Parbhani further compromised representations of the event.[15] The PCR Cell in Bombay countered that it was unlikely that the murder had taken place suddenly and wrote to the SP in Aurangabad again, on August 30, asking why Bombay had not received a detailed report, especially when the murder appeared to be an instance of anti-Dalit violence.[16]

As the wireless communication between Bombay and Aurangabad accelerated, pressure on the police investigation in Parbhani also increased: what was the cause of Sawane's murder? The response to a report of August 30, 1991, titled "Incident of murder of a kotwal belonging to a backward community in Parbhani District," sent to the additional chief secretary of the Home Department, state of Maharashtra, by the additional director general of police (Law and Order) was harsh. In a series of handwritten notes on the margin of this report, the Home Department commented:

1) Press note seems to have been clumsily prepared, and contains material that need not have been there
2) No indication whether deceased had taken a leading part in installation of Ambedkar bust and whether this was resented by caste Hindus
3) Whether such resentment manifested into altercations, or otherwise generated tension
4) Were office bearers like sarpanch, police patil, etc. involved?
5) When was village last visited and didn't police official come to know of differences/tensions
6) SP's comment that the incident blew up after 10 days—apparently there was some whispering campaign from both sides[17]

Like the newspaper reports castigating police mishandling of the case, the handwritten notes of the chief secretary, Home Department, changed the course of the inquiry. It counterposed Sawane's death on the steps of the temple against accounts of his political activism. Sawane's attempt to install an Ambedkar statue in the village now became a crucial piece of information that began to transform this case into an act of symbolic-political violence and atrocity. Significantly, the note addressed the local political context in Pimpri Deshmukh instead of focusing on Sawane's murder near the temple. Were the police *patil* and *sarpanch* involved? When was the village last visited? Political pressure and publicity lifted Sawane's murder from a purely localized context, reframing it as a more representative form of political violence, with the installation of the Ambedkar statue becoming the dominant explanation for Sawane's murder.

The national commissioner of SCs and STs, Ram Dhan, was the person most responsible for arguing that the atrocity was an act of political violence. He wrote to Chief Minister Sudhakarrao Naik about a September 3 visit he had made to Pimpri Deshmukh, and noted: "A sensational news item appeared in the *Times of India* dated 28–8-91 to the effect that a Scheduled Caste (Mahar) Police Kotwal of village Pimpri Deshmukh in Parbhani district was stoned to death by upper-caste residents on 16–8-91 for standing on the steps of a Hanuman temple in the village. That such an incident should have taken place in the year of the birth centenary of Dr. Babasaheb Ambedkar is a matter of extreme shame to the Indian society."[18] Ram Dhan pressed the significance of Sawane's murder on the Hanuman temple steps and explained it as the consequence of Sawane's position as "a young and upcoming leader of the Mahars."[19] He noted Sawane's foiled attempts to install a statue of Ambedkar on village land and associated that with his murder.

Newspapers picked up on this association between political militancy and the symbolic charge of Sawane's murder on the temple steps. The *Indian Express* reported that caste Hindus had stopped a procession celebrating Ambedkar's birthday on April 14 and noted that the *sarpanch* had prevented the installation of an Ambedkar statue in the village, even though Sawane had collected money for that purpose.[20] Political parties got involved. The Bharatiya Janata Party led a delegation to the chief minister's office to press him to visit the village, while the Republican Party of India (Athavale faction) staged a demonstration in front of the district collectorate in early September.

If the state government consistently downplayed the Ambedkar statue, Ram Dhan worked to publicize the murder as a caste atrocity, framed as retribution for Dalits' political self-representation. Ram Dhan's report emphasized the geography of violence and the contest over public space. Arguing that Sawane's murder had been preceded by a struggle over the social signification of space, he suggested that efforts to claim "public" space had invited retributive violence and had reproduced the spatial segregation that defined untouchability. Ram Dhan also historicized these tensions by asserting that public commemorations of Ambedkar had taken on powerful symbolic connotations since the *namantar* agitation.[21] Thus, Ram Dhan's report provided a *political* explanation of Sawane's murder, connecting this discrete instance of caste crime with broader upper-caste resentment of Dalits' militancy. By reframing Sawane's murder as caste atrocity, Ram Dhan also put pressure on the police to register the symbolic and political dimensions of the case: a Dalit had been bludgeoned to death on the steps of a temple because he had tried to install a statue of Ambedkar in Pimpri Deshmukh.

By the time Ram Dhan's report was issued, Sawane's murder had assumed national proportions. The Lok Sabha discussed the issue of atrocities against SCs and STs on August 19, 1991, well before news of Sawane's homicide reached the press.[22] On September 31, the prime minister wrote to all chief ministers requesting them to monitor atrocities cases.[23] The Committee on the Welfare of the Scheduled Castes and Scheduled Tribes noted "an astounding increase in the number of crimes committed against Scheduled Castes and Scheduled Tribes even after the implementation" of the POA Act, and added that the stringent punishments of the act encouraged greater cover-up through collusion between state functionaries and upper-caste leaders. The central and state governments were now responsible for addressing how a deterrent, the POA Act, was contributing to caste violence. The DIGP in Bombay noted the national concern over caste atrocities in a note to the subdivisional police officer in Parbhani, on September 2: "You are aware that DIGP PCR is looking after this subject and is required to send reports to State government as well as Central government. It is very disappointing that you failed to send a report to me till it was discussed in the Parliament though you had sent your report to other officials. Explain your failure. All Unit Commanders are again requested to keep this in mind and must endorse copy of their wireless message and reports whenever atrocities are committed on SC/STs. Similar section of PAA [Prevention of Atrocities Act] must repeat must be applied wherever necessary."[24]

As the state government became involved in Sawane's murder and the case became a state and nationwide scandal, "locality" also attained new significance. On September 3, 1991, the *Maharashtra Times* and the *Times of India* carried news about the persistence of untouchability in Marathwada's villages. Rajdeep Sardesai wrote in the *Times* that a nongovernmental organization based in Vasai and the Nirmala Niketan School of Social Work, Bombay, had conducted a survey between May 6 and May 26, 1991. The survey found that over 80 percent of Dalits did not have the right to enter temples in Marathwada, that they were barred from common water sources, performed defiling labor, and faced political discrimination. The findings questioned whether Maharashtra, the region that produced Phule and Ambedkar, could claim to be a progressive state. On September 6, the DIGP and the PCR Cell in Bombay demanded that special police officers be sent to investigate untouchability in the villages mentioned in the *Maharashtra Times* and *Times of India* articles.[25]

Another *Times of India* story on September 3 noted negligence by government functionaries: "Not only the police but the people's representatives seem very indifferent to the dastardly murder. The minister in charge of the district, Lakshmanrao Dhate, stated that he had not visited the village only because there would be an impression that he was on the side of only the Dalits." The Shiv Sena MLA [member of the Maharashtra Legislative Assembly] of Parbhani, Mr. Datta Bagade, said that he had not visited the village "only because it would create tension, for except the Dalits and the Muslims all the others are voters of the Shiv Sena."[26] Both the politics of untouchability and the struggles over political power came to be highlighted in the press.[27] As various government agencies attended to journalistic coverage, the local context of caste relations became even more significant for what it illustrated about the persistence of anti-Dalit violence.

A beleaguered note of September 19 from Parbhani to the PCR Cell
in Aurangabad noted the scandalous publicity around Sawane's murder:

> The incidence of murder of a Mahar kotwal Ambadas Sawane by caste
> Hindus at village Pimpri in Parbhani District on 16-8-91 has attracted
> huge press publicity and also visits by various V.I.P.s including Social Wel-
> fare Minister Ramdas Athwale, Parbhani District Minister Shri Madhu-
> karrao Ghate, Hon. Chief Minister of Maharashtra and Shri Ramdhan,
> Chairman SC/ST, Government of India, New Delhi followed by the visits
> of different political parties and social delegations led by Dalit Panther,
> B.J.P., S.K.P., Shiv Sena, Human rights Association, "Rachnatmak Sangarsh
> Samiti", etc. to the village. I was also present for supervising bandobast and
> security arrangements. *The press, state associations and even Parliament
> had brought the village under scrutiny over the above incident.*[28]

As the police investigation interacted with other forms of publicity,
Sawane's murder was increasingly represented as a caste atrocity, even
though the practice of untouchability was amenable to different interpretations. Some press reports in English and Marathi emphasized Sawane's
murder as a case of *mandir pravesh* (temple entry), locating the atrocity
in the murder on the temple steps. Others, like Ram Dhan, focused on the
Ambedkar statue as the occasion of a political struggle. Pratap Bhangar,
an advocate and activist of the Janata Dal, made an important statement
about party loyalty: "The police patil and the sarpanch have been politically affiliated for 10 years. At that time Ambadas and Kachru, who are
today actively involved with Dalit politics, were also with them. In fact
they were dependent on Ambadas. With the entry of the Shiv Sena two
years ago, the first seeds of discord were sown."[29] A press report identified the five men convicted of Sawane's murder as Shiv Sena activists.
Significantly, the Maharashtra State Welfare Committee noted that in their
meeting with Kachru they had learned that Muslim residents had tried to
leave Pimpri Deshmukh when the Shiv Sena came to power, but Sawane
had encouraged them to remain.[30] Sawane's murder thus came to be implicated in the broader political context of the growing power of the Shiv
Sena in Marathwada. The dual registers of the symbolic-political were differently comprehended by the law, however.

PRONOUNCEMENT: LEGAL STRUCTURES OF RECOGNITION

The transformation of raw intelligence gathered through police work into
the repetitive narrative structure of the wireless report illuminates how
governmental knowledge is vulnerable to internal and external mecha-

nisms of surveillance, the media, local activists, upper echelons of the police bureaucracy, and state and party functionaries. Police procedure and bureaucratic hierarchies joined with forms of critical publicity, which forced the police to recognize Sawane's murder as a caste crime. The jurisprudence of atrocity draws attention to how judicial knowledge is structured by political negotiations outside the framework of law, and to how judicial discourse is embedded in policing practices.[31]

As we will see in the adjudication of Sawane's murder, normalizing judicial-legislative frameworks of the postcolonial state combined with a distinct form of subalternity, Dalitness, to redefine Dalit and upper-caste identities as those of victim and perpetrator. The manner in which state, policing bureaucracy, and the judge framed Sawane's death, however, made it difficult for them to apprehend and comprehend a social world of symbolic-political violence. It was a strange juxtaposition of recognition of the "political" ramifications of Sawane's murder, itself the consequence of scandalous publicity, and the impossibility of justice that was staged in the courtroom. Herein lay the second scandal of Sawane's murder: the depoliticization of the political atrocity of anti-Dalit violence.

The Special Judge V. B. Adharkar passed judgment on Special Case No. 11/91 in the Parbhani Sessions Court on June 18, 1992.[32] I have already noted that Adharkar's judgment revealed awareness of the sociopolitical context in which Sawane's murder took place, yet it was blind to the ways in which caste sociality contaminated the police investigation and resultant publicity. It is fair to say, however, that there were problems with the POA Act itself, which assumed untouchability as the basis for the commission of caste crime, yet demanded that judges follow standard judicial procedure in bringing criminal trials to closure. The way that "untouchability" was discursively deployed in the courtroom reveals a split that disconnected the recognition of caste atrocity from the ability to address it by punishing perpetrators. The other dynamic at work in Adharkar's judgment was the way he disconnected the narrative of historic caste tension in the village from his evidentiary findings regarding intent, thereby separating aspects of the case that were integrally related to each other.

Adharkar opened his judgment by describing the geographical situation and the social structure of the village, because they explained Sawane's efforts to install an Ambedkar statue in the village and his brutal murder. He correlated space with caste power:

> As per ancient custom the untouchables reside in a separate Wasti outside the village at a distance of 300 feet towards the North side. The said Wasti

was previously known as Maharwada and now as Boudhwada. For
the sake of convenience it is referred to as Maharwada. There is a way
from the village to the Maharwada running East-West. The Maharwada
is the north side of the road and a house of . . . a caste Hindu (Mali) is to
the South of the road. The untouchables decided to install a statue of Dr.
Babasaheb Ambedkar near the house of the said [Hindu].[33]

Later the judge noted, "The said site is not in the Maharwada but in
the village" (6). Adharkar had no doubt that the installation of the
Ambedkar statue posed a powerful challenge to the symbolic division of
the village into caste Hindu and Dalit. The *sarpanch* and the police *patil*
had opposed the installation of the statue and had threatened Sawane
with dire consequences. As well, a group of villagers had tried to bribe
the Dalits with Rs. 500 to place the Ambedkar statue in the Maharwada
rather than inside the village. Adharkar drew attention to commemorative politics of space that, whether it took place in a village or in an urban slum, put Dalit selfhood on the line in a political struggle to control
the (re)signification of space. Adharkar also felt it worthwhile to add this
observation: "Sometimes the police had to go there [Maharwada] to
maintain law and order, and to see that there should not be breach of
peace" (3).

Adharkar contrasted this with the political geography of the temple
as a public place and a sacred space. Sawane's murder on the steps of
the temple was understood as an issue of temple entry because Dalits were
barred from the temple. "The untouchables were prohibited from making entry into the temple on the ground of untouchability. In this way untouchability was observed in the village." The judge mentioned a series
of events that defined the politics of this space: the upper castes denied
Sawane entry into the Maruti temple because he was a Dalit, they insulted him by calling him Mahardya (a derogatory reference to Sawane's
subcaste], and they assaulted him *on the steps of the temple*. Indeed, when
asked why Sawane was being beaten, the crowd outside the temple is
supposed to have said, "The temple has been dis-sacred! In our temple
Ambadas Mahar had come and therefore we have been beating him" (73).
Oral evidence given in court claimed that the crowd outside the temple
said to Sawane's brother, "Oh *Mahardya,* how did your brother enter
into the temple? The temple has [been] dis-sacred."[34] The fact that Sawane
was brought outside the temple and called "Mahardya" while being assaulted, constituted the public practice of untouchability.

The use of the insulting name, Mahardya, is significant, since the POA
Act considers the caste insult to be a psychic wound approaching the

severity of physical assault. When the public prosecutor emphasized that an insult was a caste crime, the defense resorted to an ingenious argument: "Because the villagers knew that Ambadas [Sawane] was Mahar by caste (whether) such person was referred to as "'Mahar Ambadas' or only 'Ambadas' has no meaning at all" (78–79). In essence, the defense argued that because Sawane was known to be a Dalit, verbal confirmation of his identity should not be taken as motive for the crime.

Judge Adharkar countered that the substance of the testimony associated Sawane's caste identity with the desecration of the temple. Furthermore, Adharkar distinguished two forms of phenomenal violence: new violent caste sociality displayed in conflict around the Ambedkar statue *and* retaliatory counterviolence that reinstated Dalits' stigmatized status. In other words, the struggle over installing the Ambedkar statue had produced counterviolence that attempted to replicate apparently archaic forms of caste sociality. Adharkar understood Sawane's murder on the temple steps—the upper castes' maintenance of the temple's purity—as such a form of retaliatory violence in service of reasserting caste privilege in the face of Dalit militancy. Dalit political militancy was met with a brutal variation on an anachronistic form, barring entry into a temple.

Though he took the caste insult seriously, as a prelude to violence, and even though he produced a narrative indicating the relevance of the sociopolitical context of caste crime, Adharkar adjudicated the case by sticking narrowly to the question of intent. Could it be said that the villagers meant to murder Sawane because he was a Dalit? Adharkar noted that the villagers had clearly meant to protect the temple from pollution but that the violence that ensued was spontaneous and unplanned. When some Dalit boys who had come to attend a wedding in Pimpri Deshmukh entered the Hanuman temple in 1985 or 1986, their families had been threatened with dire consequences if the boys weren't disciplined. But they had not been murdered (84). Could it be established, after all, that the villagers had the intent to murder Sawane? Without evidence of prior planning, Sawane's death could not be characterized as caste atrocity. Furthermore, since the assailant who threw the rock that fatally injured Sawane could not be identified, none of the men could be punished for murder. Adharkar wrote, "The sum and substance of the evidence is that deceased Ambadas sustained one fatal injury resulting in death but it could not [be] attributed to a particular accused person in this case"(84). Ironically, even though atrocity legislation assumed collective violence, as well as the existence of an unspoken (yet pervasive) caste prejudice, it was precisely the collective nature of the murder that produced Adharkar's inability to adjudicate intent.

Adharkar acknowledged repeated evidence of police negligence as well as the political motivations for Sawane's murder. He wrote, "There is no evidence that the political leaders or the Ministers brought pressure or influence on the investigation officers, but the truth is, as can be seen from the facts stated earlier, the direction of the investigation had changed [after SDPO Kolhapurkar was replaced by SDPO Parab]"(40). The judge then proceeded to simply ignore the "new" evidence produced by Parab, including evidence of the police *patil*'s involvement in the crime. Adharkar noted that the Code of Criminal Procedure did not make "provision" for recording either supplementary or "fresh statements."

Adharkar's seemingly schizophrenic judgment, at once acknowledging and refusing to include evidence of conflict around the political symbology of Dalit identity—whether the effort to install an Ambedkar statue or the murder's location on the temple steps—is exceedingly odd. The judgment is a perversion of justice if we recall that the POA Act explicitly defines as atrocities acts ranging from humiliation to economic terror and ritualized violence. At one level, perhaps the judge's deliberate and extended search for motive was simply disingenuous, the performance of what was expected of him given the enormous publicity around the case. His presentation of himself as a committed judge allowed the purposeful imposition of another judicial framework, something like *mens rea,* even when the crime specified the use of exceptional laws, that is, atrocities legislation, that obviated requirement of a specific motive. This is certainly possible, and even probable. Acknowledging collective violence and simultaneously individuating it, as Adharkar had done, was enabled by atrocities legislation. On the one hand, *all crimes* against Dalits were assumed to be acts of anti-Dalit violence. However, the adjudication of caste crime made no *procedural* accommodation for the enmity and mutual fear that was assumed by atrocities legislation as the grounds of a daily sociality between Dalits and caste Hindus. The caste civility that was the creation of governmental imagination was also a response to the structuring violence of untouchability. Judges in atrocities cases therefore had great leeway in reproducing precisely the kind of impasse we see in the adjudication of Sawane's murder. The conventions of legal redress open possibilities for escape from justice.

The law might disrespect the dead, but they are not the only actors in this drama. Compensation—the conversion of human presence into monetary value—was an important mechanism by which the living continued to engage with the state. In his report, Ram Dhan argued that caste crime had to be addressed as a human rights violation: "At present many of the State Governments are sanctioning Rs. 1 lakh as relief to the families of those who are killed in caste and communal riots. As compared to these cases, killing of SC/ST persons in cases of atrocities on them amounts to crime against humanity. Therefore the families of SC/ST persons who are killed in cases of atrocities . . . deserve an equal treatment if not a more sympathetic one."[35] However, Sawane's death attained symbolic closure through a smaller sum: Rs. 54,050 were collected from the Chief Minister's Fund, the Social Welfare Board, the Revenue Employees Welfare Fund, the district collector, and the village. Sawane's wife, Rukminibai, was offered his kotwalship at a salary of Rs. 900 per month and given a small plot of land in Pimpri Deshmukh. Having failed to punish the perpetrators, compassion now assumed the guise of compensation and further commodified Dalit pain and suffering.

POLITICS, SYMBOLIC FORM, SACRIFICE, AND COMMEMORATION

The social life of this new juridical form, the caste atrocity, is embedded in structures of caste sociality, which are in turn reproduced and distinguished along two mutually constitutive registers: atrocity as a political act that calls for Dalit response and atrocity as the performance of ritualized violence. Can we distinguish political violence from archaic rituals that reproduce Dalit stigma? Or is it that political violence becomes efficacious through the renewed symbolization of cultural forms and ritual practices associated with the (caste) body? Another crucial point of entry into the significance of Sawane's death is thus the performative context from which the atrocity of caste violence gains its intense symbolic charge.

Sawane's murder throws into relief a problematic permeability between violent acts that *reproduce* stigmatized existence and violent acts that *prevent* social and political advancement. The double valence of violence derives in part from the specific trajectories of the Dalit subject "becoming political." Structures of everyday life are politicized as a consequence of creating a new identity for the collective Dalit self through the accelerated symbolization of *Dalit* forms, such as statues of Ambedkar. But, as we saw in chapter 6, anti-Dalit violence is also enmeshed in a cultural matrix, a set of symbolic codes that devalue Dalit bodies. We can neither understand the specificity nor the peculiar intimacy of anti-

Dalit violence without considering the semiology of political subject-formation. The violent reciprocity between Sawane's involvement with an Ambedkar statue and his murder on the steps of a temple reflects caste violence in the double register of the ritual-archaic and the political. The intersecting logics of sacrifice and political commemoration together elucidate the crucial role of the political resignification of symbolic forms in Dalit subject-formation.

The ritually charged *ves*, the space demarcating the village from the public world, joins the Mahar caste to the task of guarding the village boundary. Living outside the village boundaries, the Mahar *veskar* is the outsider figure who protects the integrity of the village social unit. As *kotwal*, Sawane was vested with responsibility for a modern variant of this practice. The Mahar's central role in securing a place from which he was banished resonates with a larger set of associations around the use of the Mahar's body to consecrate physical space. This is why the suggestion that Sawane's murder was a human sacrifice, though it appears atavistic, is not farfetched. It has a basis in medieval practices of sacrifice. In the medieval Deccan, human sacrifice—often of a Mahar—was a crucial trope through which land grants and *vatandari* rights and patrimonies were either legitimized or challenged. Often, the Mahar was a surrogate for those of higher-caste status or military rank whose claims to sovereignty were understood to be incomplete without human sacrifice to strengthen acts of military incorporation. Mahars were often sacrificed at the foundations of forts or buildings that had been wrested from enemy control in order to appease the gods with an offering imbued with a "dark polluting magic," though the benefits accrued to the person on whose behalf the Mahar was sacrificed.[36]

The organization of the medieval polity around this victim-figure also became the ground for Mahars' claims to future *vatandari* rights and duties. These were livelihood claims to maintenance and the right to life, if you will, that positioned Dalits within an Old Regime habitus characterized by performances of distinguishing, demeaning, and subsuming the self, and pertained throughout contexts from worship to kingship. Sumit Guha relates the case of the eighteenth-century Civhe Kolis who advanced claims to *vatandari* rights to a fort based on a copper-plate inscription from 587 mentioning a Mahar sacrifice: Mahar surrogates, "Nathnak, son of Bahirnak Sonnak and Devaki, wife of Nathnak, were buried in the foundations of the tower. Only then could the tower be successfully completed."[37] Guha also recounts rival claims to *vatandari* rights from the years 1746–47 that resurrected the trope of burial in a building's foundation. The father of the claimant, Ramnak, was supposed to have been buried in "the Sarja tower [where] the masonry marker still exists. I am his son."[38] There are two sides to this act: one is the sacrifice itself, and the other the *vatandari* rights that emanate from Mahar sacrifice. Both signal the role of the Mahar as a surrogate emissary who transfers impurities from a place or territory through the violent expulsion of sacrificial death: power is performatively secured through the sacrifice of the Mahar body.

This sacrificial logic returns in the Mahars' origin story of the fifty-two *vatandar*'s rights. We will recall that the account of Amrutnak from the 1920s emphasized voluntary castration as the symbol of Mahars' loyalty and the origin of the charter of the fifty-two rights of the village Mahars, including the guarding of the *ves*.[39] Both sacrifice and sexuality were connected in Mahar histories of their status as virile protectors; they had virile power *because* they were also sacrificial victims.

René Girard discusses sacrifice as the ritualization of violence. The centrality of sacrifice derives from its status as an act of excessive symbolization that transforms a mimetic doubling of violence into a condensed, singular act. Though the sacrificial act gains salience through its connection to broader contexts of violent enactment, it also transcends them to become a mythic origin point, the prehistory of society or a people, for instance.[40] As Allen Feldman writes, "The central political problematic of violent reciprocity is the thin membrane of division, reversibility, and doubling that both divides and conflates 'legitimate' and 'illegitimate' violence."[41] This describes the Maratha social-political formation perfectly. Stewart Gordon describes an emergent polity defined by guerrilla warfare and the constant transformation of outlaws—including Shivaji himself—into kings.

It is precisely that moment when the legitimacy of violent acts of expropriation have to be asserted retroactively that the "necessity" for ritual violence, violence placed *outside* the space-time of everyday or political violence, becomes most pressing. As Feldman notes, "The search for legitimacy through the search for nonmimetic practice resolves into a new *cultural construction of violence.*"[42] In India this ritual reconstruction of violence also requires a culturally coded sacrificial victim, the Mahar, who personifies the community's pollution and must therefore be cast out. Sacrifice, like the "contract" of political theory, *produces* society.[43] Society in turn, like caste itself, is organized around an excluded negativity, an abandoned or absent figure, in this case the Mahar.[44]

The symbolic import of Sawane's murder on the steps of a temple was lost on no one, from the policemen who conducted the initial inquiry to Judge Adharkar. There is a clear formal resemblance between the logic of sacrifice and the murder on the temple steps. Yet the epochal socio-political changes that temporally separated the two sacrificial acts—a Mahar buried in a structure's foundation and Sawane's murder—also distorted the aura of sacrality attached to the second sacrificial event. The sacrifice of a Mahar at the foot of a military fortification was once a ritual act, while the 1991 murder of a Dalit on the steps of a temple was a criminal act. Whereas in the first case political legitimacy required a sacrificial act, in the second case a criminal act echoed *symbolic* salience because a Dalit was murdered on the temple steps. In both instances, how-ever, ill-defined boundaries between religious and political space were clarified *through violation of the Dalit's body.* The boundary-enforcing function of the Mahar *veskar* was intimately tied to this creation of boundaries through the Mahar's physical body.

The archaic imaginary is necessarily limited; it works through repeti-tion and formal resemblance. Sawane's murder on the steps of the tem-ple carried a symbolic charge derived from the resuscitation of symbolic forms still active in popular memory. These range from the medieval pro-duction of an authoritative subaltern history through the narrative sig-nature of Mahar sacrifice in a twentieth-century Dalit counterhistory locating Amrutnak's sacrifice as the source of Dalits' enforced inclusion within the hierarchy of caste.

Although Sawane's murder on the temple steps resonates with the logic of sacrifice, this logic does not completely encompass its meaning. The apparent continuities with archaic practice are formal, for Sawane's mur-der followed from his participation in a project of political assertion, namely, to commemorate a new Dalit collectivity through the installa-tion of an Ambedkar statue. Since the *namantar* movement, many Dalit struggles revolved around new acts of boundary making and destruction, from Dalits' encroachment onto *gayraan zamin* (common grazing land) leading to increased conflict with the Shiv Sena since 1985, to the visual icons of Ambedkar, Phule, and Periyar that began to dot urban and rural landscapes throughout India during the 1990s. Indeed by the late 1990s, the northern Indian state of Uttar Pradesh, under Bahujan Samaj Party (Party of the Majority; BSP) leadership, took the lead in such acts of po-litical commemoration.

What was the symbolic significance of erecting an Ambedkar statue? Wherein lay the power of its desecration? The journalist P. Sainath has observed, "Currently, there are more Ambedkar statues in India's villages than any other leader. His statues are not government installed—unlike those of the others. The poor put them up at their own expense."[45] In turn, statue defilements are acts of symbolic annihilation. Violence to and around the statue links Ambedkar's symbolization as the origin point of Dalit history with caste Hindus' perception of the proliferation of Ambedkar images as illicit acts of sacralization.[46] The particular mode of desecration thus is significant. Political desecration of religious icons goes back to the 1920s and 1930s, when Satyashodak and non-Brahmin activists occasionally garlanded Hindu deities with slippers, though this practice was more common among Self-Respecters in the south. This turned an act of veneration, garlanding the deity, into an act of desecration. Not only that, but using a defiled object, the slipper made from leather, a defiling substance, also polluted the idol. This signaled active repugnance toward caste hierarchy and religious superstition, and it was on par with burning Hindu scriptures and abusing Hindu gods and goddesses. This idiom of public desecration has since expanded to include shaming politicians by garlanding them with slippers, a transliteration from ritual to political registers.

Erecting an Ambedkar statue imitates acts venerating representations of religious and political figures, but there is a difference. The proliferation of Ambedkar statues is a claim to space within a representational economy saturated by deified nationalist icons commemorated by the state, as Sainath notes. Commodified images of Ambedkar, such as calendars, posters, buttons, and so forth, depict his life in the style of Puranic narratives, where the god's life is told through a series of ideal-typical events and encounters. There are also collages of Ambedkar's photographs across time, in which he increasingly resembles the Buddha. The most common three-dimensional representations of Ambedkar, however, portray him in a militant upright pose, dressed in a recognizable blue suit and red tie, holding the Constitution in his left hand, his right arm outstretched to make a point. In this representation, Ambedkar's role as a crucial public figure for independent India merges with his signal importance in producing a new history for the Dalit community and self. On display here is not only his singular individuality, the agentive power of self-determination to remake the Dalit self and thus challenge the social invisibility and humiliation of that community, but also the strong visual connection of Ambedkar to the constitution of the Indian polity itself.

The fact that a Dalit figure is at the center of acts of symbolic exchange does not mean that there is a shared understanding of what the figure means, however. The desecration of Ambedkar statues by non-Dalits assumes structural equivalence between Ambedkar and religious icons and symbols, and in turn enacts an enraged desymbolization and symbolic annihilation of Dalits as a community. As Dalits experiment with a new regime of signification, their acts and aspirations run the risk of being misconstrued as acts of deification precisely because some idioms of performance resemble acts of veneration. This is ironic because Dalits associate Ambedkar with *refusal* of the representational practices and ideological structures that define caste Hinduism. We must thus ask whether a political statue imbued with affective charge becomes a "sacred" object, or whether we can find other ways to describe acts of political commemoration that seek to resignify Dalits' resistance to the cultural and ideational practices of the Hindu order. It is entirely possible to read the response to the desecration of Ambedkar statues not merely as a reaction to defilement but also, and more strongly, as a response to Hindu society's persistent refusal to recognize and respect the acts of symbolization through which Dalit identity is constituted in the first place.

In Pimpri Deshmukh today, there is a bust of Ambadas Sawane next to a statue of Ambedkar. His inclusion within a recognizable tradition of political iconography creates a political biography for Sawane: his murder is commemorated as an act of martyrdom. Sawane's inclusion within this iconography suggests the capacity of semiotic technologies to expand an existing representational field by imputing contiguity between political figures and politicized symbols. The sad irony, of course, is that Sawane's commemoration comes as the result of his own failed attempts to install an Ambedkar statue in Pimpri Deshmukh.

AFTER ATROCITY: VIOLENCE AND EVERYDAY LIFE

As I have shown throughout the second part of this book, the conjugation of Dalit identity with historical suffering, on the one hand, and with legal-bureaucratic forms of protection, on the other, has produced new sites of conflict *and* new possibilities for Dalit emancipation. The interpellation of the Dalit subject into regimes of state recognition publicizes anti-Dalit violence *as atrocity* and in so doing challenges the postcolonial state's discourses of social welfare and protection. As we have seen, atrocities legislation is not merely prophylactic. Rather, by embedding agents and social practice in new frames, legal discourse also transforms the perceptual field around categories such as "untouchability" and identities such as "Dalit" or "caste Hindu," provoking new forms of social engagement and interaction. The regulatory function of law also allows law to function as a particularly potent form of publicity that creates the exception, the "case," out of the practices of everyday life.[47] When invisible forms of everyday violence—invisible because they are a structuring violence—are rendered spectacular, as during Sawane's murder and the defilement of the Sirasgaon women, new political struggles organize around violence.

Political violence unsettles symbolic forms and challenges the deep structure of the caste Hindu order. However, the resilience of everyday practices of stigmatization also conditions Dalits' continued quest for social justice and dignity. Sawane's political assertion intensified caste antagonism along the registers of the ritual-archaic and the political. In turn, these antagonisms were heightened by legal structures of recognition that emphasized the agonistic nature of caste interaction between victim and perpetrator, violator and violated, often making Dalits vulnerable to further violence. Rather than a cessation of anti-Dalit violence, efforts to legislate Dalit vulnerability out of existence have instead helped to establish violence as a public mode of recognition between upper castes and Dalits. The repertoires and targets of violence may be transformed, but violent acts responding to new forms of Dalit militancy tend to simultaneously deepen existing patterns of ritual violation and symbolic humiliation. How to understand this paradoxical aspect of Dalit emancipation?

A careful reading of the social life of the caste atrocity implicates local state functionaries in the miscarriage of justice. It also implicates the caretaking efficacy of the postcolonial state insofar as legal redress—in this case, the adjudication of murder *as* caste atrocity—reencodes vulnerability as a crucial axis of Dalit existence. The bifurcation between a definition of caste crime as violence toward a vulnerable collective and adjudication of caste crime through an individuated structure of trial and punishment makes a just social order less possible, even as it becomes all the more urgent.

This is reflected in a further irony: as the targets of anti-Dalit violence become more clearly political—through acts and symbols related to Dalit demands for economic empowerment, educational opportunities, jobs, rights to public space—repertoires of retributive violence coalesce around historical modes of Dalit stigmatization. In the postcolonial period, political symbology—flags, statues, the *namantar* movement, cultural production—objectify the memory work through which a new community identity emerges. As these acts of symbolization have drawn new objects and icons into an existing semiotic field, they have also provoked acts of desymbolization—by upper castes and policing functionaries—through practices of defilement, dismemberment, and desecration. State functionary participation extends further into the deformation of accepted legal process itself, as we have seen in this chapter and the preceding one, with efforts to protect local officials, such as the police *patil* and *sarpanch,* and with the search for exact but unprovable individual motive.

Violence has played a central role in the semiotic density and public salience that the term "Dalit" has acquired across the last century. The public violence of the Worli riots and the *namantar* agitation, and the more intimate violence of Sirasgaon and Pimpri Deshmukh, offer points at which we can historicize the relationship between political violence and symbolic politics by being attentive to the deployment of specific social and cultural forms. While each act of caste violence is distinctive, I have suggested a model of reading the atrocity across time to understand the growing salience of particular tropes and symbols.[48] By analyzing key transformations in Dalit politics over a thirty-year period, I have argued that accelerated practices of self-representation are visible not merely as a retelling of political history, but equally in the semiotics of Dalit life itself.

Is this really political? Yes, because the most powerful axis of Dalit political subject-formation has focused on remaking the caste self and the caste body—the experiential site of stigma—through acts of political resignification. The demand for rights and social recognition that defines Dalit struggle poses a fundamental challenge to the representational economy of caste Hinduism. Becoming "Dalit" is the process through which the caste subaltern enters into circuits of political commensuration and into the value regime of "the human." Because the name and bodily experience are crucial sites of political subject-formation, political violence must also address this semiotic axis as the space of politics.

Dalit Futures

My friend's elderly father, Vasantrao Kamble, had spent his working life in a government office. While speaking with him in Aurangabad in March 1997, I casually asked him about caste discrimination. His response was illuminating. He said that when caste Hindus at work came to know his caste identity, they reacted as if they had received an electric shock. The term Kamble used, *shock basane*, replaced the more common expression, *dhakka basane,* which means to experience a physical jolt.[1] By describing contact between untouchables and caste Hindus through the metaphor of electric shock, Kamble emphasized *his* impact on upper-caste persons rather than the effect of untouchability on him.[2] Instead of citing an instance of discriminatory practice as we might expect, the audacity of Kamble's statement lies in his description of social recognition as electric shock, as producing a violent sense of dislocation *for caste Hindus.*

Violence and otherization, though central to Dalit subject-formation, are invariably omitted or marginalized in scholarly accounts of caste relations. If violence is an axis for subject-formation, so too are the more quotidian practices of caste privilege and prejudice. Elements in the modern habitus of caste include the small insult, the sudden withdrawal of friendship and intimacy, and the surprised discovery of caste identity or caste-identified practices. They are eloquent testimony to the effects of inherited privilege upon those denied its protective embrace: while upper castes recess their caste identity, Dalit and lower-caste persons are burdened by the fact of caste. For instance, Kumud Pawde describes her excessive visibility and peculiar "attraction" as a Sanskit scholar:

> That a woman from a lower caste that is the lowest of the low should learn Sanskrit, and not only that, also teach it—is a dreadful anomaly to a traditional mind. And an individual in whose personality these anomalies are accumulated becomes an object of attraction—an attraction blended of mixed acceptance and rejection. The attraction based on acceptance comes from my caste-fellows, in the admiration of whose glance is pride in an impossible achievement. That which for so many centuries was not touched by us, is now within our grasp. That which remained encased in the shell of difficulty, is now accessible. Seeing this knowledge hidden in the esoteric inner sanctum come within the embrace, not just of any person, but one whom religion has condemned to vermin—that is their victory.
>
> The other attraction—based on rejection—is devastating. It pricks holes in one's mind—turning a sensitive heart into a sieve. Words of praise of this kind, for someone who is aware, are like hot spears. . . .
>
> "Well isn't that amazing! So you're teaching Sanskrit at the Government College, are you? That's very gratifying, I must say." The words are quite ordinary; their meaning is straight-forward. But the meaning conveyed by the tone in which they are said torments me in many different ways! "In what former life have I committed a sin that I should learn Sanskrit from you? All our sacred scriptures have been polluted." . . .
>
> The result is that although I try to forget my caste, it is impossible to forget. And then I remember an expression I heard somewhere: "What comes by birth, but can't be cast off by dying—that is caste."[3]

If Pawde's narrative of education and upward mobility is marred by the persistence of prejudice, it is also marked by keen awareness of the caste body. She notes that as a child, she bathed with Pears soap and her mother "rubbed Kaminia hair oil on her hair, and plaited it neatly."[4] She was cleaner and smelled better than most of her Brahmin classmates, but their mothers refused to let the children play with Pawde or to invite her into their homes. When she stood at the entrance to a wedding ceremony delighted by the Vedic chanting, she was mistaken for a poor child hoping to get food, and was shooed away with a *laddoo,* a traditional sweet. Pawde concludes with the bitter realization that her marriage to a Maratha eased her entry into the academy. "But one thought still pricks me: the credit for Kumud Somkuwar's job is not hers, but that of the name Kumud Pawde."[5] In Pawde's account, the name and the caste body speak the unspeakable and, in turn, elicit visceral practices of prejudice and discrimination. Caste cannot be forgotten because of the facticity of the caste body.

Together and separately, Kamble and Pawde describe the persistent, if hidden, signs of caste distinction that coexist with its more spectacular manifestations—caste's relentless "outing" through caste certificates, segregated housing, and anti-Dalit violence. And if Dalits bear the burden of caste, embarrassed silence is the typical response to the social visibility of caste privilege. The relative visibility and invisibility of caste in the public sphere is a sign of the differential subject positions occupied by upper and lower castes with relation to caste privilege, as well as an acknowledgment of caste as *the* public secret of secular modernity. Academics, too, have tended to ignore the complicity between secular personhood and upper-caste privilege, focusing instead on Dalits and lower castes whose identities are overdetermined by caste. The result is that the upper-caste habitus operates as a sphere of secular modernity uninfected by caste, as if a neglected Brahmin minority had followed Marx's injunction to transcend a burdensome historical religious identity.[6] Thus M. S. S. Pandian's account of that oxymoronic entity, the "secular Brahmin," is noteworthy for its glimpse into the reproduction of caste privilege. Historically, Tamil Brahmins saw no contradiction between performing their bureaucratic competence in a caste-heterogeneous environment, while vigorously reproducing their Brahminhood in the domestic sphere.[7] If the southern Indian Brahmin's divided self has historically allowed him to defend caste as a practice of the intimate self, while simultaneously claiming to be a victim of the reservations regime— now redefined as a form of reverse discrimination—this is because inherited privilege is naturalized and caste power elided.

The conceit of inherited privilege goes beyond the small minority of southern Indian Brahmins, of course. Today, upper castes typically attribute their alienation from civic life and associational institutions to the criminalization of politics, rampant corruption, and the breakdown of public civility. The implied subtext of these statements is that the reservations regime is responsible for distorting political culture. A presumed threat to inherited privilege, now recast as concern for the protection of equal opportunity, enabled the vigorous opposition of the so-called Forward Castes to the extension of reservations to the Other Backward Classes during the anti-Mandal agitations of 1989. More recently, during the second round of anti-Mandal agitations in 2006, there was massive mobilization against efforts to extend reservations to the nation's top engineering, management, and medical schools. The spectacle of quiescent upper castes rallying to protect the rule of merit and demanding an end to caste-based reservations reflects how India's secular democracy has quietly but successfully ventriloquized the hegemonic aspirations of an upper-caste minority as the voice of the social majority. Privatization, economic liberalization, and India's growing presence on the global stage have also provided fertile ground for the entrenchment of upper-caste hegemony through an increasingly diasporic and mobile Indian middle class.[8]

The invisibility of upper-caste caste privilege has to be set against Dalits' experience of intimate practices of prejudice. Indeed the twinned structure of denial and disclosure gestures to the continued relevance of a *corporeal politics,* whose enabling conditions (and limits) I have tried to specify in this book.[9] Dalit selfhood and the caste body have been historically central to the problematic of Dalit emancipation precisely because the stigma of caste is a birthmark, it is what "can't be cast off by dying." Central aspects of Dalit subject-formation therefore include efforts to find an appropriate language for describing stigmatized existence together with the translation of caste stigma into a form of political inequality.

There are at least two different experiences of the caste body at stake in this account. The political history of Dalit subject-formation and militant identity is organized around the emancipated subject. But it is also the case that the politically inadequate subject is the one who continues to experience the stubborn stigma of caste. The constitutive tension between relational and embodied identity has historically required that "the terms of exclusion on which discrimination is premised are at once refused and reproduced in the demands for inclusion."[10] This has produced new fields of power and identity that have crystallized around the Dalit, thus challenging the prevailing terms of politics.

Etienne Balibar's discussion of the epistemic rupture inaugurated by the Declaration of the Rights of Man and its vision of (political) emancipation provides a framework for historicizing the manner in which embodied identity is rendered politically salient, through a process I have termed the "politicization of politics." In a provocative set of essays on the relationship of theoretical Marxism to classical political theory, Balibar argues that "the signification of the equation man = citizen is not so much a definition of a political right as the affirmation of a *universal right to politics.* Formally at least—and this is the classic example of a form that can become a material weapon—the *Declaration* opens an indefinite sphere of politicization of rights-claims each of which reiterates in its own way the demand for citizenship, or for an institutional, public inscription of freedom and equality."[11]

In Balibar's formulation, politics is a contingent, conjunctural process punctuated by momentary resolutions reflected in political forms—for example, fascism, totalitarianism, and electoral democracy—each premised on a different relationship between state and political subject. Balibar ascribes to the Declaration the enunciation of a *right to politics* rather than a discrete set of *political rights*. Any final resolution to political conflict is, in fact, impossible. Accordingly, acts of political commensuration and equalization are acts without closure and processes without end. I take the import of Balibar's point to be the transposability of rights claims between one social field, such as labor, and another, such as sexual difference, a process integral to what he terms an "ethics of emancipation," which undergirds the right to politics, that is, the conviction that "*the emancipation of the oppressed can only be their own work,* . . . emphasizes its immediately ethical signification."[12] Such a notion of "the political" does not deny transformative junctures along multiple (and uneven) axes of social, political, and economic enfranchisement. Neither does it imply that political forms are without constraint. Instead, this perspective makes possible an account of subaltern identity formation that enabled Dalit critique and allowed stigmatized existence to become politically salient. If the Dalit subaltern brings central aspects of the Indian political into view, is there a structuring relationship between caste subalternity and Indian democracy that requires specification?

WHY "THE CASTE QUESTION"?

By the turn of the twentieth century, caste equality and the reform of untouchability were everywhere volatile issues open to debate and the interventions of colonial officials, nationalist reformers, and activists from the various untouchable communities. Untouchable reform had become central to the identity of a confessional Hinduism, on the one hand, and to the consolidation of Hindus as a political community or constituency, on the other. Standard accounts that tell the story of untouchable community formation, colonial modernity, and anticolonial nationalism trace a movement from the social reformist phase of untouchable reform to the subsequent (if ironic) politicization of untouchability as a problem for Hindus and Hinduism in the hands of M. K. Gandhi and the Indian National Congress. A political compromise between (Hindu) social reformers and Congress radicals on the issue of untouchable reform allowed Hindu upper castes to function as a political reflection of the nation as a whole. This compromise consisted of defining untouchability as a matter of hygiene and personal cleanliness while undertaking projects of religious inclusion. By refusing to address caste (especially un-touchability) as the practice of inequality, nationalists also made un-touchability the paradigmatic instance of (Hindu) "difference" that mo-tivated various strategies of inclusion, from temple- entry to the reserved electorate. This is the standard narrative against which a Dalit history of India's political modernity takes shape, in the process illuminating an alternative set of relationships between the key categories of state and community, nation and minority, and ultimately, between the religious and the political.

In Bombay, debate was especially vociferous, and it was conducted at a high level of political sophistication due to the legacy of caste radical-ism, which connected a critique of Brahminical hegemony and religious superstition with a powerful socioeconomic critique of caste as a mate-rial structure of exploitation. Jotirao Phule produced a systematic account of caste as both inhuman and inegalitarian, and he rewrote Hindu his-tory as a history of caste conflict and race war between Aryan (Brahmin) and Dravidian (Kshatriya). This became Dalit political common sense. Caste radicals more generally understood the religious and political as-pects of caste as phenomenologically distinctive, yet mutually constitu-tive. By the turn of the twentieth century, a series of dispersed shifts in Dalit life and labor had begun to crystallize around the public experi-ence of being a stigmatized subject, efforts that crucially involved the re-form of the Dalit domestic. Such efforts restructured authority within community: a new generation of Dalit advocates with a historical mem-ory of military employment and the benefits of colonial education, and centrally influenced by the tradition of Satyashodak activism, took up po-sitions of leadership within the community. They encouraged new forms of activism around public space and access to government property.

While Dalit reform drew on the considerable reformist efforts of the well-to do Mahar Dalits of Vidarbha and the Central Provinces, the idiom of segregation and civic exclusion through which Dalit activists such as Gopalbaba Valangkar, Vithal Raoji Moon Pande, and Shivram Janba Kamble criticized traditional hierarchies was distinctive, and it was dis-tinctively new. Dalit critique was the outgrowth of Dalits' experience of the spatio-temporal orders of colonial modernity as refracted through institutional sites such as schools, railways, and factories. The putative anonymity of urban life combined with the promise of social equality in colonial institutions was a bittersweet, double-edged experience for Mahar Dalits. Their entry into public spaces such as schools, streets, trains, and temples was thwarted by novel technologies of segregation that reflected the adaptation of modern disciplinary formations as conduits for the reproduction of caste norms and prejudice. More broadly, untouchability was transformed along two axes: (1) it was further interiorized as an ineffable quality of the caste body; and (2) caste exclusion and segregation were legitimized through recourse to a language derived from liberal property regimes. Recasting demands for social inclusion as claims upon private property thus enabled a legal defense of caste inequity in the language of liberalism (and not tradition). Thus, the secularization of untouchability was paradoxical: ritually inflected practices of separation inhered within liberal paradigms of exclusion and the legal discourses that justified them. Under colonial conditions, political recognition could support caste privilege and the interests of a powerful minority.

The objectified structure of existence named "untouchability" was a creation of legal modernization, but it did not remain a colonial construct. As debates about untouchability accelerated during the interwar years, a changed imperial context transformed the discursive milieu and sociopolitical frame within which those debates were embedded; mutual transformations inflected political discourses and shaped institutional strategies. Increasingly, the activities of a regionally distinctive community, Mahar Dalits, animated by the political thinking of their most significant thinker, B. R. Ambedkar, placed the problem of untouchability at the very heart of a national debate about political rights and social recognition. Dalits challenged the interpenetration of caste power with Brahminical authority, but their most crucial political demand, separate representation, failed. This demand was the first step, however, in engaging the political idioms and procedural forms, first of colonial liberalism and later of postcolonial civil rights and developmentalism. Indeed, the difficulty of resolving historical discrimination is reflected by the terms in which Indian constitutionalism conceives the problem of Dalit enfranchisement through the dual registers of exception and equalization. It is here that we see the continued salience of symbolic forms and structures of alterity.

The cultural and political history of how untouchables became Dalits is also the story of how a political universal, equality, was transformed into a historically and culturally specific entity, how equality was redefined as caste equality. One of the main contributions of *The Caste Question* is to challenge the centrality of "caste" to discourses of South Asian exceptionalism on the one hand, and to demand attention to secularism and democracy as cultural objects on the other. To make cultural categories political is to make visible the caste subaltern as an inaugural political subject. To culturalize political categories, on the other hand, is to challenge the assumption that words such as "rights," "equality," and "democracy" are universals. With this in mind, it is worth specifying the *topos* of Indian democracy in so far as it conjugates the interaction between social recognition and rights through the figure of the Dalit.

THE POLITICS OF RECOGNITION

During the last century, the humanity of the Dalit came to be predicated on arduously resignifying the apparently consensual order of caste as the practice of sanctioned discrimination and violence. The visibility of the Dalit subaltern and the political salience of embodied difference for Indian politics reflects the success of Dalit claims to human recognition. We can better evaluate how Dalits are situated on the field of recognition by exploring affinities with, and significant departures from, the paradigmatic model of recognition.

G. W. F. Hegel's account of the master-slave dialectic makes power, inequality, and terror essential to the struggle for freedom. In Hegel's account, coming to self-consciousness depends on the other's recognition and is an inherently violent process. As is well-known, the parable of recognition is inaugurated when two equal and opposite forms of self-consciousness, each desirous of the other's recognition, embark on a struggle unto death. But herein lies the problem: only one of them can win. Victory is short-lived, for it is contingent on enslaving the other so that mutual recognition becomes impossible. The master wins the first round of the struggle, but becomes dependent on the acknowledgment of an enslaved other. The slave retains the capacity for self-realization through labor and the willingness to risk his life to achieve his full human potential, to imagine freedom in its plenitude. In this account of recognition, social relations are permanently conflictual. The slave, like the proletariat or the peasant, is an inaugural subject existentially defined by negative consciousness, but carrying the seeds of revolutionary action.[13] By establishing the inseparability of subject-formation, social relations, and political processes, Hegel also reminds us, contra John Locke, for example, that there are no originary individuals who "found" society by contract or any other means. Thus, Hegel profoundly questions whether the accepted separation between individual and community and the story of their subsequent political integration is intellectually sustainable.

In Hegel's time, the Haitian Revolution played a crucial role in embedding race and slavery within the conceptual circuitry of rights and recognition.[14] The institution of slavery became an organizing figure for political thought through the paradoxes it posed for the self-identity of master and slave.[15] In India, too, at least from Phule's time, slavery was a powerful concept-metaphor for caste as a conflictual and antagonistic social structure suffused by violence. Thus, what Thomas Holt refers to as the enduring "problem of freedom" hinges on this paradoxical centrality of slavery to the imagination of freedom in the Western philosophical tradition, not to mention the historical contiguity of (plantation) slavery with the development of capitalism.[16] By explicitly linking subject-formation with the development of political forms, Hegel's model of recognition—and its significant emendation by theorists of anticolonial struggle—provides a useful template against which to address Dalit subject-formation.

It is obvious why an account that places violence and freedom at the heart of narratives of self-identity and social recognition should have provoked engagement and extension into new domains of social experience. Frantz Fanon's revision of Hegel connected subject-formation with the racial and cultural violence of colonialism. The cycle of misrecognition Fanon famously outlined in *Black Skin, White Masks* (1952) develops through a psychoanalytic rereading of Hegel that begins with the externalization of the racial self through a child's fearful gaze, "Mama, see the Negro! I'm frightened!" It ends with the Negro's identification with the white gaze, seeing himself as he is seen: "The Negro is an animal, the Negro is bad, the Negro is mean, the Negro is ugly."[17] Substituting the black man's epidermal schema, the fact of blackness, for his corporeal schema, white racism systematically misrecognized the black person.

A response to the psychic wound of racialization and the organizing logic of colonial exploitation is conceived in Fanon's famous manifesto of decolonization, *The Wretched of the Earth* (1961). Here Fanon proposed violence—rather than work, or as a specific kind of work—as the transformative activity of the colonized. In his masculinist narrative of national liberation, Fanon described decolonization in apocalyptic terms, as a moment of rebirth and the making of a new man. His solution to colonial dehumanization lay in the spectacular violence of the colonized: revolutionary violence was both necessary and purifying.

There was no endorsement of antistate violence in Ambedkar's scheme of Dalit liberation, insofar as Ambedkar stood against revolutionary violence and spoke for a territorially dispersed minority within the nation.[18] Fanon and Ambedkar creatively reinterpreted Hegel's narrative of subject-formation through historical particularity—slavery or caste—and situational possibility—revolution or postcolonial transition. Both saw subject-formation as violent per se but also as the creative basis of society. Fanon's response was to exacerbate violent antagonism to the point of revolutionary violence as political creation. The impossibility of converting Dalit minority status into the principle of nationality meant that it was the revolutionary act of constitution making that imagined a new social contract between Dalits and Hindus, between oppressors and oppressed. Ambedkar's faith that the state, via law as habit-changing technology, could effectively transform social relations and behavior reflects his intellectual proclivities.[19] As well, it was a pragmatic response to the colonial-national context within which he worked to resolve the Dalit question.

This is where the Dalit question takes a detour from the demand for a purifying violence to counter the violence of colonial exploitation and racialization. Rather than instigating violent separation, the permanent antagonism between Dalit and non-Dalit became a structuring contradiction of state practice. Ambedkar's attempts at political separation, though they failed at the level of realpolitik, underlined the fact that Dalits were a territorially dispersed minority. From then on, a principle of separation would inhere as a permanent reminder of the impossibility of justice for Dalits' historic suffering within the normal terms and conditions of political discourse.

The moment of constitution making predicated the development of the postcolonial polity on redressing caste "backwardness," now defined as a complex form of social inequality, through practices of equalization. What Marc Galanter calls policies of "compensatory discrimination" carry within them an analytics of power: they provide a diagnostic of the structural causes of sociopolitical deprivation, and they are a mechanism for its redress. What is noteworthy is the centrality of the Scheduled Castes to this vision, for their enfranchisement was conceived through the dual registers of exception and equalization. Because the *politically inadequate subject was also a socially marginal subject,* the constitutional resolution to the caste question required questions of social inequality to be addressed through political means. Strategies of equalization were thus conceived as capable of transforming social practice in addition to rendering stigmatized subjects into citizens. In this schema, national freedom and emancipation were prospective, they were promissory notes contingent on the success of time-bound measures, for example, reservations, which assumed that substantive equality and a new sociality would reign in the future. Here lies an indication of what I have termed the "politicization of politics."

The second axis of identity, resting on the rewritten Dalit history of enduring conflict between Buddhism and Brahminism, allowed Dalits to claim the political identity of non-Hindu. This challenged the Dalit's centrality to a reformed Hinduism and a recuperated upper-caste self "premised on a shared concept of humanity which means that the other is a perverted version of the self."[20] Instead, for Dalits, the right to religious belief was also the right to assert an agonistic identity counterposed to the hegemonic embrace of Hindu history. The maximal act, conversion out of Hinduism, also purposively reminded Hindus of the intimate violence of untouchability.

Such trajectories emphasize the dual problematic of Dalit emancipation: to overcome religious discrimination and political inequality simultaneously, rather than transcending religious distinction by substituting the rule of the state for the rule of religion. Dalit liberation staged the interpenetration of the religious and the political as a permanent, constitutive contradiction of the Indian social order, rather than their sublation or transcendence. The tension between a vulnerable identity derived from historically stigmatized existence and its translation into the language of state classification and protection became a structuring aspect of Dalit postcolonial existence. The interanimating tension between the "religious" and the "political" resolution of the Dalit was revealed. Therefore, challenges to the complex ritual, social, and economic inequities generated by caste Hinduism mobilized the dual registers of cultural exception and political equalization, identity and equality. They correspond to the paradoxical duality of a Dalit identity balanced between a purely relational and historical identity, on the one hand, and a more essentialist or embodied one on the other. The problem of Dalit essentialism captured in the "Buddhism versus Marxism" debates after national independence, the cultural politics of Dalit liberation, the symbolic violence of speech and word in Dalit literature, and the continued vulnerability of Dalits to ritualized structures of political violence each reflect the delicate balance of conceiving Dalit both as an identity and as political potentiality.

Alarmingly, symbolic politics and political symbology in general, and ritualized structures of anti-Dalit violence in particular, reflect the Dalit's pivotal role in *expanding the domain of politics by making manifest the relationship between violence and politics*. The increased salience of the caste body and the visibility of Dalits are mutually entailed by state structures of recognition and the politicization of public space, whether urban or rural, where the game of recognition between Dalit and non-Dalit is at least tensely, and often violently, enacted. Contemporary Dalit vulnerability is, in part, an artifact of state intervention, juridical convention, and efforts to manage the caste atrocity through the constitutionally mandated field of civil rights law to which the SCs are central. Juridical structures of protection are thus the reflex of an existing archaic structure of violence *and* the response to it.

RIGHTS, RESERVATIONS, AND REPRESENTATION

In my account of Dalit emancipation, I have consistently emphasized the transformative potential carried by the idea of rights, social recognition, redistribution, and political representation *and* their significant revision in the course of Dalit struggle. In its focus on individual reason, rights, and human equality, anticaste discourse might appear as a vernacular complement, a homegrown version of political liberalism. However the valence of these concepts was transformed when they were addressed to distinctive forms of life, that is, to caste stigma, and because they took root in a colonial context that precluded standard narratives of subject-formation and individual agency.

One way to emphasize the distinctive genealogy of Dalit subject-formation is to contrast it with the tension between group identity and individual rights in the West, where group identity is often characterized as a secondary, sometimes aberrant effect of the normative trajectories of individuation. I should clarify that my intention is not to make a point about Indian deviance or belatedness, but precisely the opposite. I want to suggest that by exploring a defining feature of Indian strategies of equalization, affirmation of individual rights through affirmation of collective identities, we might also be invited to reconsider the problematic status of group rights for late-modern Western democracies.

In the West, the consensual politics envisioned by liberal democracies has been dependent on mechanisms for casting out social forms and religio-cultural practices that offend moral dispositions, violate the freedom of others, or require some form of remedial correction. Policies and procedures for recognizing difference are typically viewed as practices of prejudice or as the introduction of particularism into a normative political field. Even when they are acknowledged to be necessary, as with the case of affirmative action policies, they carry the taint of exceptional or extraordinary measures of short duration and ostentatious modes of state intervention into civil society. Extended and inconclusive debates around the politics of identity derive in part from the fact that religious or cultural practices implicate a group or community as the bearer of identity, challenging liberal conceptions of the individual as the locus of autonomous or voluntary action and the bearer of rights.

The tension between individual and group rights is the classic impasse of liberal multiculturalism in the West. The most persuasive reading of this dilemma is articulated by Charles Taylor (1994), who argues that the politics of identity place liberal democracies in the position of managing the commitment to equality and universal rights against claims to authenticity.[21] As individuals and groups use symbols of ethnic, religious, sexual, and cultural belonging as markers of authenticity, they also deepen the public visibility of particularistic identities as the grounds for making claims upon the social collectivity for equal rights, on the one hand, and for tolerance and respect on the other. For Taylor, as for other communitarians, the *right to recognition* is understood as a claim to the *right to difference*.

The problem for a politics of identity thus becomes how to distinguish the recognition of difference from the practice and perpetuation of inequality, from the problem of the social redistribution of political and economic opportunity, on the one hand, and from support for repugnant practice on the other. Ironically, liberal tolerance might enable "liberal strategies of exclusion," to borrow Uday Mehta's apposite phrase. Moral repugnance has become a powerful defense against cultural practices, (e.g., genital cutting, veiling, or bigamy) and the legitimating ground for political intervention, often (and increasingly) in the name of human rights. In less extreme instances, the remedy for this problem is articulated as the need to contextualize each instance on its own terms, confident that liberal consensus can distinguish "good" difference from "bad." We thus return to the classic recourse to law, context, and the individual "case."

The pressing issue of social redistribution as a response to historical discrimination tends to be divorced from the social recognition of difference.[22] In this latter instance, the embarrassment around group rights manifests as a challenge to the relevance of addressing past injustice through present practices of antidiscrimination. This is buttressed by a growing consensus—certainly in recent debates over affirmative action policies in the United States—that it is preferential quotas that constitute a practice of prejudice, rather than the socioeconomic circumstances to which they respond. Demands for recognition and for equality thus mobilize divergent conceptions of history, and they enact different relationships to the state. While the politics of recognition addresses groups as fully developed, autonomous identities competing for social space, the model of discrimination assumes coeval or connected histories based on differential access to social and political power that must be remedied through state intervention.

The simultaneity of Dalit enfranchisement with postcolonial transition requires a different understanding of Dalits' political history. Recognition, redistribution, and equal representation were to be simultaneously secured through the mechanism of reservations. Thus separation, or group identity, has functioned as the modal form of political inclusion, generating a form of politics where a sociopolitically inadequate, demographic majority—for instance, lower castes—has challenged upper-caste hegemony. The limits to such a form of politics—whose logical culmination would be a system of proportional representation along caste lines—arises, however, due to the political conviction that caste is not a positive form of social organization but a historically and culturally specific form of inequality. Thus the dual impulse to recognize and to remove caste has produced an agonistic terrain of politics where caste identification is expected to lead to the annihilation of caste. The paradox of embracing universal models of progress while in practice working through caste defines the postcolonial career of Indian democracy. The gap between substantive equality and embodied difference generates a *corporeal politics* of caste.[23]

How does this happen? We might begin by noting the historic centrality of community, for like caste and religion, community was a representational construct, an effect of colonial knowledge. Community was understood to enframe caste and religious entities, however, giving them organizational regularity, coherence, and a kind of public legibility. Colonial misreading of the nomothetic character of community meant that communities were viewed as perversely political: they were affective, prepolitical entities, on the one hand, and manifestations of despotic power on the other.

While the status of community-as-constituency is an enduring legacy of colonial government, it is also true that a reductive definition of "community" was challenged from the start. Initially, Jotirao Phule's characterization of the *shudra-atishudra* as a political collectivity and an ethical unity challenged the Brahmin's hegemony through implicit use of the discourse of majority and minority at a time when the nation was yet to be passionately imagined by anticolonial thought. Unity among the Dalit and non-Brahmin communities proved impossible, however, given the economic contradictions between those who owned and those who labored, together with non-Brahmins' investment in the ritual hierarchy of caste. A consistent tension in the politics of non-Brahminism was posed to those who challenged the Brahmin's political power but accepted his ritual sacrality, versus those who imagined the caste self and the social order outside the frame of Hindu history altogether. These contradictions affected B. R. Ambedkar's efforts to enumerate a community of *non-Hindus,* their identity negatively defined through a historic antagonism to touchable Hindus, which revealed a structuring violence, a fundamental cleavage *within* the Hindu community.

The mechanism through which such negative identity was to be manifest is instructive. The separate electorate was a colonial means of commensuration that assumed qualitative equivalence between quantitatively incommensurable entities. That is, equivalence between the Hindu majority and Muslim minority was assumed on the grounds that they were both religious communities. Thus Ambedkar's efforts to use the separate electorate to define a *new minority* organized around a negative principle of social organization, untouchability, was bound to fail. In essence, Ambedkar sought to delineate a community whose very existence indicted inherited privilege as a form of caste power. The failure was instructive nonetheless, since it revealed untouchability as the glue uniting the otherwise fissiparous castes, while the visible economy of caste was secured through the dehumanization of the untouchable. This structure of a necessary yet negated existence is precisely what strategies of equalization were meant to redress.

Inherited subalternity precluded Dalits from unequivocally claiming cultural distinctiveness, for theirs was a culture of subordination, physical deformation, and the performance of degraded labor. Gandhi's sharp query whether Dalits desired to retain their stigmatized identity was prescient, but the response was complex: theirs was an identity that had to be acknowledged and refused.

Adult franchise together with the persistent politicization of caste as a sign of inequality and of "civilizational shame" has brought social forms and practices within the frame of political commensuration.[24] Though policymakers envisaged reservations as temporary measures, a decade at a time, the practice is now integral to the architecture of the postcolonial state. The seeming irony of India's democratization through ostensibly derided cultural forms and social practices associated with the "traditional" order of caste has affinity with the use of race in affirmative action policies. Unlike affirmative action policies in the United States, however, it is the demographic majority that is conceived as sociopolitically inadequate, from the superclassification of the Dalit to reservations for the OBCs.

EQUALITY AND DIFFERENCE

It was only when the national community could be aligned with the Hindu nation, that is, in the crucial years leading up to Partition and its aftermath, that the state's protection of Dalits' rights as minority rights was placed on new footing. These rights were secured through the regime of civil rights and the secularization of Hinduism.[25] The dual resolution of the Dalit question is quite distinct from the constitutional categorization of Muslims as a religious minority or, for that matter, the impasse of female enfranchisement that is recurrently staged as a conflict between state and community.

If Muslims were the modal minority in colonial India, theirs was a question of sovereignty and not of difference.[26] For this reason, Partition challenged the conceptual viability of the term "Indian Muslim," so much so that it became political common sense to define the good Muslim as one who did not self-identify as one.[27] In contrast, the Indian Constitution redefined Muslims as religious rather than political minorities. The identification of the Muslim as pure alterity has had pernicious effects, ranging from the susceptibility of Muslims to genocidal violence, to growing evidence that their indices of socioeconomic growth rank even lower than the SCs.[28]

The "secularism debates" in India have focused, however, on extending one of the fundamental precepts of the politics of identity by redefining the right to difference as the *equal right to religious difference*.[29] Partha Chatterjee has argued for the need to respect religious communities as forms of life even when they refuse to subscribe to the norms of reasoned debate, thus challenging the liberal rationality presumed by the politics of identity. By emphasizing the incommensurability of community practice with state reason, Chatterjee suggests that even when the *identity* of communities is incommensurable, they must be presumed to be commensurable (as political units) with respect to the state. Chatterjee's demand for a "strategic politics of tolerance" that respects religious difference, together with the "push for democratization from the inside" through "institutions which have representative legitimacy," is oddly redolent of the status of community in colonial thought.[30] His position has generated significant criticism by feminist scholars, who argue that it paves the way for patriarchal unfreedom.[31]

Feminist scholars, on the other hand, have been concerned with the status of women as a political collectivity. Joan Scott has argued that in the West, demands for political equality have mobilized around sexual difference as that which precludes political equality *and* as the grounds for political recognition for women. This has produced a recurrent (and unresolved) tension between difference and equality in feminist demands for rights.[32] In India the problem is complicated by the fact that women must engage state and community simultaneously, albeit differently, since sexual rights—marriage, divorce, inheritance, maintenance—are regulated by religious personal laws, while the Indian state adjudicates other aspects of women's status. Mrinalini Sinha has posited the distinctive perils for Indian feminism as a consequence of such bifurcation: feminist demands for difference were historically aligned with "the collective interests of religious communities," while demands for political equality posited women as "entirely apart and separate from all other social relations," though in practice this aligned them with the political position of upper-class, upper-caste Hindu men.[33] While Sinha's work reveals how a hegemonic feminism was ideologically aligned with mainstream nationalism, Rajeswari Sunder Rajan has brilliantly theorized the implications of this impasse for the gendered subaltern when she is also a religious minority. From "Shah Bano" to "Amina"—cases that consistently point to the failure of justice for Muslim women, whether through personal laws or criminal justice—Sunder Rajan explores the contemporary impasse of feminist theorization of the female subject when confronted with the bifurcated subjectivity of the Muslim woman as citizen-subject.[34] If "honor" is the disciplining discourse of community, Sunder Rajan's work unravels the hazards of statist discourses of "protection," a discourse Indian feminists have challenged but also implicitly reproduced through their engagements with the state.[35]

I would argue that one way out of the continued impasse of female enfranchisement as individuating yet affiliating is for feminists to mobilize dual demands—political equality vis-à-vis the state, and *sexual equality* within community—but to focus, ultimately, on rendering "community" an unstable and illegible category, as caste radicals sought to do earlier in the century through intercaste and political marriage. Rather than efforts to subsume community to the state, aligning sexual rights with political rights—and thereby challenging the stability of "community"—might be the more salient method of intervention. I say this because India's peculiar path to secular modernity has exacerbated the tension between community and state, with both conceived as static entities. Introducing sexual difference as the site of social reproduction thus poses a serious challenge to the political status of community and the hegemony of the state.

Unlike female enfranchisement, which must mediate between sexuality and community, the Dalit question is now conjoined with democracy and secularism in a unique manner. It stages political equalization and cultural exception as dual strategies for challenging the complex inequities generated by caste Hinduism. For Dalits, emancipation of self and community are simultaneous goals, since the aim is to overcome discrimination and inequality in the political and religious spheres. In turn, my theorization of anti-Dalit violence posits it as a limit to political commensuration for Dalits.

DALIT POWER

Given the long history of Dalits' resistance to Hindu incorporation, it is ironic that the caste question has become prominent as a consequence of Hindu nationalism's transformation of political culture and its challenge to extant forms of secularism.[36] The immense irony of Hindu nationalism is that it brought Dalit and Backward Caste politics to the forefront through an aggressive, inclusive Hindu nationalist casteism that accelerated lower-caste politicization while giving some a place as foot soldiers in anti-Muslim violence.[37] As Dalits have been symbolically reincorporated into the formal political arena via Hindutva politics and its anti-Muslim enactments, an emergent Dalit politics has also challenged Hinduization.

Indeed, it is not overstatement to say that the post-Mandal Dalit subject is at the heart of a democratic revolution of the Indian polity and represents another reorientation of power around electoral politics and the figure of the caste subaltern. The electoral success and populist polemics of the Bahujan Samaj Party in Uttar Pradesh, India's most populous state, spotlights the new direction. The historic election victory of the BSP in May 2006 staged "Dalit power" through a landslide victory free of past political alliances, including the Hindu nationalist Bharatiya Janata Party.[38] Scholars such as Gopal Guru and Sharad Patil have long associated the politics of the BSP—political coalition building, including with Hindu nationalists; the sharpening of caste identities; and a symbolic contempt for the upper castes—with political opportunism rather than political emancipation.[39] This time was different. Virtually ignored by mainstream media, the BSP ran a highly successful campaign that departed from the anti-Brahmin posture it had taken since its 1984 founding.[40] Mayawati, the only Dalit woman to become chief minister of an Indian state, had won the post thrice in the past, heading coalition governments. In the 2006 elections, Mayawati cultivated the Brahmin vote and a Dalit-Brahmin *bhaichara* (brotherhood) to win a BSP victory. While 80 percent of the Dalit vote went to the BSP, the votes of Brahmins and the so-called Middle Backward Classes were crucial to the landslide.[41] This was a subaltern version of the Congress strategy of winning elections through a coalition of upper castes and "core minorities." One of the tens of thousands of BSP supporters gathered in Lucknow for Mayawati's swearing-in ceremony noted the symbolic potency of the event: "Mythology . . . has recorded how Brahmin priests across the length and breadth of the country refused to perform Raj Tilak [accession of power] ceremonies for Shivaji just because he was a Maratha. . . . [Today] we are witnessing the Raj Tilak of a Dalit, and that too of a woman, virtually conducted by hundreds of thousands of Brahmins."[42]

The epochal shift was lost on no one: Dalit subalterns had captured state power and stood at the center of Uttar Pradesh's politics. The transformation of Dalits' low status into an electoral catalyst was a belated realization of Ambedkar's dream.[43] Ironically, the power of the Dalit vote was realized by emphasizing the structural similarities between Dalits and Brahmins as demographic minorities, on the one hand, and by forcing Brahmins to recognize their political dependence on the BSP, on the other. Dalit power was manifest through the BSP, but Brahmins were put in a position to name themselves *as Brahmin* and as a numerical minority to boot.

The BSP's success indicates that a subaltern transformation of the political brings with it the recognition of state power as caste power. Mayawati's shift in emphasis from the *bahujan samaj* (majority community) to *sarva samaj* (the entire society) indexes the symbolic centrality of Dalit power for transforming politics. As one journalist noted, "The BSP's victory advances the issues of equity and redistributive justice towards the top of the agenda—not just in U.P. [Uttar Pradesh] but in India as a whole."[44]

The potential transformation of the Indian polity through the centralization of Dalit power appears anomalous if judged from the perspective of Western democratic regimes. It is also the case that the egalitarian promise held out by the BSP has yet to be realized. However, the symbolic association between democracy and the Dalit has become a partial reality in India's political landscape. Mayawati's success derives from using the space of representative democracy and adult franchise to focalize Dalits' particular interests. This resembles Ambedkar's early argument regarding the possibility of using universal enfranchisement together with political safeguards to make the Dalit minority visible as a complexly subordinated group. As well, it reflects possible alliances between Dalits and other stigmatized groups, including Muslims and Christians, alliances that are not along traditional class lines, but instead require creative linkage between caste and class.[45]

These developments return us to the dual resolution of the Dalit question along the axes of the ethical and the political, of conversion and commensuration. I have argued that this resolution is in fact a recipe for the politicization of politics, for new imaginations of social justice and dignity. This derives from the impossibility of doing justice to the Dalit within existing forms of political restitution. Thus the successful accretion of political value for Dalits in one part of the subcontinent might be a portent of the future. Or, perhaps it will give way to new imaginations of the human and of human rights outside the subcontinent.[46]

The effort to imagine the contours of a shifting politics and a society that is yet to come returns us to Vasantrao Kamble's powerful metaphor of connection: the electric shock as a model of social recognition. History, politics, culture, the caste body—each has been surprisingly transformed by the demand for Dalit recognition. Dalit struggles for equality and self-respect have not been abstract thought experiments. They have been generated within the embodied space of stigmatized selfhood. By implicating Dalits and non-Dalits in its genealogy of political subject-formation, Dalit history implicates us all in the imagination of a Dalit future.

Abbreviations

ADPM	Anarya Dosh Pariharak Mandali
AIR	*All India Reporter*
AISCF	All-India Scheduled Caste Federation
ANM	Asprishyata Nivarak Mandali
BAWS	*Babasaheb Ambedkar Writings and Speeches*
BB	*Bharatishkrit Bharat*
BC	Backward Class
BDD	Bombay Development Department
BHS	Bahishkrit Hitakarini Sabha
BJP	Bharatiya Janata Party
BLR	*Bombay Law Reporter*
BSP	Bahujan Samaj Party
CID	Central Intelligence Department
CPI	Communist Party of India
DB	*Din Bandhu*
DCM	Depressed Classes Mission
DIGP	Deputy Inspector General of Police
DSP	Deputy Superintendent of Police
ED	Education Department
FIR	First Information Report

GD	General Department
ILP	Independent Labour Party
ILR	*Indian Law Reporter*
JD	Judicial Department
MSA	Maharashtra State Archives, Mumbai
OBC	Other Backward Class
PCR Act	Protection of Civil Rights Act
PES	People''s Education Society
POA Act	Prevention of Atrocities (against Scheduled Castes and Scheduled Tribes) Act
PSI	Police Subinspector
RCSCST	*Report of the Commissioner of Scheduled Castes and Scheduled Tribes*
RD	Revenue Department
RPI	Republican Party of India
RSS	Rashtriya Svayamsevak Sangh
SC	Scheduled Caste
SM	*Somavanshiya Mitra*
SP	Superintendent of Police
ST	Scheduled Tribe

Notes

AUTHOR'S NOTE

1. I take inspiration from W. E. B. DuBois, who justified his use of the term "Negro" even if it appeared "illogical" (and, one assumes, geographically imprecise) because he "believe[d] that eight million Americans are entitled to a capital letter." W. E. B. DuBois, *The Philadelphia Negro* (New York: Lippincott, 1899), 1–4.

INTRODUCTION

1. Joan Scott, "The Conundrum of Equality" (occasional paper, Institute for Advanced Study, Paper no. 2, March 1999), 3.

2. An important developmentalist account that differs from my focus on the staggered and uneven temporalities of Dalit emancipation is Eleanor Zelliot, *From Untouchable to Dalit,* 3rd ed. (Delhi: Manohar, 2005). See also Eleanor Zelliot, "Dr. Ambedkar and the Mahar Movement" (PhD dissertation, University of Pennsylvania, 1969), republished as *Dr. Babasaheb Ambedkar and the Untouchable Movement* (New Delhi: Blumoon Books, 2004).

3. For a brilliant account of these two histories, see Thomas Holt, *The Problem of Freedom: Race, Labor, and Politics in Jamaica and Britain, 1832–1938* (Baltimore, MD: Johns Hopkins University Press, 1991), 3–12.

4. Philip Abrams, "Notes on the Difficulty of Studying the State," *Journal of Historical Sociology* 1, no. 1 (1988): 58–89. See also Timothy Mitchell, "Economy and the State Effect," in *State/Culture,* ed. George Steinmetz (Ithaca, NY: Cornell University Press, 1999), 76–97.

5. Nicholas B. Dirks, *Castes of Mind: Colonialism and the Making of Modern India* (Princeton, NJ: Princeton University Press, 2001).

6. For an argument about how Christianity became the standard for evaluating other "world religions," see Talal Asad, *Genealogies of Religion: Discipline and Reasons of Power in Christianity and Islam* (Baltimore, MD: Johns Hopkins University Press, 1993). For an account of how Hinduism was reified as a consequence of India's encounter with missionary Christianity, see Peter van der Veer, *Imperial Encounters: Religion and Modernity in India and Britain* (Baltimore, MD: Johns Hopkins University Press, 2001). With regard to Christian conversion of the lower and untouchable castes in western and central India, see Saurabh Dube, *Untouchable Pasts: Religion, Identity, and Power among a Central Indian Community, 1780–1950* (Albany: SUNY Press, 1998); and Rosalind O'Hanlon, *Caste, Conflict, and Ideology: Mahatma Jotirao Phule and Low Caste Protest in Nineteenth-Century Western India* (Cambridge: Cambridge University Press, 1985).

7. Dilip Menon, *Caste, Nationalism and Communism in India: Malabar, 1900–1948* (Cambridge: Cambridge University Press, 1994); and Vijay Prashad, *Untouchable Freedom: A Social History of a Dalit Community* (Delhi: Oxford University Press, 2000).

8. Louis Dumont, *Homo Hierarchicus: The Caste System and Its Implications,* complete rev. English ed. (Chicago: University of Chicago Press, 1980); and Louis Dumont, *From Mandeville to Marx: The Genesis and Triumph of Economic Ideology* (Chicago: University of Chicago Press, 1977).

9. Michael Moffatt, *An Untouchable Community in South India: Structure and Consensus* (Princeton, NJ: Princeton University Press, 1979).

10. Robert Deliège, *The World of the "Untouchables": Paraiyars of Tamil Nadu* (Delhi and New York: Oxford University Press, 1997). Promising avenues of inquiry are found in the work of R. S. Khare, who discusses how Dalit Chamar intellectuals theorize their subalternity; Owen Lynch's study of Dalit political mobilization in Lucknow; and the work of Gyan Prakash on the Bhuinyas of Bihar, where labor servitude and ritual degradation produced a critique of caste that involved both the internalization of ritual hierarchy and its virulent rejection in favor of egalitarianism. R. S. Khare, *The Untouchable as Himself: Ideology, Identity, and Pragmatism among the Lucknow Chamars* (Cambridge: Cambridge University Press, 1984); Owen M. Lynch, *The Politics of Untouchability: Social Mobility and Social Change in a City of India* (New York: Columbia University Press, 1969); and Gyan Prakash, *Bonded Histories: Genealogies of Labor Servitude in Colonial India* (Cambridge: Cambridge University Press, 1990).

11. Nicholas B. Dirks, *The Hollow Crown: Ethnohistory of an Indian Kingdom,* 2nd ed. (Ann Arbor: University of Michigan Press, 1993). Gloria Raheja has argued for the coexistence of Kshatriya power and Brahmin dominance, but does not discuss how their intersection transforms scholarly understandings of caste power. Gloria Goodwin Raheja, "Centrality, Mutuality and Hierarchy," *CIS* 23, no. 1 (1989): 79–101.

12. Dirks, *Castes of Mind,* part 3. For a discussion of Indological and social-scientific constructions of a sociopolitically deficient "India," see Ronald Inden, *Imagining India* (Oxford: Basil Blackwell, 1990).

13. Sekhar Bandyopadhyay, *Caste, Protest, and Identity in Colonial India: The Namasudras of Bengal 1872–1947* (Richmond, Surrey: Curzon Press, 1997);

V. Geetha and S. V. Rajadurai, *Towards a Non-Brahmin Millennium: From Iyothee Thass to Periyar* (Calcutta: Samya, 1998); Menon, *Caste, Nationalism and Communism in India;* and Prashad, *Untouchable Freedom.*

14. Mark Juergensmeyer, *Religion as Social Vision: The Movement against Untouchability in Twentieth-Century Punjab* (Berkeley: University of California Press, 1982); and Khare, *The Untouchable as Himself.* Nandini Gooptu's work addresses underexplored linkages between caste-labor and urban politics in the interwar period. Nandini Gooptu, *The Politics of the Urban Poor in Early Twentieth-Century India* (Cambridge: Cambridge University Press, 2001). Antonio Gramsci defines the organic intellectual as a member of the subordinated classes who, like all dominated peoples, carries a contradictory perspective on the world that acknowledges the force and power of elite domination even as it rejects the validity of those same categories of identity and social description. Antonio Gramsci, *Prison Notebooks,* (New York: Columbia University Press, 1992).

15. Important examples include J. Duncan M. Derrett, *Essays in Classical and Modern Hindu Law,* 4 vols. (Indian repr., Delhi: Universal Book Traders, 1995), especially vol. 3, *Anglo-Indian Legal Problems,* and vol. 4, *Current Problems and the Legacy of the Past);* Marc Galanter, *Law and Society in Modern India,* ed. Rajeev Dhavan (New Delhi: Oxford University Press, 1989); and R. Lingat, *The Classical Law of India,* trans. J. Duncan M. Derrett (Berkeley: University of California Press, 1973).

16. Rachel Sturman has explored how "marginal communities"—Khojas, Memons, Mahars—had been brought under the ambit of Hindu and Muslim personal laws that were invested with "universalized and rationalized jurisdiction" during the 1930s. Rachel Sturman, "Public and Private Communities," in "Law's Subjects: Property, Personhood and Family in the Making of Modern India" (unpublished ms.).

17. Partha Chattejee, "The Nationalist Resolution of the Woman's Question," in *Recasting Women: Essays in Indian Colonial History,* ed. Kumkum Sangari and Sudesh Vaid (New Brunswick, NJ: Rutgers University Press, 1990), 233–53.

18. For recent examples, see Shahid Amin, *Event, Metaphor, Memory: Chauri Chaura 1922–1992* (Delhi: Oxford University Press, 1995); and Dipesh Chakrabarty, *Provincializing Europe: Postcolonial Thought and Historical Difference* (Princeton, NJ: Princeton University Press, 2000). Works on the gendered subaltern have identified significant lacunae in the conception of sexed subalternity and a more general refusal, on the part of the Subaltern Studies Collective, to engage the question of gender. Important examples include Uma Chakravarti, *Rewriting History: The Life and Times of Pandita Ramabai* (Delhi: Kali for Women, 1997); Indrani Chatterjee, *Gender, Slavery and Law in Colonial India* (Delhi: Oxford University Press, 1999); Charu Gupta, *Sexuality, Obscenity, Community: Women, Muslims, and the Hindu Public in Colonial India* (New York: Palgrave, 2002); Tanika Sarkar, *Hindu Wife, Hindu Nation: Community, Religion, and Cultural Nationalism* (Bloomington: Indiana University Press, 2001); Mrinalini Sinha, *Specters of Mother India: The Global Restructuring of an Empire* (Durham, NC: Duke University Press, 2006); and Rajeswari Sunder Rajan, *The Scandal of the State: Women, Law, and Citizenship in Post-*

colonial India (Durham, NC: Duke University Press, 2003). The classic text is the groundbreaking essay, Gayatri Chakravorty Spivak, "Can the Subaltern Speak?" in *Marxism and the Interpretation of Culture,* ed. Cary Nelson and Lawrence Grossberg (Urbana: University of Illinois Press, 1988), 271–313.

19. Ranajit Guha, *Elementary Aspects of Peasant Insurgency in Colonial India* (Delhi: Oxford University Press, 1983).

20. Eleanor Zelliot's pathbreaking work on B. R. Ambedkar and the Dalit movement provides the basis for important recent works, including Jayashree Gokhale's study of the Ambedkar movement and Gail Omvedt's comparative study of Dalit movements in the west and south. Zelliot, *Dr. Babasaheb Ambedkar and the Untouchable Movement*; Jayashree Gokhale, *From Concessions to Confrontation: The Politics of an Indian Untouchable Community* (Bombay: Popular Prakashan, 1993); and Gail Omvedt, *Dalits and the Democratic Revolution: Dr. Ambedkar and the Dalit Movement in Colonial India* (New Delhi: Sage Publications, 1994). The twelve-volume Marathi biography of Ambedkar, first published in 1964 by C. B. Khairmode, is a critical source for scholars of the movement. C. B. Khairmode, *Bhimrao Ramji Ambedkar Charitra,* 3rd ed. (Pune: Sugawa Prakashan, 2003).

21. For key studies that consider caste radicalism as an intellectual formation, see V. Geetha and Rajadurai, *Towards a Non-Brahmin Milennium;* and O'Hanlon, *Caste, Conflict, and Ideology.* For writings by and on Phule, see R. S. Ghadge *Amhi Pahilele Phule* [The Phule That We Saw], ed. Sitaram Raikar (Pune: Ma. Phule Samata Pratisthan, 1981); Pandharinath Sitaram Patil, *Mahatma Jotirao Phule Yanche Charitra* [A Biography of Mahatma Jotirao Phule] (Chikhali, 1927); and Dhananjay Keer and S. G. Malshe, eds., *Mahatma Phule Samagra Vangmay* [Collected Works of Mahatma Jotirao Phule] (Mumbai: Mumbai Rajya Sahitya ani Samskriti Mandal, 1969), reprinted 1991, ed. Y. D. Phadke.

22. O'Hanlon, *Caste, Conflict, and Ideology.*

23. Chatterjee, "The Nationalist Resolution of the Woman's Question."

24. Although *dalit* and *paddalit* were used in the 1920s, the terms only gained traction and came into common usage in the 1970s.

25. Gandhi attributes the term "Harijan" to the saint Narasinha Mehta. *Navajivan,* August 2, 1931; and *Young India,* August 6, 1931. Earlier, Gandhi used the term *antyaja* (last born) to refer to untouchables.

26. Thomas Blom Hansen, *Wages of Violence: Naming and Identity in Postcolonial Bombay* (Princeton, NJ : Princeton University Press, 2001), 2.

27. Allen Feldman, *Formations of Violence* (Chicago: University of Chicago Press, 1991).

28. A key example is the famous model of Sanskritization and westernization put forward by M. N. Srinivas and the unfortunate longevity of his now-dated analysis of caste assertion among political scientists. A recent example in an otherwise important account of the rise of "backward" caste and Dalit politics is Christophe Jaffrelot, *India's Silent Revolution: The Rise of the Lower Castes in North India* (New York: Columbia University Press, 2002). Though prescient in recognizing the growing political salience of caste, Srinivas's model of politics is ultimately homeostatic: it assumes that dominant castes transfer social capital and social conflict onto a new field, electoral politics. Indeed, Srinivas's

model of social transformation—"Sanskritization" and "westernization"—describes parallel forms of upward mobility: one is ritual, the other secular; one mimics the idealized power of Brahmin, the other of colonizer. The model describes perceived reality—for example, that Marathas dominate electoral politics in Maharashtra, or Gowdas in Karnataka—but it does not constitute a theory of caste power. Mysore Narasimhachar Srinivas, *Social Change in Modern India* (Berkeley: University of California Press, 1966). On caste and electoral politics, see also Lloyd I. Rudolph and Susanne Hoeber Rudolph, *The Modernity of Tradition: Political Development in India* (Chicago: University of Chicago Press, 1972).

29. R. Moore, "The Twilight of the Whigs and the Reform of the Indian Councils, 1886–1892," *The Historical Journal* 10, no. 3 (1967): 400–414.

30. R. Moore, "John Morley's Acid Test: India 1906–1910," *Pacific Affairs* 40, nos. 3–4 (1967): 333–40; and Stanley Wolpert, *Morley and India, 1906–1910* (Berkeley: University of California Press, 1967).

31. Ranajit Guha, "Discipline and Mobilize," in *Dominance without Hegemony: History and Power in Colonial India* (Cambridge, MA: Harvard University Press, 1997), 100–150.

32. C. L. R. James, *The Black Jacobins: Toussaint L'Ouverture and the San Domingo Revolution,* 2nd ed. (New York: Vintage, 1963). As Laurent Dubois has recently noted, James's exclusive focus on Toussaint L'Ouverture was polemically powerful yet historically problematic and ignored the fact that L'Ouverture's efforts to build a postemancipatory social order reinstituted the racial and economic orders of the plantation he had struggled against. Laurent Dubois, *Avengers of the New World: The Story of the Haitian Revolution* (Cambridge, MA: Belknap Press of Harvard University Press, 2004). See also David Patrick Geggus, *The Impact of the Haitian Revolution in the Atlantic World* (Columbia: University of South Carolina, 2001).

33. On the Cambridge School argument regarding the provincialization of politics, see, for example, Christopher Baker and David Washbrook, *South India: Political Institutions and Social Change* (Dehli: Vikas, 1975); and John Gallagher, Gordon Johnson, and Anil Seal, eds., *Locality, Province, and Nation: Essays on Indian Politics 1870 to 1940,* reprinted from *Modern Asian Studies* (Cambridge: University Press, 1973). For an early critique, see M. S. S. Pandian, "Beyond Colonial Crumbs: Cambridge School, Identity Politics, and Dravidian Movement," *Economic and Political Weekly* 30, nos. 7–8 (February 18, 1995): 385–91. For an important discussion of the emphasis on capitalism over colonialism in Cambridge historiography, see Dirks, *Castes of Mind,* epilogue.

34. Graham Burchell, Colin Gordon, and Peter Miller, eds., *The Foucault Effect: Studies in Governmentality* (Chicago: University of Chicago Press, 1991).

35. Abrams, "Notes on the Difficulty of Studying the State." See also Mitchell, "Economy and the State Effect."

36. Partha Chatterjee, *The Nation and Its Fragments: Colonial and Postcolonial Histories,* Oxford India Paperbacks (Delhi: Oxford University Press, 1995). See also David Scott, "Colonial Governmentality," *Social Text* 43 (Autumn 1995): 191–220.

37. Joan Wallach Scott, *Only Paradoxes to Offer: French Feminists and the Rights of Man* (Cambridge, MA: Harvard University Press, 1996).

38. Aga Khan, *Times of India*, October 6, 1906. Before Partition, one of four Indians was Muslim. Muslims were a demographic majority in Baluchistan, Sind, Bengal, Punjab, and the Northwest Frontier Provinces. See Ayesha Jalal, *The Sole Spokesman: Jinnah, the Muslim League, and the Demand for Pakistan* (Cambridge: Cambridge University Press, 1985), 2.

39. Female enfranchisement was posited either as an extension of collective community rights or as an individual right transcending social relations. Upper-caste Hindu feminists refused to demand special representation because they rejected the political separation this implied, which put them on par with Depressed Classes and Muslims. However, women were ultimately unable to elide gender specificity to claim the position of the unmarked, universal citizen. This failure intensified the schism between feminists' political identification with the universal subject of rights and their structural position as political subjects caught between communitarian and state logics of incorporation. As well, because the universalist position was historically aligned with the political interests of the Hindu upper-caste male, Indian feminists increasingly confronted the uneasy resemblance between their demands for (universal) political rights and the rhetoric of upper castes who rejected special representation for minorities. Sinha, "Ambiguous Aftermath," in *Specters of Mother India*, 197–247

40. Prime Minister Ramsay MacDonald suggested that a double vote allowed for weightage without the enforced political segregation of the Muslim separate electorate. "General Appreciation of the Communal Award," Home Political File no. 41–44 and KW Serial nos. 1–37, NAI, cited in Shabnam Tejani, "A Pre-History of Indian Secularism: Categories of Nationalism and Communalism in Emerging Definitions of India, Bombay Presidency C. 1893–1932" (PhD dissertation, Columbia University, 2002).

41. For an account of the 1935 Government of India Act as a blueprint for continuation of British rule in opposition to nationalist demands, see Carl Bridge, *Holding India to the Empire: The British Conservative Party and the 1935 Constitution*, South Asian Publications Series, no. 1 (New Delhi: Sterling Publishers, 1986).

42. David Gilmartin, "A Magnificent Gift: Muslim Nationalism and the Election Process in Colonial Punjab," *Comparative Studies in Society and History* 40, no. 3 (July 1998): 415–36.

43. Karl Marx, "On the Jewish Question," in *The Marx-Engels Reader*, 2nd ed., ed. Robert C. Tucker (New York: Norton, 1978), 26–52. On the affinities between the Jewish question in Europe and the problem of Muslim minority on the subcontinent, see Aamir Mufti, *Enlightenment in the Colony: The Jewish Question and the Crisis of Postcolonial Culture* (Princeton, NJ: Princeton University Press, 2007).

44. Dorothy Ko, *Cinderella's Sisters: A Revisionist History of Footbinding* (Berkeley: University of California Press, 2005), 41.

45. Etienne Balibar, "'Rights of Man' and 'Rights of the Citizen': The Modern Dialectic of Equality and Freedom," in *Masses, Classes, Ideas: Studies on Politics and Philosophy Before and After Marx* (London: Routledge, 1994), 46.

46. Important texts include: Arjun Appadurai, *Fear of Small Numbers: An Essay on the Geography of Anger* (Durham, NC: Duke University Press, 2006);

Urvashi Butalia, *The Other Side of Silence: Voices from the Partition of India* (New Delhi: Penguin Books India, 1998); E. Valentine Daniel, *Charred Lullabies: Chapters in an Anthropography of Violence* (Princeton, NJ: Princeton University Press, 1996); Veena Das, *Mirrors of Violence: Communities, Riots, and Survivors in South Asia* (Delhi: Oxford University Press, 1990); Ritu Menon and Kamla Bhasin, *Borders and Boundaries: Women in India's Partition* (New Brunswick, NJ: Rutgers University Press, 1998); Gyanendra Pandey, *Remembering Partition: Violence, Nationalism and History in India* (Cambridge: Cambridge University Press, 2002); and Faisal Devji, "Hindu/Muslim/Indian," *Public Culture* 5, no. 1 (1992): 1–18.

47. Jean and John Comaroff, "Criminal Justice, Cultural Justice: The Limits of Liberalism and the Pragmatics of Difference in the New South Africa," *American Ethnologist* 31, no. 2 (2004): 188–204. For an argument about the two epochs of postcolonial politics, the first defined by decolonization and development and the second by neoliberal governance and discourses of social order, see Jean and John Comaroff, "Millenial Capitalism and the Culture of Neoliberalism," *Public Culture*, 12, no. 2 (Spring 2000): 291–343; and Jean and John Comaroff, eds., *Civil Society and the Political Imagination in Africa: Critical Perspectives, Problems, Paradoxes* (Chicago: University of Chicago Press, 1999).

48. For sociological studies of caste violence, see Susan Bayly, *Caste, Society, and Politics in India: From the Eighteenth Century to the Modern Age* (Cambridge: Cambridge University Press, 1999), especially chapter 9, "Caste Wars and the Mandate of Violence"; Ghanshyam Shah, *Untouchability in Rural India* (New Delhi: Sage Publications, 2006); and Oliver Mendelsohn and Marika Vicziany, *The Untouchables: Subordination, Poverty, and the State in Modern India* (Cambridge: Cambridge University Press, 1998), especially chapter 2, "The Question of the 'Harijan Atrocity.'" An early account of this phenomenon can be found in N. D. Kamble, *Atrocities on Scheduled Castes in Post Independent India, 15th August 1947 to 15th August 1979* (New Delhi: Ashish Pub. House, 1981).

49. Examples include Uma Chakravarti, *Gendering Caste through a Feminist Lens* (Calcutta: Stree, 2003); Satish Deshpande, *Contemporary India: A Sociological View* (New Delhi: Viking, 2003); K. Ilaiah, *Why I Am Not a Hindu: A Sudra Critique of Hindutva Philosophy, Culture and Political Economy*, 2nd ed. (Calcuttta: Samya, 2005); Mary E. John, "Alternative Modernities? Reservations and Women's Movement in 20th Century India" *Economic and Political Weekly* (October 28, 2000): WS22–WS29; Dilip M. Menon, *The Blindness of Insight: Essays on Caste in Modern India*, Other Headings (Pondicherry: Navayana Pub., 2006); Aditya Nigam, *The Insurrection of Little Selves: The Crisis of Secular-Nationalism in India* (New Delhi: Oxford University Press, 2006); Chandra Bhan Prasad, *Dalit Phobia: Why Do They Hate Us?* (New Delhi: Vistar Pub., 2006); M. S. S. Pandian, *Brahmin and Non-Brahmin: Genealogies of the Tamil Political Present* (Dehli: Permanent Black, 2007); Anupama Rao, ed., *Gender and Caste: Contemporary Issues in Indian Feminism* (New Delhi: Kali for Women, 2003); and Ghanshyam Shah et. al, *Dalit Identity and Politics: Cultural Subordination and the Dalit Challenge*, vol. 2 (New Delhi: Sage Publications, 2001).

50. Dirks, *The Hollow Crown*, xxiii.

51. Thomas R. Trautmann, *Dravidian Kinship* (Cambridge: Cambridge University Press, 1981).

52. On the seventeenth- and eighteenth-century formation of regional breakaways, see Muzaffar Alam, *The Crisis of Empire in Mughal North India: Awadh and the Punjab, 1707–48* (Delhi: Oxford University Press, 1986); and Andre Wink, *Land and Sovereignty in India: Agrarian Society and Politics under the Eighteenth-Century Maratha Svarajya* (Cambridge University Press, 1986).

53. For a discussion of the resonance of Shivaji for Maratha history, see Prachi Deshpande, *Creative Pasts: Historical Memory and Identity in Western India, 1700–1960* (New York: Columbia University Press, 2007); and Daniel Jasper, "Commemorating Shivaji: Regional and Religious Identity in Maharashtra, India" (PhD dissertation, New School for Social Research, 2002).

54. R. E. Enthoven, *The Tribes and Castes of Bombay*, vol. 2 (Bombay: Government Central Press, 1922), 401–18. Interestingly, Enthoven fails to mention Mahars' involvement in military service.

55. Zelliot, "Dr. Ambedkar and the Mahar Movement," 22.

56. Chakravarti, *Rewriting History;* Sumit Guha, "An Indian Penal Regime. Maharashtra in the Eighteenth Century," *Past and Present* 147 (1995): 101–26; V. S. Kadam, "The Institution of Marriage and the Position of Women in Eighteenth Century Maharashtra," *Indian Economic and Social History Review* 25, no. 3 (1988): 341–70; and N. K. Wagle, "The Government, the Jati and the Individual: Rights, Discipline and Control in the Pune Kotwal Papers, 1766–1794," *Contributions to Indian Sociology* 34, no. 3 (2000): 321–60.

57. See Frank F. Conlon, *A Caste in a Changing World* (Berkeley: University of California Press, 1977), for the Chitpavans. On the Peshwai, see Hiroshi Fukazawa, *The Medieval Deccan: Peasants, Social Systems and States; Sixteenth to Eighteenth Centuries* (Delhi: Oxford University Press, 1991).

58. O'Hanlon, *Caste, Conflict, and Ideology,* 53.

59. Ambedkar's entry into active politics coincided with the retreat of key political leaders from the Vidarbha region, including Kalicharan Nandagavli, Kisan Fagoji Bansode, Ganesh Akkaji Gawai, and M. M. Thaware. Rejecting Ambedkar's 1935 call for conversion out of Hinduism, they supported inclusion within a reformed Hinduism. The Rashtriya Swayamsevak Sangh (National Volunteer Corps), founded in Nagpur in 1925 by K. B. Hegdewar with its commitment to Hindu nationalism, was a strong presence in the region.

1. CASTE RADICALISM

1. Scholars of north India have argued that the vernacular public sphere exacerbated Hindu-Muslim conflict, even as it enabled new constituencies to take shape within a fractured and complexly ramified public sphere. See Sandria B. Freitag, *Collective Action and Community: Public Arenas and the Emergence of Communalism in North India* (Berkeley: University of California Press, 1989); Nandini Gooptu, *The Politics of the Urban Poor in Early Twentieth-Century India,* Cambridge Studies in Indian History and Society 8 (Cambridge: Cambridge University Press, 2001); Charu Gupta, *Sexuality, Obscenity, Community: Women,*

Muslims, and the Hindu Public in Colonial India, 1st Palgrave ed. (New York: Palgrave, 2002); Kathryn Hansen, *Grounds for Play: The Nautanki Theatre of North India* (Berkeley: University of California Press, 1992); and Francesca Orsini, *The Hindi Public Sphere 1920–1940: Language and Literature in the Age of Nationalism* (New Delhi: Oxford University Press, 2002). For western India, see Veena Naregal, *Language Politics, Elites, and the Public Sphere: Western India under Colonialism* (Delhi: Permanent Black, 2001). For an important account of the articulation between music, modernity, and the Brahminizing performative sphere, see Janaki Bakhle, *Two Men and Music: Nationalism in the Making of an Indian Classical Tradition* (Oxford: Oxford University Press, 2005).

2. Gail Omvedt, *Cultural Revolt in a Colonial Society: The Non-Brahman Movement in Western India 1873 to 1930* (Bombay: Scientific Socialist Education Trust, 1976).

3. The most important scholarly account of Phule's thought is Rosalind O'Hanlon, *Caste, Conflict, and Ideology: Mahatma Jotirao Phule and Low Caste Protest in Nineteenth-Century Western India* (Cambridge: Cambridge University Press, 1985).

4. Though strapped for cash, these newspapers managed to give some continuity to a Dalit communicative public. The *Din Bandhu* (Friend of the Impoverished) was an organ of Satyashodak anti-Brahminism. The first issue of *Din Bandhu* was published in January 1877 with a circulation of 300 copies. By 1884, with a circulation of 1,650, the newspaper was second only to Tilak's *Kesari*. *Native Newspaper Report,* September 6, 1884, MSA. *Din Bandhu*'s first editor, Krishnarao Bhalekar (1850–1910), was an early member of the Satyashodak Samaj. A forceful critic of Brahmin hegemony and ritualism, he came from the village of Bhamburde, near Pune. Educated at a mission school and employed at a district court in Pune, Bhalekar had staged anti-Brahmin plays and started a school for the poor even before he met Phule in 1867. Y. D. Phadke, *Vyakti ani Vichar: Kahi Anubandh* (Pune: Srividya Prakashan, 1979), 41–64. In 1880, Narayan Meghaji Lokhande took over publication of *Din Bandhu.* Lokhande was active in the working-class movement and started the Mill Hands Association in Bombay, thus creating new linkages between the peasant base of the Satyashodak Samaj and Bombay's laboring classes. Lokhande opened the Bombay branch of the Satyashodak Samaj in 1874. Manohar Kadam, *Narayan Meghaji Lokhande: Bharatiya Kamgar Calvalice Janak,* 3rd. ed. (Mumbai: Mahatma Phule Samata Pratishthan and Akshar Prakashan, 2002). The *Somavanshiya Mitra* (Friend of the Somavanshi), started by the Poona reformer Shivram Janba Kamble, was published from 1908 to 1912. Ambedkar's first journalistic venture, the *Muknayak* (Leader of the Mute), was active from 1917 to 1920, and the *Bahishkrit Bharat* (Outcaste India) was published between 1927 and 1929. Appa Ranpise, *Dalitanchi Vrittapatra* (Bombay: Bauddha Sahitya Parishad, 1962).

5. For an account of the changing valence of Maratha history and the politics of vernacular history writing, see Prachi Deshpande, *Creative Pasts: Historical Memory and Identity in Western India, 1700–1960,* Cultures of History (New York: Columbia University Press, 2007).

6. Important revisionist accounts include Stewart Gordon, *The Marathas 1600–1818* (Cambridge: Cambridge University Press, 1993); Frank Perlin, "State

Formation Reconsidered, Part Two," *Modern Asian Studies* 19, no. 3 (1985): 415–80; and Andre Wink, *Land and Sovereignty in India: Agrarian Society and Politics under the Eighteenth-Century Maratha Svarajya* (Cambridge University Press, 1986). For the legal order, see Sumit Guha, "An Indian Penal Regime: Maharashtra in the Eighteenth Century," *Past and Present* 147 (1995): 101–26; V. S. Kadam, "The Institution of Marriage and Position of Women in Eighteenth-Century Maharashtra," *Indian Economic and Social History Review* 25, no. 3 (1988): 341–70; and N. K. Wagle, "The Government, the Jati and the Individual: Rights, Discipline and Control in the Pune Kotwal Papers, 1766–1794," *Contributions to Indian Sociology* 34, no. 3 (2000): 321–60.

   7. Frank Perlin, "Of White Whale and Countryman in the Eighteenth Century Maratha Deccan: Extended Class Relations, Rights and the Problem of Autonomy under the Old Regime," *Journal of Peasant Studies* 5, no. 2 (1978): 172–237.

   8. Hiroshi Fukazawa, "State and Caste (Jati) in the Eighteenth-Century Maratha Kingdom," *Hitotsubashi Journal of Economics* 9, no. 1 (1968): 32–44.

   9. N. K. Wagle, "Ritual and Change in Early Nineteenth Century Society in Maharashtra: Vedokta Disputes in Baroda, Pune and Satara, 1824–1838," in *Religion and Society in Maharashtra,* ed. M. Israel and N. K. Wagle (Toronto: Centre for South Asian Studies, University of Toronto, 1987), 145–81. For a non-Brahmin perspective on the Vedokta controversy and its 1830 resolution in favor of the Maratha case, see M. G. Dongare, *The Lineage of the Bhosle Family* (Kolhapur, 1905), cited in O'Hanon, *Caste Conflict and Ideology,* 33–34. For a discussion of the tension between Shahu Chatrapati's emphasis on ritual recognition within varna terms, and his commitments to the Satyashodak critiques of caste hierarchy, see Omvedt, *Cultural Revolt in a Colonial Society,* 124–36.

   10. *Peshwa* dominance coincided with Maratha incursion into Malwa, Gujarat, Delhi, and Bengal in the period 1720–40, and the annexation of Orissa in 1745. The collection of *chauth* (tribute) from Bengal and Bihar continued until 1758, when the British stopped payment after becoming de facto sovereign over Bengal, Bihar, and Orissa.

   11. N. K. Wagle, "A Dispute between the Pancal Devajna Sonars and the Pune Brahmins Regarding Social Rank and Ritual Privileges: A Case-Study of the British Administration of Jati Laws in Maharashtra, 1822–1825," in *Images of Maharashtra: A Regional Profile of India* (London: Curzon Press, 1980), 129–59.

   12. Phule's history was based on a reinterpretation of the Dasavatara, which describes the cyclical movement of the *yugas,* or ages of man, through Vishnu's ten incarnations on earth. Phule argued that the Matsya (fish) avatar foretold the invasion of the Aryan *bhat* Brahmins. He focused, however, on the defeat of Bali, the virtuous king of the Daityas, or the *asuras* (so-called demons), by Vishnu's chicanery and cunning. Vishnu, in the guise of Vamana, a Brahmin dwarf, asked Bali for a boon—the grant of all the land he could encompass in three steps. Vamana then grew to gargantuan proportions, encompassed the earth and the heavens with two steps, and placed his foot on Bali's head for the third step. This consigned Bali to the netherworld. Phule argued that Bali's defeat foretold the historic humiliation of the *shudra-atishudras.* Jotirao Phule, *Gulamgiri,* in *Samagra Vangmay: Mahatma Phule Samagra Vangmay* [Collected Works of Mahatma Jotirao Phule], ed. Dhananjay Keer and S. G. Malshe (Mumbai: Mumbai Rajya

Sahitya ani Samskriti Mandal, 1969), reprinted 1991, ed. Y. D. Phadke. On Puranic history, see Romila Thapar, *Interpreting Early India* (Delhi: Oxford University Press, 1992).

13. Joan Leopold, "The Aryan Theory of Race in India," *Indian Economic and Social History Review* 7 (1970): 271–97; and Thomas R. Trautmann, *Aryans and British India* (Berkeley: University of California Press, 1997).

14. Bal Gangadhar Tilak, *The Arctic Home in the Vedas: Being Also a New Key to the Interpretation of Many Vedic Texts and Legends* (Poona: Tilak Brothers, 1956).

15. Joan Leopold, "The Aryan Theory of Race in India, 1870–1920," *Indian Economic and Social History Review* 7 (1970): 271–97; and Thomas R. Trautmann, *Aryans and British India* (Berkeley: University of California Press, 1997).

16. V. D. Savarkar's text, *Hindutva: Who Is a Hindu* (1923), a founding text for contemporary Hindu nationalism, drew on such affective associations between language, territory, and (religious) identity, but extended the concept of Hindu beyond religious adherence to the *political identity* of anyone who claimed India, or Bharatvarsha, as *pitrabhumi* (fatherland) and *punyabhumi* (sanctified or holy land). Thus the Hindu Mahasabha over which Savarkar presided stood not for Hindu revival—a project for which the atheist Savarkar had little patience—but for the *secular nationalism of Hindus,* who were conceived as an ethnopolitical category. Arvind Rajagopal has argued for distinguishing Savarkar's brand of political Hinduism from the contemporary ideology of Hindu nationalism, though they are assumed to be identical, both in popular perception and among key thinkers of the Hindu right. Arvind Rajagopal, *Politics after Television: Hindu Nationalism and the Remaking of the Public in India* (Cambridge: Cambridge University Press, 2001).

17. There was some consensus that the Mahars were the original inhabitants of Maharashtra. R. E. Enthoven, *The Tribes and Castes of Bombay,* vol. 2 (Bombay: Government Central Press, 1922), 401–18; Alexander Robertson, *The Mahar Folk: A Study of Untouchables in Maharashtra* (Calcutta: YMCA Publishing House, 1938), chapter 4; and R. V. Russell and Rai Bahadur Hira Lal, *The Tribes and Castes of the Central Provinces,* vol. 4 (London: Macmillan, 1916), 129.

18. Phule, *Gulamgiri,* in *Samagra Vangmay,* 120.

19. Ibid., 116.

20. Ibid., 72.

21. Mahars, especially those from the Konkan region, used the term "Somavanshi" to associate themselves with the Lunar line (lit. *vamsa,* "genealogy") of Kshatriyas.

22. The newspaper *Somavanshiya Mitra* mentions the activities of "Kondiram Ramji Master," a schoolteacher and itinerant preacher, who spoke frequently at Mahar meetings in the Bombay-Poona region. *SM,* August 1, 1908; December 1, 1908; and January 1, 1909. The founder of the Depressed Classes Mission (DCM, established 1906), Vithal Ramji Shinde (1873–1944), noted that Pandit Kondiram held a meeting in front of his home on Nesbit Road in Bombay on June 5, 1910, to commemorate Cokhamela's death. See B. B. Keskar, ed., *Vitthal Ramji Shinde: Lekh, Vyakhyane va Upadesh* (Mumbai: Damodar

Savalaram and Company, 1912), 145. Shinde, who was from a Maratha family in Jamkhandi, joined the Prarthana Samaj in 1899. He went to England in 1901 to study comparative religion at Oxford with the support of Sayajirao Gaikwad of Baroda (1875–1939), whose patronage of anticaste activists extended from Phule and Valangkar to B. R. Ambedkar. Shinde returned in 1903 and worked for untouchable reform until he resigned from the DCM in 1923 over allegations of casteism by a Dalit student at one of the mission's schools and popular criticism of his support for Congress nationalism. Shinde's book on untouchability, *Bharatiya Asprusyatecha Prashna* (1933), argued for a distinctive historical identity (and Buddhist past) for the untouchable communities. Shinde's efforts at untouchability reform should be placed against those of the Brahmin reformer S. M. Mate (1886–1957), who was affiliated with the Hindu Mahasabha and supported caste endogamy through a eugenicist argument about its benefit for the "Hindu nation." Mate's book, *Asprushtancha Prashna,* also published in 1933, uses the term *asprushta* (untouched) rather than *asprushya* (untouchable) to refer to the Dalit communities. For an excellent account of Shinde's thought and activism, see G. M. Pawar, *Vithal Ramji Shinde: Jeevan va Karya* (Mumbai: Lokvangmaygriha, 2004).

23. Pandit Kondiram's *pada* (poem), verse 4, in G. B. Valangkar, "Anarya Dosh Pariharak Mandali Petition to His Excellency the Commander-in-Chief of Bombay Presidency in Poona, July 1984" (Marathi), Khairmode Collection, Bombay University.

24. Ibid., verse 5.

25. Ibid., verse 7.

26. *Laws of Manu,* trans. Wendy Doniger with Brian K. Smith (Delhi: Penguin, 1991), 10: 8–26, 50.

27. Phule, *Gulamgiri,* in *Samagra Vangmay,* 91.

28. Kamble argued that Mahars had been in the employ of virtuous Dravidian kings like Bali, Ravana, and Hiranyakashipu before they appeared in the Puranic literature as degraded *asuras. Nagpur Yethil 30 va 31 May ani 1 June 1920 Bahishkrit Bharat Parishadet Zhalele Ra. Shivram Janba Kamble Yanche Bhashan* [Shivram Janba Kamble's Speech at the Bahishkrit Bharat Parishad of May 30–31, and June 1, 1920] (Pune: Istralight Chapkhana, 1920).

29. *Maharashtra State Gazetteer, Ratnagiri District, 1880,* rev. ed. (Bombay: Diretorate of Government Printing, Stationary, and Publications, Maharashtra State, 1962), 129 (for population figures) and 206 (for Mahar land ownership).

30. On Mahar history, see N. G. Bhaware, "Marathekalin Asprushyanchi Stithi," *Asmitadarsh,* (January–March 1980); "Shivashai Ani Peshvaitil Asprushyateche Svarup," *Asmitadarsh,* Divali Ank [Divali issue] (1980); P. Gavli, *Peshvekalin Gulamgiri va Asprushyata* [Slavery and Untouchability under the Peshwa Rule] (Kolhapur: Prachar Prakashan, 1981); and Zhumbarlal Kamble, "Rainak—Thoda Itihas, Thodya Dantakatha," *Asmitadarsh* (October-December 1978). For an excellent account of Mahar demilitarization and the racial reorganization of the British Army, see Philip Constable, "The Marginalization of a Dalit Martial Race in Late Nineteenth- and Early Twentieth-Century Western India," *Journal of Asian Studies* 60, no. 2 (2001): 439–78. Constable draws on

the important work of Steven Cohen, "The Untouchable Soldier: Caste, Politics, and the Indian Army," *Journal of Asian Studies* 28, no. 3 (1969): 453–68.

31. Surya, Soma, Shesha, and Brahma were the four Kshatriya lineages. The surname Somavanshi (Lunar lineage) was also common among Mahar Dalits. Indeed, shared Maratha and Dalit surnames were an important source of Dalit claims to Kshatriya status. Early petitions from Konkan and the Vidarbha region in the name of the "Somavanshi Mahars" are common.

32. Like many Chambhar and Mahar pensioners of Dapoli, Valangkar was influenced by the radical egalitarianism and caste critique associated with the fourteenth-century weaver-philosopher from north India, Kabir. C. B. Khairmode, *Dr. Bhimrao Ramji Charitra*, vol. 1, 3rd ed. (Pune: Sugawa Prakashan, 2003), 204. Kabirpanthis, or followers of the Kabir sect, are distinguished by their use of the *kanthi*, or necklace of tulsi beads. Kabir's sayings are popularized through song form, or *pada*, as well as the aphoristic two-line *doha*, which draw from the lifeworlds of the laboring classes. Ramesh Dhavare has suggested that Valangkar was the "Kabir Panth Shudra Sadhu" with whom Phule conducted a dialogue on the religious basis for caste hierarchy. Ramesh Dhavare, "Gopal Baba Valangkar," *Mangaon Parishad: 62nd Smriti Mahotsav* [Mangaon Conference: The 62nd Anniversary Celebrations] (Kolhapur, 1980), 2–3. Vithal Ramji Shinde argued that Valangkar's thinking was influenced by the Christian convert, Baba Padmanji, in *Mazhya Athvani va Anubhav* (1958), 214. Padmanji's account of his 1854 conversion was recounted in the Christian paper *Arunodaya* [Dawn] and translated into English by the Protestant missionary J. Murray Mitchell as *Once Hindu Now Christian: The Early Life of Baba Padmanji* (1890).

33. Sitaram Raikar, ed., *Amhi Pahilele Phule* (Pune: Mahatma Jotirao Phule Samata Pratishtan, 1981), 37. See also R. S. Ghadge to P. S. Patil, Pune, May 29, 1930, P. S. Patil MSS, Shivaji University, Kolhapur.

34. Raikar, *Amhi Pahilele Phule*, 16–17.

35. *Din Bandhu* [Friend of the Impoverished], February 2, 1896. The banning of Dalit groups is also mentioned in Gangadhar Pantawane, *Vadalacha Vamshaj* [The Stormy Lineage] (Kolhapur: Prachar Prakashan, 1982), 29. However, in the following year, 1896, Phule's close associate, Krishnarao Bhalekar, presented Valangkar with a roll of honor at a Satyashodak Samaj meeting in Pune. *DB*, January 19, 1896. The *samaj* continued to be involved in Dalit reform into the 1920s, especially in the Vidarbha region.

36. Valangkar's *Vinanti Patra* of 1888 was reprinted in the journal *Purogami Satyashodak* (July–September, 1979) under the title *Vitthal Vidhwansan*. Valangkar is supposed to have written another text titled *Hindu Dharma Darpan* [Mirror of the Hindu Religion], about which no further information is available. Valangkar mentions being unable to get one of his works published in *DB*, May 10, 1894.

37. G. B. Valangkar, *Khali Lihilelya Sarkari Surveypramane Konkanatil Mahar Jati Sanbandhi Mahiti* [Information on the Mahar Caste of the Konkan According to the Government Survey Below] (n.p., August 31, 1894).

38. On the other hand, Satyashodak activists such as Pandit Dhondiram Namdev, who was from the Kumbhar, or potter caste, attacked Brahmin hypocrisy by pointing to the importance of animal sacrifice (and the role of beef)

in Vedic culture. Pandit Dhondiram asked how Brahmins, who were descended from Vedic beef eaters, could attack the Mahar Kshatriyas for eating carrion in times of hunger. Pandit Dhondiram Namdev, *Vedachar* [Thoughts on the Vedas] (Bombay, 1896). Dhondiram was a prolific writer who wrote a *Tamasha* (1897) and a dialogue titled *Ganpatrao Thorat, Gustadji Shet, Babulabudhan Va Pandit Dhondiram Namdev (Satyashodak Samaj) Yancha Samvad* (n.d., n.p.). It is most probable that he was the "Dhondiba" with whom Phule conducted the dialogue in *Gulamgiri*.

39. Valangkar noted the difficulty of raising funds for the ADPM's activities. *DB*, May 20, 1894.

40. *Kirtans* were conducted in Pune, Satara, Nagar, and Solapur. *DB*, October 13, 1895. A decade thereafter, Valangkar's ADPM successor, Ramchandraji Talsarkar, promised that the organization would go on two *kirtan* tours per year. *SM*, December 1, 1908.

41. The resolution of this issue remains unclear. See Valangkar's letters in *DB* from March 31, May 4, May 19, and June 30, 1895.

42. The military pensioners refrained from sending Valangkar's 1894 petition for fear of losing their pensions. *DB*, April 7, 1894. The ADPM sent it on April 11, 1895, after a March meeting chaired by Subhedar Major Ramchandraji Talsarkar and Subhedar Major Hon. Bahadur Kopadkar. In 1901, Subhedar Major Ramnak Chownak sent another petition to the government on behalf of the ADPM. Military pensioners in Satara, led by Shivram Govind Waiker Master, also petitioned the Bombay government in 1894 and 1895, but the government refused to interfere. *Reply from Chief Secretary to Government to Petition from Shivram Govind Waiker Master*, March 26, 1895, RD, vol. 77, 1895, MSA.

43. For the 1903 and 1905 petitions, respectively, see *Memorial from Certain Mahars from the Bombay Presidency Praying That They May Be Enlisted in the Indian Army and Employed in Large Numbers in the Police Forces, 30 June, 1905*, GD, vol. 98, 1906, MSA; and *Memorial from the Mahar Community for Employment in the Indian Army and Police, 14 December, 1910*, GD, vol. 94, 1912, MSA. This latter petition appears in the Khairmode Collection, Bombay University, as *The Conference of Deccan Mahars 1878 Cantonment Poona, Bombay Presidency, November 1910 to the Right Honorable The Earl of Crewe, K. G., C., M. A., F. S. A., Secretary of State for India, London*.

44. The 111th Mahar Regiment temporarily recruited Mahars for the war effort during World War I. B. R. Ambedkar on behalf of the BHS, "Memorial on the Disbandment of the 111th Mahar Regiment," 1922. Khairmode Collection, Bombay University.

45. On Mahar use of petitions, see for example, Shivram Janba Kamble, "Mahar Kontya Hi Babtit Halke Nahit" [Mahars Are in No Way Degraded] *DB*, August 5, 1908, republished in *Asmitadarsh*, Divali Ank [Divali issue] (1979). The benefit of British government and benevolence was another running theme in Mahar petitions. See for example, "Deva, Amchya Ingraji Rajala Udhanda Ayushya Dhya" [God, Please Give Our English Government a Long Life], *SM*, December 1, 1908.

46. Both Phule and Valangkar criticized the ninetieth hymn of the Tenth Book of the Rg Veda, called the *Purusa Sukta*, which equated the origins of

the *varnas* with different parts of Purusa's body, thus relating social function with social status, or stigma. Valangkar's distinction between a descent-based and a performance-oriented theory of caste hierarchy is discussed in the *Vinanti Patra*, 20.

47. Krishnarao Jedhe, the important non-Brahmin leader, joined the Congress in 1930. This was preceded by Vithal Ramji Shinde's efforts to join non-Brahmin politics with Gandhianism through his Nationalist Maratha Party.

48. Gail Omvedt argues for two strands of non-Brahmin politics: one radical-populist, the other drawing on the association between Marathas and kingship to assert Kshatriya status. Kolhapur was an important site of Satyashodak activism and non-Brahmin politics because of Shahu Chatrapati. Omvedt, *Cultural Revolt in a Colonial Society,* 124–36. Shahu supported key Dalit initiatives, from reservations in employment and education to funding B. R. Ambedkar's education and hosting the important Mangaon Parishad of 1920, where he declared Ambedkar the unquestioned leader of the untouchable communities. For essays on the continuities between Satyashodak and early Dalit activism, see Ramesh Dhavare, ed., *Mangav Parishad Vishesh Ank 1982* (Kolhapur: B. S. Patil for Nava Maharashtra Mudrana va Prakashan Sanstha, 1982).

49. By 1935, Congress representatives had been elected to ten out of eleven local boards in Bombay. Y. D. Phadke, *Politics and Language* (Bombay: Himalaya Publishing House, 1979). Colonial reports reveal a significant rise in Congress membership, noting a massive jump between 1936 and 1937 from 45,915 to 156,894 members. *Extract from Weekly Letter,* no. 47, November 27, 1937, Home (Special) 922(2), MSA.

50. Uma Chakravarti, "Reconceptualizing Gender: Phule, Brahminism and Brahminical Patriarchy," in *Women in Indian History,* ed. Kiran Pawar (Patiala: Vision and Venture, 1996).

51. Dipesh Chakrabarty has argued that widows' suffering was central to the self-fashioning of male reformers as both reasonable and sentimental. Dipesh Chakrabarty, *Provincializing Europe: Postcolonial Thought and Historical Difference,* Princeton Studies in Culture/Power/History (Princeton, NJ: Princeton University Press, 2000), 117–48.

52. Jotirao and Savitribai Phule publicized the house thus: "Printed notices were . . . pasted on the walls of the corners of streets, where the Brahmins reside. From its commencement up to the present time, thirty-five pregnant widows came to this house." Quoted in Rosalind O'Hanlon, "Issues of Widowhood: Gender, Discourse and Resistance in Colonial Western India," in *Contesting Power: Resistance and Everyday Social Relations in South Asia,* ed. Douglas Haynes and Gyan Prakash (Delhi: Oxford University Press, 1991), 84.

53. See Padma Anagol, "The Emergence of the Female Criminal in India: Infanticide and Survival under the Raj," *History Workshop Journal,* no. 53 (2002): 73–93, for a discussion of the Vijayalakshmi case. Anagol cites many instances of widows' sexual abuse, including the case of a Mahar woman who was turned out of her home by her lover when she became pregnant.

54. When Krishnarao Bhalekar criticized Shinde's book in 1885, Phule argued that Bhalekar's position supported the decadent lifestyle of men while binding women to domestic servitude. Phule, *Satsar 2,* in *Samagra Vangmay.* Simi-

larly, Meghaji Lokhande, the trade union leader and editor of the *Din Bandhu,* located female promiscuity as a threat to working-class families and criticized the Christian convert, Pandita Ramabai, whose book, *The High Caste Hindu Woman* (1888), like Shinde's *Stri-Purush Tulana,* engaged in a devastating critique of Brahmin patriarchy. By 1893, however, Lokhande supported Ramabai and also led a strike of four hundred female textile workers at Bombay's Jacob Mill. Kadam, *Narayan Meghaji Lokhande.*

55. *DB,* July 19, 1896.

56. Issues of property and inheritance were central to the ban on widow remarriage. The Widow Remarriage Act of 1856 legislated the right of (upper-caste Hindu) women to remarry, since women from the lower castes were customarily entitled to divorce and remarriage. By enacting universalist legislation on behalf of all Hindu women and predicating sexual emancipation on the material disenfranchisement of women—women had to give up claims to their first husband's property to remarry—the colonial government also stigmatized domestic forms and inheritance practices among lower-castes and laboring classes, where women had long held the right to remarry and to inherit property. For a brilliant account of the production of a Brahminical-Victorian patriarchal order, see Lucy Carroll, "Law, Custom and Statutory Social Reform: Hindu Widows' Remarriage Act of 1856," *Indian Economic and Social History Review* 20, no. 4 (1983): 363–88.

57. "Anna" is a colloquial term for father, especially in southern Maharashtra.

58. Mahamuni uses the term *bodki karne,* "to make bald," rather than the high Sanskrit term for tonsure, *keshavapan.*

59. Bhimrao Mahamuni, "Bodki," *Vidya Prakash,* revised and expanded 2nd ed. (Khetwadi, Mumbai: Vithal Chapkhana, 1911), 37.

60. Gangadhar Morje, "Marathi Shahirichi Badalthi Roop," *Asmitadarsh,* Divali Ank, vol. 11, no. 3 (1982): 172–73.

61. For details, see Madhavrao Bagal, *Hirak Mahotsav Granth* [Sixtieth Anniversary Souvenir of the Satyashodhak Samaj] (Kolhapur, 1933); Sambhaji Kharat, *Satyashodak Jalse* (Kolhapur, n.d.); and Krishna Kirwale, *Ambedkari Shahiri: Ek Shodh* (Pune: Nalanda Prakashan, 1992). In addition to Mahamuni, other *jalsa* books included Bhaurao Patil, *Jalsashikshak;* Pandurang Lembhya, *Jalsaprakash;* and Haribhau Chavan, *Jalshakaritha Kavitasangraha.* In Nagpur, the Mahar Dalit reformer Kisan Fagoji Bansode (1879–1946)—who also supported the theory of Aryan conquest and enslavement of Dalits and lower castes— started a Satyashodak Jalsa Mandal in 1918 and wrote farces titled *Sadhuchi Phajithi, Paratantra Vimochan Athava Antyaj Sudharanachi Marg,* and the *Manoranjan Pancharangi Tamasha.* Between 1932 and 1940 the Satyashodak Jalsa Mandal performed famous *jalsas* such as *Shethkaryanchi Vyatha* (The Suffering of the Peasantry), *Brahman Konashi Mhanave?* (Who Should Be Called a Brahmin?), and *Keshavapan* (The Tonsure of Widows).

62. Home (Special) 363(5), "Brahmans v. Non-Brahmans," MSA.

63. Mr. Moysey, District Magistrate, Satara, to Home (Pol) Secretary, RJ, no. S.D. 703, June 21, 1921, Home (Special) 363, "Brahmans v. Non-Brahmans," 1932, MSA.

64. See *Samagra Vangmay,* 327–39, for a description of the Satyashodak wed-

ding ceremony. See also Phule, *Brahmanache Kasab* [Priestcraft Exposed], in *Samagra Vangmay,* 49–54. In 1873–74, two Satyashodak marriages were reported. By the mid-1880s, many such marriages were being reported in important Satyashodak organs such as the *Din Bandhu* and the *Din Mitra,* a paper started in 1910 in Tarawade village, Ahmednagar by Krishnarao Bhalekar's son, Mukundrao Patil. *Satyashodak Samaj Parishad Baithak Tisari, Varshik Report, March 20, 1913* [Third Annual Report of the Meeting of the Satyashodak Samaj, March 20, 1913]. For Bhalekar's biography, see *Din Mitra Jubilee Ankh* (1937). In Junnar district, over 300 marriages had been performed by 1884; villagers boycotted Brahmin priests and refused to till their fields. Balaji Patil's case was the climax of the movement challenging Brahmin hegemony. *Din Bandhu,* May 25, 1884. *Native Newspaper Reports Week Ending May 31, 1884.* Near Kolhapur, 200 marriages were reported for 1912 and 266 marriages for 1913. By 1915, the rural areas of Khed *taluka* in Poona district were reporting that more than 46,000 Satyashodak ceremonies had taken place since the 1890s. A. B. Latthe, *Memoirs of His Highness, Shri Shahu Chatrapati, Maharajah of Kolhapur,* vol. 2 (Bombay: Bombay Times Press, 1924), 377–79.

65. *BB,* June 21, 1927. The Samata Sangh (comprising upper-caste reformers associated with Ambedkar's early activist efforts) and the Hindu Mahasabha, (under V. D. Savarkar's leadership) supported the performance of Vedic weddings (and thread ceremonies) for the Dalit communities. For Dalit Mahars' demand for Vedic weddings, see *BB,* July 12, 1929. Due to their social stigmatization, Dalit communities typically had separate priests, called *gosavi* or *joshi,* who performed religious rites for the community. Gopalbaba Valangkar had undertaken a campaign to replace Brahmin *joshis* with Dalit priests in the Ratnagiri district. A female *purohit* (priest) from Ratnagiri, called Phatiakka, is mentioned as performing religious rites, including marriages, as early as 1860. Urmila Pawar and Meenakshi Moon, *Amhihi Itihas Ghadavila: Ambedkari Calvalit Striyancha Sahabhag* [We Also Made History: Women's Participation in the Ambedkar Movement] (Mumbai: Stree Uvac Prakashan, 1989), 46.

66. For Self-Respect marriages, see S. Anandhi, "Women's Question in Dravidian Movement c. 1925–1948, *Social Scientist* 19:24–41; and V. Geetha, "Periyar, Women and an Ethic of Citizenship," *Economic and Political Weekly* 33 (April 25, 1998): 9–15, republished in Anupama Rao, ed., *Gender and Caste: Contemporary Issues in Indian Feminism* (New Delhi: Kali for Women, 2003). See also K. Srilata, ed., *The Other Half of the Coconut: Women Writing Self-Respect History* (New Delhi: Kali for Women, 2003).

67. Otur, a village of less than two thousand people, was the hub of Samaj activism. Phule's close associate, Krishnarao Bhalekar, was from Otur, as were Satyashodak activists Bhimrao Mahamuni, Narobaba Mahaghat Patil, and Dharmaji Ramji Dhumre Patil. Each was responsible for spreading the Satyashodak message to Vidarbha in the north, and to Kolhapur and Belgaum in the south. Mahamuni was active in Vidarbha between 1892 and 1910. Bhalekar was in Amraoti from 1900 to 1905 representing the Satyashodak Samaj and the DCM.

68. *Waman Jagannath Joshi and Others v. Balaji Kusaji Patil,* before Chief Justice Charles Sargent and Justice Candy, *ILR* 21 Bom 167.

69. Ibid. (emphasis added).

70. A suit from 1918 concerns the recovery of a *joshi*'s fees, though a man with Satyashodak affinities had performed his mother's funeral rites without calling in a Brahmin priest. *Bala Genuji Navale and Another v. Balwant Laxman Ghatpande, ILR* 17 Bom 613. By 1925, the Bhandari actvist S. K. Bole tabled a bill in the Bombay Legislative Council to abolish the *joshi vatan*. The Invalidation of Ceremonial Emoluments Act of 1926 abolished the fees and property holding that derived from the Brahmin's customary right to officiate at Hindu ceremonies. The Satyashodak activist Mahaghat Patil applauded the move in the pamphlet *Brahmananca Hakk Nahi, Yabaddal High Court Tharav* (n.p., n.d.).

71. O'Hanlon, "Issues of Widowhood," 70–72.

72. Shivram Janba Kamble wrote a series of articles that appeared in *Somavanshiya Mitra* in 1909 concerning marriage and sexuality in the Mahar community: "Adultery," January 1, 1909; "Polygamy," February 1, 1909; "Discourse on the Origins of Marriage," March 1, 1909; and "Polyandry," April 1, 1909. Robertson notes the prevalence of polygamy in *Mahar Folk*, 37.

73. To suggest that a discursive structure is gendered male does not preclude women's activism. My argument is concerned with the ideology governing political practice, and not with the sociology of protest. For an important account of Dalit women's activism and the central role women played in Ambedkar's movement (including interviews with the activists), see Pawar and Moon, *Amhihi Itihas Ghadavila.*

74. The classic text outlining the contested identity of the scribal community of Chandraseniya Kayastha Prabhus is by K. S. Thackeray, *Gramanyachya Sadhyant Itihas Arthat Nokarashiche Banda* [A Comprehensive History of Rebellion, or the Revolt of the Bureaucrats] (Mumbai: Yashwant Shivram Raje, 1919). Thackeray's text is a litany of discrimination suffered at the hands of Brahmins from the Shivaji period into the post-*peshwa* period. On the other hand, the historian V. K. Rajwade attributed to the Prabhus—and most Marathas—a miscegenated status as the product of inferior Kshatriyas and autochthonous Nagas from the Deccan. V. K. "Chandraseniya Kayastha," *Itihasacharya V. K. Rajwade Samagra Sahitya*, vols. 7–8, ed. Murlidhar Shah (Dhule: Itihasacharya V. K. Rajwade Samshodhan Mandal, 1995–98): 225–39.

75. Valangkar, *Khali Lihilelya Sarkari Surveypramane.*

76. The Sahyadrikhand, dating from the fourteenth century, is a late addition to the Skandapurana and reflects multiple (and fraught) efforts to incorporate the variety of Maharashtrian Brahmins—the Chitpavans, Deshasthas, Devarukh, and Karhades—within a genealogy of the Brahmin subcastes, which are divided between the Gauda Brahmins of the north, and the Dravidian Brahmins of the south. In the Sahyadrikhand, the Saraswat Brahmins of the Konkan are extolled, while other Brahmin subcastes, especially the Chitpavans, are denigrated. Madhav Deshpande, "Panca Gauda and Panca Dravida: Contested Borders of a Traditional Classification," published as "Panca-Gauda und Panca-Dravida: Umstrittene Grenzen einer traditionellen Klassifikation," in *"Arier" und "Draviden": Konstruktionen der Vergangenheit als Grundlage für Selbst- und Fremdwahrnehmungen Südasiens*, ed. Michael Bergunder and Rahul Peter (Halle: Das Neue Hallesche Berichte, Quellen und Studien zur Geschichte und Gegenwart Südindiens, 2002). English version obtained from Deshpande via personal com-

munication. See also N. K. Wagle, "The History and Social Organization of the Gauda Saraswat Brahmanas of the West Coast of India," *Journal of Indian History* 48, parts 1–2 (April 1970): 7–25, 295–333.

77. Treta Yuga, the second of four *yugas,* is best known for Vishnu's fifth, sixth, and seventh incarnations: as Vamana, Vishnu defeated King Bali; as Parashurama, he rid the earth of Kshatriyas; and as the god-king Rama, he vanquished the king of Lanka, Ravana. Each of these episodes was the subject of non-Brahmin histories that rewrote Hindu mythic narratives of virtuous gods versus evil demons as illustrations of Brahmin cunning and will to power.

78. V. K. Rajwade, the famous Brahmin historian, offered a eugenicist argument for the value of strategic marriages between upper-caste men and lower-caste women for gradual uplift of the lower castes. Sadanand More, introduction to *Itihasacharya V. K. Rajwade Samagra Sahitya,* vol. 10 (Dhule: Itihasacharya V. K. Rajwade Sanshodhan Mandal, 1995–98), 33. Vithal Ramji Shinde called Rajwade the modern-day Parashurama, who wanted to defeat the Marathas *twenty-two* times and denigrate them as Shudras. M. P. Mangudkar, *Shinde Lekhasangraha* (Pune: Thokal Prakashan, 1963), 185.

79. B. R. Ambedkar, *BAWS,* 16 vols., ed. Vasant Moon (Bombay: Government of Maharashtra, 1979–), *The Untouchables,* in vol. 7, 195–97.

80. See Mukundrao Patil, *Hindu ani Brahman* (Poona: Shri Shanken Chapkhana, 1914).

81. Vasudevrao Birze's book, *Maratha ani Tyanche Astitva* (Bombay: Induprakash Press, 1912), set the tone. Birze was editor of *Din Bandhu* for a brief period. He later founded the Maratha Education Conference in 1918 and was librarian to Sayajirao Gaikwad of Baroda.

82. Gopal Dajiba Dalvi, *Maratha Kulancha Itihas* (Mumbai: Induprakash Press, 1915–16).

83. *Vijayi Maratha* was published by Shripatrao Shinde, an editor committed to an inclusive non-Brahminism. *Rashtraveer* was more conservative and elitist in its outlook. Both papers carried similar marriage advertisements, which make for interesting reading as they often appear next to advertisements for farm implements and medicines for common ailments.

84. Bhaskarrao Jadhav, *Marathe Ani Tyanchi Bhasha* (Kolhapur: Dasram Book Depot, 1932), 9; Mukundrao Patil, *Hindu ani Brahman;* and Vithal Ramji Shinde, "Early Customs of the Marathas," in *Shinde Lekhasangraha,* 63–94.

85. See for example, Keshav Marutrao Jedhe, *1922–1927 Chatrapati Mela Padyasangraha* (Poona: Jedhe Mansion, 1928); Keshavrao Jedhe, *San 1924 Salchi Shri Chatrapati Melyachi Padyasangraha* (Poona: Vijayi Maratha Press, n.d.); and Keshav Marutrao Jedhe, *1928 Salchi Shri Chatrapati Melyachi Padyasangraha* (Poona: Shri Shankar Printing Press, n.d.).

86. Y. D. Phadke, *Brahmanetar Calvalitila Dhadhadiche Karyakarte Dinkarrao Javalkar Samagra Vangmay* (Pune: Mahatma Jotirao Phule Samata Pratishthan, 1984), 66.

87. Home (Special) 363(3), 1925–28, "Brahmans v. Non-Brahmans," MSA.

88. *Servant of India,* September 3, 1926.

89. The term *dasiputra* (lit. "son of a slave") was an important legal category. J. D. M. Derrett notes that *dasiputra* meant offspring that were "the result

of a personal relationship between his father and the bondswoman, a relationship resting upon a business transaction (as often as not) and not partaking of the character of a family asset." This relationship of servitude was interpreted loosely to mean a system of concubinage or "informal marriage" through which a relationship with a "kept" woman, usually lower caste, also involved a responsibility to her offspring. J. D. M. Derrett, "Inheritance By, From and Through Illegitimates at Hindu Law," in *Essays in Classical and Modern Hindu Law,* vol. 3, ed. J. D. M. Derrett (New Delhi: Universal Book Traders, 1995), 182–219. The Calcutta High Court interpreted the term *dasi* literally as a "female slave," while the High Courts of Allahabad, Bombay, and Madras interpreted *dasi* to mean a Shudra woman who was kept as a concubine. See for example, *Rahi v. Govind, ILR* 1 Bom 97. The sons of upper-caste women living in concubinage with lower-caste men were ineligible to inherit their father's property because their mother's relationship was described as causing "degeneration of the race." *Ramchandra Dodappa v. Hanamnaik Dodnaik, ILR* 37 Bom 920.

90. Introduction to Jedhe, 1922–1927 *Chatrapati Mela Padyasangraha,* 1–2.

91. See for example, Ramachandra Narayan Lad, *Marathyanche Dasiputra Arthat Paypoc Kimathiche Peshve* [The Bastards of Marathas, That Is to Say, the Useless Peshwas] (Poona: Shri Shahu Printing Press, 1927).

92. The text was printed at the Shri Shivaji Printing Press owned by the Saraswat activist R. N. Lad and published in the name of Keshavrao Jedhe, of Jedhe Mansion, Poona. Case no. 1452 of 1925, decided by Poona City Magistrate H. C. Fleming, imposed a year in prison and a fine of Rs. 250 for Javalkar and Lad. Jedhe and Bagade were fined Rs. 100 and sentenced to six months imprisonment. Javalkar was also prosecuted under Section 153-A of the Indian Penal Code for the publication of three other pamphlets (the *Chatrapati Padyasangraha*), while Lad was sentenced to nine months for writing an inflammatory article in the newspaper *Majur.* The Sessions Court acquitted the defendants on October 20, 1926, however.

93. Details of the controversy are from the report of the Oriental Translator to Government, Home (Special) 363(4)II, "Brahmans v. non-Brahmans," MSA.

94. Keshavrao Bagade, introduction to *Deshache Dushman* (n.p.: Shri Shivaji Printing Press, 1925).

95. Ibid.

96. *Deshache Dushman,* introduction.

97. K. B. Kulkarni's *Peshvyanche Paypoc* [Footwear of the Peshwas] (Poona: Hind Sevak Press, 1926) was a response to *Deshache Dushman.* This was followed by publication of R. N. Lad's *Marathyanche Dasiputra* (1927), to which D. N. Date wrote a response titled *Bepattha Bapache Bete* [Children of the Missing Father] (Poona: Hind Sevak Press, 1928). Each of the texts related contemporary caste identity with historical accounts of sexual licentiousness, conquest, and political treachery. Home (Pol), No. 10, 1928, MSA.

98. *Deshache Dushman,* 7.

99. Ibid., introduction.

100. Ibid.

101. Ibid., 56.

102. No. S.D. 1133, October 7, 1933, from D. J. Donell, Assistant Secretary

to Government of Bombay, to Secretary India, Home (Pol), Home (Special) 363(4)II, "Brahmans v. non-Brahmans," MSA.

103. Memorandum no. OT 288, dated June 17, 1926, from Oriental Translator to Secretary, Government of Bombay, Home (Special) 363(4)II, "Brahmans v. non-Brahmans," MSA.

104. *Times of India,* September 4, 1926.

105. *Mahratta,* August 22, 1926.

106. "Social Pests Condemned," *Mahratta,* September 12, 1926.

107. Reported in *Times of India,* September 6, 1926. The *Vijayi Maratha* had in mind the popular Marathi farces that were modeled on the English one-act plays performed in the Grant Road Theatre, which was inaugurated on February 10, 1846. The first Marathi farce was performed in 1856. Farces addressed a variety of themes, from historical chronicles, to pornographic or lewd performances reminiscent of *tamasha,* to critiques of social reform agendas, especially those concerned with female education. Usually farces were set within Hindu mythologicals and functioned as a moment of social realism that was set apart from the epic time of the mythological. Bhimrao Kulkarni, *Marathi Farce* (Pune: Maharashtra Sahitya Parishad, 1987).

108. Partha Chattejee, "The Nationalist Resolution of the Woman's Question," in *Recasting Women: Essays in Indian Colonial History,* ed. Kumkum Sangari and Sudesh Vaid (New Brunswick, NJ: Rutgers University Press, 1990), 233–53.

109. For a missionary feminist's description of the status of *muralis* in Bombay, see Mrs. Marcus Fuller, *The Wrongs of Indian Womanhood,* with an introduction by Pandita Ramabai (New York: Ravell, 1900). Jennifer and Marcus Fuller were both missionaries with the American Faith Mission, who opened mission branches in Akola, Berar, in 1882. Published in the year of Jennifer Fuller's death, *The Wrongs of Womanhood,* previously serialized in the *Bombay Guardian,* catalogued gender discrimination, including ritual dedication.

110. *Vaghyas* were men dedicated to the god Khandoba. Another typical figure associated with the ritual practices of the Mahar and Mang communities was the *potraj,* a devotee of the goddess Mariai. The *potraj* had long braided hair, wore ankle-length skirts and anklets, and a cowrie-shell necklace around his neck. He carried a set of stones smeared in vermilion—representing Mariai—in a box, and carried a whip in which the goddess was said to reside. Smeared in vermilion and given to dancing with the whip, the *potraj* was a fearsome figure associated with Shiva. Mentioned in Robertson, *Mahar Folk.*

111. Sharmila Rege, "Hegemonic Appropriation of Sexuality: The Case of the Erotic Lavani of Maharashtra," in *Social Reform, Sexuality and the State,* ed. Patricia Uberoi (New Delhi: Sage Publications, 1996), 23–38. For an analysis of the emergence of urban, commercial public theater in the post-1850 period and its impact on popular performative traditions, especially of female impersonation, see Kathryn Hansen, "Theatrical Transvestism in the Parsi, Gujarati and Marathi Theatres (1850–1940)," in *Sexual Sites, Seminal Attitudes: Sexualities, Masculinities, and Culture,* ed. Sanjay Srivastava (New Delhi: Sage Publications, 2004), 99–122.

112. R. B. More's autobiography contains vivid accounts of Bombay's fa-

mous Batatyachya Chawl, inhabited by prostitutes and famous *tamasgirs* (*tamasha* performers) of the time. Satyendra More, *Comrade R. B. More: Dalit va Communist Calvalicha Sashaktha Duva* (Mumbai: Paryay Prakashan, 2003), 53. More played a key role in the Mahad *satyagraha* but joined the Communist Party in 1930. He was an important union organizer affiliated with the textile, railway, dockyard, and Bombay Electric Supply and Transport (BEST) unions in Bombay. He probably went to Bombay in 1918 or 1919. By then, Dalits were an important constituency in Bombay's urban culture, as spectators and performers. *Sangeet natak* companies, which staged Hindu mythologicals, were important financial contributors to early Mahar Dalit activist efforts, including the famous Mahad *satyagraha*. R. M. Biwalkar and Zhumbarlal Kamble, *Mahadcha Mutisangram* [Mahad Freedom Struggle] (Pune: Rajhans Prakashan, 1977), 12, 47.

113. Pavalabai and Patthe lived together for a time in central Bombay during the 1920s. Patthe met B. R. Ambedkar to offer funds for the Mahad satyagraha. Ambedkar refused, accusing Patthe of making his money by exploiting Mahar women. Biwalkar and Kamble, *Mahadcha Mutisangram,* 47. The few details of Pavalabai's life can be found in Kanta Achalkhamb, "Namchand Pavala Bai," *Asmitadarsh,* Divali Ank, vol. 11, no. 3, 1982. I am also drawing from interviews held August 14 and 30, 2004, with Madhukar Nerale, owner of the Hanuman Theater, which staged *tamasha* performances between 1948 and 1994.

114. The original letter of July 1908 from the *panch* is unavailable, as this issue of the *Somavanshiya Mitra* is missing from the Khairmode Collection, Bombay University.

115. *SM,* December 1, 1908.

116. K. R. Bomanji, Collector of Bijapur, no. 3474, July 12, 1906, JD, vol. 155, no. 1559, 1909, "Murlis," MSA.

117. Bomanji noted that the practice of allowing the sons of *muralis* to inherit their mother's ancestral property was approved by GR no. 2266, dated May 5, 1874.

118. No. 290 of 1857 to H. C. Anderson, Secretary to Government, from Collector, Dharwar, February 27, 1857, JD, vol. 143, no. 2078, 1907, "Memorials," MSA.

119. K. R. Bomanji, Collector of Bijapur, no. 3474, July 12, 1906, JD, vol. 155, no. 1559, 1909, "Murlis," MSA.

120. Memorandum no. 1116 of 1873, April 11, 1874, from Collector, Dharwar, JD, vol. 140, 1874, MSA.

121. For an analysis of how the Bombay government addressed inheritance through the mother's line for the offspring of *devadasis,* as opposed to the rights of *dasiputras,* (illegitimate sons) to inherit from Sudra fathers, see Rachel Sturman, "Theorizing Rights, Morality, and Exchange in the Colonial Jurisprudence of Hindu Marriage," *Feminist Studies* (forthcoming).

122. JD, vol. 155, no. 1559 (1909), "Murlis," MSA. As chairman of the Depressed Classes Conference, Chandavarkar had pressured the Indian National Congress to clarify its position on caste, which led to the passage of Congress's 1917 Resolution on Untouchability.

123. Attachments from Madras district magistrates are found in JD, vol. 155, no. 1559, 1909, "Murlis," MSA.

124. These figures were produced in response to GR(D) no. 2843 of May 1906, sent to all district magistrates asking them to report on the practice. JD, vol. 143, no. 2078, 1907, "Memorials," MSA.

125. Chandavarkar's handwritten note of October 12, 1908, suggested passing a law applying to "all Sudras who hold watans." He downplayed the import of his suggestion by noting that existing legislation had already "set aside the order of Hindu law or inheritance" by excluding "female heirs from the right of heirship of a watan." JD, vol. 155, no. 1559, 1909, "Murlis," MSA. This Brahminizing move directly contravened an earlier finding that "amongst Sudras the right of succession undoubtedly devolves on illegitimate sons in the absence of legitimate sons, sons' sons, or sons' sons' sons." Memo from the RLA, no. 1695, December 22, 1884, JD, vol. 155, no. 1559, 1909, "Murlis," MSA.

126. R. B. More argues that the *Somavanshiya Mitra* shut down in 1912 due to lack of funds, which was the result of community resistance to *murali* reform. Satyendra More, *Comrade R. B. More*, 98.

127. In 1896, an account in the newspaper *Shetkaryancha Kaivari* noted that a young, educated girl of fourteen in the town of Yeola was getting ready to become a *murali*. Holding the girl responsible for this "decision," the paper wondered why she was not being married to a good Mahar and made to give up her evil ways.

128. *SM*, December 1, 1908.

129. *SM*, August 1, 1909.

130. *SM*, March 1, 1909.

131. It was argued that existing laws governing the sale or transfer of girls for prostitution were adequate. Parents were punishable under Section 372 of the Indian Penal Code for dedicating daughters, as were priests performing the dedication. "Procurors" could be prosecuted under Section 373. Minors were protected under the Guardians and Wards Act, which allowed that "a Collector, guardian, relative or friend of a minor can seek to protect a minor." Thus it was not new legislation so much as "public initiative" that failed to curtail the practice. Unofficial Reference from JD, no. I-M, April 20, 1909, JD, vol. 155, no. 1559, 1909, "Murlis," MSA.

132. GR no. 3866, JD, July 8, 1909, *Proclamation Issued by the Government of Bombay, on the Subject of the Custom Prevailing in the Bombay Presidency of Marrying Young Girls to Hindu Gods,* JD, vol. 155, no. 1559, 1909, "Murlis," MSA.

133. The Jejuri case is reported in *SM*, November 1, 1909; the Bombay case in *SM*, December 1, 1909. See also "Result of the trial of Kisan Sadhu Mahar who dedicated his minor daughter as a 'Murali' to the god 'Khandoba' at Jejuri, April 1909." Because Kisan's thirteen-year-old daughter Radha was dedicated in April 1909, before the law banning dedication went into effect, Kisan was sentenced on October 25, 1909, to "rising of the court and Rs. 10." JD, vol. 216, no. 687, 1910, MSA.

134. Shivram Janba Kamble, Shripatrao Ramji Thorat, and Shivram Tatyaba

Tanbate wrote to support *murali* marriage. *SM,* January 1, 1909, and July 1, 1909. The *Sudharak* also asked men to consider marrying *muralis* in an article of July 30, 1906.

135. An advertisement for a special issue of *Somavanshiya Mitra* mentions that a photograph of Shivubai and Hanumantrao Gaikwad will be included. Unfortunately, that special issue is missing in the Khairmode Collection, Bombay University.

136. A notice from July 19, 1909, noted that Vithabai, a *murali* from Kamathipura, Bombay's famous red-light district, converted to Islam to marry her partner. Thorat asked why *murali* marriages could not be supported within the Hindu religion. *SM,* August 1, 1909. The newspaper also reported that fifty-five *muralis* had been married. *SM,* July 1, 1909. A Bahishkrit Sabha in Ambarnath, in Thana district, on August 9, 1927, demanded that the age of marriage be set at twenty-two years for men and sixteen years for women as part of a broader effort to link *murali* reform with the transformation of gender relations in the community. Pawar and Moon, *Amhihi Itihas Ghadavila,* 46–47.

137. *Times of India,* June 17, 1936.

138. *BB,* September 30, 1927.

139. Ambedkar's speech on December 27, 1927, took place before "thousands of women from the surrounding area [who had] walked eight to ten miles by foot to take [Ambedkar's] darshan." Biwalkar and Kamble, *Mahadcha Mutisangram,* 73. Biwalkar and Kamble note that a makeshift changing room was erected at the conference, to teach Dalit women to tie the sari in a respectable way.

140. Pierre Bourdieu describes "habitus" as a set of culturally specific practices of bodily comportment inculcated early in life, and a form of symbolic power that works through the reproduction of bodily practice, belief, and comportment. Pierre Bourdieu, *The Logic of Practice* (Cambridge: Polity Press, 1990), 69. While Bourdieu's idea of the habitus addresses the resilience of quotidian practices of distinction, his ideas are less helpful in explaining alterations in corporeal practice.

141. Ambedkar noted, "The greatest progress we have made is to be found amongst our women folk. Here you see in this conference these 20,000–25,000 women present. See their dress, observe their manners, mark their speech. Can any one say that they are untouchable women?" *Report of the All-India Depressed Classes Conference* (Nagpur, 1942), 28–29.

142. The largest migration to Bombay was from the Ratnagiri district in the Konkan, which provided the "single largest source of industrial workers for Bombay." The district's high proportion of quit rent and grain deficits produced high levels of rural indebtedness. Baniprasanna Misra, "Factory Labour During the Early Years of Industrialisation: An Appraisal in Light of the Indian Factory Commission, 1890," *Indian Economic and Social History Review* 8, no. 3 (July–September 1975), 210. The post office (which operated out of schools) was important to the remittance economy that sustained the Konkan. Valangkar, *DB,* August 26, 1894.

143. *Census of India, 1881,* vol. 3 (London: Eyre and Spottiswoode, 1883). The 1938 figure is from Gopinath Ramchandra Pradhan, *Untouchable Workers of Bombay City* (Bombay: Karnatak Publishing House, 1938). By 1921, the pop-

ulation of untouchable castes working in Bombay's textile mills was 12 percent; this figure reached 38 percent by 1941. Morris D. Morris, *The Emergence of an Industrial Labor Force in India: A Study of the Bombay Cotton Mills, 1854–1957* (Berkeley: University of California Press, 1965). Throughout this period, untouchables represented 40 percent of the workforce in the ring-spinning department and 20.9 percent of the workforce in the winding and reeling departments, with a greater concentration of men (70 percent) in the former and a majority of women (74 percent) in the latter. Morris D. Morris, "Caste and the Evolution of the Industrial Work Force in India," *Proceedings of the American Philosophical Society* 104, no. 2 (April 1960), 128.

144. Rasiklal Cholia, *Dock Workers in Bombay* (Bombay, 1941), 41–45.

145. Valangkar, *DB*, March 31, 1895.

146. The *abhang* is a verse set to the metrical style of the *bhakthi* poetry of the Varkari saints such as Tukaram, Eknath, and the Dalit (Mahar) saint Chokhamela.

147. Valangkar, *DB*, September 30, 1894. The repeated invocation of the term *sarvajanik*, lit. "for all people," and *sabha*, "association," refers to the Sarvajanik Sabha, the regional precursor to the Indian National Congress that was formed in 1872 by the liberal M. G. Ranade.

148. "Memorial to the Hunter Commission, 1882," in *Samagra Vangmay.*

149. R. V. Parulekar, ed., *Selections from the Records of the Government of Bombay: Education, Part 1, 1819–1852* (Bombay: Asia Publishing House, 1955). See also *Extract from Report of the Board of Education, Bombay for the Years 1840 and 1841*, MSA.

150. "Report of the Director of Public Instruction," July 10, 1856, in *Bombay General Proceedings for the Year 1856–1857*, MSA.

151. Remarks by C. H. Snow, Assistant Collector, Pune, February 1, 1887, ED, vol. 45, no. 348, 1895, MSA.

152. *Report of the Indian Education Commission Appointed by Resolution of the Government of India Dated 3rd February 1882* (Calcutta: Superintendant of Government Printing, 1882), 515, MSA. Colonial officials believed that English education would have an influence on the reform of caste society. E. H. Gumperz, "English Education and Social Change in Nineteenth-century Bombay, 1858–98" (PhD diss., McGill University, 1980); and Ellen McDonald, "English Education and Social Reform in Late Nineteenth-Century Bombay," *Modern Asian Studies* 5 (1965–66): 453–70. Gauri Viswanathan's argument about a colonial genealogy for English, which developed through the links between language and Christian doctrine, complicates these earlier studies that operate with an instrumental understanding of the value of English education. Gauri Viswanathan, *Masks of Conquest: Literary Study and British Rule in India* (Delhi: Oxford University Press, 1998).

153. Lee Warner to Collector, Poona, via Commissioner, July 10, 1887, ED, Report no. 3875, July 12, 1887, vol. 45, no. 348, 1895, MSA.

154. G. F. M. Grant to Mackenzie, Satara, August 2, 1887, *Annual Administration Report of the District Deputy Collector for 1886–1887*, ED, para. 19, vol. 45, no. 348, 1895, MSA.

155. Three classes of schools received government aid: Class A schools were

supported by local, municipal, and provincial funds; Class B schools were privately managed (e.g., by missionaries), received grants-in-aid and had to open their doors to untouchable students; Class C schools, designated special schools, existed for a particular community and purpose. There was some confusion among colonial officials whether Class C schools were mandated to receive untouchables. Lee Warner to HE Gov., August 4, 1887, ED, vol. 45, no. 348, 1895, MSA.

156. Philip Constable, "Sitting on the School Verandah: The Ideology and Practice of 'Untouchable' Educational Protest in Late Nineteenth Century Western India," *Indian Economic Social History Review* 37, no. 4 (October– December 2000): 383–422.

157. R. B. More was born in Dasgaon, a few miles outside Mahad. More's father's maternal uncle was Vithal Joshi, a literate, wealthy jungle contractor in whose home Valangkar was supposed to have composed *Vitthal Vidhwansan*. In his *Vinanti Patra*, Valangkar mentions a wealthy Mahar family that built a second story for their home and invited a Brahmin priest to bless the home on September 3, 1888. The Brahmin *joshi* was excommunicated. The owner of that home was most certainly Vithal Joshi. Joshi's sons were educated by Valangkar and went on to become teachers at Mahad's Marathi school. By 1917, in response to the growing demand for education among Mahars, a relation of More's had rented his premises for a separate Mahar school (partly) funded by the government. Satyendra More, *Comrade R. B. More*, 19–25.

158. *DB*, April 15, 1894. See also "Petition from Pensioned Native Officers, Dapoli, to Nugent," February 8, 1894, ED, vol. 45, 1895, MSA. Ambedkar's father, Subhedar Ramnak Malnak, was one of the signatories to the petition. See also *DB*, October 14, 1894; and Sahasrabuddhe to Chatfield, Director of Public Instruction, November 29, 1894, ED, vol. 45, 1895, MSA.

159. My recapitulation of these events relies on Sahasrabuddhe to Chatfield, Director of Public Instruction, November 29, 1894, ED, vol. 45, 1895, MSA; and the Marathi correspondence that accompanies a letter from the Collector of Ratnagiri, W. W. Drew, to Sahasrabuddhe, April 26, 1894, ED, vol. 45, 1895, MSA.

160. Charles Selden, "A Prince and Outcast at Dinner in London," *New York Times*, November 30, 1932 (an interview with B. R. Ambedkar).

161. *DB*, January 1, 1893.

162. Petition from Pensioned Native Officers, Dapoli, to Nugent, February 8, 1894, ED, vol. 45, 1895, MSA.

163. An English letter noted that Dapoli Mahars had sent a memorial to the commissioner of the Southern Division demanding that their children be permitted to attend local schools. *DB*, April 8, 1894.

164. J. Nugent, Commissioner of the Southern Division, to W. W. Drew, Collector, Ratnagiri, May 2, 1894, ED, vol. 45, 1895, MSA.

165. J. Nugent, Commissioner of the Southern Division, to Lee-Warner, Secretary of Government, June 30, 1894, ED, vol. 45, 1895, MSA. On the municipality's recalcitrance, see also *DB*, October 14, 1894.

166. No. A 4863 of 1894–95 from Sahasrabuddhe, Education Inspector, SD, to Director, Public Instruction (Chatfield), Dharwar, November 29, 1894, vol. 45, no. 348, 1895, MSA.

167. Petition from Ramnak Chownak, President of ADPM, March 25, 1901, ED, vol. 33, 1901, MSA.

168. These figures are drawn from the *Census of India, 1911,* vol. 7 (Bombay: Government Central Press, 1911–15); *Census of India 1921,* vol. 8 (Calcutta: Superintendant of Government Printing, 1921–24); and *Census of India, 1931,* vol. 8 (Delhi: Manager of Publications, 1932).

169. The Central Provinces saw the resurgence of a second phase of Satyashodak activism at the turn of the twentieth century. The region also saw Dalit activism among literate and sometimes wealthy Dalit landowners, or *malguzars,* who endowed educational institutions and demanded representation in government. For details of reformist efforts, see H. L. Kosare, *Vidarbhatila Dalit Calvalicha Itihas* (Nagpur: Gnan Pradeep Prakashan, 1984); and Vasant Moon, *Madhyaprant-Varhadatila Dr. Ambedkarpurva Dalit Calvali* (Pune: Sugawa Prakashan, 1987).

170. For Kamble's efforts, see *SM,* June 1, 1910, October 1, 1909, and November 1, 1909. See also *Presidential Speech of His Highness the Maharajah Gaekwar at the All-India Conference on the Abolition of Untouchability, Bombay, 23 March 1918* (Bombay: British India Press, 1918). An editorial regarding Gaikwad's educational initiative appeared in *SM,* August 1, 1908.

171. Khairmode, *Dr. Bhimrao Ramji Charitra,* vol. 2, 227.

172. *SM,* March 1, 1909.

173. R. H. Craddock, *The Settlement Report of Nagpur Zilla* (n.p., 1899). Moon Pande was the grandfather of Vasant Moon, who was the editor and compiler of the *BAWS* series until his death in 2002. Vasant Moon writes that he received his grandfather's papers in 1979 when a grand-uncle handed him a bundle of papers wrapped in a large cloth. The grand-uncle had contemplated burning the papers, but remembered Moon's penchant for collecting old documents just in time. Vasant Moon, *Madhyaprant-Varhadatila Dr. Ambedkarpurva Dalit Calvali,* introduction.

174. Testimonial for Vithoba Raoji Moon Pande by Reverend W. D. Waller, Kamptee, January 1, 1916, Vasant Moon Collection, Nagpur. In 1922, Moon Pande established a Cokhamela Sudharak Mandal (Cokhamela Reform Society) to assert a positive Hindu identity for Mahars and called for the reform of practices such as eating carrion and child marriage. *Report of the Second Session of the Cokhamela Sudharak Mandal* (Ramtek, November 24, 1923).

175. At the turn of the twentieth century, Nagpur's Mahars were also demanding education, equal access to water wells, and *dharamshalas* (guesthouses). *Nagpur Mahar Mitras Sabheche Suchiputra* [Information Regarding the Meeting of the Friends of the Nagpur Mahars] (n.p., April 13, 1913).

176. Marathi petition from Vithoba Raoji Moon Pande to the Honourable Members of the Ramtek Temple Committee (n.d.), Vasant Moon Collection, Nagpur.

177. Vasant Moon, *Dr. Ambedkarpurva Dalit Calvali,* 11–12.

178. Letter no. 214 from the Gorakshan Karyalaya, Nagpur, October 26, 1903; letter from Shri Gorakshan Sabha Office, Nagpur, to the Mahar Community, October 11, 1903; letter from N. Deshmukh, Secretary of the Gorakshan Sabha, Nagpur, October 30, 1911, all in the Vasant Moon Collection, Nagpur.

179. Petition from Vithoba Sant Pande to Ramtek Temple Committee, October 28, 1908; and petition to the Gorakshan Sabha from the Mahar Community, September 20, 1907, both in the Vasant Moon Collection, Nagpur.

180. Deed of sale to Vithoba Raoji Moon Pande, March 2,1906, Vasant Moon Collection, Nagpur.

181. *The Loyal Mahar Sabha: A Brief Summary of its Record,* March 15, 1914, Vasant Moon Collection, Nagpur. A receipt in the name of the "Cokhamela Devasthan Committee (Ramtek)" mentions a fee of five annas for a *pande*'s services.

182. *Kararnama* [Testimony], March 4, 1907, Vasant Moon Collection, Nagpur.

183. *Jahir Patra* [Public Notice], November 10, 1920; and petition from Vithoba Raoji Moon Pande Sant to His Excellency, the Governor in Council, Central Provinces, Nagpur, January 4, 1924, both in the Vasant Moon Collection, Nagpur. Hindu inclusion was a strong demand among Mahars in Vidarbha.

184. *Atmaram (accused) v. King Emperor, AIR* 1 Nagpur 121. The case was decided on March 10, 1923, and reported the following year.

185. The Bombay government gave a figure of three thousand attendees at the March meeting. *Extract from Confidential Weekly Letter,* District Magistrate, Kolaba, December 10, 1927, Home (Special) 365(64)II, "Mahad Satyagraha," MSA. Dhananjay Keer estimates a crowd of ten thousand in his *Dr. Ambedkar: Life and Mission,* 3rd ed. (Bombay: Popular Prakashan, 1971), 69.

186. Twenty people were severely wounded and seventy more were badly hurt, including four women. *Dnyanprakash,* June 27, 1927. Five caste Hindus were sentenced to four months of imprisonment for rioting. "Mahadcha Khatala va Asprushyancha Jay" [The Mahad Judgment and the Untouchables' Victory], *BB,* July 1, 1927. The protection offered by Muslims in the town is noted in "Aajkalche Prashna" [Today's Questions], *BB,* April 6, 1926.

187. *Extract from Confidential Weekly Letter,* District Superintendent of Police, Kolaba, November 5, 1927, Home (Special) 365(64)II, "Mahad Satyagraha," MSA. Women's financial contributions to the *satyagraha* are mentioned in *BB,* November 4, 1927.

188. Confidential Reports on the Mahad Satyagraha, January 1, 1928, Home (Special) 365(64)II, "Mahad Satyagraha," MSA. This is surprising because Keshavrao Jedhe and Dinkarrao Javalkar had given speeches at the first *satyagraha* arguing that Marathas were responsible for oppressing Dalit communities in rural areas. Ratnakar Ganvir, *Mahad Samata Sangar* (Nagpur: Srinivas Mudranalaya, 1981), 45. B. R.Ambedkar criticized the non-Brahmin movement in his editorial, "Mahad Yethila Dharmasangar va Varishta Hinduna Jababdari" [The Religious War at Mahad and Caste Hindu's responsibility], *BB,* April 22, 1927.

189. "Aajkalche Prashna" [Today's Questions], *BB,* July 1, 1927. The first issue of *BB,* April 3, 1927, also noted retaliatory violence against Dalits. Caste Hindu retaliation is also mentioned in Biwalkar and Kamble, *Mahadcha Mutisangram,* 54.

190. The *Manusmriti* was the prime symbol of Brahmin domination for caste radicals. The text's ban on education for women and untouchables, and the prescribed ill-treatment of the Shudra castes were repeatedly challenged as symbols of Hindu tyranny.

191. B. R. Ambedkar chaired the BHS, whose board included caste Hindus and Dalits. Caste Hindu or Parsi members of the board included C. H. Setalvad (president), Meyer Nissim, G. K. Nariman, V. Chavan, R. Paranjpe, B. G. Kher (all vice presidents). The BHS's management consisted of Ambedkar (chairman of council of management), S. N. Shivtarkar (general secretary), and N. T. Jadhav (treasurer). Meetings were normally held in Damodar Hall in Bombay. *Bahishkrit Hitakarini Sabha, Niyam Patrak, Sthapana July 20 1924* [Rules of Constitution of the BHS, established July 20 1924], Khairmode Collection, Bombay.

192. *Report for 1925 of the Depressed Classes Institute,* Khairmode Collection, Bombay.

193. The BHS worked together with the Samata Sangh (Association for Equality), founded by Ambedkar in 1926. The Samata Sangh was led by Deorao Naik, a Deshastha Brahmin; Bhaskarrao Khadrekar, a Bhandari; and Bal Gangadhar Tilak's son, Sridhar Balwant Tilak. The Sangh worked among caste Hindus to stress activities such as intercaste dining, the promotion of Vedic weddings, and the wearing of the sacred thread. Its newspaper, *Samata,* was published for one year, from 1928 to 1929.

194. R. B. More notes that he organized a meeting of military pensioners in 1924 with the help of a member of the Satyashodak Samaj, a Chambhar named Maruti Agavane, to take up the water issue. The Mahar Samaj Seva Sangh (Association for Service to the Mahar Community) then decided to collect Rs. 3 from each village to support a Bahishkrit Parishad, and to invite Ambedkar to preside over it. Satyendra More, *Comrade R. B. More,* 81. An alternative narrative emerges from Surendranath Tipnis, who was chairman of the Mahad municipality when it passed the resolution opening the tank. Later known as Dalitmitra (friend of the Dalits) or Nanasaheb, Tipnis was influenced by his brother-in-law A. V. Chitre, an important member of Bombay's Social Service League. Tipnis argues that it was at Chitre's insistence that a Bahishkrit Parishad was called to test the municipality's resolution. "Interview with Shri Nanasaheb Tipnis," *Siddharth College of Law Magazine* (Bombay) (1971–73), 21; and R. M. Biwalkar, "Interview with Tipnis," *Manus* (December 8, 1973): 17–32.

2. THE PROBLEM OF CASTE PROPERTY

1. Vasant Moon, "Prantik Assemblitila Asprushya Sadasyanche Karya" [The Work of Untouchable Representatives in the Provincial Assembly], parts I and II, *Asmitadarsh,* Divali Ankh [Divali issue] (1980 and January–March 1981), Jafema (1980, 1891). Nandagavli's resolution was passed by the Central Provinces regional assembly but did not become law. H. L. Kosare, *Vidarbhatila Dalit Calvalicha Itihas* (Nagpur: Gnan Pradeep Prakashan, 1984), 461.

2. Resolution no. 4770 of August 4, 1923, quoted in Dhananjay Keer, *Dr. Ambedkar: Life and Mission,* 3rd ed. (Bombay: Popular Prakashan, 1971), 53.

3. V. Geetha and S. V. Rajadurai, *Towards a Non-Brahmin Millennium: From Iyothee Thass to Periyar* (Calcutta: Samya, 1998), 54.

4. "Satyagraha Ka Thambavila" [Why I Stopped the Satyagraha], *BB,* February 3, 1928.

5. Extract from the confidential diary of the DSP, Kolaba, for the week end-

ing August 13, 1927, Home (Special) 365(64)II, "Mahad Satyagraha," MSA. Another effort to open the Chavdar tank to all castes was voted down by a majority of the municipality's members on December 3, 1927, not long before the second *satyagraha*. Letter to Monteath from Hood, December 9, 1927, Home (Special) 365(64)II, MSA. See also "Asprushyancha Satyagraha Ani Mahadchya Chavdar Talyachi Raksha" [The Untouchables' Satyagraha and the Protection of Mahad's Chavdar Tank], *BB*, December 23, 1927.

6. Details of the Mahad civil case are as follows. The original suit, no. 405 of 1927, *Raghunath Pandurang Dharap and Others v. Bhimrao Ramji Ambedkar and Others*, was decided by G. V. Vaidya, the second-class subordinate judge of Mahad. He dismissed the plaintiffs' suit ordering each party to bear its own cost. Thereafter, B. N. Sanjana, second assistant judge of the Thana District Court, ruled on Appeal no. 32 of 1930 on January 30, 1930. He confirmed the original decision and asked each party to bear its costs. The Second Appeal no. 462 of 1933 was admitted to the Bombay High Court on August 18, 1933. The Mahad case was decided in favor of the *satyagrahis* on March 17, 1937. See *Narhari Damodar Vaidya and Others v. B. R. Ambedkar and Others*, AIR 1939 Bom 146.

7. Remembrancer of Legal Affairs, S.J. 348, February 2, 1968, Home (Special) 365(64)II, "Mahad Satyagraha," MSA (emphasis added).

8. Letter from J. R. Hood, District Magistrate, Kolaba, to Secretary to Government, Home (Pol), April 20, 1927, Home (Special) 365(64)II, "Mahad Satyagraha," MSA.

9. Home (Pol), no. S.D. 461 of May 10, 1927, from J. Monteath to all Commissioners, and reply from H. L. Painter, Commissioner Southern Division, to Secretary of the Government Home Department, no. POL 411 of October 19, 1927, MSA.

10. Letter of October 7, 1927, Order no. 4770/13055A, Home (Special) 365(64)II, "Mahad Satyagraha," MSA.

11. Appeal no. 462 of 1933, Bombay High Court, Objection no. 11. The original case papers are at the Bombay High Court archives.

12. B. R. Ambedkar, "Mahad Yethila Dharmasangar va Varishta Hinduna Jababdari" [The Religious War in Mahad and Upper-Caste Hindus' Responsibility], *BB*, April 22, 1927.

13. B. R. Ambedkar, "Mahad Yethila Dharmasangar va Ingraz Sarkarchi Jababdari" [The Religious War in Mahad and the English Government's Responsibility], *BB*, May 6, 1927. On July 1, 1927, *BB* mentioned the opening of the new Thakurdwar temple in Bombay to all castes. Ambedkar was heckled when he visited the temple, and the temple was later purified.

14. Appeal no. 462 of 1933, Bombay High Court, Objection no. 5.

15. Ibid.

16. Quoted in Pradeep Gaikwad, ed., *Dr. Babasaheb Ambedkaranchi Samagra Bhashane, Khand* 9 (Nagpur, 2001), 59–60. This is from Ambedkar's presidential speech at the Amraoti temple *satyagraha*, which was led by the prominent non-Brahmin activist Punjabrao Deshmukh and by Ganesh Akkaji Gawai, a member of the Amraoti Municipal Council. The struggle to enter the Amraoti temple in the Central Provinces fizzled out soon after a public meeting was held

at the Indrabhuvan Theatre on November 13 and 14, 1927, since efforts to negotiate with temple trustees failed.

17. Appeal no. 462 of 1933, Bombay High Court, Point no. 12. Included are three documents—a report of June 9, 1843, to the revenue commissioner, Northern Division from the collector, Kolaba; a report by the members of the municipal board to the governor-in-council, Bombay, of March 6, 1865, and a petition to the governor-in-council from the inhabitants of Mahad of July 1, 1864—that discuss tank repairs and prove that the Chavdar tank was maintained by public funds.

18. Appeal no. 462 of 1933, Bombay High Court, Point no. 22.

19. L. T. Kikani, *Caste in Courts or Rights and Powers of Castes in Social and Religious Matters as Recognized by Indian Courts* (Rajkot: Ganatra Printing Works, 1912); Janaki Nair, *Women and Law in Colonial India* (New Delhi: Kali for Women in collaboration with the National Law School of India University, 1996); and Sripati Roy, *Customs and Customary Law in British India* (repr., Delhi: Mittal Publications, 1986).

20. Appeal no. 32 of 1930, District Court of Thana; the original case papers are at the Bombay High Court archives.

21. Judge Sanjana ruled, however, that "the story of ownership of a limited number of touchables was first released at the hearing and there is nothing to support it in the pleadings on record." Regular Civil Suit no. 405 of 1927, Point no. 8; the original case papers are at the Bombay High Court archives.

22. B. R. Ambedkar accompanied the president of the Mahad municipality to the Chavdar tank on January 1, 1928, and found a stone in the southeastern *ghat* bearing the Marathi inscription, "Mahad Municipality, 1899." A similar stone was found on the southwestern *ghat*, except that someone had tried to remove the writing with a chisel. DSP, Kolaba, January 7, 1928, Home (Special) 365(64)II, "Mahad Satyagraha," MSA.

23. J. R. Hood to Commissioner, Southern Division, Belgaum M.S.C. 192 of October 14, 1927, Home (Special) 365(64)II, "Mahad Satyagraha," MSA.

24. Civil Suit Number 405 of 1927, Point no. 15. The original case papers are at the Bombay High Court archives.

25. According to *ILR* 28 Bom 161, only the owner of a trust could sue to prohibit a certain class of people from using its facilities. Caste Hindus found recourse in another case, *ILR* 7 Bom 323, which gave the beneficiaries of a trust the right to sue if trespass offended their social status.

26. Dilip Menon, *Caste, Nationalism and Communism in South India* (Cambridge: Cambridge University Press, 1994), 115.

27. N. V. Gadgil, *Kahi Mohara, Kahi Moti* (Poona, 1962), 219.

28. "Mahar *Satyagraha* to Assert Rights to Enter Changdev Temple at Edalabad in East Khandesh," letter of November 9, 1930, Home (Special) 355(64)IV-B, 1931, MSA. Temple regulation in Bombay derived from efforts to regularize *inam* lands, a catchall category describing rights to land granted to an individual, a collective, or to institutions like temples.

29. Franklin Presler, *Religion under Bureaucracy: Policy and Administration for Hindu Temples in South India* (Cambridge: Cambridge Univeristy Press, 1988), especially chapter 2, "The Temple Connection in the Nineteenth Century."

V. Geetha and Rajadurai note that Justice Party intervention into temple management and executive control in 1922 left exclusionary worship patterns untouched. V. Geetha and Rajadurai, *Towards a Non-Brahmin Millenium*, 212–16.

30. In Bombay, temples under direct government control as well as those ad-
ministered by a managing committee appointed by local government officials received government grants for temple upkeep. The sum varied with the size and
significance of the temple. *The Report of the Assistant Commissioner of Inams,*
no. 1061 RD, August 31, 1860. For example, the Budget White Book for 1933–
34 does not disaggregate figures for temple allowance, but shows that more than
Rs. 3 lakhs were paid annually as *devasthan* and mosque allowance. Tax-free
inam lands involving a *nuksan* (loss) of Rs. 9.25 lakhs to the government were
held as *warshasans* and *devasthans*. Handwritten note from RD, March 3, 1933,
Home (Pol) 800(40)(7)C, 1933, MSA. According to this note, efforts to collect
detailed information about temples through district collectors in the 1860s were
generally unsuccessful.

31. Arjun Appadurai uses the phrase "redistributive process." See Arjun Appadurai, *Worship and Conflict under Colonial Rule: A South Indian Case* (Cambridge: Cambridge University Press, 1981), 34–36. See also Carol Breckenridge,
"The Sri Minaksi Sundaresvar Temple: Worship and Endowments in South India, 1833–1925" (PhD dissertation, University of Wisconsin-Madison, 1976);
and Nicholas B. Dirks, *The Hollow Crown: Ethnohistory of an Indian Kingdom,*
2nd ed. (Ann Arbor: University of Michigan Press, 1993), especially chapter 9,
"Temples and Society," and chapter 12, "Temples and Conflict: The Changing
Context of Worship."

32. Home (Special) sent by Id. E. L. V., Secretary, May 30, 1930, Home (Special) 355(64)IV-A, part 1, MSA. The colonial government recognized public temples supported by kings, and also shrines privately owned by families and caste
groups.

33. Letter no. 2042, June 2, 1930, from Home (Special), RD, 5493/28, 1930,
"Kalaram Temple-Nasik," MSA.

34. Bhaskar Damodar, Officiating Alienation Settlement Officer, Southern Division, to W. Hart, Revenue Commissioner, Southern Division, no. 282, May 4,
1865, RD, 4477/28, 1930, "Disputes between Untouchables and High Castes
on Parvati Temple," MSA. This correspondence includes documentation regarding government management of the Parvati temple from 1818 to 1865.

35. Note from J. Ghoshal, Commissioner, Southern Division, to Secretary
(Revenue), January 20 1930, RD, 4477/28, 1930, "Disputes between untouchables and high castes on Parvati Temple," MSA.

36. Conflict between the priest and temple trustees in 1919 led to a court
case. The trustees won their rights in two lower courts, but the case went to the
Bombay High Court on appeal. *Times of India,* March 30, 1931.

37. RD, 5493/28, 1930, "Kalaram Temple-Nasik," MSA.

38. Letter U.O.R. no. S.D. 2041, from Home Secretary to Chief Secretary,
May 30, 1930, RD, 5493/28, 1930, "Kalaram Temple-Nasik," MSA.

39. The legality of custom was confirmed in the important case of *Sankara
Linga Nadar v. Raja Rajeswara Sethupathi, Law Reports* 35, Indian Appeals, p.
76. This case involved the entry of Shanars (toddy tappers) into a Meenakshi tem-

ple in the Ramnad district of the Madras Presidency in 1897. The Raja of Ramnad accepted an inter alia agreement allowing Shanars entry into the temple while
a civil suit was being decided, but later retracted Shanar's right to temple entry.

40. *Bombay Chronicle,* November 29, 1929.

41. On Kamble's role in the Parvati *satyagraha,* see H. N. Navalkar, *The Life
of Shivram Janba Kamble and Brief History of the Poona Parvati Satyagraha*
(Poona: Hanuman Press, 1930).The ANM was comprised of activists from the
Hindu Mahasabha: N. C. Kelkar, editor of B. G. Tilak's newspaper, *Kesari,* and
president of the Bombay branch of the Hindu Mahasabha; L. B. Bhopatkar, editor of the weekly *Bhala,* a strong critic of the Mahad *satyagraha;* and S. M. Mate,
who was involved in untouchable uplift in Pune.

42. Madan Mohan Malaviya was the chairman of the Anti-Untouchability
Subcommittee and Jamnalal Bajaj was its secretary. Other important members
included Swami Anand, Chakravarthi Rajagopalachari, and B. G. Kher. C. Rajagopalachari (1878–72) was a conservative Brahmin and Congress thinker from
south India, who was influenced by B. G. Tilak and Annie Besant before joining
Gandhi in 1919. Elected general secretary of the Congress in 1921, Rajagopalachari was also acting governor general of India (1947–49), and chief minister of Madras (1952–54). B. G. Kher was a member of the Samata Sangh, formed
in 1927.

43. The Chamar activist Balkrishna Januji Devrukhar tried to form a Bombay Temple Entry Satyagraha Committee on October 20, 1929, under the aegis
of the Hindu Mahasabha, with support from V. D. Savarkar. The committee took
up the issue of entry into the following temples: the Gora Ram temple in Thakurdwar, the Madhav Bagh temple, and the Mahalakshmi, Babulnath, and Mum-
baidevi temples. Devrukhar even tried to organize a meeting of fifty thousand
untouchable *satyagrahis* on November 14, 1929, to "march to the Bombay temples and demand admission." *Times of India,* November 11, 1929. These temple-
entry efforts only succeeded during Gandhi's fast-unto-death in September 1932.
Home (Special) 800(4)4-AA, part 1, MSA.

44. *Times of India,* November 11, 1929. The notice board read, "Non-Hindus
are requested not to enter the Temple." The Mang activist K. G. Patade tried to
remove the new noticeboards and threatened to return with "a hammer and chisel
and make sure of removing the board." *Time of India,* December 2, 1929. The
decision to remove the notice board was made at a meeting in the Depressed
Classes Mission Hall, Poona, on November 23, 1929, to challenge the description of Dalit *satyagrahis* as non-Hindus. *Bombay Chronicle,* December 12, 1929.
Instead, temple trustees argued that non-Hindus were barred from temple entry
per the Poona collector's orders of March 15, 1842, subsequently confirmed by
the *sarpanch* on March 5, 1894. *Dalitbandhu,* October 2, 1929.

45. M. P. Mangudkar and G. B. Nirantar, eds., *Gandhi-Rajbhoj Correspondence 1932–1946* (Poona: Bharat Dalit Sevak Sangh, 1956).

46. *Bombay Chronicle,* October 16, 1929.

47. "*Satyagraha* in Poona," *Bombay Chronicle,* October 17, 1929.

48. "Right of Entry to Poona Parvati Temple," *Times of India,* October 17, 1929.

49. Jamnalal Bajaj, *Report of the Work Done by the Anti-Untouchability Sub-
Committee, April–December 1929.*

50. Talk with a deputation on behalf of the Depressed Classes, consisting of S. M. Mate, P. N. Rajbhoj, and others in Yeravda jail, morning of September 21, 1932, in Mahadev Desai, *The Diary of Mahadev Desai*, vol. 1, *Yeravda-Pact Eve, 1932,* trans. Valji Govindji Desai (Ahmedabad: Navajivan Publishing House, 1953), 167 (emphasis added).

51. District Superintendent of Police, Weekly Letter, October 26, 1929, Poona, MSA, Home (Special) 355 (64)V, 1928. Gunjal, a member of the Legislative Council in addition to being a Parvati temple trustee, had gained notoriety by calling non-Brahmins the "Kshatriyas of Shukrawar Peth." Shukrawar Peth was the redlight district in old Poona. District Magistrate, Weekly Letter, October 4, 1925, Home (Special) 363(4)II, "Brahmans v. non-Brahmans," MSA. The association of (sexual) intimacy with caste equality is an important theme. For example, in U. R. Ananthamurthy's novel, *Bharatipura,* set in the postindependence period and focused on village temple entry, the Brahmin reformer Jagannatha addresses caste sociality through the metaphor of sexual contact: "The untouchables should desire what we want. An untouchable man should be able to desire a Brahmin girl. A Brahmin girl should want to sleep with an untouchable. . . . There should be a birth of new desire in our untouchables. A birth of jealousy." U. R. Anathamurth, *Bharatipura,* trans. P. Sreenivasa Rao (Houndmills: Macmillan, 1997), 138.

52. The next two paragraphs and quotations in them are drawn from B. R. Ambedkar, "Pune Yethila Parvati Satyagraha" [The Satyagraha in Pune], *BB,* November 15, 1927.

53. *BB,* November 21, 1927, carries a long exegesis on the concept of *satyagraha.* In 1928, Ambedkar wrote an essay, "Notice to Hinduism," about possible conversion, and also the essay, "Hindu Mahasabha and Untouchability."

54. On Rajbhoj, see G. B. Nirantar et al. eds., *Shri Bapusaheb Rajbhoj: Jeevan Va Karya* (Poona: Rajbhoj Satkar Samiti, 1956); Mangudkar and Nirantar, *Gandhi-Rajbhoj Correspondence 1932–1946,* 53–54; and Babulal Maurya, ed., *Mahatma Gandhi's Letters to P. N. Rajbhoj* (Pune: K. P. Rajbhoj, 1967).

55. Home (Special) 355(64)IV-A, part II, "Untouchables and Temple Entry: Nasik Kalaram Temple Satyagraha," MSA. For a narrative of the Nasik *satyagraha* from start to finish, see Y. D. Phadke, "Dr. Ambedkar Ani Kalaram Mandir Satyagraha" [Dr. Ambedkar and the Kalaram Temple Satyagraha], *Purogami Satyashodak* 11, nos. 3–4 (July–December 1986).

56. Diary of the DSP for the week ending November 23, 1929, Home (Special) 355(64)IV-A, part I, MSA.

57. Diary of the DSP for the week February 8, 1930, Home (Special) 355(64)IV-A, part I, MSA.

58. Letter no. C/279 from DSP to District Magistrate, Nasik, November 26, 1931, Home (Special) 355(64)IV-A, part II, MSA.

59. DSP to District Magistrate, Nasik, February 22, 1930, Home (Special) 355(64)IV-A, part I, MSA.

60. The Nasik Yuvak Sangh Sangeet Jalsa was established on October 26, 1930. Keru Arjun Ghedge (from the village Karsul in the Niphad subdistrict) and Ramachandra Bansode also led a group that performed Ambedkari *jalsas* in Nasik. There is mention of other *jalsa* groups that formed in Bombay during this period: Dinbandhu Jalsa Mandal; Naigaon Jalsa Mandal led by another balladeer

named Bhimrao Kardak; Satara Jilha Samatavadi Mandal; and Delisle Road Samata Parvatak Jalsa Mandal. There is little information about them, however. *Asmitadarsh, Divali Ank,* special issue on Dalit shahirs (1982).

61. Bhimrao Kardak and Dadasaheb Pagare, *Ambedkari Jalse: Svarup va Karya* (Mumbai: Abhinav Prakashan, 1978), 5.

62. Ibid., 14.

63. R. G. Gordon, to the Commissioner, Central Division, Letter no. 31, March 3, 1930, Home (Special) 355(64)IV-A, part I, MSA.

64. *Times of India,* February 15, 1930. The Bombay Provincial Congress Committee passed a resolution expressing their full sympathy with the untouchables, though they decided not to take part in the struggle. Letter no. C/283 from DSP to District Magistrate, Nasik, December 1, 1931, Home (Special) 355(64)IV-A, part II, MSA. The Maharashtra Pradesh Congress Committee also expressed its support. Extract from Letter no. 5729/H/3717, November, 16, 1931, from Commissioner of Police, Bombay, Home (Special) 355(64)IV-A, part I, MSA. By the end of 1932, it was clear that Congress would remain aloof from the *satyagraha* to retain caste Hindus' support. Letter no. C-277 of 1931, DSP to District Magistrate, November 23, 1932, Home (Special) 355(64)IV-A, part II, MSA.

65. Desai, *Diary of Mahadev Desai,* vol. 1, 165.

66. In a speech to Mahar leaders who met in May to discuss "the future course of the Untouchables," Ambedkar argued that Hindu inclusion was endlessly conflictual; that "as long as you are weak, you cannot survive the conflict." The only option was mass conversion. *Mumbai Ilakha Mahar Parishad* (May 1925), Khairmode Collection, Bombay University.

67. "Mandirpravesh Satyagraha Committees Madat Kara" [Help the Temple-Entry Committee], handbill, Home (Special) 355(64)IV-A, part II, MSA.

68. Another handbill, "Asprushya Bandhuna Vinanti" [Request to Untouchbale Brethren] (n.d.) said., "*Parantu satyagraha committeene je shisthanche niyam tharavile ahet, va veloveli je shisthiche niyam tharavithil tyaviruddha yathkichithi varthan karu naye* [No one is to question the disciplinary orders established by the *satyagraha* committee, or the orders they may formulate from time to time]." Home (Special) 355(64)IV-A, part II, MSA.

69. Letter from J. Ghoshal, Commissioner, Central Division, to Hotson, Home Minister, March 9, 1930, Home (Special) 355(64)IV-A, part I, MSA (emphasis added).

70. Shahid Amin, *Event, Metaphor, Memory: Chauri Chaura 1922–1992* (Delhi: Oxford University Press, 1995), 175–89.

71. Author interview with Premanand Rupawate, August 27, 2004, Mumbai; and author interview with members of the Samata Sainik Dal at *dikshabhumi* (initiation site), October 23, 2004, Nagpur.

72. *Times of India,* March 3, 1930. The Samata Sainik Dal was formed in 1927 to protect Dalits from physical attack and intimidation. Members wore khaki half-pants, a red shirt, and a khaki strip around the shins in addition to a khaki *topi,* signifying their military past.

73. Ambedkar to Bhaurao Gaikwad, March 3, 1934. Ambedkar's intentions were similar to the advice of Self-Respect leaders during temple-entry struggles

in the Tamil country: though they entered temples, activists were not to worship in them. As Self-Respecters they believed in neither the sacrality of the temple nor the god within. V. Geetha, personal communication, June 4, 2005.

74. Memorandum, Remembrancer of Legal Affairs, September 21, 1931, Home (Special) 355(64)IV-A, part II, MSA.

75. Office of the Remembrancer of Legal Affairs, February 14, 1932, Home (Special) 355(64)IV-A, part II, MSA.

76. Letter from Clayton, Commissioner, Central Division, to R. G. Gordon, December 10, 1931, Home (Special) 355(64)IV-A, part II, MSA. A case from Pathardi, Ahmednagar district, from 1926 concerned disputed shares to the Kanhoba temple, which was also known as the Hazrat Shah Ramzan dargah. This was decided under Section 147 as a dispute over religious property. Handwritten notes, G. F. S. Collins, Home Secretary, April 2, 1931, Home (Special) 355(64)IV-A, part II, MSA.

77. Letter from J. Ghoshal, Commissioner, Central Division, to Hotson, Home Minister, March 9, 1930, MSA, Home (Special) 355(64)IV-A, part I.

78. Letter of from B. K. Gaikwad, Esq., Secretary of the Satyagraha Committee, to B. R. Ambedkar, March 19, 1930, Home (Special) 355(64)IV-A, part I, MSA (emphasis added).

79. Letter from B. R. Ambedkar to the Home Minister, March 24, 1930, Home (Special) 355(64)IV-A, part I, MSA.

80. Report of the District Superintendent of Police, Reynolds, April 8, 1930, Home (Special) 355(64)IV-A, part I, MSA.

81. R. G. Gordon to Home Secretary G. F. S. Collins, March 30, 1930, Home (Special) 355(64)IV-A, part I, MSA.

82. Confidential Letter from D. Dhanarati, Office of Remembrancer Legal Affairs, to Home Department (Special), no. 72, April 25, 1930, Home (Special) 355(64)IV-A, part I, MSA.

83. L. N. Brown, District Magistrate, Nasik to Home Secretary, April 10, 1932, Home (Special) 355(64)IV-A, part II, MSA.

84. A. W. W. Mackie, who replaced J. Ghoshal as commissioner wrote to the home secretary on March 26, 1930, and noted that Gordon's handling of the *pujari* affair could be interpreted as support for caste Hindus. Gordon was issued a warning. Letter no. S.D. 674, March 30, 1930, Home (Special) 355(64)IV-A, part I, MSA.

85. G. F. S. Collins to R. G. Gordon via Commissioner, Central Division, April 1, 1930, Home (Special) 355(64)IV-A, part I, MSA.

86. G. F. S. Collins, Secretary, to R. G Gordon, no. S.D. 863, April 6, 1930, Home (Special) 355(64)IV-A, part I, MSA.

87. Minutes of April 30, 1930, Home (Special) 355(64)IV-A, part I, MSA.

88. Confidential Letter no. 84, R. G. Gordon to Home Secretary, Chandor, February 16, 1932, Home (Special) 355(64)IV-A, part II, MSA.

89. Letter from Commissioner, Central Division, Clayton to R. G. Gordon, December 10, 1931, Home (Special) 355(64)IV-A, part II, MSA.

90. L. N. Brown to Maxwell, May 23, 1932, "Proceedings under S. 147 CPC on the claims of the untouchables to bathe in the Ram Kund," Home (Special) 355(64)IV-A, part II, MSA.

91. Dilip Menon argues that by 1933 the Congress gave up temple entry, with Gandhi going so far as to argue that those who imputed a connection between the two were "wholly mistaken." Menon, *Caste, Nationalism and Communism in India: Malabar, 1900–1948*, 115. When Bhaurao Gaikwad asked P. N. Rajbhoj to lead a flagging Nasik *satyagraha* in 1934, Rajbhoj consulted Gandhi, who dissuaded him. Extract from District Magistrate's Weekly Letter, Nasik, March 21, 1934, Home (Special) 355(64)IV-A, part II, MSA. By 1935, Gandhi was arguing that he was no longer in favor of temple entry. *Bombay Chronicle*, March 22, 1935.

92. Memorandum, Remembrancer of Legal Affairs, September 21, 1931, Home (Special) 355(64)IV-A, part II, MSA.

93. Report submitted with reference to home minister's minutes of October 25, 1929, and a query of January 9, 1930. A confidential note from Home (Pol) of March 4, 1930, offers a longer history of the property issue and includes a letter from the district magistrate to the Home Department on October 21, 1929, as well as a memorandum submitted to the police commissioner, Central Division, on November 13, 1929, regarding ownership of the Kalaram temple. Home (Special) 365(IV)IV-A, part II, MSA.

94. Confidential Letter no. 4477-F/28 from R. D. Bell, Esq., Acting Chief Secretary of the RD, to Commissioner, Central Division, April 3, 1930, Home (Special) 355(64)IV-A, part I, MSA.

95. Handwritten notes, September 18, 1931, Home (Special) 365(IV)IV-A, part II, MSA.

96. Handwritten notes, September 19, 1931, Home (Special) 365(IV)IV-A, part II, MSA.

97. The first bill for the abolition of untouchability was introduced in 1921 by Hari Singh Gour. This was followed by M. R. Jayakar's Hindu Untouchable Castes (Removal of Disabilities) Bill of 1930, which stated that "no Hindu was to be incapable, by reason of his caste, of sharing the benefit of a religious or charitable trust or of a convenience, utility or service for the use of the general public." A similar bill was introduced thereafter in the Central Legislature. In the meantime, two bills were introduced in the Madras Legislative Council in November 1932: the Removal of Depressed Classes Religious Disabilities Act was introduced by Narayan Nambiar, and the Temple Entry Disabilities Removal Act was introduced by D. Subbaroyan. The governor-general refused to sanction the bills because they involved issues of all-India importance. Finally, on March 24, 1933, Ranga Iyer introduced the Hindu Temple-Entry Disabilities Removal Bill. When the Assembly was dissolved and all-India elections announced in 1934, Gandhi withdrew support for the bill and the issue of temple entry died a quiet death. N. R. Malkani, *A Critical Note on the Hindu Temple Entry (Removal of Disabilities) Bill* (Delhi: All India Harijan Sewak Sangha, 1934). See also S. R. Venkataraman, *Temple Entry Reviewed: With Acts and Bills* (Madras: Bharat Devi Publications, 1946); and C. Rajagopalachari, *Plighted Word: Being an Account of the History and Objects for the Untouchability Abolition and Temple Entry Bills* (Delhi: Servants of Untouchables Society, 1937).

98. Cornelia Sorabji, "Temple Entry and Untouchability," *The Nineteenth Century and After* 108 (1933): 698–702.

99. *Opinions on the Hindu Temple Entry Disabilities Bill*, 2 vols. (Dehli: Government of India, Legislative Department, 1934).

100. C. Rajagopalachari, *Plighted Word: Being an Account of the History and Objects for the Untouchability Abolition and Temple Entry Bills*, 2.

101. Begging for food was a particularly powerful image used by Dalit activists to conscientize village Mahars. Tarachandra Khandekar, "Nagpur-Varhadatila Ambedkarpurva Mahar" [The Situation of Mahars in Nagpur and the Central Provinces Before Ambedkar], *Asmitadarsh*, Divali Ank [Divali issue] (1975). The dependance on leftovers is a key trope in the Dalit *sahitya* (literature), which began in the 1970s. Key texts include Amitabh, *Pad* (Mumbai: Abhinav Prakashan, 1980); Shankarrao Kharat, *Bara Balutedar* (Pune: Thokal Prakashan, 1959); and Daya Pawar, *Baluta* (Mumbai: Granthali 1995).

102. Govinda is a folk reference to god, in other words, "Oh God!"

103. The term used for "beggary" is *madhukari*, a custom among poor Brahmins, especially students, to ask for food in other peoples' homes. Thus *vritti*, a traditional occupation, is associated with the servility of the Brahmin's *bhikshuki vritti*, or begging as a way of life.

104. Kardak and Pagare, "Maharkica Farce," in *Ambedkari Jalse: Svarup va Karya*, 17. The base tune for this farce is drawn from a famous nationalistic song by the reformer Sane Guruji, who led a temple *satyagraha* in Pandharpur in 1947 and who was a founder-member of the Socialist Rashtra Seva Dal.

105. Sumit Guha argues that struggles over *vatandari* rights took place in the most monetized regions of the precolonial Deccan. This is because adjudication of *vatan* claims and fines for laggard performance of the associated duties generated revenue for the state, while *vatandars* were able to extract bribes and informal labor within the village as a consequence of holding office. Sumit Guha, "Civilisations, Markets and Services: Village Servants in India from the Seventeenth to the Twentieth Centuries," *The Indian Economic and Social History Review* 41, no. 1 (2004): 73–94.

106. This is the famous Sasvad charter of the Mahars' fifty-two rights, a copy of which was reproduced in the nineteenth century. The charter associates the granting of these fifty-two rights to the Bidar *padshah*, or the Bidar king, of the Adilshah Sultanate in 1228–29 C.E. These rights included participation in ceremonial processions such as marriage, deciding boundary disputes, the right to receive bread from every home, and the grant of the *hadki* or *harola* (tax-free *inam* lands). See 1913 *Sammelana Vritta*, conference proceedings of the Bharat Itihas Samshodak Mandal, cited in P. A. Gavli, *Peshvekalin Gulamgiri va Asprushyata* (Kolhapur: Prachar Prakashan, 1981), 96ff. I am grateful to Sumit Guha for a discussion of the Mahar *vatan*. E-mail communication, July 24–26, 2007.

107. The story of Amrutnak is nowhere noted before the late nineteenth century. However, the petition for reemployment of Mahars in the military by Govind Waiker Master in 1894 mentioned the Amrutnak legend as the origin of the Mahars' fifty-two rights and dated it to Akbar's period. See also, C. B. Khairmode, *Amrutnak* (Sholapur, 1921); and N. G. Bhavare, *Maharashtratila Mahar: Ek Ladhav va Parakrami Jamat* [The Mahar of Maharashtra: A Martial and Courageous Race], in *Mangar Parishad: 62nd Smriti Mahotsav* [Mangaon Conference: The 62nd Anniversary Celebrations], ed. Ramesh Dhavare (Kolhapur, 1980).

108. The *vatan* was tied to holding office, but it also indexed forms of village sociality. Frank Perlin has argued that multiple and overlapping rights to a *vatan* were described through the metaphor of caste commensality. Shares in a *vatan* were described as "eating from the same plate." Frank Perlin, "Of White Whale and Countryman in the Eighteenth Century Maratha Deccan: Extended Class Relations, Rights and the Problem of Autonomy under the Old Regime," *Journal of Peasant Studies* 5, no. 2 (1978): 172–237.

109. Hiroyuki Kotani notes that the commutation of *deshmukh* and *deshpande vatan*s was begun in the Southern Division by S. J. Gordon and later extended to the Central and Northern Divisions. By 1873, when the Bombay Hereditary Offices Bill was introduced, most *deshmukhs* and *deshpandes* had already ceased to be classified as hereditary district officers. Hiroyuki Kotani, *Caste System, Untouchability, and the Depressed,* vol. 1, *Japanese Studies on South Asia* (New Delhi: Manohar Publishers & Distributors, 1997), 112–13.

110. Bombay Hereditary Offices Act, quoted in Kotani, *Caste System, Untouchability, and the Depressed,* 115.

111. When A. Rogers introduced Bill II of 1873 (later known as the Bombay Hereditary Offices Act) in the Bombay Legislative Council on July 23, 1873, he suggested that Mahars had taken to poisoning cattle in order to extract the maximum benefit from their "hereditary" office. For a discussion of cattle poisoning, see Ramnarayan Rawat, "Making the Chamar a Criminal: Crime of Cattle Poisoning in Nineteenth Century UP," in "Struggle for Identities: A Social History of the Chamars of Uttar Pradesh, 1881–1956" (Dissertation, Delhi University, 2005).

112. Kotani, *Caste System, Untouchability, and the Depressed,* 115.

113. T. Atre, *Gav-Gada (The Balutedars of the Village)* (Pune: Varad Books, 1915); and Harold Mann, *Land and Labour in a Deccan Village* (Bombay: Asia Publishing House, 1971).

114. *Janata,* October 16, 1937.

115. Gholap was associated with *Muknayak,* but left after a disagreement with Ambedkar in 1920 and tried to publish the newspaper independently from Satara. Gholap asked for "commutation" of the Mahar *vatan,* though he actually meant to support its incorporation into the normative property regime, known by the term "resumption," which would lead to Mahars paying taxes on their *vatan* lands.

116. Ambedkar responded to Mahars' criticisms about giving up the Mahar *vatan* in "Mahar Vatanacha Kayda va Tyat Suchavilelya Durustyanche Spashtikaran" [A Clarification about the Mahar *Vatan* Law and the Remedies Therein], *BB,* November 4, 1927; and "Mahar Vatan Billavarila Kahi Akshep" [Some Clarifications Regarding the Mahar *Vatan* Bill], *BB,* November 7, 1928.

117. Dadasaheb Pagare notes that rural Mahars were extremely afraid of boycotts for withholding village services. Mahars said that the barbers refused to shave them, the *dhobis* (washermen) refused to wash their clothes, and they had no money. The campaign to stop Mahars from eating carrion (begun in Vidarbha at the turn of the twentieth century) meant that they were unable to eat meat. The villagers who spoke with Pagare noted that their extreme dependence on caste Hindus exposed them to constant threat of violence, unlike

the Dalit city boys who had come to mobilize them. Kardak and Pagare, *Ambedkari Jalsa*, 8.

118. B. R. Ambedkar, "Mahar ani Tyanche Vatan" [Mahars and Their *Vatan*] appeared as three editorials: *BB,* September 2, September 16, and September 30, 1927.

119. B. R. Ambedkar, "Mahar ani Tyanche Vatan," *BB,* September 2, 1927.

120. B. R. Ambedkar, "Hindu Dharmala Notice" [Notice to Hinduism], *BB,* March 15, 1929.

121. M. G. Bhagat, *The Untouchable Classes of Maharashtra* (Bombay: Karnatak Printing Press, 1935).

122. *Bombay Legislative Council Debates,* vol. 8, p. 791.

123. Ibid. In June 1929, the Satyashodak Samaj, chaired by Bhaurao Patil, decided to oppose the Mahar *vatan* bill. This was another indication of increasing conflict between Mahars and Marathas as a consequence of the activities of the non-Brahmin movement. Dadumiya, *Dalitanche Rajkaran* (Bombay: Majestic Book Stall, 1974), 91.

124. *Bombay Government Gazette,* October 21, 1937.

125. W.T.N. 6/5, from J. W. Smyth, Esquire, Commissioner, Central Division (Poona), to Secretary to Government, December 23, 1937, RD, 7420/33-I, "Bombay Hereditary Offices Act: Bill by Dr. Ambedkar to Amend Certain Sections of," 1939, MSA. Smyth noted that giving Mahars the right to refuse their services conflicted with Section 16 of the Hereditary Offices Act of 1874, which gave villagers the right to demand "customary" services from village servants.

126. *Bombay Legislative Council Debates,* vol. 18, p. 723.

127. By 1940, Mahar *vatandars* were refusing to perform services unless they were treated like other government servants, who received a dearness allowance to offset inflation and economic hardship. Dadasaheb Gaikwad asked the government to clarify Mahars' status as part-time servants and to protect them from harassment. "The Mahars are harassed every moment by the caste Hindus, including village officers. That being so will they ever give permission to the Mahars to even go to the weekly bazaar once a week without giving the substitute. The wording of the circular [GR 7420/33 clarifying *vatandar* duties] is drafted so as the village officers will always get benefit of it." Letter from B. K. Gaikwad to Undersecretary, Revenue, December 29, 1944, RD, 7429/33-III, "Kaiwad, taluka Athnur on refusal of Mahars to perform services," MSA.

128. GR, Revenue, 7420/33, September 13, 1938, RD, 7420/33-I, "Bombay Hereditary Offices Act: Bill by Dr. Ambedkar to Amend Certain Sections of," 1939, MSA.

129. In Nasik, a Mahar *vatan* had been transferred, "though it was subsequently re-granted to mahar watandars as deputies performed services adequately." GR, Revenue, July 14, 1942, RD, 7429/33-III, "Kaywad, taluka Athnur on refusal of Mahars to perform services," MSA.

130. In 1929, it was calculated that a loss of Rs. 2.2 lakhs would be incurred in the Central Division alone, if the Mahar *vatandars* were paid at market rate. W.T.N. 6/5, J. W. Smyth, Esquire, Commissioner, Central Division (Poona),

to Secretary to Government, January 20, 1929, RD, 7420/33-I, "Bombay Hereditary Offices Act: Bill by Dr. Ambedkar to Amend Certain Sections of," 1939, MSA.

131. See RD, 7420–33-II, "Free Labour," MSA.

132. See, for example, speech by R. D. Bhandare, "Vatandar Gaonkar Parishad, Brahmapuri, Satara Jilha," December 25, 1949, Ramesh Shinde Collection.

133. *Narhari Damodar Vaidya and Others v. B. R. Ambedkar and Others,* AIR 1939 Bom 146.

134. Steven Pierce argues that British officials fundamentally misrecognized the meaning of "property" and "land tenure" in northern Nigeria, even as they claimed to use native conceptions of ownership to justify colonial intervention. Steven Pierce, "Inventing Land Tenure," in *Farmers and the State in Colonial Kano* (Bloomington: Indiana University Press, 2005), 79–110.

135. John Locke, *Second Treatise of Government,* ed. C. B. Macpherson (New York: Hackett Publishing Co., 1980).

136. Pierce, *Farmers and the State,* 81.

3. DALITS AS A POLITICAL MINORITY

1. Ambedkar considered conversion to Islam, but the Hindu Mahasabha enticed him to consider Sikhism by suggesting that this would allow Dalits to retain constitutional safeguards meant for (Hindu) SCs. These debates can be found in Home (Special) 800(40)(4)A-IV-B, part I, MSA. Ultimately, Buddhism's status as an indigenous alternative to Brahminism played a crucial role in Ambedkar's choice.

2. B. R. Ambedkar, *Bombay Chronicle,* October 16, 1935.

3. Vasant Moon, *Growing Up Untouchable in India: A Dalit Autobiography* (Lanham, MD: Rowman & Littlefield, 2001).

4. D. C. Ahir, *Buddhism and Ambedkar* (Delhi: B. R. Publications, 2004), 35.

5. *Akhil Mumbai Ilakha Mahar Parishad* [Mass Appeal Regarding the Mass Conversions as Suggested by Ambedkar], (n.p., 1936), Ramesh Shinde Collection.

6. *Times of India,* March 14, 1936.

7. *Bombay Chronicle,* August 8, 1936 (emphasis added). B. S. Moonje held talks with Ambedkar between July 18 and 20, 1936, to dissuade him from converting to Islam, which posed a "real danger to Hindus," and asked him to preside over the annual Mahasabha session in 1936. M. C. Rajah—who signed a pact with Moonje early in 1932 in support of reserved seats for Depressed Classes in legislative bodies—publicized the secret talks between Moonje and Ambedkar in order to criticize the Mahasabha position. See also K. Meadowcroft, "The All-India Hindu Mahasabha, Untouchable Politics, and 'Denationalising' Conversions: The Moonje-Ambedkar Pact," *South Asia* 29, no. 1 (April 2006): 9–41. By the end of 1937, Ambedkar had also given up the idea of converting to Sikhism for at least two reasons: the British refused to extend quotas to Scheduled Caste Sikh converts who faced discrimination, and the Akalis, who gained control over Sikh religious institutions and political power after 1922, opposed Scheduled Castes' mass conversion, fearing loss of their political power. H. K. Puri, "Sched-

uled Castes in the Sikh Community," *Economic and Political Weekly* 38, no. 28 (June 28, 2003): 2698.

8. M. K. Gandhi, "Limitation of Reformers," *Harijan,* March 21, 1936.

9. M. K. Gandhi, *Bombay Chronicle,* August 8, 1936.

10. Martin Fuchs, "A Religion for Civil Society? Ambedkar's Buddhism, the Dalit Issue and the Imagination of Emergent Possibilities," in *Charisma and Canon: Essays on the Religious History of the Indian Subcontinent,* ed. Vasudha Dalmia, Angelika Malinar and and Martin Christof (New Delhi: Oxford University Press, 2001), 250–73.

11. Valerian Rodrigues, "Making a Tradition Critical: Ambedkar's Reading of Buddhism," in *Dalit Movements and the Meanings of Labour in India,* ed. Peter Robb (Delhi: Oxford University Press, 1993), 299–338.

12. *Times of India,* October 16, 1935.

13. Recent studies concerning Ambedkar and Buddhism include Surendra Jondhale, *Reconstructing the World: Dr. Ambedkar and Buddhism in India* (Delhi: Oxford University Press, 2004); *Dr. Ambedkar, Buddhism and Social Change,* ed. A. K. Narain and D. C. Ahir (Delhi: B. P. Publishing, 1994); Gail Omvedt, *Buddhism in India: Challenging Brahmanism and Caste* (New Delhi: Sage Publications, 2003); and S. Theodore and M. M. Thomas Wilkinson, *Ambedkar and the Neo-Buddhist Movement,* CSRS Social Research Series (Bangalore: Christian Literature Society Madras, 1972).

14. D. R. Nagaraj, *The Flaming Feet: A Study of the Dalit Movement in India* (Bangalore: South Forum Press, 1993), 58.

15. Martin Fuchs, "Buddhism and Dalitness," in *Reconstructing the World: B. R. Ambedkar and Buddhism in India,* ed. Surendra Jondhale and Johannes Beltz (New Delhi: Oxford University Press, 2004), 289.

16. Ambedkar credited the economic historian Edward Seligman, one of the founders of the New School for Social Research, and the philosopher John Dewey as major influences on his thought. Ambedkar started the newspapers *Muknayak* (Leader of the Mute) (1918–20), *Bahishkrit Bharat* (Outcaste India) (1927–29), *Janata* (The People) (1929–55), and *Prabuddha Bharat* (The Enlightened India) (1955). These organs of mass mobilization established his preeminence as a Dalit (Mahar) leader. Between 1936 and 1956, Ambedkar established the ILP (1936), the AISCF (1942), and the RPI (1956), none of which was an effective alternative to the Indian National Congress or to various Marxist political parties. Ambedkar disliked the Congress, but he allied with the Communists on occasion and defined the *bahishkrit varga* (excommunicated classes) as a socially, ritually, and materially exploited class. The discomfort of the Communist Party's Brahminical leadership with caste analysis made such alliances episodic, however. Ambedkar was also a member of the Bombay Legislative Assembly (1937–39) and Labour Minister in the Viceroy's Executive Council (1942–46), before being nominated to the Constituent Assembly in 1949 and becoming India's first law minister in 1951. His public life, as with many well-known figures, was contradictory and controversial. Detractors—many had previously been staunch followers—called him megalomaniacal and intolerant of criticism. Mahars' competitive edge in education and employment, and Buddhist conversion—which invested the community with new civic and religious status—provoked antagonism

against the token few who benefitted from the civil rights regime to become so-called government Brahmins. English biographies of Ambedkar's life include Christophe Jaffrelot, *Dr. Ambedkar and Untouchability: Analysing and Fighting Caste* (New Delhi: Permanenet Black, 2004); and Dhananjay Keer, *Dr. Ambedkar: Life and Mission* (Bombay: Popular Prakashan, 1954).

17. *The Annihilation of Caste*, in BAWS, vol. 1, 41.

18. *Hindu Code Bill*, in BAWS, vol. 14, 1325–26.

19. The estimated figures for conversion at the *diksha* ceremony in October 1956 is 380,000, with localized conversions following soon thereafter.

20. D. R. Nagaraj argues that the 1932 conflict effected a deep transformation in Ambedkar's and Gandhi's thinking on caste. Nagaraj, "Self Purification and Self Respect," in *Flaming Feet*, 1–30. See also Nicholas B. Dirks, "The Reformation of Caste: Periyar, Ambedkar, and Gandhi," in *Castes of Mind: Colonialism and the Making of Modern India* (Princeton, NJ: Princeton University Press, 2001), 255–74; Valerian Rodrigues, "Between Tradition and Modernity: The Gandhi-Ambedkar Debate," in *Dr. Ambedkar, Buddhism, and Social Change*; and Eleanor Zelliot, "Congress and Untouchables: 1917–1950," in *Congress and Indian Nationalism: Pre-Independence Phase*, ed. Richard Sisson and Stanley A. Wolpert (Berkeley: University of California Press, 1988), 182–97.

21. *The Buddha or Karl Marx*, in BAWS, vol. 3.

22. Aniket Jaaware, "Stamping the State on Its Forehead: The Uses of Foucault and Ambedkar" (paper delivered at Jawaharlal Nehru University, March 15, 2007).

23. Ambedkar acknowledged the thematic continuities between this early essay and his later writings on caste. He regretted that he could not incorporate *Castes in India* in the third edition of *The Annihilation of Caste*. The posthumously published text, *Revolution and Counter-Revolution*, in BAWS, vol. 3, cites *Castes in India*, 296–302.

24. *Who Were the Shudras?* in BAWS, vol. 7.

25. *The Annihilation of Caste*, in BAWS, vol. 1, 75.

26. *Castes in India*, in BAWS, vol. 1, 9.

27. *Revolution and Counter-Revolution*, in BAWS, vol. 3, 320.

28. Ranajit Guha has written eloquently about the violence of the boycott and its transformation into a tool of Gandhian discipline in "Discipline and Mobilize: Hegemony and Elite Control in Nationalist Campaigns," in *Dominance Without Hegemony* (Cambridge, MA: Harvard University Press, 1998), 100–51.

29. *The Untouchables*, in BAWS, vol. 7, 266.

30. *Evidence before the Simon Commission*, in BAWS, vol. 2, 479.

31. *What Congress and Gandhi Have Done to the Untouchables*, in BAWS, vol. 9, 88.

32. The Jat-Pat Todak Mandal was established in 1922 by a group of Chamars, including Sant Ram, as a wing of the Arya Samaj in the Punjab. It broke away in 1924 due to the development of the Ad-Dharm movement. For an early account of Ad-Dharm that draws on interviews with Sant Ram, see Mark Juergensmeyer, *Religion as Social Vision: The Movement against Untouchability in Twentieth-Century Punjab* (Berkeley: University of California Press, 1982).

33. *The Annihilation of Caste*, in BAWS, vol. 1, 69.

34. Extract of Sant Ram's letter to Ambedkar, quoted in *Harijan*, August 15, 1936.

35. *The Annihilation of Caste*, in *BAWS*, vol. 1, 35.

36. Ibid., 75. Ambedkar's turn to Hindu juridicality distinguishes him from earlier caste radicals, who focused on practices of Hindu religiosity and the Puranic literature. Ambedkar was prohibited from majoring in Sanskrit at Elphinstone College, but he maintained a scholarly interest in Indology all his life, and even registered for coursework at Heidelberg University with the famous Indologist Hermann Jacobi in 1921. He never attended Heidelberg, however. Maren Bellwinkel-Schemp, "Ambedkar Studies at Heidelberg," http://www.sai.uni-heidelberg.de/saireport/2003/pdf/1_ambedkar.pdf.

37. *The Annihilation of Caste*, in *BAWS*, vol. 1, 77.

38. Ibid., 89 (emphasis added).

39. *The Untouchables*, in *BAWS*, vol. 7, 370.

40. "A Childhood Journey to Koregaon Becomes a Nightmare," in *BAWS*, vol. 12, part 1, 665–71.

41. "Back from the West and Unable to Find Lodging in Baroda," in *BAWS*, vol. 12, 673–78.

42. Frantz Fanon, *Black Skin, White Masks* (New York: Grove, 1967), 112.

43. *Slaves and Untouchables*, in *BAWS*, vol. 5, 117.

44. I am grateful to Lee Schlesinger for pushing me to clarify the analogy between the commodity form and the caste order. Personal communication, April 27, 2005. Jayashree Gokhale argues that Marx's influence is evident in the class model that dominated Ambedkar's analysis of caste during the 1930s, as he tried to create caste-class unity among the laboring poor. Gail Omvedt notes that Ambedkar revalued the Marxian base-superstructure distinction by privileging *varna* ideology but retained a mechanical reading of Marxism. See, for example, Gail Omvedt, *Dalits and the Democratic Revolution: Dr. Ambedkar and the Dalit Movement in Colonial India* (Dehli: Sage Publications, 2000), 228–29.

45. My reading draws inspiration from Jean-Joseph Goux, *Symbolic Economies: After Marx and Freud* (Ithaca, NY: Cornell University Press, 1990); Gayatri Chakravorty Spivak, *In Other Worlds: Essays in Cultural Politics* (New York: Methuen, 1987), especially the chapter "Scattered Speculations on the Question of Value." I also draw on Dipesh Chakrabarty's important essay, "The Two Histories of Capital," in *Provincializing Europe: Postcolonial Thought and Historical Difference* (Princeton, NJ: Princeton University Press, 2000), 42–71.

46. Louis Althusser, *For Marx* (London: Verso, 2005), 208.

47. Herbert H. Risley (1851–1911), commissioner of the 1901 census, is responsible for describing caste as a racial hierarchy. For an account of Risley's reversal of earlier efforts, by William Crooke, Denzil Ibbetson, and J. C. Nesfield, to define caste as an occupational ranking, see Dirks, "The Enumeration of Caste," in *Castes of Mind*, 198–228. The 1901 census emphasized a transactional model for caste reproduction and aligned caste practice with forms of civic exclusion and social segregation.

48. There was great variation in the government's enumeration of the Depressed Classes during the 1920s and the 1930s due to regional differences in

how the practice of untouchability was defined. According to the 1931 census, the Depressed Class population was 50.2 million, a number just below Risley's 1908 calculation of 50.6 million. See *RCSCST* for 1951 and 1953 (Delhi: Government of India).

49. U. N. Mukerji, *A Dying Race* (Calcutta: Mukerjee and Bose, 1909).

50. *The Tribune*, November 12, 1910.

51. *India Review,* September 1910.

52. J. H. Hutton, *Caste in India: Its Nature, Function, and Origins,* 3rd ed. (Bombay: Oxford University Press, 1961), 194.

53. Ibid., 195.

54. Judith Butler and Ernest Laclau, "The Uses of Equality," *Diacritics* (Spring 1997): 5.

55. For an argument about race, culture, and the colonial exception, see Anupama Rao and Steven Pierce, "Humanitarianism, Violence, and the Colonial Exception," in *Discipline and the Other Body: Correction, Corporeality and Colonialism,* ed. Steven Pierce and Anupama Rao (Durham, NC: Duke University Press, 2006), 1–35.

56. *Evidence before the Southborough Commission,* in *BAWS,* vol. 1, 25.

57. Congress and the All-India Muslim League boycotted the Simon Commission in 1928, and Ambedkar was accused of being a British stooge because he had given evidence before the commission, thereby recognizing its legitimacy.

58. *Evidence before the Simon Commission,* in *BAWS,* vol. 2, 479.

59. *Evidence of Dr. Ambedkar before the Indian Statutory Commission on 23rd October, 1928,* in *BAWS,* vol. 2, 465.

60. Pyarelal, *The Epic Fast* (Ahmedabad: Mohanla Bhagat, 1932), 7. Also quoted in *What Congress and Gandhi Have Done to the Untouchables,* in *BAWS,* vol. 9, 68.

61. *Supplementary Written Statement of B. R. Ambedkar,* in *BAWS,* vol. 1.

62. In debates preceding the Nehru Committee Report of August 1928, Muhammed Ali Jinnah (1876–1948) agreed to give up the separate electorate in return for the creation of a Muslim province in Sind, a higher political status for Baluchistan and the Northwest Frontier Provinces, proportional representation for Muslims in Bengal and Punjab, and a third of the seats in the Central Legislature to be reserved for Muslims. The Nehru Report did not accept these demands.

63. *Times of India,* October 6, 1906 (emphasis added).

64. *Statement concerning safeguards for the protection of interests of the depressed Classes as a minority in the Bombay Presidency and the changes in the composition of and the guarantees from the Bombay Legislative Council necessary to ensure the same under Provincial Autonomy, submitted by B. R. Ambedkar on behalf of the Bahishkrit Hitakarini Sabha (Depressed Classes Institute) to the Indian Statutory Commission, May 29 1928,* in *BAWS,* vol. 2, 438–39.

65. In his 1930 presidential address at the annual meeting of the Muslim League, Muhammed Iqbal demanded a Muslim state in India, consisting of Punjab, Sind, the Northwest Frontier Provinces, and Baluchistan. A Muslim state could be used to create parity between Hindus and Muslims and to challenge the negligible political presence of Muslims in other parts of India. Until 1940, Punjab stymied efforts to use the Muslim-majority provinces as a bargaining chip

for Muslims' demands. Ayesha Jalal, *The Sole Spokesman: Jinnah, the Muslim League and the Demand for Partition* (Cambridge: Cambridge University Press, 1994), especially chapters 1 and 2.

66. *A Report on the Constitution of the Government of Bombay Presidency, Presented to the Indian Statutory Commission*, in BAWS, vol. 2, 320, 319.

67. *Evidence before the Southborough Commission*, 250.

68. Etienne Balibar, *Masses, Classes, Ideas: Studies on Politics and Philosophy before and after Marx* (London: Routledge, 1994), especially the chapter "'Rights of Man' and 'Rights of the Citizen': The Modern Dialectic of Equality and Freedom."

69. *Communal Deadlock and a Way to Solve It*, in BAWS, vol. 1, 377.

70. Ambedkar's support for separate representation ironically coincided with the compromise between M. C. Rajah, president of the Depressed India Association and B. S. Moonje of the Hindu Mahasabha in early 1932 over reserved representation for the Depressed Classes within the general (Hindu) electorate.

71. *Memorial on Behalf of All Marathi Speaking Untouchables of the Bombay Presidency*, submitted to the Indian Statutory Commission by Dnyandev Dhruvnath Gholap, President, Satara District, Mahar Seva Sangh, May 20, 1928, Khairmode Collection, Bombay University.

72. *Evidence before the Southborough Commission*, in BAWS, vol. 1, 270.

73. *Muknayak*, February and March issues; and Vasant Moon, ed., *Source Material on Dr. Babasaheb Ambedkar and the Movement of Untouchables*, vol. 1 (Mumbai: Education Department, Governnment of Maharashtra, 1990).

74. Editorial in *BB*, May 20, 1927.

75. *What Congress and Gandhi Have Done to the Untouchables*, in BAWS, vol. 9, 90. In his critique of Dalit politics, the veteran Communist leader, B. T. Ranadive noted that the Communists had the weapon of the general strike while Dalit parties had no such weapon. *Kranti Jyoti* 2, nos. 10–12 (October–December 1979). Ranadive led the Girni Kamgar Union (Textile Workers Union) in Bombay and served as secretary of the Great Indian Peninsula (GIP) Railwaymen's Union before joining the Community Party of India (Marxist) in 1964. Like those of other Brahmin Marxists, his writings betray an inability to understand the autonomy of caste.

76. Nagaraj, *Flaming Feet*, 38.

77. Ramsay MacDonald to Gandhi, September 8, 1932, in Mahadev Desai, *The Diary of Mahadev Desai*, vol. 1, *Yeravda-Pact Eve, 1932*, trans. Valji Govindji Desai (Ahmedabad: Navajivan Publishing House, 1953), 105.

78. For an excellent discussion of Gandhi's discourse on the Bhangi, see "Harijans," in Vijay Prashad, *Untouchable Freedom: A Social History of a Dalit Community* (Delhi: Oxford University Press, 2000), especially 220–21.

79. "Letter to Rajbhoj," in *Gandhi–Rajabhoj Correspondence 1932–1946*, ed. M. P. Mangudkar and G. B. Nirantar (Pune: Bharat Dalit Sevak Sangh Prakashan, 1956). The (feminized) forms of *bhakti* (devotion) are perhaps most similar to Gandhi's affective politics. *Bhakti* was the quintessential form of submission; the devotee became abject by subjecting herself to the object of love, to god, and in the process obtained his *darshan* (divine sight) while in an ecstatic state. Dipesh Chakrabarty, "Nation and Imagination," in *Provincializing Europe,*

149–79. See also Ajay Skaria, "Gandhi's Politics: Liberalism and the Question of Ashram," *South Atlantic Quarterly* 101, no. 4 (2002): 955–86.

80. On October 26, 1932, the newly established All India Anti-Untoucha-bility League, later known as the Servants of Untouchables Society, and finally called the Harijan Sevak Sangh, was established with G. D. Birla as president and A. V. Thakkar as secretary, with a budget of Rs. 6 lakhs. "Draft Constitution of the Harijan Sevak Sangh [March 9, 1933]," in *Collected Works of Mahatma Gandhi*, vol. 59 (New Delhi: Publications Division, Ministry of Information Broadcasting, 1992). Initially a member of the League, Ambedkar resigned in disgust at the League's efforts to placate orthodox caste Hindus. Other Dalit members of the Sangh's central board included M. C. Rajah, Rao Bahadur Srinivasan, and P. Baloo. Eventually, even Congress Dalits characterized the Harijan Sevak Sangh as a caste Hindu organization working for Harijan welfare. Jagjivan Ram, *Caste Challenges in India* (New Delhi: Vision Books, 1980), 45. M. C. Rajah criticized Gandhi for surrounding himself with sycophants who behaved well in his presence but quickly forgot their "promises and obligations" when they were away from him. M. C. Rajah to Gandhi, October 17, 1938, M. C. Rajah Papers, Nehru Memorial Museum and Library, New Delhi. Rajah was most probably alluding to his encounter with C. Rajagopalachari, who refused support for Rajah's Temple-Entry Bill of 1938. On another front, the weekly, *Harijan*, began publication September–October 1932, and Gandhi went on the Harijan tour in 1933 to raise money for the Sangh. In all, more than Rs. 8 lahks were collected, to be spent on "constructive work" such as education, building houses, and digging wells. The novel fund-raising tactic for the Harijan tour was the auction, with a focus on the voluntary impoverishment of caste Hindus. Especially interesting are Gandhi's exhortations to women and young girls to divest themselves of the ritual symbols of gendered servitude by parting with their gold jewelry. Gandhi supported voluntary poverty by arguing, "In no other way can we identify ourselves with Harijans." Gandhi's day-by-day travel itinerary and an account of monies collected is available in Mukut Behari and Hari Prasad Dwevedi Varma, *History of the Harijan Sevak Sangh, 1932–1968* (Delhi: Harijan Sevak Sangh, 1971); and also in Baren Ray, ed., *Gandhi's Campaign against Untouchability, 1933–1934* (Delhi: Gandhi Peace Foundation, 1996). *Gandhi's Campaign* is a collection of the colonial government's Secret Official Reports, collated from File no. IOR/4691L/P&J/7/595, India Office, London.

81. Gandhi and R. K. Prabhu, *Caste Must Go and the Sin of Untouchability* (Ahmedabad: Navajivan Pub. House, 1964), 73–74.

82. "Varnadharma [March 19, 1933]," in *Collected Works of Mahatma Gandhi*, vol. 60, translated from the Gujarati-language *Harijanbandhu* newspaper. A similar argument about untouchables as Shudras is found in *Young India*, February 5, 1925.

83. "A Vindication of Caste by Mahatma Gandhi," in *The Annihilation of Caste*, in *BAWS*, vol. 1, 81–85.

84. *The Annihilation of Caste*, in *BAWS*, vol. 1, 47.

85. Ibid., 60–61.

86. Michel Foucault discusses the Marxian model of class struggle premised on a deeper genealogy of permanent war as the defining feature of the modern

state. Foucault notes that Marx explicitly attributed his idea of class struggle to Augustin Thierry's notion of the race wars and described Thierry as the "father of the class-struggle." Michel Foucault, *Society Must Be Defended: Lectures at the Collège de France, 1975–76* (New York: Picador, 2003), 85.

87. Bhimrao Kardak and Dadasaheb Pagare, "Congress Bhakta ani Asprushya Samvad" [Dialogue Between a Congressite and an Untouchable], in *Ambedkari Jalse: Svarup va Karya* (Mumbai: Abhinav Prakashan, 1978), 184–87.

88. Omvedt, *Dalits and the Democratic Revolution*, 190–222.

89. *Independent Labour Party Election Manifesto* (n.p., 1936). See also *Independent Labour Party: Its Formation and Its Aims*, ILP Publications no. 1 (n.p., 1937), Khairmode Collection, Bombay University.

90. In contrast, the All-India Depressed Classes League was formed in 1935 by Congress, with Jagjivan Ram as the president and the Punjabi Dalit leader, Prithvi Singh Azad, as secretary, to woo Dalits to Congress after the Poona Pact. P. N. Rajbhoj, who had been secretary, left the League to join the ILP.

91. "Svatantra Mazdoor Paksha Umedwarana Mata Dhya" [Vote for the Candidates of the ILP], *Janata*, January 30, 1937. The article notes that the Congress put up Mangs and Chambhars against the ILP candidates.

92. *Janata*, May 18, 1937.

93. Ambedkar's early economic writings, "The Problem of the Rupee," published in 1923, and *The Evolution of Finance in British India*, published in 1925, assume a state-regulated national economy capable of competing, under (fair) free-market conditions, in a global economy and criticize British monetary policy. *State and Minorities*, published in 1943, advocated "state socialism," collective agriculture, and an interventionist state dictating industrial policy.

94. *Janata*, June 26, 1948.

95. *Presidential Address to the GIP Railway Workers, Manmad, 1938* (n.p., n.d.), Khairmode Collection, Bombay University.

96. *Mumbai Municipal Kamgar Sangh, Sahava Varshik Ahval* [Bombay Municipal Workers' Organization, Sixth Report] (n.p., April 1, 1938 to March 31, 1939); *Mumbai Municipal Kamgar Sangh, Sathva Varshik Ahval* [Bombay Municipal Workers' Organization, Seventh Report] (n.p., April 1, 1939 to March 31, 1940). There were rumors, however, that the funds of the Municipal Kamgar Sangh had been embezzled. *Janata*, December 24, 1940.

97. *Janata*, June 26, 1948.

98. *Evidence before the Simon Commission*, in BAWS, vol. 2, 474.

99. BB, May 3, 1928. Gail Omvedt notes that across the 1920s and the 1930s, the All-India Kisan Sabha and the All-India Trade Union Congress refrained from engaging caste issues. Omvedt, *Dalits and the Democraic Revolution*, 180–81.

100. *Janata*, January 15, 1938; "The Illusion of the Communists and the Duty of the Untouchable Class," *Janata*, June 25, 1938.

101. In the Central Provinces and Berar, the party won four of nineteen reserved seats, while the Congress won five seats.

102. *Election Manifesto of Dr. P. G. Solanki for Kamathipura and Nagpada Areas* (n.p., n.d.). Also, Shankarrao Malharrao Patil, Chairman, Harale Samajonnathi Mandal, *Mahar Ani Chambhar* [Mahar and Chambhar] (n.p., n.d.). For a record of early efforts by Dhors, Chambhars, and Mangs to reform and or-

ganize their own communities, see *Annual Report of the Matanga Samaj Pune, Bhamburda for the year 1921–22,* and *Report of the First All-India Chambhar-Dhor Parishad,* both published by P. N. Rajbhoj, Secretary. Khairmode Collection, Bombay University.

103. *The Cabinet Mission and the Untouchables,* in BAWS, vol. 10, 539.

104. The offer was made immediately after the Cripps Mission of March 1942. Sir Stafford Cripps was a left-wing politician in Winston Churchill's War Cabinet. He came to India in March 1942 to broker a deal for Dominion status and eventual political independence if Indians supported the British war effort. Linlithgow was antagonistic to Cripps and threatened to resign when Cripps went on his mission to India in 1942.

105. *The Cabinet Mission and the Untouchables,* in BAWS, vol. 10, 538.

106. M. K. Gandhi, "The Fiction of the Majority," *Harijan,* October 21, 1939, 312.

107. Address by the president, Rao Bahadur N. Sivaraj, in *Report of the Proceedings of the Third Session of the All-India Depressed Classes Conference, Held at Nagpur on July 18 and 19, 1942* (n.p., n.d.), 24.

108. *Report of the Proceedings of the Third Session of the All-India Depressed Classes Conference, Held at Nagpur on July 18 and 19, 1942.* A conference of the Samata Sainik Dal was held on July 20, as was the second session of the All-India Depressed Classes Women's Conference.

109. Address by the president, Rao Bahadur N. Sivaraj, in *Report of the Proceedings of the Third Season of the All-India Depressed Classes Conference, Held at Nagpur on July 18 and 19, 1942,* 23. The AISCF was created at this meeting.

110. Address by B. R. Ambedkar, in ibid., 31–32.

111. Ibid., 32–33.

112. *Pakistan, or the Partition of India,* in BAWS, vol. 8.

113. *Report of the Proceedings of the AIDC Conference* (n.p., n.d.), 5. The demand arose again in on September 23, 1944, at a meeting of the Working Committee of the AISCF in Bombay.

114. According to the January 1955 AISCF constitution, officers of the AISCF Executive Committee paid an annual fee of Rs. 10, while members of the village, *taluka,* and district committees paid Rs. 5 per year.

115. *Bombay Chronicle,* March 24, 1932.

116. Chambhar leaders' support for the Rajah-Moonje pact suggests growing conflict between Mahar Ambedkarites and Chambhar supporters of the Congress. The famous cricketer P. Baloo joined the Congress during this period, as did N. S. Kajrolkar. P. N. Rajbhoj, who played an important role in the Mahad and Nasik *satyagrahas,* embraced Gandhian politics by 1932, and supported the Rajah-Moonje pact. Finally, G. M. Thaware, a Mahar leader from Vidarbha and assistant general secretary of the All-India Depressed Classes Association, who initially supported a demand for separate electorates, now criticized Ambedkar's stance. G. M. Thaware, *Report on Salvation of the Depressed Classes Lies in the Joint Electorate* (n.p., March 31, 1932), Khairmode Collection, Bombay University.

117. The Simla discussions, held June 25–July 14, 1945, were organized by Lord Wavell, viceroy for India, to consider the shape of a "transitional Govern-

ment at the Centre representative of the main political parties," namely, the Congress and Muslim League. Nicholas Mansergh, ed., *The Transfer of Power, 1942–7: Constitutional Relations between Britain and India*, vol. 5, *The Simla Conference Background and Proceedings, 1 September 1944–28 July 1945* (London: His Majesty's Stationery Office, 1974), 39.

118. *What Congress and Gandhi Have Done to the Untouchables*, in BAWS, vol. 9, 90.

119. Eleanor Zelliot argues that Ambedkar's political duties as Labour member of the Viceroy's Executive Council might have caused him to neglect campaigning for the 1945–46 elections. Eleanor Zelliot, *Dr. Babasaheb Ambedkar and the Untouchable Movement* (New Delhi: Blumoon Books, 2004), 198. The AISCF polled higher than the Congress in primaries in Madras, Bombay, and the Central Provinces, but it was soundly defeated during the 1946 elections. In Bombay the AISCF lost all fifteen reserved seats. Fourteen went to Congress and one to the Independent candidate. *The losses were hugely significant because election results were the basis for participation in the Constituent Assembly.* In 1948, Ambedkar lost a bid for election to the Constituent Assembly from Bombay and in 1952 lost a seat in the Lok Sabha to the Congress Chambhar candidate, N. S. Kajrolkar. Thus, at a crucial point, the SCs found themselves without independent representation in the Constitution-making body. Ramnarayan Rawat's painstaking analysis of the 1946 election results confirms Ambedkar's critique of the Poona Pact in almost every detail: the two-tier structure of electing SC candidates worked almost always to the advantage of Congress. Ramnarayan Rawat, "Making Claims for Power: A New Agenda in Dalit Politics of Uttar Pradesh 1946–48," *Modern Asian Studies* 37, no. 3 (2003): 585–612.

120. Qualifications for SC voters had been reduced to include literacy or previous performance of inferior village servant duties. Government of India Bill, *Instruments of Instructions to the Governor-General and Governors* (1935), cited in Zelliot, *Dr. Babasaheb Ambedkar and the Untouchable Movement*, 188.

121. Lani Guinier has argued that racist societies experience "qualitative vote dilution" through the one person-one vote principle. As an antidote, Guinier suggests a system of distributed voting where "voters get the same number of votes as there are seats or options to vote for, and they can then distribute their votes in any combination to reflect their preference." Lani Guinier, *The Tyranny of the Majority: Fundamental Fairness in Representative Democracy* (New York: Free Press, 1994), 7.

122. Ambedkar's ILP and Periyar's Self-Respect movement in the Tamil country lost the support of Communists, who gravitated toward Congress between 1937 and 1940. By 1948, the CPI's "Political Thesis" described Ambedkar as an antinational separatist and a pro-British opportunist. Omvedt, *Dalits and the Democratic Revolution*, 182–83. During the 1952 elections, Jawaharlal Nehru accused Ambedkar and the AISCF of being "communal." Mamidipudi Venkatarangaiyya, *The General Election in the City of Bombay, 1952* (Bombay: Vora, 1953), 32–34, 37.

123. K. Santhanam, *Ambedkar's Attack: A Critical Examination of Dr. Ambedkar's Book "What Congress and Gandhi Have Done to the Untouchables"*

(New Delhi: Hindustan Times Press, 1946), 2–3. Santhanam, a Congress activist from 1920 to 1942, was a member of the All-India Congress Committee and the Tamil Nadu Congress Committee. He was a Congress member of the Central Assembly when he resigned his post in 1942.

124. Chakravarti Rajagopalachari, *Ambedkar Refuted* (Bombay: Hind Kitabs, 1946), 5–6.

125. Ibid., 8–9.

126. Santhanam, *Ambedkar's Attack*, 20.

127. Ibid., 33–34.

128. *Lord's Debate on India: Text of Secretary of State's Speech*, GI, Home (Pol), no. 51/2/1946, NAI, quoted in Sekhar Bandhyopadhyay, "Transfer of Power and the Crisis of Dalit Politics in India, 1945–1947," *Modern Asian Studies* 34, no. 4:922.

129. The Purusha Sukta, the famous ninetieth hymn of the tenth book of the Rg Veda, was at the center of controversy. The text addressed the mythic creation of the *varna* order through the dismemberment of Purusha, the Original Man. The Shudras (and by extension, the untouchables) were said to have sprung from the feet, a "most ignoble part of the human frame," as Ambedkar noted. Phule, Valangkar, and Ambedkar argued that the Purusha Sukta was a recent addition to the Rg Veda, since the Rg Veda made no mention of a fourth, degraded caste, the Shudras. Dhananjay Keer and S. G. Malshe, eds., *Mahatma Phule Samagra Vangmay* [Collected Works of Mahatma Jotirao Phule] (Mumbai: Mumbai Rajya Sahitya ani Samskriti Mandal, 1969), reprinted 1991, ed. Y. D. Phadke, 74, 77, 83–84, 95–97, 120–21; Valangkar, *Vinanti Patra* (1888), 20, reprinted in *Purogami Satyashodak* (July–September 1979) as *Vitthal Vidhwansan*; B. R. Ambedkar, *Who Were the Untouchables?* in BAWS, vol. 7, 31–32.

130. Ambedkar was influenced by Vithal Ramji Shinde (1873–1944), founder of the DCM, who argued that Buddhism was based on a rational and humanitarian philosophy and that the Dalit communities were originary Buddhists vanquished by Brahmins. M. P. Mangudkar, *Shinde Lekhasangraha* (Pune: Thokal Prakashan, 1963), 53–54.

131. Scholarly research on Buddhism was started by a group of Bengali scholars at the turn of the twentieth century. However, the Maha Bodhi Society, founded by Anagarika Dharmapala in Ceylon in 1891, was the most important vehicle for research in Buddhism across the Indian subcontinent, Ceylon, and Nepal. In Bombay, R. G. Bhandarkar became interested in Buddhism in 1878, and his associate, K. B. Pathak, began working on Buddhist texts in 1894. The most famous Buddhist scholar from western India was Dharmanand Kosambi (1876–1948), father of the Marxist historian D. D. Kosambi. Dharmanand Kosambi was ordained as a *bhikku* in 1902, started a Pali Language Department at the University of Bombay, and taught Pali at Poona's Fergusson College (1912–18). Ambedkar was greatly influenced by Kosambi's book, *Bhagvan Buddha* (1940), and before that by a Marathi biography of Buddha that was presented to him in 1898 by its author, K. A. Keluskar, a teacher at the Wilson High School. Ambedkar's interest in Buddhism also coincided with a resurgence of intellectual interest in Buddhism and long-standing identification in the Tamil country between Buddhism and *adi-Dravida* identity. Ambedkar also wrote an intro-

duction to the third edition of Tamil Buddhist Lakshmi Narasu's book, *The Essence of Buddhism* (1948), first published in 1907. See Eleanor Zelliot, "The Indian Rediscovery of Buddhism, 1855–1956," in *Studies in Pali and Buddhism: A Memorial Volume in Honor of Bhikkhu Jagdish Kashyap,* ed. A. K. Narain and Leonard Zwilling (Delhi: B. R. Publishing Corp., 1979), 398–405.

132. Ambedkar drew upon the 1936 People of India survey, which distinguished two Aryan races, the brachycephalic and the dolichocephalic (short-headed and long-headed) peoples, who were distributed along India's interior and exterior, respectively. This became the basis for Ambedkar's reinterpretation of the Rg Veda, which had been read by Indologists, including the famous P. V. Kane, as outlining the defeat of the agrarian Dasyus by the pastoral Aryans.

133. *Who Were the Shudras?* in BAWS, vol. 7, 97.

134. Ambedkar notes that the Rg Veda makes no mention of the Shudra, while the Shanti Parvan mentioned Paijavana, a Shudra king. He used this evidence to support his thesis regarding the emergence of the Shudra as a historical category coeval with the rise of Puranic Hinduism.

135. Phule believed that the thread ceremony and the chanting of the Gayatri Mantra were constitutive of Brahmin power. Non-Brahmins were ritually excluded from these practices. In the 1920s, the Hindu Mahasabha and the Samata Sangh held functions to invest Dalits and non-Brahmins with the sacred thread. For instance, the Samata Sangh invested four thousand people with the sacred thread at a Depressed Classes conference in Ratnagiri, which was attended by over six thousand people. *Bombay Chronicle,* May 25, 1928.

136. *Castes in India,* in BAWS, vol. 1, 8.

137. D. D. Kosambi, "Marxism and Ancient Indian Culture: Review of S. A. Dange's *India from Primitive Communism to Slavery,*" *Annals of the Bhandarkar Oriental Research Institute* (Poona), vol. 29 (1949): 271–77.

138. For a critique of anticololonial nationalists' nostalgia for a Vedic golden age, see Uma Chakravarti, "Whatever Happened to the Vedic Dasi? Orientalism, Nationalism and a Script for the Past," in *Recasting Women: Essays in Indian Colonial History,* ed. Kumkum Sangari and Sudesh Vaid (New Brunswick, NJ: Rutgers University Press, 1990), 27–87.

139. Sharad Patil, *Dasa-Shudra Slavery* (Pune: Sugawa Prakashan, 1991).

140. *Revolution and Counter-Revolution in Ancient India,* in BAWS, vol. 3, 373.

141. Early works on Shivaji portrayed him in a populist vein, as a Shudra king. See Rajaram Shastri Bhagwat, *The Life of Shivaji* (n.p., 1889); Arjunrao Keluskar, *The Life of Shivaji Maharaj* (Bombay: Manoranjan Press, 1921); and Jotirao Phule, *Chatrapati Shivaji Raja Bhosale Yanca Powada* [The Ballad of Chattrapathi Shivaji], in *Samagra Vangmay.* Bhagwat was a reformist Brahmin who supported non-Brahmins' access to Vedic knowledge.

142. *Who Were the Shudras?* in BAWS, vol. 7, 179.

143. Ibid., 178.

144. "Caste and Class," in *The Essential Writings of B. R. Ambedkar,* ed. Valerian Rodrigues (New Delhi: Oxford University Press, 2002), 105.

145. See also B. R. Ambedkar, "Hindu Dharmala Notice" [Notice to Hinduism], *BB,* March 15, 1929.

146. *Report on Akhil Mumbai Ilakha Mahar Parishad* [Mass Appeal Regarding the Mass Conversions as Suggested by Ambedkar] (n.p., 1936).

147. For a powerful reading of the multiple valences of Dalit conversion, see Gyanendra Pandey, "The Time of Conversion," *Economic and Political Weekly* 41, no. 18 (May 6, 2006): 1779–88.

148. *The Buddha or Karl Marx,* in BAWS, vol. 3, 457.

149. Ibid., 462.

150. Gauri Viswanathan, *Outside the Fold: Conversion, Modernity, and Belief* (Princeton, NJ: Princeton University Press, 1998), 231.

151. Louis Althusser, *For Marx,* trans. Ben Brewster (New York: Penguin, 1969).

152. Louis Althusser and Etienne Balibar, *Reading Capital,* 1st American ed. (New York: Pantheon, 1971). I do not wish to collapse Ambedkar's eclectic and wide-ranging intellectual interests to a preoccupation with Marxist thought. I do believe, however, that we scant Ambedkar's critical relationship to Marxist thought if we reduce it to debates about the relationship between caste and class, or to evidence of Ambedkar's episodic alliance with the Communists.

153. Even during this period of political rapprochement, clashes between Congress and AISCF supporters continued in Bombay's working-class neighborhoods of Worli, Naigaon, De Lisle Road, and Mazgaon in the summer of 1946. *Bombay Chronicle* May 25, May 30, May 31, June 1, and July 4, 1946. AISCF supporters took a *morcha* (peaceful march) to Gandhi's residence in Poona on July 10 and staged a *satyagraha* outside the Bombay Legislative Assembly from July 11 to 18. *Bombay Chronicle,* July 11–18, 1946. By July 29, when the assembly decided to adjourn, over eleven hundred AISCF supporters, including one hundred women, had been arrested for agitating against the Congress. *Bombay Chronicle,* July 29, 1946. In the meantime, Ambedkar, who had lost in the 1945 Bombay election, was elected to the Constituent Assembly from east Bengal through the activism of the Namashudra Dalit leader, Jogendranath Mandal. Because Ambedkar stood to lose his seat in the Constituent Assembly after Partition, Congress offered him a seat from Bombay in April 1947, which was vacated by M. R. Jayakar of the Hindu Mahasabha. For a violent and intellectually misinformed attack on Ambedkar as a British collaborator and antinationalist who was marginal to the drafting of the Indian Constitution, see Arun Shourie, *Worshipping False Gods: Ambedkar, and the Facts which Have Been Erased* (New Delhi: Harper Collins, 2001). For a critique of Shourie's position, see S. M. Gaikwad, "Ambedkar and Indian Nationalism," *Economic and Political Weekly* 33, no. 10 (March 7, 1998): 515–18. For a compelling account of this debate, and an argument supporting Ambedkar's critical role in the Constitution's Drafting Committee, see Christophe Jaffrelot, *Dr. Ambedkar and Untouchability* (Delhi: Permanent Black, 2004), 98–114.

154. Bandhyopadhyay tackles a crucial missing link in Ambedkar scholarship: to explain Ambedkar's virulent criticism of Congress and his subsequent volte-face in accepting Congress nomination for a seat in the Constituent Assembly. Sekhar Bandhyopadhyay, "Transfer of Power and the Crisis of Dalit Politics in India, 1945–47," *Modern Asian Studies* 34, no. 4 (October 2000): 893–942. Gail Omvedt has explained Congress dominance by arguing that the

Congress's Depressed Classes League made significant inroads into the Dalit base. Omvedt, *Dalits and the Democratic Revolution,* 304. M. S. Gore argues merely that Congress sought to co-opt Dalit politics in the aftermath of Partition. M. S. Gore, *Social Context of an Ideology: Ambedkar's Political and Social Thought* (New Delhi: Sage Publications, 1993), 180–83.

155. G. Aloysius, *Nationalism without a Nation in India* (Delhi: Oxford University Press, 1997). Ambedkar's critique of the village as a "den of ignorance" and "narrow-mindedness," and the AISCF's poignant demand for separate villages, reflect the impasse. In contrast, Ambedkar's argument about the relationship between (Muslim) nationality, sovereignty, and territoriality in *Pakistan, or the Partition of India,* in *BAWS,* vol. 8, is nonideological, by which I mean that he traces the logical implications of a stated position to its culmination in making the case *for* Pakistan.

156. Dhananjay Keer, *Dr. Ambedkar: Life and Mission* (Bombay: Popular Prakashan, 1962), 166–67. Ambedkar's comment was occasioned by Gandhi saying that he had "been thinking over the problem of Untouchables ever since my schooldays—when you [Ambedkar] were not even born. You may perhaps be knowing what enormous amounts of efforts I had put in to incorporate this problem in the programme of the Congress. . . . The Congress has spent not less than rupees twenty lakhs on the uplift of the Untouchables" (165).

4. LEGISLATING CASTE ATROCITY

1. M. K. Gandhi to Samuel Hoare, Secretary of State for India, March 11, 1932, quoted in Mahadev Desai, *The Diary of Mahadev Desai,* vol. 1, *Yeravda-Pact Eve, 1932,* trans. Valji Govindji Desai (Ahmedabad: Navajivan Publishing House, 1953), 301.

2. Gandhi undertook a fast in support of striking millworkers in Ahmedabad, fasted in response to the Jallianwala Bagh massacre of 1919, and fasted when riots erupted in response to the massacre. These were brief fasts of personal atonement. A 1922 fast for "personal cleansing" was a response to the Chauri Chaura incident. However, the fast-unto-death against the Communal Award, like the twenty-one day fast of 1924 that was undertaken to promote Hindu-Muslim amity in the aftermath of riots during the Khilafat movement, had the explicit aim of disciplining errant subjects.

3. Reginald A. Reynolds, *Gandhi's Fast: Its Cause and Significance* (London: No More War Movement, n.d.), 17.

4. Desai, *Diary of Mahadev Desai,* vol. 1, March 10, 1932.

5. Desai, "Shock Treatment," in *Diary of Mahadev Desai,* vol. 1, August 21, 1932, 301.

6. See, for example, Joseph Alter, *Gandhi's Body: Sex, Diet, and the Politics of Nationalism* (Philadelphia: University of Pennsylvania Press, 2000).

7. M. K. Gandhi to George Joseph, April 12, 1924, *Collected Works of Mahatma Gandhi,* vol. 23 (New Delhi: Publications Division, Ministry of Information Broadcasting, n.d.), 420.

8. M. K. Gandhi, "Confession and Repentance," *Young India,* February 16, 1922.

9. Not everyone could undertake such penance. The Congress volunteer Kelappan was warned to desist from undertaking "imitative fasts" during the Vaikom *satygraha*. Cited in Dilip Menon, *Caste, Nationalism and Communism in South India* (Cambridge: Cambridge University Press, 1994), 114. Ashram members were prohibited from undertaking penitential fasts without Gandhi's permission. "The Institution of Fasting," *Harijan*, March 13, 1939.

10. B. R. Ambedkar, "Pune Yethil Parvati Satyagraha" [The *Satyagraha* in Pune], *BB*, November 15, 1927.

11. Nagaraj, *Flaming Feet*, 31

12. *What Congress and Gandhi Have Done to the Untouchables*, in BAWS, vol. 9.

13. *The Annihilation of Caste*, in BAWS, vol. 1, 75.

14. Walter Benjamin, "Critique of Violence," in *Reflections: Essays, Aphorisms, Autobiographical Writings* (New York: Schocken Books, 1978).

15. Marc Galanter, "Hinduism, Secularism, and the Indian Judiciary," in *Secularism and Its Critics*, ed. Rajeev Bhargava (Delhi: Oxford University Press, 1998): 268–96.

16. I should make it clear that I am not offering a political history of constitution making, but a reading of constitutional "effects" on institutional contexts and discursive fields. For the history of constitutionalism, see Granville Austin, *The Indian Constitution: Cornerstone of a Nation* (Delhi: Oxford University Press, 2000). See also Shiva Rao, *The Framing of India's Constitution, A Study*, vol. 5 (New Delhi: Indian Institute of Public Administration, 1967).

17. Ambedkar introduced the Hindu Code Bill to the Constituent Assembly by noting that it was an effort to "codify the rules of Hindu law which are scattered in innumerable decisions of the High Courts and the Privy Council, which form a bewildering motley to the common man." Because Hindu law was essentially personal law governing the Hindu domestic, the amended bill contained a set of measures—equal property rights for women, abolition of customary law, grounds for divorce—that articulated the principle of gender justice. Though the Constituent Assembly had accepted the principle of equality and absence of discrimination between the sexes, the effort to reform personal law provoked violent resistance, support for superstitious practices, assertion of patriarchal sentiment, and finally, repugnance for the Dalit minister who would reform religious law. The Constituent Assembly debates are filled with oblique references to Ambedkar's caste identity, as well as explicit manifestations of caste prejudice. BAWS, vol. 17. For a discussion of Hindu prejudice, see Gyanendra Pandey, "The Time of Conversion," *Economic and Political Weekly* 41, no. 18 (May 6, 2006): 1779–88.

18. *Balaji v. State of Mysore* was one of the first cases in which caste was defined in this dual manner. *AIR* 1963 S.C. 649.

19. Austin Granville, *Working on a Democratic Constitution: The Indian Experience* (New York: Oxford University Press, 1999). For studies of minority identity and the Constituent Assembly debates, see Iqbal Ansari, "Minorities and the Politics of Constitution Making in India," in *Minority Identities and the Nation State,* ed. D. L. Sheth and G. Mahajan (Delhi, 1999), 113–37; Rochana Bajpai, *Minority Rights in the Constituent Assembly Debates, 1946–1950*, QEH Working Paper Series no. 30 (Oxford: University of Oxford, November 30, 1999);

James Chiriyankandath, "Constitutional Predilections," *Seminar,* no. 484 (December 1999); Shefali Jha, "Secularism in the Constituent Assembly Debates, 1946–1950," *Economic and Political Weekly* 37, no. 30 (July 27, 2002): 3175–80; and Ralph Retzlaff, "The Problem of Communal Minorities in the Drafting of the Indian Constitution," in *Constitutionalism in Asia,* ed. R. N. Spann (London: Asia Publishing House, 1963), 55–73. Also see Faisal Devji, "Hindu/Muslim/Indian," *Public Culture* 5, no. 1 (1992): 1–18; and Gyanendra Pandey, "Can a Muslim Be an Indian?" *Comparative Studies in Society and History* 41, no. 4 (1999): 608–29.

20. For a discussion of the relationship between colonial categories and the emergence of a national sociology of caste, see Nicholas B. Dirks, *Castes of Mind: Colonialism and the Making of Modern India* (Princeton, NJ: Princeton University Press, 2001).

21. An important case challenging Article 17 via Article 26 is *Chinamma v. D. P. I., AIR* 1964 Andhra Pradesh 277. For judgments arguing that Article 26 permits excommunication rights, see also *Venkataramana Devaru v. State of Mysore, AIR* 1958 S.C. 255; *Sarup Singh v. State of Punjab, AIR* 1959 S.C. 860; and *Saifuddin v. State of Bombay, AIR* 1962 S.C. 853 (869, 873, 875).

22. Gyanendra Pandey, *The Construction of Communalism in Colonial North India* (New Delhi: Oxford University Press, 1990); and Jha, "Secularism in the Constituent Assembly Debates, 1946–1950."

23. In *Sangannagonda v. Kallangonda, AIR* 1960 Mysore 147, the court held that assigning *varna* status to individuals is neither religious discrimination nor a denial of equal rights.

24. Key readers on secularism include Rajeev Bhargava, ed., *Secularism and Its Critics* (Delhi: Oxford University Press, 1998); Niraja Gopal Jayal, *Democracy and the State: Welfare, Secularism, and Development in Contemporary India* (Delhi: Oxford University Press, 1999); and Anuradha Dingwaney Needham and Rajeswari Sunder Rajan, eds., *The Crisis of Secularism in India* (Durham, NC: Duke University Press, 2005).

25. Early cases, such as *State of Kerala v. N. M. Thomas,* interpreted the equal opportunity intent of the reservations regime to also require "equality of result" when free and fair play of market forces prevails. *State of Kerala v. N. M. Thomas, AIR* 1976 S.C. 490.

26. Marc Galanter, *Competing Equalities: Law and the Backward Classes in India* (Delhi: Oxford University Press, 1984), 361. A more recent evaluation of the reservations regime can be found in Marc Galanter, "The Long Half-Life of Reservations," in *India's Living Constitution: Ideas, Practices, Controversies,* ed. Zoya Hasan, E. Sridharan, and R. Sudarshan (New Delhi: Permanent Black, 2002), 306–18. See also Lelah Dushkin, "Scheduled Caste Policy in India: History, Problems, Prospects," *Asian Survey* 7, no. 9 (September 1967): 626–36.

27. G. S. Ghurye, *Caste, Class and Occupation* (Bombay: Popular Book Dept, 1961).

28. Galanter, *Competing Equalities: Law and the Backward Classes in India,* 154–79.

29. For a discussion of the postcolonial politics of caste as it relates to Mandal, see Dirks, *Castes of Mind,* 231–54, and 275–96.

30. For an early exploration of this issue, see Marc Galanter, "The Abolition of Disabilities: Untouchability and the Law," in *The Untouchables in Contemporary India*, ed. J. M. Mahar (Tucson: University of Arizona Press, 1972), 227–314.

31. Legislation against caste crime was enabled by a generous interpretation of Article 15(4), allowing special provisions for the "advancement" of SCs and STs. Under Article 35(a)(ii), all legislation penalizing untouchability must be enacted by Parliament. The *RCSCST* for 1952–53 noted that late-colonial legislation abolishing caste disabilities was ineffective: "The pity . . . is that even where such offenses are made cognisable, these legislations have not been of any material help to those for whom they were enacted."

32. *Devarajiah v. Padmanna, AIR* 1958 Mysore 84 (para. 4; emphasis added).

33. Two cases held that the Untouchability (Offences) Act did not cover "private" places, including sites of worship: *Benudhar Sahu and Another v. State, ILR* 1962 Cuttack Series 256; and *Kandra Sethi v. Metra Sahu and another, ILR* 1963 Cuttack Series 455.

34. R. G. Karmarkar, *The Protection of Civil Rights Act, 1955 [Act 22 of 1955]* (Pune: N. R. Bhalerao Law Book-Sellers and Publishers, 1978), 13.

35. See, for example, *Lok Sabha Debates*, August 26, 1954, 408; August 27, 1954, 451; August 31, 1954, 709; April 27, 1955, 6608, 6664, 6650, 6660–61, 6668–69.

36. The bill that became the 1955 Untouchability (Offences) Act was first introduced in the Lok Sabha in March 1954. It went to a joint committee of Lok Sabha and Rajya Sabha members, whose comments were discussed in the Lok Sabha in April 1955. A major change suggested by the joint committee was to delete the definition of "untouchable" in clause 2 of the bill.

37. These discussions occurred in the Lok Sabha on April 27 and 28, 1955. The amended bill was passed on April 28.

38. M. Gurupadaswamy, in *Lok Sabha Debates*, August 27, 1955, 6650. Also see Govind Ballabh Pant, in *Lok Sabha Debates*, August, 27, 1955, who argued: "So far as the definition of an expression which has not been defined in the Constitution itself is concerned, we have to submit to that word without defining it further" (6668–69).

39. Basudeb Barman, in *Lok Sabha Debates*, August 27, 1955, 6660–61.

40. *Lok Sabha Debates*, August 26, 1954, 408 (emphasis added).

41. *Lok Sabha Debates*, August 27, 1954, 6608.

42. *Lok Sabha Debates*, August 31, 1954, 672–73 (emphasis added).

43. Discussions to amend the Untouchability (Offences) Act began in 1962 and culminated in 1974–75. Major issues included debates about the extent of punishment, noncompoundable offenses, the status of private temples, and whether persons convicted of caste crime could be barred from running for central government office. With the passage of the amended PCR Act in 1976, the practice of untouchability was defined to consist of acts such as prohibiting entry into places of worship, denying access to shops and other public places, denying access to any water supply, prohibiting entry into hospitals, refusing to sell goods or render services, and insulting someone on the basis of his or her caste. Section 7(1)(d) of the amended PCR Act of 1955 classified the boycott, spoken

or written incitement to practice untouchability, and insults against an SC person as offenses punishable by a minimum two-year sentence and a fine. A PCR Cell was established at an all-India level to respond to the lack of convictions under atrocities legislation.

44. The POA Act focused on transacted violence, gave the complainant more weight—there is no mechanism for anticipatory bail, and atrocities are non-bailable offenses—and provided stringent punishment for police negligence. The last was a consequence of broader concerns with police corruption, reflected in the twenty-second chapter of the *Third Report of the National Police Commission* (New Delhi: Government of India, 1980). The nineteenth chapter of this report addresses conflict between BCs and Dalits as a new phase in caste violence. By 1995, the government of India enacted accompanying rules for the POA Act that took up amounts and timetables for compensating victims of caste crime. Rules 16 and 17 called for the constitution of state- and district-level vigilance and monitoring committees comprising official and nonofficial members to review efficacy of the POA Act, victim relief and rehabilitation, and the conduct of different officers and agencies charged with the act's implementation.

45. Drawing on the philosopher J. L. Austin and legal theorist Robert Cover, Judith Butler argues that linguistic performatives blur the distinction between word and deed. Performatives, according to Austin, are words that behave as if they are deeds; these words produce physical effects simultaneously with their utterance. For Butler, hate crimes in the United States are one such powerful instance of performatives that produce "linguistic vulnerability," making harmful words equivalent to the infliction of a physical wound. Judith Butler, *Excitable Speech: A Politics of the Performative* (New York: Routledge, 1997).

46. The Department of Social Welfare was itself ignored within government. A Lok Sabha member noted, "Nobody takes the decisions of this department into consideration and no other department cares for this department." Baidhar Behara, in *Lok Sabha Debates* 16, no. 50, April 25, 1968, 3152.

47. See *Economic and Political Weekly* 13 (July 28, 1978): 1159, for an analysis of this oddity.

48. *Enforcement of Untouchability (Offences) Act 1955—A Survey* (New Delhi: Bureau of Police Research and Development, 1976). See also *Syndicate Study on Implementation of the Protection of Civil Rights Act* (Hyderabad, 1980), found at the Sardar Vallabhai Patel National Police Academy. The Untouchability (Offences) Act gave maximum punishment of six months imprisonment and/or a Rs. 500 fine. The 1976 PCR Act enforced jail sentences between one and six months and levied fines between Rs. 100 and Rs. 500. First, second, and third offenses committed under both acts were bailable until 1989. Public servants refusing to recognize untouchability offenses could be charged under the amended PCR Act of 1976.

49. *Broken People: Caste Violence against India's "Untouchables"* (New York: Human Rights Watch, 1999), 191, http://www.hrw.org/legacy/reports/1999/india.

50. Michel Foucault, *The History of Sexuality*, trans. Robert Hurley (New York: Vintage, 1988).

51. As Wendy Brown argues, efforts to protect those with injury-forming identities may also entrench those aspects of their identity and produce a repetitive

structure of ressentiment as the necessary complement to a politics of identity. I extend (and amend) Brown's insight to examine how such mechanisms of subject-formation create new arenas of conflict and new forms of political engagement. Wendy Brown, *States of Injury: Power and Freedom in Late Modernity* (Princeton, NJ: Princeton University Press, 1995), 21.

52. Oliver Mendelsohn and Marika Vicziany, *The Untouchables: Subordination, Poverty, and the State in Modern India* (Cambridge: Cambridge University Press, 1998); and N. D. Kamble, *Atrocities on Scheduled Castes in Post Independent India, 15th August 1947 to 15th August 1979* (New Delhi: Ashish Publishing House, 1981).

53. According to the *Oxford English Dictionary,* "atrocity," from the Latin *atrocitatem,* means: "1. savage enormity, horrible or heinous wickedness; 2. Fierceness, sternness, implacability; 3. An atrocious deed, an act of extreme cruelty and heinousness; and finally, 4. *colloq.* with no moral reference: A very bad blunder, violation of taste or good manners, etc."

54. Cited in S. K. Awasthi, *The Scheduled Castes and Scheduled Tribes (Prevention of Atrocities) Act, 1989* (Alahabad: Premier Publishing Co., 1994), 159.

55. Elayaperumal Report (1969), 56.

56. Ibid.

57. In suggesting that the practice of untouchability was produced, in large meaure, by the laws meant to abolish untouchability, I am inspired by Philip Abrams's argument about the state as an "effect" of practices of power that give it a centralizing legitimacy, rather than the origin of centralized power. Philip Abrams, "Notes on the Difficulty of Studying the State," *Journal of Historical Sociology* 1, no. 1 (1988): 58–89.

58. Slavoj Žižek, "The Supposed Subject of Ideology," *Critical Quarterly* 39, no. 2 (Summer 1997): 39–59.

59. Saurabh Dube, *Stitches on Time* (Durham, NC: Duke University Press, 2004), chapter 3.

60. Robert Cover, "Violence and the Word," in *Narrative, Violence and the Law,* ed. Martha Minow, Michael Ryan, and Austin Sarat (Ann Arbor: Univesity of Michigan Press, 1995), 216.

61. Allen Feldman, *Formations of Violence* (Chicago: University of Chicago Press, 1991).

62. For two important works that theorize delocalization, see Akhil Gupta, "Blurred Boundaries: The Discourse of Corruption, the Culture of Politics, and the Imagined State," *American Ethnologist* 22, no. 2 (1995): 375–402; and Steven Pierce, "Looking Like a State: Colonialism and the Discourse of Corruption in Northern Nigeria," *Comparative Studies in Society and History* 48, no. 4 (October 2006): 887–914.

5. NEW DIRECTIONS IN DALIT POLITICS

1. Thomas Blom Hansen, *Wages of Violence: Naming and Identity in Post-colonial Bombay* (Princeton, NJ: Princeton University Press, 2001), 43.

2. Maharashtra ranked second in the number of complaints regarding anti-Dalit violence during the 1960s. Elayaperumal Report (1969), 163.

3. Autobiographies by men note that their mothers often resisted, wrapped the idols, and kept them in a corner or refused to throw them away. Daya Pawar, *Baluta*, 6th ed. (Mumbai: Granthali, 1995); and Narendra Jadhav, "Sonu," in *Outcaste: A Memoir* (Delhi: Penguin, 2003), 174–92.

4. Bhimrao Kardak and Dadasaheb Pagare, *Ambedkari Jalse: Svarup va Karya* (Mumbai: Abhinav Prakashan, 1978), 111–12. For a discussion of the use of popular cultural forms, including the *tamasha*, see Gopal Guru, *Dalit Cultural Movement and Dialectics of Dalit Politics in Maharashtra* (Mumbai: Vikas Adhyayan Kendra, 1997).

5. *Charitras* are often sung. Collections called *Bhim gita* (songs to Bhim) can be found at roadside stalls and in cassette form. Like the Ambedkari *jalsas* of the 1930s, set to popular musical tunes, *Bhim gita* are often sung to popular Hindi film tunes. Many are also set to devotional music and sung as *bhajans*.

6. Christopher Emmrich, with Adele Fiske, "The Use of Buddhist Scriptures in Dr. B. R. Ambedkar's 'The Buddha and his Dhamma,'" in *Reconstructing the World: Dr. Ambedkar and Buddhism in India*, ed. Surendra Jondhale and Johannes Beltz (Delhi: Oxford University Press 2003), 114.

7. Ibid., 115. For an excellent discussion of Ambedkar imagery, see Gary M. Tartakov, "Art and Identity: The Rise of a New Buddhist Imagery," *Art Journal* 49, no. 4 (Winter 1990): 409–16.

8. *Report on the Constitution of the Bauddha Jana Panchayat Samiti* (n.p., n.d.), Ramesh Shinde Collection.

9. Visits to the Koregaon memorial in Pune predate these pilgrimages. The Koregaon memorial commemorates the crucial battle against Peshwa Bajirao II on January 1, 1818, in which twenty-two Mahar men (recognized by the suffix *nak*, usually attached to Mahar names) died fighting for the British. The memorial became the site of Mahar pilgrimage from the 1920s. Shivram Janba Kamble convened a Depressed Classes Conference on January 1, 1927, at the Koregaon War Memorial—built to commemorate victory of British troops against the *peshwa*'s forces in 1818—where Ambedkar spoke about the Mahar military past.

10. B. R. Ambedkar, "Mahad Yethila Dharmasangar va Varishta Hinduna Jababdari" [The Religious War at Mahad and Caste Hindu's Responsibility], *BB*, April 22, 1927. Ambedkar long maintained that Dalits were caught in the middle of Marathas, immediate rural oppressors, and Brahmin nationalists with a questionable commitment to caste reform. He argued that Brahmin and upper-caste Communist leaders resisted organizing around caste even when they were sympathetic to the experiences of lower-caste laborers.

11. Ambedkar's critique of linguistic states began with a discussion of "the consolidation of the North and the balkanization of the South" that was produced by the States Reorganization Commission. He then argued for the necessity of balancing states created on a linguistic principle against territorial size and economic development, and favored a balance between majority and minority interests. It was from this perspective that he suggested the creation of four Maharashtrian states, including a Bombay City State that was "an asylum, a place of refuge where [minorities] can be free from the tyranny of the majority." *Thoughts on Linguistic States*, in *BAWS*, vol. 1, 148, 158.

12. Dadasaheb Gaikwad, *Samyukta Maharashtra Samitiche Dusre Adiveshan* (n.p., October 14–16, 1960), Ramesh Shinde Collection. The 1957 alliance was effective, winning the RPI national, state and local seats. See Shiv Lal, ed., *Election Archives 10* (New Delhi: Shiv Lal, 1988).

13. *Prabuddha Bharat,* April 14, 1959, contains the RPI manifesto written by Shankarrao Kharat, onetime vice chancellor of Marathwada University. N. Shivraj's speech on the RPI is reported in *Prabuddha Bharat,* May 16, 1959. On the ILP, see R. K. Kshirsagar, *Bharatiya Republican Paksha* (Aurangabad: Nath Prakashan, 1979), 36.

14. B. K. Gaikwad, or Dadasaheb Gaikwad (1902–71), was moderately educated, came from a rural background, and led the Nasik *satyagraha.* Described by Ambedkar as his "right hand" and a man of "24 carat gold," Gaikwad was de facto leader of the RPI. For biographies of Gaikwad, see Bhavana Bhargave, *Padmashri Dadasaheb Gaikwad* (Pune: Kalpana Mudranalaya, 1968); Girish Ramchnadra Jadhav, *Karmaveer Dadasaheb Bhaurao Krishnarao Gaikwad Yanche Jeevan Charitra* (Nasik: Kashiram Runjaji Gaware, 1961); and Ramsh Shinde, ed., *Karmaveer Dadasaheb Gaikwad* (Pune: Sugawa Prakashan, 2002).

15. Jayashree Gokhale, *From Concessions to Confrontation: The Politics of an Indian Untouchable Community* (Bombay: Popular Prakashan, 1993), 255.

16. B. C. Kamble, *Dr. Babasaheb Ambedkaranchya Communist Nindemagil Rahasya va Artha Bodh* [The Secret Behind Dr. Babasaheb Ambedkar's Reproach of the Communists and Its Important Lesson (for the Dalit Movement)] (Bhoiwada, Mumbai: Messrs D. B. Bhaskar Jadhav, 1965), 25. Kamble was also referring to prior conflict between the AISCF and the Communists over the 1952 elections for the Bombay Legislative Assembly, when Ambedkar allied with the Praja Socialists. The Communist Party put out a pamphlet accusing Ambedkar of being antinational and was alleged to have asked its cadre to cast blank votes for the reserved-seat candidate instead of voting for Ambedkar. Ironically, all the candidates—Ambedkar, Mehta, and Dange—lost to the Congress. Author interview with Madhu Shetye, July 28, 2008, Mumbai. The contradictory pull of egalitarian ideology and resistance to caste issues is poignantly discussed in the biography of Dalit Communist R. B. More. Satyendra More, *Comrade R. B. More: Dalit va Communist Calvalicha Sashaktha Duva* (Mumbai: Paryay Prakashan, 2003).

17. Raosaheb Kasbe, "Dalit Calval: Kahi Prashna" [The Dalit Movement: Some Questions], *Sadhana,* December 13, 1980. Such antagonism hides the fact that the majority of SC government employees occupy the lowest rungs of bureaucracy while better positions remain vacant. For an important evaluation of SC public sector employment, see Christophe Jaffrelot, *India's Silent Revolution: The Rise of the Lower Castes in North India* (New York: Columbia University Press, 2002). For Maharashtra-focused studies of social mobility, see Vasant Deshpande, *Towards Social Integration: Problems of Adjustment of Scheduled Caste Elite* (Pune: Shubhada-Saraswat Prakashan, 1978); Govind Gare and S. Limaye, *Marashtratil Shodha Ani Bodh* (Bombay: Sahadhyayan Prakashan, 1970); R. S. Gawai, *The Caste War over Reservations* (Nagpur: Maharashtra State Republican Party, 1981); Sunanda Patwardhan, *Change among India's Harijans- Maharashtra, a Case Study* (Delhi: Orient Longman, 1973); Sachidananda, *The Harijan Elite*

(New Delhi: Thomson Press, 1977); and Vasant Sathe, *Buddha Zhala Mahar* (Pune: Dvanda Prakashan, 1981).

18. R. D. Bhandare was active with the Municipal Workers' Union since the 1930s, and worked with Communists and Socialists in Bombay to organize mill labor. He split from the RPI in 1960. Barrister Khobragade, who broke away in 1974, had organized *bidi* workers in Nagpur.

19. See Anthony Carter, *Elite Politics in Rural India: Political Stratification and Political Alliances in Western Maharashtra* (London: Cambridge University Press, 1974); David Hardiman, "The Indian 'Faction': A Political Theory Examined," in *Subaltern Studies 1* (New York: Oxford University Press, 1982), 192–232; Henry Orenstein, *Gaon: Conflict and Cohesion in a Maharashtrian Village* (Princeton, NJ: Princeton University Press, 1965); Rajni Kothari, ed. *Caste in Indian Politics* (New York: Gordon and Breach, 1970).

20. Julia Eckert, *The Charisma of Direct Action: Power, Politics and the Shiv Sena* (New Delhi: Oxford University Press, 2003); Dipankar Gupta, *Nativism in a Metropolis: The Shiv Sena in Bombay* (Delhi: Manohar Books, 1997); Hansen, *Wages of Violence*; Mary Fainsod Katzenstein, *Ethnicity and Equality: The Shiv Sena Party and Preferential Policies in Bombay* (Ithaca: Cornell University Press, 1979); Jayant Lele, "Saffronisation of the Shiv Sena," in *Bombay: Metaphor for Modern India*, ed. Sujata Patel and Alice Thorner (Bombay: Oxford University Press, 1995), 185–212.

21. Lakshman Mane, "Dalitanchya Bhashanace Bhandval," *Maharashtra Times*, June 14, 1976.

22. For instance, Panther Sayyed Nizami was described as a *goonda* from Nagpada who ran with a gang. Some Panthers may have engaged in petty thievery. Lata Murugkar, *Dalit Panther Calval* (Pune: Sugawa Prakashan, 1995). On the lumpenproletariat as a sartorial category in Marx, see Peter Stallybrass, "Marx and Heterogeneity: Thinking the Lumpenproletariat," *Representations* 30 (1990): 69 95.

23. "The Worli Report," *Secularist* 37–38 (January–April 1976): 27.

24. For every Rs. 100 earned, members were to pay annual dues of Rs. 1, of which 0.50 was sent to the central body treasurer, 0.25 to the district, 0.13 to the subdistrict office, and 0.12 to the *chhavni*. *Dalit Pantherchi Ghatana ani Karyakram* [Panthers Constitution and Activities] (n.p., n.d.), Gangadhar Pantawane Collection.

25. By 1974, Raja Dhale told a scholar of the Dalit Panthers that there were 1,000 registered Panthers in each *taluka*, and 200,000 members spread across seventy-five *chavanis* in Bombay. Murugkar, *Dalit Panther*, 79. Statistics are hard to come by, but it was generally the case that youth supported the Panthers, while their parents supported the RPI. The Panthers' assertive displays and challenge to the status quo was recognized, even when there was criticism of the Panther's organizational anarchy and discomfort with their vitriolic speech.

26. Namdeo Dhasal, "Dalit Pantherchi Ganagaulan" [Ballad of the Dalit Panthers]; *Abkadai*, Divali Ank (1974): 117.

27. *Dalit Pantherchi Bhumika* [The Dalit Panthers' Position], in Arjun Dangle, *Dalit Sahitya: Ek Abhas* [Dalit Literature: A Study] (Mumbai: Maharashtra Rajya Sahitya Sanskriti Mandal, 1978).

28. Ibid., 5.

29. Vasant Dhamankar, with a foreword by Raja Dhale, *Gair Republican Pudhari, Bichari Paddalit Janata, Ani Dalit Panther* [Corrupt Republican Leaders, Unfortunate Oppressed Dalits, and the Dalit Panthers] (n.p., 1974), 7. This pamphlet was published in response to B. C. Kamble, *Republican Paksha-Aikya, Tikakarana Uttara, Mhanje Bharatiya Rajkaranacha Dhavatha Adhava* (n.p., n.d.).

30. Dhamankar, *Gair Republican Pudhari*, 5.

31. Kamble, *Dr. Babasaheb Ambedkaranchya*, 7.

32. The Buddhist population went from 141,426 in the 1951 census to 3,206,142 in 1961.

33. *Prabuddha Bharat*, June 29, 1957.

34. P. N. Rajbhoj, Narayan Kajrolkar, and Jagjivan Ram—all non-Mahar Dalits of Congress persuasion—opposed reservations for Buddhists.

35. R. D. Bhandare, *The Problem of the Buddhists: What Category? Memorandum Submitted to Committee on Reservations for Backward Classes in the Services* (Bombay, 1964), 204.

36. This double bind arose in two major cases involving the right of Buddhist candidates to be elected to reserved seats, *Karwad v. Shambharkar* (1958) and *Ganpat v. Presiding Officer* (1975). Both cases illustrated the difficulties of proving public conversion to Buddhism and distinguishing Buddhist practices from the range of sectarian differences accommodated under the legal definition of Hinduism. When conversion was proved, as happened in *Punjabrao v. Meshram* (1964), candidates lost the right to constitutional safeguards and protections.

37. *Bauddha Houn Maharac Rahile* [They Became Buddhist but Remained Mahars] (n.p., n.d.), Gangadhar Pantawane Collection.

38. The Government of India recognized Buddhists in the (President's) Scheduled Caste Order in 1990. *Times of India*, May 8, 1990.

39. *Blitz* carried news of the Panther split on July 20, 1974, followed by *Maratha* on July 23, 1974.

40. Dhale and Dhasal were initially associated with Communists and Socialists, respectively; their first formulations of the Dalit were in materialist terms. Many scholars and activists associated with the left believed that the Panthers had radicalized Dalit politics with their "total critique" and that "if there had been an autonomous, grass-roots Dalit leadership, then the seeds of revolution would have sprouted amongst the Panthers." Gail Omvedt, "Varga Ladha Ki Jati Yuddha," *Kranti Jyoti*, Varsha 2, Ank 10, 11, 12 (October–December 1979): 58.

41. Raja Dhale, *Dr. Ambedkar and Revolution* (Bombay, 1976).

42. Raja Dhale, *Eknistha Communist: Eknishta Ki Eknishtha* [The Determined Communist: Egotistical or Dedicated] (Bombay, 1974). The title is a clever play on words: there is a subtle difference between *eknishta*, used ironically to mean "arrant" or "extreme," and *eknishtha*, which means "determined." Dhale is playing on the difference between commitment to a cause and self-serving politics.

43. Dhamankar, *Gair Republican Pudhari*.

44. Dhasal slowly moved away from Marxism. He supported Indira Gandhi

during the emergency years (1975–77) and embraced her brand of authoritarian populism. He joined the Shiv Sena in 1997.

45. Hansen, *Wages of Violence*, 65.

46. Anne Philips, *The Politics of Presence* (Oxford: Oxford University Press, 1995).

47. The first Panther meeting, in Siddharthnagar, central Bombay, on July 9, 1972, discussed caste atrocities and was important in publicizing the boycott against Dalits in Bawda, Poona district, and the assault on two Dalit women in Brahmangaon.

48. Dhasal, "Dalit Pantherchi Ganagaulan." 108–18, 136–50.

49. The Panthers filed a report on November 4, 1972, that *sainiks* were disturbing their speeches and taunting supporters. Murugkar, *Dalit Panther,* 151.

50. Baba Adhav interview in Murugkar, *Dalit Panther,* 104.

51. K. S. Thackeray, known as "Prabodhankar," was a central figure in the development of non-Brahmin polemics, which were discussed in chapter 1. His son, Shiv Sena supremo Bal Thackeray's rhetoric and command over the idiomatic and expressive registers of Marathi accord with this tradition, though his political extremism is distinctive.

52. Early English accounts of Marathi Dalit *sahitya* (literature) can be found in the *Times of India* supplement, "Dalit Literature: Voices of the Oppressed," vol. 4, no. 17, November 25, 1973, compiled by Dileep Padgaonkar; *Vagartha*, no. 12 (1977), ed. Meenakshi Mukherjee; and the special issue of *Journal of South Asian Literature* 27, no. 1 (Winter–Spring 1982), ed. Philip Engblom and Eleanor Zelliot. See also Arjun Dangle. ed., *Poisoned Bread: Translations from Modern Marathi Literature* (Hyderabad: Orient Longman, 1992). For a recent account of Dalit *sahitya* that also engages with writing in other Indian languages, see Eleanor Zelliot, "Dalit Literature, Language and Identity," in *Language in South Asia,* ed. Braj Kachru and S. N. Sridhar (Cambridge: Cambridge University Press, forthcoming); Jayashree Gokale, "Bhakti or Vidroha: Continuity and Changes in Dalit Sahitya," *Journal of Asian and African Studies* 5, no. 2 (1988): 29–42; Arjun Dangle, *Dalit Sahity: Ek Abhyas* (Pune: Sugawa, 1998); Yeshwant Manohar, *Dalit Sahitya: Siddharth va Svarup* (Aurangabad: Prabodhan Prakashan, 1987); and Shankarrao Kharat, *Dalit Vangmay: Prerana va Pravritti* (Pune: Inamdar Bandhu Prakshan, 1978).

53. Dhasal, "Dalit Pantherchi Ganagaulan," 117.

54. Literary representations of the Dalit pose difficult questions of responsibility, witnessing, and the fine line between testimony and aesthetic experimentation. There is no study of Dalit *sahitya* that attends to the circulation of texts and how they transformed the reading practices of progressive, middle-class Marathi readers. Aniket Jaaware has argued that Dalit *sahitya* is not merely ethnographic or historical evidence about Dalit life, but that it occupies a critical position in the history of Marathi literary modernism as a distinctive mode of literary experimentation. Aniket Jaaware, "Eating and Eating with, the Dalit: A Reconsideration Touching upon Marathi Poetry," in *Indian Poetry: Modernism and After,* ed. K. Satchidanandan (New Delhi: Sahitya Akademi, 2001), 262–93.

55. See the frontispiece in Pawar, *Baluta.* Next to this short poem is a line

from Jack London: "This stone, which was removed from the structure of a building, is therefore rendered useless."

56. Prahlad Chendwankar, "White Collar Brahmin," in *Audit* (Bombay: Abhinav Prakashan, 1976), 29–30.

57. Neera Adarkar and Meena Menon, *One Hundred Years, One Hundred Voices: The Millworkers of Girangaon: An Oral History* (Calcutta: Seagull Books, 2004); and Rajnarayan Chandavarkar, *Imperial Power and Popular Politics: Class, Resistance and the State in India, C. 1850–1950* (Cambridge: Cambridge University Press, 1998).

58. Rajnarayan Chandavarkar, *Origins of Industrial Capitalism in India: Business Strategies and the Working Classes in Bombay, 1900–1940* (Cambridge: Cambridge University Press, 1994), 212–18. On the relationship between *tamasgirs* and gymnasiums, see N. G. Bhaware, "Dr. Babsaheb Ambedkaranchya Dalitoddhar Calvalitil Dalit Shahir" [Dalit Performers in Dr. Ambedkar's Dalit Uplift Movement], *AD*, Divali Ank (1982): 25–34.

59. Hansen, *Wages of Violence*, 185–193.

60. Quoted in S. P. Punalekar, "Dalit Literature and Dalit Identity," in *Dalit Identity and Politics,* ed. Ghanshyam Shah (Dehli: Sage Publications, 2001), 228.

61. J. P. Orr, *The Bombay City Improvement Trust from 1898 to 1909* (Bombay: Times Press, 1911), quoted in A. R. Burnett-Hurst, *Labour and Housing in Bombay: A Study in the Economic Conditions of the Wage Earning Classes in Bombay* (London: P. S. King and Son, 1925), 31. The 1896 Bombay plague epidemic, which prompted an exodus of half the city's population, foreshadowed the demolition of most of the inner city north of the fort area by the Bombay City Improvement Trust (BIT). The development of modern Bombay through wide-ranging reforms in the urban core grew out of urban elites' fear that disease was spreading to their bungalows from overcrowded inner city slums. Ruthlessly demolishing tenements and seizing lands in the name of public health and open spaces, the BIT planned and developed most of the Island City. The 1918 textile mill strike and the food riots of 1919 renewed fears of social unrest. The government responded by creating an independent body, the BDD, which operated between 1920 and 1926. The BDD was charged with building five hundred thousand one-room tenements using the cheapest materials and methods of building possible. Ninety-four percent of the chawls remained vacant in 1926. By 1937, 52 percent were vacant. Only in 1949 were the BDD chawls fully inhabited. For an analysis of how plague management provided the BIT with cover for aggressive urban planning, see Prashant Kidambi, *The Making of an Indian Metropolis: Colonial Governance and Public Culture in Bombay, 1890–1920* (London: Ashgate, 2007), 49–114. On failed efforts to institute housing for the working poor, see Sandip Hazareesingh, "Colonial Modernism and the Flawed Paradigms of Urban Renewal: The Uneven Development of Bombay City, 1900–1925," *Urban History* 28, no. 2 (2001): 235–55. For a brief history of the BDD chawls, see Vanessa Caru, "The Worli BDD Chawls: A Case Study, 1922–1947" (unpublished paper).

62. Distance from the workplace and surveillance of workers' political activities contributed to the continued problem of vacant chawls: in 1925 a repre-

sentative of the Bombay Millowners Association complained that 76 percent of the chawls stood empty. Dick Kooiman, *Bombay Textile Labour: Managers, Trade Unionists and Officials, 1918–1939* (Amsterdam: Free University Press, 1989), 17.

63. "Concealed Fascism," *Economic and Political Weekly* 9, nos. 1–2 (January 12, 1974): 1; "Attack on Dalit Panthers," *Economic and Political Weekly* 9, no. 3 (January 18, 1974): 51–52. See also Dinu Ranadive, "Worli Dangalichi Parshvabhumi Va Rajakiya Paksha," *Maharashtra Times,* February 22, 1974; and Dinu Ranadive, "Worli Dangaline Balamnavar Anishtha Parinam," *Maharashtra Times,* February 22, 1974.

64. "Dalit Panthers: Another View," *Economic and Political Weekly* 9 (May 4, 1974): 715–16.

65. *Navakal,* February 18, 1973. Until 1977, the Panthers boycotted elections as symbols of state corruption. The Communist-affiliated Girni Kamgar Union, established in 1938, was a powerful presence in Bombay's working-class neighborhoods until its decline in the 1950s and its final demise after the historic 1982 textile mill strike led by Dada Samant. Rajni Desai, *The Long Haul: The Historic Bombay Textile Strike.* (Bombay: BUILD Documentation Centre, 1987). The GKU played a key role in the 1974 election.

66. Anil Avchat, "Angry Pantherchi Zunj" [Angry Panthers' Combat], *Manohar,* September 25, 1974.

67. A similar situation occurred more than a decade later in 1987, when the Bombay government published *The Riddles of Rama and Krishna,* which criticized inconsistencies in the Vedas and depicted Hindu gods as cruel and lascivious. As demands grew for banning this book, ten thousand Dalits staged a rally in November 1987. The Sena burnt copies of the book and there were altercations between Dalits and *sainiks* in many parts of Bombay. Dalit youth damaged the Hutatma Chowk, which commemorates the martyrs of the Samyukta Maharashtra movement. In response, Chagan Bhujbal, an OBC leader of the Shiv Sena, had the structure purified, inflaming Dalit sentiment.

68. A *lathi* charge is a crowd-control tactic in which police rush at crowds armed with *lathis,* or thick wooden staffs.

69. The Naigaum and Delisle Road chawls are geographically proximate to private chawls constructed by millowners.

70. S. B. Bhasme, *Report of the Commission of Inquiry on the Worli and Naigaum B.D.D. Chawls Disturbances* (Mumbai: Government of India, 1976), 12 (hereafter Bhasme Report). The commission collected statements from the public between September 23 and November 28, 1975. Legal arguments concluded on February 19, 1976. In all, forty-six police witnesses, seventy party witnesses, and two special commission witnesses were questioned. Subsequent quotations from commission findings are from this report unless otherwise noted.

71. Ibid., 192.

72. Ibid., 222–23.

73. Ibid., 2.

74. Witness 47, Gangubai Ganpat Jagtap, with regard to the incidents of January 6, 1974, Bhasme Report, 55.

75. C.W. [Criminal Witness] 109, Vishnu Gopal Mahadik, with regard to the incidents of January 18, 1974, Bhasme Report, 150.

76. Witness 52, Chindu Hari Bhalerao, with regard to the incidents of January 9, 1976, Bhasme Report, 56.

77. C.W. 13, Assistant Police Inspector Chavan, Bhasme Report, 77.

78. The anti-Sikh riots of 1984 reflect a similar pattern of targeting Sikh neighborhoods with the tacit cooperation of government ministers and local police. More troubling is the impact of anti-Muslim violence—from the Bhiwandi riots of 1970 to the Bombay riots of 1993—followed by sustained patterns of social segregation. The recent Gujarat pogroms of 2002 provide the most chilling evidence of a state-sponsored strategy of "Muslim cleansing." *We Have No Orders to Save You* (New York: Human Rights Watch, 2002), http://hrw.org/reports/2002/india.

79. Bhasme Report, 318.

80. Balsara, then assistant commissioner of police, police witness, with regard to the events of January 18 and 19, 1974, Bhasme Report, 73.

81. The reporter, Anil Avachat, noted that the police seemed to know where the Sena supporters were stationed: "So somehow or the other they [the police] wanted to disperse the morcha. Either they knew that there was going to be trouble near Laxmi Cottage or they had arranged for the trouble." Anil Avachat, "Dalit Pancheri Zunj," *Manohar*, September 27, 1974, reprinted as evidence in the Bhasme Report, 66–68.

82. Dhasal noted that the Panthers started using Molotov cocktails during the Worli riots. Dhasal, cited in Anil Avachat, "Dalit Pantherchi Zhunj," *Manohar*, September 27, 1974, 141.

83. Bhasme Report, 315.

84. Ibid., 263.

85. Ibid., 190.

86. Ibid., 189.

87. Ibid.,165–66. The Shiv Sena was already notorious for interfering with police appointments and having troublesome policemen dismissed. At least one *matka* manufacturer mentioned in the Bhasme Report was associated with the Shiv Sena and was a member of the Police Advisory Board. The Sena and the Dalit Panthers controlled gangs in working-class neighborhoods.

88. "In the 1970s, a complete terminology and set of narrative frames derived from the American gangster terminology became ever more popular in descriptions of Bombay's underworld." Hansen, *Wages of Violence*, 188. The focus on gangs was evident in the Worli riots. Bhasme noted that, "although disturbances assumed communal form to a certain extent, it was sheer goondaism." Bhasme Report, 165.

89. In a 1960s study of working-class neighborhoods in the heart of Bombay, workers were asked how they spent their leisure time. They often said they went "roaming," which they considered "a mode of relaxation." K. Patel, *Rural Labour in Industrial Bombay* (Bombay: Popular Prakashan, 1963), quoted in Chandavarkar, *Imperial Power and Popular Politics*, 172.

90. Partha Chatterjee, *Politics of the Governed* (New York: Columbia University Press, 2004), 14.

91. Ibid., 40–41.

92. Hansen, *Wages of Violence*, 49.

93. Allen Feldman, *Formations of Violence* (Chicago: University of Chicago Press, 1991), 5.

94. There was agitation in 1972 over the administration of the Employee Guarantee Scheme. Again in 1974, the Vikas Andolan led huge demonstrations in the Aurangabad, Nanded, and Parbhani districts demanding regional development on parity with other parts of the state.

95. *Report on Population of Scheduled Castes and Nava Bauddhas in Districts of Maharashtra, Maharashtra, 1975–1976* (Bombay: Government of Maharashtra, 1977). The figures in this report are based on the 1971 all-India census.

96. D. L. Soman, "Vidyarthi Andolan: Aurangabad," *Manus*, March 1, 1974, 2. See also, *Caste Violence in Marathwada* (Aurangabad: Jagruti Publications, July 1979), a revised version of the submission to the Ramdhan Committee, which visited Marathwada on September 23, 1978. The caste and demographic breakdown of university students can be found in *District-Wide Distribution of SC Students Enrolled in Univ. Departments and Affiliated Colleges, 1977–1978* (Marathwada University, n.d.), appendix 1.

97. *Peoples Education Society Silver Jubilee Report, 1945–1973*, in *People's Education Society* (Bombay, 1974), quoted in Gokhale, *From Concessions to Confrontation*, 195. The PES received much of its funding from central and state governments. In Bombay, the PES founded its first institution, the Siddharth College of Arts and Sciences, in 1946. The Siddharth College of Commerce and Economics, the Siddharth College of Law, and the Dr. Ambedkar College of Commerce and Economics soon followed. The Bombay PES also operated a high school and a student hostel. By 1973, there were twenty-nine PES institutions in Bombay, Pune, Aurangabad, Mahad, Dapoli, and Pandharpur cities and in Dhulia, Jalgaon, and Parbhani districts. The PES also ran BC hostels in Gujarat and Karnataka.

98. The PES received land from His Highness the Nizam of Hyderabad on a long-term lease. The Nizam also provided funds to start colleges. Milind College, the first PES institution in Marathwada, was established in 1958.

99. Gokhale, *From Concessions to Confrontation*, 198.

100. Ashok M. and Jayant M. Baile, *Marathwada Udrekacha Itihas* [A History of the Marathwada Uprising] (Mumbai, n.d.), 16 (emphasis added). Marathwada University had the most caste-diverse student body.

101. *RCSCST, 25th Report, 1977–1978* (Dehli: Government of India, 1978), part 2, appendix 64.

102. Gokhale, *From Concessions to Confrontation*, 200.

103. A commentator drew attention to echoes of Mao's Long March. Interestingly, he also equated the Long March with the Varkari *samata dindi*, a procession for equality. Narendra Kukade and Subhash Joshi, *Namantar: Samata Sangharshache Nave Parva* (Kolhapur, n.d.), 5. The Varkari *dindis*, comprising small groups of devotees from around the region, gathered at Pandharpur on Ashadha Ekadashi. They thus reenacted the ritual of migration on foot toward Vithoba, the god of the Dhangar shepherds (also signified as the "Krishna" of the Puranic pantheon), performing the *abhangs* of Eknath Janabai, Namdev, and Tukaram along the way. By associating the Long March with cosmological time and the importance of pilgrimage for the Varkari tradition, the authors of this pamphlet gestured to the university as a ritually charged space.

104. R. S. Morkhandikar, "Marathwada Riots 1978: Dilemmas of a Dalit Movement," *Punjab Journal of Politics* 9, no. 1 (January–June 1985): 42.

105. Raja Dhale headed Mass Movement, Namdev Dhasal headed the Dalit Panthers, and Arun Kamble and Gangadhar Gade led the Aurangabad unit. The Panthers had decided to launch a statewide agitation to secure support for the renaming of the university. The Nagarik Vidyarthi Kriti Samiti (Student and Citizens Action Committee) was composed of the pro-*namantar* faction led by Govindbhai Shroff and Anant Bhalerao. The latter was editor of the newspaper *Marathwada*.

106. Chief Minister Vasantdada Patil initially supported the renaming, but backtracked and argued that educational institutions should not be named after individuals. By July 27, 1978, the new chief minister, Sharad Pawar, who headed a coalition ministry, proposed the name Dr. Babasaheb Ambedkar Marathwada University.

107. Moin Shakir, "Marathwada-Pawar's Christening in Blood," *Weekly Sunday*, n.d.

108. Anonymous, interviewed in *Research Team Investigating the Marathwada Riots* (n.p., n.d.).

109. M. B. Chitnis, *Namantaraviruddha Athyachari Andolan: Kahi Prashna* [Anti-Namantar Violence: Some Questions] (Aurangabad: Modern Printing Press, 1978), 10.

110. R. S. Gawai, quoted in D. N. Sandanshiv, *Reflections on the Counter-Revolution in Marathwada* (Aurangabad: Anand Publications, 1978). Sandanshiv's text was submitted to the members of the Parliamentary Committee who visited Aurangabad during the riots. The original quotation appears to be from the *Illustrated Weekly*.

111. *Maharashtra Times*, August 16, 1978.

112. "Marathwada Vidyapeeth Namantar: Dusri Bazu Hi Samzhun Ghya!" [Renaming Marattwada University: Understand the Other Side], *Mumbai Sakal*, October 26, 1978.

113. Morkhandikar, "Marathwada Riots 1978."

114. Sulabha Brahme, G. K. Brahme, and S. H. Pore, *Regional Planning: A Case Study of Marathwada Region* (Poona: Gokhale Institute of Political Economy, 1975); and Sulabha Brahme and Anant Phadke, *Dalit-Savarna Tanav: Ek Mulgami Vishleshan* [Dalit-Caste Hindu Tension: A Radical Analysis] (Pune: Shankar Brahme Samaj Vignan Granthalaya, 1972).

115. *Caste Violence in Marathwada*, 3.

116. Sandanshiv, *Reflections on the Counter-Revolution in Marathwada*, 25. A PES study found 330 affected villages, with 1,725 houses destroyed and 15,250 houses affected. V. D. Gaikwad, *Marathwada Vidyapeeth Namantar Atyachari Andolan: Ek Abhyas* (Aurangabad, n.d.). The home minister said that 900 households in 70 villages were affected, comprising 6,370 people. S. Punalekar, *Marathwada Riots: Aspects of Caste and Class in Social Tension* (Surat: Centre for Social Studies, 1981).

117. Chitnis, *Namantaraviruddha Athyachari Andolan*, 10.

118. Morkhandikar, "Marathwada Riots 1978," 48.

119. *Manohar*, August 20–26, 1978, 6–7.

120. Morkhandikar, "Marathwada Riots 1978," 40.

121. Brahme and Phadke, *Dalit-Savarna Tanav: Ek Mulgami Vishleshan*, 15.

122. *Report of the Commission on the Welfare of Scheduled Castes and Scheduled Tribes, Presented to the Lok and Rajya Sabhas on the 30th of April, 1979* (Delhi: Government of India, 1979). This report called on the state government to institute a judicial inquiry into the riots in Marathwada. The government of Maharashtra turned down the request "in the public interest."

123. In the 1980s, struggles over *gaayran zamin* (common grazing lands) became a major site of conflict between Dalits and Shiv Sena in Marathwada. *Sainiks* let out cattle on Dalit lands, cut off physical access, or instigated economic and social boycotts against Dalits to challenge their economic independence. For a sophisticated analysis of the meaning of caste violence, see Gopal Guru, "Dalit Killings in Marathwada," *Economic and Political Weekly* 26, no. 51 (December 21, 1991): 2926–30. See also Amrita Abraham, "A Report from Marathwada," *Economic and Political Weekly* 13, no. 36 (September 9, 1978): 1536–40; and Atyachar Virodhi Samiti, "The Marathwada Riots: A Report," *Economic and Political Weekly* 14, no. 19 (May 12, 1979): 845–52.

124. *Report of the Commission on the Welfare of Scheduled Castes and Scheduled Tribes*, 1979.

125. Ibid.

126. As a result of anti-Dalit violence, there were demands for separate Dalit villages and calls for Dalits to take up arms. R. K. Kshirsagar, *Dalitancha Jahirnama* (Aurangabad: Anand Prakashan, 1978). Also see Gail Omvedt, "Class Struggle or Caste War," *Frontier* 2 (September 30, 1978).

127. *Marathwada*, July 27, 1978.

128. Govindbhai Shroff, "Why Namaantar Alone?" in *Marathwada Nagarik Samiti* (n.p., n.d.), 33.

129. *Illustrated Weekly*, September 10–16, 1978.

130. Sandanshiv, *Reflections on the Counter-Revolution in Marathwada*, 18.

131. For popular accounts of the *namavistar*, see Venkat Balande, *Namantar Sangarsh Parva* (Latur: Amit Publications, 1995); Sukhdev Navale, *Namantar te Namavistar: Kahi Ghatana, Kahi Ghadamodi* (Pune: Vasant Vyakhyanmala, 1994); and Anil Nitanware, *Namantar: Swapna ani Satya* (Amraoti: Amol Prakashan, 1992). For a genealogy of the violence, see Gopal Guru, "Violence against Dalits in Marathwada," *Economic and Political Weekly* 29, no. 9 (February 26, 1994): 469–72.

132. The Sena's efforts controverted law and contrasted with Dalit victims' experience of the legal system. In 1996, there was a five-year delay in the disposal of atrocity cases. Of the 875 cases registered under the act, 692 were pending investigation; 1,918 of the 1,921 cases registered in 1993 were pending, and 1,066 of the 1,449 cases registered in 1992 were pending. "Failure to Meet Domestic and International Legal Standards to Protect Dalits," chapter 10 in *Broken People: Caste Violence against India's "Untouchables"* (New York: Human Rights Watch, 1999), http://www.hrw.org/legacy/reports/1999/india.

133. Author's field notes, April 17, 1996.

134. Louis Althusser, "Ideology and Ideological State Apparatuses," in *Notes*

toward an Investigation: Lenin and Philosophy and Other Essays (London: New Left Books, 1971), 127–88.

135. Feldman, *Formations of Violence*, 259. My arguments in this section are inspired by Feldman's brilliant theorization of political and symbolic violence.

136. *Research Report on Holocaust in Marathwada, 1978* (Pune: Pune University, School of Interdisciplinary Studies, 1978).

137. Chitnis, *Namantaraviruddha Athyachari Andolan*, 11.

138. The organized left argued that Dalit leaders were preventing a broader caste-class coalition. See Chandragupta Chaudhari, *Marathwadyachi Dangal: Kahi Prashna, Kahi Uttare* (Bombay: Maharashtra Council Press, Communist Party of India [Marxist], n.d.). Gail Omvedt argues that "overall the left has not understood economic, social, and religious issues together. And they have tended to form single-caste organizations." Omvedt, "Varga Ladha Ki Jati Yuddha," 58. Sharad Patil's unique effort to write a heterogeneous history of capital through a new synthesis of Phule, Marx, and Ambedkarvad addresses Brahminism as a distinct social form and *gulamgiri* (enslaved or bonded caste labor) as its perverse instantiation. Patil has throughout tried to embed Indian (Hindu) history within the universal narrative of capital and to distinguish its exemplary particularity, *caste labor*. Sharad Patil, *Dasa-Shudra Slavery* (Pune: Sugawa Prakashan, 1991).

139. Gokhale, *From Concessions to Confrontation*, 291.

6. THE SEXUAL POLITICS OF CASTE

1. Ann Laura Stoler, "'In Cold Blood': Hierarchies of Credibility and the Politics of Colonial Narratives," *Representations*, no. 37 (Winter 1992): 151–89.

2. *Yadu and Others v. the State of Maharashtra* was filed in Gangapur *taluka* as case number 768/64. It was shifted to the Aurangabad District and Sessions Court when both parties alleged that there was undue pressure and interference in the case. The *taluka* court ruled on December 28, 1964, under the supervision of Judicial Magistrate First Class P. E. Vani. The case was filed in Aurangabad District and Sessions Court as Criminal Appeal no. 5/1965 on January 16, 1965. The sessions court passed judgment on June 30, 1965, under the supervision of Judge C. J. Dighe. The case then went to the Bombay High Court as Criminal Revision Application no. 622/1965, and Justice V. M. Tarkhunde ruled on March 29, 1966. Both the sessions court and the Bombay High Court upheld the judgment passed by the judicial magistrate, with slight modification.

3. Ranajit Guha, "Chandra's Death," in *Subaltern Studies: Writings on South Asian History and Society,* vol. 5, ed. Ranajit Guha (Delhi: Oxford University Press, 1988), 140.

4. The representation of the social world as objective fact is inextricable from our perception of social distinction and difference as transparent or real. I use the term "publicity" to refer to those evidentiary practices and knowledge protocols that mediate or enframe social representation *as information*. I draw here on Timothy Mitchell's resonant description of "enframing" as the ideological work of rendering concept into image, of materializing or visually condensing

emergent structures of knowledge and power. See also his more recent arguments about the transformation of information into expertise. Timothy Mitchell, *Colonising Egypt* (Berkeley: University of California Press, 1991), and *Rule of Experts* (Berkeley: University of California Press, 2003).

5. *Marathwada* focused on regional underdevelopment from the 1960s onward, and articulated a distinctive Marathwada *asmita* (identity) formed in opposition to the Nizam of Hyderabad, who had ruled over the region until 1948. Given its Socialist leanings, the newspaper framed its opposition to feudal rule, rather than formulating this as an explicitly anti-Muslim position.

6. *MLA Debates,* vol. 12, part 2, March 11–April 3, 1964, 693–703 (discussion under a cut motion); and *MLC Debates,* vol. 12, no. 3, February 14–April 3, 1964.

7. Aurangabad District and Sessions Court, Judgement ón Criminal Appeal no. 5/1965, judgment of June 30, 1965, under the supervision of C. J. Dighe.

8. Ibid.

9. For the etiology of scandal as a specific form of publicity, see Nicholas B. Dirks, *The Scandal of Empire: India and the Creation of Imperial Britain* (Cambridge, MA: Belknap Press of Harvard University Press, 2006); Anupama Rao, "Problems of Violence, States of Terror: Torture in Colonial India," in *Discipline and the Other Body: Correction, Corporeality and Colonialism,* ed. Steven Pierce and Anupama Rao (Durham, NC: Duke University Press, 2006), 151–85; and Rajeswari Sunder Rajan, *The Scandal of the State: Women, Law, and Citizenship in Postcolonial India* (Durham, NC: Duke University Press, 2003).

10. *Marathwada,* January 5, 1964, front page.

11. Aurangabad District and Sessions Court, Criminal Appeal no. 5/1965, judgment of June 30, 1965, under the supervision of C. J. Dighe.

12. Ibid.

13. D. R. Nagaraj, *The Flaming Feet: A Study of the Dalit Movement in India* (Bangalore: South Forum Press, 1993), 38.

14. *Taluka* court judgment, December 28, 1964, under the supervision of Judicial Magistrate First Class P. E. Vani (emphasis added).

15. Judge Dighe noted that Dalit women had been carrying water through the village for two years, indicating that they were banned from doing so earlier.

16. Saurabh Dube, *Untouchable Pasts: Religion, Identity, and Power among a Central Indian Community, 1780–1950* (Albany: SUNY Press, 1998).

17. *Taluka* court judgment, December 28, 1964, under the supervision of Judicial Magistrate First Class P. E. Vani.

18. Aurangabad District and Sessions Court, Criminal Appeal no. 5/1965, judgment of June 30, 1965, under the supervision of C. J. Dighe.

19. Ibid.

20. Ibid. (emphasis added).

21. Ibid. (emphasis added).

22. It is important that S., picking up on statements by the perpetrators, recalled access to water as the source of the Sirasgaon conflict.

23. Aurangabad District and Sessions Court, Criminal Appeal no. 5/1965, judgment of June 30, 1965, under the supervision of C. J. Dighe.

24. Ibid. (emphasis added).

25. See E. Valentine Daniel, *Charred Lullabies: Chapters in an Anthropography of Violence* (Princeton, NJ: Princeton University Press, 1996), 81–83.

26. Lee Schlesinger notes that a village usually has one *ves* in each cardinal direction. Personal communication, March 21, 1998. In Sirasgaon there was only one *ves*, and it was in ruins.

27. We have already seen that *muralis'* marriages were advertised in the pages of *Somavanshiya Mitra*. The following intercaste marriages were noted in *Bahishkrit Bharat:* a Mahar girl named Shevanti with a Mang boy named Narayan Kunde, in Bhamburde, Pune, BB, May 20, 1927; Lakshmibai Kamble, a Dalit Mahar, with Dattaram Rangnath Upasak, a Maratha, BB, November 12, 1928; Devikabai Gaikwad, a Dalit woman, with a Brahmin with the last name Sathe, in Pune, April 12, 1929. The editor of *Janata,* the Deshashta Brahmin B. R. Kadrekar, was married to a Dalit woman. The editor of *Muknayak,* Pandurang Bhatkar, had married a Brahmin woman. Activist D. G. Jadhav was married to Kamlakant Chitre's daughter. Chitre, a member of the Social Service League, was involved in the Mahad *satyagraha. Janata* often carried congratulatory notices on these intercaste marriages.

28. Accounts of men and women lynched for engaging in intercaste relationships or eloping to marry are continued evidence of the political volatility of sexual relations that transgress caste boundaries. For an analysis of elopement in colonial and postcolonial perspective, see Prem Chowdhry, *Contentious Marriages, Eloping Couples: Gender, Caste and Patriarchy in Northern India* (New Delhi: Oxford University Press, 2007). Famous cases include the "Bodi riots," which took place from September to October 1989 after a Dalit woman was sexually abused and killed in southwest Tamil Nadu. As Dalit activists called for the abduction of upper-caste women, a caste riot ensued, leading to thirty deaths, mass injuries, and damage to property. In Chundur, a village in Andhra Pradesh, at least eight (and up to fifteen) people were hacked to death on August 6, 1991, due to unsubstantiated rumors that a Dalit boy had molested a young woman from the dominant Reddy caste at a movie theater. On September 22, 1992, Bhanwari Devi, a grassroots worker (*sathin*) in the Rajasthan government's Women's Development Programme, was gang-raped in front of her husband for reporting a child marriage. The police refused to register the case, arguing that she was too old and unattractive to have been raped by anyone. The trial judge acquitted the accused, noting, "An upper-caste man could not have defiled himself by raping a lower-caste woman." "Attacks on Dalit Women: A Pattern of Impunity," in *Broken People: Caste Violence against India's "Untouchables"* (New York: Human Rights Watch, 1999), 176–77, http://www.hrw.org/legacy/reports/1999/india; K. Balagopal, "Chundur and Other Chundurs," *Economic and Political Weekly* 26, no. 42 (October 19, 1991): 2399–2405; Gabrielle Dietrich, "Dalit Movements and Women's Movements," in *Reflections on the Women's Movement: Religion, Ecology, Development* (New Delhi: Horizon India, 1992), 73–93; Kancha Iliah, "The Chundur Carnage: The Struggle of Dalits," in *At Cross-Roads: Dalit Movement Today,* ed. Sandeep Pendse (Bombay: Vikas Adhyayan Kendra, 1994); and Samata Sanghatana Report, "Upper Caste Violence: Study of Chunduru Carnage," *Economic and Political Weekly* 26, no. 36 (September 7, 1991): 2079–84. We see here that the overdetermination of sexual violence as caste pun-

ishment forecloses the possibility of cross-caste desire, which runs the risk of being misrecognized as violence. Or else, that sexual desire is always already aligned with patriarchal power, as in the case of Dalit men's desire for upper-caste women, as a recent study argues. S. Anandhi, J. Jeyaranjan, and Rajan Krishnan, "Work, Caste and Competing Masculinities: Notes from a Tamil Village," *Economic and Political Weekly* (October 26, 2002). Intercaste marriage thus remains a biopolitical frontier for caste emancipation.

29. Ambedkarite politics was shaped by negotiations with the colonial state and Indian nationalism, and worked through institutional forms such as the caste association. Between 1917 and 1927, three national women's organizations had emerged—the Women's India Association, the National Council of Women in India, and the All-India Women's Conference, with the latter emerging as the premier women's organization by 1940. Dalit women's organizations grew out of this conjuncture, which saw the emergence of the woman activist as a distinct figure. Two women, Savitribai Borade and Ambubai Gaikwad, were appointed to *Janata* in 1930. By 1930, Mahila Parishads, or Women's Conferences, were being organized, and in 1936 the Mahila Parishad resolved to reserve one of three seats for SC women in provincial legislative councils. The ILP years—which saw increased militancy around caste labor more generally—saw demands for equal wages for female mill workers, support for compulsory education for Dalit girls through scholarships, and programs to encourage young women to finish their education before getting married. Urmil Pawar and Meenakshi Moon, *Amhihi Itihas Ghadavila: Ambedkar Calvalit Striyancha Sahbhag* [We Too Made History: Women's Participation in the Ambedkar Movement] (Mumbai: Stree Uvac Prakashan, 1998), 73. Anjana Deshbratar noted the social segregation of Dalit women at the 1938 meeting of the All-India Women's Congress in Nagpur. This led to support for separate organization of Dalit women. The All-India Untouchable Women's Conference was formed in 1942, along with the AISCF. Women's employment and education was a focus throughout. Pawar and Moon, *Amhihi Itihas Ghadavila*, 80. Women also played a critical role in the black flag demonstrations in 1946 and the landless struggles of 1956 and 1964. Ibid., 81–84, 100–21.

30. For a discussion of Dalit feminism along with excerpts from selected texts, see Anupama Rao, ed., *Gender and Caste: Contemporary Issues in Indian Feminism* (New Delhi: Kali for Women, 2003).

31. Quoted in Dube, *Untouchable Pasts*, 171. For a moving account of Muli, who pimped Dalit women for a living, see James M. Freeman, *Untouchable: An Indian Life History* (London: George Alien and Unwin, 1979). In *Kolhatyache Por* (Child of the Kolhatis), Kishore Shantabai Kale writes of being born in the community of *tamasha* performers to a mother who abandons him to negligent relatives. The autobiography is an extended meditation on coerced sexual labor and social illegitimacy. Kishore Shantabai Kale, *Against All Odds*, trans. Sandhya Pandey (Delhi: Penguin, 2000).

32. Feminist critiques of Lévi-Strauss's position on marriage as gift exchange are numerous and date to a period in disciplinary anthropology dominated by feminist debates about the geohistorical limits (and theoretical relevance) of "gender" as a category of analysis. The two critiques I find particularly useful are

Gayle Rubin, "The Traffic of Women: Notes on the Political Economy of Sex," in *Towards an Anthropology of Women*, ed. Rayna Reiter (New York: Monthly Review Press, 1975), 157–210; and Marilyn Strathern, *The Gender of the Gift: Problems with Women and Problems with Society in Melanesia* (Berkeley: University of California Press, 1990). Rubin theorizes limits to Marxist, psychoanalytic, and anthropological conceptions of sex/gender, while Strathern revisits the theory of the gift by examining the dangers of Western social categorization occluding Melanesian paradigms of gendered sociality. A sophisticated exploration of the relationship between European social theory and the social history of colonialism in constituting gendered subalternity can be found in Gayatri Chakravorty Spivak, "Scattered Speculations on the Theory of Value," and "Breastgiver," in *In Other Worlds: Essays in Cultural Politics* (New York: Routledge, 1988), 154–78, 222–40.

33. Carole Pateman, *The Sexual Contract* (Stanford, CA: Stanford University Press, 1998), 19–76.

34. Susie Tharu, "The Impossible Subject: Caste and the Gendered Body," in *Gender and Caste*, 261–75.

35. In her brilliant study of the paradoxes of sexual subjugation in the antebellum South, Saidiya Hartman explores how the legal bifurcation of slave as person and property enabled the disappearance of "sexual violence" from the law. Since sexual violence neither incapacitated the slave for work nor inflicted damage to the slave as *value-producing property,* rape and molestation did not figure in the regime of partial commodification that defined chattel slavery. Another enabling paradox, the assumption of the slave's passion (and black sexuality) as provoking consensual sex, also served to occlude sex as violence. Neither the laws of property nor personhood allowed recognition of the constitution of female slave subjectivity through violation. Saidiya Hartman, "Seduction and the Ruse of Power," in *Scenes of Subjection: Terror, Slavery and Self-Making in Nineteenth Century America* (New York: Oxford Unverity), 79–114.

36. Fact-finding report of the Vidarbha Jan Andola Samiti, which visited Khairlanji on October 6, 2006, "Kherlanji Other Reports: A Buddhist Family Massacred," along with other fact-finding and newspaper reports available at Atrocity News, http://atrocitynews.wordpress.com/manuski-centre-khairlanje-report.

37. Anand Teltumbe, "Khairlanji and Its Aftermath: Exploding Some Myths," *Economic and Political Weekly* 42, no. 12 (March 24, 2007): 1019–25.

38. Bhaiyyalal, a witness to the violence (and sole survivor of the Bhotmange family), failed to get the case registered with police. The case was initially dismissed as the handiwork of Maoist extremists; the special inspector general of police was bribed; and government doctors failed to check for sexual assault while conducting the postmortems. No visits from state functionaries or upper-level police were forthcoming. The bodies of the two women were exhumed and a second autopsy conducted on October 5 due to mounting public pressure. *Organised Killings of Dalits in Khairlanji Village, Tal. Mohadi, Dist. Bhandara* (Pune: YASHADA, November 2006).

39. *The Hindu*, September 16, 2008.

40. Smriti Koppikar, quoting Nagsen Sonware, president of the Ambedkar Center for Peace and Justice, in "Beat the Drum," *Outlook,* December 18, 2006.

41. Dalit feminism is agonistic, not antagonistic, to a mainstream Indian feminism that has typically addressed caste as antimodern and antisecular. Like the critique of race and gender by African American feminists who connect racialization with sexual violence, and sexual control with the reproduction of white privilege, Dalit feminists emphasize the role of sexual violence in reproducing caste privilege. For instance, the founding statement of the National Federation of Dalit Women notes that Dalit women are negatively defined within the framework of a hegemonic Brahminical patriarchy that privileges caste and sexual purity. On the other hand, says the National Federation of Dalit Women, Dalit women are also claimed as the sexual property of their community and are subject to bourgeois notions of respectability that are the consequence of the modern patriarchy of the Dalit family. Anupama Rao, introduction to *Gender and Caste*, 1–47.

42. A report by the CID tabulated 1,166 offenses against SCs in 2007, compared to 1,053 during 2006, signifying an increase of 10.73 percent. The report notes an 83.91 percent increase in caste violence between 2002 and 2007. *The Hindu*, September 27, 2008.

7. DEATH OF A *KOTWAL*

1. Given the recent occurrence of this atrocity—it was on appeal at the Aurangabad High Court in 1997 when the police wireless (radio) reports and case documents were procured—the names of individual policemen and the judge have been changed.

2. Giorgio Agamben and Carl Schmitt discuss the logic of exception with regard to the relationship between law and sovereignty. For Agamben, the sovereign's power is reflected in his ability to place himself outside the laws he enacts. Giorgio Agamben, *Homo Sacer: Sovereign Power and Bare Life* (Stanford, CA: Stanford University Press, 1998). Schmitt argued that situations like Germany's constitutional crisis of the 1930s manifest a situation of political emergency that require the abeyance of law to restore political order. The difference between Agamben and Schmitt lies in the former's description of a political paradox, while the latter argues that legal exceptionalism is constitutive of political sovereignty. Carl Schmitt, *The Crisis of Parliamentary Democracy*, trans. Ellen Kennedy (Cambridge, MA: MIT Press, 1985). I suggest that legal exceptionalism is an enduring feature of colonial and postcolonial law, from legislation meant to control collective crime such as Thuggee in the 1830s and 1840s, to racial regulation and postcolonial legislation on domestic violence and caste atrocities. For an argument about the colonial exception, see Anupama Rao and Steven Pierce, "Humanitarianism, Violence, and the Colonial Exception," in *Discipline and the Other Body: Correction, Corporeality and Colonialism*, ed. Steven Pierce and Anupama Rao (Durham, NC: Duke University Press, 2006), 1–35.

3. A case proceeds as follows: (1) the FIR is filed and receives a crime record (CR) number; (2) the police organize the account into the categories of A (where evidence has not been collected), B (registration of a false case), and C (no offense committed); (3) the charge sheet is filed; and (4) the case receives a court case (CC) number once it is sent to the court.

4. SP, Parbhani, to the DIGP, Aurangabad Range, Wireless no. 5023/DSB/91, August 19, 1991 (emphasis added).

5. "Who Killed Ambadas Savne?" *Illustrated Weekly,* September 14, 1991.

6. In "Suggestions for Effective Policing in Rural Areas," Onkar Sharma observed that *patils* and *kotwals* were decaying functions, falling prey to political machinations. "The present set-up of the Village Police is only nominal and its utility nearly nil," he wrote. "This Village Police agency is not in a position to meet the policing requirements of the villages efficiently and satisfactorily." Sharma's discussion about police intervention in the village explicitly recognizes policing as a political issue. *Proceedings of the Eighth Police Science Congress* (Hyderabad, 1970), 239.

7. Wireless no. 4372/DSB/91. Vivek Pandit's *Handbook on Prevention of Atrocities: Scheduled Castes and Scheduled Tribes* (n.p.: Vidhayak Sansad, 1995) was meant to aid activists in understanding the intricacies of the PoA Act. In his introduction, Pandit writes: "On 16th August 1991, Ambadas Savane, a Dalit Kotwal of Pimpri Deshmukh village in Parbhani district of Marathwada, was stoned to death by the upper castes for taking shelter in the temple premises during a heavy shower. I read a small news item in a local newspaper about this gruesome death. I was deeply affected, and fought for justice on his behalf. I could pursue the case using the SC/ST (Prevention of Atrocities) Act."

8. The *Enforcement of Untouchability (Offences) Act 1955: A Survey* (1976) and the *Syndicate Study on Implementation of the Protection of Civil Rights* (1980) are regional studies of the act's effectiveness (the reports can be found at Sardar Vallabhbhai Patel Police Academy, Hyderabad). The reports reflect the perspective of highly placed administrators who trained and sensitized police officers to respond to caste violence. Both reports offer sociological accounts of untouchability and represent it as a social evil that has existed "since time immemorial."

9. Wireless no. 4372/DSB91.

10. This is also noted in SP, Parbhani, to the DIGP, Aurangabad Range, Wireless no. 5023/DSB/91, September 19, 1991.

11. Pimpri Deshmukh was classified as a sensitive village in 1971, according to a confidential report of the CID, noted in ibid. Villages were classified according to the history of caste and communal violence and reports of "terrorist" activity in the area.

12. SP, Parbhani, to the DIGP, Aurangabad Range, Wireless no. 5023/DSB/91, August 19, 1991.

13. A detailed report of the Sawane murder appeared in *Loksatta* on August 28, 1991, twelve days after the murder, which appears to have accelerated inquiries from Bombay.

14. SP, Parbhani, DIGP, Aurangbad, from DIGP (PCR), Wireless no. PCR/M-6/Parbhani/91, August 27, 1991.

15. A supplementary FIR was filed indicating that Kishore Marathe, the police *patil,* was accused in Sawane's murder.

16. Wireless no. 4372/DSB/91, August 19, 1991.

17. PCR Cell Headquarters to Additional Chief Secretary, Government of Maharashta, Wireless no. PCR/M-6/Parbhani/91, August 30, 1991 (notes scribbled on letter).

18. *Report on the spot enquiry by Shri Ram Dhan, Chairman, National Commission SC/ST into the killing of a Scheduled Caste Village Police Kotwal in Village Pimpri Deshmukh, Taluka and District Parbhani (Maharashtra) on 16-8-91,* in PCR Cell documents.

19. Ibid.

20. SP, Parbhani, to the DIGP, Aurangabad Range, Wireless no. 5023/DSB/91, September 19, 1991. It was alleged that Kachru did not mention the installation of the statue and the ensuing tension in his FIR, in the supplementary information gathered on August 30, 1991, or in his deposition before the judicial magistrate first class on October 1, 1991. These are not available with the court documents, so the allegation could not be verified.

21. *Report on the spot enquiry by Shri Ram Dhan, Chairman.*

22. "Motion re: Atrocities Being Committed on the Scheduled Castes and Scheduled Tribes and Other Weaker Sections in the Country," *Lok Sabha Debates,* vol. 3, August 19–22, 1991, 225–94. This debate took about four hours and considered issues ranging from the socioeconomic weakness of SC/ST communities, to the persistence of untouchability as a social practice, to making laws more stringent and effective. Besides the eclectic speaking styles of some members, what stands out is the range of "evidence" they mobilized: stories from the Mahabharata about Eklavya's sacrifice of his thumb to illustrate the historic oppression of Dalits; invocations of Ambedkar's and Gandhi's arguments against untouchability; social and political evidence of the failure to implement reservations effectively; and the destitute conditions under which most members of the SCs and STs lived. Speakers consistently highlighted society's "lack of resolve," as one member put it.

23. Committee on the Welfare of Scheduled Castes and Scheduled Tribes, *Tenth Lok Sabha Report on Atrocities on Scheduled Castes and Scheduled Tribes and Patterns of Social Crimes Towards Them* (n.p., 1992–93), 13. The prime minister also convened a meeting of chief ministers in October to discuss the atrocities issue.

24. Wireless no. PCR/M-6/Parbhani D/T, September 2, 1991.

25. Wireless no. PCR/M-3/Aurangabad 91 D/T, September 6, 1991. The note was sent to all police stations in Marathwada (under the ranges of Beed, Latur, Nanded, Osmanabad, Parbhani); to the DIGP of the Aurangabad Range; to the DSP (PCR) in Aurangabad; and to the special inspector general of police (Crime) in Pune.

26. *Times of India,* September 3, 1991.

27. The Maharashtra state government's *Anusuchit Jati Kalyan Samiti* (Scheduled Caste Welfare Committee) addressed Sawane's murder in two reports: the 1991–92 *Cautha Ahval* (Fourth Report) and the 1995–96 *Pahila Ahval* (First Report). The 1991–92 report noted that the Welfare Committee had conducted a survey of the Dalits (*magasvargiya,* lit. "Backward Class") in Pimpri Deshmukh to propose welfare schemes to build Dalits' confidence (*athmavishwas vadhavinyasathi*) in government.

28. SP, Parbhani, to the DIGP, Aurangabad Range, Wireless no. 5023/DSB/91, August 19, 1991 (emphasis added).

29. "Who Killed Ambadas Savne?" *Illustrated Weekly,* September 14, 1991.

I met Bhangar on July 27, 1996. Though he was a Janata Dal activist when Sawane was murdered, he had since joined the Shiv Sena. His wife accompanied me on my first visit to Pimpri Deshmukh and told me that Bhangar (who came from the OBC community) did not like the Sena ethos but had chosen to go with the party because they gave him a ticket to contest local elections.

30. Scheduled Caste Welfare Committee, *Cautha Ahval* [Fourth Report] (Mumbai: Maharashtra State Government, 1991–92), 6.

31. This expands Upendra Baxi's critique of the Subaltern Studies Collective's failure to engage rigorously with the work of law. Upendra Baxi, "The State's Emissary: The Place of Law in Subaltern Studies," in *Subaltern Studies,* vol. 7 (Delhi: Oxford University Press, 1992), 147–164.

32. Under the POA Act, the sessions court functions as a special court for hearing atrocities cases and the sessions judge acts as special judge.

33. Judgement in respect of C.R. 40/91, delivered on June 18, 1992, by Special Court, Parbhani, p. 3. Subsequent quotations are from this judgment, with page numbers, if any, noted in parentheses.

34. Ibid. The case judgment is in English. I surmise that "dis-sacred" translates the term that was probably used, *brasht* (polluted, or desecrated.)

35. *Report on the spot enquiry by Shri Ram Dhan, Chairman.*

36. Sumit Guha, "Recovering Subaltern History in Western India" (paper prepared for the conference Postcolonialism and the State of South Asian Studies, University of Pennsylvania, Philadelphia, April 20, 2007). I am grateful to Professsor Guha for making this paper available to me and for e-mail exchanges (July 24–26, 2007) that clarified questions regarding Mahar ritual sacrifice. For an early critique of the practice of burying Mahars alive, see Dhananjay Keer and S. G. Malshe, eds., *Samagra Vangmay: Mahatma Phule Samagra Vangmay* [Collected Works of Mahatma Jotirao Phule] (Mumbai: Mumbai Rajya Sahitya ani Samskriti Mandal, 1969), reprinted 1991, ed. Y. D. Phadke, 160.

37. Ganesh Chimnaji Vad, *Selections from the Government Records in the Alienation Office Poona: Sanads and Letters,* ed. Purshotam Vishram Mawjee and D. B. Parasnis (Poona: P. V. Mawjee, 1913), 7–8, quoted in Guha, "Recovering Subaltern History in Western India," 6.

38. Shankar Narayana Khare and Ganesh Hari Joshi, eds., *Sivacaritrasahitya,* vol. 3 (Pune: Bharata Itihasa Samshodhaka Mandala, 1930), 197–98, quoted in Guha, "Recovering Subaltern History in Western India," 14–15.

39. P. Gavli, *Peshvekalin Gulamgiri va Asprushyata* [Slavery and Untouchability under the Peshwa Rule] (Kolhapur: Prachar Prakashan, 1981), 96.

40. René Girard, *The Scapegoat* (Baltimore: Johns Hopkins University Press, 1986).

41. Allen Feldman, *Formations of Violence* (Chicago: University of Chicago Press, 1991), 258.

42. Ibid. (emphasis added).

43. Sacrifice is distinctive precisely because it elaborates a structure of mimetic violence and displays the reversibility of sacred and profane, unlike the contract, a legitimating fiction that is future oriented and premised on a structure of forgetting that recasts originary violence as law.

44. For a brilliant reading relating Agamben's work on law and bare life

to the anthropology of sacrifice, see Rey Chow, "Sacrifice, Mimesis and the Theorizing of Victimhood (A Speculative Essay)," *Representations* 94 (2006): 131–49.

45. P. Sainath, "The Fear of Democracy of the Privileged," *The Hindu*, December 8, 2006.

46. When an Ambedkar statue in the Ramabai chawls of the Mumbai suburb of Ghatkopar was desecrated with a garland of slippers in 1997, Dalits protested vehemently. Police shooting killed ten people, wounded at least twenty-six others, and initiated a government inquiry. S. D. Gundewar, Judge, Bombay High Court, *Report of the Committee of Inquiry into Desecration of Dr. Ambedkar Statue Violence, Police Firing on 11th July, 1997 at Ghatkopar, Mumbai* (Bombay: Government of Maharashtra, 1998).

47. Rajeswari Sunder Rajan, "The Ameena Case," in *The Scandal of the State: Women, Law, and Citizenship in Postcolonial India* (Durham, NC: Duke University Press, 2003), 41–71.

48. While I do not focus on the statistical increase or decrease of caste violence per se, the figures allow us to address when and why "caste violence" became an important category of record keeping and whether activism around the atrocity might have also renewed attention to the practice. For a discussion of a similar phenomenon, see Lata Mani, "Contentious Traditions: The Debate on Sati in Colonial India," in *Recasting Women: Essays in Indian Colonial History*, ed. Kumkum Sangari and Sudesh Vaid (New Brunswick, NJ: Rutgers University Press, 1990), 88–126.

EPILOGUE

1. The Marathi verb *basane* means "to sit," or "to fit."

2. Scholars have long noted the reorganization of sense perception as one of the most important transformations of modernity. For the now classic work on the perceptual shifts wrought by European modernity, see Walter Benjamin and Rolf Tiedemann, *The Arcades Project* (Cambridge, MA: Belknap Press of Harvard University Press, 1999). Also important is Wolfgang Schivelbusch, *The Railway Journey: Trains and Travel in the 19th Century* (New York: Urizen Books, 1979). For a brilliant account of technology in the colonies, see Rudolf Mrázek, *Engineers of Happy Land: Technology and Nationalism in a Colony* (Princeton, NJ: Princeton University Press, 2002).

3. Arjun Dangle, ed., *Poisoned Bread: Translations from Marathi Dalit Literature* (Hyderabad: Orient Longman, 1992), 96–97.

4. Ibid., 99.

5. Ibid., 106.

6. Vivek Dhareshwar, "Caste and the Secular Self," *Journal of Arts and Ideas*, no. 25–26 (1993): 115–26; and Anupama Rao, introduction to *Gender and Caste: Contemporary Issues in Indian Feminism* (New Delhi: Kali for Women, 2003), 1–47.

7. M. S. S. Pandian, "Brahmin Hybridity," in *Brahmin and Non-Brahmin* (New Delhi: Permanent Black, 2007), 60–101.

8. See the discussion of the Bhopal White Paper, which demanded reserva-

tions in private sector employment, in Aditya Nigam, "In Search of a Bourgeoisie: Dalit Politics Enters a New Phase," *Economic and Political Weekly* 37, no. 13 (March 30, 2002): 1190–93. Nigam's important article addresses how liberalization has affected debates about caste equity. See also *The Bhopal Document: Charting a New Course for Dalits for the 21st Century* (Bhopal: Government of Madhya Pradesh, 2002); and P. G. Jogdand, ed., *New Economic Policy and Dalits* (Jaipur: Rawal Publications, 2000).

9. I use the term "corporeal politics" to specify the manner in which demands for political recognition have intersected with ongoing debates about caste embodiment. Though inspired by Foucault's account of the body as a key site of regulation and control and as material artifact of racialization and sexual differentiation, my arguments ought to be distinguished from ongoing debates around "biopolitics," a term coined by Foucault and used rather differently by the philosopher Giorgio Agamben. Foucault's view of biopolitics is essentially productive: it is a command to *live*, albeit in highly particular ways. For Agamben, biopower is essentially a politics of death produced by a rule of law that expels certain subjects into the domain of "bare life." From this follows Foucault's long-standing interest in technologies of life, and the discourses and evidentiary rules through which subjects are historically constituted. In contrast, Agamben focuses on how law and sovereignty subtend citizenship to produce the biological human. The European genealogy of biopolitics—its association with forms of state racism and massified violence practiced under totalitarianism and (especially) National Socialism—makes this a difficult term to transpose to other contexts without emendation. See Giorgio Agamben, *Homo Sacer: Sovereign Power and Bare Life* (Stanford, CA: Stanford University Press, 1998); Michel Foucault, *The History of Sexuality*, vol. 1 (New York: Vintage, 1980), and *The Birth of Biopolitics: Lectures at the College de France*, trans. Graham Burchell (New York: Palgrave Macmillan, 2008). For a powerful argument about how biopolitics relates to colonial corporeality, see Ann Laura Stoler, *Race and the Education of Desire: Foucault's History of Sexuality and the Colonial Order of Things* (Durham, NC: Duke University Press, 1995).

10. Joan Scott, "The Conundrum of Equality" (occasional paper, Institute for Advanced Study, Paper no. 2, March 1999), 3.

11. Etienne Balibar, "'Rights of Man' and 'Rights of the Citizen': The Modern Dialectic of Equality and Freedom," in *Masses, Classes, Ideas: Studies on Politics and Philosophy Before and After Marx* (London: Routledge, 1994), 49.

12. Ibid.

13. Michel Foucault's account of permanent war as the model for the modern state traces the contiguity between the antagonistic structures of race war and class war in Marx. Foucault notes that Marx explicitly attributed his idea of class struggle to Augustin Thierry's discussion of the race wars and described Thierry as the "father of the class-struggle." Michel Foucault, *Society Must Be Defended: Lectures at the Collège de France, 1975–76*, trans. David Macey (New York: Picador, 2003), 85.

14. C. L. R. James, *The Black Jacobins: Toussaint L'Ouverture and the San Domingo Revolution*, 2nd ed. (New York: Vintage, 1963).

15. Hegel's *Phenomenology of Spirit* (1807) was written soon after this first

successful slave revolt of the modern world. Though it remains underacknowl-edged by the philosophical traditions that took up his parable of recognition, Hegel's description of the master-slave dialectic signals the impact of historico-political events on German idealist thought. See Susan Buck-Morss, "Hegel and Haiti," *Critical Inquiry* 26, no. 4 (Summer 2000): 821–65.

16. Thomas Holt, *The Problem of Freedom: Race, Labor, and Politics in Jamaica and Britain, 1832–1938* (Baltimore, MD: Johns Hopkins University Press, 1991).

17. Frantz Fanon, *Black Skin, White Masks* (New York: Grove Press, 1982). Judith Butler offers a brilliant account of the centrality of the master-slave dialectic to French philosophical and psychoanalytic appropriations of Hegel via Alexandre Kojève's 1933–39 lectures on the *Phenomenology of Spirit* at the École des Hautes Études. See Judith Butler, *Subjects of Desire: Hegelian Reflections in Twentieth-Century France* (New York: Columbia University Press, 1999).

18. India's decolonization, defined as a "transfer of power," was also a longer-term process by which a Western-educated, largely upper-caste elite assumed the mantle of agents of development and modernization for a national state that re-tained colonial infrastructure and bureaucracy. Fanon's model of revolutionary transformation is thus not an accurate descriptor of India's path to decolonization.

19. It is precisely this focus on the state as the ultimate guarantor of Dalits personhood that distinguishes Ambedkar from Marx, who challenged the as-sumption that the state is "the only 'universal' that can be posited against the particularity of competing private interests." Dipesh Chakrabarty, *Rethinking Working-Class History: Bengal 1890–1940* (Dehli: Oxford University Press, 1989), 227.

20. D. R. Nagaraj, *The Flaming Feet: A Study of the Dalit Movement in India* (Bangalore: South Forum Press, 1993), 40.

21. Charles Taylor, *Multiculturalism: Examining the Politics of Recognition,* ed. Amy Gutman, with comments by Kwame Anthony Appiah, Jurgen Haber-mas, Stephen C. Rockefeller, Michael Walzer, and Susan Wolf (Princeton, NJ: Princeton University Press, 1994).

22. T. H. Marshall's stageist argument about rights is relevant here, as it out-lines a progression from political citizenship to claims to social and economic citizenship. T. H. Marshall, "Citizenship and Social Class," in *The Welfare State Reader,* ed. C. Pierson and F. G. Castles (Cambridge: Polity Press, 2003), 32–41. More recently, Nancy Fraser has traced a genealogy of feminist claim-making from its focus on social and economic redistribution to cultural recognition. Nancy Fraser, "Mapping the Feminist Imagination: From Redistribution to Recognition to Representation," *Constellations* 12, no. 3 (2005): 295–307; I would note that the ideological disaggregation of claims for redistribution from demands for recognition allows states to distinguish demands for racial equal-ity from those for sexual equality or cultural rights by differentiating subjects making those claims. See the special issue of *Constellations* 7, no. 4 (2004), with essays by Wendy Brown, Caroline Emcke, Patchen Markell, and James Tully.

23. I distinguish the politicization of the caste body from Foucault's argu-ment about the politicization of "life" that falls under the rubric of biopolitics. I do so for two reasons: first, to distinguish my efforts from Foucault's focus on

the technological management of life at the level of biology, of life itself; second, to challenge the broad distinctions between governmentality and population that have emerged in the wake of Foucauldian analyses of the social. I am interested in historicizing the effects of social differentiation and political categorization.

24. The phrase "civilizational shame" is used by Nicholas Dirks to describe the politicization of caste resulting from efforts to redress caste inequality. Nicholas B. Dirks, "Caste Politic and the Politics of Caste," in *Castes of Mind: Colonialism and the Making of Modern India* (Princeton, NJ: Princeton University Press, 2001), 275–96.

25. I am drawing here on Marc Galanter's argument regarding the emergence of Hinduism as a legal construct. See Marc Galanter, "Hinduism, Secularism, and the Indian Judiciary," in *Secularism and Its Critics,* 268–96.

26. Aamir Mufti, *Enlightenment in the Colony: The Jewish Question and the Crisis of Postcolonial Culture* (Princeton, NJ: Princeton University Press, 2007).

27. Gyanendra Pandey, "*Remembering Partition,* and Faisal Devji, Hindu/Muslim/Indian," *Public Culture* 5, no. 1 (1992): 1–18.

28. See, for example, the recommendations of the Sachar Committee Report. The committee was set up on March 9, 2005, with a mandate to study the socioeconomic and educational status of Muslims. The report is available at the Ministry of Minority Affairs website, http://minorityaffairs.gov.in/newsite/sachar/sachar.asp.

29. For an engagement with the key interlocutors and arguments in this debate, see David Scott, "Culture in Political Theory," *Political Theory* 31, no. 1 (February 2003): 93–116.

30. Partha Chatterjee, "Secularism and Tolerance," in *Secularism and Its Critics,* ed. Rajeev Bhargava (Delhi: Oxford University Press, 1998), 375–76, 378.

31. Nivedita Menon, "State/Gender/Community: Citizenship in Contemporary India," *Economic and Political Weekly,* January 31, 1998, PE3–PE10; Rajeswari Sunder Rajan, "Women between Community and State: Some Implications of the Uniform Civil Code Debate in India," *Social Text* 18, no. 4 (2000): 55–82. For a discussion of demands for reservations for women as they affect the rights of Dalit and lower-caste women, see Mary E. John, "Alternative Modernities? Reservations and Women's Movement in 20th Century India," *Economic and Political Weekly,* October 28, 2000, WS22–WS29.

32. Joan Scott, *Only Paradoxes to Offer: French Feminists and the Rights of Man* (Cambridge: Harvard University Press, 1996).

33. Mrinalini Sinha, *Specters of Mother India: The Global Restructuring of an Empire* (Durham, NC: Duke University Press, 2006), 245.

34. Zakia Pathak and Rajeswari Sunder Rajan, "Shah Bano," *Signs: Journal of Women in Culture and Society* 14 (Spring 1989): 558–82; and Rajeswari Sunder Rajan, "The Ameena 'Case': The Female Citizen and Subject," in *Scandal of the State: Women, Law and Citizenship in Postcolonial India* (Durham, NC: Duke University Press, 2003), 41–71.

35. Sunder Rajan, *Scandal of the State.*

36. Arvind Rajagopal, *Politics after Television: Religious Nationalism and the Reshaping of the Indian Public* (Cambridge: Cambridge University Press, 2001).

37. The participation of Dalit and Adivasi or so-called "tribal" communities in the 2002 Gujarat pogroms is a noteworthy comment on the near-total ghettoization of Muslims in many parts of India today.

38. I take the phrase "Dalit power" from an article of the same name, Venkatish Ramakrishnan, "Dalit Power," *Frontline* 24, no. 10 (May 19–June 1, 2007), http://www.hinduonnet.com/fline/fl2410/fl241000.htm.

39. Gopal Guru, *Kanshi Ram Yanca Bahujanvad* [Kanshi Ram's Bahujan Politics] (Pune: Samajvignan Academy, 1994); Sharad Patil, "Democracy: Brahminical and Non-Brahminical," *Frontier* (September 30–October 21, 1995): 42–46. Guru and Patil argue against the identitarian politics of number that dominates BSP political strategy. Instead, they suggest that a radical Dalit politics ought to annihilate caste through political identification with (and the eventual transcendence of) caste subalternity. Other commentators argue that compromising with caste enemies in view of electoral constraints ought to be seen nonideologically, as apprehension of the deep divisions and persistent prejudice that render commitment to a stated political ideology unrealistic, perhaps politically suicidal, for Dalits. See the exchange between Anand Teltumde ("A Mayawati Revolution in UP: Challenging the Imputed Social Revolution of the BSP Victory") and Chitti Babu ("Mayawati and the Meaning of Her Victory") at Kafila, "The Meaning of Mayawati for the Dalit Movement," http://kafila.org/2007/06/11/.

40. Founded by Kanshi Ram in 1984, the BSP has explicitly focused on the capture of state power by Dalits, along with Muslims and Bahujans, or lower castes. In the past, the BSP ran on slogans such as "*Jat todo, samaj jodo* [Break caste and unite society]" or "*Vote hamara, raj tumhara, nahi chalega, nahi chalega* [Our vote, your rule, this can't go on]," which emphasized the necessity of the Dalit-Bahujan vote to upper-caste parties. Another BSP slogan reversed the contempt for and symbolic degradation of Dalits by the castes mentioned: "*Tilak, tarazu aur talwar, inko maro joote char* [Beat the Brahmins, Banias (monelylenders), and the Thakurs (a Kshatriya non-Brahmin community) with shoes]."

41. Praful Bidwai, "Creating History," *Frontline* 24, no. 10 (May 19–June 1, 2007), http://www.hinduonnet.com/fline/fl2410/stories/20070601003209800.htm.

42. Ramakrishnan, "Dalit Power."

43. It should come as no surprise that *The Chamcha Age* (1984), written by BSP founder Kanshi Ram, addressed the continued consequences of the Poona Pact for the realization of Dalit power.

44. Bidwai, "Creating History." Unfortunately, restitutive justice goes together with retributive justice. Today, Dalit power is challenged by the rise of the BCs and OBCs, who are at the forefront of anti-Dalit violence in many parts of India. The numerical dominance of these middle and lower-middle castes and their entry into the reservations regime, together with competition for state protection, presages new axes of political contradiction and violence.

45. Sudha Pai, *Dalit Assertion and the Unfinished Democratic Revolution* (New Delhi: Sage Publications, 2002).

46. Dalit groups are increasingly participating in a transnational discourse of human rights. In 2001, the International Campaign for Dalit Human Rights (ICDHR) petitioned to include anti-Dalit discrimination as a form of racism at

the United Nations World Conference against Racism, Racial Discrimination, Xenophobia and Related Intolerance (WCAR). This came on the heels of a stand-off between Dalit groups and nongovernmental organizations working with Dalit communities, on the one hand, and the Indian government on the other, about the implications of defining caste discrimination as racism. The Indian government argued that focusing on caste "diluted" the aims of the WCAR, implying that caste discrimination was "better" than the entrenched racial formations of the United States and South Africa, with their interpersonal violence and institutionalized exclusion. Instead, Dalit groups encouraged the comparison and defined racism as any form of historical discrimination, labor exploitation, or social stigmatization based on descent, including untouchability. For work that draws on a Dalit human rights paradigm, see *A Public Hearing on Atrocities against Dalits with Specific Reference to Dalit Women* (n.p., n.d.), a report from hearings organized in March 1994 by Women's Voice and the Asian Women's Human Rights Council; and *Report on the National Public Hearing on Atrocities against Dalits in India* (Madurai, 1999). See also Aloysius Irudayam, Jayashree Mangubhai, and Joel Lee, *Report on Dalit Women Speak Out: Violence against Dalit Women in India*, 3 vols. (New Delhi: Campaign for Dalit Himan Rights, 2006); and *Broken People: Caste Violence against India's "Untouchables"* (New York: Human Rights Watch, 1999), http://www.hrw.org/legacy/reports/1999/india; and *Hidden Apartheid: Caste Discrimination against India's Untouchables* (New York: Human Rights Watch, 2007), www.hrw.org/reports/2007/india0207.

Index

Italicized page numbers refer to figures.

Text: 10/13 Sabon
Display: Sabon
Compositor: Integrated Composition Systems
Printer: Thomson-Shore, Inc.